MW00886646

SHORT, SIMPLE and SNAPPY

TASTE WITH NO TIME TO WASTE

By

MARIA McRAE

Copyright 2010
Library of Congress
Washington, D. C.

Printed by CreateSpace

To my Readers

Thank you for inviting me into your kitchen.

FOREWORD

The motto is: SHORT, SIMPLE and SNAPPY.

The Aim   Invite you to be creative and improvise without having to stick to given amounts. Present you with ideas you can interpret "your way".

Help you whip up meals with ingredients you have on hand.

Incite you to acquire a flair for new combinations of foods and flavors. Give you self-confidence to take off on your own.

The Reach   Busy People who don't have much time to spend in the kitchen, particularly at the end of a long day.

Beginners, young couples, those on a tight budget, and of course all Food Lovers.

The Recipes Avoid lengthy preparations, long lists, large amounts of ingredients.

"The ambition of every good cook must be to make something very good with the fewest possible ingredients."

Urbain Dubois

QUANTITIES AND INGREDIENTS ARE FLEXIBLE.

My project started with: "I don't have much time to spend in the kitchen!"

"Give me ideas. I have ham, what do I do without having to go through long fancy recipes?"

"I'm broiling a piece of fish for two. How do I pizzazz it? Real quick!"

"I have fish and rice. What's short and simple for a risotto?"

My concept was to liven up the routine of everyday cooking by creating recipes with flexibility in amounts and ingredients. Recipes where, a shrimp pasta could appeal to different cultures, by its variation of components and seasonings.

My cookbook is also a reference book of ideas.

The recipes are simple. Ingredients can be substituted with ones you already have or others you prefer. Seasonings can be substituted with Ethnic Flavors. A list of them is included.

Most recipes serve two. They can be doubled or tripled. Easier than dividing large amounts.

Quantities are average. They can be increased or decreased according to appetites.

However, in certain sauces and ethnic recipes, it is advisable to follow the amounts indicated in the recipe. Seasonings can be altered to taste.

Available cooked foods such as rotisserie chicken, turkey, ham, cured meats, shrimp, and all kinds of leftovers, open the way for speedy and savory meals.

There is no chapter on Appetizers, Pastas or Soups. They come in under the main ingredient in their composition, such as Fish, Poultry, Vegetables, or other.

Preceding each chapter is an index of the recipes included in that chapter. Thereby helpful in selecting a dish with the main ingredient you are planning to use.

"BASIC RECIPES" are formulas: like Frittata, Quiche, Soufflé. As long as you stick with the formula, you can add any Fillings or Seasonings you wish.

Ingredients are written in capital letters, or headed with a capital letter, thus easy to find when scanning a page and looking for an item.

Having lived on three continents, and traveled to many countries, I've included some of my favorite recipes from around the world. Adjusting to the title of this book, they are simplified versions of classics, with some unusual highlights you might enjoy.

A few are lengthy but worth it!

A word of encouragement: some of the "best cooks" have never been to cooking school. Many of us remember someone in our family as "the best cook".

Be daring in your exploration of foods and flavors. Cooking is an art. It has no limits.

Raid your refrigerator for leftovers. That holiday ham and turkey, or the cold piece of roast, can go ... a tasty way.

IMPORTANT   Prepare all ingredients, wash, trim, cut, before starting your cooking.
                 This can be done ahead and ingredients refrigerated until ready to use.

TO SAVE TIME   Get organized.

Bon appétit!

P. S.   Please read the whole recipe before starting your cooking.

"Have no fear of perfection - you'll never reach it."

Salvador Dali

CONTENTS

INTERNATIONAL CELEBRITIES
Some with simplicity

Some with a sweet tooth

* Many recipes.   ** Recipes with variations.

WEIGHTS

OUNCES		GRAMS
1/2-oz	=	14
1	=	28
1-1/2	=	42
2	=	57
2-1/2	=	71
3	=	85
3-1/2	=	99
4	=	114
4-1/2	=	128
5	=	142
5-1/2	=	156
6	=	170
7	=	199
8	=	226
9	=	254
10	=	283
11	=	311
12	=	340
13	=	368
14	=	396
15	=	425
16	=	453 = 1 lb
35-1/4	=	1000 = 1 Kilo
2 lbs + 3-1/4 oz	=	1 Kilo

LIQUIDS - METRIC CONVERSIONS

1 liter	=	1000 milliliters (ml)
	=	100 centiliters (cl)
	=	10 deciliters (dl)
1 dl	=	3.2 oz (fluid oz)
1 liter	=	1.05 quart US

FLUID OUNCES		cl	=	ml	=	dl
1/4-cup	=	0.06	=	0.065		
1/2-cup	=	0.12	=	0.125		
3/4-cup	=	0.18				
1 cup	=	0.24	=	0.240	=	2.4
1-1/4 cups	=	0.30				
1-1/2 cups	=	0.36				
1-3/4	=	0.42				
2 cups	=	0.47	=	1 pint US		
3	=	0.72				
4	=	0.94	=	1 quart US		

		cl		TB		oz
1/8-cup	=	3 cl	=	2 TB	=	1 oz
1/4-cup	=	6 cl	=	4 TB	=	2 oz
1/3-cup	=	8 cl	=	5 TB	+	1 tp
3-1/3 oz	=	10 cl	=	1 dl		
1/2-cup	=	12 cl	=	8 TB	=	4 oz
3/4-cup	=	18 cl	=	12 TB	=	6 oz
1 cup	=	24 cl	=	16 TB	=	8 oz
1-1/2 cups	=	36 cl	=	24 TB	=	12 oz
1-3/4	=	42 cl	=	28 TB	=	14 oz
1 pint	=	47 cl	=	32 TB	=	16 oz
1 pint + 1 oz	=	50 cl	=	1/2-liter		

OUNCES		GRAMS		LITERS		SPOONS		MILLILITERS		
1/6	=	5	=	0.005	=	1 tp	=	5		
1/3	=	10	=	0.010	=	2 tp	=	10 ml	=	1 cl
1/2-oz	=	15	=	0.015	=	1 TB	=	15 ml	=	1.5 cl
1	=	28	=	0.03	=	2 TB	=	30 ml	=	3 cl
8	=	226	=	0.24	=	1 cup	=	240 ml	=	24 cl

SPOONS		CUPS	FLUID
1 pinch	=	1/8 tp	
3 tp	=	1 TB	1/2-oz
1-1/2 tp	=	1/2-TB	
1 tp	=	1/3-TB	
2 TB	=	1/8-cup	1 oz
4 TB	=	1/4-cup	2 oz
5 TB + 1 tp	=	1/3-cup	2.60 oz
8 TB	=	1/2-cup	
10 TB + 2 tp	=	2/3-cup	
12 TB	=	3/4-cup	
16 TB	=	1 cup	8 oz
32 TB	=	2 cups	16 oz
		4 cups	1 quart
		16 cups	4 qts = 1 gallon

U.S. LIQUIDS		ENGLISH
1-1/4 cups	=	1/2-pint - 10 fluid ounces
2-1/2 cups	=	1 pint - 20 fluid ounces
5 cups	=	1 quart
5 quarts	=	1 gallon

FAHRENHEIT		CELSIUS	rounded
100	=	38	
125	=	52	
150	=	66	
175	=	79	
200	=	93	
212	=	100	
			rounded
225	=	107	110
250	=	121	120
275	=	136	140
300	=	149	150
325	=	163	160
350	=	177	180
375	=	191	190
400	=	204	200
425	=	219	220
450	=	232	230
475	=	246	245
500	=	260	260
525	=	274	275

INGREDIENT WEIGHTS and MEASURES

BACON

3 oz = 6 strips

BUTTER

1 stick	=	8 TB	=	4 oz	=	1/2-cup	=	114 grams
1/2-stick	=	4 TB	=	2 oz	=	1/4-cup	=	57 grams
1/4-stick	=	2 TB	=	1 oz	=	1/8-cup	=	28 grams

CHEESE

Grated 1 oz = 1/4-cup

FLOUR

1 lb	=	4-1/2 cups
1 cup	=	3-1/2 oz

SUGAR

1 lb	=	2-1/2 cups
1 cup	=	6-1/2 oz
Confectioners 1 cup	=	2-3/4 oz

EGGS

3 lge raw	=	2/3-cup
1 lge raw	=	3 TB + 2tp
1 chopped	=	4 TB

RICE

1/2-lb	=	1 cup
1 cup raw	=	3 cups cook ed

HAM *chopped*

4 oz	=	1-1/3 cups
1 oz	=	5-1/3 TB

FRUIT and VEGETABLE CANS

Small	=	6 to 8-1/4 oz
Medium	=	7 to 10 oz
Large	=	15 to 20 oz

PASTA SAUCE JARS

26 to 28 oz

UNCOOKED PASTA

2 oz per p.	=	main course
2 oz small Pasta	=	1 cup
2 oz cooked	=	1-1/2 cups

SOUP and BROTH CANS

10.5 oz reg. Size

TUNA FISH CANS

Small	=	3 oz
Medium	=	6 oz
Large	=	12 oz

TOMATOES - CANNED

Paste	=	6 oz small
Sauce	=	8 oz small
Peeled	=	26 to 28 oz

CUT FRUIT and VEGETABLES *(approx)*

diced	medium Apple	=	1 cup
diced	2 large Apples	=	3 cups
trimd	med. Asparagus	=	1/4-cup
diced	med. Bell Pepper	=	1 cup
diced	large Carrot	=	1/3-cup
diced	Kirby Cucumber	=	2/3-cup
cubed	1 lb Eggplant	=	4 cups
slcd	Endive 4 oz	=	1 cup
slcd	Leek 3 oz	=	1cup
slcd	Mushrooms 3 oz	=	1 cup
diced	1/4-medium Onion	=	1/4-cup
diced	Potato 4 oz	=	1 cup
shred	Radicchio 8 oz	=	4 cups
diced	med. Plum Tomato	=	1/3-cup
cubed	large Turnip	=	1-1/2 cups
diced	med. Zucchini	=	2/3-cup

VEGETABLE WEIGHTS *(approx)*

medium Apple	=	7 to 8 oz
medium Asparagus	=	1 oz
large Bell Pepper	=	8 to 9 oz
small Bell Pepper	=	4 oz
large Carrot	=	5 oz
Kirby Cucumber	=	3 to 4 oz
Baby Eggplant	=	4 to 6 oz
medium Eggplant	=	1 lb
large Eggplant	=	1-1/4 lbs
med. Belgian Endive	=	4 oz
Fennel Bulb trimmed	=	8 oz
trimmed 1" thick Leek	=	3 oz
2-1/2 cups Mushrooms	=	8 oz
medium Onion	=	7 to 8 oz
large baking Potato	=	9 to 10 oz
4 med. Potatoes	=	1 lb
8 Shallots	=	10 oz
Small Tomato	=	5 oz
medium Tomato	=	6 to 7 oz
large Tomato	=	8 oz
4 small Zucchini	=	1 lb
medium Zucchini	=	5 oz

OTHER

Juice of 1 Lemon	=	3 to 4 TB
1 lb Potatoes	=	2 cups mashed

ETHNIC FLAVORS and INGREDIENTS

AFRICAN

ALLSPICE
CHILIES
CINNAMON
COCONUT MILK
COCONUT shredded
CORIANDER
CUMIN
MANGO
PEANUTS
PINEAPPLE
RAISINS
RED HOT PEPPER

CARIBBEAN

ALLSPICE
BANANAS
BELL PEPPER
BLACK and RED BEANS
CAPERS
CHILIES hot
CILANTRO
CINNAMON
CLOVES
COCONUT
CUMIN
MANGO
PAPAYA
PIMIENTOS
PLANTAINS
PINEAPPLE
RUM
TABASCO
VANILLA

CHINESE

BAMBOO SHOOTS
BEAN CURD
BEAN SPROUTS
BOK CHOY
BROWN-BEAN SAUCE
CELLOPHANE NOODLES
CHILI-GARLIC PASTE
CILANTRO
DUCK SAUCE
HOISIN SAUCE
OYSTER SAUCE
PLUM SAUCE
SOY SAUCE
EGG NOODLES
GARLIC
GINGER ROOT
MUSHROOMS dried
PEPPERCORNS Sichuan
RED-BEAN PASTE
RICE WINE
RICE glutinous
SESAME SEEDS
SESAME-SEED OIL
SNOW PEAS
WATER CHESTNUTS
WONTON WRAPS

GREEK

ALLSPICE
ANISE
CINNAMON
CLOVES
FETA CHEESE
KASERI CHEESE
KEFALOTIRI CHEESE
MANOURI CHEESE
GARLIC
MINT dried, fresh
OKRA
OLIVES
OLIVE OIL for cooking
EXTRA-VIRGIN OLIVE OIL
OREGANO dried
OUZO
PHYLLO DOUGH
PINE NUTS
RETSINA WINE
ROSE WATER
TARAMA carp roe paste
TARAMOSALATA carp roe dip
THYME
YOGURT

INDIAN

CARDAMON
CHILIES hot
CHUTNEY
CINNAMON
CLOVES
COCONUT grated, shredded, milk
CORIANDER
CURRY POWDER
FENNEL SEED
GARAM MASALA spice mixture
GARLIC
GINGER
MINT dried, fresh
PEANUTS
RICE Basmati
ROSE WATER
SAFFRON
TURMERIC
YOGURT

ITALIAN

ANCHOVIES
ARBORIO RICE
BALSAMIC VINEGAR
BASIL fresh, dried
CAPERS
EXTRA-VIRGIN OLIVE OIL
GARLIC
MARSALA WINE
MOZZARELLA
OREGANO dried
PARMESAN
PEPERONCINI hot pepper flakes
SAFFRON
VERMOUTH dry, sweet

JAPANESE

BAMBOO SHOOTS
BEAN CURD
BEAN SPROUTS
BROWN-BEAN SAUCE
BUCKWHEAT NOODLES
CELLOPHANE NOODLES
CILANTRO
DAIKON white radish
GINGER ROOT
HIYAMUGI thin noodles
MIRIN sake for cooking
MISO soybean paste
RICE Japanese
RICE VINEGAR
SAKE
SEAWEED WRAPS nori
SHITAKE mushrooms
SOMEN thin noodles
SOY SAUCE
TERIYAKI SAUCE
TOFU
UDON wide noodles
WASABI MUSTARD

MEXICAN, LATIN AMERICAN

ANCHO CHILIES
AVOCADO
BEANS all colors
CAYENNE
CHILIES hot
CHORIZO
CILANTRO
CLOVES
CORIANDER SEEDS
CUMIN
GARBANZOS
JALAPEÑOS
MASA FLOUR
NOPALITOS pear cactus
OLIVE OIL
PALM HEARTS
PINE NUTS
PLANTAINS
QUESO BLANCO
TOMATILLOS
TORTILLAS

MIDDLE EASTERN

ALLSPICE
ANISE
BURGHUL cracked wheat
CORIANDER ground
CUMIN ground
MINT dried, fresh
NUTMEG
PHYLLO DOUGH
PINE NUTS
PITA BREAD
SAFFRON
TAHINI sesame paste
YOGURT

NORTH AFRICAN

ANISE
CARAWAY SEEDS
CARDAMON PODS
CAYENNE
CILANTRO
CINNAMON
CLOVES
CORIANDER seeds and ground
COUSCOUS
CUMIN ground
DATES fresh and dried
HARISSA hot chili pepper paste
LEMONS preserved, pickled
MINT fresh, dried
NUTMEG ground
OLIVES
OLIVE OIL
ORANGE FLOWER WATER
PAPRIKA also sweet paprika
PEANUT OIL for cooking
ROSE WATER
SAFFRON
TAGINE PASTE ready-made
TURMERIC

PORTUGUESE and SPANISH

ANGULAS baby eels
BACALAO salt cod
BASIL fresh and dried
CAYENNE
CHORIZO
CILANTRO
CINNAMON
CUMIN
DRY SHERRY for cooking
EXTRA-VIRGIN OLIVE OIL
GARBANZOS chick peas
HOT RED PEPPERS
NUTMEG
OLIVE OIL for cooking
OLIVES
PAPRIKA
PIMIENTOS also in a jar
PINE NUTS
ROSEMARY
SAFFRON
SERRANO HAM
THYME

RUSSIAN

BASTURMA dried garlicky beef
BLINIS buckwheat pancakes
CAVIAR
DILL
KASHA buckwheat groats
LIVER PÂTÉ
PICKLED HERRING
SALMON ROE
SOUR CREAM
VODKA

Try a shot of VODKA in a
Steak Tartare. Unforgettable!

Add VODKA to a Pasta Sauce.

BASIC INGREDIENTS

It is helpful and time-saving to stock your pantry and refrigerator with Basic Ingredients.

BALSAMIC VINEGAR
CHAMPAGNE VINEGAR
RED WINE VINEGAR
WHITE WINE VINEGAR

EXTRA-VIRGIN OLIVE OIL
COOKING OLIVE OIL
COOKING VEGETABLE OIL
COOKING SPRAY

BUTTER
MARGARINE

BREADCRUMBS
CROUTONS

CHEESE to taste
PARMESAN for grating

EGGS
SOUR CREAM
YOGURT

GARLIC
SHALLOTS
ONIONS

HERBS dried, fresh

HORSERADISH
MAYONNAISE
MUSTARD

NUTS

DRIED BEANS

OLIVES
PICKLES
RELISH

PASTA
PASTA SAUCE

RICE

RAISINS

SPICES to taste
SEEDS celery, fennel, other

SAUCES ready-made, to taste
ASIAN SAUCES
TABASCO
HOT SAUCES to taste
RED PEPPER FLAKES to taste

TOMATOES canned
TOMATO PASTE
TOMATO SAUCE

CANNED FOODS to taste

LIMES, LEMONS A zest grater

ARROWROOT POWDER *
FLOUR **
CORNSTARCH

* ARROWROOT POWDER thickens a Sauce or Gravy and leaves it transparent.

- For 1 cup of Sauce or Gravy, use 1-1/2-to-2 teaspoons of Arrowroot Powder.
- Dissolve by pouring into it 2-to-4 Tablespoons of cold Water or Broth.

- Use more or less Arrowroot, according to consistency of Sauce at the start.

- Do not use Arrowroot for Sauces with a Milk or Cream base.

** FLOUR or CORNSTARCH thickens a Sauce or Gravy and renders it opaque and milky.

HELPFUL HINTS

ASPARAGUS

Wrap fresh ASPARAGUS in moist paper towels, seal in plastic bag, refrigerate.
If trimmed ahead of time, store the same way to prevent Asparagus from drying.

BREADCRUMBS

Cut DRY BREAD into pieces. Grate in food processor.
Mix several kinds of breads (optional). Store in a jar or can. Refrigerate.
Also process store-bought seasoned Croutons.

BUTTERED: In a skillet melt 1 TB BUTTER per 1/2-cup Breadcrumbs. Stir them into
the melted Butter until it has been absorbed. Optional: toast lightly.

IN OIL: In a skillet, heat 1 TB OLIVE or PEANUT OIL. Toast in it 1 cup Breadcrumbs.

CROUTONS   Preheat oven to 350°.

Baked   Cut DRY BREAD into small cubes and place them in a shallow baking pan.
Sprinkle with OLIVE or VEGETABLE OIL, SALT, PEPPER, HERBS.
Or place the cubes in a plastic bag, add Seasonings and shake.
Bake until golden or golden brown.

Fried   Heat in a skillet: VEGETABLE or EXTRA-VIRGIN OLIVE OIL, or SEASONED OIL.
Fry Croutons, adding Seasonings to taste.

Crouton Seasonings - shake them in a plastic bag with Seasonings, before frying.

CELERY SALT	DILL	NUTMEG	PARMESAN grated
CINNAMON	GARLIC powder, salt	ONION powder, salt	SWEET BASIL dried
CURRY powder	GINGER ground	OREGANO dried	TARRAGON dried

GARLIC - rub the Bread slices with a GARLIC CLOVE before cutting them into cubes.

CLARIFIED BUTTER

Cut Butter into patties. Melt it over low heat, do not brown. Turn off heat.
Skim and discard the foam off the top.

DRIED FRUIT - Soak in APPLE CIDER or JUICE, TEA, or BROTH. Add BRANDY or RUM.

EGG WASH GLAZE   Beat 1 EGG with 1 TB Water or Milk. Before baking, brush it on Pastry.

FAT - REMOVING IT FROM A LIQUID SURFACE

When Stock is warm, float on its surface large LETTUCE LEAVES. Cool. Refrigerate.
The fat clings to the lettuce. Remove when it has cooled and hardened.
Or freeze the Stock for an hour or two.. Remove the Fat with a slotted spoon.
To remove slight Fat from a sauce or stew: when still warm, crumple a paper towel,
hold it over the liquid surface and absorb the fat. It may take several paper towels.

FETA CHEESE *(before refrigerating)*

Place the Feta in a plastic container to store it in BRINE: prevents it from drying.
Measure how many cups of bottled Water you are adding until the Feta is covered.
Add 1-1/4 teaspoons of SALT for every cup of Water to maintain saltiness balance.
If you want it less salty, use less Salt in the water. Water draws Salt from the Feta.

GARLIC   To peel, mash the clove with the flat side of a knife. The skin comes off easily.

8

GARLIC OIL   For frying and Salads.

> Pour the Oil in a jar. Per 1/2-cup add 3 cloves Garlic. Seal, refrigerate at least 1 day.

GRATED CHEESE

> HARD CHEESE - use a fine-grate blade.
> SEMI SOFT CHEESE - use a coarse-grate blade, or a shredder blade.
> Rinse utensils in cold water first. Hot water will melt Cheese on them.

HONEY   Loosen crystallized Honey by putting the jar in a bowl and let hot water run over it.

NUTS   SKINNED: Blanch a minute or two. Pinch Almond skins, the Almond will pop out.

> ALMOND PURÉE: Soak for 15 minutes a 1/2-cup of blanched Almonds in a 1/2-cup of boiling water. Pour Almonds and water in blender. Blend at high speed into a purée.

> TOASTED: Preheat oven to 350°. Spread the Nuts in a shallow baking pan.
> Sprinkle with dry Seasoning, optional.   Bake until golden, 7-to-10 minutes. Stir once.
> Or, toast in a hot skillet over medium heat, stirring the Nuts.

ONIONS   Onion rings that hang down on a fork are awkward to eat. I halve or quarter them,
> then thinly slice them. If rings are needed, use small or medium size Onions.

ORANGE and GRAPEFRUIT

> With a sharp or paring knife slice off the peel at both ends.
> Sit fruit on a plate or board. Slice away the peel and white pith from top to bottom.
> Trim off any pith that's left after peeling. The fruit is ready for slicing.
> Wedges: use a sharp knife to cut them away from either side of the membrane.
> After removing the wedges, squeeze the membrane to collect the juice.

OVEN   Unless otherwise instructed, always bake on middle rack of oven.
> BAKING DISHES: use a size to fit the Meat. It avoids juice from spreading and drying.
> GLASS OVEN DISHES - if refrigerated, bring to room temperature, before baking.

PARMESAN   Do not buy it already grated, it usually is not of the best quality.

> Buy a good piece, wrap it in wax paper, store in a container, refrigerate.
> Grate when needed. When all the Cheese has been grated, do not discard the rind.
> Cut it up into pieces and use them in soups or stews, then discard.

PASTA   Uncooked: 2 ounces per person (as a main course). Or according to appetites.

1.   Cook Pasta in a large pot of salted boiling water over high heat. It prevents it from sticking together. Per quart of water use 1 teaspoon of Salt for 4 ounces of Pasta. To avoid overflowing, do not fill the pot with water to the brim. Leave about one inch. Cook partially covered to avoid overflowing and stir the Pasta once in a while. Never break long Pasta. Put it in boiling water, bend it with a wooden spoon.

2.   "Al dente" means the Pasta should be firm to the bite. Cooking time depends on the type and cooking directions on the package. To avoid overcooking, test by tasting it. When draining the Pasta, save a 1/2-cup of the Water. You may need it to moisten the Pasta or to thin the Pasta Sauce. Pasta must be served immediately.

3   ADDING OIL to the cooking Water is acceptable only if Pasta is served plain. Sauce won't stick to oily Pasta. It'll run off the Pasta and end up at the bottom of the dish. ADD OIL to partially cook Lasagne, Manicotti, large Shells. This will prevent them from sticking, as you handle them.

FRESH PASTA   Add a little Olive Oil to the water to prevent it from sticking together.

PECANS and WALNUTS in SALADS

Add them before serving. If they remain in the Salad too long, they may discolor into the mayonnaise or onto ingredients like apples or endives.

PIE CRUST SHELL - FROZEN and UNCOOKED

You can either bake it in its aluminum pan or proceed as follows:

Transfer to a mold   Invert the frozen Crust on wax paper, thaw 5-to-10 minutes.

Remove the pan. Carefully invert the Crust. Put it in an oven-proof pie dish or pan with a removable base, that fits the Crust shape and size.
Let it thaw completely for 10 more minutes. It will soften. Shape it into the dish.
Leave enough dough around to cover the edge. Freeze until ready to bake.

To bake the empty Pie Crust Shell   -   Stick it randomly a few times with a fork.

Line the Crust base with foil or wax paper. Fill with dried beans.
Place it on a cookie sheet and bake according to package directions.
After 10 minutes take it out of the oven. Gather the liner around the beans and lift them out. Return to oven and bake to a golden brown.

RADISHES as garnish   In the shape of a flower.

Trim greens, wash thoroughly. Cut deep incisions from top to bottom. Or petals around the radish. Soak them in cold water until they open up.

RICE   To loosen sticky Rice, like Chinese, steam it. Loosen it with a fork as it steams. For the recipes in this book, the amount of Liquid used to cook the Rice is based on the Uncle Ben's Rice chart. For other brands, always consult their chart.

SEEDS   Like Cardamon, Celery, Dill, Fennel. Toast in a skillet for about 2 minutes.

SKEWERS

Bamboo: to prevent them from burning in the oven or on the grill, soak them in water for 30 minutes before threading the Ingredients.
Metal: oil slightly for Ingredients not to stick to them during baking or grilling.

SKILLET MEASUREMENTS

The ones given in the recipes are for the base diameter. Top diameters vary according to side inclination: a 10-inch Frittata is the size of the base diameter.

SLICED COLD MEATS - JULIENNE

Stack the slices and roll them. Slice the roll thinly to obtain thin strips.

SPOONS   Use wooden ones to cook. Not metal. It will scratch pots and skillets.

STRAWBERRIES

Wash them first, then remove the stems. Rinse once more.
They get soggy if they stay in a juice too long.

VANILLA SUGAR   For 1 pound of Regular Sugar.

Mix in 2 or 3 Vanilla Pod seeds. Seal tightly. Allow 4 or 5 days for flavors to blend.

IMPORTANT - Keep a note-pad in the kitchen to jot down amounts to remember.

I

BASIC RECIPES

A BASIC RECIPE is a formula.

As long as you stick to the formula,

you can add any Fillings or Seasonings you wish.

A BOUQUET GARNI

Is a fresh Herb bunch tied in cheesecloth
and removed after the cooking is done.

Usually it will include 1 or 2 sprigs of Parsley,
a sprig of Thyme and a Bay Leaf.

Other Herbs can be used, as well as a Garlic clove.

"There is no love sincerer than the love of food."

George Bernard Shaw

BASIC RECIPES

ASPIC

An Aspic is a jellied dish in a molded shape. It is made with Clarified Stock and Gelatine.

THE STOCK FISH, CLAM JUICE, SEAFOOD, CHICKEN, MEAT, VEGETABLE JUICE or BROTH.
Or a combination of Stock and Juice.
It must be completely degreased and clarified with Egg White and Egg Shell.
Strained through a fine sieve lined with 4 or 5 layers of damp cheesecloth.

Optional Add DRY SHERRY, WHITE WINE, MADEIRA WINE or VERMOUTH.

Sweet Aspics are prepared with FRUIT JUICE.

THE FILLING Chicken, Cured Meats, Fish, Seafood, Poached Eggs, Vegetables, Fruit.

ASPIC STOCK PREPARATION

CLARIFYING THE STOCK   *Yields 4 cups of Aspic Stock*

Heat	[4-1/4 cups	STOCK degreased, seasoned, strained
Wash	[1	EGG
Break and separate	[	White and Yolk (discard the yolk)
Crush	[	Egg shell into bits
Slightly beat	[	Egg White mix shell bits into it

Stir EGG White and Shell into the hot Stock or Broth.
Bring slowly to boiling point, stirring constantly with a wire whip.
When boiling point has been reached, stop stirring. Let the Stock simmer for 3 minutes.

The Egg will rise to the surface. Turn off heat. Let stand for 15-to-20 minutes.
Strain through a fine sieve lined with 4 layers of damp cheesecloth.
Approximately a 1/4-cup of Stock will evaporate.

NOTE - To obtain 2 cups of Clarified Stock: use as above 1 EGG and 2-1/4 cups of STOCK.

THE WINE	Add to the	[	CLARIFIED STOCK
	Optional, to taste	[	DRY SHERRY, DRY WHITE WINE, MADEIRA WINE, or VERMOUTH

ADDING THE GELATINE	Dissolve in a	[1/2-cup	cold CLARIFIED STOCK
		[2 TB	UNFLAVORED GELATINE
	Bring to boiling point	[3-1/2 cups	CLARIFIED STOCK

Stir into the boiling Stock the 1/2-cup of
Stock with the Gelatine.
Mix well. Turn off heat. Add Seasonings.
Cool before using in Aspic preparations.

For 2 cups of Clarified Stock dissolve in	[1/2-cup	cold CLARIFIED STOCK
	[1 TB	UNFLAVORED GELATINE
Mix it into	[1-1/2 cups	hot CLARIFIED STOCK

ASPIC STOCK WITH CANNED BROTH OR BOUILLON

Canned CHICKEN BROTH is greasy. It is also salty. Use FAR FREE and lightly salted.

Canned BEEF BROTH or BOUILLON is clear, Fat Free and salty.
With Water added, it can be used for Aspic Stock and does not need to be clarified.

Per 2 cups of BROTH: dissolve in a   [1/2-cup   cold BROTH
                                             [1 TB   UNFLAVORED GELATINE

                             Heat [1-1/2 cups   BROTH

When the Broth is hot, add the cold Broth with Gelatine. Stir. Set aside to cool before using.

ASPIC - MOLDED PREPARATION

Measure in cups the content of mold or ramekins. Plan accordingly amount of ASPIC STOCK and FILLING. About 1/3-Stock, the rest for the Filling. Or to taste.

Line the bottom of the mold with Aspic Stock: 1/4-inch deep. Refrigerate until set.

Arrange on top decoratively a layer of Ingredients. It will be the top of the Aspic.
Pour a little Aspic Stock over it. Refrigerate until set.

Repeat adding Ingredients and Aspic Stock. Refrigerate after each layer, until set.
Cover mold(s) with foil or plastic wrap. Refrigerate. Prepare a day ahead.

To UNMOLD   Place mold(s) for a few seconds in hot water. Set on a towel and dry.
Cover with an inverted plate(s). Grasp plate and mold, invert.
Lift the mold. If Aspic doesn't slide out, rap the plate on the counter.
Or cover the mold for a minute with a hot wet towel. Or return to hot water.

GARNISH THE ASPIC and (optional) fill the center of the jellied mold with creamy Salad or other.

ASPIC as a GARNISH

Spread in an ice-cube tray a layer, 1/2-inch deep, of ASPIC STOCK. Refrigerate until stiff.

Cut the Aspic into dice about a 1/2-inch in size. For smaller dice, spread a thinner layer.

ASPIC with TOMATO JUICE, V 8 JUICE or BLOODY MARY MIX

                            Stir into [1/2-cup of   cold JUICE
                                       [1 TB   UNFLAVORED GELATINE

   In a saucepan, over medium low heat, heat [1-1/2 cups of JUICE

When it simmers, add the Juice/Gelatine.
Set aside to cool before using .
                            Add any of [to taste   SALT, PEPPER, CELERY SALT
                                        [WORCESTERSHIRE SAUCE
                                        [TABASCO, LEMON JUICE
Use the JELLIED JUICE to prepare Aspics.

BROTH and STOCK

Use a large Pasta Cooker which comes with a removable strainer, or a wire basket that fits into your stockpot. Solids are thus easy to separate from Liquid.

CHICKEN BROTH

For a lean Broth, remove skin and fat. Wash and dry the Chicken with paper towels. Make sure there are enough bones with the meat.

Yields 5-to-5/12 cups after evaporation

Combine in the saucepan	[1 lb	CHICKEN cut into large pieces
	[1 medium	CARROT cut into large chunks
	[1 small	ONION quartered
	[1 rib	CELERY cut up
	[2 sprigs	PARSLEY or a BOUQUET GARNI
	[7 cups	WATER
	[4-to-6	PEPPERCORNS or to taste
Optional	[1 or 2	GARLIC CLOVES
	[a pinch	SALT (add more with recipe)

Bring to a boil then reduce heat to low.
Cover and simmer for about 3 hours or until the Chicken falls apart from the bone.
First hour skim foam, scum with a fine mesh strainer every 15 minutes, then every half hour.

When the Broth is ready, turn off heat and let it stand until cool.
Remove strainer or wire basket with the Chicken/Vegetables, let it drain over a bowl.
Set over another bowl a fine sieve lined with 3 layers of damp cheesecloth. Strain the Broth as well as the one drained from the Chicken. Discard solids.

Cover the bowl, refrigerate overnight. The next day skim solidified Fat.

For small quantities when needed, freeze in ice cube trays

COURT-BOUILLON for POACHED FISH and SEAFOOD

Combine in a saucepan	[2 cups	WATER
	[2/3-cup	DRY WHITE WINE or GOOD RED
	[1 medium	ONION finely sliced
	[1 small rib	CELERY chopped
	[1 small	CARROT thinly sliced
	[1/4-tp	SALT
Add a BOUQUET GARNI of	[2 sprigs	PARSLEY, 3 sprigs THYME
	[1	BAY LEAF, 2 or 3 PEPPERCORNS

Bring to a boil, then reduce heat to low, cover and simmer for about 30 minutes.
Strain through a fine sieve lined with three layers of damp cheesecloth. Discard solids.

POACHING   Half-fill a skillet with cool Court-Bouillon. Add 2 or 3 slices of peeled Lemon.
Place the Fish in it. It must not be submerged with the Liquid.
Bring to a simmer, continue to simmer until the Fish is cooked. Cooking time
will depend on thickness of Fish. Baste it with Court-Bouillon as it simmers.

WITHOUT WINE   Use instead: 3 cups WATER + 3 TB WHITE WINE VINEGAR.

FISH STOCK   *4-1/2-to-5 cups after evaporation*

Use a Pasta Cooker with a removable strainer, or a wire basket that fits into your stockpot.
Wash in a colander under cold water, head, bones and trimmings from a lean Fish (not oily).

In the stockpot, bring to a simmer	[1 lb	FISH TRIMMINGS
with	[6 cups	COLD WATER
or	[5 cups	COLD WATER
	[1 cup	WHITE WINE

Skim foam and scum.

After 10 minutes add	[4	PEPPERCORNS
	[1 small	ONION or LEEK coarse-chopped
	[1 small	CARROT 1/2-inch pieces
	[1	CELERY STALK 1/2-inch pieces
	[1 sprig	PARSLEY
	[3 slices	LEMON peeled
	[1	BAY LEAF
	[a pinch	SALT (add more with recipe)

Bring to a boil. Reduce heat to low, cover leaving a slit for the steam to escape.
Simmer for 45 minutes. Skim froth and scum until liquid is clear.
Let cool. Drain the strainer with the Fish over a bowl.

Set over another bowl a fine sieve lined with 3 layers of damp cheesecloth.
Strain the Stock, as well as the Stock drained from solids. Discard solids.

SPEEDY FISH STOCK

Bring to a boil	[2 cups	WATER
	[1 cup	CLAM JUICE
	[1 small	ONION quartered

Reduce heat to low, simmer for about 30 minutes. Strain and cool. Season according to recipe.

LOBSTER STOCK   *4-1/2-to-5 cups after evaporation*

When cooking Lobster, save, shells, coral and trimmings. Dining out, bring them home!
Crush the shells, freeze them with trimmings, until you are ready to make the Stock.

In a heavy saucepan, sauté in	[2 TB	BUTTER
	[1 medium	ONION coarsely chopped
	[1 small	CARROT thinly sliced
When Onion is translucent, add	[3 cups	SHELLS, CORAL, trimmings
	[sprinkle	SALT, GROUND BLACK PEPPER
Sauté Shells until Onion begins to		
brown, then add	[2/3-cup	DRY WHITE WINE
or any of	[4 TB	DRY SHERRY, BRANDY, COGNAC
Stir until Liquor evaporates, and add	[6 cups	COLD WATER
	[1	BAY LEAF, a dash CAYENNE

Bring to a slow boil. Reduce heat to low.
Cover leaving a slit for steam to escape. Simmer for 1-1/2 hours. Turn off heat, let cool.

Strain the Stock through 3 layers of damp cheesecloth, crushing Shells with a wooden spoon.
Store the Stock in a sealed container. Freeze until ready to use. Season according to recipe.

SHRIMP STOCK   *4 cups after evaporation*

When you prepare Shrimp, freeze the Shells, cooked or raw. Use them to prepare a Stock.

In a heavy saucepan, sauté in	[2 TB	BUTTER + 1 tp VEGETABLE OIL
	[1 small	ONION coarsely chopped
	[1 small	CARROT thinly sliced
When Onion is translucent, add	[2 cups	SHRIMP SHELLS crushed
		(1 lb shells = about 2 cups)
Sauté until Onion begins to brown, then add	[1/2-tp	SALT, PEPPER to taste
	[2/3-cup	DRY WHITE WINE
Stir until Wine entirely evaporates, then add	[5 cups	COLD WATER

Bring to a slow boil. Reduce heat to low. Simmer for 1 hour. Turn off heat, let Stock cool.
Strain the Stock through a fine sieve lined with 3 layers of damp cheesecloth.
Crush the Shells with a wooden spoon, squeezing out the Stock. Let stand until well drained.
Store in a sealed container. Refrigerate or freeze.

SIMPLE SHRIMP BROTH   *2 cups after evaporation*

Empty into a small saucepan	[1 can	CHICKEN BROTH
Add	[1-1/2 cans	WATER
	[1 oz	SHRIMP SHELLS
Optional	[to taste	DRY WHITE WINE or BRANDY

Bring to a boil, reduce heat to low, simmer for 45 minutes. Taste, add Salt and Pepper.
Let the Broth cool. Drain through a sieve lined with cheese cloth. Use for Rice or Sauces.

MEAT STOCK   *4-to-4-1/2 cups after evaporation*

Bring to a boil, simmer over medium heat	[1/2-lb	BONES cut into 3-inch pieces
	[1/2-lb	LEAN MEAT, TRIMMINGS cut up
	[6 cups	COLD WATER

Remove scum with a fine mesh strainer.

When scum ceases to rise, add	[1 small	ONION cut in half
	[1 medium	CARROT scraped, cut into chunks
	[1 small	CELERY STALK cut into chunks
	[2	SPRIGS PARSLEY
	[4 to 6	PEPPERCORNS or to taste
	[1	BAY LEAF
	[1/2-tp	SALT
	[1 or more	GARLIC CLOVE(S) optional

Add Water, if needed, to cover by 1-inch.
Bring to a boil then simmer for 3-to-4 hours. Keep removing the scum to prevent a build-up.
Do not allow the liquid to boil as it alters the flavor. Keep covered partially
As Liquid evaporates, add cold Water to keep ingredients covered by 1-inch.
Cool. Strain. Refrigerate. Degrease if needed

BROWN STOCK

In the stock pot, sear and brown BONES and MEAT. Add and brown ONION. Proceed as above.

CRÊPES

A nonstick skillet   - 6-to-6-1/4 inches at its base. For a larger Crêpe use an 8-inch skillet.

To prepare the skillet   - Melt in it 1/4-tp BUTTER. Spread and wipe it off with a paper towel.

Measuring the Batter   6-to-6-1/4 inch Crêpe   = 3 TB of Batter   Add 1 TB for a thicker Crêpe
                              8-inch Crêpe   = 4 TB   Add 1 TB

Measure 3 TB of Batter in a shot glass. Mark off the measure with a thin stroke of nail polish.
Fill the shot glass from the Batter in the blender as you make the Crêpes. Use a small ladle.
For 4 or 5 TB of Batter, use a small glass and mark off the measure in the same way.

To freeze or refrigerate Crêpes - For each Crêpe cut a piece of wax paper into a 6-inch square.

To freeze   You must brown the Crêpes on both sides. If not, the wax paper will stick to
                  the un-browned side, and will tear the Crêpes when you remove it.

                  Spread on a plate or flat surface a sheet of foil, big enough to wrap the Crêpes.
                  Place in its center a square of wax paper. Place on it the Crêpe. Top it with
                  another square of wax paper. Repeat until all the Crêpes are in a stack.

                  Fold the foil carefully into a package. Place it in a plastic box, seal and freeze
                  Or use a disposable aluminum pie pan. Wrap it with heavy foil to freeze it.

To refrigerate   Place package of newly-made Crêpes in the refrigerator until ready to use.

To thaw   Unwrap the foil. Let frozen Crêpes thaw at room temperature.

The Filling   Prepare it first if you intend to fill the Crêpes as you make them.
                  Or stack them with wax paper in between. Fill them right away.

DESSERT CRÊPES   Must be browned on both sides.

BASIC RECIPE

Batter yields about 2-1/4 cups for 12 Crêpes, using 3 TB of batter for a 6-to-6-1/4 inch Crêpe.

Mix in a blender   [1-1/4 cups   MILK cold or room temperature
                        [3/4-cup   FLOUR all purpose
                        [1 large   EGG
                        [2   EGG YOLKS
                        [1 TB + 1 tp   BUTTER melted
                        [a pinch   SALT (SUGAR for sweet Crêpes)

Make Crêpes as soon as Batter is blended.
If you are making them later, refrigerate the Batter in the blender. Blend again before using.

1.   Heat the greased skillet over medium heat. Pour the Measure of Batter into it.
        Tilt the skillet, roll the Batter quickly around, covering the base. It will cook fast.
        When the edges begin to brown, loosen them around with a thin rubber spatula.

2.   Shake the skillet to loosen the Crêpe. Lift with the spatula, check underside.
        When golden brown, slide the Crêpe to the edge of the skillet. Pick it up with
        your fingers, flip it. Brown a few seconds. Or use a large spatula to flip it.

3.   Slide the Crêpe onto a plate or on a cool surface. At this point you can fill it, or
        keep making the Crêpes. If the skillet gets dry, grease it again lightly.

FILLING CRÊPES

THE FILLING   2-1/4 cups of FILLING makes 12 Crêpes of 6-to-6-1/4 inches in diameter.

After preparing the Filling, cover its surface with plastic wrap to prevent it from drying. Refrigerate for 2 or 3 hours, or overnight. The Filling is easier to work with when cold.

Use 2-1/2 to 3 TB of Filling per Crêpe.

1.   An oven-proof dish 11-3/4 x 7-1/2 x 1-3/4, will hold 2 rows of 12 filled Crêpes. Brush the dish with melted Butter, or spray it with a mist of Cooking Spray.

2.   With a knife split the Filling in four. Use each quarter for a quarter of the Crêpes.

3.   Set the Crêpe on a plate. Spread the Filling across at 1-1/2 inches from bottom edge. Leave 1-inch on the sides.
Fold in left and right sides. Fold bottom over the Filling. Roll towards the top.

4.   Place Crêpes in the oven-proof dish, seam side down, facing the same direction. Their long sides barely touching each other. Slightly flatten each Crêpe.
Wrap foil tightly over the dish. Refrigerate. (Can be prepared a day ahead).

To heat   Bring the dish to room temperature. Do not remove the foil.
Heat in oven preheated to 300° for 15-to-20 minutes, or according to Filling.

To serve   Remove the foil, serve hot. Optional: top with a Sauce or serve on the side.

Crêpes with a WHITE SAUCE or CHEESE TOPPING: heat them in the oven. Remove the foil. Pass under the broiler, brown lightly.

VARIATIONS

HERB CRÊPES   Add to batter   [1 tp or more   minced PARSLEY, CHIVES, HERBS, other

[a pinch   CAYENNE, CURRY POWDER, CHILI POWDER, CUMIN, GROUND GINGER, PAPRIKA

SWEET CRÊPES   [a pinch   GROUND CINNAMON or GINGER, or to taste

GIANT CRÊPE

1.   Preheat oven to 350°. Grease lightly a baking tray or large oven-proof skillet.

2.   Spread the Crêpe batter in it. Bake until sides touching the pan turn golden brown. Watch it, it bakes fast.

3.   Slide the Crêpe on a board. Add the Filling. Fold in the sides and roll.
Or spread the Filling all over the Crêpe, fold in the sides and roll.

Fillings   - LEFTOVERS. Top with a Sauce.

Sweet Fillings - FRUIT, FRUIT PRESERVES or SAUCE, WHIPPED CREAM, CHOCOLATE MOUSSE.

Top with   - SYRUP, BERRIES, BUTTERSCOTCH, CONFECTIONER'S SUGAR.

20

CROQUETTES

BÉCHAMEL BASE   [1-3/4-to-2 cups   cooked MEATS or FISH
                           [1 cup   VERY THICK BÉCHAMEL   (see "SAUCES")
                           [1 EGG   + 2 YOLKS

POTATO BASE   [see "VEGETABLES"   POTATOES

SHAPING and FRYING with a BÉCHAMEL BASE

Refrigerate the Croquette Mixture. When cold, form the Croquettes.
Shapes: small balls (hors-d'oeuvres), 2-inch cylinders (appetizer size), patties or flat cakes.

In a bowl beat [1   EGG   Put in a plate   [FLOUR
         with [1 TB   MILK   In another plate   [BREADCRUMBS

Roll the Croquettes in Flour. Shake off excess. Dip in beaten Egg. Roll in Breadcrumbs.
Place on a cookie sheet. Allow to dry. Cover with plastic wrap, refrigerate until ready to fry.
Deep fry in hot VEGETABLE OIL (390°) to a golden brown. Drain on paper towels.

SHAPING and FRYING with a POTATO BASE

Refrigerate Croquette Mixture. Shape into small balls (hors-d'oeuvres) or cylinders.
Or small Patties the size of a 1/2-inch thick silver dollar. Place them on a cookie sheet.

In a bowl beat [1   EGG   Put in a plate   [FLOUR
         with [1 TB   VEGETABLE OIL   In another plate   [BREADCRUMBS

Roll the Croquettes in Flour. Shake off excess. Dip in beaten Egg. Roll in Breadcrumbs.
Place them on a cookie sheet. Cover with plastic wrap and refrigerate until ready to fry.

DEEP FRY   Small Croquettes in hot oil (390°) to a golden brown. Drain on paper towels.
                  Large Potato Croquettes will absorb a lot of Oil.

SKILLET FRY   Skillet-fried Patties absorb less Oil. Heat VEGETABLE OIL - 1/4-inch deep.
                  Fry the Patties on both sides to a golden brown. Drain on paper towels.
                  When adding more Oil, wait until it is very hot before adding more Croquettes.

Croquette recipes see FISH, SEAFOOD, CHICKEN, HAM, BEEF, POTATO.

CROSTINI and BRUSCHETTA   (bruce-ketta)

CROSTINI
                          Cut diagonally   [BAGUETTE into 1/4-inch thick slices
Lay it on cookie sheet. Brush or sprinkle with   [EXTRA-VIRGIN OLIVE OIL
             Optional, rub first with a   [GARLIC CLOVE

Bake at 350°. Turn, color both sides to golden brown. Crostini must be crisp through.
Add Toppings: Vegetables, Fish, Seafood, Cured Meats. Serve as Hors-d' oeuvres.

BRUSCHETTA   - Use Ciabatta or any other Bread. Cut slices, 1/2-to-3/4-inch thick.
                   - Brush or sprinkle with the Olive Oil on both sides. Bake as the Crostini.
                   - The Bread should be crisp golden brown on both sides, soft in the middle.
                   - Add Toppings. Serve as a snack, or even as a light meal.

EGGS

HARD-COOKED   To obtain a bright yellow yolk without a greenish circle around it:

- Place the Eggs in a saucepan and cover them with cold water.
- Leave saucepan uncovered and bring the water to a boil.
- As soon as the water boils, turn off heat and cover with a lid.
- Leave the Eggs in for <u>exactly 15 minutes.</u>
- Pour out the water. Run cold water over the Eggs. Peel when cool.

Never cook EGGS over high heat.

SOFT-COOKED   Bring the Eggs to room temperature.

- Place enough water in a saucepan to cover the Eggs. Bring to a boil.
- With a spoon lower each Egg into the water. Turn off heat. Cover.
- Let Eggs stand from 4-to-6 minutes, according to desired doneness.

POACHED   If you do not have an egg poacher: break each Egg into a saucer or cup.

- Fill a saucepan with Water 3 inches deep. Add per quart 1 TB Vinegar.
- Bring Water to a simmer. Slide the Eggs, one at a time, into the Water.
- With a wooden spoon, gently fold the white over the yolk to cover it.
- Simmer 4 minutes. Remove with skimmer/slotted spoon. Serve at once.

<u>For later use</u> - Before poaching have ready a bowl of COLD WATER.

- Lift poached Egg with skimmer or slotted spoon, slide it into the WATER.
- The poached Eggs may remain in the Cold Water until needed.

<u>For a neat shape</u> - Such as filling Aspics or Artichoke Bottoms:

Lay poached Egg on a cutting board, pat dry with paper towel. Use a knife
to trim the white around it. Set it on a plate, or in cold Water, refrigerate.

<u>To reheat</u> - Bring poached Eggs to room temperature.

- With slotted spoon lower the Eggs into a saucepan of <u>simmering water</u>
  (not boiling), for 30 seconds to 1 minute, remove with the slotted spoon.
- Holding the Egg in the slotted spoon, pat it dry with a paper towel.

SCRAMBLED   Beat the Eggs with a fork.

- Add Milk: 1 TB per Egg. With Cream: 1 TB per 2 Eggs.   Add Seasonings.
- Melt Butter (1 tp per Egg) in a nonstick skillet. Or use Vegetable Oil.
- To cook the Eggs evenly, skillet must be wide enough to stir them around.
- Add the Eggs, cook over low heat. With a flexible spatula stir, fluff them.
- Pull in from the sides until the Eggs thicken into creamy soft curds.

SHIRRED   <u>Method 1</u>   Place oven rack at top of oven. Preheat oven to 500°.

In shallow oven-proof individual dishes spread [Cooked Ingredients like BEANS, VEGETABLES
                                              [Garnishes like shredded CHEESE, SAUCE
                          Break on top [1 or 2   EGGS
                            Top with [a little   melted BUTTER, SALT, PEPPER

Bake on top rack of oven until the Eggs are set: 4-1/2-to-5 minutes.

            <u>Method 2</u>   Bake the Eggs in a slow oven: 250° to 300°, on the middle rack.

DEVILED EGGS

BASIC FILLING

For	[2	HARD-COOKED EGG YOLKS
start with	[1/2-TB	MAYONNAISE
	[1/4-tp	MUSTARD or to taste
To taste	[minced	ONION, CHIVES, PICKLES, CAPERS
	[to taste	CAYENNE, CURRY, PAPRIKA, HERBS
	[to taste	CHILI SAUCE, KETCHUP, SOY SAUCE
		TABASCO, WORCESTERSHIRE, other

Mince and add to taste any of:

[ANCHOVIES, CAVIAR, SHRIMP,
[SMOKED SALMON, TUNA

[HAM, PROSCIUTTO, SALAMI

Add to Mayonnaise, or substitute Mayonnaise with   [CREAM CHEESE, MASCARPONE, SOUR CREAM

For a coarse texture, mash with a fork. Use about 1-1/2 TB of FILLING per Egg half.
For a smooth Purée, use a processor. With a pastry bag, pipe the Purée into the Egg Whites.

PLAIN OMELET

Beat with a dinner fork, into a shallow bowl	[2	EGGS
	[a pinch	SALT and PEPPER
	[to taste	HERBS and OTHER SEASONINGS
Optional	[1 tp	WATER or MILK
For a sweet Omelet	[1 TB	GRANULATED SUGAR

Heat a 4-1/2-to-5-inch heavy nonstick skillet,
then, over medium heat, add [1/2-TB   BUTTER (up to 1 TB, to taste)

1. When the Butter sizzles, swirl it around to coat the skillet, do not let it brown.
    Pour in the Eggs. Swirl the Eggs and tilt the skillet to coat it evenly with the Eggs.
    With a fork, scramble lightly to fluff the Eggs.

2. Then with a spatula lift the edges to allow uncooked Eggs to flow underneath.
    The Omelet is ready when underside is golden and the center creamy and fluffy.
    NOTE: do not brown an Omelet. It should be pale to a very light golden yellow.

3. Run the spatula around the Omelet to separate the cooked edges from the skillet.

4. Tilt the skillet away from you. With the spatula fold over one half of the Omelet.
    Tilt the skillet and slide the Omelet onto a warm plate.
    OPTIONAL: sprinkle a little grated or shredded Cheese over the top, then fold.

    Fold in three a large Omelet: fold left side to the center; right side to the center.
    Tilt the skillet to turn the Omelet upside down onto the plate.

    Also see FRUIT - SOUFFLÉ OMELET in the chapter "FRUIT and FRUIT DESSERTS".

OMELET with FILLINGS

For a 2 Egg Omelet use 1/3-to-1/2 cup of Filling

When the surface is creamy, spread the Filling evenly on one half of the Omelet.
Fold the plain half of the Omelet, as in Step 4 above, over the Filling.
Or center the Filling and fold in three.

Gently slide the Omelet to the center of the skillet by tilting it or using the spatula.
Allow the Filling to get hot, Cheese to melt. Turn off heat, let set for a few seconds.

FONDUES

A FONDUE is a casual way to entertain. Conversations become lively around the Fondue Pot.

The Fondue is cooked in the Pot. It is then brought piping hot to the table and placed on the Metal Stand over the Heating Unit. The Sterno candle isn't enough to keep the Fondue hot after many "Dunks". During the dinner, you may have to return the Pot to the stove.

THE FONDUE SET includes:

A FONDUE POT	- heat resistant.
A METAL STAND	- which supports the Cooking Pot and HEATING UNIT.
A HEATING UNIT	- select CANNED HEAT, such as a STERNO candle.
A TRAY	- to hold the set and prevent drippings on your table.
FONDUE FORKS	- 10-to-11-inches long, for each one of your guests.

THE TABLE SETTING   Use a washable tablecloth, individual plates and fondue forks.
For a buffet table Fondue, use disposable bamboo skewers.

THE "DUNKS"   Fish, Seafood, Meats, Poultry, Breads, Vegetables cut into bite-size.
Arrange them in dishes within reach of the guests.
Dunks are speared on the Fondue Forks and swirled into the Fondue.

BASIC FONDUE RECIPE

1 lb	[	CHEESE diced or shredded, or a combination of Cheeses.
1-3/4-to-2 cups	[	LIQUID: any of: Wine, Beer, Ale, Champagne, Milk, canned Soup.
2 TB	[	CORNSTARCH or FLOUR.
Optional: 2-to-4 TB	[	any of: APPLEJACK, DRY RUM, KIRSCH, BOURBON, BRANDY, SHERRY
	[	SEASONINGS

The Cheese Crust "la religieuse" which sticks to the pot is delicious. Do not discard it.

CLASSIC CHEESE FONDUE   *Serves 4 to 5*

Mix in a bowl with	[2 TB	CORNSTARCH or FLOUR
Diced or shredded	[1 lb	GRUYÈRE or SWISS
Pour into the Fondue Pot	[2 cups	DRY WHITE WINE or CIDER
	[1	GARLIC CLOVE crushed
		(or rub the pot with it, discard)

Over medium heat, bring Wine to a simmer.
Simmer for 1 minute (do not boil).
Reduce heat to low.

| Remove Garlic, add | [1 TB | LEMON JUICE |

With a wooden spoon stir in the Cheese.
Adding it a handful at a time.

When the Fondue is smooth, stir in	[2 to 4 TB	KIRSCH to taste
Turn off heat and add	[to taste	NUTMEG grated
	[to taste	SALT, GROUND BLACK PEPPER
The "Dunks"	[	CRUSTY BAGUETTE, HAM, SAUSAGE

FONDUE VARIATIONS

Mix 2/3-of the semi-hard Gruyère with 1/3-of another Cheese.

SEMI-HARD CHEESES

APPENZELLER	GOUDA (smoked)	
CANTAL	GRUYÈRE	
CHEDDAR mild/sharp	MANCHEGO	
COLBY	MONTEREY	
EDAM	MONTEREY JACK	
EMMENTHAL	RACLETTE	
FONTINA	TILSIT	

HIGHLIGHT
amount to taste

BLEU DE BRESSE	PARMESAN
BLUE CHEESE	PECORINO
BOURSIN	ROMANO
CAMEMBERT	ROQUEFORT
DANISH BLUE	PROVOLONE
GORGONZOLA	STILTON

Mix Flour or Cornstarch with

CHILI POWDER
CREOLE SEASONING
CUMIN (ground)
CURRY POWDER
DRY MUSTARD

Season to taste with chopped or minced

BACON crumbled
CAPERS
CHIVES
CORNICHONS
DILL, BASIL, TARRAGON

GREEN ONIONS
HORSERADISH
JALAPEÑOS
ONION
WORCESTERSHIRE

Season with Cured Meats cooked, chopped

CHORIZO
HAM
PROSCIUTTO
SALAMI
SAUSAGE

Substitute Kirsch with

APPLE JACK   RUM dark, white
BRANDY   SHERRY
GRAPPA   TEQUILA
PEAR BRANDY   VODKA flavored

WINES

CHABLIS
NEUFCHATEL
RIESLING
SAUTERNE

Wine Substitutes

ALE
BEER
CIDER
GINGER ALE

CHAMPAGNE

Do not use any
other alcohol
with it.

To thin the Fondue, add gradually any of: (at room temperature)

WINE   -   MILK   -   LIGHT CREAM   -   BEER   -   CIDER   -   GINGER ALE

WELSH RAREBIT   A Beer/Cheddar Fondue   *Serves 4 to 5*

Mix	[2 TB	CORNSTARCH or FLOUR
with	[1/4-to-1/2 tp	DRY MUSTARD to taste
Mix Cornstarch/Mustard into	[1 lb	CHEDDAR mild, sharp, mixed
Pour into the Fondue Pot	[1-1/2 cups	BEER or ALE room temperature

Over medium heat, bring Beer to a simmer.
(Do not boil). Reduce heat to low.
With a wooden spoon stir in the Cheddar, a
handful at a time, until smooth.

Add	[to taste	WORCESTERSHIRE SAUCE
	[	PAPRIKA or CAYENNE, SALT

If needed, thin with a little Beer or Ale.

THE "DUNKS"   - BREADS, CURED MEATS, POULTRY, raw/cooked VEGETABLES, FRUIT.

Serve   - In a chafing dish, as a DIP, with TORTILLA CHIPS.
             - On hot CORN TORTILLAS spread with BEANS, AVOCADO, JALAPEÑOS.
             - On TOAST -   Broil until the Cheese is bubbly and the edges crisp.

As a SAUCE   - With Fish, Meats, Pancakes, Vegetables. Reduce recipe. Thin with Beer, Ale.

CARIBBEAN FONDUE

Serves 4 to 5

In a bowl, mix	[2 TB	CORNSTARCH or FLOUR
with	[1/2-tp	DRY MUSTARD
Then mix it into	[1 lb	CHEDDAR sharp, mild, mixed
Pour into the Fondue Pot	[2 cups	GINGER ALE room temperature

Over medium heat bring Ginger Ale to a simmer and add [1 TB LEMON JUICE

Reduce heat to low.
With a wooden spoon stir in the Cheddar,
a handful at a time, until smooth.

Add	[to taste	WORCESTERSHIRE SAUCE
	[2 TB	DARK RUM or more to taste
Turn off heat and add	[to taste	GROUND CINNAMON
	[	SALT, GROUND BLACK PEPPER

If too thick, add a little Ginger Ale.

The "DUNKS"

Meats and Seafood	CHICKEN TURKEY	HAM, SAUSAGE		BARBECUE PORK	LOBSTER SCALLOPS	SHRIMP
Vegetables and Fruit	AVOCADO CANTALOUPE	CARROTS braised HONEYDEW		MANGO POTATOES	PAPAYA PEARS	PINEAPPLE YAMS

CURRY FONDUE

Serves 4 to 5

Mix	[2 TB	CORNSTARCH
with to taste	[1 tp	CURRY POWDER mild, 1/2-tp hot
Stir the CURRY/CORNSTARCH into	[1/2-lb	SWISS shredded
mixed with	[1/2-lb	MANCHEGO or RACLETTE
Pour into Fondue Pot	[2 cups	DRY WHITE WINE or GINGER ALE
	[1 or 2	GARLIC CLOVES minced *(or rub the pot with it, discard)*

Over medium heat, bring Wine to a simmer
for 1 minute, reduce heat to low and add [1 TB LEMON JUICE

With a wooden spoon stir in the Cheese, a
handful at a time, until smooth.

Bring to a simmer and stir in	[1/2-tp	LEMON ZEST grated
	[2 TB	CHIVES
	[2 TB	COCONUT grated or flaked
	[	SALT, PEPPER, or CAYENNE

Turn off heat.

     Serve sprinkled with [COCONUT

The "DUNKS"

BEEF	SAUSAGE	BAY SCALLOPS	POTATOES	BROCCOLI sautéed	BANANA
LAMB	CHICKEN	SHRIMP	YAMS	CAULIFLOWER	MANGO
PORK	DUCK			EGGPLANT	PAPAYA
HAM	TURKEY	SOURDOUGH		MUSHROOM CAPS	PINEAPPLE

GORGONZOLA or BLUE CHEESE FONDUE   *Serves 4 to 5*

Serve as a side-dish with Steaks on the grill. Steam POTATOES and VEGETABLES.
Guests cut their own Vegetables and dunk them into the Fondue.

In a bowl, mix	[12 oz	SWISS diced or shredded
with	[4 oz	GORGONZOLA or BLUE CHEESE
		crumbled
Add	[3 TB	FLOUR
Rub Fondue Pot with	[1 clove	GARLIC and discard
Pour into it	[2 cups	DRY WHITE WINE

Over medium heat bring the Wine to a small
bubble. Reduce heat to low.

Add	[1 TB	LEMON JUICE

With a wooden spoon stir in the Cheese,
a handful at a time, until smooth

Bring to a simmer and stir in	[3 TB	PEAR BRANDY (like "Williams")
Turn off heat and add	[to taste	PEPPER, SALT if needed

SEAFOOD FONDUE   *Serves 4 to 5*

Mix	[2 TB	CORNSTARCH
with	[1/4-tp	CAYENNE PEPPER or to taste
Stir the Cornstarch into	[12 oz	SWISS diced or shredded
mixed with	[4 oz	CHEDDAR shredded
Rub the Fondue Pot with	[1 clove	GARLIC and discard
Add	[2 cups	DRY WHITE WINE

Over medium heat bring the Wine to a simmer
for 1 minute. Reduce heat to low.

Add	[1 TB	LEMON JUICE

With a wooden spoon stir in the Cheese,
a handful at a time, until smooth.

Bring to a simmer and stir in	[1 or 2 TB	BRANDY or to taste
	[1 TB	CHIVES
	[1/2-tp	DRIED TARRAGON optional

When smooth, turn off heat.

Add	[to taste	SALT and WHITE PEPPER

The "DUNKS"   - OYSTERS, CLAMS, MUSSELS, SCALLOPS, LOBSTER, SHRIMP.

- Steamed or sautéed   BROCCOLI, CAULIFLOWER, BRUSSELS SPROUTS,
CARROTS, MUSHROOMS, PEARL ONIONS.
- Boiled or steamed   POTATO chunks, NEW POTATOES, FINGERLINGS.

- Crusty BAGUETTE.

Optional   - Serve a green Salad on the side.

VARIATIONS   - Omit Cayenne, mix with Cornstarch 1/4-tp CREOLE SEASONING, or to taste.
or 1/4-tp SAFFRON THREADS crushed

FRITTATA

A thin flat omelet with added Ingredients.   It is cooked over low heat then passed under the broiler. Served hot, warm, at room temperature, as a light meal, or hors-d'oeuvre wedges.

Frittata skillets are available. They look like double skillets and allow you to flip the Frittata without having to pass it under the broiler.

<u>Use a heavy skillet with an oven-proof handle that can go under the broiler</u>

Skillet sizes	7 - 8 inches	for	2 EGGS	plus	other Ingredients
	9 "		3	+	
	10		4	+	
10 - 12			5 or 6	+	

Approximate way to calculate the amount of Ingredients

Eggs		Cooked Ingredients		Onion for flavor		Optional
		to		to		
For 2	use	3/4 - 1 cup	1	-	1-1/2 TB	To increase Egg volume
3		1 - 1-1/4	1-1/2	-	2	add to beaten Eggs:
4		1-1/2 - 1-3/4	2	-	3	
5		2 - 2-1/4	3	-	3-1/2	1 TB LIGHT CREAM
6		2-1/2 - 3	3-1/2	-	4	per 1 or 2 Eggs

Take into consideration the volume after cooking. Example: 1 cup of Onions = 1/2-cup cooked.

<u>BUTTER or OIL to cook the Frittata</u> -   or both: adding a little Oil prevents Butter from burning.

For a skillet:	7-to 8-inches	use	2 TB	10-inches	use	3 TB
	9-inches	-	2-1/2 TB	12-inches	-	3-1/2 TB

<u>CHEESE</u> -   Grated Cheese, beyond adding flavor, will bind and firm up the Frittata.

BASIC RECIPE

With Leftover CHINESE VEGETABLES

In a nonstick skillet, over medium heat, heat	[1 TB	VEGETABLE OIL
When a light haze forms, sauté	[1/4-cup	ONION finely chopped
When Onion begins to color, stir in	[2 cups	CHINESE VEGETABLES drained, coarsely chopped

Sauté for 1 minute. Drain in a sieve, let cool.
Preheat broiler.

In a bowl, whisk	[4 large	EGGS
When well blended, whisk in	[1/4-cup	CHEDDAR coarse-grated
	[1 TB	PARSLEY finely chopped
Add the CHINESE VEGETABLES and	[to taste	SALT, GROUND BLACK PEPPER

In a 10-inch skillet, over medium heat, heat	[2-1/2 TB	BUTTER + 1/2-TB OLIVE OIL

When it sizzles, add the EGG MIXTURE. Spread it evenly with a spatula. Reduce heat to low. Cook slowly to avoid burning the underside of the Frittata. It should be lightly browned. When the Eggs are almost set, the surface creamy, with a spatula loosen around the Frittata.

Place the skillet under the broiler, for 30 seconds or longer, to cook the top, brown it lightly. Slide the Frittata onto a platter. Serve hot, warm, at room temperature. Even cold.

GRATIN

A GRATIN   is a baked dish of raw or semi-cooked Ingredients, covered with a White Sauce, topped with grated Cheese, and/or Breadcrumbs, and dotted with Butter.

The crusty golden brown top is "THE GRATIN". It can be improved by passing it under the broiler. The Gratin takes longer to cook than the Gratinée.

A GRATINÉE   consists of cooked Ingredients, with/without White Sauce. Topped with Cheese, and/or Breadcrumbs, dotted with Butter, briefly baked, passed under the broiler.

BASIC GRATIN RECIPE - POTATO GRATIN DAUPHINOIS

Serves 4 to 6	[2 lbs	YUKON GOLD POTATOES
	[1/4-cup	MILK mixed with
	[1 cup	HEAVY CREAM
	[1 clove	GARLIC cut in half
	[2 slices	BUTTER 1/2-TB each slice
	[4 oz (1 cup)	SWISS CHEESE coarse-grated
Optional	[a dash	NUTMEG grated

THE POTATOES - Wash, peel. With a mandolin slice them 1/8-inch thick. Dry in a dish towel.
         - Do not soak in water. It would remove the starch needed to tie the Gratin.

THE DISH   - A 1-1/2 quart, 1-3/4 inch deep, baking dish.
         - Rub it well with the GARLIC CLOVE. Discard the Garlic.
         - Spray it with Cooking Spray or brush it lightly with melted Butter.
         - Do not fill to the top. Leave 1/3-inch of space to prevent overflow.

         - As you layer the POTATOES, sprinkle with SALT, PEPPER, 3/4-of the CHEESE.

THE GRATIN   - Preheat oven to 375°. Bring to a boil the MILK/CREAM. Add NUTMEG.
         - Pour it over the Potatoes. Smooth the top. Sprinkle remaining CHEESE.
         - Dot with the diced BUTTER. Let set 10-to-15 minutes before baking.
         - Can be prepared ahead, refrigerated. Bring to room temperature.
         - Bake 45 minutes to 1 hour, until Potatoes are tender, creamy, all Liquid has been absorbed and the top light golden brown. Optional, pass under broiler.

PAELLA

Speedy recipe. Serves 3

Heat	[2-1/4 cups	CHICKEN BROTH
Dissolve in it	[1/4-tp	SAFFRON THREADS or to taste
In a 10-to-12-inch cast-iron skillet heat	[2 TB	EXTRA-VIRGIN OLIVE OIL
Sauté	[1 medium	ONION finely chopped
When Onion softens, add	[2 cloves	GARLIC finely chopped
	[1 medium	RED BELL PEPPER diced
When Bell Pepper softens add	[1 cup	LONG GRAIN WHITE RICE
Stir and add	[2 medium	TOMATOES peeled, seeded, diced
Add the CHICKEN BROTH and	[1/2-cup	FROZEN PEAS

Bring to a boil. Cover reduce heat to low,
   simmer for 15 minutes then add any of   [raw SHRIMP, cooked CHORIZO, SAUSAGE, HAM
   When the Rice is cooked you can add   [cooked CLAMS, MUSSELS, PORK, CHICKEN

PHYLLO

A Greek and Middle Eastern dough, tissue-paper-thin, used to wrap Fillings, then baked and served as hors-d'oeuvre, appetizers, main courses, or desserts soaked in syrup.

Phyllo is available frozen. The one pound package contains about 22 sheets: 14 x 18 inches.

Before using, thaw the package at room temperature, for 1 hour. Or refrigerate 2-to-3 hours.

PHYLLO PREPARATION - FIRST FIVE STEPS

1. Melt in a small pan 3 or 4 tablespoons BUTTER. Melt more, if needed, as you go along,

2   Brush lightly a cookie sheet or baking dish with the BUTTER. Or use COOKING SPRAY.

3. Before unfolding the dough, dampen a dish towel or cloth.

4. Unfold the PHYLLO on a working surface, resting it on its wrapping paper.

    NOTE - PHYLLO dries fast and crumbles, cover it immediately with wax paper,
              and top the wax paper with the dampened towel or cloth.
          - Every time you remove a layer, cover the remaining Phyllo.

5. Place a sheet of PHYLLO on a pastry board.
    With a pastry brush, brush across lightly at random, with BUTTER.

    Do not brush the whole surface, it would make it too greasy.

    Top with a second sheet of Phyllo. Repeat as needed, brushing randomly with Butter.

PHYLLO ROLLS - APPETIZER SIZE

The size of an egg roll but puffier - about 2-1/2-to-3 TB of Filling

1. Follow the FIRST FIVE STEPS of the PHYLLO PREPARATION.

2. Use a sharp knife. If needed, as a guide use a light ruler or paper strip.
    Cut 2 buttered sheets downward into 3 Strips about 6 x 14 inches.

3. At 2 inches from the bottom end of Strip spread about 2-1/2-to-3 TB of Cooked Filling.
    Leave one inch of space left and right.

4. Fold the bottom edge over the Filling and roll half way up.

5. Fold in the left and right sides and continue rolling all the way up.

6. Place Rolls on the cookie sheet, or in the baking dish seam side down.
    Leave a 1-inch space between them. Brush lightly with melted Butter.
    Poke each with a toothpick 8 times (5 for small rolls).

7. Cover with plastic wrap or foil, refrigerate until ready to bake.
    If the Rolls are in a glass baking dish, bring to room temperature before baking.

8. Preheat oven to 350°, or at temperature indicated on Phyllo package.
    Bake until golden crisp.
    Serve hot. Whole or sliced in half diagonally.

PHYLLO ROLLS - FINGER FOOD SIZE

The thickness of a small cigar - 1 TB of Stuffing

1. Follow directions as in ROLLS - APPETIZER SIZE. Serve the finger food size whole.

2. Cut the two buttered sheets in half <u>crosswise</u> into: 2 Strips 9 x 14 inches.
   Cut each Strip <u>downward</u> into: 3 Strips 4-1/2 x 9

3. At 1-1/2 inches from the bottom end of the Strips spread 1 TB of Filling.
   Leave a 3/4-inch space left and right. Follow steps <u>4 to 8</u> for APPETIZER ROLLS.

<u>NOTE</u>   To freeze Rolls, Triangles, put them in a container with wax paper between layers.
   Seal tight the container. Bake them frozen.

PHYLLO - STRUDEL

1. Spray a cookie sheet with a mist of Cooking Spray.

2. Place on it a sheet of Phyllo. Brush it <u>randomly</u> with melted Butter.
   Do not brush all over, the result would be too greasy.
   Repeat to form a stack of 6 layers.

3. At 3-inches from edge nearest you, spread 3 cups of FILLING in a 3-inch wide heap.
   Leave 2-inches of space left and right.

4. Fold the edge nearest you over the stuffing and roll one turn up.
   Fold in the left and right sides and continue rolling all the way up.

5. Slide the Strudel to the center of the cookie sheet, seam side down.
   Brush it with melted Butter. With a sharp knife make 3 diagonal gashes on top.

6. Bake at 350°, or as indicated on Phyllo package, until crisp golden brown.
   Sprinkle with Confectioners' Sugar.

PHYLLO - COLD STRUDEL

The Filling goes between pre-baked layers, like a large Napoleon. It may consist of fresh or cooked Fruit, Custard, whipped Cream. Assemble before serving to avoid sogginess.

FOR A STRUDEL WITH 1 CENTER LAYER OF FILLING - YOU NEED 2 STACKS OF PHYLLO

- Follow steps 1 and 2, as in above recipe, with 6 layers of Phyllo.
- Cut the Phyllo to obtain 2 portions, to the width and length desired.
- Place them on a greased cooking sheet, with space in between
- Bake until crisp and golden brown. Let cool in a dry place.
- Spread the Filling between the baked layers. Sprinkle with Confectioner's Sugar.

FOR A STRUDEL WITH 2 LAYERS OF FILLING - YOU NEED 3 STACKS OF PHYLLO

The middle stack should be thinner. Use 4 sheets only.

PHYLLO - NAPOLEONS

- Brush a cookie sheet with melted Butter. Prepare on it 5 buttered sheets of Phyllo.
- Cut into rectangles, to desired size of Napoleons. Rounds can be cut with a cookie cutter.
- Let cool. Assemble before serving, with Filling between baked rectangle layers.

PHYLLO - TRIANGLES

<u>APPETIZER SIZE</u>   -   1 TB of FILLING.   Cut 2 buttered sheets into 4 Strips: 3-1/4 x 18 inches.

<u>HORS-D'OEUVRE SIZE</u>   -   1 full teaspoon of Filling.   Strips: 2-1/4 x 14 inches.

1.   Place 1 TB of the Filling close to the bottom left corner of the Strip.

2.   Lift the right corner of the Strip and fold it over the Filling to form a triangle.
      Lift the left point of that triangle, fold it again into another triangle.
      Repeat all the way up. Trim end of the Strip, for the seam to be under the triangle.

3.   Place triangles, seam side down, on a greased cookie sheet or pan.
      Brush them lightly with melted Butter. Poke them 3 times with a toothpick.
      Cover with plastic wrap and refrigerate until ready to bake. Bake until golden brown.

PHYLLO - PIE SHELLS

1.   Butter 8 layers of Phyllo. Lift and center them into a buttered oven-proof dish or pan.
      Let the edges hang outside of the dish or pan. If it is round, trim off the corners.

2.   Roll edges outward. Crumple them into a border around the dish, resting on its edge.

3.   Add the FILLING. Optional: cover it with a buttered 6 sheet stack. Bake at 350°.

      <u>TO OBTAIN AN EMPTY COOKED PIE SHELL</u> - when the Filling needs no cooking.

      - Poke the base a few times with a toothpick. Cover with a round piece of wax paper
        to fit the base. Spread on it Dry Navy Beans. Bake until the Phyllo begins to color.
      - Remove from oven. Slide Beans towards the center of paper, carefully lift the paper
        with the Beans. Return to oven until the Shell is crispy and light golden brown.

      - Let cool. Carefully lift the Shell, place it on a serving platter. Fill it before serving.

PHYLLO - NESTS   *Appetizers or Desserts*

1.   Butter 3 layers of Phyllo. Cut them downward into 3 equal sections: 6 x 14 inches.
      Then cut in half across to obtain 6 equal pieces.

2.   Spray a muffin tray (1 cup size) or individual ramekins with Cooking Spray.
      Fit each Phyllo section into a muffin cup or ramekin. Let corners hang. When using
      muffin trays, leave an empty cup in-between. Poke the base 5 times with toothpick.

3.   Cut 4" squares of foil. Place on each 2 TB of DRY NAVY BEANS. Roll it into a ball.
      Place each foil ball into a Phyllo cup. This will prevent the bottom from rising as it
      bakes. Save the Bean balls for the next time.

4.   Bake in oven preheated to 350°, or as indicated on Phyllo package.
      When the Phyllo begins to color, remove the Bean balls. Finish baking until the Phyllo
      turns to a light golden brown. Let the Nests cool before removing them.

      Place them on a cookie sheet and set aside, in a dry place, until ready to use.
      Fill the Nests before serving, with cold Ingredients, or at room temperature, or hot.

5.   <u>To serve hot PHYLLO NESTS</u> with Seafood, Vegetables, Cheese toppings, other:

      Place baked Nests on a cookie sheet lined with parchment or foil. Fill before serving.
      Warm in oven preheated to 325°, until the Filling is hot and the Cheese has melted.

PHYLLO - PIE

Phyllo casseroles turn out and look better in rectangular or square oven-proof dishes or pans.

1.   Butter randomly 8 layers of Phyllo.
      Lift and center them into a buttered oven-proof dish or pan.
      With a sharp knife trim off excess Phyllo. It must fit exactly into the bottom.

2.   Spread into it the FILLING: 3/4-to one inch thick for Spinach, Vegetables, Meats.*

3.   Butter another 8 layers of Phyllo.
      Lift and center them on top of the Filling.
      Trim off excess Phyllo, for the layers to fit exactly in the dish, on top of the Filling.

4.   Brush the top with melted Butter.

5.   Chill the casserole for 30 minutes. It will be easier to cut the surface into a pattern.**

6.   Cut *only* the top layers of Phyllo into a pattern.
      Bake in oven preheated to 350° until the Pie colors to a light golden brown.

7.   Let the Pie cool for 10 minutes. Then cut outlined pattern all the way to the bottom.

      Serve hot or at room temperature Spinach, Vegetable or Meat Pies.

*BAKLAVA WITH NUT FILLING   - Spread over 6 buttered layers a thin layer of Filling.
                            - Top with 2 layers of Buttered Phyllo.
                            - Repeat until all the Stuffing is used. Top with 6 layers.
                            - Or spread 1/2-inch layer of Filling between 2 stacks of Phyllo.
See further SWEET FILLING.

** DESIGNING a pattern of SQUARES or RECTANGLES on the TOP LAYERS

- With a ruler or paper strip, measure the pan crosswise to form columns about 2 inches wide.
- With a sharp pointed knife, cut the top layers of Phyllo into the 2-inch wide columns.
- Be careful not to cut the bottom layers of Phyllo.
- Measure lengthwise and repeat, designing squares or rectangles.

** DESIGNING DIAMONDS

   To obtain an X cut the surface diagonally from: Top left corner to bottom right corner.
                                  And from: Top right corner to bottom left corner.

   Follow the diagonals and cut the surface into even diamonds. Use a ruler or paper strip.

HONEY SYRUP   For Baklava   *For a 9 x 12 x 1-3/4 baking dish*

                  Combine in a saucepan   [3 cups   GRANULATED SUGAR
                                          [2 cups   WATER
                                          [1 TB   LEMON JUICE
Over medium heat bring to a boil.
Reduce heat to low, simmer until the Syrup
reaches medium-thick consistency.
                         Stir in [1/3-cup   HONEY

Remove from heat. When the Syrup has cooled, pour it over the Baklava.
Important - The Baklava must cool completely before pouring the Syrup over it.

33

FILLINGS for PHYLLO ROLLS and TRIANGLES

CHEESE

For about 35 hors-d'oeuvre Triangles, with 1 full teaspoon of Filling.
For a Pie in an 8 x 12 x 1-3/4 baking dish, double the recipe.

	[1/2-lb	PHYLLO
	[8 oz	BUTTER melted
Beat in processor until fluffy	[2	EGGS
Add	[4 oz	COTTAGE CHEESE
	[4 oz	CREAM CHEESE cut small pieces
Process until smooth, then add and process	[8 oz	FETA CHEESE crumbled
	[1/4-cup	PARMESAN grated
	[1 TB	DRIED MINT crumbled
	[a dash	NUTMEG grated
	[	WHITE or BLACK PEPPER

Process until well mixed and smooth.
The Cheese Filling is now ready. Refrigerate. It will be easier to handle.

FISH and SEAFOOD

About 1-1/2 cups of Filling = about 35 full teaspoons.

Beat in processor until fluffy	[1	EGG
Add	[3 oz	CREAM CHEESE
Process until smooth, then add and process	[1-1/4 cups	cooked FISH or SHRIMP
	[2 TB	CHIVES finely chopped
When smooth, season to taste with	[	SALT, GROUND BLACK PEPPER
Process and add to taste	[any of	CREOLE or CURRY POWDER, NUTMEG, TOMATO PASTE

Process to blend Seasonings. Refrigerate.

HAM

About 1-1/2 cups of Filling = about 35 full teaspoons.

Chop in processor to obtain	[1 cup	HAM finely chopped
Remove Ham. Beat in processor until fluffy	[1	EGG
Add	[3 oz	CREAM CHEESE
	[1/4-cup	PARMESAN grated
When smooth, add	[	the Ham
	[to taste	GROUND BLACK PEPPER

Process until smooth. Refrigerate.

SMOKED SALMON

About 1-1/2 cups of Filling = about 35 full teaspoons.

Chop coarsely in processor	[8 oz	SMOKED SALMON

Remove from processor.

Beat in processor until fluffy	[1	EGG
Add	[5 oz (1 pkg)	GARLIC HERB BOURSIN CHEESE
When smooth, add	[	the Smoked Salmon
	[2 TB	PARSLEY or DILL finely chopped

Process until smooth. Refrigerate.

34

SPINACH FILLING

Makes 1 Pie in a baking dish measuring 9 x 12 x 1-3/4.
Or about 50 Triangles (for less reduce amounts by half)

Steam separately, in microwave, for 6 minutes [3 pkg -10 oz each FROZEN CHOPPED SPINACH

Combine all the Spinach in a colander, let cool.

In a large nonstick skillet, medium heat, heat	[2 TB	EXTRA-VIRGIN OLIVE OIL
When a light haze forms, sauté	[1 cup	ONION slice 1/4-inch thick, chop
	[1/4-cup	GREEN ONIONS thinly sliced
When Onion is translucent, add	[	the Spinach

Stir and sauté for 2 minutes or until moisture
has evaporated.

Mix in	[3 TB	DILL snipped or 1/2-tp DRIED
	[3 TB	FLAT LEAF PARSLEY finely chop
	[to taste	SALT, GROUND BLACK PEPPER

Turn off heat. Push aside the Spinach and
tilt the skillet. Soak up any Oil left with a
paper towel.

Beat in processor until fluffy	[4	EGGS
Add and process until smooth	[1 lb	FETA CHEESE cut into pieces

Then add gradually through feeder tube	[4 oz	COTTAGE CHEESE cream-style
	[4 oz	CREAM CHEESE
	[1/2-cup	PARMESAN grated
	[1/4-tp	NUTMEG grated or ground
	[to taste	GROUND BLACK PEPPER, no Salt

Process the Mixture until smooth.
Transfer it into a large bowl. Fold in the SPINACH. Cover and refrigerate until ready to use.

FOR AN 8 x 8 BAKING-DISH   Use:

[1 TB + 1 tp	OIL	[2 pkg	SPINACH	[3	EGGS	[3 oz	COTTAGE CHEESE
[2/3-cup	ONION	[2 TB	DILL	[11 oz	FETA	[3 oz	CREAM CHEESE
[3 TB	GREEN ONION	[2 TB	PARSLEY			[1/3-cup	PARMESAN

NOTE - Any remaining Spinach Mixture can be frozen. Thaw in a fine sieve. Drain if needed.

INGREDIENTS THAT CAN BE ADDED TO PHYLLO FILLINGS

CRISPY BACON crumbled	CHIVES	HORSERADISH	PINE NUTS toasted
CAPERS minced	FRESH DILL	JALAPEÑOS minced	RAISINS minced
CHEDDAR shredded	GINGER grated	PARMESAN grated	SALAMI minced
CHEESE grated	HERBS	PARSLEY minced	SPICES
GARLIC, ONIONS, SHALLOTS	GROUND MEAT with ONIONS		SAUSAGE MEAT

SWEET FILLING - NUTS

For a 9 x 12 x 1-3/4 baking dish

Chop, not too finely in processor	[2 lbs	WALNUTS or PISTACHIOS, or BLANCHED ALMONDS, or mixed

Transfer to a bowl and mix in	[1/4-cup	GRANULATED SUGAR
	[1 tp	GROUND CINNAMON or to taste
	[1 tp	ROSE PETAL WATER or more

Use this FILLING for small Phyllo rolls, or for Baklava. Refrigerate any remaining Filling.

QUICHE

A QUICHE consists of a baked PIE SHELL with a FILLING and a CUSTARD.

THE FILLING   - Must be prepared first and left to cool.

THE PIE CRUST   - Ready-made, uncooked, frozen. Comes in 9-inch pans of aluminum foil.
- Whisk the EGGS for the Custard.
- Remove from freezer the PIE SHELL. Brush it lightly with the beaten Eggs.
- Set it in preheated oven for 2 minutes only. Let cool. Add the Filling.

THE CUSTARD   - Eggs and any of Heavy or Light Cream, Sour Cream, Milk, Half and Half.
- Cheese, which ties the Custard and gives it a delicious flavor.
- The Cheese is grated, crumbled or diced, according to its texture.

BAKING   - Place the QUICHE in its foil pan on a cookie sheet, on middle rack of oven.
- Bake for 40-to-50 minutes. When golden, insert a knife through its center.
  If it comes out clean, it's ready. If sticky, cook a few more minutes.
- Cool on a wire rack. It can be refrigerated. Heat it in a warm oven.

TO SERVE   - Place the foil pan, in a pie dish. Serve at room temperature.

FORMAL   - Invert the frozen PIE CRUST on wax paper. Thaw for 5-to-10 minutes.
- Remove the aluminum pan and discard. Carefully invert the CRUST.
- Place it in a pie baking-dish to fit its size, or in a pan with removable base .
- Let it thaw completely for 10-to-15 minutes. It will soften.
- Shape it into the dish or pan, with enough dough to cover the edge.
- Cover gently the Pie Crust with plastic wrap. Freeze until ready to fill.

BASIC RECIPE FOR THE CUSTARD   [3   EGGS
                                  [1 cup   CREAM, MILK, HALF and HALF
                                    [4 oz   CHEESE can be a mixture

FOR THE FILLING   [1-1/2-to-2 cups of INGREDIENTS

MINI QUICHES (crustless) - BASIC RECIPE

Hors-d'oeuvre

Spray a Tray of 12 small Muffin cups (1/4-cup size) with Cooking Spray. Preheat oven to 375°.

Spread into each Muffin Cup   [1 TB + 1 tp COOKED INGREDIENTS   chopped
(also use Leftovers)

THE CUSTARD   In a bowl, whisk   [4   EGGS
                       Whisk into the Eggs   [1/4-cup   HEAVY CREAM
                                 add   [2 oz   GRATED CHEESE
                                       [1/4-tp   SALT, GROUND BLACK PEPPER
                                       [1/4-tp   GROUND NUTMEG or other
                                       [2 to 3 TB   PARSLEY or any other Herbs

- Use a 1/8-cup measure to pour 1/8-cup of Egg Mixture into each muffin cup. Fill 3/4-way up.
- Stir the Ingredients in each cup. Bake 10-to12 minutes on middle rack, until light golden.
- Insert a thin knife or skewer into one or two Quiches. If it comes out clean, they are ready.
- Let cool. They unmold easily. Serve at room temperature. Reheat in foil, in a warm oven.

For a 24 cup mini-muffin tray use   [1-1/2 tp   COOKED INGREDIENTS chopped

Add the CUSTARD, fill 3/4-way up. Bake for 8-to-10 minutes.

RISOTTO

Method   The Rice is stirred constantly, Hot Broth added gradually and absorbed before adding more. Risotto must be creamy, the grains tender but firm to the bite.

THE RICE   Several Italian brands are available. 1 cup of Arborio Rice weighs 7 oz.
Some brands absorb more BROTH than others. Have extra Broth available.
It is always advisable to follow the amounts given on the package directions.

THE BROTH   Usually CHICKEN Broth. Or FISH/SEAFOOD Broth for a Fish/Seafood Risotto.
Keep it on the back burner over low heat, simmering.

UTENSILS   A large heavy skillet, 7-to-12-inches at its base, depending on the amount of Rice to be cooked, allowing plenty of space for the Rice to be well stirred.
Use a wooden spoon to stir the Rice.

BASIC RISOTTO PREPARATION

Over medium heat, heat until very hot [	VEGETABLE OIL or BUTTER (or both)
Sauté until soft and translucent [	ONION
Reduce heat and add [	RICE

RICE and ONION   - Stir for 3 minutes, until grains are coated and glisten.

WINE   - If using, add it now. Stir until it has evaporated. Add Hot Broth.

HOT BROTH   - Add a ladle (1/2-cup) at a time. Stir, letting the Rice absorb it before adding more Broth. Plan to always have extra Broth.
                 - Some Ingredients will absorb Broth: like Mushrooms, Raisins, Nuts.

COOKED VEGETABLES - Add them about 10-to-15 minutes into the cooking.

COOKED SEAFOOD   - Add it 20 minutes into the cooking. Use Fish/Seafood Broth.
                 - Or add to Chicken Broth a little Clam Juice.

COOKED MEATS, POULTRY   - Add them when the Risotto is almost ready.

When all the Broth has been absorbed, the Risotto should be ready, about 25-to-30 minutes.

- Turn off heat. If the Risotto is too sticky, loosen it with 1 or 2 Tablespoons of hot Broth.
- Stir in the BUTTER, then the grated PARMESAN, GRANA or ROMANO.
- After adding the Cheese adjust Salt and Pepper. Serve grated Cheese on the side.

For a creamier Risotto, add to taste 1 or 2 TB, or more, of MASCARPONE CHEESE.

BASIC AMOUNTS

Serves 2 as a main course		*Serves 3 as a main course*	
Serves 3 as an appetizer		*Serves 4 as an appetizer*	
[1 cup	ARBORIO RICE = 7 oz	[1-1/2 cups	ARBORIO RICE
[4 cups	BROTH + 1/2-cup if needed	[6 cups	BROTH + 1/2-cup
[2 TB	BUTTER	[3 TB	BUTTER
[1 TB	VEGETABLE OIL	[1-1/2 TB	VEGETABLE OIL
[2 to 8 TB	ONION or SHALLOT finely chopped	[3 to 8 TB	ONION, SHALLOT
[2 to 4 TB	DRY WHITE WINE	[4 to 8 TB	DRY WHITE WINE
[1 TB	BUTTER stir into cooked Risotto	[1-1/2 TB	BUTTER
[2 TB	GRATED PARMESAN	[3 to 4 TB	GRATED PARMESAN

NOTE   -   If you are adding other IMPORTANT INGREDIENTS, reduce the amount of RICE.

RISOTTO alla MILANESE
Serves 2 as a main course, 3 as an appetizer

Bring to a simmer	[4 cups	CHICKEN BROTH lightly salted (+ 1/2-cup more if needed)
In a small saucepan, pour	[1 cup of	the simmering Broth
Dissolve in it	[1/4-tp	SAFFRON THREADS l et simmer
In a 7-to 8-inch skillet, medium heat, heat	[2 TB	BUTTER + 1 TB VEGETABLE OIL
When it sizzles, sauté	[1/4-cup	ONION finely chopped
When Onion begins to color, add	[1 cup	ARBORIO RICE
Stir until grains are coated and glisten, add	[1/4-cup	DRY WHITE WINE

- Stir until the Wine evaporates.
- Add a 1/2-cup of the SAFFRON BROTH.
  When it has been absorbed, keep adding
  the Broth, <u>a ladle</u> (1/2-cup) at a time.

- When 3 cups of Broth have been absorbed,
  add the rest of the SAFFRON BROTH.
- When it has been absorbed, the Rice should
  be tender but firm and creamy.
  Only add more Broth, if needed.

Turn off heat and stir in	[1 TB	BUTTER soft, diced small
Mix well and add	[2 TB	GRATED PARMESAN
Taste and adjust	[	SALT and PEPPER

Cover, let Risotto set for 5 minutes.   Serve [grated PARMESAN on the side

<u>NOTE</u> - This Risotto can be prepared with a Light Beef Broth. Or mixed Chicken and Beef.
     - Or sauté in Butter 2 oz Beef Marrow. Stir it into the Risotto made with Chicken Broth.

RISOTTO PRIMAVERA - BASIC RECIPE
Serves 3 as appetizer

In a small saucepan simmer	[4 cups	CHICKEN BROTH lightly salted (+ 1/2-cup more if needed)
In a 10-inch heavy skillet, medium heat, heat	[3 TB	BUTTER + 1 TB VEGETABLE OIL
When it sizzles, sauté	[2 TB	ONION finely chopped
	[1/2-cup	CARROTS finely diced
	[1/4-cup	CELERY finely diced
When Carrots and Celery have softened, add	[1/2-cup	ZUCCHINI quarter longwise, dice
Stir for 3 minutes and add	[1 cup	ARBORIO RICE
Stir until grains are coated and glisten. Add	[2 TB	DRY WHITE WINE

Stir until the Wine evaporates.
Add <u>one ladle</u> (1/2-cup) at a time of BROTH.

When 2 cups have been absorbed, add	[1/4-cup	FROZEN GREEN PEAS thawed

Keep adding the Broth until 4 cups have been
absorbed. The Rice should be tender, firm
and creamy.

Turn off heat and mix in	[1 TB	BUTTER soft, diced small
	[2 TB	GRATED PARMESAN or to taste
	[	GROUND PEPPER, SALT if needed

ROUX, SOFFRITO and MIREPOIX

WHITE ROUX Is the base for White Sauces. It consists of BUTTER and FLOUR stirred over medium heat. Then BROTH or MILK are added. See "SAUCES".

YELLOW ROUX Is cooked until the mixture turns yellow. For Cheese and Vegetable Sauces.

BROWN ROUX Cooked until light brown or rust. For Gravies, Brown Sauces, Curries, Stews.

THE SOFRITO is used to flavor sauces and dishes in Spanish, Latin and Caribbean cuisine.

In a heavy nonstick skillet, heat	[2 TB	VEGETABLE OIL
Over medium heat, sauté	[1 cup	ONION finely chopped
	[1 TB	GARLIC minced
	[2 medium	BELL PEPPERS finely diced
Optional	[to taste	HOT CHILE minced
When the Vegetables are soft , add	[1 cup	TOMATOES canned, drain, chop
	[2 tp	CILANTRO finely chopped
	[1 tp	GROUND CUMIN
Reduce heat, cover, simmer for 30 minutes until the Sofrito thickens. Season to taste	[	SALT, GROUND BLACK PEPPER

- Cool in a bowl, refrigerate. Or freeze in an ice cube tray. Store cubes in plastic bag, freeze.
- According to the recipes you may need from one to several tablespoons of Sofrito in a recipe.

ITALIAN SOFRITO and FRENCH MIREPOIX   Base for Braising, Sauces, Soups, Stews.

Basic - 1 part CARROT   Example - 1/4-cup Carrot diced   Sauté in Oil or Butter, or both
       - 1 part CELERY   - 1/4-cup Celery
       - 2 parts ONION   - 1/2-cup Onion   1 TB per cup of Vegetables

LOUISIANA MIREPOIX   Substitute the Carrot with Bell Pepper.

SOUFFLÉ

THE SOUFFLÉ DISH 1-1/2 quart round oven-proof porcelain casserole with vertical outside ribs or individual 1-1/4-cup ramekins.

- Brush generously with melted UNSALTED BUTTER, or rub with the stick of BUTTER.
- Add 1-1/2 TB of grated PARMESAN or BREADCRUMBS, or SUGAR. Per ramekin: 1-1/4 tp.
- Shake and roll the dish around to coat it on all sides with Cheese, Breadcrumbs, or Sugar.
- Turn the dish upside down, tap it on the counter to rid of excess. Refrigerate until needed.

THE COLLAR   Prevents the Soufflé from overflowing. You may or may not use it. With or without it, allow 1-1/4 inches above the Mixture to avoid overflow.

- Cut a 9-inch wide strip of wax paper, long enough to encircle the casserole, with a 2-inch overlap. Fold in two longwise. From the fold down, Butter a 3-inch wide strip across.
- Dust with Cheese, Breadcrumbs, or Sugar. Wrap it around the dish, buttered side inside.
- Stand it 3-inches higher than the rim of the dish. Tie it tightly around with trussing string.

UTENSILS   To cook the Mixture   a 1-1/2 quarts SAUCEPAN.
           To beat Egg Whites   a large STAINLESS STEEL BOWL , an ELECTRIC BEATER.
           To beat the Yolks   a WIRE WHIP, a LARGE RUBBER SPATULA to fold Eggs.

SOUFFLÉ BASIC RECIPE   *For 1-1/2 quart soufflé dish (serves 4 to 6) or 4 ramekins.*

1 cup	[CREAMY BÉCHAMEL - see "SAUCES". Prepared with Milk or Broth.
4 EGG YOLKS	[Must be at room temperature when used.
OTHER INGREDIENTS	[3/4-cup finely chopped or puréed Fish, Meat, Vegetables, Fruit.
CHEESE	[1/3-to-1/2-cup grated.
5 EGG WHITES	[At room temperature. No Egg Yolk particles in them.
CREAM OF TARTAR	[Add 1/8-tp
	[Beat the Whites until stiff. Gather some on the whip, hold it upright.
	[If a peak forms, they are ready. If not, beat longer, but do not dry.

CHEESE SOUFFLÉ   *Serves 4 to 6*

1.   Rub a 1-1/2 quart soufflé dish with   [BUTTER
(Or use 4 soufflé ramekins)   Dust with   [1-1/2 TB   PARMESAN grated. Refrigerate.
                                                                    (1-1/4 tp per ramekin)

2.   Set out at room temperature   [5   EGGS you need 5 Whites, 4 Yolks

3.   In a heavy nonstick skillet, prepare   [1 cup   CREAMY BÉCHAMEL ("SAUCES")

- When Béchamel thickens, remove from heat.
- Break 1 EGG, drop the WHITE into stainless
  steel bowl. The YOLK into the Béchamel.
- With a wire whip beat it into the Sauce.
- Repeat with 3 more Yolks, one at a time.
- Return saucepan to stove. Over <u>low heat</u>
  stir for 1 minute to bind the Eggs.

         Turn off heat. Stir into it, until melted   [2/3-cup   SWISS or CHEDDAR grated,
                                                                        reserve 1 TB, for ramekins 4 tp

                                        Add   [3 TB   PARMESAN   grated
                                                    [1/2-tp   SALT, WHITE PEPPER to taste
                                                    [to taste   NUTMEG   grated

- Set aside to cool. Can be prepared ahead to
  this point. Cover the surface with wax paper.
- Warm barely before adding the EGG WHITES.

4.   Preheat oven to 400°. Set out soufflé dish.

Add to the 4 EGG WHITES 1 EGG WHITE and   [1/8-tp   CREAM OF TARTAR

a)   Beat the EGG WHITES until stiff and glossy, but not dry.
   - Add one ladle of WHITES to the BÉCHAMEL. Gently fold them in with a rubber spatula.
   - Then gently pour the BÉCHAMEL into remaining EGG WHITES.
   - Fold in with the spatula, scooping from the bottom towards the top as you turn the bowl.
   - Do not fold too much, it would keep the Soufflé from rising well. White spots do no harm.

b)   Pour MIXTURE into the soufflé dish(es). Smooth the surface with a spatula.
   - Sprinkle with the reserved 1 TB of CHEESE. Or for each ramekin 1 tp.

c)   Place on middle rack of oven. Immediately reduce heat to 375°. Bake 25-to-30 minutes.
   - Less time for the ramekins. Don't open the oven door until the Soufflé is well puffed.
   - Test by inserting a thin knife or metal skewer. If it comes out clean, the Soufflé is ready.
     If not, cook 5 minutes longer. It should have a light brown crust and creamy center.

40

TORTILLAS

<u>To heat TORTILLAS</u>   - Wrap them in a double sheet of foil, place them in a warm oven.
                          - Or, heat one at a time in a lightly greased skillet, flipping it for
                            10 seconds on each side.

<u>BURRITOS</u>

- Fill one warm Tortilla at a time. Keeping the others under wrap.
- Place the Filling in the center. Just enough for flaps to overlap.
- Fold like a package: flip the right side on top of the Filling. Then the left side.
- Fold over the bottom and top sides. Hold flaps together with a toothpick.

- Place the Burritos in a sprayed oven-proof dish. Toothpick side up.
- To prevent Tortillas from drying as you work, keep them covered with a napkin.
- Cover the dish with foil. Warm in oven preheated to 325°. Serve with Salsa.

<u>CHALUPAS</u>

Shaped like small boats (chalupas). Crunchy and fried. Available ready-made.
They are served as hors-d'oeuvres: filled with mashed Beans, Cheese, Guacamole, other.

<u>ENCHILADAS</u>

- Fill one warm Tortilla at a time. Keeping the others under wrap.
- Spread the Filling at 1-1/2 inches from the edge. Fold the edge over, roll into a tube.
- Lay the Enchiladas seam side down, into a sprayed oven proof dish. Cover with foil.

- TO SERVE: Top with a Cream Sauce. Sprinkle with plenty of shredded Cheese.
- Bake in oven preheated to 350° until the Cheese melts. Pass under the broiler.
- Or top with a thick Gravy. Serve with Rice, refried Beans, grilled Vegetables.

<u>FAJITAS</u>

Wrap the hot Tortillas in a napkin, place them in a bread basket, or a special Tortilla basket.
The Fillings are presented in a variety of small dishes. Roll your own Tortillas at the table.

<u>QUESADILLAS</u>

A Quesadilla is a toasted Tortilla Sandwich with a Cheese (Queso) Filling.

- Place the Cheese and other trimmings on one half of Tortilla.
- Fold other half over the Filling and press edges to seal.
- In a nonstick skillet, over medium heat, cook the Tortilla from 1-to-2 minutes on
  each side. Or use a griddle. Serve cut in half or in wedges.

<u>TACOS</u>

Are available ready-made. They are hard Tortilla Shells folded in half with enough space left
for the Filling. No cooking is required.
Taco Shells are also available in the shape of individual Pie Shells.

<u>TOSTADAS</u>

Fried crispy Tortillas. Toppings are added. The smaller size is served as hors-d'oeuvres.

<u>CONDIMENTS AND SOME FILLINGS</u> *for any of the above*

BEANS mashed	GUACAMOLE	OLIVES sliced or chopped	SOUR CREAM
CHEESE shredded	JALAPEÑOS pickled	ONIONS chopped	TOMATILLOS
CILANTRO chopped	LETTUCE shredded	SALSA red or green	TOMATOES diced

THE VICHYSSOISE

THE VICHYSSOISE is a cold Leek and Potato Soup. Before serving a little Cream may be added.
Served hot it is called a LEEK and POTATO SOUP.

Use it as a BASE to add cooked Vegetables. It makes easy and delicious Soups.
For recipes see "VEGETABLES" : ARTICHOKES, BEETS, CAULIFLOWER.

BASIC RECIPE

Trim and separate the Leek sections, white and light green parts only. Wash thoroughly.
Gather the sections and thinly slice them. Peel, wash, dry, cut Potatoes into 1-inch cubes.

In a heavy saucepan combine in equal parts	[2 cups	LEEKS
	[2 cups	POTATOES
Add their total	[4 cups	WATER or BROTH very lean
	[	SALT to taste

1.　Cover the saucepan, bring to a boil.
　　Reduce heat to low. Simmer until the Vegetables are tender. About 45 minutes.

2.　With a slotted spoon remove the Vegetables and put 2 cups of them in a blender.
　　Add a 1/2-cup of the Cooking Liquid. Blend until smooth.
　　Add gradually more of the Cooking Liquid until the desired consistency is obtained.
　　It should be thick and creamy but still run off the spoon.

3.　Empty the blender into a bowl. Proceed the same way with remaining Vegetables.
　　Reserve remaining Cooking Liquid. If you run out of it, use bottled or filtered Water.

4.　Add Salt and Pepper to taste. Let the Vichyssoise cool. It thickens when cold.
　　Cover, refrigerate. To thin it, use the Cooking Liquid or bottled Water,

5.　Store in sealed containers. Refrigerate or freeze for later use.
　　When thawed, it is lumpy. Return it to blender and liquefy. Or heat it.

To serve hot	Before serving add to taste [	LIGHT CREAM a little, optional
	Top with any of [	CHIVES, PARMESAN, CROUTONS
To serve chilled	Top with [	CHIVES or WATERCRESS finely chopped
	and/or a scoop of [	SALMON ROE CAVIAR optional

CANNED POTATO and LEEK SOUP	[	If you like its flavor use it as a base.
	[	Add any cooked Vegetables, and blend.

AVOCADO VICHYSSOISE

Cut in half and scoop out the pulp of	[2	AVOCADOS medium size
Put it in a blender and add	[2 cups	VICHYSSOISE BASE
	[1 TB + 1 tp	LEMON JUICE
Blend until smooth and creamy. Add	[to taste	SALT, PEPPER or TABASCO

If needed, thin by adding gradually a little cold Water.
This Vichyssoise must be thinner than a custard, but thick enough to barely run off the spoon.
Keep it in the blender. Press plastic wrap on the surface. Refrigerate. Blend before serving.

Chop finely and top with any of	[	CHIVES, CILANTRO, WATERCRESS
Optional, add	[	a dollop of SALMON ROE CAVIAR

II

DIPS and SPREADS

Dips add an extra relish to Hors-d'oeuvre.

Serve them with Crudités.
Stick a variety of "Dunks" on toothpicks.

Enhance Sandwiches and Canapés with savory Spreads
rather than Butter, Mayonnaise or Mustard.

CRUDITÉS and DUNKS

Finger Food

Crudités

Asparagus
Baby Carrots
Belgian Endive
Bell Pepper strips
Broccoli Florets
Carrot sticks
Cauliflower Florets
Celery
Coconut sticks
Fennel
Jicama
Lemon Peel candied
Radish
Squash sticks
Zucchini sticks

On Toothpicks

Shrimp
Smoked Mussels
Smoked Oysters
Smoked Salmon

Chorizo
Ham
Prosciutto
Salami
Sausage

Barbecue
Meatballs

On Toothpicks

Fruit and Vegetables

Artichoke Bottoms canned, cubed
Baby Brussels Sprouts cooked
Cherry Tomatoes
Dried Apricots
Ginger strips, rolled
Grapefruit chunks
Grapes
Kiwi
Lichee Nuts canned
Mango
Mellon Balls
Mushroom Caps
Palm Hearts
Papaya
Pineapple
Strawberries
Sweet Potato, Yams, cubed

Pickles

*Skewer on toothpicks
then add other items.*

Baby Corn
Cornichons
Dill and Sour
Marinated Mushroom Caps
Okra
Olives   pitted
Onions
Pimientos

DIPS and SPREADS

DIPS   46

Avocado	Goat Cheese
Black Beans	Green Goddess
Blue Cheese	Horseradish
Capers	Pineapple
Chili Sauce	Roquefort
Crabmeat Thousand Island	Salmon Roe Caviar
Curry Mayonnaise	Sardines
Curry Yogurt	Smoked Ham
Feta Cheese	Smoked Trout

ETHNIC DIPS   47

Bagna Cauda
Guacamole
Tahini (Babaghanoush)
Tahini Hummus
Taramosalata

SEASONED BUTTERS and MAYONNAISE   48

SPREADS for SANDWICHES and CANAPÉS

Asparagus Tips 49	Lemon Celery 50
Avocado	Lemon Pimiento
Beans	Mint Radish
Blackeyed Peas	Mustard Relish
Cream Cheese Cucumber	Navy Beans
Cream Cheese Pimiento	Red Beans
Cream Cheese Radish	Ricotta Capers
Cream Cheese Salmon	Ricotta Olives
Cream Cheese Sardines	Roquefort Cream Cheese
Egg Tartare	Tomatillo Tartare
Feta Cheese Mint	Tomatoes Garlic
Feta Cheese Oregano	Tomatoes Green Onion
Ginger Watercress	
Goat Cheese Cornichons	
Goat Cheese Olives	Anchoïade
Horseradish Sour Cream	
Hummus	Anchovy Tapenade
Ketchup Mayonnaise	Olive Tapenade

"Imagination is more important than knowledge.
Knowledge is limited. Imagination encircles the world."

Albert Einstein

DIPS

Mix Ingredients and add Salt and Pepper according to taste.

AVOCADO mash with

[MAYONNAISE or SOUR CREAM
[GREEN ONIONS minced
[LEMON JUICE
[CILANTRO or PARSLEY minced

BLACK BEANS mash with

[SOUR CREAM
[GROUND CUMIN
[ONION minced
[TABASCO, optional GARLIC

BLUE CHEESE mash with

[SOUR CREAM
[PECANS chopped
[GREEN ONION or FRESH BASIL minced
[RADISH grated

CAPERS mince and mix with

[SOUR CREAM
[ANCHOVIES mashed
[HARD-COOKED EGGS chopped
[PARSLEY minced

CHILI SAUCE mix with

[CREAM CHEESE
[GREEN ONION minced
[RELISH

CRAB MEAT chopped, mix with

[AVOCADO mashed
[LEMON JUICE
[GREEN ONION minced

CURRY MAYONNAISE

[MAYONNAISE/SOUR CREAM equal amounts
[CURRY POWDER
[SCALLIONS minced
[RAISINS minced
[COCONUT grated

CURRY YOGURT

[YOGURT mix with CURRY POWDER
[GARLIC minced, or GARLIC POWDER
[CILANTRO minced
[RED BELL PEPPER minced

FETA CHEESE crumble, mash with

[SOUR CREAM half amount of Feta
[SCALLIONS
[MINT fresh or dried

GOAT CHEESE mash with

[CRÈME FRAÎCHE
[BASIL or TARRAGON finely chopped
[PIMIENTOS minced
[GARLIC minced, or POWDER a touch

GREEN GODDESS DRESSING mix with

[CRÈME FRAÎCHE or SOUR CREAM
[CELERY grated
[SCALLIONS minced
[HARD-COOKED EGGS chopped

HORSERADISH mix with

[CRÈME FRAÎCHE or SOUR CREAM
[SCALLIONS minced
[RAISINS minced
[PARSLEY

PINEAPPLE crushed, drained, mix with

[COTTAGE CHEESE
[FRESH GINGER grated
[GREEN ONION minced
[SOY SAUCE

ROQUEFORT SALAD DRESSING mix with

[CREAM CHEESE
[WATERCRESS finely chopped
[PECANS chopped

SALMON ROE CAVIAR mix with

[SOUR CREAM
[SCALLIONS minced
[HARD-COOKED EGG YOLK chopped

SARDINES mash with

[TARTARE SAUCE
[KETCHUP a little, or TOMATO PASTE
[LEMON JUICE
[GREEN ONION minced
[CELERY finely chopped

SMOKED HAM mince in processor with

[SOUR CREAM
[MUSTARD
[CHIVES
[KOSHER PICKLE minced

SMOKED SALMON mince, mix with

[SOUR CREAM or CRÈME FRAÎCHE
[LEMON JUICE
[GREEN ONION minced, CAPERS minced

ETHNIC DIPS

BAGNA CAUDA   Hot Anchovy Dip   (Italy)   *Yields about 1 cup*

In a nonstick skillet, over medium heat, heat	[1/2-cup	EXTRA-VIRGIN OLIVE OIL
with	[3 TB	BUTTER
As soon as it sizzles, add	[4 large	GARLIC cloves , mashed
Stir until the Garlic begins to soften, then add	[8	ANCHOVY FILLETS chopped

Reduce heat to low. With a wooden spoon mash Garlic with Anchovies, until dissolved.
Do not boil or let the Butter/Oil brown. When the Sauce is well combined, turn off heat.

Serve warm, in a small chafing dish over a flame, with Crudités and toasted Bread dunks.

GUACAMOLE

Mash	[2 ripe	LARGE AVOCADOS or 3 medium
Mix in	[1 TB	LIME JUICE or more, to taste
	[2 TB	WHITE ONION minced, or more
	[2 TB	FRESH CILANTRO minced
	[1/4 tp	SALT or more to taste
	[optional	SERRANO CHILI seed, finely chop

Cover surface with plastic wrap. Refrigerate.

TAHINI EGGPLANT   BABAGHANOUSH   (Middle East)   *Yields about 1-1/2 cups*

Char a	[1 lb	EGGPLANT see "VEGETABLES"
Combine in a blender and blend	[3 TB canned	TAHINI see "SAUCES" on how to remove it from can
	[4 TB	LEMON JUICE freshly squeezed
	[2 TB	WATER
Over blender mash with garlic press and add	[1 clove	GARLIC
	[1/4-tp	GROUND CUMIN
	[1/4-tp	SALT, GROUND BLACK PEPPER

Blend to obtain a creamy paste.
If too thick add Water by Tablespoon. Mix TAHINI into EGGPLANT, mashing it with a fork.
Adjust Seasonings to taste. Refrigerate.
Sprinkle with minced Parsley. Serve with Pita Bread, toasted Pita Bread chips, Crudités.

TAHINI HUMMUS   (Middle East)   *Yields about 1-1/2 cups*

Mash in processor	[1 cup	CHICK PEAS canned, rinse, drain
Add prepared	[3/4-cup	TAHINI SAUCE see "SAUCES"
When well blended, add to taste, if needed	[	LEMON JUICE
	[	SALT, GROUND BLACK PEPPER
	[	GROUND CUMIN
	[to taste	GARLIC CLOVE or POWDER

Mix well to obtain a smooth texture.

To serve	[drizzle with	OLIVE OIL, minced PARSLEY

TARAMOSALATA   Available ready-made. A Greek Spread of Carp Roe (TARAMA).

As a Dip, beat it with a little	[	CRÈME FRAÎCHE or WHIPPED CREAM
Optional, mix in a few	[	BLACK OLIVES minced
Serve sprinkled with	[	PARSLEY minced

SEASONED BUTTERS and MAYONNAISE

For SANDWICHES and CANAPÉS

Use UNSALTED BUTTER. Bring to room temperature before using.
Store Mixtures in crocks or plastic containers. Refrigerate. Allow time for flavors to blend.

Add to BUTTER or MAYONNAISE any of the following combinations. Mince finely the Ingredients.
Mix amounts and Seasonings according to taste.

ANCHOVIES   mashed

[LEMON JUICE
[PARSLEY or DILL finely chopped

BLUE CHEESE (with Butter)

[or ROQUEFORT, or GORGONZOLA
[WALNUTS   crumbled

CAPERS

[PICKLED ONIONS
[DRIED SWEET BASIL

CHILI POWDER

[CORNICHONS

CREOLE POWDER

[DRIED OREGANO
[DILL   snipped

CHIVES

[PAPRIKA

CHIVES or PARSLEY

[HORSERADISH
[DILL

CHIVES or PARSLEY

[MUSTARD
[ALMONDS   toasted, ground

CHIVES

[CURRY POWDER

CILANTRO

[LEMON ZEST grated
[CHIVES

DILL PICKLES

[KETCHUP
[ONION

GINGER   fresh, grated

[GREEN ONION
[CILANTRO

LUMPFISH ROE

[RED ONION
[PARSLEY

LUMPFISH ROE

[WHITE ONION
[LEMON JUICE

OLIVES (black or green)

[DRIED OREGANO
[SCALLIONS

ONION   white or red

[DRIED GARDEN MINT

ONION

[DRIED or FRESH TARRAGON
[RED PEPPER FLAKES

ONION JUICE

[DRIED or FRESH BASIL

PARMESAN   grated (with Butter)

[NUTMEG   grated
[FRESH BASIL

PARSLEY

[CEKERY SALT
[CAYENNE

RAISINS   minced

[CURRY POWDER

RED SWEET PIMIENTOS

[GROUND CUMIN
[CHIVES

SARDINES   mashed

[LEMON JUICE
[ONION

SCALLIONS

[SOY SAUCE
[GINGER   grated

48

SPREADS for SANDWICHES and CANAPÉS

Bring Cheese to room temperature before mixing it with other Ingredients.
Cream Cheeses can be thinned with a little Cream or Milk.
With SMOKED FISH double Creamy Cheese: Example: 4 oz Smoked Trout, 8 oz creamy Cheese.

Mince finely Ingredients. Mix amounts and Seasonings according to taste.

ASPARAGUS TIPS (canned) mash with

[MAYONNAISE
[PIMIENTOS
[CHIVES

AVOCADO mash with

[LEMON JUICE a few drops
[MAYONNAISE
[CILANTRO

BEANS any kind mash or purée

[BALSAMIC VINEGAR
[WHITE ONION
[CRISPY BACON crumbled

BLACKEYED PEAS mashed

[JALAPEÑOS minced or JUICE
[RED ONION
[CILANTRO

CREAM CHEESE - CUCUMBER

[Mix CHEESE with CUCUMBER seeded, grated
[ONION or ONION JUICE
[DRIED MINT

CREAM CHEESE - PIMIENTO

[Mash CHEESE with PIMIENTO minced
[GREEN ONION   minced
[POPPY SEEDS
[PICKLE RELISH

CREAM CHEESE - RADISH

[Mash CHEESE with RADISH grated
[HAZELNUTS toasted, finely chopped
[BLACK GROUND PEPPER

CREAM CHEESE - SALMON

[Mash CHEESE with SMOKED SALMON   minced
[GREEN ONION   minced
[PARSLEY   minced

CREAM CHEESE SARDINES

[mash Cheese with SARDINES
[GREEN ONION   minced
[LEMON JUICE

EGG TARTARE

[TARTARE SAUCE
[HARD-COOKED EGGS   minced
[CHIVES

FETA CHEESE - MINT

[mash the CHEESE with OLIVE OIL
[ONION minced or ONION JUICE
[GARDEN MINT   dried

FETA CHEESE - OREGANO mash

[with OLIVE OIL
[BLACK OLIVES   minced
[OREGANO   dried

GINGER WATERCRESS

[MIRACLE WHIP
[FRESH GINGER   grated
[WATERCRESS
[SOY SAUCE

GOAT CHEESE - CORNICHONS

[Mash CHEESE with SOUR CREAM
[CORNICHONS   minced
[SUN-DRIED TOMATOES   minced

GOAT CHEESE - OLIVES

[Mash CHEESE with MASCARPONE
[OLIVES   minced
[PAPRIKA

HORSERADISH mix with

[SOUR CREAM
[SCALLION
[FRESH BASIL
[GREEN OLIVES   minced

HUMMUS   see Ethnic Dips

[RED or GREEN ONION
[PARSLEY

KETCHUP MAYONNAISE

[mix KETCHUP with MAYONNAISE
[HORSERADISH
[GREEN ONION

LEMON CELERY

[Mix MAYONNAISE with
[LEMON ZEST
[CELERY   grated
[CHIVES

LEMON PIMIENTO

[Mix TARTARE SAUCE with
[LEMON ZEST
[HOT or SWEET PIMIENTO

MINT RADISH

[Mix SOUR CREAM with
[RADISH   grated
[MINT   fresh or dried
[CHIVES

MUSTARD RELISH mix with

[SOUR CREAM
[CELERY   finely chopped
[CHIVES

NAVY BEANS mash with

[KETCHUP
[CHEDDAR   grated
[WHITE ONION
[PICKLES
[CILANTRO

RED BEANS mash with

[SOUR CREAM
[WHITE ONION
[PARSLEY
[CUMIN
[TABASCO

RICOTTA mash with

[SUN-DRIED TOMATOES
[DRIED OREGANO
[CAPERS   minced
[GREEN ONION

RICOTTA mash with

[SUN-DRIED TOMATOES
[FRESH BASIL
[BLACK OLIVES
[GREEN ONION

ROQUEFORT CREAM CHEESE

[mash ROQUEFORT with
[CREAM CHEESE
[CHIVES
[PECANS   finely chopped
[DRY SHERRY

TOMATILLOS TARTARE

[canned TOMATILLOS, mince and
[mix with TARTARE SAUCE
[CHEDDAR   grated
[CILANTRO

TOMATOES GARLIC

[TOMATOES   peeled, seeded
[mash with OLIVE OIL
[GARLIC   minced
[FRESH DILL or BASIL

TOMATOES GREEN ONION

[TOMATOES   peeled, seeded
[mash with OLIVE OIL
[DRIED OREGANO
[GREEN ONION

ANCHOÏADE

Purée in processor:

[8 canned   ANCHOVY FILLETS   drained
[1 clove   GARLIC
[1/2-tp   TOMATO PASTE
[1-1/2 TB   EXTRA-VIRGIN OLIVE OIL
[1 tp   LEMON JUICE   or add more to taste
[to taste   GROUND BLACK PEPPER

ANCHOVY TAPENADE

Purée in processor:

[8 canned   ANCHOVY FILLETS
[1 clove   GARLIC
[1 TB   CAPERS   rinsed
[1-1/2 TB   EXTRA-VIRGIN OLIVE OIL
[1/2-tp   LEMON JUICE
[to taste   GROUND BLACK PEPPER

OLIVE TAPENADE

Chop in processor to obtain a coarse texture:

[8 oz   BLACK OLIVES   pitted
[3 or 4   ANCHOVY FILLETS
[1 small   GARLIC CLOVE
[2TB   CAPERS   rinsed
[1 TB   LEMON JUICE
[4 TB   EXTRA-VIRGIN OLIVE OIL
[1/4-tp   DRIED THYME/ TARRAGON

III

SANDWICHES

SANDWICHES

In the following recipes, you can substitute Ham with Chicken or Turkey.
Chicken or Turkey with Ham or Meat.

For BUTTERS, MAYONNAISE and SPREADS see "DIPS and SPREADS".

CANAPÉS and FINGER SANDWICHES

BREADS FOR SANDWICHES and OPEN-FACE SANDWICHES

Bagels	Ciabatta	Rolls onion
Baguette	Croissant	Rolls variety
Buckwheat	Country Bread	Rye
Buns	English Muffin	Sourdough
Brioche	Pita Bread	Wholewheat
Challah	Pumpernickel	Wraps

Also for open-face Sandwiches:

Foccaccia   Potato Blini   Waffles

"I don't need music, lobster or wine
Whenever your eyes look into mine;
The things I long for are simple and few:
A cup of coffee, a sandwich - and you!"

Billy Rose

SANDWICHES

Sandwiches can be baked, fried, or toasted in a sandwich maker or grill.
If you don't have a sandwich grill, oil lightly and heat a grilling pan. Place the Sandwich in it.
Weight it down with a small cast iron skillet. Grill one side, then grill other side the same way.

CROQUE-MONSIEUR

The classic CROQUE-MONSIEUR is filled with Ham and Gruyère Cheese, then fried or grilled.
A real CROQUE-MADAME has Cheese only. A fancy Croque-madame can have anything in it,
and on it, including a Béchamel Sauce and a fried Egg on top.

To fry the Croque-monsieur in a skillet, it must be tied like a package, with trussing string, to
prevent it from falling apart when turned over. No trussing needed in a sandwich grill.

> Cut Bread slices about 3/8- thick.
> Cut Meats to fit Bread slices. Cut smaller slices of Cheese, it spreads when it melts.
>
> Spread lightly the BUTTER on both sides. Or on the side in contact with the skillet.
> Spread the inside, in contact with the Filling, with a SEASONED BUTTER.
> Or one "in side" with Seasoned Butter, the other with Mustard.
>
> Lay the FILLING on the bottom slice. Cover with top slice, press down, truss it.
> Can be prepared ahead, wrapped in plastic wrap, refrigerated until ready to fry.

FRY   In a nonstick skillet, over medium heat, melt 2 teaspoons Butter. Spread it.
       When the Butter turns golden (not brown), fry the Croque-monsieur. When the
       bottom slice turns golden brown, with tongs and spatula turn the Croque-monsieur
       and golden brown the other side. Add BUTTER if skillet gets too dry.

       Cut and remove gently the trussing string. Serve hot, cut in half or triangles.
       As an hors-d'oeuvre, cut into small squares and fasten each with a toothpick.

Some Cheeses for Croque-Monsieur

AMERICAN CHEESE	BRIE	EDAM	GOUDA	MOZZARELLA
APPENZELLER	CAMEMBERT	EMMENTHAL	GRUYÈRE	PORT-SALUT
BEL PAESE	CHEDDAR	FONTINA	MONTEREY JACK	SWISS CHEESE

CROUSTADE

A CROUSTADE is a fried or baked slice of Bread used for open-face Sandwiches.

TO FRY   Cut the slices about a 1/2-inch thick. The Crust can be left or trimmed.
             Heat the skillet. Melt in it BUTTER, FAT or OIL, enough to cover the base.
             When it sizzles, fry the slices on both sides until golden brown.
             Place them on a cookie sheet. Top with Ingredients, then the Cheese.
             Pass under the broiler until the Cheese has melted. Serve immediately.
             NOTE: some toppings may not need to go under the broiler.

TO BAKE   Preheat oven to 375°. Brush the slices with BUTTER, FAT or OIL.
             Place them in a pan. Bake on both sides until golden brown.
             Top with cooked Ingredients. Pass under the broiler if needed.

THE TOPPINGS - Creamed Mixtures of Fish, Seafood, Poultry, Cured Meats, scrambled Eggs.

PITA BREAD

Sandwiches can be served cold, warm, baked, broiled or fried.
They can be split in half and served as appetizers, hearty meals, light lunches.
Fried and cut into small wedges, they make lovely hors-d'oeuvres.
Bring Pita Bread to room temperature before using it.

To soften before using wrap in foil. Preheat oven to 300°. Heat 4 or 5 minutes.

SANDWICHES WITH COLD FILLINGS

Cut Pita in half. Or make a slit on the side large enough to insert the FILLING.
Wrap foil half-way up the Sandwich. It will be easier to hold and prevent drippings.

BAKED SANDWICHES   Preheat oven to 350°.

With a sharp pointed knife cut carefully an X on top side of Pita to make 4 flaps.
Lift Flaps, stuff the Pita. Press down gently. Brush the top with a little OLIVE OIL.

Line an oven tray with foil. Place the stuffed Pita on it. Turn on broiler.
Broil 3-to-5 minutes to crust the top. Turn off the broiler and bake at 350°, or
longer, depending on the Filling. With Cheese, wait until it has melted.

FRIED SANDWICHES

Brush top and bottom of Sandwiches with OLIVE OIL. Rub with the OIL a nonstick
skillet. Heat the skillet, fry the Sandwich in it, on both sides, until crisp.

TOASTED PITA   Preheat oven to 350°.

Cut the Pita in half. Detach the pocket sides. Cut them into 2 or 3 triangles.
Place on a cookie sheet, inside facing up. Bake without turning until golden brown.
Optional: brush inside with OLIVE OIL. Cut triangles. Sprinkle Salt, Spices, bake.

HAM - ASSORTED SANDWICHES

Add HAM or PROSCIUTTO to the following combinations.

APPLE SAUCE	BRIE CHEESE	CREAM CHEESE	MOZZARELLA
[CAPERS minced	[PEAR	[RAISINS minced	[ROASTED PEPPERS
[GOUDA thinly sliced	[CORNICHONS	[RELISH	[CHIVES
[PARSLEY minced	[WATERCRESS	[PIMIENTO STRIPS	[ARUGULA
ARTICHOKE BOTTOMS	**CAMEMBERT**	**CREAM CHEESE**	**MOZZARELLA**
[MAYONNAISE mix with	[DRIED FIGS sliced	[CUCUMBER	[TOMATOES
[CHIVES	[PECANS chopped	[OLIVES	[FRESH BASIL
[CAPERS	[FRESH DILL	[GREEN ONION	[OLIVES
ASPARAGUS TIPS	**CHÈVRE**	**EMMENTHAL**	**PROVOLONE**
[TARTARE SAUCE	[TOMATOES	[CRANBERRY SAUCE	[TOMATOES
[WATERCRESS	[CHIVES	[PICKLED ONIONS	[CAPERS or CHIVES
BRIE CHEESE	**CREAM CHEESE**	**EMMENTHAL**	**RICOTTA**
[CUCUMBER	[PINEAPPLE	[APPLE grated	[HORSERADISH
[CHIVES, WATERCRESS	[CAPERS	[WORCESTERSHIRE	[WATERCRESS

HAM - CROQUE-MONSIEUR

CLASSIC Butter both sides of BREAD with [PLAIN BUTTER

Spread on bottom slice a good layer of [GRUYÈRE or SWISS sliced or shredded
Top with sliced [HAM
Add [GRUYÈRE or SWISS CHEESE
Cover with top slice.

AVOCADO Butter outside of slices with [PLAIN BUTTER
Spread on inside of slices [MAYONNAISE mix with CURRY POWDER

Top CURRY MAYONNAISE with [CHUTNEY
[AVOCADO thinly sliced
[HAM
Cover with top slice.

FETA Butter outside of slices with [PLAIN BUTTER

Spread on inside of both slices [FETA CHEESE mashed with
a little [EXTRA-VIRGIN OLIVE OIL
add [CHIVES or GREEN ONION minced

Top Feta with [HAM and chopped BLACK OLIVES
Cover with top slice.

HAM or PROSCIUTTO - CROUSTADES

Toppings that go under the broiler.

ASPARAGUS TIPS

Spread [HERB BOURSIN on Croustade
top with [HAM minced, or PROSCIUTTO
[ASPARAGUS TIPS cooked
[CREAMY BÉCHAMEL *
[PARMESAN grated

BRIE CHEESE

Spread [SOUR CREAM and
[HORSERADISH on Croustade
top with [SHALLOTS sautéed
[HAM or PROSCIUTTO
[BRIE CHEESE sliced

BROWNED ONIONS

Brown [ONION
in [BUTTER
Add [SALT, PEPPER
Spread [MUSTARD on Croustade
[BROWNED ONIONS
[HAM sliced
[GRUYÈRE or SWISS sliced

* See "SAUCES".

EGGS

Spread [KETCHUP on Croustade
mix [HAM chopped, with
[CAPER BÉCHAMEL * and
[HARD-COOKED EGGS chopped
top with [CHEDDAR shredded

GOAT CHEESE

Spread [GOAT CHEESE on Croustade
top with [TOMATO sliced
[FRESH BASIL
[HAM or PROSCIUTTO
[MOZZARELLA sliced

MUSHROOMS

Sauté [MUSHROOMS sliced
with [GARLIC minced
and [TARRAGON dried
Add [HAM finely diced
[PARMESAN grated
A little [HEAVY CREAM
Spread [the Mixture on Croustade
top with [GRUYÈRE or SWISS shredded

56

Toppings that do not go under the broiler.

AVOCADO

Mash	[AVOCADO
with	[LEMON JUICE a little
and	[JALAPEÑOS minced
top with	[HAM sliced or PROSCIUTTO
and	[TOMATO sliced
	[CILANTRO finely chopped

OLIVE TAPENADE **

Mix	[TAPENADE w/MAYONNAISE
	[Spread it on Croustade
top with	[GREEN ONION minced
	[CUCUMBER sliced
	[HAM sliced or PROSCIUTTO
	[FRESH BASIL finely chopped

CREAMED CORN

Heat	[CREAMED CORN
add	[CHEDDAR shredded
Spread	[on Croustade
top with	[RED ONION minced
	[HAM, SAUSAGE or PROSCIUTTO
top with	[CREAMED CORN

RÉMOULADE SAUCE ***

Mix with	[RÉMOULADE SAUCE
	[CORNICHONS minced
	[TOMATO diced
top with	[HAM or PROSCIUTTO
	[a little more Sauce
	[PARSLEY minced

** Tapenade - see "DIPS and SPREADS".   *** Rémoulade - see "SAUCES" - COLD.

HAM or PROSCIUTTO in PITA BREAD - BAKED

CHINESE VEGETABLES leftovers

[EGGS scramble with
[CHINESE VEGETABLES chopped, and
[HAM chopped. Fill Pita.
[Top with CHEDDAR shredded

CREAMED SPINACH

[TOMATO diced
[HAM or PROSCIUTTO
[PARMESAN grated
[MOZZARELLA shredded

PINEAPPLE thinly sliced

[CILANTRO finely chopped
[PICKLES chopped
[HAM
[CHEDDAR shredded

CREAMED CORN

[SWEET PIMIENTO strips (in a jar)
[HAM
[FRESH DILL snipped
[BRIE CHEESE thin slices

MUSHROOMS sauté with

[GARLIC and
[BASIL finely chopped
[HAM or PROSCIUTTO
[MOZZARELLA or SWISS

SAUERKRAUT drained

[ONIONS smothered
[RAISINS
[HAM
[CHEDDAR shredded

SALAMI / SAUSAGE - ASSORTED SANDWICHES

Add SALAMI or SAUSAGE to the following combinations.

CHÈVRE (Goat Cheese)

[ARUGULA
[TOMATO sliced
[PICKLES or OLIVES

EGG SALAD

[PALM HEARTS
[CHIVES
[WATERCRESS

MELTED CHEESE top with

[RAISINS chopped
[ONIONS sauteed
[ALFALFA

CREAM CHEESE mix with

[PESTO SAUCE
[CUCUMBER or TOMATO
[LETTUCE

MELTED CHEESE

[TOMATILLO SAUCE
[KIWI sliced
[CILANTRO

SOUR CREAM mix with

[BLACK BEANS
[GREEN ONION
[CHEDDAR

MUFFULETTA   The New Orleans Sandwich   *Grilled in a sandwich grill or grilling pan.*

Spread [	ROUND ROLL or BUN halves with OLIVE TAPENADE (see "Dips and Spreads")
Top with all [	MORTADELLA, HAM, SALAMI, PROVOLONE. Cover with top part of Roll.

SALAMI / SAUSAGE - CROUSTADES

Toppings that go under the broiler - Place Ingredients in the order they are listed.

BAKED APPLE   leftover

Spread   [BAKED APPLE   chopped
on   [CROUSTADE
top with   [CURRANTS or RAISINS
           [SAUSAGE   sliced
           [CHEDDAR   slices

BAKED BEANS

Spread   [BAKED BEANS
top with   [FRIED ONIONS   canned
           [SAUSAGE sliced, or SALAMI
           [AVOCADO   thinly sliced
           [MOZZARELLA   slices

CREOLE

Spread   [MAYONNAISE   thinly
top with   [BANANA   thinly sliced
           [SAUSAGE   sliced
           [SPICY STEWED OKRA   canned
           [MONTEREY   shredded

MOZZARELLA

Spread   [TOMATO SAUCE   thinly
top with   [MOZZARELLA   slices
           [SALAMI   plenty
           [FRESH BASIL   minced
           [MOZZARELLA

Toppings that do not go under the broiler.

CREOLE

Sauté   [ONION and
           [GREEN BELL PEPPER   strips
add   [TOMATO   diced
sprinkle   [CREOLE SEASONING   to taste

Spread   [CREAM CHEESE   on Croustade
top with   [SAUSAGE   sliced, or SALAMI
           [Sautéed VEGETABLES
sprinkle   [SPICY PECANS   chopped

HAWAIIAN

Sauté   [ONION   with
           [SAUSAGE MEAT   and
           [RAISINS
Add   [CAPERS   minced
A little   [MAPLE SYRUP

Spread   [MUSTARD   on Croustade
top with   [PINEAPPLE   sliced
top with   [SAUSAGE MEAT MIXTURE

SALAMI / SAUSAGE in PITA BREAD - BAKED

LENTILS

Mix   [LENTILS
with   [SOUR CREAM   and
           [GREEN ONIONS   minced
Add   [SALAMI or SAUSAGE
top with   [MOZZARELLA   shredded

MUSHROOMS

Sauté   [MUSHROOMS
with   [ONIONS
Add   [PARSLEY
           [SALAMI or SAUSAGE
top with   [SWISS   shredded

STIR-FRY

Stir-fry   [BELL PEPPERS and ONIONS
Add   [SAUSAGE   diced
           [PESTO SAUCE   to moisten
Mix in   [PARMESAN   grated
top with   [MOZZARELLA   sliced

STIR-FRY

Stir-fry   [SNOW PEAS and ONIONS
Add   [SAUSAGE
           [TERIYAKI SAUCE   to moisten
           [SESAME SEEDS   toasted
top with   [CHEDDAR   shredded

EGGS in PITA BREAD - BAKED

           [EGGS   scrambled with
any of   [CHEESE, BELL PEPPER, ONIONS
           [MUSHROOMS, TOMATOES
Add   [HAM, PROSCIUTTO, SALAMI
           [SAUSAGE, TUNA, SEAFOOD

Stuff Pita with scrambled Eggs and bake.

FETA in PITA BREAD - FRIED

Mash   [FETA CHEESE
with a little [EXTRA-VIRGIN OLIVE OIL

Optional   [MINT or BASIL   finely chopped
           [GREEN ONION   minced

Stuff Pita with Feta Cheese and fry.

FISH SANDWICHES   *The following make good combinations with Fish.*

CHEESE   -   Boursin Garlic/Herbs, Boursin Pepper, Cream Cheese, melted Cheddar, Swiss.

SAUCES/DIPS   -   Aïoli, Hummus, Salsa, Seasoned Mayonnaise, Soy, Tartare, Guacamole.

VEGETABLES   -   Asparagus, Bean Sprouts, shredded Carrots, Cucumber, Onions, Tomato.

FRUIT   -   Avocado, Kiwi, Pineapple.

FLAVORS   -   Capers, Herbs, grated Ginger, Olives, Pickles, Relish, Sun-dried Tomatoes.

OTHER   -   Beans, Caponata, Egg Salad or hard-cooked, Ratatouille, roasted Bell Pepper.

In the following recipes, all amounts are flexible. Use canned SALMON and TUNA.

SALMON - CELERY

Mix   [6 oz   SALMON finely flaked
          [3 TB   TARTARE SAUCE ready-made
          [2 TB   CELERY finely chopped
          [1 TB   GREEN ONION minced
          [1 tp   CAPERS rinse, drain, mince
          [PEPPER, SALT if needed

          [garnish   ALFALFA or LETTUCE

SALMON - FENNEL

Mix   [6 oz   SALMON finely flaked
with   [2 TB   SOUR CREAM
        [1 TB   MAYONNAISE or to taste
        [3 TB   FENNEL diced or grated
        [1 TB   CHIVES or to taste
        [garnish   WATERCRESS

TUNA - ARTICHOKES

Chop coarsely in processor:

          [3 oz   TUNA drained
          [2 oz   ARTICHOKE HEARTS
Then
add   [2 TB   EXTRA-VIRGIN OLIVE OIL
          [2 TB   LEMON JUICE
          [1 TB   MAYONNAISE
          [garnish   WATERCRESS

TUNA - NIÇOISE

Mix   [3 oz   TUNA drained, flaked
          [2 TB   MAYONNAISE
          [a little   LEMON JUICE
          [1 small   TOMATO seeded, diced
          [4 TB   BELL PEPPER finely chopped
          [ANCHOVIES to taste, mashed

Rub   [Bread with   GARLIC CLOVE
          [spread with   OLIVE TAPENADE ("Dips and Spreads")
          [top with   TUNA MIXTURE

SALMON - CURRY

Mix   [3 TB   MAYONNAISE
                  [CURRY POWDER to taste

Stir it into   [6 oz   SALMON finely flaked
Add   [3 TB   BELL PEPPER diced
                  [1 tp   ONION or to taste
                  [LEMON JUICE to taste
                  [grated   FRESH GINGER to taste

SALMON - PINEAPPLE

Mix   [6 oz   SALMON finely flaked
                  [3 TB   MAYONNAISE
                  [SOY SAUCE a dash
                  [4 TB   PINEAPPLE diced
                  [CAPERS to taste

Or substitute Capers with DILL PICKLED diced

TUNA - CELERY

Mix   [3 oz   TUNA drained, flaked
                  [2 TB   TARTARE SAUCE
                  [2 TB   CELERY finely chopped
                  [RED ONION to taste
                  [RELISH to taste
                  [garnish   CILANTRO finely chop

TUNA - RADISH

Mix   [3 oz   TUNA drained, flaked
                  [2 TB   MIRACLE WHIP
                  [LEMON JUICE a little
                  [3 TB   RED RADISH grated
                  [2 TB   GREEN ONION minced
                  [1/2-of   HARD-COOKED EGG
                                     chopped
                  [garnish   ARUGULA

SMOKED SALMON - CROQUE-MONSIEUR

Butter both sides with	[PLAIN BUTTER
Sprinkle inside with	[FRESH DILL snipped
Top with	[BRIE thinly sliced pieces
	[SMOKED SALMON
	[LEMON JUICE a few drops
	[CHIVES, a little more BRIE

SMOKED SALMON - CROUSTADE

Spread on Croustade	[BRIE
Melt under broiler.	
Top with	[SMOKED SALMON
Sautéed	[MUSHROOMS
	[SHALLOT BÉCHAMEL
	[PARSLEY minced

SMOKED SALMON SANDWICHES   *Combine the Salmon with any of:*

CHEESE	-	Bel Paese, Garlic Boursin, Brie, Feta, a variety of Goat Cheese, Mascarpone.
SAUCES	-	(See "SAUCES") Green Goddess, Horseradish Cream, Rémoulade, Tartare.
VEGETABLES	-	cooked Beets, Endive, Cucumber, Fennel, Green Onion, grated Radish.
FLAVORS	-	Capers, Chives, Cornichons, Dill, Horseradish, Lemon Juice, Olive Tapenade.
OTHER	-	Avocado, scrambled Eggs with Onion, Egg Salad, mashed Navy Bean Salad.

*Use a 1/4-cup of Sauce per Croustade. * See "SAUCES".*

SMOKED TROUT - CROUSTADE

Trim		[SMOKED TROUT
		verify there are no bones left
Prepare	1 cup	[SHALLOT BÉCHAMEL *
Add	1 TB	[PARSLEY finely chopped
	2	[BOILED EGGS chopped
Cover		
to keep it warm.		
Prepare		[CROUSTADES
Top with		[AVOCADO mashed
Top with		[Smoked Trout
Top with		[Shallot Béchamel

Serve immediately.

SARDINES - CROUSTADE

Prepare		[LEMON EGG SAUCE *
		Turn off heat. Cover.
Flake		[SARDINES skinless, boneless,
		drained
Prepare		[CROUSTADES
Top with		[sardines
Prepare		[EGG soft-cooked or poached

- Warm the Sauce during Egg preparation.
- Top Sardines with Eggs. Cover with Sauce.

Sprinkle	[PARSLEY finely chopped

TUNA MELT - CROUSTADE

Mix	3 oz can	[TUNA FISH drain, flake
	1-1/2-TB	[MAYONNAISE or to taste
	1/2-tp	[LEMON JUICE or to taste
Add to taste		[CAPERS rinse, mince
	or	PICKLED JALAPEÑO minced
To taste		[GREEN ONION minced
		[PAPRIKA, SALT if needed
Spread on	2	[CROUSTADES
Top with		[CHEDDAR shredded

Pass under the broiler until the Cheese melts.

VARIATION   -   Substitute Cheddar with:

WELSH RAREBIT. ("BASIC RECIPES" - FONDUE)
Serve it over the Tuna. Do not pass under the broiler.

TUNA MELT - GRILLED SANDWICH

Spread	[BREAD SLICES
with	[BUTTER and MUSTARD
Top with	[slices CHEDDAR, or ASIAGO,
	MANCHEGO, EDAM
Top with	[TUNA MIXTURE for Croustade
Cover with	[slices of the CHEESE

- Top with a slice of the buttered BREAD.
- Press down.
- Grill in a sandwich grill, or as described in
  the beginning of this chapter.

SEAFOOD - CROUSTADES

They make lovely appetizers. Serve them in a baking dish or in individual oven-to-table dishes.
Use Breads with flavors like Cheese, Jalapeño, Olive, Onion.   *A 1/4-cup of Sauce per Croustade.*

Toppings that go under the broiler.

ALFREDO

Toss   [CRABMEAT
with   [ALFREDO SAUCE *
add   [PARSLEY   minced
Place   [ASPARAGUS TIPS on Croustade
top with [CRABMEAT/ALFREDO SAUCE
top with [SWISS   shredded. Broil golden.

CAPER BÉCHAMEL for FISH

Toss   [CRABMEAT
with   [CAPER BÉCHAMEL **
Place   [SHREDDED CHEDDAR   on Croustade
top with [CARAMELIZED ONIONS
          [CRABMEAT with CAPER BÉCHAMEL
          [SHREDDED CHEDDAR

FLORENTINE

Sauté   [MUSHROOMS   sliced
with   [GARLIC   minced
          [Spread them on Croustade
top with [OYSTERS
          [CREAMED SPINACH
          [PARMESAN   grated

PESTO

Mix   [PESTO   ready-made
with   [ALFREDO SAUCE *
Place   [CRISPY BACON STRIPS
          [on Croustade
top with [SHRIMP
          [PESTO/ALFREDO SAUCE
top with [FONTINA CHEESE coarse-grated

Toppings that do not go under the broiler.

CHAMPAGNE or WHITE WINE SAUCE

Trim   [FENNEL, shred in food processor
Prepare   [CHAMPAGNE or WHITE WINE SAUCE **

When the Sauce is ready, add to it the Fennel.
For 1 cup of Sauce use 1/3 cup Fennel.

Place   [SLICED PALM HEARTS on Croustade
          [LOBSTER or CRABMEAT
          [CHAMPAGNE or WHITE WINE SAUCE

LEMON EGG SAUCE

Mix   [AVOCADO   diced
with   [LEMON JUICE   a little

Add   [CAPERS   minced
to   [LEMON EGG SAUCE **

Place   [SEAFOOD on Croustade
top with [AVOCADO
and   [LEMON EGG SAUCE

CREAMY CAVIAR

Add to   [MEDIUM WHITE SAUCE **
to taste [SALMON ROE CAVIAR drain if needed
          [CHIVES

Lay on   [CROUSTADE
          [ARTICHOKE BOTTOMS   thinly sliced
top with [SCALLOPS   sliced, sautéed
top with [CAVIAR SAUCE

MUSSELS MARINARA

Sauté   [2 TB   ONION   minced
          [2 TB green BELL PEPPER
          [2 TB   CELERY   minced
          [GARLIC to taste
Add   [1/2-cup   MARINARA SAUCE*

When hot add [MUSSELS steamed and shelled
Serve on   [CROUSTADES

CREAMY CURRY

Mix   [CREAMY CURRY SAUCE **
with   [SCALLOPS   sautéed, sliced, or SHRIMP
Brown   [APPLE   thinly sliced
in   [BUTTER, then place on Croustade
top with [SEAFOOD in CURRY SAUCE

SHALLOT BÉCHAMEL

Add to   [SHALLOT BÉCHAMEL **
          [PARSLEY   minced, CHIVES
Place   [CRABMEAT on Croustade
top with [FRIED or POACHED EGG
top with [SHALLOT BÉCHAMEL

* Ready-made or see "SAUCES".   ** See "SAUCES".

ASSORTED SANDWICHES

Add Meats and Seasonings to the following combinations.

BEEF and BARBECUE

EGG TARTARE SPREAD *

[ARTICHOKE BOTTOMS   thinly sliced
[PAPRIKA
[WATERCRESS

GINGER WATERCRESS *

[TOMATO sliced
[WATER CHESTNUTS sliced
[LETTUCE

GOAT CHEESE CORNICHONS *

[BEETS   thinly sliced
[GREEN ONION   minced
[LETTUCE

HERDEZ canned Mexican Sauce

[AVOCADO   thinly sliced
[SUNFLOWER SEEDS
[CHEDDAR or AMERICAN sliced

HORSERADISH SOUR CREAM *

[CHIVES
[CUCUMBER slice lengthwise
[ALFALFA

SAUERKRAUT - CROUSTADE

[SAUERKRAUT   prepared
[CORNED BEEF
[WELSH RAREBIT

LEG of LAMB in PITA BREAD

AÏOLI **

[TOMATO   sliced
[BLACK OLIVES   sliced
[ALFALFA

AVOCADO mashed

[RED ONION   finely chopped
[TOMATO   thinly sliced

BEANS   (Navy or Lima) mashed

[TAHINI **
[TOMATO   sliced

CREAM CHEESE CUCUMBER *

[TOMATO
[BLACK OLIVES

CURRY MAYONNAISE **

[ROASTED BELL PEPPER
[GREEN ONION

CURRY MAYONNAISE **

[Mix MAYONNAISE with CURRY POWDER
[CHUTNEY
[APPLE   thinly sliced

EGGPLANT

[Broiled EGGPLANT slices ***
[HUMMUS spread on Pita
[RED ONION   very thinly sliced

FETA CHEESE MINT *

[CUCUMBER thinly slice lengthwise
[BLACK OLIVES   pitted, chopped

GARLIC MAYONNAISE **

[HARD-COOKED EGG   sliced
[WATERCRESS

GREEN LENTILS with MINT ***

[CUCUMBER thinly sliced lengthwise
[CHIVES

HUMMUS * or ready-made

[RED ONION   thinly sliced
[TOMATO   sliced

MINT YOGURT

[Mix DRIED MINT with YOGURT
[GREEN ONION   finely chopped
[RADISHES   thinly sliced

* See "DIPS and SPREADS".   ** See "SAUCES".   *** See "VEGETABLES".

62

ROAST PORK

CHILI MAYONNAISE

Mix [MAYONNAISE
with [CHILI POWDER
and   [DRIED APRICOTS   chopped
Top   [with PORK
      [ALFALFA

GRATED APPLE   mix with

         [CREAM CHEESE
         [RAISINS   chopped
         [GROUND CINNAMON   a sprinkle
Top with [PORK
         [WATERCRESS

GINGER WATERCRESS SPREAD *

[PINEAPPLE   sliced
[RADISH   grated
[PORK
[CILANTRO   chopped

ORANGE MARMALADE   mix with

[MUSTARD PICKLES   minced
[KIWI   thinly sliced
[PORK
[ALFALFA

ROAST VEAL

CREAM CHEESE RADISH SPREAD *

Layer [SWEET PIMIENTO STRIPS (in a jar)
       [VEAL
       [HARD-COOKED EGGS   sliced
       [ARUGULA

LEMON CELERY MAYONNAISE SPREAD *

[PEAR   thinly sliced
[VEAL
[CAPERS   minced
[BLUE CHEESE   crumbled

KETCHUP MAYONNAISE SPREAD *

[VEAL
[AVOCADO
[CHEDDAR   thinly sliced

ROQUEFORT CREAM CHEESE SPREAD *

[VEAL
[FENNEL   grated or shredded
[CAPERS   minced

* See "DIPS AND SPREADS".

CHICKEN and TURKEY SANDWICHES

CREATE A SANDWICH

The following Ingredients make good combinations with Chicken and Turkey.

SPREADS **	CHEESE	VEGETABLES	HERBS	FRUIT
Aïoli	Bel Paese	Alfalfa	Basil	Avocado
Cranberry Sauce	Blue Cheese	Arugula	Chives	Banana
Guacamole	Camembert	Bean sprouts	Cilantro	Kiwi
Horseradish	Chavrie	Cucumber	Watercress	Pineapple
Hummus	Chèvre	Bell Pepper		
Olive Tapenade	Colby	also Roasted	SAUCES	
Pesto	Cream	Mushrooms		
Salsa	Gruyère	Vidalia Onion	Asian	
Tartare Sauce	Stilton	Radish	Chili	

FLAVOR - Capers, Chutney, Cornichons, Ginger, Jalapeño, Olives, Pickles.

OTHER - Mashed Beans, Egg Salad, Lentil Salad, mixed green Salad in Pita Bread.

** Also see "DIPS and SPREADS".

CHICKEN / TURKEY - CROQUE-MONSIEUR

BRIE

Spread both sides of	[	BREAD SLICES
with	[	PLAIN BUTTER
Top with	[	BRIE CHEESE
	[	CRISPY BACON crumbled
	[	CHICKEN / TURKEY
A dash	[	WORCESTERSHIRE SAUCE
	[	BRIE CHEESE

Cover with top slice.

CARIBBEAN

Spread outside with	[	PLAIN BUTTER
Process in processor into a fluffy texture	[	CHICKEN or TURKEY
Transfer to a bowl and mix to taste with	[	CRUSHED PINEAPPLE canned, drained
	[	TINY CAPERS or HOT CHILLIES
Spread inside of BREAD SLICES with	[	RED or BLACK BEANS mash
Top with	[	MONTEREY JACK shredded
	[	Pineapple Mixture
	[	MONTEREY JACK

Cover with top slice.

CLASSIC

Spread both sides with	[	PLAIN BUTTER
Spread inside with	[	MUSTARD
Top with	[	SWISS or GRUYÈRE sliced
	[	CHICKEN / TURKEY sliced or shredded
	[	SWISS or GRUYÈRE

Cover with top slice.

SAN REMO

Spread both sides of	[	BREAD SLICES
with	[	PLAIN BUTTER
Season inside with	[	MUSTARD
Top Mustard with	[	MOZZARELLA sliced, or PROVOLONE
	[	PROSCIUTTO or SALAMI
	[	CHICKEN / TURKEY sliced or shredded
	[	FRESH BASIL chopped
	[	MOZZARELLA or PROVOLONE

Cover with top slice.

TEX-MEX

Spread both sides with	[	PLAIN BUTTER
Mash to taste	[	REFRIED BEANS
with	[	SALSA or PICKLED JALAPEÑOS chopped

Spread it on bottom slices.

Top with	[	RED ONION chopped, or AVOCADO sliced
	[	CILANTRO finely chopped
	[	CHICKEN / TURKEY
	[	MONTEREY JACK shredded or grated

Cover with top slice.

CHICKEN / TURKEY - CROUSTADES

Place Ingredients in the order they are listed.

Toppings that go under the broiler

ASPARAGUS TIPS

```
[ ASPARAGUS TIPS
[ CHICKEN / TURKEY
[ MEDIUM WHITE SAUCE *
[ CHEDDAR
```

AVOCADO

Mash   [AVOCADO
top with [CHICKEN / TURKEY thinly sliced
A dash   [WORCESTERSHIRE SAUCE
          [BROWNED ONIONS
          [CHEDDAR

CORDON BLEU

```
[ GRILLED HAM
[ CHICKEN / TURKEY  thinly sliced
[ GRUYÈRE  sliced or shredded
```

CREAM of CORN

Spread   [MUSTARD on Croustade
top with [CHICKEN / TURKEY
          [CREAM of CORN
          [GRUYÈRE or SWISS slices

CURRY BÉCHAMEL *

Spread   [CARAMELIZED ONIONS
top with [BANANA thinly sliced
          [CHICKEN / TURKEY
          [CURRY BÉCHAMEL
          [COCONUT grated
          [CHEDDAR shredded

HARD-COOKED EGGS chopped, mix with

         [MEDIUM WHITE SAUCE *
         [CHIVES
Top   [CHICKEN / TURKEY with Sauce
and   [SWISS CHEESE shredded

ONIONS - CARAMELIZED

Spread   [SWISS shredded
top with [CARAMELIZED ONIONS
          [CHICKEN / TURKEY
          [CARAMELIZED ONIONS
          [SWISS shredded

MUSHROOMS sautéed with Shallot

         [MUSHROOMS
         [CHICKEN / TURKEY
         [ALFREDO SAUCE
top with [SWISS shredded

PESTO

         [MASCARPONE spread lightly
         [CHICKEN / TURKEY
         [PESTO SAUCE
         [MOZZARELLA shredded

SPINACH - CREAMED

         [PARMESAN grated
         [SPINACH
         [CHICKEN / TURKEY
         [PARMESAN
         [SPINACH
top with [GRUYÈRE or SWISS shredded

Toppings that do not go under the broiler

AÏOLI *

Sauté   [ONIONS minced
and   [RED BELL PEPPERS diced
in   [OLIVE OIL
Let cool.
Mix in   [CHICKEN /TURKEY diced
         [AÏOLI
         [PARSLEY minced

EGGS

Sauté   [ONION chopped
and   [TOMATO diced
Add   [CHICKEN / TURKEY chopped

Spread on [CROUSTADE
top with [EGG fried or poached

* See "SAUCES".

HOLLANDAISE *

Sauté   [ONIONS thinly sliced
         [MUSHROOMS sliced
         [DRIED TARRAGON
Spread on [CROUSTADE
top with [CRISPY BACON
         [CHICKEN / TURKEY sliced
         [HOLLANDAISE SAUCE

PIZZAIOLA *

Spread   [MASCARPONE on Croustade
top with [PARMESAN grated
         [FRESH BASIL finely chopped
         [CHICKEN / TURKEY sliced
         [PARMESAN grated
         [PIZZAIOLA SAUCE

PAN BAGNAT

Pan (bread) Bagnat (bathed) in French dialect means "soaked bread". This Sandwich originated in the South of France. Pronounced "pahn-baan'-yah". It consists of Vegetables and Garnishes, moistened with a Salad Dressing, or with Olive Oil and Seasonings.

SALAD LEFTOVERS, make delicious Pan Bagnats. They can be stuffed into Pita Bread, hollowed out Bun or Baguette, or even between thick Bread slices.

HARD-COOKED EGGS, CHEESE, PICKLES, FISH, TUNA, SEAFOOD, CURED MEATS can be added.

Wrap filled Pan Bagnats in foil and flatten them out with a weight, for a few minutes.
The foil will make the Sandwich easier to hold and prevent the Dressing from dripping.

CLASSIC MEDITERRANEAN

Remove partially inside crumb from [	BAGUETTE or HAMBURGER BUN
Rub the inside with a [	GARLIC CLOVE split in half
Moisten with a little [	EXTRA-VIRGIN OLIVE OIL
Fill with [	TOMATOES sliced
Drizzle Tomatoes with [	EXTRA-VIRGIN OLIVE OIL
Sprinkle with Salt, Pepper. Top with [	BELL PEPPER strips
[	MOZZARELLA sliced
Drizzle Mozzarella with [	EXTRA-VIRGIN OLIVE OIL
[	FRESH BASIL LEAVES
[	HARD-COOKED EGG sliced
[	ANCHOVIES or SARDINES
[	OLIVES pitted and sliced

CAESAR SALAD

Toss in a bowl	[ROMAINE LETTUCE
	[HARD-COOKED EGG chopped
	[ANCHOVIES
	[PARMESAN grated and shavings
Moisten with	[OIL and LEMON DRESSING

GREEK SALAD

Toss in a bowl	[LETTUCE
	[TOMATOES
	[CUCUMBER
	[ONION
	[FETA CHEESE
	[BLACK OLIVES
Moisten with	[VINAIGRETTE DRESSING

SPINACH SALAD in PITA BREAD

Toss in a bowl [	BABY SPINACH
[	HARD-COOKED EGGS chopped
[	RAW MUSHROOMS sliced
[	CRISPY BACON crumbled
[	PINE NUTS toasted
Season with a [	VINAIGRETTE

TABBOULEH

Drain the leftover [	TABBOULEH - see "SALADS"
Adjust its seasoning, adding a little [	LEMON JUICE, SALT and PEPPER
Fill PITA with Tabbouleh, optional, add any of [	ANCHOVIES, SARDINES, SHRIMP, TUNA,
[	FETA or HALOUMI CHEESE, OLIVES

CANAPÉS and FINGER SANDWICHES

Select BUTTERS, MAYONNAISE and SPREADS - see "DIPS and SPREADS".

ANCHOVIES mash with

[SOUR CREAM
[SCALLIONS
[HARD-COOKED EGG   sliced

CRABMEAT

[CREOLE MAYONNAISE *
[PICKLES   minced

HERRING

[SOUR CREAM
[CAPERS   minced
[CHERRY TOMATO   sliced

* See "SAUCES".

SARDINES

[SCALLION   minced
[LEMON JUICE
[CORNICHONS   minced

SHRIMP

[RÉMOULADE * mix with
[PINEAPPLE   grated

SMOKED SALMON

[GOAT CHEESE
[GREEN ONION
[LEMON JUICE

SMOKED TROUT

[CUCUMBER
[SOUR CREAM mix with
[HORSERADISH

TARAMOSALATA

[CUCUMBER
[BLACK OLIVES   minced

TUNA FISH - (Sashimi)

[WASABI MUSTARD
[GINGER   bits or grated
[CILANTRO   finely chopped

CURED MEATS

BRESAOLA

[UNSALTED BUTTER mix with MUSTARD
[BRESAOLA   sprinkle with a little
[OLIVE OIL and LEMON JUICE
[CORNICHONS   slice in a fan shape

CHORIZO

[MAYONNAISE season to taste with
[HORSERADISH and CILANTRO   minced
[CHORIZO
[PIMIENTO OLIVES   sliced

HAM / CURRY

[SOUR CREAM mix with CURRY POWDER
[HAM
[PINEAPPLE   shavings
[Sprinkle with PAPRIKA

PROSCIUTTO / ARTICHOKES

[MAYONNAISE mix with DRIED BASIL
[and CAPERS minced. Spread on Bread.
[ARTICHOKE BOTTOMS   thinly sliced
[PROSCIUTTO   sprinkle with CHIVES

PROSCIUTTO / CANTALOUPE

[UNSALTED BUTTER mix with
[PARMESAN   grated. Spread on Bread.
[PROSCIUTTO   top with
[SMALL CANTALOUPE BALL   cut in half

SALAMI / GOAT CHEESE

[GOAT CHEESE   mash with a little
[HORSERADISH and spread on bread.
[SALAMI
[MARINATED MUSHROOM CAPS

VEGETABLES

CUCUMBER   thinly sliced

[FETA CHEESE mashed with CHIVES
[CUCUMBER
[FRESH MINT   finely chopped

KIWI thinly sliced

[BLUE CHEESE mix with BUTTER and CHIVES
[KIWI
[top with SPICY PECAN   halves

KIWI

[MAYONNAISE mixed with GINGER grated
[KIWI, SALTED PEANUTS   chopped

PAPAYA thinly sliced

[GOAT CHEESE   spread
[CILANTRO   finely chopped
[PAPAYA sprinkle with CHILI SAUCE

PEACH   thinly sliced

[CAMEMBERT   thinly sliced
[PEACH
[CHIVES

PINEAPPLE

[STILTON   mashed with BUTTER
[PINEAPPLE, PECANS   chopped

GARNISHES for CANAPÉS and OTHER FOOD PRESENTATIONS

ANCHOVIES

Rinse. Cut into thin strips.
Roll strips. A caper in the center.

ASPARAGUS TIPS (thin)

Cut in half lengthwise. Use one piece,
or both, side by side. Place across
Asparagus a thin Pimiento strip.

AVOCADO

Scoop out small balls, cut in half. Or
dice finely. Sprinkle with Lemon Juice.

BACON

Crispy fried and crumbled.
Raw: wrap around Vegetables or Fruit.
Secure with wooden toothpick, broil.

BEETS

Minced or diced finely.
Thinly sliced: make cut-outs.

BLUEBERRIES

Cut in half. Use as polka dots.

CAPERS

Drain, rinse, dry. Whole or minced.

CELERY

Thinly sliced. Grated or shredded.

CHEESE

Crumbled or grated.
Or cut thin slices into triangles,
stars. With a corer cut rounds.

CHERRIES Maraschino

Sliced or cut in half.

CHERRY TOMATOES

Cut in half. Or slice into half moons.

CHIVES

Sprinkle lightly.

CORNICHONS (small)

Slice thinly crosswise or mince.
Slice lengthwise in three, leave one end
uncut, spread in a fan shape.

CUCUMBER (a thin size)

Dent lengthwise the skin with a fork.
Thinly slice.

EARS OF CORN - PICKLED (small)

Cut in half lengthwise

GRAPES (seedless)

Cut in half or slice crosswise.

GREEN PEAS

Use on creamy toppings.

GINGER - FRESH

Grated or thinly shredded.

HARD-COOKED EGGS

Mince separately whites and yolks.
Slice thinly: rounds or half moons.

HERBS

Fresh: mince. Dried: crumble.
Use leaves to create a design.

HORSERADISH (prepared)

Tiny dots.

JALAPEÑOS   Pickled

Cut into thin strips, or minced.

KETCHUP

Tiny dots.

KIWI

Slice thinly. Cut into small wedges.

LEMON or LIME

Zest: grated. Or tiny julienne.
Slice thinly pulp. Cut into wedges.

(continued)

LUMPFISH   Black, Orange Red or Golden.

Tiny dots or a small mound in center.

MAYONNAISE

Use a pastry bag and small cone to squeeze out Mayonnaise into zig-zags or other designs.

MUSHROOMS

Sliced. Brush lightly with Dressing. Marinated caps.

MUSTARD

Tiny dots.

NUTS

Chopped, ground, sliced, slivered.

OLIVES

Halved, minced or sliced. Pimiento and Manzanilla Olives.

ONIONS - PICKLED (small)

Whole or cut in half.

PAPRIKA

Sprinkle for color.

PECANS and SPICY WALNUTS

Halves or chopped.

PICKLES

Any kind. Sliced or minced.

PINE NUTS

Toasted.

POMEGRANATE SEEDS

Give color.

QUAIL EGGS

Slice in half lengthwise. Slice into rounds. Or cut into wedges.

RADISH

Cut red peel into petals or other forms.

RAISINS

Soak in Water, Apple juice or Brandy. Use whole or chopped.

SALMON ROE CAVIAR

Use as dots. Or center into a small mound.

SEEDS

CARAWAY, FENNEL, POPPY, SESAME. Sprinkle over Canapés. Salted: SUNFLOWER.

SHRIMP (tiny)

Whole, with a Sweet Pimiento strip twisted around it. Split in half lengthwise.

SPICES

CINNAMON, CUMIN, CURRY, NUTMEG. Sprinkle lightly.

SUN-DRIED TOMATOES

Mince finely.

SWEET PIMIENTOS (in a jar)

Cut into thin strips. Use strips in crisscross designs. Roll strips into a curl.

SWEET RELISH

Use on spicy food.

TOMATO SAUCE or PASTE

Tiny dots.

TURMERIC

Sprinkle for yellow color.

WATER CHESTNUTS

Very thinly sliced.

NOTE   -   Prepare ahead of time Garnishes that need preparation and cutting. Store them in a sealed container, plastic wrap or foil. If needed, refrigerate until ready to use.

FRENCH TOAST

Remove the crust from [6 slices   BREAD of your choice
Cut it 3/4-inch thick.

In a shallow dish, beat [2   EGGS
with [1 cup   MILK
[1/4-tp   SALT

Dip Slices into the Egg Mixture, let excess drip,
place them on a tray or cookie sheet.

In a nonstick skillet, melt until it subsides [just enough   BUTTER   to cover the skillet base
or [a light   VEGETABLE OIL
Sauté the Slices to a golden brown.

Top them with   -   Eggs and Bacon, Ham, Sausage, Maple Syrup.
   -   Chicken or Ham Hash, Leftovers in Cheese Sauce, Fish/Seafood in a Sauce.

GARLIC TOAST

Version 1   Toast on both sides [BREAD SLICES

Rub the Toast with [GARLIC CLOVE   split in half
Drizzle with [EXTRA-VIRGIN OLIVE OIL
To taste [SALT, PEPPER, DRIED HERBS

Version 2   Use a pastry brush to brush [one side of BREAD SLICES
with [EXTRA-VIRGIN OLIVE OIL
Toast in oven at 350° until golden brown.

Rub toasted slices with [GARLIC CLOVE
Sprinkle with [SALT, PEPPER, DRIED HERBS

Version 3   Brush Bread slices with [EXTRA-VIRGIN OLIVE OIL
Sprinkle with [GARLIC POWDER
or rub with a [GARLIC CLOVE
[SALT, PEPPER, add HERBS   after baking
Toast in oven at 350° until golden brown.

WRAP SANDWICHES and CRISPS

WRAPS are flat Breads available in a variety of flavors. Wrap Sandwiches can be hot or cold.

- To serve hot, place the filled Sandwich in a sandwich grill and press the lid down to flatten it.
- Or wrap it in foil, flatten down, bake in oven preheated to 350° until heated through.

CRISPS   Brush lighter side of WRAPS with [EXTRA-VIRGIN OLIVE OIL

Cut into squares or rectangles, place
on a cookie sheet and sprinkle with [SALT, ZAA'TAR *, other

Bake at 350° until crisp: 12-to-15 minutes.

* A Middle Eastern Spice Mixture. Or use ground CUMIN, GARLIC SALT, ground CINNAMON.

IV

PIZZAS

In Italy Pizza-making is a tradition often handed down through generations. Their creations are called an Art.

Pizzas have become part of our culture.

They symbolize the fast pace at which we live and lack of time for home-cooked meals. Their greatest appeal is turning up at the mere touch of a number.

If we find the time, a home-made Pizza can become a delicacy with toppings not found by phone.

It can also be a simple and tasty way of using the Leftovers awaiting a bright inspiration.

With pre-cooked Crusts, Pizza is one of the easiest and quickest treats to prepare.

"The real voyage of discovery consists not in seeking new landscapes, but in having new eyes."

Marcel Proust

PIZZAS

NOTE

Amounts in Pizza recipes are flexible. Use more or less according to taste and availability.

PIZZAS

To experiment for future preparations, buy a ready-made Crust. Cut it into quarters and test your oven, following the label temperature directions. Bake a quarter topped with Ham and shredded Cheese. It will give you an idea of the amount of Ingredients to use.

- Have all Ingredients ready, at room temperature, to assemble the Pizza.
- First toast the Crust if you prefer a crunchy Pizza.
- Add the toppings and bake. In a half hour or less, the Pizza is on the table.
- It would take longer if raw Ingredients are involved.

UNCOOKED STORE-BOUGHT PIZZA DOUGH

I do not use it in the recipes. The purpose of this book is to use shortcuts.

However, if you choose to use it, first sprinkle your pastry board with Flour. Use a rolling pin to roll out thinly the Dough, about 1/4-inch thick. For cooking, follow the package directions.

Bake until it starts to color, then add the toppings and finish baking. This will prevent the toppings from drying, unless the Ingredients are raw and need to cook with the Pizza.

PIZZA CRUST - READY-MADE and PRECOOKED

A variety of brands is available. I use for my recipes the one(s) with the thinner Crust.

Amounts in the recipes apply to a 12-inch Pizza Crust. (You can use more or less according to taste). For an 8-inch Crust, reduce amounts by one third, or use a little more than half.

Package directions usually indicate to top the Pizza Crust with the Ingredients and bake it. By doing so, to avoid overcooking the toppings, the Crust remains chewy. I like a crunchy Crust.

CRUNCHY PIZZA CRUST

1. Place cookie sheet in the oven. Preheat oven following the package directions.

2. Place the ready-made, precooked Pizza Crust on the cookie sheet, browned side under.

   Option 1   Bake the Crust 6 minutes. Flip it over and bake one more minute.

   Option 2   Pour a little EXTRA-VIRGIN OLIVE OIL in a saucer. With a pastry brush, brush lightly with Oil the top "un-browned side" of the Crust. Bake the Crust for 6 minutes. Do not flip over.

   To taste   Before oiling rub the Crust with a Garlic clove split lengthwise.

3. - The bottom will be toasted. The crispy top will soften when Ingredients are added, but it won't get soggy. All ovens are not the same.
   - Cut a Pizza Crust into six wedges. Experiment the toasting time by baking each piece separately. A thicker Crust may take longer to toast.

4. - Take the Crust out of the oven. Top it with the Ingredients.
   - At this point, place a piece of foil under the Pizza. Some Ingredients and Cheese may run. The foil will prevent them from sticking and burning on the cookie sheet.

5. - Return Pizza to oven and bake it for 6-to-8 minutes.
   - If the Ingredients need no cooking, bake long enough for the Cheese to melt.

PIZZA TOPPINGS

Ready Toppings that can be used on a Pizza Crust:

HAM cooked	SEAFOOD canned	ASPARAGUS canned	RATATOUILLE, CAPONATA
CURED MEATS	SEAFOOD cooked	ARTICHOKES canned	MUSHROOMS canned
SAUSAGES cooked	TUNA canned	AVOCADO	MUSHROOMS raw, sliced
SMOKED TURKEY	ANCHOVIES	BELL PEPPERS roasted	TOMATOES
SMOKED FISH	SARDINES	CORN KERNELS canned	VEGETABLES canned
CHEESE	PICKLES	SUN-DRIED TOMATOES	PASTA SAUCES
CHIVES, HERBS	PIMIENTOS	SWEET ONIONS	BOTTLED SAUCES

CHEESE
Is easier to shred, slice or dice, when cold.
Shred or grate Leftover bits. Mix them, use them on your Pizzas.
Use semi-soft Cheese besides Mozzarella. Thinly slice or dice it.

Shredded Cheese melts in 5-to-6 minutes in oven at 450°.
Spread on a crispy Crust it will barely soften it, if the Crust is taken out of the oven as soon as the Cheese has melted.

Sliced, it takes 6-to-8 minutes, depending on thickness.

POULTRY
Add it after the Pizza with its other Ingredients has been baked.
(Re-cooked Poultry has an unpleasant taste.)

SAUCES
Should be spread sparingly on the Crust. They will soften the Crust anyway.
After the Pizza has been baked with Ingredients, if you are adding a topping such as Chicken in a Sauce, it must be hot. Do not return to oven.
Use a slotted spoon not to overload the Pizza with Sauce.

THE CRUST
Seasoning it can be done before adding the other Ingredients.

Brush the Crust with Olive Oil, sprinkle with Spice before toasting.
Do not sprinkle with Herbs, then toast. The Herbs would dry and burn.
After toasting the Crust, sprinkle with Herbs then add other Ingredients.

SPICE SEASONINGS

ALLSPICE	CHILI POWDER	CUMIN ground	DRY MUSTARD	PAPRIKA
CAYENNE	CINNAMON ground	CURRY POWDER	NUTMEG	PEPPER

SWEET PIZZA
When using the Crust as a base for Fruit or a Custard, brush it with melted unsalted Butter, not Oil. Sprinkle with Sugar, ground Cinnamon or Ginger.

MINI PIZZAS

Spray a cookie sheet with a mist of [VEGETABLE OIL

Sprinkle your pastry board with [FLOUR

Use a rolling pin to roll out [UNCOOKED PIZZA DOUGH 1/4-inch thick

Use a cookie cutter to cut the Dough into small rounds. Place them on the cookie sheet.
Bake until the Mini Pizzas start to color then add the Cooked Toppings and Cheese.
Bake for 8-to-10 minutes longer.

NOTE - Prepare ahead of time the Mini Pizzas. Place them on a cookie sheet, cover loosely with plastic wrap. Before serving, bake and add Toppings as above.

FISH PIZZAS

SMOKED SALMON -   becomes flaky when cooked. To maintain its texture, lay the Smoked Salmon on the Pizza after it is out of the oven.

SIMPLE SMOKED SALMON

Brush lightly a	[12-inch	PIZZA CRUST precooked
with	[	EXTRA-VIRGIN OLIVE OIL

Bake to golden brown.

Spread on baked Pizza	[	SOUR CREAM
Sprinkle with	[	CHIVES
Top with	[	SMOKED SALMON thinly sliced

Following the recipe on page 74 prepare the "CRUNCHY PIZZA CRUST"

SMOKED SALMON with BRIE CHEESE

Spread over the	[12-inch	CRUNCHY PIZZA CRUST
	[	BRIE CHEESE thinly sliced
Sprinkle over the Brie	[3 TB	CHIVES
	[	CAPERS drained, rinsed, minced

Bake until Brie has melted into a cream.

Remove Pizza from oven, sprinkle with	[2 TB	FLAT LEAF PARSLEY finely chop
Top it with	[4 oz	SMOKED SALMON

Serve immediately.

SMOKED SALMON with RED ONIONS and DILL

Spread over the	[12-inch	CRUNCHY PIZZA CRUST
	[to taste	RED ONION sliced, loosen rings
Top with	[shredded	MOZZARELLA
	[4 oz	SMOKED SALMON
Sprinkle with	[	FRESH DILL snipped
	[	GROUND BLACK PEPPER
Cover with	[shredded	MOZZARELLA

Bake the Pizza until the Mozzarella melts into a cream. Serve immediately.

SMOKED SALMON with WHITE ASPARAGUS   Or use green Asparagus

Spread over the	[12-inch	CRUNCHY PIZZA CRUST
	[shredded	SWISS and MOZZARELLA mixed
Top with	[4-to-5 oz	SMOKED SALMON
	[	WHITE ASPARAGUS cooked firm
Cover with plenty of	[shredded	MOZZARELLA and SWISS

Bake until the Cheese has melted.   To serve [sprinkle   PARSLEY   finely chopped

Following the recipe on page 74 prepare the "CRUNCHY PIZZA CRUST"

SARDINES - MARINARA

In a small skillet, over very low heat, warm	[1 cup	MARINARA SAUCE ready-made
Stirring with a fork, mix in	[2 TB	TOMATO PASTE
	[1 TB	BALSAMIC VINEGAR
	[2 tp	LEMON JUICE
	[3 TB	FRESH BASIL
Drain from their oil	[3 cans	SARDINES (4-1/2 oz each can)
Spread them on the	[12-inch	CRUNCHY PIZZA CRUST
Top with	[	the Marinara Sauce
Top with	[	RED ONION very thinly sliced
Plenty of	[shredded	MOZZARELLA

Bake until Mozzarella has melted.

TUNA - CALABRIA

In a large nonstick skillet heat	[2 TB	EXTRA-VIRGIN OLIVE OIL
Sauté until fragrant	[1 clove	GARLIC mashed and minced
Then add	[4 large	RIPE TOMATOES (about 2 lbs) Peel, seed, coarsely chop.

Stir the Tomatoes. Mash them with a wooden spoon. Cook until moisture has evaporated and the Tomatoes form a thick paste.

Stir in	[3 TB	FRESH BASIL minced

Remove from heat.

Drain, flake with a fork	[9 oz	TUNA FISH (3 oz can + 6 oz can)
Stir Tuna Fish into the Tomatoes and add	[2 TB	ANCHOVY FILLETS minced
	[1/3-cup	BLACK OLIVES chopped
	[1/3-cup	GREEN OLIVES chopped
	[1 TB	TINY CAPERS drained, rinsed
	[	GROUND BLACK PEPPER
Top the	[12-inch	CRUNCHY PIZZA CRUST
with	[	the Tuna Mixture
	[shredded	MOZZARELLA

Bake until the Mozzarella has melted.

TUNA MELT

Drain, place in a bowl	[(2) 6 oz-cans	TUNA FISH
Flake the Tuna with a fork and mix in	[3 TB	DILL PICKLE finely chopped
	[3 TB	GREEN ONION minced
	[2 medium	TOMATOES peeled, seeded, diced
	[1/4-cup	CHEDDAR shredded
Brush lightly a	[12-inch	PIZZA CRUST precooked
with	[	EXTRA-VIRGIN OLIVE OIL
Sprinkle	[to taste	DRY MUSTARD

Bake 6 minutes. Take out.

Top with	[	Tuna Mixture
and	[shredded	CHEDDAR

Bake until the Cheddar has melted.

SEAFOOD PIZZAS

RAW SEAFOOD	Cook it on the Pizza from 10-to-15 minutes at 450°. In this case do not toast the Crust before.	
COOKED SEAFOOD	Place it on the Crunchy Pizza Crust with just enough time for the Cheese to melt. Sliced Cheese takes longer to melt.	
PARTIALLY COOKED	Cook it on the Pizza for 7-to-10 minutes. Toast the Crust before.	

Following the recipe on page 74 prepare the "CRUNCHY PIZZA CRUST"

CRABMEAT - CREOLE

In a nonstick skillet, over medium heat, heat	[1 TB	VEGETABLE OIL
When a light haze forms, sauté	[1/2-cup	ONION coarsely chopped
When it softens, add	[1 clove	GARLIC mashed and minced
When Onion begins to color, add	[1 cup	GREEN BELL PEPPER thin strips
When the Bell Pepper is tender, stir in	[3 medium	TOMATOES peeled, seeded, diced
	[1 TB	TOMATO PASTE
	[1/4-tp	LEMON JUICE
	[1/4-tp	CREOLE SEASONING or to taste
	[1 TB	TINY CAPERS rinsed, drained
	[2 TB	PARSLEY minced
Cover, simmer for 5 minutes, add	[to taste	SALT, GROUND BLACK PEPPER
Spread the VEGETABLE MIXTURE on the	[12-inch	CRUNCHY PIZZA CRUST
Top with	[1-1/2 cups	LUMP CRABMEAT or more
Cover with	[shredded	MOZZARELLA

Bake until Mozzarella has melted.

SALMON ROE CAVIAR

On the	[12-inch	CRUNCHY PIZZA CRUST
sprinkle	[4 TB	CHIVES
Top with	[plenty of	MOZZARELLA slices

Bake until Mozzarella has melted.

Top with	[	SALMON ROE CAVIAR

SHRIMP - OLYMPUS

In a nonstick skillet, over medium heat, heat	[2 TB	EXTRA-VIRGIN OLIVE OIL
When a light haze forms, sauté	[2 medium	ONIONS coarsely chopped
When the Onions turn golden, add	[2 large	TOMATOES peeled, seeded, diced
Stir for 2 minutes and mix in	[1 tp	DRIED OREGANO
Turn off heat and stir in	[1/2-cup	FETA CHEESE crumbled
	[	GROUND BLACK PEPPER
Spread the TOMATO MIXTURE on the	[12-inch	CRUNCHY PIZZA CRUST
Lay on top	[24 medium	SHRIMP cooked, deveined
Scatter	[1/3-cup	BLACK OLIVES pitted, halved
Top with	[shredded	MOZZARELLA

Bake until Mozzarella has melted.

CHICKEN PIZZAS

Always add the Chicken when the Pizza is cooked and out of the oven.

Following the recipe on page 74 prepare the "CRUNCHY PIZZA CRUST"

ALFREDO

In a nonstick skillet, over medium heat, heat	[2 TB	VEGETABLE OIL
When a light haze forms, sauté	[2 medium	ONIONS thinly sliced
When Onions begin to color, sprinkle with	[	SALT, GROUND BLACK PEPPER
Add	[1 can	small ARTICHOKE HEARTS
		drained, quartered

Stir, cook until Onions turn golden brown.
Turn off heat.

In another skillet, over low heat, warm	[1 cup	ALFREDO SAUCE ready-made
When the Sauce is hot, stir in	[2 cups	CHICKEN cut into small pieces

Turn off heat and cover.

Sprinkle the	[12-inch	CRUNCHY PIZZA CRUST
with	[	PARMESAN grated

Spread on it the ARTICHOKES/ONIONS		
and sprinkle with	[2 TB	FLAT LEAF PARSLEY
		finely chopped
Cover with	[shredded	MOZZARELLA

Return Pizza to oven.
Heat the Chicken in Alfredo Sauce.
When the Mozzarella has melted, take the Pizza out of the oven.
Top the Pizza with the hot Chicken Alfredo Mixture. Serve immediately.

CACCIATORE

In a nonstick skillet, over medium heat, heat	[1 TB	VEGETABLE OIL
When a light haze forms, sauté	[1/2-cup	ONION coarsely chopped
Optional	[1 or 2	GARLIC CLOVES mashed, minced
When Onion is translucent, add	[1 medium	GREEN BELL PEPPER thin strips
When Bell Pepper softens, add	[1 cup	TOMATO SAUCE FOR PASTA
	[1 tp	DRIED OREGANO or to taste
	[3 TB	BLACK OLIVES chopped
	[4	ANCHOVY FILLETS chopped
When Sauce is hot, add	[2 cups	CHICKEN cut into small pieces

Stir to heat through. Turn off heat and cover.

Spread over the	[12-inch	CRUNCHY PIZZA CRUST
	[	MOZZARELLA slices

Bake until Mozzarella has melted.

Top with	[	the Chicken Mixture

Serve immediately.

TURKEY PIZZAS

Following the recipe on page 74 prepare the "CRUNCHY PIZZA CRUST"

ALFREDO

In a nonstick skillet, over medium heat, heat	[2 TB	VEGETABLE OIL
When a light haze forms, sauté	[2 cloves	GARLIC mashed and minced
When Garlic is fragrant discard it. Add	[1 medium	ONION quartered, thinly sliced
When Onion begins to color, add	[8 oz	MUSHROOMS thinly sliced
	[1 TB	PARSLEY finely chopped
When Mushrooms are cooked, stir in	[1 cup	ALFREDO SAUCE ready-made
When Alfredo Sauce is hot, add	[2 cups	TURKEY bite-size pieces

Stir and turn off heat.

Sprinkle the	[12-inch	CRUNCHY PIZZA CRUST
with	[1/2-cup	PARMESAN grated
Top with	[	MOZZARELLA shredded

Bake until Mozzarella has melted.
Meanwhile heat the Turkey and Mushrooms.
When the Mozzarella has melted top it with the TURKEY MIXTURE. Serve immediately.

Alla MARGHERITA

Splash the	[12-inch	CRUNCHY PIZZA CRUST
with	[	TOMATO SAUCE
Spread with	[	MOZZARELLA shredded
Add in the order they are listed	[	RED PEPPER FLAKES optional
	[2 cups	TURKEY bite-size pieces
	[4 medium	TOMATOES peel, seed, slice
Sprinkle with	[	GROUND BLACK PEPPER
	[	FRESH BASIL LEAVES
Cover with	[shredded	MOZZARELLA

Bake until Mozzarella has melted, not longer.

Al PESTO

Heat	[1/2-cup	PESTO SAUCE ready-made
When Pesto is hot, stir in	[2 cups	TURKEY bite-size pieces

Turn off heat.

Spread over the	[12-inch	CRUNCHY PIZZA CRUST
	[	MOZZARELLA shredded
Top with	[4 medium	TOMATOES peel, seed, slice
Sprinkle with	[	SALT, GROUND BLACK PEPPER
Top with	[shredded	MOZZARELLA

Bake until the Mozzarella melts.
Meanwhile heat the Turkey and Pesto.
Top the melted Mozzarella with it.

Sprinkle with	[grated	PARMESAN

Serve immediately.

HAM and PROSCIUTTO PIZZAS

Oven-cooked Prosciutto looks like dried Bacon. Under other Ingredients it remains moist.
To maintain its texture, when other Ingredients have baked, add it and bake for 1 more minute.

Following the recipe on page 74 prepare the "CRUNCHY PIZZA CRUST"

HAM - MEXICANA

Spread over	[12-inch	CRUNCHY PIZZA CRUST
	[shredded	MEXICAN CHEESE MIXTURE
Top the Cheese with	[	AVOCADO slices
Scatter	[	PICKLED JALAPEÑO chopped
Sprinkle with	[3 TB	CILANTRO finely chopped
Top with	[	HAM overlapping slices
	[	CHEESE MIXTURE

Bake until the Cheese has melted.

HAM - OLYMPIA

Rub the	[12-inch	CRUNCHY PIZZA CRUST
with	[1 clove	GARLIC split in half

Bake for 6 minutes.

Sprinkle with	[	DRIED OREGANO to taste
Scatter	[1 cup	FETA CHEESE crumbled
and	[	BLACK GREEK OLIVES chopped
Top with	[	HAM overlapping slices
Top the Ham with	[3 medium	TOMATOES peel, seed, slice
Sprinkle with	[	GROUND BLACK PEPPER
	[	DRIED OREGANO to taste
Cover with	[	MOZZARELLA shredded

Bake until the Cheese has melted.

PROSCIUTTO - MUSHROOMS al PESTO

In a nonstick skillet, over medium heat, heat	[2 TB	EXTRA-VIRGIN OLIVE OIL
When a light haze forms, sauté	[1 lb	SLICED MUSHROOMS
When browned and tender, stir in	[1/2-cup	PESTO SAUCE ready-made
Spread the MUSHROOMS over the	[12-inch	CRUNCHY PIZZA CRUST
Top with	[6 oz	PROSCIUTTO thinly sliced
Cover with	[	MOZZARELLA shredded

Bake until Mozzarella has melted.

PROSCIUTTO - TRATTORIA

In a large nonstick skillet, heat	[2 TB	EXTRA-VIRGIN OLIVE OIL
Sauté to golden brown	[3 medium	SWEET ONIONS thinly sliced
	[to taste	SALT, GROUND BLACK PEPPER
Spread over the	[12-inch	CRUNCHY PIZZA CRUST
	[thin coat of	TOMATO PASTA SAUCE
Sprinkle with	[	PARMESAN grated
Spread over it the ONIONS, top with	[	MOZZARELLA shredded
Bake until Mozzarella has melted. Top with	[6 oz	PROSCIUTTO

SALAMI PIZZAS

You can use 2 or 3 kinds of SALAMI on the same Pizza. Combine it with PEPPERONI SAUSAGE.

Or combine SALAMI and COOKED SAUSAGE. And don't forget MORTADELLA.

Following the recipe on page 74 prepare the "CRUNCHY PIZZA CRUST"

Alla NAPOLITANA

Splash the	[12-inch	CRUNCHY PIZZA CRUST
with	[	PASTA or MARINARA SAUCE
Sprinkle with	[	DRIED OREGANO
Scatter a few	[	ANCHOVY FILLETS whole or chop
To taste	[2 TB	TINY CAPERS drained, rinsed
	[	FRESH BASIL LEAVES
Top with overlapping	[	SALAMI slices
Cover with	[shredded	MOZZARELLA

Bake until Mozzarella has melted.

Al PROVOLONE

Sprinkle the	[12-inch	CRUNCHY PIZZA CRUST
with	[	DRIED SWEET BASIL
Spread with a layer of	[	SMOKED PROVOLONE thin slices
Sprinkle	[optional	RED PEPPER FLAKES
Top with overlapping	[	SALAMI slices
Scatter on top	[	MARINATED ARTICHOKE HEARTS
		cut into wedges
Top with	[	SMOKED PROVOLONE

Bake until Provolone has melted.

SURF and TURF

Spread over the	[12-inch	CRUNCHY PIZZA CRUST
	[	MOZZARELLA thinly sliced
Sprinkle over one half	[	FRESH PARSLEY finely chopped
Sprinkle over the other half	[	CHIVES finely chopped
Top the Parsley with	[sliced	ARTICHOKE BOTTOMS canned
Top the Chives with	[red	* ROASTED BELL PEPPER strips
Top the Artichokes with	[	LUMP CRABMEAT
Top Roasted Bell Peppers with	[	SALAMI thinly sliced
Cover the whole with	[shredded	MOZZARELLA

Bake until the Mozzarella has melted. You can also prepare two Pizzas: one Surf and one Turf.

* See "VEGETABLES".

82

SAUSAGE PIZZAS

Do not use raw Sausage on Pizzas. The Pizza doesn't stay long enough in the oven to cook it.

Following the recipe on page 74 prepare the "CRUNCHY PIZZA CRUST"

CHORIZO ACAPULCO

In a nonstick skillet , heat and swirl	[1 TB	VEGETABLE OIL
When hot, fry until well-cooked, lightly brown	[8-to-10 oz	CHORIZO thinly sliced
Drain on paper towels. Sprinkle a	[12-inch	CRUNCHY PIZZA CRUST
with	[to taste	GROUND CUMIN and CAYENNE
Spread on it	[	CHEDDAR shredded
Sprinkle with	[4 TB	TORTILLA CHIPS crumbled
Top with	[1 or 2	AVOCADOS thinly sliced
Drain on paper towel and scatter	[canned	TOMATILLOS thinly slice
Top with CHORIZO and cover with	[shredded	MONTEREY JACK

Bake until the Cheese has melted.

Alla RUSTICA

Splash the	[12-inch	CRUNCHY PIZZA CRUST
with	[ready-made	ROASTED GARLIC PASTA SAUCE
Spread on it	[plenty of	PARMESAN shavings
Top with	[	COUNTRY SAUSAGE
Scatter	[	FRESH BASIL LEAVES
Cover with	[	MOZZARELLA shredded

Bake until Mozzarella has melted.

SUPER BOWL I

Prepare ahead   Thinly slice into rings [1 large   SPANISH ONION   per Pizza
(or more to taste)

Scatter them in a sprayed pan.
Broil to golden brown. It won't take long.
Let Onions cool in pan. Cover loosely with
a paper napkin.

Spread ONIONS over the	[12-inch	CRUNCHY PIZZA CRUST
Top with slant-cut 1/4-inch thick slices of	[cooked	JUMBO FRANKS or KNOCKWURST
Scatter	[sliced	DILL PICKLE pat dry
Sprinkle with plenty of	[shredded	CHEDDAR and/or MOZZARELLA

Bake until the Cheese has melted.

SUPER BOWL II

Cover the	[12-inch	CRUNCHY PIZZA CRUST
with	[	AVOCADO thinly sliced
Top with	[	MONTERREY JACK shredded
Top with slant-cut 1/4-inch thick slices of	[cooked	JUMBO FRANKS
	[	TOMATOES peel, seed, slice
	[	BLACK PEPPER, TABASCO
Top with	[	MONTEREY JACK shredded

Following the recipe on page 74 prepare the "CRUNCHY PIZZA CRUST"

Bake Pizzas until the Cheese has melted

SUPER BOWL III

Splash the	[	12-inch	CRUNCHY PIZZA CRUST
with	[		MARINARA SAUCE ready-made
Sprinkle with	[		DRIED SWEET BASIL
Top with	[	slices of	PEPPERONI SAUSAGE
Sprinkle with	[		GREEN OLIVES coarsely chopped
Top with	[		SMOKED GOUDA sliced

SUPER BOWL JUNIORS

On	[	12-inch	CRUNCHY PIZZA CRUST
splash	[		TOMATO PASTA SAUCE
Top with	[	2 cups	FRESH PINEAPPLE diced
Top with	[		CHEDDAR shredded
Top with slant-cut slices of	[	cooked	FRANKFURTERS
and	[		CRISPY BACON strips
Cover with	[	plenty of	CHEDDAR shredded

PIZZA VESUVIO

In a nonstick skillet, heat and swirl	[	1 TB	EXTRA-VIRGIN OLIVE OIL
When a light haze forms, sauté	[	1 cup	ONION finely chopped
When Onion is translucent, add	[	2 cups	GREEN & RED BELL PEPPER diced
and	[	10 oz	ITALIAN SAUSAGE
			(removed from casing)

Break up lumps, sauté the Meat until cooked,
lightly browned. Drain in a sieve to rid of fat.

Transfer Mixture into a bowl. Mix in	[	4 TB	MARINARA or PASTA SAUCE
	[	6 TB	PARMESAN grated

Spread the Mixture on the	[	12-inch	CRUNCHY PIZZA CRUST
Cover with	[		MOZZARELLA shredded

GRILLED VEGETABLES

Spread over the CRUNCHY CRUST	[		GOAT CHEESE thinly sliced
Top with	[		GRILLED VEGETABLES
Sprinkle with	[		FRESH BASIL finely chopped
Top with	[		MOZZARELLA shredded / sliced

CLASSIC MARGHERITA

*Created in 1889 by a Naples restaurateur,
in honor of Queen Margherita of Savoia.
Red, white and green match the Italian flag.*

Splash over "CRUNCHY PIZZA CRUST"	[	plenty of	THICK TOMATO SAUCE
Top randomly with	[	slices of	MOZZARELLA
Garnish with	[		FRESH BASIL LEAVES
	[	a drizzle of	EXTRA-VIRGIN OLIVE OIL

Bake until the Cheese has melted.

V

SAUCES

A NOTE

In COLD and YOGURT SAUCES,
amounts are flexible according to taste.

"In the orchestra of a great kitchen, the sauce chef is a soloist."

Fernand Point

SAUCES

LA BÉCHAMEL White Sauces

Thin White Sauce 88
Velouté White Sauce
Medium White Sauce
Béchamel for Puff Pastry Fillings
Creamy Béchamel
Very Thick Béchamel
Variations 89
Caper for Fish, for Meat and Poultry
Cheese
Four Cheese
Mascarpone
Mustard and Cheese
Onion 90
Pernod
Shallot, Shallot with Herbs
Shrimp with Milk
Shrimp / Lobster with Stock
Tomato
Velouté Cream Sauce

SAUCES

Alfredo and Fettuccine Alfredo 91
All'Amatriciana
All'Arrabiata
Avogolemono 92
Béarnaise, Tomatée
Blue Cheese 93
Bolognese (Speedy Recipe)*
Brown Sauce
Butter Sauce
Champagne or White Wine Cream Sauce
Cream Gravy 94
Creamy Caviar
Creole
Curry,
Curry Coconut 95
Curry Raisin
Hollandaise 96
Lemon Egg
Marinara
Pesto with Basil or Parsley 97
Pizzaiola
Provençale
Puttanesca
Red Wine 98
Tomato
Tuna Fish Sauce for Pasta
Vodka

COLD SAUCES

Aïoli 99
Avocado
Blue Cheese
Caper Mayonnaise
Chili   -
Creole   -
Curry   -
Dijon/Herbs Mayonnaise 100
Dried Fruit   -
Garlic Roasted -

* Bolognese also see "BEEF" - GROUND BEEF

COLD SAUCES *continued*

Ginger Mayonnaise 100
Green Goddess
Green Sauce (Italian Salsa Verde)
Honey Mustard 101
Honey Soy
Horseradish Cream
Ketchup Mayonnaise
Ketchup Orange
Lemon Mayonnaise
Mayonnaise like Real Mayonnaise
Mayonnaise - Yolkless 102
Mint Capers
Mint Sauce
Mustard Sour Cream
Peanut Coconut
Pineapple Capers 103
Pineapple Red Onion
Red Onion in Vinegar
Rémoulade
Rémoulade for Celery Root
Salsa Cruda   -   Caribbean
                 -   Pico de Gallo
                 -   Tomatillo
Soy Sauce Mayonnaise
Tartare
Tomato Mayonnaise
Tuna Mayonnaise 104

ETHNIC SAUCES

Skordalia 104
Tahini 105
Tzatziki Beets
Tzatziki Cucumbers

YOGURT SAUCES

Curry 105
Dill
Dill Curry 106
Dill Mint

SWEET SAUCES - MEATS and POULTRY

Apple	-	Allspice	106
	-	Chutney	
	-	Cinnamon	
	-	Ginger	
	-	Horseradish	
	-	Raisin	
Cranberry	-	Coconut	
	-	Ginger	
	-	Ginger	
	-	Jalapeños	
	-	Orange	
	-	Tarragon	
Pineapple	-	Bell Pepper	
	-	Capers	
	-	Coconut	
	-	Ginger	
	-	Horseradish	
	-	Raisin	

LA BÉCHAMEL

THIN WHITE SAUCE   Basic Preparation   *Yields 1 cup*

In a heavy nonstick skillet, medium heat, heat [1 TB   BUTTER
When it sizzles, add [1 TB   FLOUR
Use a wooden spoon.
Stir until smooth and white-pale-yellow, about
2 minutes. Remove from heat.

With a wire whisk beat in gradually [1 cup   MILK or BROTH hot, not boiling
(or a mixture of both)
- Mix well to smooth out the lumps.
- Return to medium high heat, whisk until the Sauce reaches the boiling point and thickens
  into a smooth and creamy texture. Turn off heat. Season according to recipe

Too thick add a little Milk. Too thin stir longer. Lumpy pass through a sieve or stir in blender.

Cheese - Besides adding flavor, it thickens the Sauce. Use fine or coarse-grated Cheese.

VELOUTÉ WHITE SAUCE   *Yields 1 cup*   *Sauces, Soups, Gratins, Gratinées*

[1 TB   BUTTER   Gratin, Gratinée: for 1 cup of Sauce
[1-1/2 TB   FLOUR
[1 cup   MILK or BROTH   use [1-to-1-1/2 oz CHEESE

MEDIUM WHITE SAUCE   *Yields 1 cup*   *Scalloped dishes, Gratins, Gratinées*

[2 TB   BUTTER   [CHEESE   1-to-1-1/2 oz
[2 TB   FLOUR
[1 cup   MILK or BROTH   [Without, use 2-1/2 TB FLOUR

BÉCHAMEL for PUFF PASTRY SHELL FILLINGS   *Thickens to yield 3/4-cup*

[2-1/2 TB   BUTTER
[3 TB   FLOUR
[1 cup   MILK   [FILLING   1-1/2 cups Fish, Poultry, other

CREAMY BÉCHAMEL   *Yields 1 cup*   *Soufflés, Crêpe Fillings. Also see Sweet Soufflés.*

[3 TB   BUTTER
[3 TB   FLOUR
[1-1/4 cups MILK or BROTH

Stir until the Sauce has well thickened and reduced to 1 cup. Cold, it's like a custard.

VERY THICK BÉCHAMEL   *Base for Croquettes.*   *Yields about 3-1/4 cups*

[4 TB   BUTTER   Beat [2   EGG YOLKS   COOKED INGREDIENTS [2 cups
[4 TB   FLOUR   [1   WHOLE EGG
[1-1/4 cups MILK   with [2 TB of the hot Sauce

- Keep stirring with wooden spoon until the Sauce becomes very thick. Reduce heat to low.
- Add the EGGS. Stir until they are well incorporated. Add COOKED INGREDIENTS.
- Stir until Mixture separates from the skillet, like dough. Transfer to a greased dish.
- Cover tightly with plastic wrap to prevent a skin from forming. Let cool. Refrigerate.

BÉCHAMEL VARIATIONS

1.   For 1 cup of Sauce, mix with the FLOUR, before cooking, any of the following:

1/2-teaspoon   [CHILI POWDER   1/4-teaspoon   [GROUND GINGER   or to taste
               [CURRY POWDER   or   [NUTMEG   grated, to taste
               [CREOLE SEASONING   [ONION or GARLIC POWDER
               [DRY MUSTARD   [SAFFRON dissolve in Broth or Milk

2.   When the Sauce is ready, add any of the following and stir to mix well.

To taste   [CAPERS   minced   To taste   [HORSERADISH
           [GREEN PEPPERCORNS   [OLIVES   chopped
           [HARD-COOKED EGG chopped   [PIMIENTO   minced
           [FRESH HERBS minced   [WORCESTERSHIRE SAUCE

A "NOTE" ON THE FOLLOWING SEASONED BÉCHAMEL SAUCES

- Make the White Sauce as in Basic Preparation: thin, velouté, medium, creamy, or as needed.
- AFTER adding all other Seasonings, add SALT and PEPPER. Note that some Broths are salty.

CAPER BÉCHAMEL   For Fish, Seafood

Make the BÉCHAMEL with:

[1 cup   FISH STOCK, CLAM JUICE, or mixed,
                      or mix either with Milk
When it thickens, add:

[1 TB   CAPERS   rinsed, dried, minced
[1 TB   PARSLEY   minced
[1/2-tp   LEMON JUICE

CAPER BÉCHAMEL   Meats, Poultry

Make the BÉCHAMEL with:

[1 cup   CHICKEN BROTH or MILK

When it thickens, add:

[1 TB   CAPERS   minced
[1 TB   PARSLEY   minced

CHEESE BÉCHAMEL   Per cup of Sauce

When the Sauce thickens, stir in until melted the
Cheese: grated, shredded, crumbled. Any of:

[2 to 4 TB   BLUE CHEESE, GORGONZOLA,
                       ROQUEFORT
[4 to 8 TB   CHEDDAR   shredded
[4 to 6 TB   EMMENTHAL , GRUYÈRE, SWISS
[4 to 6 TB   PARMESAN   grated

CHEESE SAUCE DIP

Add to:

[1 cup   MEDIUM WHITE SAUCE
[2/3-cup   CHEDDAR   shredded, or
                       combine with other Cheese

When smooth, turn off heat.
Serve hot in a chafing dish.

FOUR CHEESE BÉCHAMEL   Per cup

When the Sauce thickens, stir in until melted:

[1 TB   EMMENTHAL or SWISS   shredded
[2 TB   FONTINA   coarse-grated
[2 TB   PARMESAN   grated
[1 TB   PECORINO   grated

If too thick, add Milk gradually. Season to taste.

MASCARPONE BÉCHAMEL

Add to:

[1 cup   WHITE SAUCE
[4 flat TB   MASCARPONE
[SALT, PEPPER
[to taste   NUTMEG
[HERBS
[or seasoning   HOT SAUCE, other

MUSTARD and CHEESE BÉCHAMEL

Per 1 cup of Sauce: add to the FLOUR   [1/4-tp   DRY MUSTARD   or more to taste
When Sauce thickens, add per 1-cup of Sauce   [1/4--cup   CHEDDAR or SWISS coarse-grate
Stir until Cheese melts. Add   [to taste   WORCESTERSHIRE SAUCE

ONION MILK for BÉCHAMEL

Over medium heat, bring to a boil [1cup + 3 TB MILK (3 TB of Milk added, allow
for evaporation)
and [1-1/2 oz   ONION chunks
Cover and simmer for 20 minutes.
Strain through a sieve. Discard Onions. Use Onion Milk to prepare the BÉCHAMEL.

PERNOD BÉCHAMEL

Boil [1/3-cup   CHICKEN BROTH
and [2 TB   PERNOD
Reduce Liquid by half.
Pour it into a measuring cup. Add MILK or BROTH to obtain 1 cup or 1-1/4 cups.
Use Pernod Milk to prepare a Béchamel for FISH and SEAFOOD.

SHALLOT BÉCHAMEL   *Use Butter, Flour, Milk, as per: Velouté, Medium, etc.*

In a heavy skillet, over medium heat, heat [BUTTER
When it sizzles, sauté but do not brown [SHALLOTS finely chopped
1 or 2 TB *per cup of Sauce*

When Shallots are limp, stir in [FLOUR

When Mixture turns smooth and pale-yellow,
remove from heat and stir in [MILK or BROTH

Return to heat, smooth out lumps. Continue following directions in Béchamel recipe.

WITH HERBS   *Per cup of Sauce, any of* [1-to-2 TB PARSLEY, TARRAGON, BASIL, other

SHRIMP BÉCHAMEL with MILK

Wash, dry, combine in a saucepan [1 cup   UNCOOKED SHRIMP SHELLS
or   COOKED SHRIMP SHELLS
[1-1/2 cups   COLD MILK
[half of a   SMALL ONION   chopped
A dash [SALT, WHITE PEPPER

[1/4-cup   DRY WHITE WINE   optional
Over medium heat, bring to a boil.
Cover partially. Simmer for 1 hour. Stir often. Let cool.
Strain through 2 layers of cheese cloth. Crush shells with a wooden spoon to extract juices.
Use SHRIMP MILK to prepare the Béchamel.

SHRIMP / LOBSTER BÉCHAMEL with STOCK

Prepare the Béchamel with   [SHRIMP SHELL STOCK
or LOBSTER SHELL STOCK

Optional, use per cup of Béchamel Sauce [2 TB   DRY WHITE WINE
[or DRY VERMOUTH

Example   -   Pour Wine or Vermouth into a measuring cup. Add Stock to obtain 1 or 1-1/4 cups
of Sauce, according to recipe. Use this Stock to prepare the Béchamel.

Use for   -   Fish Crêpes, Seafood, Seafood Pasta, in Crêpe Fillings, Soufflés.

90

TOMATO BÉCHAMEL

When the Béchamel thickens, add to taste:

	[	TOMATO PASTE 1/4-tp at a time
or	[	TOMATO PASTA SAUCE to taste
Any of	[	BASIL, CAPERS, CHIVES, DILL,
		OREGANO, PARSLEY, TARRAGON

VELOUTÉ CREAM SAUCE

Make a VELOUTÉ SAUCE.

When it thickens reduce heat to low.

Gradually add HEAVY CREAM until desired consistency is obtained. Add Seasonings.

SAUCES

ALFREDO SAUCE   Also available ready-made   *About 1-3/4 cups*

For best results, prepare this Sauce just before using it.

In a 7-inch nonstick skillet, low heat, heat	[4 TB	BUTTER
Before it sizzles, add	[1 cup	HEAVY or LIGHT CREAM
		or HALF AND HALF, or a mixture

Simmer, do not boil. Stir until the Sauce
begins to thicken.

Mix in until melted	[1/2-cup	PARMESAN CHEESE grated
	[1/4-cup	ROMANO CHEESE grated
Add	[to taste	SALT, BLACK PEPPER, NUTMEG

FETTUCCINI ALFREDO

Prepare the Sauce in an 8-inch skillet. Optional, rub the skillet with a Garlic clove.
Toss the cooked Fettuccini into the Sauce. Serve on the side grated Parmesan.

ALL'AMATRICIANA   Pasta Sauce   *About 2-1/2 cups*

In a nonstick skillet, over medium heat, heat	[3 TB	OLIVE OIL
When a light haze forms, sauté	[1/2-cup	ONION finely chopped
and	[8 strips	BACON coarsely chopped
When Onion is translucent, add	[2 cups	CHOPPED TOMATOES canned,
		with liquid
	[1/2-tp	SUGAR
	[to taste	CRUSHED RED PEPPER or BLACK

Stir, bring to rapid boil, reduce heat to low.
Simmer for 20 minutes or longer. When the Sauce thickens and oil appears on the surface, it
is ready. Add SALT to taste. Serve the Pasta with grated PECORINO ROMANO on the side.

ALL'ARRABBIATA   Pasta Hot Sauce   *About 1-3/4 cups*

In a nonstick skillet, over medium heat, heat	[4 TB	OLIVE OIL
Sauté	[2 whole	GARLIC CLOVES

When fragrant, discard.

Stir into the Oil	[2 cups	TOMATOES canned, chopped
		with liquid
	[1/2-tp	SUGAR
	[to taste	CRUSHED RED HOT PEPPER
	[2 TB	FRESH BASIL finely chopped
Bring to a rapid boil. Add to taste	[	SALT

Reduce heat to low. Simmer for 30 minutes,
stirring occasionally.

Turn off heat, stir in	[2 TB	FRESH BASIL finely chopped

AVGOLEMONO SAUCE   Egg Lemon Sauce   (Greece)   *About 1-1/4 cups*

See "SAUCES". Prepare	[1 cup	VELOUTÉ WHITE SAUCE
with	[	hot CHICKEN BROTH

Remove from heat.

In 3 small cups put	[3	EGG YOLKS one in each cup
With a fork beat each Egg Yolk, adding	[3 TB	warm BROTH : 1 TB per Egg Yolk

Whisk into SAUCE, one at a time, the Yolks.
Return skillet to stove over <u>low heat</u>.

Whisk for 3 minutes, adding gradually	[2 TB	LEMON JUICE

Do not boil, or Eggs will curdle. Whisk until
the Sauce thickens to the smooth consistency
of a light custard. Turn off heat.

Add	[to taste	SALT and WHITE PEPPER
According to the use of the Sauce, add	[	PARSLEY finely chopped, or DILL

If desired a little more lemony, (with Fish), add a few more drops of Lemon Juice.

<u>Serve with</u> - Asparagus, stuffed Cabbage or Zucchini, stuffed Grapevine Leaves, steamed or
sautéed Vegetables, poached Eggs. Fish, Chicken Breasts, Lamb, Veal.

BÉARNAISE   A Butter Mayonnaise   *About 1-1/3 cups*

In 1-quart heavy saucepan, over medium heat, bring to a boil	[4 TB	TARRAGON VINEGAR
	[4 TB	DRY WHITE WINE
	[1 TB	SHALLOTS finely chopped
	[3	PEPPERCORNS crushed
	[1 TB	FRESH TARRAGON finely chop

Reduce heat to low. Simmer until Liquid is
reduced to barely a film on the bottom.
Remove from heat. <u>Cool completely</u>.

Quarter lengthwise and dice	[2 sticks	BUTTER (8 oz) leave at room temperature
Add to Shallot Mixture in the saucepan	[3	EGG YOLKS
With a wire whip beat until blended, then add	[2 TB	WATER

- When blended, set saucepan over <u>low heat</u>
  in a skillet of barely simmering water.
  (If the heat is too hot, the Yolks will curdle)
- Beat the Mixture until it thickens.

- Now start gradually whisking in the BUTTER,
  <u>1 dice at a time</u>. It must be absorbed by the
  Yolks before adding more.
- When all of it has been absorbed and the
  Sauce is thick and creamy, remove from heat.

Add	[1 TB	FRESH TARRAGON finely chop
	[to taste	SALT and WHITE PEPPER

Serve as is, or rub through a fine sieve.
Keep warm by immersing the saucepan in a pan of hot water.

BÉARNAISE TOMATÉE   Add to taste TOMATO PURÉE   The Sauce should be light pink.

BLUE CHEESE SAUCE

About 1-3/4 cups

In a non-stick skillet, stir over low heat, in	[1/2-cup	MILK
	[3 oz	BLUE CHEESE crumbled
When the Cheese has melted, add	[1/2-cup	HEAVY CREAM
	[4 TB	GRATED PARMESAN
Stir until Sauce is smooth and thickens. Add	[to taste	GROUND BLACK PEPPER

If too thick, thin with a little Milk. Serve with Pasta, Cheese Ravioli, Tortellini, over Croustades.

BOLOGNESE SAUCE   Speedy recipe   *Yields about 3-3/4-to-4 cups*

In large nonstick skillet, medium heat, heat	[2 TB	EXTRA-VIRGIN OLIVE OIL
When a light haze forms, sauté	[1 medium	ONION finely chopped
When Onion is translucent, add	[1 lb	LEAN GROUND ROUND
With a wooden spoon, break up the lumps, stir, cook until lightly browned and add	[28-oz jar	TOMATO or MARINARA SAUCE
	[1/4-tp	ALLSPICE or to taste
	[to taste	GROUND BLACK PEPPER, SALT

Bring to a boil. Cover, reduce heat to low, simmer for 30 minutes. Refrigerate overnight.

BROWN SAUCE

About 1 cup

In a heavy skillet, over medium heat, heat	[2 TB	BUTTER
Before it sizzles stir in	[2 TB	FLOUR
Stir until Mixture turns to golden brown, add	[1 cup	BEEF BROTH
Stir until Sauce thickens. Add	[to taste	BROWNING & SEASONING SAUCE

BUTTER SAUCE

Mix in processor	[1 stick (4 oz)	UNSALTED BUTTER room temp.
	[3 TB	PARSLEY coarsely chopped
To taste	[1 or 2	GARLIC CLOVES chopped
Optional	[1/4-tp	SALT or to taste
	[	GROUND BLACK PEPPER

Process until the Mixture is smooth.
With a spatula heap it onto a sheet of wax paper, fold it over the Butter. Refrigerate.
After 30 minutes, roll the Butter in the wax paper, shape it into a log about 1-1/4 inches thick.
Transfer the Butter log to plastic wrap, roll, twist ends, freeze. Use slices when needed.

Serve with Escargots, Fish, Vegetables. As a Dip for Artichoke Leaves. A patty on hot Steaks.

CHAMPAGNE or WHITE WINE CREAM SAUCE   *About 1 cup*

In nonstick 7-inch skillet, medium heat, melt	[1 TB	BUTTER
Add	[1 TB	SHALLOT finely chopped
Stir until the Butter begins to sizzle, add	[1/4-cup	CHICKEN BROTH
	[1/4-cup	CHAMPAGNE or WHITE WINE

Bring to a boil until Liquid has reduced by half.
Strain through a fine sieve into a bowl, then
return to skillet.

Add	[1 cup	HEAVY CREAM

Stir over medium high heat.
When the Sauce thickens into a light cream add to taste Salt and White Pepper.

CREAM GRAVY

Yields about 1-3/4 cups

Prepare a WHITE SAUCE with	[2 TB	BUTTER or PAN DRIPPINGS
	[2 TB	FLOUR
	[3/4-cup	CHICKEN or BEEF STOCK
When smooth, gradually stir in	[1 cup	LIGHT CREAM

Over medium heat smooth out lumps. When boiling point is reached reduce heat to medium low, stir until the Sauce thickens and add Seasonings to taste.

CREAMY CAVIAR SAUCE *Prepare before serving* *Yields about 1-1/2 cups*

In heavy nonstick skillet, medium heat, heat	[1/4-cup	MILK + 1/4-cup HEAVY CREAM
When hot add	[3 oz	PHILADELPHIA CHEESE in bits
Stir until the Cheese melts, add	[2 TB	SOUR CREAM
Stir to smooth, turn off heat, add	[3-1/2 oz	SALMON ROE CAVIAR
	[to taste	WHITE PEPPER, SALT if needed

Thin with hot Milk, to desired texture.
Toss into hot Pasta. Serve with Fish, Vegetables, Croustades, Pancakes.

CREOLE SAUCE

Yields about 2-1/2 cups

In an 8-inch skillet, over medium heat, heat	[2 TB	VEGETABLE OIL
When a light haze forms, sauté	[1/2-cup	ONION finely chopped
	[1 medium	GREEN BELL PEPPER diced
	[1/4 cup	CELERY chopped
	[2 cloves	GARLIC mashed, minced
	[1 tp	CREOLE SEASONING POWDER
When Vegetables are tender, add	[2 cups	CHOPPED TOMATOES (canned)
	[1/2-tp	SUGAR
	[1	BAY LEAF
	[1/2-tp	LEMON JUICE
	[to taste	SALT, CAYENNE PEPPER

Bring to a boil. Reduce heat to low. Simmer for 15 minutes.   Adjust Seasonings and add   [1 TB   DRY SHERRY   or to taste

Simmer for 10-to-15 minutes. Turn off heat. Let cool. Can be refrigerated. Simmer to reheat.

CURRY SAUCE

About 2 cups

In a 1-quart saucepan, medium heat, heat	[2 TB	BUTTER
When it sizzles, sauté	[1/2-cup	ONION finely chopped
When Onion softens add	[1 clove	GARLIC mashed and minced
When Onion begins to color add	[2 TB	FLOUR mixed with
	[2 TB mild	CURRY POWDER or 1 TB hot
Stir until Onions turn golden brown, mix in	[1 TB + 1 tp	RED WINE VINEGAR
Gradually add	[2-1/3 cups	BROTH Beef, Chicken or other

- Smooth out lumps.
- When Sauce reaches boiling point, reduce heat to medium low and stir until it thickens.
- When thickened, turn off heat.

Stir in	[2 tp	LEMON JUICE or more to taste
	[to taste	SALT, PEPPER *(continued)*

94

Optional, strain through a fine sieve. Cover the surface with wax paper. Let cool.
This Sauce tastes better the next day. Store in a sealed container, refrigerate or freeze.

For a VEGETABLE CURRY   *Follow the Curry Sauce recipe*

In a 2-quart saucepan sauté the	[1/2-cup	ONION + 2 cloves GARLIC
Add and sauté	[2 cups	VEGETABLES diced or cubed
When Vegetables begin to soften, stir in	[3 TB	FLOUR + 3 TB CURRY mild
Stir for 1 minute to blend and add	[2 TB	RED WINE VINEGAR
	[3-1/3 cups	BROTH

Stir until the Sauce thickens. Bring to a boil.
Cover. Simmer until Vegetables are cooked.

Turn off heat, stir in	[1 TB	LEMON JUICE or more to taste

Condiments

ALMONDS sliced, toasted	COCONUT flaked	PEANUTS	POPADUMS fried
AVOCADO diced, sprinkle Lemon Juice	CHUTNEY	PINEAPPLE	WALDORF SALAD
BANANAS slice just before serving	RAISINS	PINE NUTS	

CURRY COCONUT SAUCE

About 3 cups

In a 1-quart saucepan, medium heat, heat	[1 TB	BUTTER + 1 TB MARGARINE
When it sizzles (using a wooden spoon) sauté	[1 cup	ONION finely chopped
When the Onion softens, add	[3 TB	FLOUR mixed with
	[3 TB mild	CURRY POWDER or 2 TB hot
Stir until Onions are golden brown, then add	[1-1/2 cups	CHICKEN BROTH
	[1 can	COCONUT MILK (13.5 oz)

Stir until the Sauce thickens. Reduce heat to
low. Cover, simmer 15-to-20 minutes.   Add   [to taste   SALT

Pass through a fine sieve. Cover with wax
paper. Let cool. Refrigerate overnight.

Simmer to re-heat. Add	[1 tp	LEMON JUICE (before serving)

Serve with Raisin and Pine Nut Rice, Chicken, Fish, Shrimp.

WITH VEGETABLES   - Sauté the Vegetables sprinkled with Curry Powder. Add to the Sauce.

WITH LAMB   - Season and sprinkle cubed Lamb with Curry Powder. Brown and cook
                            the Lamb. Add it to the Sauce and refrigerate overnight.

CURRY COCONUT RAISIN SAUCE

About 1 cup

In a small nonstick skillet, heat	[1/2-TB	BUTTER
Sauté	[2 TB	ONION finely chopped
When Onion turns lightly golden, add	[3 TB	GOLDEN RAISINS chopped
	[a dash	CINNAMON

Sauté for 1 more minute, turn off heat.

Prepare a MEDIUM WHITE SAUCE with	[2 TB	FLOUR mixed with
	[1 TB mild	CURRY POWDER or 1/2-TB hot
Use	[1/2-cup	COCONUT MILK + 1/2-cup MILK
When the Sauce thickens, add	[	the Raisin Mixture
Stir for 1 minute, turn off heat, add	[to taste	SALT, GROUND BLACK PEPPER

HOLLANDAISE SAUCE

About 1-1/4 cups

Quarter lengthwise and dice	[2 sticks	BUTTER (8 oz) Leave at room temperature.
In a double boiler, with a wire whip beat	[3	EGG YOLKS
When the Yolks become very thick, add	[1 TB	WATER
	[1 TB	LEMON JUICE

- Beat until well blended. About 1 minute.
- Over low heat and barely simmering water,
  beat the Yolks until thick and smooth.

  (If the heat is too hot, the Yolks will curdle).

- Now start gradually whisking in the BUTTER,
  2 dice at a time. It must be absorbed by
  the Yolks before adding more.
- When all of it has been absorbed and the
  Sauce is thick and creamy remove from heat.

Add	[to taste	SALT, WHITE PEPPER or CAYENNE
	[to taste	more Lemon Juice (by drops)

Transfer to heated bowl, serve immediately.
Or put it into a fireproof bowl, in a skillet of hot water, for a few minutes, until ready to serve.

BLENDER HOLLANDAISE - Consists of drizzling hot Butter into the Yolks while blending.
                     - This method is easy but the Yolks are not *"cooked enough"*.

LEMON EGG SAUCE

About 1 cup

Prepare	[1 cup	VELOUTÉ WHITE SAUCE
When it thickens, remove from heat, whisk in	[1	EGG YOLK beaten with
	[1 TB	warm MILK
Over low heat whisk to boiling point (do not boil, or Egg will curdle) then add	[1 TB	LEMON JUICE or more to taste
Turn off heat. Add	[to taste	SALT, WHITE PEPPER
	[optional	CAPERS minced

Serve with Fish, Seafood, Chicken, Lamb, Veal, Vegetables. Reheat in a double boiler.

MARINARA SAUCE

About 3 cups

In a large nonstick skillet, medium heat, heat	[4 TB	EXTRA VIRGIN OLIVE OIL
When a light haze forms, sauté	[1/2-cup	ONION finely chopped
When translucent, add	[2 cloves	GARLIC mashed, minced
When Onion turns golden, add 1 can	[26-to-28 oz	CHOPPED TOMATOES with liquid
Stir with wooden spoon. Add	[1 tp	SUGAR
	[1 TB	TOMATO PASTE
	[2 TB	PARSLEY finely chopped
	[to taste	DRIED OREGANO crumbled
	[	SALT, GROUND BLACK PEPPER

Bring to a boil. Reduce heat to low.
Simmer uncovered 15-to-20 minutes, or until the Sauce thickens.

PESTO SAUCE   *Serve with hot or cold foods.*   *About 3 cups*

Process in blender or processor [2 cups   BASIL LEAVES   well packed
                                 [2 or 3   GARLIC CLOVES   or to taste
                                 [1/2-cup   PINE NUTS
                                 [1 cup   EXTRA-VIRGIN OLIVE OIL

Transfer to a bowl and add   [1/2-cup   PARMESAN   grated
                                 [to taste   SALT, GROUND BLACK PEPPER
To thin use Olive Oil, Pasta Water, Broth.

VARIATION - Basil/Mint, Parsley/Mint. With Fish, Salads, add Lemon Juice, Balsamic Vinegar.

PIZZAIOLA SAUCE   *About 2-3/4 cups*

In a large nonstick skillet, medium heat, heat [3 TB   EXTRA-VIRGIN OLIVE OIL
                                        Sauté   [2 cloves   GARLIC   mashed and minced
When Garlic turns golden, add 1 can   [26-to-28 oz CHOPPED TOMATOES with liquid
Stir with wooden spoon. Add   [2 tp   SUGAR
                                                [to taste   SALT, GROUND BLACK PEPPER
Bring to a boil, reduce heat, simmer covered
for 30 minutes or longer. Stir once in a while.

When the Sauce has thickened, stir in [1 or 2 TB   DRIED OREGANO or to taste
Stir 2 more minutes. Adjust   [Seasonings

Refrigerate overnight, allowing flavors to blend. Serve with Pasta, Eggs, Fish, Poultry, Veal.

PROVENÇALE SAUCE   *About 2-3/4 cups*

In a large non-stick skillet, heat   [2 TB   BUTTER + 1 TB VEGETABLE OIl
Over medium heat, when it sizzles, sauté   [1 cup   ONION   finely chopped
When translucent, add   [1 clove   GARLIC   mashed and minced
When Onions turn golden, add 1 can   [26-to-28 oz CHOPPED TOMATOES with liquid
                                            [1/2-tp   DRIED THYME
                                            [2 TB   FRESH BASIL   finely chopped
                                            [1   BAY LEAF
                                            [1/4-tp   SUGAR
                                            [to taste   SALT, GROUND BLACK PEPPER
Bring to a boil, simmer for 25 minutes, then
stir in   [1 TB   FRESH BASIL   finely chopped

PUTTANESCA SAUCE   *About 3 cups*

In large nonstick skillet, medium heat, heat [1/4-cup   EXTRA-VIRGIN OLIVE OIL
                                      Sauté   [3 cloves   GARLIC   mashed and minced
When Garlic softens, add and mash with it   [4 or 5   ANCHOVY FILLETS
Sauté for 1 minute. Stir in 1 can   [26-to-28 oz WHOLE TOMATOES drain, chop

Bring to a boil, crushing the Tomatoes. Keep
stirring until the Sauce thickens, then add   [2 TB   TINY CAPERS   rinsed, or more
                                               [1/3-cup   BLACK OLIVES   chopped
Finely chopped   [2 TB each   FRESH BASIL   and   PARSLEY
Simmer 15 minutes. Stir occasionally, add   [to taste   SALT, CRUSHED RED PEPPER

VARIATION - Add to taste canned Tuna, drained and flaked.

RED WINE SAUCE

About 1-1/2 cups

In a small heavy saucepan, bring to a boil   [1/2-cup   DRY RED WINE
                                                                     [2 TB   SHALLOTS   minced
                                                                      [1/8 tp   DRY THYME

Reduce by half. Strain through 2 layers of cheese cloth.
Prepare 1 cup BROWN SAUCE. Gradually stir in the Wine. Simmer until the Sauce thickens.

TOMATO SAUCE

About 3-1/2 cups

In a heavy saucepan, medium heat, heat   [2 TB   EXTRA-VIRGIN OLIVE OIL
When a light haze forms, sauté   [2 cloves   GARLIC
When fragrant, discard the Garlic and sauté   [1 medium   YELLOW ONION   coarsely chop
When translucent, add   [1   CARROT   coarsely chop
   [1 stalk   CELERY trim, coarsely chop
Sauté for 2 minutes and add <u>1 can</u>   [26-to-28 oz   CHOPPED TOMATOES with liquid
Bring to a boil, adding   [6-to-8   BASIL LEAVES
   [1/4-cup   FLAT LEAF PARSLEY no stems
   [1/2 tp   SUGAR

Simmer, uncovered, for 30 minutes.
Strain through a fine sieve, mashing solids
with wooden spoon.
Back to saucepan, add   [to taste   SALT, PEPPER, ALLSPICE
and   [1/4-cup   EXTRA-VIRGIN OLIVE OIL
Simmer for another 15 minutes.

TUNA FISH SAUCE for PASTA

About 2-1/2 cups

In a nonstick skillet, medium heat, heat   [2 TB   EXTRA-VIRGIN OLIVE OIL
When a light haze forms, sauté   [1/4 cup   ONION   finely chopped
When translucent, add   [1 clove   GARLIC   mashed and minced
When Onion turns golden, stir in   [2 cups   CHOPPED TOMATOES   canned,
                                                                              with liquid
Bring to a boil and add   [1 TB   DRY VERMOUTH
   [1 TB   CAPERS rinsed, drained
Reduce heat to low, simmer for 15 minutes
and add   [6 oz-can   TUNA FISH in OLIVE OIL flaked
Stir, add   [to taste   SALT, GROUND BLACK PEPPER
Cover, simmer 15 more minutes.
Add   [2 TB   FLAT LEAF PARSLEY   finely chop

VODKA SAUCE

Yields about 2-1/2 cups

In a nonstick skillet, fry soft, do not crisp   [8 strips   SMOKED BACON coarsely chop
                                                                             Drain on paper towels.
Pour out the Fat and add to skillet   [2 TB   VEGETABLE OIL
Sauté   [1 TB   SHALLOT   minced
   [1 TB   SCALLION   minced
When Shallot softens, add the BACON and   [1-1/2 cups   CHOPPED TOMATOES (canned)
                                                                              with liquid
Add   [1/2-cup   HEAVY CREAM
   [SALT, GROUND BLACK PEPPER
Over medium low heat cook 15 minutes or
until the Sauce thickens. Then pour in slowly   [1/3-cup   VODKA

Stir 3 or 4 minutes to let Vodka evaporate. Adjust Seasonings. Serve with Pasta, Poultry, Fish.

COLD SAUCES

AÏOLI (South of France)

For less servings, reduce amounts by half.

A Garlic Mayonnaise with raw Egg Yolks, substituted here with ready-made Mayonnaise.

Pour into blender [2 TB   EXTRA-VIRGIN OLIVE OIL
Mash in presser over blender, then add them [4 large   GARLIC CLOVES

Blend into a purée.

Whip with a fork [1 cup   MAYONNAISE   ready-made
adding gradually [1 TB   EXTRA-VIRGIN OLIVE OIL
[1 tp   LEMON JUICE

When smooth, add GARLIC.

Smooth, and add [to taste   SALT and WHITE PEPPER
Seal tight.
Refrigerate overnight.

For a pink Aïoli add [1/4-tp   TOMATO PASTE

Serve with Fish, Seafood, Lamb, cold Roast. As a Dip with Crudités or French Fries.

AVOCADO SAUCE

Purée in processor:

[1 large   AVOCADO
[2 TB   MAYONNAISE   ready-made
[2 TB   EXTRA-VIRGIN OLIVE OIL
[1 TB   LIME or LEMON JUICE
[a dash   TABASCO or JALAPEÑO JUICE
[1 tp   ONION grated
[to taste   SALT, more Lime or Lemon Juice
[if too thick   add a little more Oil

BLUE CHEESE SAUCE

Mix in processor:

[1/2-cup   SOUR CREAM
[1/2-cup   MAYONNAISE ready-made
[1/2-cup   BLUE CHEESE
[2 TB   CHIVES

If too thick, thin with Milk

Before serving add 2 TB PECANS chopped

For the following Sauces, whip with a fork:

1/2-cup ready-made MAYONNAISE   +   2 tp EXTRA-VIRGIN OLIVE OIL

CAPER MAYONNAISE

Mix in, one Ingredient at a time:

[1/2-tp   YELLOW PREPARED MUSTARD
[1 TB   SCALLIONS   minced
[1 TB   CAPERS   rinse, drain, mince
[to taste   SALT and WHITE PEPPER

VARIATION - substitute Capers with Pickles.

CHILI MAYONNAISE

Mix in, one Ingredient at a time:

[to taste   CHILI POWDER / SAUCE
[1/8-tp   CINNAMON or NUTMEG
[1 finely chop   HARD-COOKED EGG
[1 TB minced   SWEET PICKLE /RELISH

Substitute Cinnamon with Cumin.

CREOLE MAYONNAISE

Mix in, one Ingredient at a time:

[1/2-tp   REGULAR AMERICAN MUSTARD
[1/4-tp   CREOLE SEASONING or more
[1 TB   GREEN ONION   minced
[2 TB   GREEN BELL PEPPER   finely chopped
[SALT, TABASCO

CURRY MAYONNAISE

Mix in, one Ingredient at a time:

[1/4-tp   CURRY POWDER   or more
[to taste   LEMON JUICE or ZEST
[1 TB minced   RED ONION   or to taste
[or   GREEN ONION
[1 TB   GOLDEN RAISINS chopped

DIJON / HERBS - MAYONNAISE

Purée in blender or processor:

[3/4-cup   MAYONNAISE
[1 TB   OLIVE OIL
[1-1/2 tp   DIJON MUSTARD   or more
[1/4-cup   tightly packed, any of
[BASIL, CHERVIL, TARRAGON, other
[a touch of HONEY optional

DRIED FRUIT MAYONNAISE

Mince [APRICOTS, CRANBERRIES, RAISINS

Chop   [PINE NUTS, PEANUTS, ALMONDS

[Mix with MAYONNAISE
[any of   GINGER, CINNAMON, ALLSPICE
[to taste DILL or PARSLEY finely chopped
[a dash   BRANDY or DRY SHERRY

GARLIC MAYONNAISE

Purée in blender:

[1 head of ROASTED GARLIC - see "VEGETABLES"
[1/2-cup   MAYONNAISE
[2 TB   EXTRA-VIRGIN OLIVE OIL
[2 TB   FRESH BASIL chopped

[to taste   SALT and PEPPER

GINGER MAYONNAISE

Whip with a fork:

[1/2-cup   MAYONNAISE
[1 tp   SUNFLOWER OIL
[1 tp   SOY SAUCE   or to taste
[2 TB   GINGER grated
[optional   GARLIC POWDER a dash
[optional   CILANTRO finely chopped

GREEN GODDESS

Whip with a fork:

[1/2-cup   MAYONNAISE
[2 tp   SUNFLOWER OIL a teaspoon at a time

When smooth, add:

[1 tp   LEMON JUICE
[1 tp   TARRAGON VINEGAR
[1 TB   FRESH TARRAGON minced, 1 tp DRIED
[1 TB   PARSLEY minced
[1 TB   WATERCRESS or CHERVIL finely chopped
[1 TB   CHIVES
[SALT and WHITE PEPPER
[1/8-tp   GARLIC CLOVE or POWDER optional

PINK GODDESS

Add to GREEN GODDESS:

[1 TB   KETCHUP

Optional, substitute Tarragon Vinegar with:

[1 tp   RED WINE VINEGAR

Substitute Fresh Tarragon with:

[1 TB   CILANTRO   finely chopped
[or   FRESH DILL snipped

GREEN SAUCE   SALSA VERDE   (Italy)

This Salsa Verde is served with BOLLITO MISTO (Mixed Boiled Meats). See "MEATS" - BEEF.

In a bowl, mix well [2 TB   SCALLIONS finely chopped
                 or   SHALLOTS finely chopped
                    [5   ANCHOVY FILLETS   mashed
                    [2 TB   CAPERS rinsed, drained, minced
                    [1/2-tp   GARLIC   minced
       Then add   [3 TB   FLAT LEAF PARSLEY finely
                                                   chopped
Mix well and add   [1 tp   RED WINE VINEGAR
                    [1/2-cup   EXTRA VIRGIN OLIVE OIL
                    [to taste   GROUND BLACK PEPPER, SALT
                                                   if needed

Optional: add to taste more Vinegar. Seal and refrigerate overnight.

To serve with FISH - Substitute Vinegar with 1-1/2 TB LEMON JUICE, or more to taste.
To serve with LAMB - Substitute Parsley with FRESH MINT LEAVES.

100

HONEY MUSTARD SAUCE

[6 TB   HONEY
[2 TB   DIJON MUSTARD or to taste
[1-1/2 tp RICE WINE VINEGAR
[optional CAPERS minced

HONEY SOY SAUCE

[1/4-cup   HONEY
[1 TB   SOY SAUCE
[to taste WASABI MUSTARD
[1 tp   SESAME SEEDS

With Fruit   In a skillet, over low heat, toss Fruit Chunks with one of the above Sauces.
              Stir until the Fruit is glazed with the Sauce.
              Serve with Ham, Pork, Cured Meats, Chicken, Duck, Turkey.

With a Salad Mix some of the Honey Mustard or Honey Soy Sauce with a little Salad Oil.
              Toss into a FRISÉE, BITTER GREENS or RADICCHIO.
              Add any of: Bacon, Blueberries, Croutons, Ham, Papaya, Peaches, Pears.

HORSERADISH CREAM

Whip with a fork until smooth:

[1/2-cup   SOUR CREAM or CRÈME FRAÎCHE
[1 TB   PREPARED HORSERADISH   or more
[1 TB   CHIVES   minced
[1 TB   CAPERS rinsed, drained, minced
[LEMON JUICE   a few drops
[SALT to taste
[2 TB   RAISINS   minced (optional)

KETCHUP MAYONNAISE

Whip with a fork until smooth:

[1/2-cup   MAYONNAISE ready-made
[1/2-tp   AMERICAN MUSTARD
[2 tp   EXTRA-VIRGIN OLIVE OIL
                      Add:
[2 TB   KETCHUP   or to taste
[1/2-tp   DRIED OREGANO
[1 TB   DILL PICKLES   fine chop

KETCHUP ORANGE MAYONNAISE

Whip with a fork until smooth:

[1/2-cup   MAYONNAISE   ready-made
[2 tp   EXTRA-VIRGIN OLIVE OIL
[1/2-tp   AMERICAN MUSTARD
[2 TB   KETCHUP
[1 TB   ORANGE JUICE or grated ZEST to taste
[2 TB   CHIVES
[1 TB   CILANTRO minced, or more to taste

LEMON MAYONNAISE

Whip with a fork until smooth:

[1/2-cup   MAYONNAISE ready-made
[1 tp   EXTRA-VIRGIN OLIVE OIL
[1/2-tp   DIJON MUSTARD
[1 TB   LEMON JUICE   or more
[1/2-tp grated LEMON ZEST   or to taste
[1 tp minced   ANY FRESH HERBS
[a pinch   GARLIC POWDER   optional

Serve with Poultry, Seafood, Fruit, Vegetable Salads.

MAYONNAISE - LIKE REAL MAYONNAISE

REAL CLASSIC MAYONNAISE is prepared with raw Egg Yolks, Oil, Vinegar and Mustard.

Nowadays, raw Eggs may carry bacteria. I use the commercial ready-made Mayonnaise. It doesn't "run off the spoon" like Real Mayonnaise, but can be prepared to look and taste like it.

            Whip with a fork [1/2-cup   MAYONNAISE   ready-made
When smooth and creamy, stir in [2 tp   SUNFLOWER OIL a teaspoon at a time
                                 [or EXTRA-VIRGIN OLIVE OIL

            Add and whip [1/2-to-1 tp   REGULAR YELLOW AMERICAN MUSTARD
                          [or   regular yellow DIJON

Store in an empty Mayonnaise glass jar and refrigerate.
Seasonings can be added to this base, like: ANCHOVY or TOMATO PASTE, PESTO, SOY SAUCE.

MAYONNAISE - YOLKLESS

Yields about a 1/2-cup

It looks like Mayonnaise, it tastes like Mayonnaise, but has no Egg Yolks in it.

Cut in half, remove the Yolks, weigh the   [whites of 3   HARD-COOKED EGGS

Anything above 3 oz of Whites, remove.
Chop coarsely the 3 oz of WHITES.

Combine in a blender these exact amounts   [6 TB + 1 tp   SUNFLOWER OIL *
  [1-1/2 tp   CHAMPAGNE VINEGAR (no other)
  [2 TB   BOTTLED WATER
  [1 tp   AMERICAN YELLOW MUSTARD
  [3 oz of   chopped Egg Whites

- Turn blender on slowly, accelerate to WHIP. Whip and stop. Stir with spatula. Whip, stop.
- Repeat, until you obtain the smooth texture of thick Custard. Like a commercial Mayonnaise.

- At this point sprinkle with SALT. Blend again. To taste add Salt or a few drops Vinegar.
- Blend again. To thin it, add Water, a few drops at a time.
- With a spatula transfer the Mayonnaise into a plastic or glass container.
- Refrigerate. It will last quite a while, without spoiling.
- To use, spoon the Mayonnaise into a bowl, if needed thin with a few drops of Water.
- Add Seasonings to taste.

*   Do not use any other, except for a stronger flavor use EXTRA-VIRGIN OLIVE OIL.

For a LEMON MAYONNAISE   Substitute, to taste, Vinegar with LEMON JUICE.
Lemon Juice Mayonnaise has to be used within 2 or 3
days. After that the Lemon will loose its fresh flavor.

Seasonings: Herbs, Creole/Curry Powder, Spices, Ketchup, Tomato Paste, Soy, Onions, Pickles.

MINT CAPERS

Pulse in processor:

[1/2-cup   FRESH MINT LEAVES
[1/4 cup   PARSLEY LEAVES
[1 TB   CHIVES
[1 TB   CAPERS   rinsed, drained

With motor running slowly dribble:

[1/4-cup   EXTRA-VIRGIN OLIVE OIL or more
[then add   SALT and GROUND BLACK PEPPER

Serve with Fish, Lamb, boiled Beef.

MINT SAUCE

Whip with a fork:

[4 TB   SOUR CREAM
[1 TB   COLD WATER or more for a
  thinner Sauce
When smooth add to taste:

[1 TB minced   MINT LEAVES   or more
[or 1 tp DRIED MINT LEAVES
[to taste   ONION or GARLIC POWDER
[SALT

Serve with cold Fish, Lamb, Vegetables.

MUSTARD SOUR CREAM

Whip with a fork:

[1/2-cup   SOUR CREAM
[1 TB   DIJON MUSTARD   or more
[1 TB   CHIVES   minced
[to taste   DRY SHERRY or BRANDY

PEANUT COCONUT SAUCE

Mix in blender:

[1/3-cup   PEANUT BUTTER
[1/2-cup   COCONUT MILK
[a pinch   GARLIC POWDER
[to taste   SOY SAUCE   optional

Then add [2 TB   YOGURT
  or [1 TB   SOUR CREAM

PINEAPPLE CAPERS

[8 oz-can   CRUSHED PINEAPPLE do not drain
[2 TB   MAYONNAISE
[2 TB   SOY SAUCE or CHILI SAUCE   to taste
[1 TB   CAPERS minced, or DILL PICKLE
[1 TB   LEMON JUICE or more to taste
[2 TB   CHIVES

RED ONION in VINEGAR   condiment

Combine in a glass jar, seal, refrigerate overnight:

[RED ONIONS finely chopped
[RED WINE VINEGAR   enough to cover Onions

Serve over Collard and Mustard Greens, cooked
Vegetables, as a touch in Soups.

SALSA CRUDA - CARIBBEAN

Substitute the Tomatoes, in the Pico de Gallo
with two 8 oz-cans of CRUSHED PINEAPPLE
drained.

Substitute Cilantro with FRESH MINT to taste.

SALSA CRUDA - PICO de GALLO

[1-1/4 lbs   RIPE TOMATOES peel, seed, dice
[1/2-cup   ONION finely diced
[1/4-cup   CILANTRO finely chopped
[1 tp canned   SERRANO CHILLI drain, rinse,
                 mince, or more to taste
       or   JALAPEÑO minced
[1 TB   LIME JUICE or more to taste
[1 TB   EXTRA-VIRGIN OLIVE OIL
[SALT to taste
[Optional   GARLIC CLOVE mashed, minced

Refrigerate until ready to use. *Yields about 2 cups.*

SOY SAUCE MAYONNAISE

Whip with a fork:

[1/2-cup   MAYONNAISE

Add to taste:

[SOY SAUCE
[GARLIC POWDER
[FRESH GINGER grated
[GREEN ONION minced
[WASABI MUSTARD

PINEAPPLE RED ONION

[8 oz-can   CRUSHED PINEAPPLE
[1/2-cup   MAYONNAISE
[2 TB   GINGER grated, or more
[4 TB   RED ONION minced
[3 TB   CILANTRO minced

RÉMOULADE

Whip with a fork:

[1/2-cup   MAYONNAISE
[2 tp   SUNFLOWER OIL
[1 tp   LEMON JUICE
[1 tp   CAPERS rinsed, minced
[1 tp   CORNICHONS
[2 tp   TARRAGON finely chop
[1 tp   PARSLEY minced

For CELERY ROOT

[1/2-cup   MAYONNAISE
[2 tp   SUNFLOWER OIL
[1 tp   TARRAGON VINEGAR
[1 tp   DIJON MUSTARD

SALSA VERDE - TOMATILLO

Chop finely in food processor:

[1 lb   TOMATILLOS

Transfer to a bowl, mix in:

[1/2-cup   ONION minced
[1 or more   GARLIC CLOVES minced
[to taste   JALAPEÑO seeded, minced
[4 TB   CILANTRO finely chop
[2 TB   EXTRA-VIRGIN OLIVE OIL
[to taste   SALT, PEPPER

TARTARE SAUCE

Whip with a fork:

[1/2-cup   MAYONNAISE
[2 tp   SUNFLOWER OIL
[1 TB   CAPERS minced
[2 tp   CORNICHONS minced
[2 tp   TARRAGON minced
[or   1/2-tp DRIED
[1 tp   PARSLEY minced
[1 tp   ONION grated
       or   ONION JUICE to toaste

TOMATO MAYONNAISE

[1/2-cup   MAYONNAISE
[2 tp   SUNFLOWER OIL
[2 tp   TOMATO PURÉE
[1/2-tp   LEMON JUICE or more to taste
[1 TB   CHIVES
[1 TB   BLACK OLIVES minced
[or   GREEN OLIVES
[any of   BASIL, OREGANO

TUNA MAYONNAISE

Yields about 2-1/4 cups

In a bowl, whip with a fork	[1 cup	MAYONNAISE ready-made
	[1-1/2 TB	EXTRA-VIRGIN OLIVE OIL
To soften intensity of Mayonnaise flavor, add	[2 TB	MASCARPONE or Crème Fraîche
Pulse in processor to a creamy texture	[6-to-7 oz-can	ITALIAN TUNA with its Olive Oil
	[1-1/2-TB	LEMON JUICE
	[4 TB	EXTRA-VIRGIN OLIVE OIL
	[3	ANCHOVY FILLETS
	[1-1/2 TB	TINY CAPERS rinsed, drained
Stir TUNA into the MAYONNAISE. Add	[to taste	PEPPER, adjust Seasonings

Refrigerate. Use as a Dip or Spread. Also see VEAL - COLD ROAST "VITELLO TONNATO".

ETHNIC SAUCES

SKORDALIA   Garlic Potato Sauce   (Greece)   *Yields about 3-to3-1/4 cups*

Wash and boil until very tender	[1-1/2 lbs	BAKING POTATOES skin on
Meanwhile, liquefy in a blender until smooth	[1-1/2 TB	GARLIC finely chopped
	[1 tp	SALT
	[4 TB	EXTRA-VIRGIN OLIVE OIL
When smooth add and continue with	[1/2-cup	EXTRA-VIRGIN OLIVE OIL
	[3 TB	LEMON JUICE *
	[a dash	WHITE PEPPER

Leave Mixture in blender.
When cool enough to handle, do not let Potatoes get cold, peel them, cut into chunks and purée in processor until smooth. (The hot Potatoes will absorb the oil easily).

Through the feeding tube of processor pour slowly and gradually into the purée the GARLIC MIXTURE as you continue processing. Potatoes must absorb the Oil before adding more.

- When the Potatoes have absorbed the Garlic mixture, and no trace of Oil shows, taste and adjust Seasonings. If needed, add to taste, more Lemon Juice, a few drops at a time.
- The Sauce should be thick enough to hold its shape in a spoon.

Seal tight, refrigerate. Serve at room temperature. (To thin, add gradually a little water).

*   If preferred, White Wine Vinegar. Start with 2 TB. Add more to taste after adding Potatoes.

AS A DIP   Serve with CRUDITÉS and other DUNKS.

AS A SAUCE   Serve in a sauceboat: with fried or broiled Fish, fried Seafood, fried
                    Zucchini, tempura Vegetables, or steamed Vegetables.

AS A LIGHT PURÉE   Add a little more mashed Potato and Seasonings.

Spread it on a platter. Top with any of the following, raw cooked or roasted

ARTICHOKES	BELL PEPPERS	CUCUMBERS	TOMATOES	SEAFOOD
ASPARAGUS	BROCCOLI	MUSHROOMS	ZUCCHINI	MEATS
BEETS	CAULIFLOWER	ONIONS	FISH	POULTRY

Drizzle with	[	EXTRA-VIRGIN OLIVE OIL.
Sprinkle with minced	[	PARSLEY or any other FRESH HERBS

TAHINI   (Middle East)   *Yields about 1 cup*

Tahini is a Sesame Paste, available canned, and sold in Middle Eastern food stores.
Preheat oven to 300°. Place the Tahini can on top of stove, near heat emanation, to warm it.
The paste will be easier to stir and spoon out. Open carefully the can, the Oil is to the brim.
Mix before using.

Combine in blender	[5 TB	TAHINI
	[5 TB	LEMON JUICE
	[6 TB	WATER
	[1/2-tp	SALT, PEPPER to taste
	[1/4-tp	GROUND CUMIN or more to taste
With a garlic press, mash over blender, add	[1 clove	GARLIC or more to taste
	[or	GARLIC POWDER to taste

Blend to obtain a creamy smooth Mixture. If too thick, add a Tablespoon of Water at a time.
When desired consistency is obtained, taste the Sauce and adjust Seasonings. Refrigerate.

AS A DIP   - Drizzle with Olive Oil and minced Parsley. Serve with Crudités and Pita Chips.
AS A SAUCE - Serve with grilled Beef, Lamb, Shish-Kebab, Fish, Vegetables.

TZATZIKI - BEETS   Dip and Sauce (Greece)   *Yields about 1-2/3 cups*

Grate, using medium holes to obtain	[2/3-cup	BOILED BEETS peeled
Mix with a fork	[1-1/2 tp	EXTRA-VIRGIN OLIVE OIL
	[1 tp	LEMON JUICE
	[1 small	GARLIC CLOVE mashed, minced
	or	GARLIC POWDER to taste
When mixed, beat in	[1 cup	PLAIN THICK YOGURT
Add	[1 or 2 TB	GREEN ONION finely chopped
When smooth, mix in	[	grated Beets
	[to taste	SALT and PEPPER

Serve with Fish, Chicken, Vegetables.

TZATZIKI - CUCUMBERS   Dip and Sauce (Greece)   *Yields about 1-2/3 cups*

In a bowl, mix with a fork	[1-1/2 tp	EXTRA-VIRGIN OLIVE OIL
	[1-1/2 tp	LEMON JUICE
	[1 small	GARLIC CLOVE mashed, minced
When mixed, beat in until smooth	[1 cup	PLAIN THICK YOGURT
	[2 tp	FRESH DILL or 1 tp DRIED MINT
Peel, seed and grate to obtain	[2/3-cup	KIRBY CUCUMBERS

Mix CUCUMBERS into the YOGURT. Refrigerate. If you wish to add Salt, do so before serving.

YOGURT SAUCES

CURRY YOGURT

Whip	[1 cup	YOGURT + 2 tp WATER
Add	[1/4-tp	CURRY POWDER or more
	[a dash	GARLIC POWDER to taste
	[2 TB	CRUSHED PINEAPPLE drained

DILL YOGURT

Whip	[1 cup	YOGURT + 2 tp WATER
Add	[3 TB	FRESH DILL snipped
	[1 TB	CHIVES or SCALLIONS
	[	SALT

DILL CURRY YOGURT SAUCE

Whip	[1 cup	YOGURT + 2tp WATER
Add	[1/4-tp	CURRY POWDER or more
	[2 TB	FRESH DILL snipped
	[1 TB	PARSLEY minced
	[	LEMON JUICE a few drops

DILL MINT YOGURT SAUCE

Whip	[1 cup	YOGURT + 2 tp WATER
Add	[2 TB	FRESH DILL snipped
	[2 TB	MINT minced
	[1 TB	CHIVES or more

SWEET SAUCES for CURED MEATS, MEATS, GAME, POULTRY

Use ready-made APPLE SAUCE, CRANBERRY SAUCE, canned CRUSHED PINEAPPLE.

Mix Ingredients to taste.

Add to APPLE SAUCE:

ALLSPICE

[ALLSPICE
[TINY CAPERS
[RED ONION finely chopped
[CILANTRO finely chopped

CINNAMON

[GROUND CINNAMON
[BRANDY
[ALMONDS roast, chop

CHUTNEY

[CURRY POWDER
[CHUTNEY finely chopped
[PEANUTS chopped

GINGER

[FRESH GINGER grated
[MUSTARD
[PEANUTS chopped

HORSERADISH

[HORSERADISH
[RED PIMIENTO
[PARSLEY minced

RAISIN

[RAISINS whole/chopped
[CORNICHONS minced
[SOY SAUCE

Add to CRANBERRY SAUCE:

GINGER

[FRESH GINGER grated
[CHIVES
[PARSLEY minced

COCONUT

[COCONUT
[RUM
[DILL

JALAPEÑOS

[JALAPEÑO PICKLES mince
[CHIVES
[CILANTRO minced

ORANGE

[ORANGE ZEST grated
[GREEN OLIVES chopped
[PISTACHIOS chopped

TARRAGON

[FRESH TARRAGON mince
[CELERY chopped
[SPICY WALNUTS chopped

Add to drained CRUSHED PINEAPPLE:

BELL PEPPER

[RED BELL PEPPER diced finely
[RED ONION minced
[DILL PICKLES chopped
[PICKLE JUICE a little

COCONUT

[COCONUT grated
[FRESH MINT minced
[SWEET-and-SOUR SAUCE

CAPERS

[CAPERS minced
[CURRY POWDER
[MAYONNAISE ready-made
[SCALLIONS minced

GINGER

[FRESH GINGER grated
[SCALLIONS minced
[SOY SAUCE

HORSERADISH

[HORSERADISH
[GREEN ONION minced
[RED PIMIENTO
[CELERY finely chopped

RAISIN

[RAISINS whole/chopped
[DILL PICKLES chopped
[MUSTARD
[CILANTRO finely chopped

Use Pineapple Syrup to adjust the Sauce consistency.

VI

DRESSINGS

A good Salad Oil and a good Vinegar
are the first steps to a good Salad.

SALAD OILS

EXTRA-VIRGIN OLIVE OIL
FLAVORED OILS
SESAME
HAZELNUT
SAFFLOWER
SUNFLOWER
TRUFFLE OIL   delicate, no Vinegar
WALNUT   strong, good in some Salads

Avoid CANOLA, CORN, PEANUT. They are preferable for cooking.

RED VINEGARS	WHITE VINEGARS
BALSAMIC	CHAMPAGNE
FLAVORED VINEGARS	CIDER
RED WINE	COGNAC and SHERRY
TARRAGON (white, red)	FLAVORED Herbs, Fruit
	RICE WINE
	WHITE WINE

Prepare Dressings ahead to allow flavors the time to blend.

Store in glass jars or plastic sealed containers. Refrigerate.

Double or triple the recipes to make sure you have enough.

INGREDIENTS USED IN DRESSINGS

Dairy

SOUR CREAM
YOGURT

Condiments and Seasonings

CAPERS
CHUTNEYS
MUSTARDS
PEPPER   many varieties
PEPPERS   mild and hot
PICKLES and RELISHES
POWDERS   Chili, Creole, Curry
ROOTS   Ginger, Horseradish
SAUCES   Ketchup, Peanut, Soy, other
SEASONED SALTS
SEEDS   Caraway, Celery, Dill, Poppy
SPICES
TABASCO
ZESTS   Lemon, Orange

Herbs and Flavor Vegetables

BASIL
CHERVIL
CHIVES
CILANTRO
DILL
GARLIC
LEMON
LIME
MINT
ONION
OREGANO
PARSLEY
SCALLION
SHALLOT
SUN-DRIED TOMATOES
TARRAGON

And of course MAYONNAISE

"The olive tree is surely the richest gift of Heaven."

Thomas Jefferson

DRESSINGS

EGG DRESSINGS

Contrary to the original Caesar Salad Dressing, no raw Egg Yolks are used.
Prepare the Dressing in the Salad bowl. Optional, rub it with a GARLIC CLOVE.

CAESAR
Recipes yield about 2/3-cup

Beat with a fork [1   SOFT-COOKED EGG (3 min.)
or [3 TB   MAYONNAISE   ready-made

Add [3 TB   EXTRA-VIRGIN OLIVE OIL
[4 TB   LEMON JUICE
[4   ANCHOVY FILLETS mashed
[1/4-tp DIJON MUSTARD or more
To taste [WORCESTERSHIRE SAUCE
[GROUND BLACK PEPPER

HARD-COOKED EGG

Mix [5 TB   EXTRA-VIRGIN OLIVE OIL
[3 TB   LEMON JUICE

Add [1/2-tp DIJON MUSTARD
[3   ANCHOVY FILLETS mashed
[3   YOLKS hard-cooked, mince
[to taste WORCESTERSHIRE SAUCE
[Optional   Add to Salad some of
[the Egg Whites, minced

LEMON and LIME JUICE

Refrigerated Fresh Lemon Juice or Dressing should be used within 2 or 3 days. If kept longer, the Lemon loses its fresh taste. For later use, freeze Juice or Dressing.

At certain times of the year, Lemons and Limes can be bought at a better price.
This is the time to stock up on Lemon or Lime Juice and freeze it.

1.   Wash Lemons/Limes. If refrigerated, put them in a bowl of hot water for 15 minutes or let hot water run over them. It will soften and render them easier to squeeze.

2.   Dry two at a time, leaving the others in hot water. Cut the Lemons in half and make an X incision in the pulp of each half. Remove seeds.

3.   Squeeze one half at a time. Leave the pulp in the juice, it enhances the flavor.

4.   Fill, with the juice and pulp of each Lemon half, the compartment of an ice cube tray. Start another with any juice left. Repeat, so that each cube will have some pulp.

5.   Freeze. Store the cubes in a plastic freezer bag. Each cube makes 2 Tablespoons.

OIL AND LEMON DRESSING

Whip with a fork [3 TB   SALAD OIL
[2 TB   LIME or LEMON JUICE (1 cube)
Add [to taste   SALT, BLACK GROUND PEPPER

Yields 5 TB of Dressing which is enough for 3 cups of Salad.

Basic   -   3 parts Oil to 2 parts Lemon Juice. Use more Oil if you like it less lemony.

INGREDIENTS THAT CAN BE ADDED TO AN OIL AND LEMON DRESSING

Minced		Seasonings		Miscellaneous	
ANCHOVIES	JALAPEÑO	CELERY SALT	HORSERADISH	BLUE CHEESE	PEPERONCINI
CORNICHONS	OLIVES	DILL SEED	MUSTARD	KETCHUP	PICKLES
CAPERS	ONIONS	FENNEL SEED	ONION powder	LUMPFISH	SESAME SEEDS
EGGS	PIMIENTOS	GARLIC powder	PAPRIKA	MAYONNAISE	TAHINI
GARLIC	SHALLOTS	HERBS	POPPY SEEDS	PARMESAN	TOMATO PASTE

CREAMY DRESSINGS - BLENDER-MIXED

Ingredient amounts are flexible. Salt and Pepper to taste. Use ready-made Mayonnaise.

BASIL

[1/3-cup   BASIL LEAVES   minced
[1/3-cup   MAYONNAISE
[1 TB   EXTRA-VIRGIN OLIVE OIL
[to taste   GARLIC POWDER
[or 1/2 of GARLIC CLOVE   mashed

CAPER

[1/2-cup   MAYONNAISE
[1 TB   EXTRA-VIRGIN OLIVE OIL
[1 TB   CAPERS
[1 tp   DRIED TARRAGON
[1 TB   CHIVES

CHILI

[1/2-cup   SOUR CREAM
[1 TB   CHILI SAUCE   or more to taste
[1/4-cup   CILANTRO minced
[1 TB   PICKLED JALAPEÑO minced

CREOLE

[1/2-cup   MAYONNAISE
[1 TB   EXTRA-VIRGIN OLIVE OIL
[to taste   DIJON MUSTARD
[1/4-tp   CREOLE SEASONING or more
[1/2-tp   DRIED SWEET BASIL

CUMIN

[1/2-cup   MAYONNAISE
[1 TB   EXTRA-VIRGIN OLIVE OIL
[1/4-tp   CUMIN POWDER   or more to taste
[1 tp   SWEET RELISH

CURRY

[1/2-cup   YOGURT
[1 tp   WATER
[1/2-tp   CURRY POWDER   or to taste
[1 TB   FRESH DILL   snipped
[1 small   GARLIC CLOVE   minced

CURRY

[1/2-cup   MAYONNAISE
[1 TB   ASIAN PEANUT SAUCE
[2 tp   ONION chopped
[1/4-tp   CURRY POWDER   or to taste
[1/2-tp   CAPERS minced

DRIED MINT

[1/2-cup   YOGURT
[1 tp   WATER
[1 tp   DRIED MINT
[2 tp   CHIVES
[optional   GARLIC POWDER or GARLIC minced

LEMON

[1/2-cup   MIRACLE WHIP
[1 TB   LEMON JUICE
[1 TB   SWEET RELISH
[1/2-tp   LEMON ZEST
[1 TB   GREEN ONION minced

MUSTARD

[1/4-cup   MAYONNAISE
[1/4-cup   SOUR CREAM
[2 TB   PICKLED ONIONS chopped
[1-1/2 TB   MUSTARD
[2 tp   DRIED TARRAGON

ONION   green, red, or white

[1/2-cup   MAYONNAISE
[1 TB   EXTRA-VIRGIN OLIVE OIL
[to taste   ONION minced
[GROUND CUMIN

PINEAPPLE

[1/4-cup   MAYONNAISE
[1/4-cup   SOUR CREAM
[2 TB   CRUSHED PINEAPPLE drain
[1 TB   CILANTRO minced, or more
[1 TB   PEANUTS chopped

SOY SCALLION

[1/2-cup   MAYONNAISE
[1 TB   SOY SAUCE   or more
[1 tp   GINGER grated
[1 TB   SCALLION minced

TAHINI   (see "SAUCES")

[1/3-cup   TAHINI SAUCE
[2 TB   MAYONNAISE
[1 TB   EXTRA-VIRGIN OLIVE OIL
[2 TB   PARSLEY minced
[1 TB   SCALLION minced

TOMATO

[1/2-cup   MAYONNAISE
[1 tp   EXTRA-VIRGIN OLIVE OIL
[1/2-tp   TOMATO PASTE
[1 tp   CAPERS minced
[1 tp   DRIED OREGANO

TROPICAL

[1/2-cup   MAYONNAISE
[2 or 3 TB CRUSHED PINEAPPLE drain
[1 TB   RED ONION chopped
[1 tp   LIGHT RUM   or more
[1/2-tp   CAPERS minced

111

CREAMY DRESSINGS - HAND-MIXED

Serve with Fish, Seafood, cold Meats, Salads, Pasta, Fruit Salads.

Mix Ingredient amounts according to taste. Thin SOUR CREAM and COTTAGE CHEESE with Milk.

ANCHOVY

[TARTARE SAUCE ready-made
[ANCHOVIES (canned) minced
[PICKLED ONIONS minced
[PARSLEY minced

ASIAN PEANUT SAUCE

[MAYONNAISE ready-made
[ASIAN PEANUT SAUCE
[GINGER grated or minced
[GREEN ONION finely chopped

BACON

[SOUR CREAM
[FRIED BACON crumbled
[PARSLEY minced
[CHIVES

BLUE CHEESE

[SOUR CREAM
[BLUE CHEESE crumbled
[DILL snipped
[WALNUTS chopped
[Add before serving

CRANBERRY

[MAYONNAISE ready-made
[CRANBERRY SAUCE
[CORNICHONS minced
[DRIED TARRAGON

CUCUMBER YOGURT

[SOUR CREAM
[CUCUMBER seeded, minced
[LEMON JUICE
[CHIVES

FETA CHEESE

[OIL AND LEMON DRESSING
[FETA CHEESE crumbled
[RED ONION minced
[BLACK OLIVES minced

FETA CHEESE

[COTTAGE CHEESE
[FETA CHEESE crumbled
[CILANTRO or DRIED OREGANO
[CHIVES

OLIVES

[MAYONNAISE ready-made
[KETCHUP a little
[GREEN / BLACK OLIVES chopped
[CAPERS minced

PADDLEFISH ROE

[SOUR CREAM
[PADDLEFISH ROE
[WHITE ONION minced
[PARSLEY minced

SALMON CAVIAR

[SOUR CREAM
[SALMON ROE CAVIAR
[CHIVES
[LEMON JUICE a little

SMOKED SALMON

[SOUR CREAM thin with Milk
[SMOKED SALMON minced
[WHITE ONION minced
[CAPERS minced
[LEMON JUICE a few drops

SMOKED OYSTERS

[MIRACLE WHIP
[SMOKED OYSTERS minced
[OIL FROM SMOKED OYSTERS
[LEMON JUICE and CHIVES

SOY GINGER

[MAYONNAISE ready-made
[SOY SAUCE
[FRESH GINGER grated or minced
[PEANUTS chopped

STILTON CHEESE

[CRÈME FRAÎCHE
[STILTON CHEESE crumbled
[FRESH DILL snipped
[PECANS chopped

SUN-DRIED TOMATOES

[TARTARE SAUCE ready-made
[SUN-DRIED TOMATOES minced
[FRESH BASIL minced
[POPPY SEEDS

CLASSIC VINAIGRETTE

Mix in a blender   [1 TB   VINEGAR
                 [1 tp   MUSTARD   Dijon or other
As blender turns, pour slowly   [4 TB   SALAD OIL

When blended, add to taste   [SALT, PEPPER, SEASONINGS

Blend once more.

Yields 5 TB of Dressing which is enough for 3 cups of Salad.

Optional, drop into the Vinaigrette a whole GARLIC CLOVE.   Let it marinate overnight or longer.

Or beat with a fork   [MUSTARD and VINEGAR
Gradually drizzle in   [SALAD OIL
Add   [Seasonings

WITH NO MUSTARD

OIL		VINEGAR		
4 TB	to	1 TB	-	mild
4 TB	-	2 TB	-	more tart
1/3-cup	-	1/4-cup	-	add HONEY
1/2-cup	-	1/3-cup	-	same

INGREDIENTS THAT CAN BE ADDED TO A VINAIGRETTE

According to the type of Ingredients, add them before or after blending.

Minced Herbs		Seasonings	Other (minced)	
BASIL	OREGANO	CELERY SALT	ANCHOVIES	ONION
CHERVIL	PARSLEY	CURRY POWDER	CAPERS	PICKLES
CHIVES	ROSEMARY	GINGER grated, ground	EGGS	PIMIENTO
CILANTRO	SAGE	PEPERONCINI	GARLIC	PICKLES
DILL	SWEET BASIL	SEASONED SALTS	GHERKINS	RELISH
FENNEL	TARRAGON	SPICES	JALAPEÑO	SCALLIONS
MINT	THYME	ZESTS - LEMON, ORANGE	OLIVES	SHALLOTS

VARIATIONS

Blend   [1-1/2 TB   VINEGAR   +   1-1/2 tp   MUSTARD
        [6 TB   SALAD OIL

Remove from blender, and add:

CORNICHONS

[1 tp   CORNICHONS
[1 tp   SHALLOT
[1 TB   WATERCRESS

MINT and CAPERS

[2 TB   FRESH MINT
[1 tp   CHIVES
[2 tp   CAPERS   minced

PECAN and CINNAMON

[2 TB   PECANS
[1/2-tp   HONEY
[a dash   CINNAMON

HERB and OLIVE

[1 tp   DRIED TARRAGON
[1 tp   DRIED SWEET BASIL
[2 TB   OLIVES   minced
[1 TB   PINE NUTS   roasted

ONION and DILL

[1 TB   WHITE ONION
[1 TB   DILL   snipped
[1/4-tp   POPPY SEEDS or
[1/2-tp   SESAME SEEDS

RAISIN and GINGER

[1 TB   RAISINS mince
[1 TB   GINGER grated
[1 TB   CHIVES
[1/2-tp   SESAME SEEDS

VINAIGRETTE VARIATIONS - BLENDER-MIXED

Ingredient amounts are flexible. Add Salt and Pepper according to taste.

ANCHOVY

[4 TB	SALAD OIL
[2 TB	WHITE WINE VINEGAR
[1 tp	ONION finely chopped
[1 or 2	ANCHOVY FILLETS
[1/2-tp	CAPERS

AVOCADO

[1/2-cup	EXTRA VIRGIN OLIVE OIL
[half of	AVOCADO small
[2 TB	LEMON JUICE
[1 TB	ONION finely chopped
[2 TB	CILANTRO finely chopped
[a little	PREPARED HORSERADISH

CURRY

[3 TB	SALAD OIL
[1 TB	TARRAGON VINEGAR
[1/4-tp	CURRY POWDER or to taste
[half	SMALL GARLIC CLOVE
[1 TB	CHUTNEY

GREEN ONIONS and OLIVES

[5 TB	EXTRA VIRGIN OLIVE OIL
[2 TB	BALSAMIC VINEGAR
[2 TB	GREEN ONIONS minced
[1 tp	DRIED OREGANO
[1 tp	SAVORA MUSTARD or other
[1 TB	BLACK OLIVES chopped

HORSERADISH

[5 TB	EXTRA VIRGIN OLIVE OIL
[1 TB	SHERRY or CIDER VINEGAR
[1 tp	MUSTARD
[1 tp	HORSERADISH
[1 tp	RELISH
[1 tp	PARSLEY minced
[to taste	WORCESTERSHIRE SAUCE

JALAPEÑO

[4 TB	EXTRA VIRGIN OLIVE OIL
[1 TB	WHITE WINE VINEGAR
[1 tp	COARSE GRAIN MUSTARD
[1/4-tp	GROUND CUMIN
[1 tp or more	PICKLED JALAPEÑO minced
[1 tp	ONION minced

KETCHUP ALLSPICE

[4 TB	SALAD OIL
[2 TB	WHITE WINE VINEGAR
[1 TB	KETCHUP
[1 TB	RED ONION minced
[1/4-tp	ALLSPICE or more to taste
[1 TB minced	DILL PICKLE add after blending

KETCHUP

[4 TB	SALAD OIL
[1 TB	BALSAMIC VINEGAR
[1 tp	ONION finely chopped
[1 TB	KETCHUP
[1 TB minced	BLACK OLIVES after blend

MUSTARD PICKLES

[5 TB	EXTRA VIRGIN OLIVE OIL
[2 tp	BALSAMIC VINEGAR
[2 TB	MUSTARD PICKLES
[2 tp	GREEN ONION finely chop
[1 tp	HONEY
[1 tp	DRIED TARRAGON or more

PICKLED ONION

[5 TB	SALAD OIL
[1 TB	PICKLED ONIONS minced
[1 TB	WHITE WINE VINEGAR
[1 TB	SWEET RED PIMIENTO
[1 TB	PARSLEY minced

SHALLOT

[4 TB	EXTRA VIRGIN OLIVE OIL
[2 TB	CIDER VINEGAR
[1 TB	SHALLOT minced
[2 tp	PARSLEY minced
[1/4-tp	DRIED TARRAGON
[or	DRIED SWEET BASIL

SOY SAUCE and GINGER

[4 TB	SESAME SEED OIL
[1 TB	RICE WINE VINEGAR
[1 TB	SOY SAUCE
[1 minced	GARLIC CLOVE optional
[2 tp	CILANTRO finely chopped
[1 tp	GINGER grated
[1/4-tp	BROWN SUGAR optional

SPICES

[4 TB	EXTRA VIRGIN OLIVE OIL
[2 TB	RICE WINE VINEGAR
[2 TB	ALMONDS roasted, chopped
[1 tp	FRESH DILL snipped
[1/2-tp	HONEY
[to taste	CINNAMON or CUMIN

TAHINI   (see "SAUCES")

[4 TB	EXTRA VIRGIN OLIVE OIL
[2 TB	RED WINE VINEGAR
[2 TB	TAHINI SAUCE
[1 TB	RED ONION minced
[1/4-tp	ALLSPICE
[1 TB	PARSLEY minced

DAIRY DRESSINGS

DAIRY INGREDIENTS THAT CAN BE USED IN DRESSINGS

BUTTERMILK   HALF and HALF   LIGHT CREAM CHEESE   SOUR CREAM
COTTAGE CHEESE   HEAVY CREAM   MASCARPONE   YOGURT and YOGURT CHEESE
CRÈME FRAÎCHE   LIGHT CREAM   RICOTTA   WHIPPED CHEESE SPREADS

Combine Cream Cheese and Light Cream, Light Cream and Mascarpone,
Yogurt and Cottage Cheese, Sour Cream and Ricotta.

Thin with a little Milk if needed. Add Herbs finely chopped.

In the following combinations, Ingredient amounts are flexible. Add Salt and Pepper to taste.

COTTAGE CHEESE and BUTTERMILK

[1 cup   COTTAGE CHEESE
[add   BUTTERMILK to taste
[HORSERADISH to taste
[CILANTRO finely chopped

COTTAGE CHEESE and YOGURT

[1/2-cup   YOGURT beat with a fork
[1/2-cup   COTTAGE CHEESE
[CHIVES
[FRESH MINT finely chopped

CRÈME FRAÎCHE and LIGHT CREAM

[1/2-cup   CRÈME FRAÎCHE
[1/4-cup   LIGHT CREAM
[1-1/2 TB   TARRAGON VINEGAR or more
[1 TB   CHIVES
[1 TB   PARSLEY minced

CRÈME FRAÎCHE and SOUR CREAM

[1/4-cup   SOUR CREAM
[1/4-cup   CRÈME FRAÎCHE
[1 or 2 TB LEMON JUICE to taste
[1 TB   SCALLIONS minced
[1 TB   DILL minced

HEAVY CREAM and BLUE CHEESE

[1/2-cup   HEAVY CREAM
[2 TB   LIGHT CREAM
[to taste   BLUE CHEESE crumbled
[CHIVES

HEAVY CREAM and MAYONNAISE

[1/4-cup   HEAVY CREAM
[add   MAYONNAISE to taste
[HARD-COOKED EGG chop
[FRESH BASIL minced

BASIC - Mix 1/4-cup SOUR CREAM and 1/4-cup MAYONNAISE. Add Seasonings to taste.

BACON FAT VINAIGRETTE

Fry the   [BACON chopped, diced or strips
Remove with a slotted spoon.
Drain on paper towels.

Keep in the skillet [3 TB   BACON FAT
Over low heat, stir in [1 TB   BALSAMIC VINEGAR
                                or TARRAGON VINEGAR
                     [1 tp   DIJON MUSTARD or other

When hot toss into Salads [MIXED GREENS, ESCAROLE, MESCLUN,
                                    SPINACH and RAW MUSHROOMS

Or serve with cooked Vegetables [ARTICHOKES, BROCCOLI, CABBAGE,
                                    CAULIFLOWER, STRING BEANS

115

MISCELLANEOUS DRESSINGS

GARLIC - RAW

[4 TB   MAYONNAISE
[4 TB   SOUR CREAM
[1 or 2   GARLIC CLOVES mashed, minced
[1 TB   FRESH BASIL minced
[1 TB   CHIVES

GARLIC - ROASTED

[4 TB   MAYONNAISE
[4 TB   SOUR CREAM
[4-to-6 cloves ROASTED GARLIC mashed
[2 TB   FRESH TARRAGON minced
[1 TB   CHIVES

SALMON ROE - CAPERS

[Mix according to taste:
[
[SOUR CREAM
[SALMON ROE CAVIAR
[LEMON JUICE a few drops
[CAPERS minced
[WATERCRESS minced

SALMON ROE - CORNICHONS

[Mix according to taste:
[
[SOUR CREAM
[SALMON ROE CAVIAR
[GREEN ONION minced
[CORNICHONS minced
[minced   HARD-COOKED EGG

SUN-DRIED TOMATOES - OLIVES

[4 TB   MIRACLE WHIP
[4 TB   SOUR CREAM
[2 TB   SUN-DRIED TOMATOES chopped
[1 TB   OLIVES chopped, or more
[1/4-tp   DRIED OREGANO or more

SUN-DRIED TOMATOES - RAISINS

[4 TB   MIRACLE WHIP
[4 TB   SOUR CREAM
[2 TB   SUN-DRIED TOMATOES
[2 TB   RAISINS minced
[1 TB   FRESH DILL snipped

WASABI MUSTARD - COCONUT

[5 TB   SOUR CREAM
[3 TB   MIRACLE WHIP
[1/2-tp   WASABI MUSTARD or more
[2 TB   DRY COCONUT grated
[1 tp   CHIVES or more
[1 TB   CILANTRO minced, or more

WASABI MUSTARD - GREEN ONION

[5 TB   SOUR CREAM
[3 TB   MAYONNAISE
[1/2-tp   WASABI MUSTARD or more
[2 TB   GREEN ONION minced
[to taste   GINGER grated
[1 TB minced   WATERCRESS or more

SWEET DRESSINGS

To add sweetness to Dressings, add a touch of Honey.

In certain Dressings you can even add a touch of Orange Marmalade.

"If you see a tree as blue, then make it blue".

Paul Gauguin

VII

SALADS

SALADS

RICE HORS-D'OEUVRE and SALADS

HORS-D'OEUVRE

Stuffed Cucumber   - Caviar 132
- Shrimp
- Smoked Oysters
- Smoked Salmon
- Prosciutto
- Smoked Ham

SALADS

Molded Rice Salad 133
Asian Crab Meat
Asian Shrimp
Caribbean Shrimp
Caribbean Fish
Creole Seafood 134
Indian Chicken
Mediterranean Beef
Mexican Ham or Shrimp
Moroccan Chicken
Southern Chicken or Turkey

CITRUS SALADS

Avocado 134
Blueberries
Papaya

SPECIAL SALADS

Caesar 135
Chef's
Cobb
Egg
Fattoosh
German Potato 136
Greek
Niçoise
Salade Russe
Tabbouleh 137
Thanksgiving 138
Waldorf
Yogurt Cucumber

ETHNIC HORS-D'OEUVRE

Greek Mezedes 139
Octopus Salad
Italian Antipasti
Middle Eastern Mezzé 140
Spanish Tapas
Miscellaneous

"A world without tomatoes is like a string quartet without violins."

Laurie Colwin

NOTES ON THE SALADS

APPETIZER   -   1-1/2 cups. With added Meats, Fish, Seafood, use 1-to-1-1/4 cups of Salad.
SIDE-DISH   -   With an Entrée: calculate approximately 1-to-1-1/4 cups per person.
BUFFET SALAD   -   About 3/4-cup per person. Unless it is a main dish. Add extra for seconds.
MAIN COURSE   -   Let's say for lunch, at least 2 cups, including Meats, Fish or Seafood.

INGREDIENT AMOUNTS   indicated in the recipes are flexible.

     Use more or less of any according to availability, taste and size of appetites.
     Amounts where indicated, show a balance of the Ingredients used.
     For example: 2 cups of Arugula is a main Ingredient in the Salad.

THE DRESSING   Prepare ahead, refrigerate. Add it gradually. You may not need all of it.

IMPORTANT   Salt draws water from Vegetables and Fruit. Add Dressings before serving.
                   Add CUCUMBERS and TOMATOES before serving.

BLANCHING VEGETABLES   See "VEGETABLES" - BLANCHING.

     The number of minutes for "blanching" depends on the crunchiness desired.
     Blanch first one piece to estimate the time.
     Test crunchiness before removing Vegetables from blanching water.

CANNED BEANS, GARBANZOS, BLACKEYED PEAS, GREEN PEAS

     Drain. Rinse under running cold water, drain for a while. Pat dry if watery.
     If they need cooking for tenderness, cook them in their liquid, drain.

ONIONS   To avoid a strong lingering taste, blanch them from 3-to-5 minutes.
                   Rinse under cold water and pat dry.
                   Blanched whole, the outside layers will be milder than the inside ones.
                   You can cut the Onion in half, separate the layers and blanch as many as
                   you need. In that case it will only take 1 or 2 minutes of blanching.

PICKLED LEMONS

Wash, scrub with a brush and dry	[5 or 6	LEMONS quarter them longwise
Add to	[1 pint	STERILE MASON JAR
	[1 TB	COARSE SEA SALT CRYSTALS
Fill 1/3-of jar with LEMON quarters, add	[2 TB	COARSE SEA SALT CRYSTALS
Repeat with	[	Lemons and Salt
Squeeze the Juice from	[6-to-8 large	LEMONS or more if needed

Fill the jar to the top with the LEMON JUICE.
Seal tightly, refrigerate for three weeks.
Tilt once in a while to redistribute the Juice.

Optional, scatter between Lemon quarters	[any, or all	4 CLOVES, 5 CORIANDER SEEDS,
		4 or 5 BLACK PEPPERCORNS

NOTE   -   Before serving the Lemons, rinse them under cold Water, pat dry with paper towels.

120

FISH and SEAFOOD SALADS

Combine amounts to taste.

FISH - GRAPEFRUIT

[ESCAROLE
[GRAPEFRUIT   chunks
[AVOCADO   diced
[RED BELL PEPPER   julienne
[FISH   bite-size pieces
[CAPERS   rinsed, drained, pat dry

[add CHIVES to a Dressing of your choice

FISH - LENTILS

[Prepare LENTILS for Salad ("VEGETABLES")

    Mix into LENTILS:

[WHITE ONION   blanched and finely chopped
[CELERY   thinly sliced or finely chopped
[CARROT   grated
[FISH   bite-size pieces

[Add to WHITE WINE VINEGAR VINAIGRETTE
[FRESH BASIL   finely chopped

FISH - POTATOES

[BOILED POTATOES   diced
[SCALLIONS   finely chopped
[TOMATOES   seeded, diced
[FISH   flaked or bite-size pieces
[ANCHOVY FILLETS (drained from oil) chopped
[CUCUMBERS   seeded, diced
[FRESH MINT   finely chopped

[OIL and LEMON DRESSING.

FISH - WATERCRESS / ENDIVE

[ENDIVE   sliced
[WATERCRESS   trimmed
[RED APPLE   diced
[FISH
[PECANS   chopped

[Add to OIL and LEMON DRESSING
[CHIVES

SALMON - À LA RUSSE

[COOKED BEETS   diced
[BOILED POTATOES   diced
[BROCCOLI   blanched, chopped
[RED ONION   finely chopped
[SOUR PICKLES   chopped
[SALMON   cooked or canned, drained

[VINAIGRETTE or SEASONED MAYONNAISE

FISH - GREEN BEANS

[FRENCH CUT GREEN BEANS *al dente*
[COOKED ASPARAGUS 1-inch pieces
[TOMATO   seeded, cut into large dice
[GREEN ONION   finely chopped
[FISH   bite-size pieces

[Add to   OIL and LEMON DRESSING
[SWEET BASIL or TARRAGON

FISH - NAVY BEANS

[Prepare NAVY BEANS for Salads
                              ("VEGETABLES")
    Mix into NAVY BEANS:

[WHITE ONION   blanched, finely chopped
[TOMATOES   seeded and diced
[PARSLEY   finely chopped
[FISH   bite-size pieces

[Add to   OIL and LEMON DRESSING
[CHIVES

FISH - RADICCHIO

[RADICCHIO   shredded or thinly sliced
[APPLES   diced
[CELERY   thinly sliced
[FISH   bite-size pieces
[RAISINS
[PINE NUTS
[FRESH DILL   snipped

[a CREAMY DRESSING

FISH - WATERCRESS/RADISH

[WATERCRESS   trimmed
[RADISHES   thinly sliced
[KIRBY CUCUMBERS   thinly sliced
[FISH
[PINE NUTS   toasted

[Add to   OIL and LEMON DRESSING
[GREEN ONIONS   minced

SALMON - ASIAN

[SNOW PEAS   blanched, crunchy
[ENOKI MUSHROOMS
[EDAMAME BEANS   cooked
[WATER CHESTNUTS   thinly sliced
[SALMON   cooked or canned, drained
[FRESH GINGER   grated

[SOY GINGER DRESSING ("Dressings")

121

SALMON - FENNEL

Mix in a bowl:

[1 cup   FENNEL   thinly sliced
[1/2-cup   WATERCRESS   finely chopped
[2/3-cup   KIRBY CUCUMBER   diced
[1 cup   SALMON   cooked or canned

The DRESSING

Whip [1/3-cup   SOUR CREAM
        [2 TB   MAYONNAISE
        [1 TB   CHIVES
        [2 TB   FRESH DILL   snipped
        [1 TB   EXTRA-VIRGIN OLIVE OIL
        [SALT and BLACK PEPPER

Refrigerate the DRESSING. When ready to use, if too thick, thin with a little cold water.

SALMON - GREEN BEANS

[FRENCH CUT GREEN BEANS   "al dente"
[YELLOW BELL PEPPER   thin strips
[SCALLIONS   minced
[BLACK OLIVES   chopped
[ROASTED ALMONDS   slivered
[SALMON cooked or canned, drained

[OIL and LEMON DRESSING + HORSERADISH

SALMON - NEW POTATOES

[ESCAROLE
[NEW POTATOES   boiled, diced
[COOKED ASPARAGUS   1-inch pieces
[SALMON   cooked or cannded, drained
[GREEN ONION   thinly sliced
[PARSLEY   finely chopped

[CREAMY DRESSING   add   CHIVES

SALMON - LEEKS

Arrange on a platter or plates:

[LEEKS see "VEGETABLES" - LEEKS for SALADS
[ARTICHOKE BOTTOMS   thinly sliced
[SALMON   cooked or canned, drained

[Select a   CREAMY DRESSING, sprinkle with
[FRESH DILL   snipped

SMOKED SALMON - WATERCRESS

[1 bunch   WATERCRESS   trimmed
[1 or 2   TOMATOES   seeded, diced
[1 or 2   HARD-COOKED EGGS   chop
[RED ONION   minced
[CAPERS   rinsed, drained
[tidbits   SMOKED SALMON

[Select a Dressing.

SMOKED TROUT - RADICCHIO and APPLES

In a nonstick skillet, heat:

           [2 TB   BUTTER
           [2 TB   EXTRA-VIRGIN OLIVE OIL
Sauté   [2   GREEN APPLES   thin wedges
           [2 tp   BROWN SUGAR

When golden brown, drizzle with BALSAMIC VINEGAR

Toss the hot Apples into a bowl with:

[RADICCHIO   thickly shredded
[SALT, GROUND BLACK PEPPER

Serve with   SMOKED TROUT

TUNA - NIÇOISE

[COOKED WHITE RICE
[TOMATO   bite-size chunks
[GREEN BELL PEPPER   thin strips
[TUNA FISH   canned, drained, flaked
[GREEN or RED ONION   finely chopped
[BLACK OLIVES
[PARSLEY   finely chopped
[HARD-COOKED EGGS   wedges, to garnish

[OIL AND LEMON DRESSING

VARIATION

Substitute Tuna with SALMON.
Or with SHRIMP or other SEAFOOD.

TUNA in STUFFED TOMATOES

[TOMATOES - cut off caps, scoop out
                                            the pulp.
[Turn upside down on paper towels

[Mix   COOKED RICE
[TUNA   canned, drained, flaked
[CELERY   finely diced
[YELLOW BELL PEPPER   finely diced
[GREEN ONION   finely chopped
[SUN-DRIED TOMATOES (in Oil)
[BLACK OLIVES   chopped
[PARSLEY   finely chopped

[Use a CREAMY DRESSING

Fill Tomatoes a half hour before serving.
Refrigerate.

122

SEAFOOD - ASIAN

[BEAN SPROUTS
[GREEN ONIONS   thinly sliced
[YELLOW BELL PEPPER   thin strips
[MUSHROOMS   sliced
[CHERRY TOMATOES   sliced
[GINGER   grated
[CILANTRO   trimmed, finely chopped
[SESAME SEEDS   toasted

     Add any of:
[CLAMS, MUSSELS, OYSTERS, SCALLOPS

[Add to   OIL and LEMON DRESSING,
[SOY SAUCE and GARLIC   minced

SEAFOOD - CAJUN

[BABY SPINACH
[CHERRY TOMATOES   cut in half
[GREEN BELL PEPPER   thin strips
[VIDALIA ONION   quarter, thinly slice
[CELERY   thinly sliced
[PICKLED OKRA   cut if too long
[CAPERS   rinsed, drained, minced

     Add any of:
[CRAB MEAT, CRAWFISH, OYSTERS

[CREOLE CREAMY DRESSING   see
                          "DRESSINGS"
[Or OIL and LEMON DRESSING

SEAFOOD - CARIBBEAN

[MANGO   bite-size chunks
[AVOCADO   bite-size chunks
[RED ONION   finely chopped
[CILANTRO   finely chopped
[COCONUT   shredded

[Add any of: CLAMS, MUSSELS, OYSTERS, SCALLOPS,
                  CRAB MEAT, LOBSTER, SHRIMP
[Add to OIL and LEMON: ALLSPICE

SEAFOOD - HAWAIIAN

[PINEAPPLE   bite-size chunks
[PAPAYA
[RED ONION   finely chopped
[SWEET PIMIENTOS   (or hot)
[PARSLEY   finely chopped

[Add any of: SEAFOOD as in CARIBBEAN

[Add to OIL and LEMON: POPPY SEEDS

SEAFOOD - STUFFED GRAPEFRUIT   Serves 2

Cut in half   [1 large   PINK GRAPEFRUIT

Cube the wedges. Scrape, wash, dry the Shells. Refrigerate.

[Combine   GRAPEFRUIT
[1 cup   CRAB MEAT, or LOBSTER, or SHRIMP
[1/2-cup   AVOCADO   diced
[1/4-cup   RED BELL PEPPER   diced
[2 TB   WATERCRESS   finely chopped
[1 TB   TINY CAPERS   rinsed, drained

Add the DRESSING gradually, you may not need all of it.
Heap Mixture into Shells. Refrigerate .

The DRESSING   Mix in a blender:

[1/3-cup   MAYONNAISE
[1 TB   EXTRA-VIRGIN OLIVE OIL
[1 TB   LEMON JUICE
[2 TB   CHIVES

[Garnish   WATERCRESS   finely chopped

SHRIMP SALAD in ARTICHOKE BOTTOMS   Or substitute with Crab Meat.

Add to cooking water   [LEMON JUICE
Cook until very tender   [ARTICHOKE BOTTOMS

Drain upside down on paper towels.
Canned: cook in their Liquid until tender).

Yields about 2 cups

[1-1/4 cups   COOKED SHRIMP diced
[1/2-cup   AVOCADO diced
[1/4-cup   CELERY finely chopped
[1 TB   GREEN ONION finely chopped
[2 TB   RED SWEET PIMIENTO chopped
[1 TB   TINY CAPERS rinsed, drained

The DRESSING   Whip in a bowl:

[1/2-cup   MAYONNAISE
[1 tp   EXTRA-VIRGIN OLIVE OIL
[1/4-tp   MUSTARD or more to taste
[2 TB   RED RADISH grated
[1 TB   PARSLEY finely chopped

Add the DRESSING gradually, you may not need all of it. Refrigerate.
Fill Artichoke Bottoms. Refrigerate. Garnish with minced Parsley or Watercress.

SHRIMP - GAZPACHO SALAD   *Yields about 5 cups*

Combine in a salad bowl, leave separated:

[1 cup   YELLOW BELL PEPPER   diced
[4 TB   SPANISH ONION finely   chopped
[2   KIRBY CUCUMBERS   seeded, diced
[1-1/2 cups   SHRIMP bite-size pieces

Cover, refrigerate.
Before serving, add   [1 cup TOMATOES   diced

The DRESSING

Rub a bowl with 1 clove GARLIC. Mix in it:

[1/4-cup   EXTRA-VIRGIN OLIVE OIL
[3 TB   TOMATO JUICE
[2 TB   LEMON JUICE   with Pulp
[1 TB   RED WINE VINEGAR
[1/4-tp   GROUND CUMIN
[to taste   SALT, PEPPER, TABASCO

Toss the Salad, adding the DRESSING gradually, you may not need all of it. Serve on a bed of GREENS.

SHRIMP - GREEN GODDESS

[ASPARAGUS   cut into 1-inch pieces
[ARTICHOKE BOTTOMS   canned, drain, large dice
[CELERY   thinly sliced
[GREEN ONION   finely chopped
[WATERCRESS coarsely chopped
[SEEDLESS GREEN GRAPES   cut in half
[SHRIMP   bite-size pieces
[SLIVERED ALMONDS
[CAPERS   minced

[OIL and LEMON DRESSING

SHRIMP - JAMBALAYA

[1 cup   TOMATOES   large dice
[1/2-cup   GREEN BELL PEPPER   diced
[1/4-cup   CELERY   thinly sliced
[1/2-cup   COOKED WHITE RICE
[1 TB   WHITE ONION   finely chop
[2 TB   GREEN ONION   thinly sliced
[2 TB   PARSLEY   finely chopped
[1/4-tp   GARLIC   minced, or more
[1 cup   SHRIMP   bite-size pieces

[MAYONNAISE with CREOLE SEASONING

SHRIMP - MANGO

[MANGO   diced
[PALM HEARTS   sliced
[RED BEANS   canned, drained
[RADISH   grated
[COCONUT   shredded
[SALTED PEANUTS   chopped
[SHRIMP   bite-size pieces

[Select a Dressing.

SHRIMP - ORIENTAL

[BEAN SPROUTS
[RED BELL PEPPER   thin strips
[GREEN BELL PEPPER   thin strips
[SEEDLESS WHITE GRAPES   cut in half
[GREEN ONION   finely chopped
[WATER CHESTNUTS   thinly sliced
[SHRIMP   bite-size pieces

[Add to   OIL and LEMON: SOY SAUCE

SHRIMP - PINEAPPLE

[1 cup   PINEAPPLE   chunks
[1/2-cup   RED or BLACK BEANS
[1/3-cup   CILANTRO or BASIL   chopped
[1 cup   SHRIMP   bite-size pieces, or more
[to taste   VIDALIA ONION   thinly sliced
[to taste   CAPERS   whole or minced

[Use a   CURRY VINAIGRETTE ("DRESSINGS")
[or a   BALSAMIC VINEGAR VINAIGRETTE

SHRIMP - TAHITI

[CARROTS   shredded
[BLUEBERRIES
[COCONUT   shredded
[SHRIMP   bite-size pieces
[RED ONION   finely chopped
[PECANS or SALTED PEANUTS

[Add to   OIL and LEMON DRESSING
[a little   MAYONNAISE, ALLSPICE

SHRIMP - TAVERNA PLAKA

[STRING BEANS "al dente"
[TOMATOES   seeded, large dice
[SHRIMP   bite-size pieces
[SCALLIONS   finely chopped
[FETA CHEESE   crumbled
[BLACK OLIVES

[Add to OIL and LEMON DRESSING, dried OREGANO

SHRIMP - WHITE BEANS

[NAVY BEANS for SALADS ("VEGETABLES")
[TOMATOES   seeded, diced
[SHRIMP   bite-size pieces
[WHITE ONION   blanched, minced
[PARSLEY   finely chopped

[Add to   OIL and LEMON DRESSING
[a pinch   GROUND CUMIN

124

CHICKEN and TURKEY SALADS

Add CHICKEN or TURKEY to the following combinations:

AFRICANA

[PAPAYA   diced
[AVOCADO   diced
[SWEET POTATO   diced
[RED ONION   minced
[GOLDEN RAISINS
[PEANUTS   roasted

   The Dressing: *yields about 1/3-cup*

[1/3-cup   MAYONNAISE
[1 TB   EXTRA-VIRGIN OLIVE OIL
[1/2-tp   MUSTARD   or more
[1 TB   PARSLEY   minced
[to taste   ALLSPICE or CINNAMON
[optional   HOT CHILIES   minced

CAESAR

Rub salad bowl with GARLIC CLOVE.

Prepare in it the CAESAR SALAD DRESSING
            (see "DRESSINGS")

[ROMAINE LETTUCE   bite-size pieces
[PALM HEARTS   sliced
[SEEDLESS GRAPES, or CHERRY TOMATOES
[CHICKEN / TURKEY   bite-size pieces
[PARMESAN   grated
[CROUTONS and PARMESAN   shavings

FRISÉE - WILTED

Crisp fry   [4   BACON STRIPS

Heat in skillet [2 TB   EXTRA VIRGIN OLIVE OIL
                 [1 TB   BALSAMIC VINEGAR
                 [1 TB   SOY SAUCE
When hot, add   [2 cups FRISÉE LETTUCE

Coat well with Dressing.
Over medium low heat cover, cook 2 minutes.

MOROCCAN

Rub salad bowl with GARLIC CLOVE.

[NEW POTATOES   boiled, cubed or sliced
[RED ONION   finely diced
[CILANTRO   finely chopped
[CARROT   shredded
[RAISINS or BLACK CURRANTS
[SESAME SEEDS   toasted
[PICKLED LEMONS   diced or large
[BLACK or GREEN OLIVES

[Add to   OIL and LEMON DRESSING
[CUMIN, ALLSPICE or CINNAMON

BITTER SWEET

[RADICCHIO   thickly shredded
[APPLE   diced
[FENNEL   thinly sliced
[BLUE CHEESE

[a VINAIGRETTE DRESSING

BOCCONCINI

[ARUGULA
[CARROT   shredded
[MOZZARELLA BOCCONCINI
[GREEN ONION   finely sliced
[PINE NUTS

CHOPPED SALAD

Chop in processor:

[3/4-cup   CARROT   shredded
[3 stalks   CELERY   cut into pieces
[1 cup   ARUGULA or WATERCRESS
[2   SCALLIONS
[to taste   KOSHER PICKLE
[or   PITTED BLACK OLIVES
[1 cup   CHICKEN / TURKEY or more

[Select a DRESSING.

Toss into the Frisée:

[1/3-cup   GOAT CHEESE   diced

   Turn of heat.
   Cover. Let stand 2 minutes.

[add   BACON   crumbled
[CHICKEN / TURKEY bite-size pieces
[SALT, GROUND BLACK PEPPER

OLIVIER   (Russia)

[3 boiled   NEW POTATOES   diced
[2   HARD-BOILED EGGS   chop
[2 TB   RED ONION   finely chopped
[1 TB   CAPERS   rinsed, minced
[1 TB   DILL   or more, snipped
[1 cup   CHICKEN / TURKEY chopped
[2 TB   SOUR DILL PICKLES   chop

   Add gradually the DRESSING:

[1/4-cup   SOUR CREAM
[1/4-cup   MAYONNAISE
[SALT, PEPPER

TROPICANA

The DRESSING mix in a blender:

[1/3-cup   MAYONNAISE
[1/4-cup   SOUR CREAM
[2 TB   CHIVES
[2 TB   PEPPER RELISH
[to taste   GINGER   grated

  Mix in a bowl:

[2 cups   CHICKEN / TURKEY   diced
[1 cup   HAM   diced   (optional)
[Mix gradually   the DRESSING

Arrange on a platter:

[LETTUCE LEAVES
In the center [CHICKEN / TURKEY Mixture
Surround with [HONEYDEW MELON
[MANGO   sliced
[AVOCADO   sliced
[PALM HEARTS   rounds
[VIDALIA ONION   thin rings

  Sprinkle with

[COCONUT   grated, CAPERS
[CILANTRO   finely chopped

DUCK SALADS

Also substitute Duck with Chicken or Turkey.

ORANGE   Serves 2

[1   NAVEL ORANGE   small cubes
[1-1/2 cups   ARUGULA
[1 cup   DUCK   bite-size pieces
[2 TB   RED ONION   finely chopped
[to taste   CAPERS   rinsed, whole or minced
[1 TB   SUNFLOWER SEEDS   toasted

[Add to   GINGER VINAIGRETTE
[2 TB   MAYONNAISE or more to taste

ORANGE and ROMAINE

[ROMAINE LETTUCE   bite-size pieces
[ORANGES   small cubes
[KIWI   diced
[DUCK   bite-size pieces
[CRANBERRIES or DRIED APRICOTS   chop
[PECANS or HAZELNUTS   coarsely chopped
[GREEN OLIVES or FRESH GINGER   grated

[HORSERADISH VINAIGRETTE

STRING BEANS

Version 1

[FRENCH CUT STRING BEANS   *al dente*
[CARROTS   shredded
[WATER CHESTNUTS   sliced
[DUCK   bite-size pieces
[SLIVERED ALMONDS   toasted
[GOLDEN RAISINS

[Add to   OIL and LEMON DRESSING
[CHIVES

Version 2

[REGULAR STRING BEANS
[CARAMELIZED ONIONS   thinly sliced
[BEETS   diced
[DUCK   bite-size pieces
[SLIVERED ALMONDS plain
[CAPERS

[Add to   MUSTARD VINAIGRETTE
[DRIED TARRAGON

CURED MEAT SALADS

HAM - AMBROSIA

[FRESH PINEAPPLE   chunks
[MINIATURE MARSHMALLOWS
[HAM   bite-size pieces
[CELERY   thinly sliced
[RAISINS
[SOUR DILL PICKLES   minced

[DIJON HERBS MAYONNAISE ("SAUCES")

Serve on a bed of   [LETTUCE
Sprinkle on top   [COCONUT   shredded

AMBROSIA VARIATION

[ORANGE   1/2-inch slices cut into cubes
[BLUE CHEESE   crumbled
[HAM   bite-size pieces
[CELERY   thinly sliced
[BLUEBERRIES
[SPICY WALNUTS

[TARTARE SAUCE ("SAUCES")

Serve on a bed of   [LETTUCE
Sprinkle on top   [WATERCRESS   minced

HAM - ASPARAGUS

[COOKED ASPARAGUS   1-inch pieces
[RAW WHITE MUSHROOMS   sliced
[CELERY   thinly sliced
[HAM   diced or julienne
[CHIVES

[Add to   OIL and LEMON DRESSING
[DRIED TARRAGON

HAM - AVOCADO

[FRISÉE LETTUCE
[AVOCADO   diced
[RED or YELLOW BELL PEPPER   diced
[HAM   diced or julienne
[GREEN ONION   thinly sliced

[Add to   OIL and LEMON DRESSING
[MAYONNAISE

HAM - BELGIAN ENDIVE

[BELGIAN ENDIVES   sliced
[PEARS   small cubes
[HAM   diced or julienne
[BLUE CHEESE   crumbled

[Select a DRESSING.

HAM - BELL PEPPER

[RED and YELLOW BELL PEPPERS   strips
[FENNEL   thinly sliced
[HAM   diced or julienne
[PARMESAN   shavings

[Select a DRESSING.

HAM - CHOPPED SALAD

Chop separately in processor hard Ingredients and soft Ingredients. Mix them into the same bowl.
Use Ingredient amounts according to taste and Salad size.

Chop   [CARROTS   Chop coarsely   [HAM
       [CELERY   [CHEDDAR or GRUYÈRE
       [RED / SWEET ONION   [HARD-COOKED EGGS
       [RADISH   [WATERCRESS
       [ZUCCHINI
       [DILL PICKLE   Mix all and add   [FRIED BACON   crumbled
                                              Use a   [CREAMY DRESSING

HAM - NIÇOISE   *Amounts are flexible*

[2 cups   ROMAINE LETTUCE
[1/2-cup   STRING BEANS
[1/2-cup   BOILED POTATOES   diced
[2 medium   TOMATOES   seeded, diced
[2   GREEN ONIONS   finely sliced
[4   ANCHOVY FILLETS   chopped
[1/2-cup   BLACK OLIVES   or more
[1 cup   HAM   or more, bite-size pieces

[Garnish with   HARD-COOKED EGGS   wedges
[MUSTARD HERB VINAIGRETTE

HAM - PEARS / AVOCADO

Serve on a bed of GREENS:

[PEARS   sliced
[AVOCADO   sliced
[Sprinkle with a little LEMON JUICE

[HAM   sliced
[BLUEBERRIES

[Spoon over a   CREAMY DRESSING
[Garnish with   WATERCRESS

PROSCIUTTO - ARTICHOKE

Arrange on a platter or individual plates:

[WATERCRESS   trimmed
[ARTICHOKE BOTTOMS   thinly sliced

[Drizzle with   TRUFFLE OIL
[Top with   PROSCIUTTO
[Drizzle with   TRUFFLE OIL
[Top with   PARMESAN   shavings

VARIATION

[Substitute Artichokes with COOKED ASPARAGUS.

PROSCIUTTO - ARUGULA

Arrange on individual plates:

[1 cup   ARUGULA
[1 cup   FENNEL   thinly sliced
[2 TB   GOLDEN RAISINS
[2 tp   PINE NUTS   toasted

[Toss with   BALSAMIC VINAIGRETTE
[Top with   PEACHES / PEARS   sliced
[Top with   PROSCIUTTO

PROSCIUTTO - BELGIAN ENDIVE

[BELGIAN ENDIVE   sliced 1/2-inch thick
[PEARS   small cubes
[HAZELNUTS   toasted, coarsely chopped

[Select a CREAMY DRESSING

[Toss the Salad with Dressing.
[Top with PROSCIUTTO

PROSCIUTTO - PINEAPPLE

[RADICCHIO
[PINEAPPLE   small cubes
[PECANS   coarsely chopped

[Add to   WHITE WINE VINAIGRETTE
[CHIVES and HORSERADISH
[
[Top the Salad with PROSCIUTTO

SALAMI - BROCCOLI

[BROCCOLI FLORETS   blanched, cut up
[RAW MUSHROOMS   sliced
[PARSLEY   finely chopped
[GREEN ONION   thinly sliced
[SALAMI   diced
[CAPERS   rinsed, dried, whole or minced

[BALSAMIC VINEGAR VINAIGRETTE.

SALAMI - CAULIFLOWER

[CAULIFLOWER FLORETS   blanched, sliced
[RED BELL PEPPER   thin strips
[FRESH BASIL   chopped
[GREEN ONION   thinly sliced
[SALAMI   diced
[CAPERS   rinsed, dried, whole or minced

[WHITE WINE VINEGAR VINAIGRETTE

SALAMI - VESUVIO

[ARUGULA
[ZUCCHINI   diced
[ROASTED BELL PEPPERS ("VEGETABLES")
[GOAT CHEESE   bits
[RED ONION   quartered, thinly sliced
[SALAMI   diced
[RED PEPPER FLAKES   whole or crushed

[BALSAMIC VINEGAR VINAIGRETTE

SALAMI - VIVA NAPOLI

[ARUGULA
[TOMATOES   seeded, chunks
[CUCUMBERS   seeded, diced
[MOZZARELLA BOCCONCINI half or quarters
[GREEN ONION
[SALAMI   diced
[FRESH BASIL   coarsely chopped

[BALSAMIC VINEGAR VINAIGRETTE

SAUSAGE - APPLE

[MESCLUN   bite-size pieces
[RED APPLE   diced
[FENNEL   very thinly sliced
[GREEN ONION   thinly sliced
[SAUSAGE or FRANKFURTERS   sliced
[KOSHER PICKLES   chopped

[Select a DRESSING.

SAUSAGE - AVOCADO

[AVOCADO   diced
[YELLOW BELL PEPPER   diced
[TOMATOES   seeded, diced
[VIDALIA ONION   quartered, thinly sliced
[SAUSAGE or CHORIZO   sliced or bits
[MANZANILLA OLIVES   sliced

[Select a DRESSING.

SAUSAGE / CHORIZO - CAULIFLOWER   *Select a Dressing*

Spread in a nonstick skillet [	OLIVE OIL enough to cover the base
Sauté for 3 minutes [1	GARLIC CLOVE

Discard Garlic.

Sauté [	BLANCHED CAULIFLOWER FLORETS sliced
When golden, but still crunchy, add [	SALT and GROUND BLACK PEPPER

Mix in a bowl sautéed FLORETS and [	BABY SPINACH
[	RED RADISH thinly sliced
[	SAUSAGE or CHORIZO tidbits or diced
[	MARINATED MUSHROOMS thinly sliced

128

MEATS in SALADS

BEEF - AUSTRIAN

[BOILED POTATOES   diced
[BABY SPINACH
[CAULIFLOWER FLORETS   blanched crunchy, sliced
[BEETS cooked or canned, sliced or diced
[SOUR DILL PICKLE   finely chopped
[STEAK or ROAST BEEF   bite-size, thinly sliced

[VINAIGRETTE DRESSING with HORSERADISH

BEEF - PESTO

[BOILED POTATOES   small cubes
[BOILED BEEF   bite-size pieces
[TOMATOES   seeded, diced
[YELLOW BELL PEPPERS   diced
[TINY CAPERS   rinsed, drained, dried

[Thin to taste   PESTO SAUCE
[with   EXTRA-VIRGIN OLIVE OIL
[To taste   LEMON JUICE

LAMB and LENTILS

Prepare   LENTILS IN OLIVE OIL ("VEGETABLES")

Dressing with   [GROUND CUMIN
                [GARLIC   minced or POWDER

Center LENTILS on a platter.

Top with   [FETA CHEESE
Surround with   [LAMB and TOMATO slices
                [HARD-COOKED EGGS   wedges

PORK - PEACHES

[BABY SPINACH
[PEACHES   cubed or diced
[PORK   bite-size pieces
[GOAT CHEESE   bits
[CURRANTS
[PECANS chopped

[Add to   WHITE WINE VINEGAR VINAIGRETTE
[DRIED or FRESH TARRAGON finely chopped

VEAL - ARUGULA

[ARUGULA
[BELGIAN ENDIVE   1/2-inch slices
[FENNEL   very thinly sliced
[RED APPLE   cubed small
[PINE NUTS   toasted
[CHIVES

[Select a DRESSING.
[Serve with sliced COLD VEAL.

BEEF - MACÉDOINE

[BOILED POTATOES   diced
[COOKED CARROTS   diced
[COOKED BEETS   diced
[COOKED GREEN PEAS
[FLAT LEAF PARSLEY   finely chopped
[BEEF   bite-size pieces

[Add ONION to a CREAMY DRESSING

BEEF - SALSA VERDE   Italian

[BOILED POTATOES   cubed
[BOILED CABBAGE   coarsely chopped
[COOKED CARROTS   sliced
[COOKED STRING BEANS   1-inch pieces
[CAULIFLOWER FLORETS
[BEEF, other MEATS, CHICKEN, SAUSAGE

[Toss with   GREEN SAUCE (SALSA VERDE)
                  see "SAUCES" - COLD

Drizzle over the Lamb and Tomatoes:

[EXTRA-VIRGIN OLIVE OIL
[to taste GROUND BLACK PEPPER

Garnish with:

[BLACK and GREEN OLIVES
[RED ONION   finely chopped
[PARSLEY   finely chopped

PORK - PEARS

[BELGIAN ENDIVE   sliced a 1/2-inch
[PEARS   cubed or diced
[PORK   bite-size pieces
[BLUE CHEESE   crumbled
[CRANBERRIES
[PECANS chopped, CAPERS optional

[Add to   WHITE WINE VINAIGRETTE
[FRESH BASIL   finely chopped

VEAL - ASPARAGUS

[COOKED ASPARAGUS   1-inch pieces
[SMALL BUTTON MUSHROOMS   sautéed
[ARTICHOKE BOTTOMS   canned, diced
[FRESH BASIL   finely chopped
[SLIVERED ALMONDS
[GREEN ONION   finely chopped

[Select a DRESSING.
[Serve with sliced COLD VEAL.

PASTA SALADS

Dressings will not cling to smooth Pastas. Choose Pastas for their shape and ability to retain the Dressing. Such as medium SHELLS, SPIRALE, hollow ribbed shapes like PENNE.

Pasta should be cooked *al dente* and cooled at room temperature before being added to Salads.

> Salt the Water in which the Pasta will cook (see "HELPFUL HINTS").
> Do not add Oil to the Water. If the Pasta is slippery, the Dressing won't stick.
> 1 cup of un-cooked Pasta = about 1-1/2 cups cooked.
>
> If Pasta is the main component, use: 1/2-of Pasta, 1/2-of other Ingredients.
> If it is not the main component, use 1/3 Pasta and 2/3 of other Ingredients.
>
> Pasta will absorb plenty of Dressing. Make sure you have enough.
> Add it gradually. Let it be soaked up, then add more. Refrigerate Salads.
>
> CREAMY DRESSINGS or COLD SAUCES are a good choice for Pasta Salads.
>
> Toss in TOMATOES and CUCUMBERS before serving.

ARTICHOKE and ASPARAGUS

Steam *al dente* [	ASPARAGUS 1-inch pieces
Drain and pat dry [	SMALL ARTICHOKE HEARTS canned
	Quarter them.
Sauté ASPARAGUS and ARTICHOKES in [	EXTRA-VIRGIN OLIVE OIL
[	SALT, GROUND BLACK PEPPER to taste
Combine in a salad bowl [	PASTA
[	ASPARAGUS and ARTICHOKES
[	PARSLEY finely chopped
[	PINE NUTS toasted
[	CHIVES

Select a CREAMY DRESSING.

VARIATION - Also serve as a hot Pasta Dish. Omit Dressing. Serve with grated PARMESAN.

CAULIFLOWER and BACON   *Serves 2*   *Select a Dressing*

Blanch for 3 minutes [	1-1/2 cups	CAULIFLOWER FLORETS
Cool and slice.		
Fry brown but not crisp [	4 strips	BACON coarsely chopped
Drain on paper towel.		
Add to Drippings [		EXTRA-VIRGIN OLIVE OIL
		enough to cover base of skillet
Over medium heat sauté [	3 TB	SHALLOTS finely chopped

When they soften, add CAULIFLOWER and
sauté to a golden brown.

Combine [	1 cup	FRISÉE LETTUCE coarse-chop
[	1 cup	COOKED PASTA
Add CAULIFLOWER, BACON and [	2 TB	PINE NUTS toasted
[	1 TB	TINY CAPERS rinsed, dried

PASTA SALADS *continued*

Use Ingredient amounts according to taste. Select DRESSINGS or SAUCES.

ALLA CAPRESE

[PASTA of your choice
[CHERRY TOMATOES   halved
[SMALL YELLOW TOMATOES
[MOZZARELLA   diced
[FRESH BASIL
[GREEN ONION a little,   finely chopped
[CAPERS

A LA NIÇOISE with TUNA FISH

[PASTA SHELLS
[STRING BEANS cut into 1-inch pieces
[TOMATOES   seeded, large dice
[TUNA FISH   canned, drained, flaked
[ANCHOVY FILLETS   chopped, optional
[GREEN ONION   minced
[BLACK and GREEN OLIVES
[BASIL or TARRAGON   finely chopped

ALLA SICILIANA with SALAMI

[PASTA of your choice
[CHERRY TOMATOES   halved
[GREEN PEAS
[ASSORTMENT of SALAMI diced or julienne
[ANCHOVY FILLETS minced, optional
[RED ONION   minced
[PARSLEY   finely chopped
[CAPERS   rinsed, drained
[BLACK or GREEN OLIVES

FRANKFURTERS and CORN

[FARFALLE (Butterflies: Bow ties)
[CORN KERNELS
[FRANKFURTERS   thinly sliced or diced
[GREEN BELL PEPPER julienne
[RED BELL PEPPER julienne
[CELERY   thinly sliced
[PARSLEY   minced
[GARLIC   in the Dressing, optional

HAM and EGGS

[PASTA SHELLS (main component)
[HAM   julienne or tidbits
[HARD-COOKED EGGS   chopped
[BROCCOLI FLORETS   blanched, chopped
[GREEN ONION   minced
[CAPERS

HAM and PESTO

[ORZO PASTA cooked in Chicken Broth
[HAM julienne or tidbits
[COOKED ASPARAGUS   1-inch pieces
[RAW WHITE MUSHROOMS   sliced
[WATERCRESS   chopped
[PINE NUTS   toasted
[Add   PESTO to VINAIGRETTE DRESSING

PASTA FAGIOLI - Shrimp / Turkey

Combine in equal amounts:
[PASTA and RED KIDNEY BEANS

Add [SHRIMP or SMOKED TURKEY
[CELERY   trimmed, diced
[MARINATED ARTICHOKES   thin wedges
[PARSLEY   finely chopped

PASTA FAGIOLI - PROSCIUTTO

Combine in equal amounts:
[PASTA SHELLS
[NAVY or CANNELLINI BEANS

Add [PROSCIUTTO   chopped
[FRESH BASIL   finely chopped
[GREEN ONION   finely chopped
[TOMATOES   seeded, diced

PICKLED HERRING

[PASTA SHELLS
[PICKLED HERRING   chopped
[RED APPLE   diced
[CELERY   thinly sliced
[WHITE ONION   blanched, finely chopped
[SOUR or DILL PICKLES   minced

Mix [MAYONNAISE, SOUR CREAM equal amounts
Add [FRESH DILL   plenty, snipped

SALMON or CRABMEAT

[PASTA SHELLS
[AVOCADO   diced
[SALMON cooked or canned, or CRAB MEAT
[CELERY   thinly sliced
[GREEN ONION   finely chopped
[WATERCRESS   chopped
[CORNICHONS   minced
[or CAPERS

SHRIMP or LOBSTER

[PASTA of your choice
[ASPARAGUS   cut into 1-inch pieces
[ARTICHOKE BOTTOMS   thinly sliced
[SHRIMP or LOBSTER
[WATERCRESS   finely chopped
[CHIVES

MUSSELS or SCALLOPS

[PASTA of your choice
[FRENCH CUT GREEN BEANS   *al dente*
[FENNEL   julienne
[RAW WHITE MUSHROOMS   thinly sliced
[MUSSELS or SCALLOPS (slice Scallops)
[FRESH TARRAGON   finely chopped
[Add   GARLIC to VINAIGRETTE DRESSING

131

RICE HORS-D'OEUVRE and SALADS

Rice Salads can be a creative way of using Leftovers. Also, leftover Rice can make a great Salad.

A mixture of WILD and WHITE RICE is an interesting combination. Cook separately, then mix.
BASMATI and JASMINE RICE have an aromatic flavor which works well with Asian combinations.
UNCLE BEN'S RICE goes with everything.

FISH, SEAFOOD   - Add Shrimp Stock or a Bouillon cube to the Rice cooking Water.

SAFFRON RICE   - Add 1/4-tp pulverized Saffron Threads to every 2 cups of hot Broth.
                  - First sauté minced Onion, then stir in the Rice, then add the Broth.

CHINESE RICE   - Its glutinous texture is a good base for hors-d'oeuvre Stuffings.
                    Stuffing Mixtures must stick together.
                    For a Salad: first loosen leftover Rice in a steamer, a little at a time.

YELLOW RICE   - Add a small pinch of TURMERIC to the water in which the Rice is cooking.

BROWN RICE   - Brown the Rice lightly when coating it with Oil, before adding the Water.

PINK RICE   - Add 1/4 teaspoon of Tomato Paste to every 2 cups of Water.

Cook Rice according to package directions. Let it cool completely before mixing it into a Salad.
Refrigerate Salads for an hour or two, allow flavors to blend. Serve cool or at room temperature.

Watery Ingredients   Add CUCUMBERS, TOMATOES, cooked ZUCCHINI, before serving.

STUFFED CUCUMBERS with CHINESE RICE

Select straight CUCUMBERS, thick enough to hold the Stuffing. Slice off ends, pare them.
Remove seeds with a corer, and a little of the flesh, leaving a cavity with firm edges.

- Stand a cored Cucumber, fill it with the plain cooked Rice. Push the Rice out into a bowl.
- Measure in Tablespoons the Stuffing. Basic: to 2 TB of Rice, add 2 TB of other Ingredients.
- Do not add Salt, it would render the Cucumbers watery.
- Wrap each Stuffed Cucumber in plastic wrap and refrigerate. Serve sliced into 3/4-inch pieces.

CAVIAR - SALMON ROE or LUMPFISH

[	4 TB	CHINESE RICE
[	3 TB	SALMON ROE or LUMPFISH
[	2 tp	SOUR CREAM
[	to taste	LEMON JUICE, CHIVES

SHRIMP

[	4 TB	CHINESE RICE
[	4 TB	SHRIMP chopped
[	2 tp	MAYONNAISE
[	to taste	SOY SAUCE, CHIVES

SMOKED OYSTERS (canned)

[	4 TB	CHINESE RICE
[	a few drops	OIL from SMOKED OYSTERS
[	3 TB	SMOKED OYSTERS chopped
[	a few drops	LEMON JUICE
[	to taste	CILANTRO finely chopped

SMOKED SALMON

[	4 TB	CHINESE RICE
[	a few drops	EXTRA-VIRGIN OLIVE OIL
[	3 TB	SMOKED SALMON tidbits
[	1/2-tp	CAPERS minced, or more
[	to taste	DILL snipped

PROSCIUTTO

[	4 TB	CHINESE RICE
[	3 TB	PROSCIUTTO chopped
[	1-1/2 tp	MASCARPONE, CHIVES

SMOKED HAM

[	4 TB	CHINESE RICE
[	4 TB	SMOKED HAM chopped
[	2 tp	MAYONNAISE, CHIVES

MOLDED RICE SALAD

Arrange decoratively Ingredients on the bottom of a ring mold.

Add DRESSING sparingly to the RICE SALAD.
Do not use watery Vegetables like Cucumbers, Tomatoes or cooked Zucchini.

Fill the mold with the Rice Salad. Stash it down with the back of a large spoon.

Refrigerate for 2 or 3 hours, or longer. Unmold on a serving platter.
Place in the center of the ring Greens, Seafood, Vegetables. Surround with Garnish.

If you are serving a Dressing on the side and the Rice Mixture is rather dry, brush
lightly the mold with Salad Oil before filling it with the Rice Mixture.

RICE SALADS

VINAIGRETTES, OIL and LEMON DRESSINGS work best with Rice Salads: grains remain separated.

Creamy Dressings, unless they are thinned, will tend to make the grains stick together.
A little Cream or Mayonnaise can be added to Vinaigrettes and Oil and Lemon Dressings.

To serve the Rice Salad with a Creamy Dressing, mix it partially into the Salad and serve the
rest on the side, in a sauceboat.

In the following combinations, use ingredient amounts according to taste. After all it's a Salad!

ASIAN - CRAB MEAT

[WHITE RICE   cooked
[SHELLED EDAMAME BEANS   boiled
[CRABMEAT
[CILANTRO   chopped
[SCALLIONS   minced
[WATER CHESTNUTS
[GINGER   grated

[OIL and LEMON DRESSING
[Add Dressing before serving and toss in
[CUCUMBER   diced

   Variation: substitute Crab Meat with Salmon.

ASIAN - SHRIMP

[WHITE RICE   cooked
[SHELLED EDAMAME BEANS   boiled
[BEAN SPROUTS   chop into small pieces
[CELERY HEART   thinly sliced
[MUSHROOMS
[RED RADISH   grated
[SCALLIONS   minced
[WATER CHESTNUTS   thin slices
[PALM HEARTS   3/8-inch slices
[WATERCRESS   chopped
[SHRIMP   small or bite-size pieces
[SEAWEED   shredded or chopped, optional

[SOY GINGER VINAIGRETTE ("DRESSINGS")
   Use: Sesame Seed Oil - Cider Vinegar

CARIBBEAN - SHRIMP

[PINK RICE   (page 132)
[BLACK BEANS   canned, rinsed, drained
[SHRIMP   bite-size pieces
[ROASTED RED BELL PEPPERS   strips
[FRESH PINEAPPLE   diced
[COCONUT   shredded
[CILANTRO   finely chopped
[CAPERS   whole or minced
[HOT RED PEPPER   optional

[Add GROUND CUMIN to VINAIGRETTE

   Variation: substitute Shrimp with HAM.

CARIBBEAN - FISH

[YELLOW RICE   (page 132)
[RED BELL PEPPER   diced
[CELERY   thinly sliced
[AVOCADO   diced
[ANY WHITE FISH or SHRIMP
[FRESH PINEAPPLE   diced
[RAISINS   soaked (in Rum)
[COCONUT   shredded
[PARSLEY   minced
[SWEET PIMIENTOS (in jar) strips
[GREEN OLIVES   chopped
[HOT RED PEPPER   optional

[Add to   SHERRY VINEGAR VINAIGRETTE
[ALLSPICE or GROUND CUMIN

CREOLE - SEAFOOD

[WHITE RICE   cooked
[RED KIDNEY BEANS   canned, drained
[GREEN BELL PEPPER   finely chopped
[MUSSELS
[CLAMS
[SCALLOPS   diced or thinly sliced
[RED ONION   minced, to taste
[PARSLEY   minced
[CAPERS   minced
[TOMATOES   seeded, diced, add before serving
[HOT RED PIMIENTO   minced, optional

[Add to   CIDER VINEGAR VINAIGRETTE
[CREOLE SEASONING

MEXICAN - HAM or SHRIMP

[WHITE RICE   cooked
[GARBANZOS   canned, drained
[AVOCADO   diced
[CELERY   finely chopped
[SMOKED HAM julienne or SHRIMP bite-size
[RED ONION   minced
[RED PIMIENTO   minced
[CILANTRO   finely chopped
[CHEDDAR CHEESE   shredded
[JALAPEÑOS   chopped
[TOMATOES   diced, add before serving

[Add to   OIL and LEMON DRESSING
[a little   MAYONNAISE

INDIAN - CHICKEN

[BASMATI RICE   browned lightly
[LENTILS FOR SALADS ("VEGETABLES")
[CARROTS   grated
[CAULIFLOWER FLORETS   blanched crisp, chopped
[CHICKEN   bite-size or shredded
[GOLDEN RAISINS
[GREEN ONION   minced
[CILANTRO   finely chopped
[PISTACHIOS or SLIVERED ALMONDS   toasted

[Add to   CIDER VINEGAR VINAIGRETTE
[GROUND CUMIN, GARLIC minced/powder

MOROCCAN - CHICKEN

[WHITE RICE or COUSCOUS
[CORN KERNELS
[ICEBERG LETTUCE   shredded
[CHICKEN   bite-size or shredded
[SWEET ONION   thinly sliced
[CILANTRO   finely chopped
[RAISINS   soaked
[WALNUTS   chopped
[ORANGE ZEST   grated

[Add to   WHITE WINE VINEGAR VINAIGRETTE
[GROUND CUMIN and CINNAMON

MEDITERRANEAN - BEEF

[SAFFRON RICE   (page 132)
[GREEN PEAS
[FENNEL shredded
[RED BELL PEPPER   diced
[BEEF   shredded, boiled or stew
[MARINATED ARTICHOKES   thin wedges
[CHIVES
[WATERCRESS   finely chopped

[RED WINE VINEGAR VINAIGRETTE

SOUTHERN - CHICKEN/TURKEY

[WILD RICE   cooked
[BLACKEYED PEAS
[CELERY   thinly sliced
[RED BELL PEPPER   diced
[AVOCADO   diced
[BERMUDA ONION   sliced and diced
[CHICKEN   shredded or bite-size pieces
[PARSLEY   finely chopped

[WHITE WINE VINEGAR VINAIGRETTE

CITRUS SALADS

For Citrus use CREAMY DRESSINGS or COLD SAUCES.

AVOCADO

[ROMAINE
[BLOOD ORANGE   chunks
[AVOCADO   cubed or diced
[COCONUT   shredded
[FRESH BASIL minced
[CAPERS

BLUEBERRIES

[MESCLUN
[PINK GRAPEFRUIT
[BLUEBERRIES
[CILANTRO   finely chopped
[GINGER   grated
[ROASTED PEANUTS   chopped

PAPAYA

[BABY SPINACH
[PINK GRAPEFRUIT
[PAPAYA large dice
[CELERY thinly sliced
[GREEN ONION
[PINE NUTS

SPECIAL SALADS

CAESAR SALAD   Version I

Prepare CAESAR SALAD DRESSING * in salad bowl.

Add [ROMAINE LETTUCE bite-size pieces
[CROUTONS
[GRATED PARMESAN to taste

   Toss and sprinkle with:

[PARMESAN shavings or grated

* See "DRESSINGS".

Version II

Arrange on plates	[ROMAINE LETTUCE spears
Pour over	[CAESAR SALAD DRESSING
Top with	[CROUTONS
Sprinkle with	[PARMESAN grated
Optional	[CAPERS, FRIED BACON

Version III as in Version I

Top with	[grilled or pan-fried FISH
Or	[PROSCIUTTO
	[COLD CHICKEN

CHEF'S SALAD

Layer in salad bowl:

[ICEBERG and BIBB LETTUCE
[or MIXED GREENS
[STRING BEANS al dente, cut in half
[CHICKEN or TURKEY julienne strips
[HAM diced or julienne
[SALAMI julienne
[SMOKED TONGUE   diced or julienne
[SWISS CHEESE diced or shredded

   Garnish with:

[HARD-COOKED EGGS wedges
[TOMATOES wedges, seeded
[WATERCRESS finely chopped

[Serve DRESSING in a sauceboat.
[Toss the Salad with it at the table.

COBB SALAD

Chop in processor:

[	1 cup	BIBB LETTUCE
[	1 cup	ROMAINE LETTUCE
[	1 bunch	WATERCRESS leaves only
[	1 cup	CHICKEN

Add to chopped mixture:

[	1	TOMATO seeded, diced
[	1 small	AVOCADO diced
[		CRISPY BACON crumbled
[	1 or 2	EGGS chopped
[	to taste	BLUE CHEESE crumbled
[	or	CHEDDAR shredded
[		PICKLES chopped
[	Add to	VINAIGRETTE DRESSING
[	2 TB	CHIVES

EGG SALAD

With a fork mix:

Add	[	1-1/2 TB	MAYONNAISE plain or Seasoned
	[	1 tp	MUSTARD or more
	[	2 large	HARD-COOKED EGGS chopped
	[	to taste	SALT and PEPPER, or CAYENNE
	[	1/2-to-1 tp	GREEN or WHITE ONION optional

Yields about a 1/2-cup

Optional, add any of:

[CHICKEN, BACON, HAM
[FISH, SEAFOOD, CAVIAR
[PICKLES, HERBS, SPICES
[TABASCO, WORCESTERSHIRE

FATTOOSH   Pita Bread Salad   (Middle East)   Amounts are flexible

Toast [2 loaves PITA BREAD - see "BASIC RECIPES". Break it into large bite-size pieces.

Combine in a salad bowl:

[	1	HEART ROMAINE LETTUCE bite-size pieces
[	3 medium	TOMATOES seeded, bite-size chunks
[	2	KIRBY CUCUMBERS peeled, halved, sliced
[	3 or 4	GREEN ONIONS thinly sliced
[	1/2-cup	FLAT LEAF PARSLEY coarsely chopped
[	1/2-cup	FRESH MINT coarsely chopped

The DRESSING   Mix in blender:

[	1/3-cup	EXTRA-VIRGIN OLIVE OIL
[	3 TB	LEMON JUICE
[	1 clove	GARLIC mashed
[	2 tp	DRIED MINT or more
[	1/4-tp	SALT, PEPPER to taste
[	1/2-tp	SUMAC SPICE optional

Before serving add gradually the Dressing, you may not need all of it.
Last add the PITA BREAD. It absorbs a lot of Dressing and will get soggy if added too soon.

GERMAN POTATO SALAD

Yields 3-1/2 to 4 cups

| | Drop into plenty of boiling water to cover | [1 lb | NEW POTATOES   washed and scrubbed |

Drop into plenty of boiling water to cover   [1 lb   NEW POTATOES   washed and scrubbed

When tender firm, drain, cover, keep warm.

In a nonstick skillet, fry until browned   [2 oz   BACON SLAB   finely diced

Remove with slotted spoon, drain on paper towels. Save in the skillet 1 TB BACON FAT.

The DRESSING   Heat the FAT, sauté in it   [1/2-cup   ONION   finely chopped
When translucent, add   [3 TB   CHICKEN BROTH   lightly salted
[2 TB   CIDER or WHITE WINE VINEGAR

- Stir for 2 minutes, turn off heat.
- Slice the hot Potatoes, 1/4-inch thick, into a salad bowl, gradually add the hot DRESSING and BACON.

Mix well, and add   [2 TB   FLAT LEAF PARSLEY   finely chop
Add a little more Broth or Vinegar if needed   [to taste   SALT, GROUND BLACK PEPPER
[optional   SOUR or DILL PICKLES chopped

Serve warm or at room temperature.

GREEK SALAD

Amounts are flexible. Add gradually the Dressing.

[1 head   HEARTS of ROMAINE LETTUCE   bite-size pieces
[2   KIRBY CUCUMBERS   sliced 1/4-inch thick
[2 or 3   TOMATOES   seeded, wedges or chunks
[1   GREEN BELL PEPPER   thin strips
[1   SMALL RED ONION   thinly sliced
[4-to-6 oz   FETA CHEESE   crumbled
[4 oz   KALAMATA OLIVES

The DRESSING

[5 TB   EXTRA-VIRGIN OLIVE OIL
[2 TB   RED WINE VINEGAR
[2 tp   DRIED OREGANO   or more
[SALT, BLACK PEPPER

NIÇOISE SALAD

Amounts are flexible. Add gradually the Dressing.

[1 cup   BOILED POTATOES   diced or cubed
[1 cup   STRING BEANS *al dente*, cut in half
[1 cup   TOMATOES   seeded, cubed
[1 or 2   RED or GREEN BELL PEPPERS   small strips
[6 oz-can   TUNA IN OLIVE OIL   drained
Include Tuna Oil in the Dressing
[5 or 6   ANCHOVY FILLETS   rinse, drain, chop
[1/2-cup   BLACK OLIVES   pitted or whole

[Garnish with   HARD-COOKED EGGS   wedges

The DRESSING

[add to TUNA FISH OIL
[enough EXTRA-VIRGIN OLIVE OIL
to obtain a 1/2-cup
Add:

[5-1/2 TB LEMON JUICE
[1 TB   DRIED TARRAGON
[SALT, BLACK PEPPER

SALADE RUSSE   (Russia)   *Yields about 6 cups*

[1 cup   BOILED POTATOES   diced
[1 cup   BEETS (boiled or canned) drained, diced
[1 cup   CARROTS   boiled or steamed, diced
[1 cup   GREEN PEAS
[1 cup   RADISHES   diced
[3   HARD-COOKED EGGS   chopped
[to taste   GHERKINS or SOUR PICKLES   chopped
[1/4-cup   FRESH DILL   snipped

The DRESSING

[1 cup   MAYONNAISE
[1 tp   YELLOW MUSTARD
[1 TB   EXTRA-VIRGIN OLIVE OIL

Mix in gradually.
Add more Mayonnaise as needed.

[Optional, add any of: ANCHOVIES, CRAB MEAT, SHRIMP, HAM, SAUSAGE.

NOTE - Amounts are flexible. Combine to taste according to the number of servings.

TABBOULEH   (Middle East)   *Recipe for 4 to 6 servings*

It consists mainly of PARSLEY, FRESH MINT, a small amount of BULGUR and lots of LEMON JUICE.
Commercial preparations consist mostly of Bulgur (Cracked Wheat) and very few Vegetables.

TABBOULEH is not a Salad that can be served alone, let's say, as an Appetizer. It accompanies
Meat, Fish or Poultry. It goes well with Lamb, grilled Lamb Chops, Meat Kebabs, spicy Sausage.

It does not go with Wine Sauce preparations, as its highlight is a strong Mint and Lemon taste.

It can also be served as an Hors-d'oeuvre, with a variety of others. See page 140.

THE DRESSING

[2	BUNCHES PARSLEY (regular, not Flat Leaf)	
[4	GREEN ONIONS medium size	
[2	KIRBY CUCUMBERS	
[1	MEDIUM TOMATO	
[4 TB	BULGUR # 2 medium	
[3/4-cup	FRESH MINT cut off stems	
[1/3-cup	DRIED GARDEN MINT	

[6 TB   EXTRA-VIRGIN OLIVE OIL
[6 TB   LEMON JUICE
[SALT, BLACK PEPPER

Add the Dressing gradually. Taste.
Add more according to taste.

The following preparations can be done a day ahead.

PARSLEY - Hold the bunch close to the leaves and cut off the long stems.
         - Untie, wash well in a large bowl under running cold water. Drain.
         - Soak in a bowl of cold water for at least an hour, to crisp it.

         - Drain well in a colander. Spread on a kitchen towel. Lightly pat dry.
         - Return to dry colander. Cover with a plate. Refrigerate on lower shelf.

         - Later, or the next day, pick the leaves off the stems. Place them in a
            sealed plastic container and refrigerate.

FRESH MINT LEAVES - Wash, drain, dry on a kitchen towel. Pick the leaves. Add them to the
                      Parsley and refrigerate.

On Tabbouleh day - Prepare ahead of time and refrigerate:

BULGUR - Place it in a fine sieve and rinse it well under running cold water.
        - Put it in a measuring cup and cover it with twice as much cold Water.
        - Soak for 30 minutes or longer. It will more than double.
        - Increase quantity if you like more Bulgur in the Salad.
        - Drain in the fine sieve. Press to release water. Refrigerate in the sieve.

PARSLEY/FRESH MINT - Put 2 handfuls at a time in processor. Pulse 3 seconds. Stir, repeat
                       2 or 3 times, until finely chopped and fluffy. Return to container.

DRIED GARDEN MINT - Crumble and mix it with the chopped Parsley/Mint. Seal container.

GREEN ONIONS - Trim. Wash, dry. Cut lengthwise. Slice very thinly.
              - Spread over the Parsley/Mint. Seal container. Refrigerate.

KIRBY CUCUMBERS - Pare. Cut in four lengthwise. Slice off seeds.
                 - Cut each quarter lengthwise and dice finely. Place in separate container.

TOMATO - Seed, drain, dice finely. Refrigerate with Cucumbers. Do not mix.

Assemble the Tabbouleh Salad just before the meal. Keep refrigerated until ready to serve.

- Place Parsley Mixture in the salad bowl. Add Cucumbers, Tomatoes and Bulgur.
- Mix in the Dressing. Taste. If needed, add more Lemon Juice, Salt and Ground Black Pepper.

THANKSGIVING SALAD
Serves 8 to 10

Prepare Ingredients and store in plastic bags or containers. Assemble and add the Dressing before serving. Mushrooms and Asparagus are the base for this Salad.

	[8 oz	SLICED RAW MUSHROOMS
Steam in microwave for 1-1/2 minutes	[8 oz	THIN ASPARAGUS
		Slant-cut into 1-inch pieces.
Slant-cut crosswise into 1/4-inch thick slices	[6 oz	CELERY HEART STALKS
Thinly slice white and light green part of	[4 or 5	THIN GREEN ONIONS
Boil following package directions	[1 cup	FROZEN EDAMAME BEANS
	[1 cup	GRAPE TOMATOES
As is, or toasted	[1/3-cup	SLIVERED ALMONDS
	[1/2-cup	CRANBERRIES
The DRESSING	[6 TB	LEMON or LIME JUICE
	[10 TB	EXTRA-VIRGIN OLIVE OIL
	[to taste	SALT, BLACK PEPPER

WALDORF SALAD
Serve with Curries and hot Foods.   *Yields 1-3/4 cups*

Soak for 20 minutes in Water, drain and dry	[1/4-cup	PECAN or WALNUT HALVES

Chop coarsely in processor.

Mix	[1 cup	RED APPLES diced small
	[1/2-cup	CELERY STALKS diced small
	[1 tp	LEMON JUICE
Add gradually to taste	[	MAYONNAISE ready-made
	[	or a SEASONED MAYONNAISE
		(see "SAUCES")
	[optional	BLUE CHEESE crumbled

Stir to coat well Ingredients. Refrigerate.
Before serving, add the NUTS. If added early, they may discolor and stain the Apples.

YOGURT CUCUMBER SALAD
Yields about 1-1/2 cups

Pare and slice paper thin	[2	KIRBY CUCUMBERS
Place in a shallow bowl. Sprinkle, mix with	[	SALT

- Press on them an upside-down small plate
  and weight it with a heavy can. Refrigerate.
- Let stand 30 minutes.
- Hold down the Cucumbers with the plate,
  pour out the water. Refrigerate.
- Repeat until Cucumbers have rendered as
  much water as possible.

Beat with a fork	[3/4-cup	PLAIN YOGURT + 1 TB WATER
When smooth, add	[2 tp	DRIED MINT crumbled, or more
	or 2 TB	FRESH MINT finely chopped
Optional	[a sprinkle	GARLIC POWDER
	[	or GARLIC minced

Add Cucumbers to the Yogurt.
Refrigerate. Before serving add Salt if needed.
<u>Serve with</u>   Fish, Lamb, Kebab, grilled Meats, grilled Lamb chops, Rice, Vegetables.

138

ETHNIC HORS-D'OEUVRE

GREEK MEZEDES   Served with Beer, Ouzo, or Wine.

DOLMADES	-	Grape Vine leaves stuffed with Rice, Herbs, in Oil (available canned). Sprinkle with a little Lemon Juice.
BABY EGGPLANT	-	"Imam Bayaldi": stuffed with Rice, Onion, Herbs (available canned).
FETA CHEESE	-	Drizzle with Extra-Virgin Olive Oil.
KEFTEDAKIA	-	Spicy little Meatballs. (see "MEATS" - GROUND BEEF MEATBALLS)
OCTOPUS SALAD	-	Baby octopus in a Dressing with Herbs.
OLIVES	-	Kalamata black Olives and any other kind, black or green.
PHYLLO SHELLS	-	Tiny Phyllo cups, available frozen. Fill with Feta, Taramosalata, other.
SKORDALIA	-	Mashed Potato/Garlic Dip. (see recipe in this chapter)
SPANAKOPITA	-	Small Phyllo triangles with Spinach and Feta. (available frozen)
TARAMOSALATA	-	Cod Roe Dip/Spread (available ready-made, in a jar - refrigerated).
TYROPITA	-	Small Phyllo triangles stuffed with Feta Cheese (available frozen).
TZATZIKI	-	Cucumber Yogurt Dip. See "SAUCES" - YOGURT SAUCES.

OCTOPUS SALAD   BABY OCTOPUS is available in fish markets, cleaned and ready to cook.

- Wash it under cold water. Place it in a saucepan with plenty of water. Boil until it turns dark red and very tender. Drain. Pat dry. Peel off the skin.
- Cut tentacles into bite-size pieces or thin rounds. Cut body into thin strips.

- Prepare a VINAIGRETTE with RED WINE VINEGAR, EXTRA-VIRGIN OLIVE OIL and mashed minced GARLIC. Add to taste minced PARSLEY, OREGANO, and DILL.
- Mix Octopus with Dressing and refrigerate.
- Or use an OIL and LEMON DRESSING with GARLIC and the Herbs.

ITALIAN ANTIPASTI

ANCHOVIES	-	and SARDINES. Fresh, marinated, or canned
ARTICHOKES	-	Marinated Artichoke Hearts.
BAGNA CAUDA	-	Hot Anchovy and Garlic Dip. ("DIPS and SPREADS" - ETHNIC DIPS)
BELL PEPPERS	-	Roasted and Marinated. See "VEGETABLES".
CALAMARI	-	Salad with an Oil and Lemon Dressing.
CAPONATA	-	Eggplant Appetizer. See "VEGETABLES" - EGGPLANT.
CHEESE	-	Smoked Provolone, Parmesan chunks.
CROSTINI	-	See "BASIC RECIPES": toasted Bread with a variety of Toppings.
CURED MEATS	-	Bresaola drizzle with Olive Oil, Mortadella, Prosciutto, Salami.
FRITTATAS	-	A variety of thin Omelets, cut into wedges.
MEATBALLS	-	See recipes: "MEATS" - GROUND BEEF.
MELON and FIGS	-	Bite-size Cantaloupe balls, or Fig wedges, wrapped with Prosciutto.
MOZZARELLA	-	Bocconcini in Olive Oil, Mozzarella di Buffala with sliced Tomatoes.
MUSHROOMS	-	Marinated Button Mushrooms or stuffed Mushroom Caps.
OCTOPUS	-	Salad with an Oil and Lemon Dressing.
OLIVES	-	A variety of Black and Green Olives.
PEPERONATA	-	Bell Pepper Appetizer. See "VEGETABLES" - BELL PEPPER
PIZZAS	-	Hot and cut into wedges. Mini Pizzas are available frozen.
SEAFOOD	-	A large variety: fried, grilled, prepared in their shells, in salads.

MIDDLE EASTERN MEZZÉ

The table is spread with a variety of small dishes. ARAK is the Mezzé drink (tastes like Ouzo).

BABAGANOUSH	-	Eggplant and Tahini Dip. (see "DIPS and SPREADS")
BASTURMA	-	Garlicky Dried Beef.
CHEESE	-	String Cheese, Haloumi. Feta Cheese, also served in the Middle East.
GRAPE LEAVES	-	Stuffed with Rice.
HUMMUS	-	Chick Pea and Tahini Dip. (see "DIPS and SPREADS")
KAFTA	-	Meatballs. Also served as Kebab on skewers. (See "MEATS" - BEEF)
LABNE	-	Yogurt Cheese: KEFIR. Drizzle with Olive Oil, a sprinkle of Zaatar.
MEAT PIES	-	Cocktail-size Pizza style. (See "MEATS" - GROUND BEEF)
OLIVES	-	A variety of black and green.
PICKLED TURNIPS	-	Bite-size chunks. (Beets in the marinade color them pink.)
RAW KIBBEE	-	Middle Eastern version of steak Tartare, prepared with ground Beef or a mixture of Beef and Lamb. (See "MEATS" - GROUND BEEF)
SPICY SAUSAGES	-	Cocktail size or sliced.
PHYLLO	-	Hot triangles, rolls filled with Haloumi Cheese, or Spinach and Feta.
TABBOULEH	-	See recipe in this chapter. Serve with Lettuce Leaves on the side.
TAHINI	-	A Sesame Sauce or Dip. (see "SAUCES")
LETTUCE LEAVES	-	To scoop up the Tabbouleh.
PITA BREAD	-	To scoop up the Dips.

SPANISH TAPAS

Served with Beer, a variety of Spanish Wines, Dry Sherry, Manzanilla.

ANCHOVIES	-	Marinated.
ANGULAS	-	Baby Eels in sizzling Olive Oil.
CHEESE	-	A variety of Spanish Cheese is available on the market.
CHORIZO	-	And Sobrasada, are spicy Sausages. As well as a variety of others.
CROQUETTES	-	Chicken, Fish or Ham (with a Béchamel Base).
CROQUETTES	-	Crispy Potato Croquettes.
EGGS	-	Cooked Mushroom caps filled with scrambled Eggs.
EMPANADAS	-	Fried Meat pies stuffed with Chicken or Meat.
FISH	-	Tiny fried Fish. Salted Cod with Tomatoes.
FRITTERS	-	Finger food size of Salted Cod or Vegetables, with an Aïoli Sauce.
HAM	-	Serrano (like Prosciutto) and Iberico.
MUSHROOMS	-	Cooked with Seafood, Ham. Grilled with Garlic, scrambled with Eggs.
OLIVES	-	Of all colors, sizes, flavors and stuffings.
REBANADAS	-	Rustic Bread Canapés topped with melted Cheese and a slice of Meat.
SEAFOOD	-	A large variety: raw, marinated, steamed, fried, or sautéed in Garlic. Served with an Aïoli Sauce (Garlic Sauce) see "SAUCES".
TORTILLA	-	Potato Omelet. Also with other Fillings. (See "VEGETABLES")
TOSTADAS	-	Toasted Canapés topped with Seafood, Fish, Meats, Cheese.

MISCELLANEOUS

BELGIAN ENDIVE	-	Spread spear tips with Steak Tartare, mashed Gorgonzola and Cream.
COUNTRY PÂTÉ	-	Cubed, skewered on toothpicks between Cherry Tomato halves.
MINI QUICHES	-	Add your choice of Fillings. See "BASIC RECIPES".
MUSHROOM CAPS	-	Fill with a minced Ham mixture, Smoked Salmon, Tuna.

VIII

AFTER HOURS

"Looking forward to things is half the pleasure of them."

Lucy Maud Montgomery

AFTER HOURS

LIGHT LATE SUPPERS

Beef   -   Meatloaf Caesar   144
           -    Roast Beef Horseradish
           -    Salad Parmentier
           -    Steak Brussels Sprouts
Chicken -   Apples and Frisée
           -    Poached Egg Aspic 145
Foie Gras or Duck Galantine
Ham / Prosciutto / Chicken - Asian Pears 146
Ham and Turkey Caprese
Salmon - White Asparagus
Smoked Salmon   -   Napoleon
                    -    Poached Egg Aspic 147
                    -    Prosciutto with Avocado
Shrimp and Crab Meat with Avocado Salsa
           -    Mussels "Al Pesto"
Trout Florentine 148
Smoked Trout à la Russe
Tomato Toasts
Vitello Tonnato

MIDNIGHT PASTAS

Alla Calabrese 149
Alla Greca
All'Italiana
Alla Piemontese
Bella Napoli
Luigi's Bar
Villa d'Este

SIMPLE YUMMIES

Chicken and Arugula 150
      - Leeks
      - Tomatoes
Pork Roast and Papaya
Veal Roast and Green Beans

LIGHT LATE SUPPERS

Prepare Ingredients ahead of time and refrigerate until ready to serve.

BEEF MEATLOAF - CAESAR

Separate in a mixing bowl [	ROMAINE LETTUCE bite-size pieces
Cooked [	MOREL or CHANTERELLE MUSHROOMS

Cover. Refrigerate.

To serve, toss with [	CAESAR DRESSING see "DRESSINGS"
Add [	CROUTONS
Sprinkle with [	PARMESAN grated
Serve on the side [	COLD MEATLOAF sliced

ROAST BEEF - HORSERADISH

Separate in a mixing bowl [	FRENCH CUT GREEN BEANS *al dente*
[	BOILED NEW POTATOES diced
[	FENNEL shredded
[	SLIVERED ALMONDS toasted
[	FRESH DILL snipped

Cover. Refrigerate.

To serve, toss with [	HORSERADISH CREAMY DRESSING
	(see "DRESSINGS")
Serve on the side [	COLD ROAST BEEF sliced

BEEF SALAD PARMENTIER

Combine in a bowl [	BOILED POTATOES cut into small cubes
[	COLD STEWED BEEF small cubes
[	PARSLEY finely chopped
[	CAPERS or CORNICHONS minced

Toss with a VINAIGRETTE DRESSING. Use [	TARRAGON or RED WINE VINEGAR
Add to taste a little [	ROSEMARY and/or THYME

Cover. Refrigerate.

Serve on the side sliced [	TOMATOES drizzle with OLIVE OIL

BEEF STEAK - BRUSSELS SPROUTS

Separate in a mixing bowl [	ARUGULA
[	BRUSSELS SPROUTS blanched, cut in half
Sprinkle with [	CHIVES
[	PINE NUTS toasted

Cover. Refrigerate.

To serve, toss with [	DRESSING of your choice
Top with [	COLD STEAK sliced

CHICKEN - APPLES and FRISÉE

Mix in a salad bowl [	APPLES diced
with a little [	OIL and LEMON DRESSING
Top Apples with [	FRISÉE LETTUCE cut into small pieces
[	GOAT CHEESE diced

Do not toss. Cover and refrigerate.

When ready to serve, toss into the Salad [	WALNUTS chopped
[	OIL and LEMON DRESSING + Seasonings
Serve on the side [	COLD CHICKEN

CHICKEN with POACHED EGG ASPIC   ASPIC see "BASIC RECIPES"

Let cool.	Prepare ASPIC STOCK with	[	CHICKEN BROTH
	Optional	[	add a little DRY SHERRY
	Boil, refrigerate until ready to use	[	NEW POTATOES
	Prepare POACHED EGGS	[	See "BASIC RECIPES" - EGGS. Refrigerate until ready to use.

Pour into ramekins [ASPIC STOCK a 1/4-inch thick layer
Refrigerate.

When jellied, place a [POACHED EGG in each ramekin
Surround the Egg with [FRESH TARRAGON or WATERCRESS
finely chopped

Add a little more [ASPIC STOCK
Refrigerate until set.

When jellied, surround the Egg with 2 rows [AVOCADO cut into thin slivers
Add more [ASPIC STOCK leaving space for a layer of
Potatoes and Aspic Stock to top them
Refrigerate.

When jellied, top with a layer of [BOILED NEW POTATOES thinly sliced

Overlap the Potato slices in concentric circles.

Cover with [ASPIC STOCK
Refrigerate until set.
Unmold onto individual plates. Refrigerate.

To serve   Surround Aspic with [FRISÉE LETTUCE
Top Lettuce with [COLD CHICKEN boned, trimmed, sliced
and [TOMATO SLICES
Drizzle over Lettuce, Chicken and Tomatoes [DRESSING of your choice

VARIATION   -   Substitute Chicken with HAM or FISH.

FOIE GRAS or DUCK GALANTINE

Salad I   Combine to taste [FRENCH CUT GREEN BEANS
[ASPARAGUS TIPS   steamed *al dente*
[ARTICHOKE BOTTOMS thinly sliced
[WHITE MUSHROOMS   thinly sliced
[HAZELNUTS   toasted, chopped

Cover. Refrigerate.
The Vinaigrette [SUNFLOWER OIL   (no Mustard)
[SHERRY VINEGAR
[SALT and GROUND BLACK PEPPER

Toss the Salad with the Vinaigrette.

Serve it on individual plates with a slice of [FOIE GRAS or DUCK GALANTINE
On the side [BRIOCHE, CHALLAH, or WHITE BREAD
toasted

Salad II   Combine to taste [BELGIAN ENDIVE thinly sliced
[RED APPLES   diced
A little [GREEN ONION   thinly sliced
[PECANS   chopped

Use the same DRESSING.

145

HAM / PROSCIUTTO / CHICKEN - ASIAN PEARS

Slice into thin wedges	[	ASIAN PEARS
Coat them with a	[	MAYONNAISE SAUCE or DRESSING

Cover. Refrigerate.

To serve	Spread on platter or salad plates	[	MESCLUN or FRISÉE LETTUCE
	Drizzle with	[	MAYONNAISE SAUCE or DRESSING

Top half of Lettuce with PEARS, sprinkle with	[	BLUE CHEESE crumbled
	[	CHIVES
	[	SUNFLOWER SEEDS toasted, salted

Top other half of Lettuce with	[		HAM or PROSCIUTTO (roll the slices)
	[	or	COLD CHICKEN, or a combination of any

HAM and TURKEY - CAPRESE

Arrange on a platter or salad plates	[	HAM thinly sliced
and	[	SMOKED TURKEY BREAST
Overlap and arrange in between	[	BEEFSTEAK TOMATOES sliced
and	[	MOZZARELLA DI BUFFALA
	[	OLIVES and PICKLES
Drizzle with	[	EXTRA-VIRGIN OLIVE OIL
	[	GROUND BLACK PEPPER
Sprinkle with	[	FRESH BASIL LEAVES

VARIATION Substitute Ham and Turkey with	[	sliced ROAST BEEF or ROAST VEAL

SALMON - WHITE ASPARAGUS

Combine in a bowl	[	WHITE ASPARAGUS cut into 1-inch pieces
	[	BOILED POTATOES diced
	[	CHIVES
	[	FRESH DILL snipped

Cover. Refrigerate.

To serve	Toss Asparagus Mixture with a	[	CHAMPAGNE VINEGAR VINAIGRETTE
	Arrange on plates	[	FRISÉE LETTUCE
		[	ASPARAGUS SALAD
		[	COLD SALMON steamed or grilled
	Sprinkle with	[	FRESH DILL snipped

SMOKED SALMON - NAPOLEON

Serve on salad plates, layered	[	BOILED POTATOES thinly sliced
	[	SMOKED SALMON
A few drops	[	LEMON JUICE
	[	PALM HEARTS thinly sliced lengthwise
	[	SMOKED SALMON
	[	ASPARAGUS TIPS split lengthwise
Spread between layers and top with	[	CAPER MAYONNAISE see "SAUCES"

146

SMOKED SALMON with POACHED EGG ASPIC

Prepare the POACHED EGG ASPIC - see previous recipe: CHICKEN - POACHED EGG ASPIC.

Surround unmolded Aspic with	[	ALFALFA and FENNEL shredded
Drizzle with	[	CAPER CREAMY DRESSING
		(see "DRESSINGS")
Top Fennel with	[	SMOKED SALMON
Sprinkle with	[	CAPERS rinsed, drained, dried

SMOKED SALMON and PROSCIUTTO with AVOCADO

Cut in half and peel	[	AVOCADOS (or substitute with Pears)
Cut halves into 4 wedges brush them with	[	OIL and LEMON DRESSING
Wrap some Avocado wedges with	[	SMOKED SALMON thinly sliced
Others with	[	PROSCIUTTO thinly sliced
Spread on a platter or individual plates	[	WATERCRESS
Arrange on top	[	WRAPPED AVOCADO WEDGES
Sprinkle with	[	BLUEBERRIES
	[	PINE NUTS toasted

Cover with plastic wrap, refrigerate.

To serve Drizzle with	[	WATERCRESS CREAMY DRESSING
		(see "DRESSINGS")

SHRIMP and CRAB MEAT with AVOCADO SALSA

Arrange on a platter a bed of	[	MIXED GREENS
Center on the mixed Greens	[	LUMP CRAB MEAT
Surround with	[	SHRIMP
Surround Shrimp with	[	PAPAYA slices

Cover with plastic wrap and refrigerate.

Combine in a bowl	[	AVOCADO diced
with	[	SALSA mild or hot

Cover. Refrigerate.

To serve Pour over the Salsa. Sprinkle with	[	CILANTRO finely chopped

SHRIMP and MUSSELS "AL PESTO"

Rub mixing bowl with	[	GARLIC CLOVE mashed, discard
and combine in it	[	COLD SHRIMP bite-size, cut if large
	[	COLD STEAMED MUSSELS no shells
	[	BOILED NEW POTATOES diced
	[	SMALL WHITE MUSHROOMS thinly sliced
	[	CELERY thinly sliced
	[	GREEN ONION thinly sliced
	[	PINE NUTS toasted
Add gradually to taste to	[	OIL and LEMON DRESSING
	[	PESTO SAUCE ready-made

Mix the Dressing into the Seafood Salad.
Refrigerate. Serve on a bed of GREENS. Substitute with any other Seafood.

TROUT FILLETS FLORENTINE   Or any other Fish Fillets   *Serves 2*

Steam in microwave for 6 minutes	[10 oz-pkg	FROZEN LEAF SPINACH

Let cool. Transfer to a plate, chop coarsely
using a knife and fork.

Combine in a bowl	[	the Spinach
	[to taste	GREEN ONION thinly sliced
	[to taste	OIL and LEMON DRESSING

Cover. Refrigerate.

To serve   Spread Spinach on 2 individual

plates, top with	[	COLD POACHED TROUT FILLETS trimmed
		or poached Fish of your choice
Garnish with	[	ARTICHOKE BOTTOMS thinly sliced
	[or	ARTICHOKE HEARTS cut into wedges
Drizzle with	[	OIL and LEMON DRESSING
sprinkle with	[	WATERCRESS finely chopped

SMOKED TROUT à la RUSSE

Mix	[	LETTUCE shredded
with	[	FENNEL shredded
Spread them on a platter and sprinkle with	[	CRANBERRIES
and	[	SOUR PICKLES finely chopped
Place in the center	[	SMOKED TROUT FILLETS skinned, boned
Surround with overlapping thin slices of	[	BEETS
	[	BOILED POTATOES
and	[	CUCUMBERS seeded, diced
Sprinkle with	[	ONION blanched, sliced, finely chopped
Cover with	[	CRÈME FRAÎCHE SOUR CREAM DRESSING
		(see "DRESSINGS" - DAIRY)

TOMATO TOASTS

In the chapter "VEGETABLES" see under TOMATOES, a variety of SNACK TOASTS.

Serve as is or with cold Chicken, Turkey, Ham, Prosciutto.
Or with a Seafood Salad, cold poached fillets of Fish.

Also see BELL PEPPERS - BRUSCHETTA PEPERONATA.

VITELLO TONNATO   Veal Tuna Mayonnaise   See "MEATS" - COLD ROAST VEAL

Arrange on a platter or individual plates	[	COLD ROAST VEAL slices
Spread over them the	[	TUNA MAYONNAISE see "SAUCES"

Cover with plastic wrap, refrigerate.

Garnish with	[	PARSLEY minced
	[	HARD-COOKED EGG sliced
	[	CAPERS, OLIVES

Serve with a green SALAD.

148

MIDNIGHT PASTAS

Mix amounts according to taste and number of servings.

ALLA CALABRESE

Drain and toss	[	SPAGHETTI
with	[canned	TUNA FISH flaked with its OIL
Add	[a few leaves	FRESH BASIL tear by hand
	[	TINY CAPERS rinsed, drained
	[	FRESH TOMATOES seeded, diced
	[	GREEN OLIVES chopped
	[drizzle with	EXTRA-VIRGIN OLIVE OIL

ALLA GRECA

Drain and toss	[	SPAGHETTINI
with	[	EXTRA-VIRGIN OLIVE OIL
Add	[	PARSLEY coarsely chopped
Stir in	[crumbled	FETA it will melt into the Pasta
	[canned	ANCHOVIES drained, finely chop
	[chopped	KALAMATA or ALFONSO OLIVES
	[	TOMATOES seeded and diced
	[	GROUND BLACK PEPPER

ALL'ITALIANA

Drain and toss	[	TAGLIATELLE white or green
with	[	EXTRA-VIRGIN OLIVE OIL
Add	[a few leaves	FRESH BASIL tear by hand
Stir in	[diced	MOZZARELLA it will melt in Pasta
	[plenty of	PARMESAN grated
	[	TOMATOES seeded and diced
	[	GROUND BLACK PEPPER

ALLA PIEMONTESE

Drain and toss	[	FETTUCCINI or fresh EGG NOODLES
with	[heated	FOUR CHEESE SAUCE
	[diced	HAM or PROSCIUTTO chopped
	[cooked	ASPARAGUS 1-inch pieces
	[	FLAT LEAF PARSLEY finely chop

BELLA NAPOLI

Rub the Pasta bowl with	[1 clove	GARLIC
Drain and pour into it	[	SPAGHETTI or SPAGHETTINI
Toss with a	[well heated	TOMATO PASTA SAUCE
	[diced	MOZZARELLA
	[diced	SALAMI or SAUSAGE
	[	TINY CAPERS rinsed, drained
	[	PARMESAN grated

LUIGI'S BAR

Drain and toss	[	GREEN TAGLIATELLE
with	[well heated	ALFREDO SAUCE ready-made
	[	SMOKED SALMON chopped
	[	CAPERS rinsed, finely chopped
	[a little	FRESH DILL snipped

VILLA D'ESTE

Drain and toss	[	FETTUCCINI or fresh EGG NOODLES
with	[heated	ALFREDO SAUCE ready-made
Mix in	[	LOBSTER bite-size pieces
	[	PINE NUTS toasted

Uncork the Champagne!

SIMPLE YUMMIES

CHICKEN and ARUGULA

Spread on platter or plates [	ARUGULA trimmed
Top with thinly sliced [	VIDALIA or BERMUDA ONION rings
Drizzle with [	HERBS VINAIGRETTE see "DRESSINGS"
Top with [	COLD CHICKEN boned, trimmed, sliced
Drizzle with [	HERBS VINAIGRETTE

CHICKEN and LEEKS

LEEKS see "BASIC RECIPES"

Serve on individual plates [	LEEKS "Prepared for Salads"

Cover with wrap.
Refrigerate. Before serving pour out
rendered Liquid.

Top with [	COLD CHICKEN boned, trimmed, sliced
Pour over [	STILTON CHEESE CREAMY DRESSING
	(see "DRESSINGS")

CHICKEN and TOMATOES

Arrange on individual plates [	TOMATOES sliced
[	COLD CHICKEN boned, trimmed, sliced
Drizzle all over [	EXTRA-VIRGIN OLIVE OIL
[	SALT and GROUND BLACK PEPPER
Sprinkle with [	PARSLEY or FRESH BASIL finely chopped

FISH and BOILED POTATOES

Center on a plate [	FISH FILLETS cold
Surround with [	BOILED POTATOES sliced
Top with [	TOMATOES seeded, diced
[	CAPERS
[	FRESH BASIL finely chopped
Drizzle with [	OIL and LEMON DRESSING

PORK ROAST and PAPAYA

Overlap on plates or platter slices of [	PORK ROAST
[	PAPAYA
[	BOILED or ROASTED SWEET POTATO
[	AVOCADO
(See "DRESSINGS") Drizzle with [	CUMIN or MUSTARD CREAMY DRESSING

VEAL ROAST and GREEN BEANS

Arrange on one side of platter, sliced [	VEAL ROAST or PORK ROAST
On the rest of the plate or platter [	TOMATOES sliced
[	BOILED POTATOES sliced
[	FRENCH CUT GREEN BEANS al dente
(See "DRESSINGS") Drizzle with [	HORSERADISH or SHALLOT VINAIGRETTE

150

IX

FISH

A NOTE

Wash thoroughly fresh Fish under running cold water and pat it dry with paper towels.

Packed frozen Fish is clean and ready to use. Thaw and pat dry.

"The fact is I simply adore fish,
But I don't know a perch from a pike;
And I can't tell a cray from a crawfish,
They look and they taste so alike."

William Cole

FISH

COOKING METHODS

Cooked Fish must be tender but firm. Do not overcook, it will fall apart.

BAKED The easiest way to cook Fish. Cooking time depends on weight, thickness, toughness.

Large Fish: 3 lbs or more	- Preheat oven to 425°.	Bake for 10 minutes.
	- Reduce heat to 350°.	Allow 10 minutes per pound.
Fillets, steaks: 1-inch thick	- Preheat oven to 375°.	Bake from 12-to-14 minutes.

- Rub the whole Fish with Salt and Lemon. Brush with Olive/Vegetable Oil. Add Pepper, Herbs.
- If you are stuffing it, secure the opening after stuffing with trussing thread or needles.
- Brush Steaks, Fillets with Olive Oil or other. Sprinkle Salt, Pepper. Bake Fillets skin side down.

- Brush an oven proof dish or pan with Olive or Vegetable oil. Optional, first line it with foil.
- Optional: spread in it any of sliced Onion, fresh Herb sprigs, shredded Fennel, Lemon slices.
- Lay on top Steaks, Fillets or whole Fish. Dot with diced Butter, unless they're brushed with Oil.

- Potatoes and Vegetables must cook partially before adding the Fish. Estimate their cooking time and the time needed to cook the Fish, according to its weight.

BOILED

- In a saucepan, bring to boiling point enough Water to cover the Fish. Season the Water with Salt, a teaspoon or more of Lemon Juice or Vinegar, a slice of Onion, and Herbs to taste.
- With a slotted spoon lower the Fish into the Water. Reduce heat to medium low, simmer from 5-to-15 minutes, depending on thickness, size, toughness of flesh. Remove with slotted spoon.
- For large Fish or large slices, place them in a wire basket and lower them into the Water.

BROILED   Also an easy way to cook Fish.

- Rub it with Salt and Lemon. Brush lightly with Olive or Vegetable Oil. To taste, Pepper, Spice.
- Grease a shallow pan with Cooking Spray or Vegetable Oil. Or line the pan with foil.
- Place the Fish in it, skin side up. Brown the skin under the broiler. Turn, cook the other side for 6-to-12 minutes, depending on thickness and toughness of flesh.

- If the Fish has skin on both sides, brown both sides.
- Broil 1-inch thick skinless Fillets and Steaks, from 4-to-5 minutes on each side.

FRIED   Unless the ventilation is good in your kitchen, the odor will linger for long.

SAUTÉ	- in a skillet, with a little Vegetable Oil or Butter, or a mixture of both.
IN A BATTER	- dip in Milk, roll in Flour and deep fry.
SOUTHERN	- dip in Milk, roll in Corn Meal and deep fry, or skillet fry.
OR	- roll in Bread Crumbs, dip in beaten Egg, roll in Crumbs. Deep fry or skillet fry.

POACHED

- Half fill a skillet with Water, add Seasonings: Salt, Onion slice, Celery rib, Pepper Corns, Herbs, Bay Leaf, dry white Wine, Lemon Juice. Or use Fish Stock, Court Bouillon ("BASIC RECIPES").
- Bring to a boil, add the Fish then immediately reduce heat to medium low and simmer.
- Depending on thickness, poach from 5-to-15 minutes, or longer. Remove with slotted spoon.
- The Cooking Liquid can be strained in a fine sieve and used to prepare a Sauce.

- Also poach in Milk with seasonings, Herbs. In Sauces: Marinara, Creole, Provençale, Tomato.

STEAMED

- Use a collapsible colander or a steamer. If desired, season the Fish. Lay it on the colander.
- In a large skillet, bring Water to a boil. Place the colander in it. The Water must not touch it.
- Cover with a large lid. Steam from 10-to-15 minutes, or longer, depending on thickness.

ANCHOVY - CROSTINI
Hors-d'oeuvre   Yields about a 1/2-cup

In a nonstick skillet, over medium heat, heat	[1 TB	EXTRA-VIRGIN OLIVE OIL
Sauté in it	[1 clove	GARLIC or more, mash, mince
When the Garlic softens, mash with it	[6 canned	ANCHOVY FILLETS
	[1/2-tp	CAPERS rinsed, dried, minced
	[1 TB	SUN-DRIED TOMATOES minced

Transfer to a bowl let Mixture cool.

| Mix in | [optional | FETA CHEESE   crumbled |

| See "BASIC RECIPES". Prepare Crostini with | [| BAGUETTE |

| Spread Mixture on Crostini. Sprinkle with | [| FRESH BASIL   finely chopped |

| *VARIATION* I   Top Crostini with | [| MOZZARELLA   thinly sliced |

| Warm in oven. When Mozzarella begins to melt, remove from oven and top with | [| Anchovy Mixture |

ANCHOVY - DEVILED EGGS
EGGS - DEVILED - see "BASIC RECIPES"

| Split in half lengthwise, remove Yolks from | [4 large | HARD-COOKED EGGS |

Mash in a bowl the	[4	Egg Yolks
with	[2 tp	MAYONNAISE
	[1/2-tp	MUSTARD prepared
	[1 tp	KETCHUP
	[2 TB	ANCHOVY FILLETS minced
	[1 tp	CAPERS rinsed, dried, minced
	[2 tp	CHIVES

Adjust Seasonings.

| Heap Mixture into Egg Whites. Sprinkle with | [| PARSLEY   finely chopped |

FISH in ARTICHOKE BOTTOMS
Cold Appetizer

| Place in a saucepan and cook in their Liquid | [| ARTICHOKE BOTTOMS   canned |
| | [| LEMON JUICE   a few drops |

When fork tender, drain, set on paper towels.
Let cool.

| Brush them lightly with | [| OIL and LEMON DRESSING |

Cover, refrigerate until ready to fill them.

| THE FILLING   Quantity depends on size and number of Artichokes | [| *2 to 4 TB per Artichoke* |

Mix in a bowl to taste	[	ANY COOKED WHITE FISH flaked
	[	AVOCADO diced
	[	HARD-COOKED EGG chopped
	[	CELERY finely chopped
	[	TARTARE SAUCE ready-made

Fill Artichokes. Refrigerate.

| To serve   Surround each Artichoke with | [| ALFALFA and chopped PARSLEY |

155

FISH in ARTICHOKE BOTTOMS

Hot Appetizer

See "SAUCES". Prepare a	[	CAPER BÉCHAMEL for FISH
Cook as in previous recipe	[canned	ARTICHOKE BOTTOMS drain
Place Artichoke bottoms side-by-side in an oven-proof dish brushed lightly with	[melted	BUTTER
In a nonstick skillet, medium low heat, heat	[1 TB	BUTTER (per 1 cup of Fish)
When Butter begins to turn golden add	[1/2-tp	LEMON JUICE
Brown lightly in the Butter	[1 cup	COOKED FISH bite-size pieces
Spoon the Fish into Artichokes, cover with	[	Caper Béchamel
and top with	[	BREAD CRUMBS

Bake in oven preheated to 425°, until Crumbs turn a light golden brown. Serve immediately.

FISH with ARTICHOKE HEARTS

Serves 2

Pour into a measuring pitcher the Liquid from	[14 oz-can	ARTICHOKE HEARTS small size
Add to it	[	COLD WATER to obtain 1 cup
Dissolve in a 1/2-cup of this Liquid	[1 TB	FLOUR
In a small saucepan, heat	[1 tp	VEGETABLE OIL
Sauté until limp (do not brown)	[1 small	ONION quartered, thinly sliced
Pour over Onion the	[	Artichoke Liquid/Water Mixture
and the	[	Mixture with the dissolved Flour
	[1/4-tp	LEMON JUICE

Stir. When Liquid thickens, add Artichokes.
Cover, cook over low heat for 10 minutes.

When Artichokes are fork tender stir in	[1/2-tp	CAPERS rinsed, drained, minced
	[1 tp	PARSLEY minced
Season to taste	[	WHITE PEPPER, SALT if needed
Serve	[	COOKED FISH
over	[	RICE or MASHED POTATOES
Top with	[	Artichoke Hearts and Sauce

FISH with ASPARAGUS GRATINÉE

Serves 2

See "SAUCES". Prepare	[1 cup	VELOUTÉ WHITE SAUCE
When it thickens remove from heat, stir in	[3 TB	SWISS CHEESE coarse-grated
	[1 TB	PARMESAN grated
In a greased shallow oven-proof dish, spread	[2 servings	FISH FILLETS raw
Top with	[2 servings	COOKED ASPARAGUS *al dente*
Cover with VELOUTÉ SAUCE and top with	[	BREAD CRUMBS
Dot Breadcrumbs with	[1/2-TB	BUTTER cut into tidbits

Bake in oven preheated to 375° for 10-to-15 minutes, according to thickness of Fillets.
Pass under the broiler to brown the top. Serve immediately.

FISH ASPIC in GRAPEFRUIT SHELLS
Per Shell use 1 cup of Filling and a 1/4-cup of Aspic Stock.

See "BASIC RECIPES". Prepare the [ASPIC STOCK with CHICKEN STOCK
[to taste   DRY SHERRY

Cut in half [large   GRAPEFRUIT   *One half per person*

- Scoop out the Pulp, cut it into bite-size chunks, place in a bowl, refrigerate.
- With scissors remove membranes. Scrape SHELLS with a grapefruit spoon.
- Rinse them out. Dry and refrigerate until ready to fill.

- Heap the FILLING into SHELLS. Pour over each a 1/4-cup of ASPIC STOCK.
- Refrigerate. Serve sprinkled with FLAT LEAF PARSLEY finely chopped.

THE FILLING   - Combine with the GRAPEFRUIT chunks cooked FISH and/or SEAFOOD.
               - Add to the Mixture any of the following:

AVOCADO	CANTALOUPE	MANGO	TOMATILLO	CAPERS	COCONUT	MINT
BELL PEPPER	CELERY	PAPAYA	GREEN ONION	CHIVES	shredded	PARSLEY
BLUEBERRIES	CRANBERRIES	PINEAPPLE	RED ONION	PIMIENTOS	CILANTRO	WATERCRESS

FISH ASPIC in a RING MOLD
ASPIC see "BASIC RECIPES"

Line the bottom of the ring mold with [ASPIC STOCK. Refrigerate until set.
Cover with a layer of [GREEN PEAS   *al dente*
Add to hold them, just enough [ASPIC STOCK. Refrigerate until set.

Mix with [MAYONNAISE
[COOKED FISH   flaked
[SMOKED SALMON   chopped

Spread it on top of the Peas. Leave 1/3-inch
all around. Fill with [ASPIC STOCK. Refrigerate until set.
Top with overlapping slices of [KIWI
Cover with [ASPIC STOCK. Refrigerate until set.

FISH ASPIC with SALMON ROE CAVIAR

Line ramekins with [a layer of   ASPIC STOCK   1/4-inch deep
Refrigerate until set.

Start with [a layer of   SALMON ROE CAVIAR
Top with [dabs of   SOUR CREAM
Sprinkle with [CHIVES
Cover with [a little   ASPIC STOCK
Refrigerate until set.

Place in center [FISH flaked
[mixed with   a little MAYONNAISE
[and   GRATED RADISH
Leave 1/4-inch around the Fish Mixture for
the Aspic Stock.
Cover with [ASPIC STOCK
Refrigerate until Aspic sets.

Top with [a layer of   SALMON ROE CAVIAR
Fill with [ASPIC STOCK
Refrigerate until set.

Unmold, garnish with [CUCUMBER   thinly sliced

FISH - BOUILLABAISSE   Mediterranean Fisherman's Soup   *Serves 6*

Use a stockpot in which you can insert a metal strainer, or a Pasta Cooker with removable strainer.

The FISH   Wash under running cold water   [1 lb   LEAN FISH TRIMMINGS heads, bones

Also wash under running cold water a   [3 lb   variety of lean white Fish, any of:
                                                     BASS, COD, HAKE, HALIBUT,
                                                     YELLOW PIKE, RED SNAPPER, other

Cut Fish into 2-inch pieces. Remove bones.

The SOUP   In the pot, over low heat, heat   [5 TB   OLIVE OIL for cooking
                                        Stir in   [4 oz   ONION halve, slice 1/4-inch thick
                                                  [1/2-cup   LEEKS   white part, thinly sliced

Cook slowly 4 minutes, stirring often. Add   [4 cloves   GARLIC   mashed in presser
                                              [9 oz   TOMATOES   thick wedges
Stir in the FISH TRIMMINGS. Sprinkle with   [1/4-tp   SAFFRON THREADS   crushed
                              Stir and add   [6-1/2 cups   WATER
                                             [1 cup   CLAM JUICE (has Salt don't add)
                                             [1 sprig   PARSLEY, 1 BAY LEAF
                                             [1/2-tp   FENNEL SEEDS
                                             [1/4-tp   DRIED THYME
                                             [1-inch wide   FRESH or DRIED ORANGE PEEL
                                             [GROUND BLACK PEPPER

- Bring to a boil and cook uncovered, over
  medium heat, for 30 minutes. Let cool.
- Put a sieve lined with 2 layers of cheesecloth
  over a large bowl. Strain the Soup, pressing
  down solids to extract Juices. Discard solids.

Rinse the stockpot and return the Soup to it   [adjust   SALT and GROUND BLACK PEPPER

Soup preparation can be made in advance.

Before cooking the Fish   Toast   [slices of   COUNTRY BREAD

COOKING the FISH   (*NOTE* - When the Fish is cooked, it must be served right away).

First place into the metal strainer the firm-fleshed Fish and thicker pieces which take longer to cook.

    - Over high heat bring the Soup to a boil. Plunge the strainer with the Fish.
    - Cook for 5 minutes. Add the rest of the Fish, which takes less time to cook.
    - Bring to a boil. Cook for another 5-to-10 minutes, depending on type of Fish.
    - Lift the strainer onto a pan. Arrange the Fish on a platter.
    - Pour the Soup and drippings from the strainer into a tureen.
NOTE   - To add MUSSELS or CLAMS, steam them separately in some of the Broth.
         - Strain the Broth through 3 layers of cheesecloth and add it to the Soup.

The ritual   Soup is ladled into individual soup plates. Diners mix in a 1/2-tp of ROUILLE.
             Then break the Bread into their Soup and add Fish and Seafood.

The ROUILLE   Rouille - meaning rust, is the Sauce served on the side with Bouillabaisse.

Ahead of time, boil until tender   [a small   RED CHILI

Discard stem and seeds. Cut its flesh into pieces.

Whilst the Soup is cooking, place in a shallow dish   [2 oz of   WHITE BREAD CRUMB
Soak the Bread Crumb with a few Tablespoons of   [clear   Soup Liquid   *(continued)*

158

After a few minutes, pour out the Liquid. Squeeze the CRUMB to remove excess Liquid.

Put the CRUMB in processor with the CHILI	[	a pinch	SAFFRON dissolve in 1 tp hot Water
	[	2 cloves	GARLIC mashed
	[	3/4-cup	EXTRA-VIRGIN OLIVE OIL
	[	1/4-tp	TOMATO PASTE
Process into a smooth Sauce. Add	[	to taste	SALT

CRÊPES see "BASIC RECIPES"

FISH CRÊPES with ASPARAGUS   *Filling yields about 2-1/4 cups*

See "SAUCES". Prepare	[	2 cups	LEMON EGG SAUCE omit Capers
THE FILLING In a nonstick skillet, heat	[	1 TB	BUTTER + 1 tp VEGETABLE OIL
When it sizzles, sauté	[	1/4-cup	ONION finely chopped
When Onion turns golden, add	[	1/2-cup	ASPARAGUS *al dente* sliced into 1/4-inch bits
Stir for 1 minute and add	[	1-1/4 cups	COOKED FISH flaked, or SALMON
Transfer to a bowl, immediately mix in	[	3 oz	PEPPER BOURSIN CHEESE bits
	[	4 TB	LEMON EGG SAUCE
			Refrigerate remaining Sauce

Cover the FILLING surface with plastic wrap, refrigerate.
Bring to room temperature *filled* Crêpes. Heat them in oven preheated to 300° for 20 minutes.
Warm the Sauce in double boiler. Splash a little over the Crêpes. Serve the rest on the side.

FISH CRÊPES FLORENTINE   *Filling yields about 2-1/4 cups*

THE FILLING Mix in processor	[	3/4-cup	CREAMED SPINACH
With the Cheese (cut into bits)	[	5 oz-pkg	HERB AND GARLIC BOURSIN
Transfer to a bowl and add	[	8 oz	COOKED FISH flaked
	[	1 oz	GRUYÈRE or SWISS coarse-grate
	[	to taste	SALT, GROUND BLACK PEPPER

Heat Crêpes as in previous recipe.

To serve	[	sprinkle	PARMESAN grated
	[	on the side	ALFREDO SAUCE

FISH CRÊPES - MARINARA   *Filling yields about 2-1/4 cups*

See "SAUCES". Prepare	[	1 cup	CREAMY BÉCHAMEL
When it thickens, add to taste	[		TOMATO PASTE
Season to taste and stir in	[	2 TB	FRESH BASIL finely chopped
THE FILLING In a nonstick skillet, heat	[	1 TB	BUTTER + 1 tp VEGETABLE OIL
When it sizzles, sauté	[	1/4-cup	ONION finely chopped
When Onion begins to color, add	[	3 oz	MUSHROOMS chopped
Sauté until browned and add	[	1-1/4 cups	COOKED FISH flaked
Transfer to bowl, immediately mix in	[	1/4-cup	MOZZARELLA coarse-grated
	[	4 TB	CREAMY TOMATO BÉCHAMEL
	[	2 TB	PARMESAN grated

Cover the surface with plastic wrap, refrigerate.
Refrigerate remaining Sauce. Heat Crêpes in oven preheated to 300° for 20 minutes.
THE SAUCE: Heat remaining Béchamel, add to taste TOMATO SAUCE. Serve it on the side.

FISH CROQUETTES - BÉCHAMEL BASE

CROQUETTES
see "BASIC RECIPES"

Yields 3-1/4 cups

Mix in a bowl	[2 cups	COOKED FISH seasoned, flaked
	[1 TB	PARSLEY finely chopped
	[1 tp	LEMON JUICE

See "SAUCES". Prepare	[1-1/4 cups	MILK as in ONION BÉCHAMEL

Use this MILK to prepare a	[	VERY THICK BÉCHAMEL
with	[4 TB	BUTTER
	[4 TB	FLOUR
	[1-1/4 cups	Onion Milk
	[1 whole	EGG + 2 EGG YOLKS

- When the Eggs are well incorporated, mix in the FISH. Adjust Seasonings to taste.
- Stir with wooden spoon until the Mixture separates from the skillet. Transfer to a buttered dish.
- Spread it. Cover with plastic wrap to prevent skin from forming on the surface. Refrigerate.
- Shape and fry Croquettes following directions in "BASIC RECIPES".

Hors-d'oeuvre   -   Serve small Croquettes with AÏOLI Dip or seasoned MAYONNAISE Dip.
Appetizer, main course -   Serve large Croquettes with a Salad.

FISH CROQUETTES - POTATO BASE   *Yields about 4 cups*

See "VEGETABLES " - POTATOES. Prepare	[	CROQUETTE BASE (2 cups)
Adding to the beaten Eggs	[a dash	WORCESTERSHIRE SAUCE

In a nonstick skillet, over medium heat, heat	[1 TB	BUTTER
When it sizzles, sauté	[2 TB	SHALLOT finely chopped
When the Shallot turns golden, stir in	[2 cups	COOKED FISH or SALMON flaked
Turn off heat, add	[1 TB	PARSLEY finely chopped
	[	SALT, GROUND BLACK PEPPER

Mix well the FISH and CROQUETTE BASE.
Spread Mixture in a buttered dish. Cover with plastic wrap. Refrigerate.
Shape and fry Croquettes following directions in "BASIC RECIPES".

Serve hot   -   As hors-d'oeuvre with a MAYONNAISE Dip ("DIPS and SPREADS" or "SAUCES").
            -   As an appetizer, form into patties, serve with a Salad.

FISH - SHIRRED EGGS FLORENTINE   EGGS see "BASIC RECIPES"

Sauté in lightly-browned	[	BUTTER
	[	ANY WHITE FISH cooked, flaked
Sprinkle with a few drops of	[	LEMON JUICE
Turn off heat and season lightly with	[	SALT, GROUND BLACK PEPPER

In oven-proof individual dishes, spread	[	CREAM CHEESE a few bits, diced
Top with a layer of	[	CREAMED SPINACH seasoned
Top Spinach with FISH. Break on top of each	[1 or 2	EGGS
Top Eggs with	[a little	melted BUTTER, SALT, PEPPER

Bake on top rack of oven preheated to 500° until the Eggs are set: 4-1/2 to 5 minutes.

160

FISH - SHIRRED EGGS TEX-MEX   EGGS see "BASIC RECIPES"

Warm in a skillet	[	BAKED or REFRIED BEANS
moistened with a little	[	EXTRA-VIRGIN OLIVE OIL
	[to taste	CUMIN, PICKLED JALAPEÑO bits

Spread the Beans in 2 individual oven dishes.

In a nonstick skillet, heat	[1 TB	EXTRA-VIRGIN OLIVE OIL
When a light haze forms, sauté	[2 TB	ONIONS finely chopped,
When the Onions turn golden, stir in	[1 cup	ANY COOKED WHITE FISH
	[	LEMON JUICE 1 tp per cup of Fish
	[to taste	FRESH CILANTRO finely chopped
	[	SALT, GROUND BLACK PEPPER

Spread the Fish Mixture on the Beans and

break on top of each	[1 or 2	EGGS
Top Eggs with a little	[	melted BUTTER, SALT, TABASCO

Bake on top rack of oven preheated to 500° until the Eggs are set: 4-1/2 to 5 minutes.

FISH - SCRAMBLED EGGS in PORTOBELLOS   *Filling: 2 cups*

See "VEGETABLES" - MUSHROOMS	[	"Prepare for cooking" PORTOBELLO CAPS
Brush them inside and out with	[	EXTRA-VIRGIN OLIVE OIL
Sprinkle with	[	SALT, GROUND BLACK PEPPER

Grill or broil until tender.

Heat	[1 TB	BUTTER + 1 tp VEGETABLE OIL
Sauté in it	[3 TB	ONION finely chopped
When Onion turns golden brown, stir in	[3/4-cup	COOKED FISH flaked
Turn off heat and add	[	SALT, GROUND BLACK PEPPER
Beat	[4	EGGS
Add	[2 TB	PARSLEY finely chopped
	[a pinch	SALT, GROUND BLACK PEPPER

Mix the Fish Mixture with the beaten Eggs.
In a nonstick skillet heat Butter and Vegetable Oil. Scramble the Egg Mixture.
Fill Portobello Caps with the Scrambled Eggs and serve. Servings according to the size of caps.

FISH FILLETS au GRATIN   *Serves 2 or 3*   GRATIN see "BASIC RECIPES"

Drain from their LIQUID	[1 can	ARTICHOKE BOTTOMS
Pour LIQUID into a measuring cup, and add	[enough	MILK to obtain 1 cup
See "SAUCES". Use this Milk to prepare	[1 cup	SHALLOT MEDIUM WHITE SAUCE
When it thickens, turn off heat, stir in	[1-1/2 TB	SWISS CHEESE coarse-grated
	[1/2-TB	PARMESAN grated
Place in a sprayed baking dish, side-by-side	[raw	FISH FILLETS *2 or 3 servings*
Top with	[	Artichoke Bottoms thinly sliced
Cover with the SHALLOT SAUCE. Sprinkle	[lightly	PARMESAN or SWISS
	[	BREADCRUMBS
Dot with	[1 TB	BUTTER cut into bits

Preheat oven to 375°.
Bake 10-to-15 minutes, according to thickness of Fillets. Pass under the broiler, brown the top.

FISH FLAN

Serves 6 as an appetizer   *(To serve 8 to 10)**

Drain in a sieve	[10 oz-can	SLICED BUTTON MUSHROOMS

POACH the FISH   Half fill 8-inch skillet with [WATER

Add	[1/2-cup	DRY WHITE WINE
	[1 slice of	ONION about 1/4-inch thick
	[1 slice	LEMON
	[a pinch	SALT
	[1/4-tp	PEPPERCORNS
When the Liquid begins to boil, add	[1 lb	FLOUNDER FILLETS

- Reduce heat. Simmer for 5 minutes.
- Remove Fillets with a slotted spoon.
- Drain on paper towels. Transfer to a plate.
- With a fork flake into small pieces.

The MOLD   Spray a 1-1/2 quart ring mold   [with   COOKING SPRAY rub it all over
the mold

Seal in a plastic bag   [2 oz   SEASONED HERB CROUTONS
(avoid Cheese Croutons)

Place the bag on a counter. Beat with a can
to crumble Croutons. Do not pulverize.

Layer in the mold some of the CROUTONS.
Top at random with the FISH, MUSHROOMS
and remaining CROUTONS.

The CUSTARD   In a heavy saucepan, heat

[2-1/3 cups	MILK
[1-1/2 cups	SHRIMP SHELLS raw or boiled
[quarter of a	SMALL ONION
[a pinch	SALT, WHITE PEPPER

- Bring the Milk to a slow boil. Reduce heat to
  low, simmer for 30 minutes. Turn off heat.
- Place a fine sieve, over a bowl. Line it with
  2 layers of cheese cloth. Strain the Milk.
- If you have less than 2 cups, add Milk to
  obtain 2 cups.

In a large bowl beat with a wire whip   [3   EGGS

- Beat into the Eggs 2 Tablespoons of hot MILK.
- Add 2 or 3 more Tablespoons and beat.
- Add gradually the rest of the Milk and beat.

Set the ring mold on a cookie sheet to go into the oven. Gently ladle the Custard into it.

To BAKE   Preheat oven to 350°. Bake for 1 hour and 5 minutes. The Flan will
shrink around the edges. Insert a metal skewer, if it comes out clean
the Flan is ready. If sticky bake a little longer. Place on wire rack to cool.

To UNMOLD   - When cold shake the mold gently to ensure the Flan is loosened.
- Run a thin knife around the edge. Top the mold with a platter. Tap the
  mold on the counter two or three times, turn upside-down and unmold.
- Wash the mold and cover the Flan with it until ready to serve.
- Refrigerate. Bring to room temperature before serving.

To serve
warm or hot   - Unmold the Flan in an oven-proof dish or platter. Cover it with the
clean mold. If refrigerated, bring to room temperature.
- Keep covered and heat in a warm oven, for about 20 minutes. *(continued)*

| The **SAUCE** | Heat | [1 can | SHRIMP or LOBSTER BISQUE |
| | Add to taste | [optional | DRY SHERRY, LIGHT CREAM |

Serve the hot Sauce on the side. It makes a contrast with the cold or warm Flan.

* Use 2-1/2 quart ring mold   -   1-1/2 lbs Fish Fillets, 1 can Mushrooms + 1 small can.
                            -   Double all other amounts.

FISH - GRATINÉE   *Sauce yields about 1-1/2 cups*

Use oven-proof porcelain shells, or abalone shells. If you don't have any, use oven-proof ramekins.

See "SAUCES". Prepare	[1 cup	MEDIUM WHITE SAUCE
mixing into the FLOUR	[1/4-tp	DRY MUSTARD or CURRY
	[1/8-tp	ONION POWDER

When smooth and creamy, turn off heat and
stir into the Sauce until melted	[1 oz	SWISS CHEESE coarse-grated
	[2 TB	MAYONNAISE ready-made
	[1 tp	LEMON JUICE
	[1 large	HARD-COOKED EGG finely chop

Place the shells or ramekins on a cookie sheet.

| Allow room for the Sauce, spread into shells | [| COOKED FISH or SEAFOOD |
| Cover with the SAUCE. Top with | [| BREADCRUMBS, dot with BUTTER |

Bake in oven preheated to 350° for 15 minutes. Pass under the broiler. Serve immediately.

FISH OMELET al PESTO   *Serves 2*   EGGS see "BASIC RECIPES"

THE FILLING	In a nonstick skillet, warm	[1 cup	COOKED FISH
	with	[1 tp	LEMON JUICE
	and	[2 TB	PESTO SAUCE or more to taste
		[1/4-cup	TOMATOES seeded, diced

| THE SAUCE | In another nonstick skillet, heat | [4 TB | PESTO SAUCE |
| | Stir into it | [2 TB | MASCARPONE or more to taste |

THE OMELET	In a bowl, beat with a fork	[4 large	EGGS
	with	[1 TB	COLD MILK
		[1/4-tp	SALT, GROUND BLACK PEPPER

| In a 6-to-6-1/2-inch nonstick skillet, heat | [1 TB | BUTTER + 1 tp OLIVE OIL |
| When it sizzles, sauté | [1/4-cup | ONION   finely chopped |

When Onion begins to color add the EGG MIXTURE. Cook the Omelet and add the FILLING.
Heat the Pesto Sauce and serve it over the folded Omelet.

FISH OMELET al POMODORO   *Serves 2*

THE FILLING	Brown in 2 tp OLIVE OIL	[1/2-cup	ONIONS coarsely chopped
	Mix in	[1 cup	COOKED FISH
		[1/4-cup	TOMATOES seeded, diced
		[2 TB	TOMATO or MARINARA SAUCE

Cook Omelet as above, top with MARINARA.

163

FISH and PASTA - AGLIO OLIO   Garlic and Oil   *Serves 2*

In nonstick 8-inch skillet, medium heat, heat	[4 TB	EXTRA-VIRGIN OLIVE OIL
When a light haze forms, sauté	[6 cloves	GARLIC thinly sliced lengthwise
When the Garlic turns golden brown, add	[1 cup	ANY WHITE FISH small pieces
Reduce heat to low, stir to heat the Fish, add	[to taste	SALT, GROUND BLACK PEPPER
Turn off heat and toss into the skillet	[4 oz	COOKED SPAGHETTINI
Sprinkle to taste	[	RED PEPPER FLAKES
Mix in	[1 TB	FRESH BASIL finely chopped
Drizzle with	[	EXTRA-VIRGIN OLIVE OIL
Serve with	[	GARLIC BREAD

FISH and PASTA - FISHERMAN'S POTLUCK   *Serves 4*

In a large nonstick skillet, medium heat, heat	[3 TB	EXTRA-VIRGIN OLIVE OIL
When a light haze forms, sauté	[1 cup	RED ONION diced
When Onion begins to color, add	[2 or 3	GARLIC CLOVES mashed, minced
Stir for 1 minute and add	[10 oz-can	RED KIDNEY BEANS rinse, drain
Cook, stirring for 4 minutes, then add	[1 can	CHOPPED CLAMS and their Liquor
	[1 can	WHOLE CLAMS and their Liquor
Stir. When the Liquid bubbles, add	[1 cup	RIPE TOMATOES seeded, diced
Stir the Tomatoes for a minute, add	[1 can	SARDINES skinless, boneless, drained and coarsely chopped
	[1 cup	ANY WHITE FISH small chunks
	[10 leaves	FRESH BASIL coarsely chopped
	[2 tp	TINY CAPERS rinsed, drained
	[	SALT, GROUND BLACK PEPPER
When all Ingredients are hot, turn off heat.		
Drain and toss into the skillet with Mixture	[8 oz	SPAGHETTI or SPAGHETTINI
	[serve with	GARLIC BREAD

FISH and PASTA - PRIMAVERA   *Serves 2 as a main course*

Version 1	Mix:		*Version* 2	Mix:
[2	VINE RIPE TOMATOES seeded, diced		[2	VINE RIPE TOMATOES
[1/4-cup	ARUGULA chopped		[1/4-cup	BASIL finely chopped
[1	SCALLION thinly sliced		[1/4-cup	RED ONION finely diced
[1 cup	COOKED FISH small chunks		[1 cup	COOKED FISH
[2 TB	EXTRA-VIRGIN OLIVE OIL		[3 or 4	ANCHOVIES minced
[1-1/2 tp	LEMON JUICE		[1 tp	CAPERS rinsed, drained
[	GROUND BLACK PEPPER		[2 TB	EXTRA-VIRGIN OLIVE OIL
[a pinch	GARLIC POWDER or Clove minced		[1/2-tp	LEMON JUICE
			[	GROUND BLACK PEPPER

Let sit at room temperature for 30 minutes.
Before serving add Salt if needed.

Add to salted boiling water	[4 oz	PENNE or FUSILI

Drain the Pasta, transfer to heated serving bowl. Immediately toss into it the Tomato Mixture.
This is a very refreshing luncheon dish on a spring or summer day. Serve with GARLIC BREAD.

FISH in PUFF PASTRY SHELLS

Filling about 1/3-cup per Shell

Wash, trim, steam in microwave for 2 minutes [6 medium   ASPARAGUS

Cut off Tips and set aside for later.
Slant-cut Asparagus into 1/2-inch pieces.

In a nonstick skillet, over medium heat, heat	[1-1/2 TB	BUTTER + 1 tp VEGETABLE OIL
When it sizzles, sauté	[2 TB	SHALLOTS finely chopped
When Shallots begin to color, add	[	the Asparagus
Sauté for 1 minute and add	[1 cup	COOKED WHITE FISH or SALMON
	[1 TB	PARSLEY finely chopped
	[1/2-tp	LEMON JUICE
	[to taste	WHITE or BLACK PEPPER

Turn off heat.

          See "SAUCES". Prepare a [BÉCHAMEL for
                                              PUFF PASTRY SHELL FILLINGS

When the Sauce thickens and is smooth, add	[2 TB	SWISS CHEESE coarse-grated
	[1 TB	CHEDDAR coarse-grated
	[1 TB	PARMESAN grated
When melted, turn off heat, mix in	[2 tp	CAPERS drained, rinsed, minced

Stir FISH and ASPARAGUS into the Sauce.
Let cool. Cover the surface with plastic wrap.
Refrigerate until ready to use.

          Bake following package directions [1 pkg   PUFF PASTRY SHELLS 6 Shells

1.   - A HELPFUL HINT: preheat oven to 400°, reduce heat to 350°, Shells will bake better.
            - When they turn golden, take them out. Remove the lids with a fork and set aside.
            - Scoop out with a fork the inside uncooked dough, discard it. Return to oven 4 minutes.
            - Take Shells out and arrange them in an oven-proof serving dish.

2.   - Heat well the FISH MIXTURE. It must be hot, but not boiling.
            - Use a soup spoon to fill the Shells, separating Fish and Asparagus from excess Sauce.
            - Divide the Filling evenly into the Shells, then add more Sauce as needed to fill them.
            - Top each with an ASPARAGUS TIP. Cover partially with lids, allow TIPS to show.

The *filled* Shells can be kept in a <u>warm</u> oven from 5-to-10 minutes. Longer, they'll get soggy.

FISH QUESADILLAS

Toasted Tortilla Sandwiches with Cheese (Queso) Filling.

For each Quesadilla, mix	[2 TB	FETA CHEESE crumbled
and	[1 TB	MOZZARELLA grated
Use a pastry brush to spread	[lightly	SALSA
over each	[	TORTILLA leave a 1/2-inch around the edge
Sprinkle over the Salsa, on each Tortilla	[	CILANTRO finely chopped
	[	the Cheese Mixture
Top the Cheese, on one half of Tortilla, with	[	COOKED FISH bits
	[a little	SALSA
	[chopped	OLIVES or PICKLED JALAPEÑOS

- Fold the Tortilla, press the edges to seal it.
- Brush a nonstick skillet with a little Vegetable Oil. Over medium heat, heat the skillet, and
  toast the Quesadillas for 1 minute on each side. Or use a griddle.
- Cut Quesadillas in half. Serve immediately.

FISH QUICHE - TAVERNA MYKONOS

In a nonstick skillet, heat	[1 TB	EXTRA-VIRGIN OLIVE OIL
When a light haze forms, sauté	[1/2-cup	RED ONION halved, thinly sliced
Optional	[1 clove	GARLIC mashed and minced
When the Onion turns golden, add	[2 medium	TOMATOES peeled, seeded, diced
Stir until Tomatoes melt into a paste. Add	[2 cups	COOKED FISH flaked
	[3 TB	KALAMATA OLIVES chopped
Stir well, turn off heat and season to taste	[	SALT, GROUND BLACK PEPPER

Let the Mixture cool.
Preheat oven to 375°.

In a large bowl beat	[3	EGGS
Brush with a little of the beaten Eggs a	[9-inch	FROZEN UNCOOKED PIE SHELL

Set in the oven for 2 minutes only. Let cool.

Whisk into the Eggs	[3/4-cup	HEAVY CREAM
	[1/4-cup	MILK
	[1 oz	SWISS CHEESE grated
	[3 oz	FETA CHEESE crumbled
	[2 TB	FRESH DILL snipped
	or	PARSLEY finely chopped
	[1/4-tp	GROUND BLACK PEPPER

To assemble   - Place the Pie Shell, in its foil pan, on a cookie sheet.
  - Spread the FISH MIXTURE into it.
  - Ladle the CUSTARD on top. Smooth the surface with the back of a spoon.

To bake   - Slide cookie sheet with Quiche into the oven. Reduce heat to 350°.
  - Bake following directions in "BASIC RECIPES".

FISH - MINI QUICHES

Spray a tray of 12 small muffin cups (1/4-cup size) with Cooking Spray. Preheat oven to 375°.

Spread into each muffin cup	[1 TB + 1 tp	COOKED FISH finely flaked
In a bowl whisk	[4	EGGS
Whisk into the Eggs	[1/4-cup	HEAVY CREAM
	[3 TB	PESTO drain from Oil in a small sieve
	[2 TB	PARMESAN grated
	[1 tp	CAPERS rinsed, drained, minced
	[1/4-tp	SALT, GROUND BLACK PEPPER

- Use a 1/8-cup measure to pour 1/8-cup of Egg Mixture into each muffin cup. Fill 3/4-way up.
- With a fork stir evenly the Ingredients in each cup.
- Bake for 10-to-12 minutes, on middle rack of oven, until they turn to a light golden color.
- Insert a thin knife or skewer in one or two Quiches. If it comes out clean, they are ready.
- Let cool. They unmold easily. Serve at room temperature. Reheat in foil, in a warm oven.

For a 24 cup mini-muffin tray use   [1-1/2 tp   COOKED FISH   in each cup

VARIATION   - Substitute the Fish with canned TUNA FISH, packed in Olive Oil, drained.

FISH with RICE - CARIBBEAN STYLE

Yields about 11 cups.
Serve as a buffet dish.

To cook Rice as per package directions add to	[1 cup	COCONUT MILK
	[enough	WATER to obtain right amount
	[1/4-tp	SALT

In a heavy saucepan, medium heat, heat	[1 TB	VEGETABLE OIL
When a light haze forms, sauté	[1/2-cup	ONION finely chopped
When Onion softens, stir in	[1 cup	UNCOOKED WHITE RICE
Stir for 1 minute to coat grains with Oil, add	[	Coconut/Milk Mixture
and	[1/3-cup	UNSWEETENED COCONUT flaked

Bring to a boil. Cover, reduce heat to
low and simmer until the Rice is cooked.

Meanwhile, in a nonstick skillet, heat	[1 TB	EXTRA-VIRGIN OLIVE OIL
When it sizzles, sauté	[1/2-cup	ONION finely chopped
When soft and translucent, stir in	[15 oz-can	BLACK BEANS drain, rinse
	[15 oz-can	RED PINTO BEANS drain, rinse

- Stir until Onion turns golden. Turn off heat.
- Just before the Rice finishes cooking, with a
  little Liquid still left, stir in the Beans.
- Cover, continue to simmer.

Prepare	[1-1/2 cups	PAPAYA finely diced
Mix it with	[1/4-cup	CILANTRO finely chopped
	[a sprinkle	WHITE PEPPER

| When the Rice is cooked, stir in | [3 cups | WHITE FISH or more, bite-size |

Transfer the Rice into a large bowl. Fluff it, stir in the Papaya Mixture. Serve at room temperature.

VARIATION - Substitute Papaya with Pineapple. Or just before serving add diced Avocado.

FISH with RICE - MIDDLE EASTERN STYLE

Appetizer
Serves 4

| In a heavy saucepan, medium heat, heat | [2 TB | VEGETABLE OIL |
| When a light haze forms, sauté | [1-1/4 cups | ONION slice 1/4-inch thick, dice |

| When Onion turns golden, stir in | [1 cup | UNCOOKED WHITE RICE |
| | [1/4-cup | PINE NUTS |

Stir the Rice and Pine Nuts until the Rice is
toasted to a golden brown.

Stir in	[1-1/4 tp	GROUND CUMIN
	[1/4-tp	GROUND ALLSPICE
and add	[	* FISH BROTH as per Rice package directions
	[1/4-cup	GOLDEN RAISINS
	[	GROUND BLACK PEPPER

Bring to a boil, cover the saucepan, reduce
heat to low, simmer until the Rice is cooked.

Meanwhile, in a nonstick skillet heat	[4 TB	BUTTER
When it sizzles, add	[2 cups	COOKED FISH bite-size pieces
Sprinkle with	[	SALT if the Fish is not salted
Stir until the Butter begins to brown. Add	[a few drops	LEMON JUICE

Stir and turn off heat.
Spread the Rice in a shallow dish. Top it with the Fish and its Brown Butter. Serve immediately.

167

FISH - RISOTTO MILANESE   RISOTTO see "BASIC RECIPES"

Serves 2 as a main course

1.   Wash dry and cut off ends of [2 (4-oz each) ZUCCHINI quarter lengthwise
and dice

In a nonstick skillet, over medium heat, heat [1-1/2 TB   BUTTER
[2 tp   EXTRA-VIRGIN OLIVE OIL
When it sizzles, sauté [2 TB   SHALLOT finely chopped
When Shallot softens add [the Zucchini

Sauté until tender and light golden brown.
Turn off heat.
Stir in [1 cup   COOKED FISH small pieces
[SALT, GROUND BLACK PEPPER

2.   In a small saucepan simmer [4 cups   CHICKEN BROTH lightly salted
(+ 1/2-cup if needed)

In another small saucepan pour [1 cup of   the simmering Broth
and dissolve in it [1/4-tp   SAFFRON THREADS
Keep Broth simmering.

3.   In an 8-inch heavy nonstick skillet,
over medium heat, heat [2 TB   BUTTER + 1 TB VEGETABLE OIL
When it sizzles, sauté [2 TB   SHALLOT finely chopped
When Onion begins to color, add [1 cup   ARBORIO RICE
Stir until grains are coated and glisten. Add [1/4-cup   DRY WHITE WINE

- Stir until the Wine evaporates.
- Add a 1/2-cup of the SAFFRON BROTH.
- When it has been absorbed, continue
  adding the Broth, a 1/2-cup at a time.

When 3 cups have been absorbed, stir in [the Zucchini and Fish

Add the remaining 1/2-cup of SAFFRON BROTH.

When it has been absorbed, the Rice should
be tender but firm and creamy.

Turn off heat and mix in [1 TB   BUTTER diced small
[2 TB   PARMESAN grated
[SALT, GROUND BLACK PEPPER
Cover, let the Risotto set for 5 minutes.

FISH - SANTORINI   *Serves 2 as an appetizer*

In a nonstick skillet, over medium heat, heat [1 TB   EXTRA-VIRGIN OLIVE OIL
When a light haze forms, sauté [1-1/4 cups RED ONION thinly sliced
When the Onion browns, reduce heat, stir in [1 cup   COOKED WHITE FISH
[1 TB   OUZO or more to taste
Stir until Ouzo evaporates, then turn off heat.

Spread into 2 individual oven-proof dishes [wedges of ROASTED RED BELL PEPPERS
Top with the FISH MIXTURE. Spread on it [TOMATOES seeded, chopped
Sprinkle with [FRESH PARSLEY finely chopped
Top with [plenty of   FETA CHEESE crumbled

Place under the broiler until the Feta melts. Serve immediately with CRUSTY BREAD.

FISH - SOUFFLÉ   *Serves 4 to 6*   SOUFFLÉ see "BASIC RECIPES"

1. ONION MILK   In a heavy saucepan, over
medium heat, bring to a boil   [1-1/2 cups   MILK
[1/3-cup   WHITE ONION   chopped

- Reduce heat to low, cover, simmer for
30 minutes. Liquid will reduce to 1-1/4 cups.
- Strain through a sieve. Discard Onions.

2.   Rub a 1-1/2 quarts soufflé dish with   [BUTTER
(or use 4 soufflé ramekins)   Dust with   [1-1/2 TB   PARMESAN   refrigerate the dish
(1-1/4 tp per ramekin)

3.   Set out at room temperature   [5   EGGS you need 5 Whites, 4 Yolks

4.   In a heavy nonstick skillet, prepare a   [CREAMY BÉCHAMEL ("SAUCES")
with   [1-1/4 cups   of the Onion Milk

- When Béchamel thickens, remove from heat.
- Break 1 EGG, drop the WHITE into stainless
steel bowl. The YOLK into the Béchamel.
- With a wire whip beat it into the Sauce.
- Repeat with 3 more Yolks, one at a time.
- Return saucepan to stove. Over low heat
stir for 1 minute to bind the Eggs.

Turn off heat. Stir into it, until melted   [2/3-cup   SWISS CHEESE coarse-grated
(less reserve 1 TB, for ramekins 4 tp)

Then add   [3/4-cup   COOKED FISH   chop in processor
[1 TB   FRESH DILL snipped
[or 1/2-tp Dried Dill
[1/2-tp   LEMON ZEST   grated
[1/8-tp   WHITE PEPPER, SALT to taste

- Set aside to cool. Can be prepared ahead to
this point. Cover the surface with wax paper.
- Warm barely before adding the EGG WHITES.

5. Preheat oven to 400°. Set out soufflé dish(es).

Add to the 4 EGG WHITES 1 EGG WHITE and   [1/8-tp   CREAM OF TARTAR

a) Beat the EGG WHITES until stiff and glossy, but not dry.
- Add one ladle of WHITES to the BÉCHAMEL. Gently fold them in with a rubber spatula.
- Then gently pour the MIXTURE into the remaining Egg Whites.
- Fold in with the spatula, scooping from the bottom towards the top as you turn the bowl.
Do not fold too much, it would keep the Soufflé from rising well. White spots do no harm.

b) Pour MIXTURE into soufflé dish(es). Smooth the surface with a spatula.
- Sprinkle with the reserved 1 TB of CHEESE. Or for each ramekin 1 tp.

c) Place on middle rack of oven. Immediately reduce heat to 375°. Bake for 25-to-30 minutes.
- Less time for the ramekins. Do not open the oven door until the Soufflé is well puffed.
- Test by inserting a thin knife or metal skewer. If it comes out clean, the Soufflé is ready.
If not, cook 5 minutes longer. It should have a light brown crust and creamy center.
- Remove the Collar, if it has one. Serve immediately.

SHRIMP SOUFFLÉ   For the BÉCHAMEL: mix into the FLOUR: 1/4-tp DRY MUSTARD.
Finely chop the Shrimp in processor.

169

FISH - STIR-FRY with RICE and LENTILS   *Yields about 5 cups*

In a 1-1/2 quart heavy saucepan, heat	[1 TB	VEGETABLE OIL
Medium heat, when a light haze forms sauté	[1/2-cup	ONION finely chopped
with	[1/2-tp	GROUND CUMIN
When Onion is translucent, add	[1/2-cup	UNCOOKED LENTILS
Stir to mix them with Onion and add	[	WATER as per Lentil package
Also add	[	WATER to cook a 1/2-cup Rice as per package
Bring to a boil and add	[1 cube	CHICKEN BOUILLON crumbled

Cover.
Cook the Lentils for 20 minutes.   Stir in [1/2-cup   UNCOOKED WHITE RICE

Bring to a boil. Cover, reduce heat to low,
simmer until the Rice is done, Liquid absorbed.
Let set for 10 minutes then fluff it with a fork.

In a skillet heat	[1-1/2 TB	BUTTER
When the Butter begins to color, brown in it	[1-1/2 cups	COOKED FISH small pieces
Then sprinkle with	[a little	LEMON JUICE
	[a pinch	SALT, GROUND BLACK PEPPER
Heat, over high heat, a large skillet or wok, and pour into it	[1 TB	VEGETABLE OIL + 1 TB BUTTER
Swirl Oil around, reduce heat to medium, add	[4 oz	MUSHROOMS coarsely chopped
Brown Mushrooms, cook until tender, stir in	[	the Rice and Lentils
	[3 TB	CHIVES finely chopped
Stir-fry the Rice for 3 minutes. Moisten with	[3 TB	CHICKEN BROTH
Mix in	[	the Fish

Serve immediately.

FISH - STUFFED TOMATOES   Appetizer   *Filling yields about 2-1/2 cups.*
Amounts are flexible.

Slice off the caps, scoop out seeds and pulp, leaving enough flesh to keep firm	[medium	TOMATOES

Turn upside down on paper towels to drain.
Refrigerate.

Mix in a bowl	[3/4-cup	COOKED COUSCOUS
	[1/4-cup	CELERY finely diced
	[1/4-cup	RED ONION finely chopped
	[1/4-cup	BLACK OLIVES chopped
	[1 cup	COOKED WHITE FISH flaked
	[3 TB	FRESH BASIL finely chopped
	[moisten with	OIL and LEMON DRESSING

Refrigerate. Fill the Tomatoes before serving.

MEXICAN STYLE			MOROCCAN STYLE	
[3/4-cup	COOKED COUSCOUS		[3/4-cup	COOKED COUSCOUS
[1/4-cup	RED BELL PEPPER finely diced		[1/4-cup	GREEN BELL PEPPER diced
[1/4-cup	GREEN ONIONS finely chopped		[1/4-cup	CARROT grated
[1 or 2 TB	PICKLED JALAPEÑOS chopped		[2 TB	PICKLED LEMONS chopped
[3/4-cup	ANY WHITE FISH flaked		[3/4-cup	ANY WHITE FISH flaked
[2 TB	CILANTRO finely chopped		[2 TB	CILANTRO finely chopped
[2 TB	TORTILLA CHIPS pulverized		[2 TB	BLACK OLIVES chopped
[Add to	OIL and LEMON DRESSING		[Add to	OIL and LEMON DRESSING
[to taste	GROUND CUMIN		[to taste	GROUND CUMIN

FISH TACOS

Heat in a nonstick skillet	[	EXTRA-VIRGIN OLIVE OIL	Layer into	[TACO SHELLS
Sauté to a golden brown	[	ONION thinly sliced		[FISH MIXTURE
Stir in	[	ANY COOKED FISH		[CILANTRO chopped
Sprinkle to taste	[	GROUND CUMIN		[SALSA
	[	PICKLED JALAPEÑO finely chopped		[CHEDDAR shredded
				[SOUR CREAM

FISH TART - SAN REMO

QUICHE see "BASIC RECIPES"

In a nonstick skillet, over medium heat, heat	[1/2-TB	BUTTER + 1/2-tp VEGETABLE OIL
When it sizzles, sauté until golden brown	[1 cup	ONIONS sliced 1/4-inch thick, coarsely chopped

Set aside.
Preheat oven to 375°.

In a bowl, whisk	[3	EGGS
Brush with a little of the beaten Eggs a	[9-inch	FROZEN UNCOOKED PIE SHELL

Set in the oven for 2 minutes only. Let cool.

Whisk into the Eggs	[1 cup	HALF-and-HALF
	[3 oz	GRUYÈRE or SWISS grated
	[1 oz	PARMESAN grated
Add the sautéed ONIONS and	[1/4-tp	SALT, GROUND BLACK PEPPER to taste

To assemble
- Place the PIE SHELL, in its foil pan, on a cookie sheet.
- Pour the CUSTARD into it. Smooth the surface with the back of a spoon.

To bake
- Slide cookie sheet with Pie into the oven. Reduce heat to 350°
- Bake following directions in "BASIC RECIPES" and until the top turns golden.
- Let the Tart cool. Optional: carefully unmold it onto a platter.

To serve Mix	[1 cup	COOKED WHITE FISH bite-size
	[1 cup	COOKED SHRIMP bite-size
Moisten well with	[	PESTO SAUCE
	[a few drops	LEMON JUICE

Spread the FISH MIXTURE over the Quiche.

Overlap on top in concentric circles	[thinly sliced	TOMATOES
Garnish with	[chopped	BLACK OLIVES

HERRING in AVOCADO HALVES

- Prepare the HERRING FILLING. Refrigerate.

- Before serving, cut in half, pit and peel AVOCADOS.
- Brush a little Lemon Juice all over the Avocados.
- Heap the FILLING into Avocados. Serve on a bed of Greens

Mix	[SMOKED HERRING flaked
with	[LEMON JUICE a little
Add	[SOUR CREAM
	[RED RADISH grated
	[SCALLION finely chopped
	[PICKLES chopped

HERRING (smoked) - CROSTINI

CROSTINI see "BASIC RECIPES"

Mix to taste	[SMOKED HERRING flaked
with	[EXTRA-VIRGIN OLIVE OIL
	[LEMON JUICE
	[WATERCRESS finely chopped
	[CAPERS rinsed, dried, minced

Optional, add a little MAYONNAISE.

Spread Mixture on CROSTINI.

Garnish: HARD-COOKED EGG finely chopped

HERRING (smoked) - PASTA BELL PEPPERS   *Serves 2*

In an 8-inch skillet, over medium heat, heat	[4 TB	EXTRA-VIRGIN OLIVE OIL
When a light haze forms, sauté	[1/2-cup	ONION quartered, thinly sliced
	[1/2-cup each	BELL PEPPERS red, yellow and orange, thin strips
Cook until Bell Peppers are tender crunchy, reduce heat to low, stir in, warm through	[1/2-cup	SMOKED HERRING cut into bits
	[1/2-tp	LEMON JUICE or more to taste
	[2 TB	PINE NUTS toasted
	[2 TB	CHIVES
	[1/2-tp	TINY CAPERS rinsed, drained
	[to taste	SALT, GROUND BLACK PEPPER
Drain and toss into the skillet	[3 oz	COOKED SPAGHETTINI
Mix well and stir in	[1 TB	FRESH BASIL finely chopped
Drizzle to taste with	[	EXTRA-VIRGIN OLIVE OIL

SALMON with ARTICHOKE SAUCE   *Sauce yields about 1-1/2 cups*

Pour into a measuring cup the Liquid from	[1 can	ARTICHOKE BOTTOMS
Add to this Liquid	[enough	CHICKEN BROTH to get a 1/2-cup
In a nonstick skillet, over medium heat, heat	[2 TB	BUTTER + 1 tp VEGETABLE OIL
When it sizzles, sauté	[2 TB	ONION finely chopped
When Onion is translucent, add	[	Artichokes cut into pieces
Sauté for 2 minutes then add the	[1/2-cup of	BROTH / ARTICHOKE LIQUID
	[1/4-tp	LEMON JUICE

Bring to a rapid boil. Simmer for 10 minutes.

Transfer Artichokes to a blender. As it spins, drizzle gradually through the feeding tube	[to taste	LIGHT CREAM a little

Blend until smooth, and until the desired

Sauce thickness is obtained. Taste and add	[	WHITE PEPPER, SALT if needed
When ready to serve, warm Sauce and stir in	[1 or 2 TB	DILL snipped, or PARSLEY

To Serve Top	[	MASHED POTATOES
with	[	SALMON steamed or grilled
and	[	Artichoke Sauce

SALMON - ASPIC   *4-cup ring mold or 4 ramekins*   ASPIC see "BASIC RECIPES"

Prepare	[2 cups	ASPIC STOCK with FISH BROTH Optional, add Dry Sherry
Set on a plate, remove skin, bones from	[7.50 oz-can	SALMON drained
Mix in a bowl the flaked SALMON with	[2 TB	SWEET PIMIENTOS chopped
	[1/2-cup	CELERY finely diced
	[2 TB	GREEN ONION finely chopped
	[2 TB	PARSLEY finely chopped
	[1 tp	LEMON JUICE
Mix well all Ingredients and then mix in	[5 TB	TARAMOSALATA ("Ethnic Dips")
	[to taste	GROUND BLACK PEPPER

Top with plastic wrap, refrigerate. *(continued)*

Line the ring mold or 4 ramekins with [a layer of   ASPIC STOCK   1/4-inch deep

Refrigerate until set.   Overlap around edge [PALM HEARTS   thinly sliced
                             and [GREEN OLIVES   thinly sliced
            Add a 1/4-inch layer [ASPIC STOCK
Refrigerate until set.

For the ramekins divide SALMON MIXTURE
into 4 equal parts. Spoon it into ramekins
leaving 1/3-inch around for the Aspic Stock [cover with   ASPIC STOCK. Refrigerate.

- For the ring mold, spread around in it the
  SALMON. Leave 1/4-inch around all sides
  for the Aspic Stock. Cover with the Stock.
- Refrigerate until set.
                Cut in half and peel [2   AVOCADOS
- Slice thinly crosswise.
- In one layer arrange them decoratively
  over the Aspic.
                     Cover with [ASPIC STOCK
Refrigerate until set.
To serve surround unmolded Aspic with Greens tossed in Oil and Lemon Dressing.

SALMON à la NEWBURG   *Serves 2*

       See "SAUCES". Prepare a [VELOUTÉ WHITE SAUCE
                      with [1 TB   BUTTER
                             [1-1/2 TB   FLOUR + 1/4-tp DRY MUSTARD
                             [1/2-cup   MILK
                             [1/2-cup   HEAVY CREAM
When the Sauce is thick and smooth remove
from heat.
              Beat with a fork [2   EGG YOLKS
       Gradually add, beating [2 TB   of the hot Sauce

Whisk the YOLKS into the Sauce.
Over low heat stir until the Yolks are well
incorporated.
         Stir in until melted [4 TB   PARMESAN   grated
              Add any of [1 TB   BRANDY, DRY SHERRY, MADEIRA
                           [SALT and WHITE PEPPER
            Then add [2 servings   POACHED SALMON
                                       Whole or cut up.
Baste to heat through. Turn off heat.

Serve   -   With White Rice, Pasta, Mashed Potatoes, Asparagus, Brussels Sprouts, Mushrooms.
         -    If the Salmon is in bite-size pieces serve in ramekins, over Croustades, in Phyllo Nests.

VARIATION I   Spread in an oven-proof dish [1-1/2 cups   COOKED PENNE
                        Mix with [SALMON à la NEWBURG
                 Sprinkle with [BREADCRUMBS
                     Dot with [BUTTER   bits
Pass under the broiler to brown.

VARIATION II   -   Lay ARTICHOKE BOTTOMS in a sprayed baking dish. Fill with Salmon Newburg.
               -   Sprinkle with BREADCRUMBS, dot with BUTTER. Brown under the broiler.

VARIATION III   Substitute Salmon with   [CRAB MEAT, LOBSTER, SHRIMP

SALMON PASTA - PARADISO

Serves 4 as an appetizer

Prepare a VELOUTÉ WHITE SAUCE with [1 TB   BUTTER
   [1-1/2 TB   FLOUR + 1/8-tp DRY MUSTARD
   [1/2-cup   MILK + 1/2-cup LIGHT CREAM

Stir until the Sauce is thick and smooth.

Reduce heat to low and add, to taste [1 TB   DRY VERMOUTH
Stir for 1 minute, add [SALT and WHITE PEPPER

Turn off heat and stir into the Sauce [1-1/2 cups   SALMON cooked or canned, drain
   [1/2-cup   AVOCADO diced small
   [1 TB   FRESH DILL snipped

Cover to keep warm.

Meanwhile cook [6 oz   FETTUCCINI

Drain the Fettuccini, transfer to a heated serving bowl, toss in the Salmon. Serve immediately.

VARIATION - substitute Salmon with Crab Meat or Lobster.

SALMON with SALSAS   See "VEGETABLES" - VEGETABLE and FRUIT SALSAS

Keep Salsas refrigerated until ready to serve.
Serve them on the side in a glass bowl.

SALSA HAWAIIANA

[BOILED POTATOES sliced   Arrange on individual plates or platter
[SALMON cold

SALSA INDIANA

[SALMON warm
[WILD RICE hot

SALSA IBERIANA

[SALMON warm
[SAFFRON RICE hot

SALSA TROPICANA

[SALMON cold
[a bed of GREENS

SMOKED SALMON - CRÊPES   CRÊPES see "BASIC RECIPES"

Filling yields about 2-1/4 cups

Chop in processor, not too finely [10 oz   SMOKED SALMON if using scraps
   weigh after trimming skin and fat

In a bowl, mix well the SALMON with [6 TB   ALFREDO SAUCE ready-made
   [4 oz   HERB/GARLIC BOURSIN CHEESE

TO FILL CRÊPES   Cut into thin strips [1   AVOCADO
Brush strips lightly with [LEMON JUICE

- Place 2-to-3 TB of Mixture on each CRÊPE.
- Top with 1 or 2 Avocado strips.
- Roll, put the Crêpes in a sprayed oven-dish.
- Cover with foil. Refrigerate.
- Heat, covered, in 350° oven, 15-to-20 minutes.

SUGGESTED SAUCE   Heat in small saucepan [1 can   LOBSTER BISQUE SOUP
Thin if needed with [a little   LIGHT CREAM

Serve on the side.

SMOKED SALMON - DEVILED EGGS à LA RUSSE

Slice lengthwise and remove Yolks from	[4 large	HARD-COOKED EGGS
Purée in processor	[2 oz	SMOKED SALMON
	[2 TB	SOUR CREAM
	[the 4	Cooked Egg Yolks
	[1/2-tp	LEMON JUICE
	[1/2-tp	HORSERADISH
Transfer the Mixture into a bowl and stir in	[2 TB	SALMON ROE CAVIAR drained
	[1 TB	CHIVES

Adjust Seasonings.
Heap Mixture into Egg Whites.   Sprinkle with   [WATERCRESS finely chopped

SMOKED SALMON - DEVILED EGGS ATHENA

Slice lengthwise and remove Yolks from	[4 large	HARD-COOKED EGGS
Purée in processor	[2 oz	SMOKED SALMON
	[3 TB	FETA CHEESE mashed
	[1 TB	MAYONNAISE
	[the 4	Cooked Egg Yolks
	[1/2-tp	LEMON JUICE
	[1 TB	FRESH MINT finely chopped
	[1 TB	CHIVES finely chopped

Adjust Seasonings.
Heap Mixture into Egg Whites.   Top with   [KALAMATA OLIVES halves

SMOKED SALMON DIP or SPREAD   *Yields about 1-1/2 cups*

Pulse in processor to a smooth cream	[3 oz	PHILADELPHIA CREAM CHEESE
	[2 TB	SOUR CREAM
	[2 TB	MAYONNAISE
	[1 TB	LEMON JUICE or more to taste
	[2 TB	GREEN ONION minced
	[2 TB	DILL snipped or PARSLEY
	[1 TB	PREPARED HORSERADISH or more
Transfer the Mixture into a bowl and fold in	[2 oz	SMOKED SALMON finely chopped in processor

Thin with a little Light Cream, if needed. Adjust Seasonings.

SMOKED SALMON and scrambled EGGS   *Serves 2*

In a bowl, beat	[4	EGGS
with	[2 TB	MILK or HALF-AND-HALF
	[1 TB	FRESH BASIL finely chopped
When the Eggs are well blended, stir in	[2 oz	SMOKED SALMON coarsely chop
	[	GROUND BLACK PEPPER
In nonstick 8-inch skillet, medium heat, heat	[2 TB	BUTTER
When it sizzles sauté	[2 TB	ONION finely chopped
When the Onion turns golden, add	[1 medium	TOMATO peeled, seeded, diced

Stir Onion and Tomato for 1 minute and pour into skillet the Egg/Salmon Mixture.
Scramble until soft and creamy. Serve immediately on TOAST.

SMOKED SALMON FRITTATA with ARTICHOKES   *Serves 4*

Drain	[10 oz-can	ARTICHOKE BOTTOMS small or medium size

Over low heat flip Artichokes in a skillet to dry outside moisture.

Halve them, thinly slice crosswise to obtain	[1-1/2 cups	of sliced Artichokes
In a large bowl, whisk	[5 large	EGGS
When well blended whisk in	[2 TB	CHIVES
	[1/4-cup	SWISS CHEESE coarse-grated
	[1/4-cup	PARMESAN grated
	[to taste	GROUND BLACK PEPPER
Stir in the ARTICHOKES and	[4 oz sliced	SMOKED SALMON coarsely chop in processor
In a 10-inch skillet that can go under the broiler, over medium heat, heat	[2-1/2 TB	BUTTER + 1/2-TB VEGETABLE OIL

When it sizzles, pour in the EGG MIXTURE. Spread it evenly with a spatula. Reduce heat to low.
Cook and pass the Frittata under preheated broiler following directions in "BASIC RECIPES"

SMOKED SALMON FRITTATA with ZUCCHINI   *Serves 2 to 4*

Scrape any blemishes, wash, dry, cut ends of	[3 medium	LIGHT GREEN ZUCCHINI slice into 1/4-inch thick rounds
In a nonstick skillet, over medium heat, heat	[3 TB	VEGETABLE OIL
When hot, sauté until it begins to color	[1/2-cup	ONION halved and thinly sliced
Add and sauté to a light golden brown	[	the Zucchini
Then sprinkle with	[	SALT, GROUND BLACK PEPPER

Transfer to a sieve to cool.

Whisk	[5 large	EGGS
	[	GROUND BLACK PEPPER
When well blended, whisk in	[1/4-cup	SWISS CHEESE coarse-grated
	[2 TB	PARMESAN grated
	[1 TB	FRESH DILL snipped
Stir in the ZUCCHINI and	[3 oz sliced	SMOKED SALMON coarsely chop in processor
In a 10-inch skillet that can go under the broiler, over medium heat, heat	[2 TB	BUTTER + 1 TB VEGETABLE OIL

When it sizzles, pour into skillet the EGG MIXTURE and proceed as in above recipe.

SMOKED SALMON - PASTA with ASPARAGUS

In a nonstick skillet, heat ready-made	[	ALFREDO SAUCE 1/3-cup per person
Do not boil the Sauce. Stir into it	[cooked	ASPARAGUS 3 or 4 per person slant-cut into 1-inch pieces
	[chopped	SMOKED SALMON to taste
Drain, transfer into a heated serving bowl	[	LINGUINE
Toss into the Linguine	[	the Asparagus/Salmon Sauce

SMOKED SALMON - PASTA alla CARBONARA

Appetizer
Serves 2

Whisk in a small bowl	[1	EGG
	[1/4-cup	LIGHT CREAM
	[1/4-cup	PARMESAN grated
	[a pinch	SALT, GROUND BLACK PEPPER
Drain and transfer to a heated bowl	[3 oz	FETTUCCINI

Toss into them Egg Mixture. *

Add	[2 or 3 oz	SMOKED SALMON coarsely chop
Toss again and add to taste	[	GROUND BLACK PEPPER, SALT if needed

* The hot Fettuccini cook immediately the Egg.

SMOKED SALMON - PASTA with GREEN PEAS

Appetizer
Serves 4

In a large nonstick skillet, medium heat, heat	[2 TB	BUTTER
When it sizzles, sauté	[2 TB	SHALLOT finely chopped
	[1 clove	GARLIC mashed, optional
When the Onion begins to color, remove and discard the Garlic, stir in	[1 cup	FROZEN GREEN PEAS thaw, drain
When the Peas are tender, reduce heat, add	[1 cup	HEAVY CREAM
	[4 oz	SMOKED SALMON coarsely chop
	[1 TB	PARSLEY finely chopped
	[2 TB	PINE NUTS toasted
	[	GROUND BLACK PEPPER

Heat, do not boil.

Turn off heat, toss in	[6 oz	TAGLIATELLE or FETTUCCINI

Serve immediately.

VARIATION		
Substitute the Peas with	[1 cup	FROZEN CHOPPED BROCCOLI
Substitute the Pin Nuts with	[2 TB	PECANS chopped

SMOKED SALMON - QUICHE à la REINE

In a nonstick skillet, over medium heat, heat	[1 TB + 1 tp	VEGETABLE OIL
When it sizzles, sauté and brown	[14 oz	YELLOW ONIONS coarsely chop
When browned, sprinkle with	[	SALT, GROUND BLACK PEPPER

Set aside.
Preheat oven to 375°.

In a large bowl beat	[3	EGGS
Brush with a little of the beaten Eggs a	[9-inch	FROZEN UNCOOKED PIE SHELL

Set in the oven for 2 minutes only. Let cool.

Whisk into the Eggs	[3/4-cup	HEAVY CREAM
Crumbled	[4 oz	HERB/GARLIC BOURSIN CHEESE
	[1/4-tp	GROUND BLACK PEPPER
Mix well then add, after trimming	[6 oz	SMOKED SALMON coarsely chop in processor

To assemble
- Place Pie Shell on a cookie sheet. Spread in it the ONIONS.
- Ladle over the CUSTARD. Smooth the surface with the back of a spoon.

To bake
- Slide cookie sheet with Quiche into the oven. Reduce heat to 350°.
- Bake until golden following directions in "BASIC RECIPES".

177

SMOKED SALMON - QUICHE with ASPARAGUS

Trim, wash, steam in microwave 2 minutes	[6 medium	ASPARAGUS 1/2-inch slant-cut
In a nonstick skillet, over medium heat, heat	[1 TB	BUTTER + 1 tp VEGETABLE OIL
When it sizzles, sauté	[8 oz	YELLOW ONIONS coarsely chop
When Onion colors, add ASPARAGUS, stir	[sprinkle	SALT, GROUND BLACK PEPPER

Set aside.
Preheat oven to 375°.

In a large bowl beat	[3	EGGS
Brush with a little of the beaten Eggs a	[9-inch	FROZEN UNCOOKED PIE SHELL

Set in the oven for 2 minutes only. Let cool.

Whisk into the Eggs, cut into bits	[4 oz	PHILADELPHIA CREAM CHEESE
	[3/4-cup	HEAVY CREAM
	[1/4-tp	GROUND BLACK PEPPER
Mix well, then add, after trimming	[4 oz	SMOKED SALMON coarsely chop
		in processor

Spread ASPARAGUS in the Pie Shell. Add the CUSTARD. Bake as in previous recipe.

SMOKED SALMON - MINI QUICHES

Spray a tray of 12 small muffin cups (1/4-cup size) with Cooking Spray. Preheat oven to 375°.

Spread into each muffin cup	[1 TB + 1 tp	SMOKED SALMON chopped
In a bowl whisk	[4	EGGS
	[1/4-cup	LIGHT CREAM
	[2 oz	HERB/GARLIC BOURSIN CHEESE
	[1/4-tp	WHITE or BLACK PEPPER

- Use a 1/8-cup measure to pour 1/8-cup of Egg Mixture into each muffin cup. Fill 3/4-way up.
- Bake for 10-to-12 minutes on middle rack of oven, until they turn to a light golden color.
- Insert a pointed knife or skewer in one or two Quiches. If it comes out clean, they are ready.

For a 24 cup mini-muffin tray use	[1-1/2 tp	SMOKED SALMON in each cup

SMOKED SALMON - RISOTTO   RISOTTO see "BASIC RECIPES"

Serves 2 as a main course

In a small saucepan bring to a simmer	[4 cups	CHICKEN BROTH lightly salted
		(+ 1/2-cup more if needed)
THE SALMON In a 6-inch nonstick skillet,		
over medium heat, heat	[2 TB	BUTTER
When it sizzles, stir in	[3 oz	SMOKED SALMON coarsely chop
		in processor
Sauté the Salmon for 1 minute and stir in	[3 TB	TOMATO PASTA SAUCE

Reduce heat to low, simmer for 4 minutes.

Turn off heat then mix in	[3 oz	HEAVY CREAM *(continued)*

178

THE RISOTTO   In an 8-inch heavy nonstick
                    skillet, over medium heat, heat   [2 TB   BUTTER + 1 TB VEGETABLE OIL
                    When it sizzles, sauté   [1 TB   SHALLOT   finely chopped

                    When the Shallot softens, add   [1 cup   ARBORIO RICE
Stir until grains are coated and glisten. Add   [1/4-cup   DRY WHITE WINE

Stir until the Wine evaporates.
Add one ladle (1/2-cup) at a time of BROTH.

            When 4 cups of Broth have been absorbed,
            and the Rice is tender and creamy, stir in   [the Salmon Mixture
                    Turn off heat. Add   [to taste   GROUND BLACK PEPPER

* *To serve 4 as an appetizer:*   THE SALMON   -   2-1/2 TB Butter, 4 oz Smoked Salmon,
                                    4 TB Pasta Sauce, 4 oz Cream

                    THE RISOTTO   -   3 TB Butter, 1-1/2 TB Vegetable Oil,
                                    1-1/2 cups Rice, 6 cups Broth

SMOKED SALMON - TARTARE   *Yields about 1 cup*

            Chop coarsely in processor   [4 oz   SMOKED SALMON

Transfer the Salmon into a bowl and mix in   [2 tp   GREEN ONION   finely chopped
                                [1 tp   PARSLEY   finely chopped
                                [1/2-tp   FRESH DILL   finely chopped
                                [1 tp   CAPERS   minced
                                [1/2-tp   LEMON JUICE
                                [1/2-tp   EXTRA-VIRGIN OLIVE OIL
                                [GROUND BLACK PEPPER

Taste. Adjust Seasonings.

                                [serve with   PUMPERNICKEL   thinly sliced

SARDINES - CROSTINI   CROSTINI see "BASIC RECIPES"

BELL PEPPERS   Mix to taste: **GOAT CHEESE**   Mash to taste:

[RED ROASTED BELL PEPPERS   chopped   [To taste, mash   SARDINES canned, drained
[SARDINES canned in OIL, drained, chopped   [with   RED ONION   minced
[GREEN ONION   minced   [PARSLEY   finely chopped
[CAPERS   rinsed, drained, chopped   [BLACK OLIVES   minced
[LEMON JUICE   [LEMON JUICE   a little

  Spread Mixture on Crostini or Bruschetta.   Spread Mixture on Crostini or Bruschetta.

[Drizzle with   EXTRA-VIRGIN OLIVE OIL   [Top with   GOAT CHEESE   thin slices
[Garnish with   FRESH BASIL finely chopped   [Sprinkle with   SEASONED BREADCRUMBS

                        Pass under the broiler until the Cheese
                        has melted.

EGG SALAD   Mix with Egg Salad: **FETA CHEESE**   Mash to taste:

[SARDINES canned in OIL, drained, chopped   [To taste, mash   SARDINES canned, drained
[CELERY   finely chopped   [with   FETA CHEESE
[RED PIMIENTOS   [minced   CHIVES or GREEN ONION
[CHIVES   [dried   OREGANO or GARDEN MINT
   or
[GREEN BELL PEPPER   finely diced   Moisten with OLIVE OIL and LEMON JUICE
[BASIL   finely chopped
[CHIVES

SARDINES - PASTA alle SARDE   (Sicily)   *Serves 4 as a main course*

Soak in Water 15-to-20 minutes, and drain	[2 TB	BLACK RAISINS or CURRANTS
Toast in a small skillet	[1/3-cup	PINE NUTS see "HELPFUL HINTS" - NUTS
In oven preheated to 350°, toast for 4 or 5 minutes, in a small pan	[1/2-cup	PLAIN BREADCRUMBS
Dissolve in	[1 cup [1/4-tp	LIGHT CHICKEN BROTH hot SAFFRON THREADS
Cut off base and tops (set Fronds aside) of	[2	FENNEL BULBS (about 1 lb)

- Discard outer tough sections. Wash and dry
  sections. Feed them gradually into processor.
- Pulse rapidly several times to chop finely,
  (do not mush), to obtain 2 cups.

In a 10-inch skillet, over medium heat, heat	[1/3-cup	EXTRA-VIRGIN OLIVE OIL
When a light haze forms, add	[1 clove	GARLIC split in half lengthwise
Sauté Garlic until fragrant, then discard, add	[1/2-cup	ONION finely chopped
	[4	ANCHOVIES chopped
With wooden spoon mash the Anchovies, add	[2 cups of	chopped Fennel
Cook the Fennel until wilted and tender. Add	[2 cans	SARDINES in OLIVE OIL and their Oil (Skinless and boneless)
Stir, breaking up the Sardines. Add	[	Saffron Broth
	[2 TB	FRONDS washed, snipped finely
Bring to a boil, reduce heat to medium low, stir until half of Liquid has evaporated, add	[[	Raisins and Pine Nuts GROUND BLACK PEPPER

Reduce heat to low, cover the skillet, simmer
for 5 minutes. Turn off heat.

Meanwhile, add to salted boiling water	[8 oz	BUCATINI long hollow Pasta or other of your choice

Cook "al dente" the Bucatini.   Drain, transfer to heated bowl.
Toss into them the SARDINE MIXTURE. Add BREADCRUMBS, toss again. Serve immediately.

SARDINES - PASTA FRITTATA

FRITTATA see "BASIC RECIPES"
Serves 4 as an appetizer

In a large bowl whisk	[4 large	EGGS
	[1/4-tp	SALT, BLACK PEPPER to taste
When well blended whisk in	[2 cans	SARDINES in OLIVE OIL (skinless and boneless) Drained, chopped.
	[1-1/2 cups	COOKED SPAGHETTINI cut up
	[2 TB	PARSLEY finely chopped
	[1 TB	CAPERS rinsed, drained, chopped
	[1/4-cup	BLACK OLIVES chopped
In a 10-inch skillet that can go under the broiler, over medium heat, heat	[2-1/2 TB	BUTTER + 1/2-TB OLIVE OIL
When it sizzles, sauté until golden	[1/4-cup	ONION finely chopped

Pour in the EGG MIXTURE. Spread it evenly with a spatula. Reduce heat to low.
Cook and pass the Frittata under preheated broiler following directions in "BASIC RECIPES".

SMOKED TROUT NAPOLEONS   _Appetizer_

See "BASIC RECIPES" - PHYLLO - NAPOLEONS. Follow directions to prepare and bake rectangles.

	Cut into 3 x 2-1/2-inch rectangles	[3 layers of	BUTTERED PHYLLO (3 rectangle stacks per Napoleon)
Cream Mixture	Pour into blender and whip	[4 oz	WHIPPING CREAM
		[2 tp	LEMON ZEST grated
		[1 tp	HORSERADISH
Per Napoleon	Flake finely	[1/4-cup	SMOKED TROUT (no bones)
	Fold in	[4 TB of	the Cream Mixture

- Before serving lay on appetizer plate a Phyllo rectangle. Spread on it half of Trout Mixture.
- Top with second rectangle. Spread the rest of Mixture. Top with the third rectangle.
- Pipe over Napoleons a little Cream Mixture.

	[sprinkle	SLICED ALMONDS toasted
Optional, surround with a few	[steamed	WHITE or GREEN ASPARAGUS

TUNA - PASTA à la PROVENÇALE   _Serves 2 as a main course_

In a nonstick skillet, medium heat, heat	[1 TB	EXTRA-VIRGIN OLIVE OIL
When a light haze forms, sauté	[1/2-cup	ONION finely chopped
When it softens add	[1 clove	GARLIC mashed and minced
When Onion turns golden, add	[1 cup	CHOPPED TOMATOES canned, drained
	[1/4-tp	DRIED THYME

Stir until Tomatoes thicken into a Purée.

Add	[6 oz-can	TUNA in OLIVE OIL with its Oil
Flake the Tuna as you heat it. Mix in	[3 TB	BLACK OLIVES chopped
Turn off heat and add	[1 tp	TINY CAPERS rinsed, drained
Pour into a heated serving bowl	[3 or 4 oz	COOKED PASTA of your choice
Toss with the TUNA MIXTURE and	[2 TB	FRESH BASIL finely chopped

TUNA - PASTA del POPOLO   _Serves 2 as a main course_

Soak for 15 minutes a	[1/4-cup	SUN-DRIED TOMATOES not in Oil
with enough	[	BOILING WATER to cover them

Drain, pat dry, cut into strips.

In a nonstick skillet, over medium heat, heat	[2 TB	EXTRA-VIRGIN OLIVE OIL
When a light haze forms, sauté	[1 small	ONION halved and thinly sliced
When Onion is translucent, add	[2 cloves	GARLIC mashed and minced
When Onion colors add Sun-dried TOMATOES	[1/2-cup	cooked BEANS, Cannellini, Navy (if canned, drain, rinse, drain)
	[6 oz-can	TUNA in OLIVE OIL with its Oil
Flake the Tuna with a fork and add	[5 TB	PESTO SAUCE ready-made
	[2 TB	EXTRA-VIRGIN OLIVE OIL
Stir until heated through and toss the Tuna Mixture into	[3 or 4 oz	hot LINGUINE

181

TUNA QUICHE - NIÇOISE

QUICHE see "BASIC RECIPES

Drain	[1 can	ANCHOVY FILLETS chop coarsely
Peel, cut into 1/3-inch thick slices and seed	[2 medium	TOMATOES
In a nonstick skillet, heat	[2 tp	EXTRA-VIRGIN OLIVE OIL
Sauté until golden brown	[1 cup	ONION 1/2-inch thick slices, coarsely chopped

Preheat oven to 375°.

In a bowl, whisk	[3	EGGS
Brush with a little of the beaten Eggs a	[9-inch	FROZEN UNCOOKED PIE SHELL

Set in the oven for 2 minutes only. Let cool.

Whisk into the Eggs	[3/4-cup	HEAVY CREAM + 1/4-cup MILK
Drained and finely flaked	[6 oz-can	TUNA in OLIVE OIL
	[3 oz	SWISS CHEESE grated
	[2 TB	PARSLEY finely chopped
	[3 TB	BLACK OLIVES finely chopped
	[2 tp	TINY CAPERS drain, rinse, dry
	[	GROUND BLACK PEPPER

To assemble - Place the Pie Shell, in its foil pan, on a cookie sheet. Spread in it the ONIONS.
 - Top with the sliced TOMATOES. Sprinkle over the chopped ANCHOVIES.
 - Top with the CUSTARD. Smooth the surface with the back of a spoon.
To bake - Slide Quiche into oven. Reduce heat to 350°. Bake as per "BASIC RECIPES".

TUNA - TORTILLA DE PATATA

POTATO OMELET see "VEGETABLES"
Serves 4 to 6

Peel, wash, dry and cut in half lengthwise	[1 lb	YUKON GOLD POTATOES slice paper thin, with a mandolin
In a 10-inch skillet, over medium heat, heat	[1/4-cup	EXTRA-VIRGIN OLIVE OIL
When a light haze forms, add	[	the Potatoes
Stir with a wooden spoon. When soft, add	[6 oz	ONION finely chopped
	[sprinkle	SALT, GROUND BLACK PEPPER

Cook, drain Potatoes/Onions as in the recipe
for POTATO OMELET.

In a large bowl, beat	[4 large	EGGS
	[1/4-tp	SALT, BLACK PEPPER to taste
When well blended, stir in	[6 oz-can	TUNA in OLIVE OIL drain, flake
and	[	the cooked Potatoes/Onions

Let it set for 10 minutes.

In a 6-1/2 inch skillet, that can go under the broiler, over medium heat, heat	[1-1/2 TB	EXTRA-VIRGIN OLIVE OIL

Cook the Tortilla following directions in the POTATO OMELET recipe.

For one serving as a main course - or for 2 as an appetizer:

[8 oz POTATO	[2 TB OLIVE OIL	[2 EGGS	[4-1/2-inch skillet
	[3 oz ONION	[3 oz-can TUNA	[1 TB OLIVE OIL

VARIATION - Substitute Tuna with chopped Ham, Prosciutto, Salami, Sausage, Smoked Salmon.

182

X

SEAFOOD

"As I ate the oysters with their strong taste of the sea and their faint metallic taste that the cold white wine washed away, leaving only the sea taste and the succulent texture, and as I drank their cold liquid from each shell and washed it down with the crisp taste of the wine, I lost the empty feeling and began to be happy, and to make plans."

Ernest Hemingway

"It is not a matter of indifference if we like oysters or clams, snails or shrimp, if only we know how to unravel the existential significance of these foods."

Jean Paul Sartre

SEAFOOD

PREPARING and COOKING SEAFOOD

CLAMS AND MUSSELS

IN SHELLS
- Wash and soak in a basin of water for one hour. Wash again under running cold water, scrubbing with a hard brush to rid of sand, grit.
- With a sharp knife scrape off Mussel "beards". Discard Mussels that float to the surface, they are not live.

STEAMED
- In Shells. After steaming discard Clams and Mussels that haven't opened.

SHUCKED CLAMS Reserve their Liquor. 1 pint Littlenecks = 24 with their Liquor.

POACHED CLAMS Shucked. Add their Liquor to Poaching Liquid. Boil then simmer, add the Clams, poach 4-to-6 minutes, depending on their size.

OYSTERS

SHUCKED
- Use their Liquor for a Broth or Sauce. 1 pint = 12 medium large with Liquor.

PAN ROASTED
- Sauté for 2 minutes in Butter.

POACHED
- In their Liquor, or add Broth. Boil then simmer, add Oysters, poach from 2-to-4 minutes, according to size, until they plump up, curl around the edges.

SCALLOPS

SHUCKED
- Wash well under cold water, drain and dry on paper towels.

PAN ROASTED
- Over medium high heat, sauté in Butter on both sides until golden brown and opaque. Per side: 3-to-4 minutes. Remove from skillet with slotted spoon.

POACHED
- Simmer in Broth 3-to-4 minutes. Just long enough for them to turn opaque. Cooking longer would render them rubbery.

SHRIMP

WITH SHELLS
- Wash in cold water, shell, devein, wash again, drain. Dry on paper towels.

BOILED
- With/without shells. Throw them in salted boiling water. Cover, turn off heat.
- Let sit for 3 minutes: medium size. 4-to-5 minutes: large. Remove with a slotted spoon, drain on paper towels. Freeze Shells, use them to make Broth.

GRILLED
- Shelled, deveined, washed, dried. Brush with Extra-Virgin Olive Oil. Salt and Pepper. Grill or sauté for 2 minutes on each side.

STEAMED
- Shelled. Curl cleaned Shrimp on a collapsible colander. Place it in a skillet with 1-inch of boiling water. Base of colander must not touch the water.
- Cover with a lid. Steam 3 or 4 minutes until pink. Dry on paper towels.

RAW SHELLS
- Save them to prepare a Broth or Stock (see "BASIC RECIPES").

DRIED SHRIMP
- The tiny ones. Wash in a sieve. Soak for 30 minutes in twice their amount of warm water. Or use half water, half Dry Sherry. Or soak in Chinese Rice Wine.
- Drain, dry on paper towels. Save Soaking Liquor to prepare a Sauce.
- Add water to Soaking Liquor, for a Broth. Use it to cook Rice, a Risotto.

CAVIAR VARIETIES

AMERICAN   Medium grain. Pearly gray-black. Mild flavor. Farm-raised.
                  There are also farm-raised overseas brands.
                  <u>Serve</u> - Traditional presentation. Also on Canapés.

GOLDEN WHITEFISH Small grain. Gold color. Mild flavor.
                  <u>Serve</u> - on Canapés, in Spreads, as a Garnish.

LUMPFISH   Pressed. Small egg. Black (dyed), golden or red (dyed). Strong
                  flavor. Use in Dips, Dressings, Sauces, Garnishes.
                  <u>Before using</u> remove Lumpfish from jar, place it in a fine sieve,
                  over a bowl. Refrigerate in the sieve, let drain. Allow 45 minutes.

SALMON ROE   Large egg. Red orange color. Strong flavor.
                  <u>Serve</u> - Traditional presentation, or on Canapés, with Egg dishes.

                  <u>Before using</u> - if it comes in a jar, turn the jar on its side on a plate,
                  place under it a folded paper towel, let the juice run out.

                  If the Caviar is very salty, place it in a fine sieve and gently run cold
                  water over it for a few seconds. Let it drain before using.

STURGEON
High Quality   SEVRUGA   Small grain. Deep-gray to black.
                  OSETRA   Medium grain. Gray to deep gray-black.
                  BELUGA   Large grain. Pearl-gray to gray-black.

WHITEFISH, PADDLEFISH   Small black egg. Strong flavor. Use in Dips, Garnishes, Sauces.

<u>NOTE</u> - Dyed Caviars, particularly the pressed ones, will discolor into Mixtures and Sauces.
        Add them just before serving.
     - Caviar can be frozen in its tin or in a plastic container. Thaw in the refrigerator.
        Do not freeze glass jars, unless they've been opened and some contents removed.

TRADITIONAL PRESENTATION   Caviar must be chilled.

Put the Caviar into a glass bowl, or leave it in its tin, and place it in a large bowl with crushed ice.

       Serve with [WHITE BREAD - thinly sliced, crust trimmed, toasted.
            or   [BLINIS - potato pancakes.
                   [SOUR CREAM or CRÈME FRAÎCHE. Optional: LEMON WEDGES.

WHITE ONION   Avoid serving it with high quality Caviar. It overpowers the Caviar flavor.
              But, it can be used with strong flavored Caviars, or Caviars of poor quality!

EGGS   Chopped whites and yolks are decorative but bring nothing to high quality
              Caviar. Use them with strong flavored Caviars to smoothen the flavor.

CAVIAR with CRÊPES   *Appetizer*   CRÊPES see "BASIC RECIPES"

          Spread the Crêpes with [CREAM CHEESE or SOUR CREAM or a
                                                                       mixture
       Spread on one half of the Crêpe [CAVIAR
                       Add if you wish [other Ingredients

Fold over the other half, and then again into a triangle. Top with a little Caviar.

CAVIAR - DEVILED EGGS   EGGS - DEVILED - see "BASIC RECIPES"

Use Crème Fraîche or Sour Cream instead of Mayonnaise. Omit the Mustard. Garnish with Caviar.

CAVIAR - DIPS with WHITEFISH CAVIAR   Serve with CRUDITÉS

1.   Purée in processor [5 oz-pkg   BOURSIN PEPPER CHEESE
                                                                       It is a very mild Cheese.
                                    with [3 TB   MILK
                                          [2 TB   GREEN ONION   minced
                             Optional [1 TB   VODKA   or more, to taste
                                                       (with Vodka use 2 TB Milk)
         Transfer to a bowl. Before serving, mix in [to taste   WHITEFISH CAVIAR

2.   Purée in processor [1 cup   CREAMED COTTAGE CHEESE
                                    with [2 TB   SOUR CREAM + 2 TB MILK
                                          [1 or 2 TB   GREEN ONIONS   minced
                                          [1 TB   LEMON JUICE   or more
         Transfer to a bowl. Before serving mix in [to taste   WHITEFISH CAVIAR

CAVIAR with JELLIED CONSOMMÉ

Serve the Consommé in elegant soup cups. Optional - add to Consommé Stock, Dry Sherry.
Top the Consommé with a scoop of good quality CAVIAR. Serve with thin Toast triangles.

CAVIAR in MINIATURE PHYLLO SHELLS   Shells are available frozen

Place Phyllo Shells on a cookie sheet. Crisp them in the oven. Let cool and fill them with:

SOUR CREAM	GUACAMOLE	CAVIAR	TARAMOSALATA Greek Carp Roe Dip
and	and	and	and
CAVIAR	SALMON ROE CAVIAR	QUAIL EGG halved	SALMON ROE or LUMPFISH CAVIAR

CAVIAR - MINI QUICHES   Hors-d'oeuvre   MINI QUICHE see "BASIC RECIPES"

Spray a tray of 12 small Muffin cups (1/4-cup size) with Cooking Spray. Preheat oven to 375°.

                         In a bowl, whisk [4   EGGS
                         Whisk into the Eggs [1/4-cup   HEAVY CREAM
                                          [2 oz   HERB GARLIC BOURSIN
                                          [2 TB   GREEN ONIONS finely chopped
- Fill cups 3/4-way up with the Egg Mixture.
- Bake for 10-to-12 minutes, on middle rack of oven, until they turn a light golden color.
- Insert a thin knife or skewer in one or two Quiches. If it comes out clean, they are ready.

To serve - Arrange the Mini Quiches on a serving platter.

                    Spread on each Mini Quiche [a little   SOUR CREAM
                              Top with [SALMON ROE or AMERICAN CAVIAR

CAVIAR with NEW POTATOES

Boil SMALL NEW POTATOES with their skin. Cut them in half lengthwise.
Scoop out some of the center, fill with SOUR CREAM and top with CAVIAR.

CAVIAR PASTA

Serves 2 as an appetizer

Add to salted boiling water   [3 or 4 oz   FETTUCCINI

In a nonstick skillet, over medium heat, heat   [1/2-TB   BUTTER
When it sizzles, lightly brown   [1 TB   SHALLOTS   finely chopped
Add and heat through   [2/3-cup   ALFREDO SAUCE   ready-made
Drain the Fettuccini.
Transfer to a heated bowl.

Toss in the SAUCE. Mix in   [2 oz   SALMON ROE CAVIAR   or more
  or GOLDEN WHITEFISH CAVIAR
Add to taste Ground Black Pepper. Serve immediately.

VARIATION   -   Omit Butter, Shallots. Toss into Fettuccini the hot Alfredo Sauce and black Caviar.

CAVIAR SAUCE - SHALLOT BÉCHAMEL

See "SAUCES". Prepare   [1 cup   SHALLOT VELOUTÉ WHITE SAUCE
Before seasoning add   [2 chopped   HARD-COOKED EGGS
  [to taste   GOLDEN WHITEFISH
  or SALMON ROE

Stir with a wooden spoon, turn off heat add   [1 TB   PARSLEY   minced
  [WHITE PEPPER, SALT if needed

Serve hot over Fish, Seafood, steamed Vegetables. Or over Croustades of Fish and Seafood.

CAVIAR - SALMON ROE in ARTICHOKE BOTTOMS

Place in a saucepan and cook in their liquid   [1 can   ARTICHOKE BOTTOMS
  [a few drops   LEMON JUICE
When Artichokes are fork tender, drain,
set upside down on paper towels. Let cool.
Cover, refrigerate until ready to fill them.

Spread into each Artichoke   [SALMON ROE CAVIAR
Spread over the Caviar   [SOUR CREAM
Sprinkle the Sour Cream with   [CAPERS   rinse, drain, mince
Top with a dollop of   [SALMON ROE CAVIAR
Sprinkle with   [CHIVES
Serve with thin Toast.

CAVIAR - SALMON ROE EGG SALAD in ARTICHOKES

See SPECIAL SALADS. Add to an EGG SALAD   [1 tp   ONION   finely chopped
and   [1 tp   CAPERS   rinsed, minced

Fill with EGG SALAD the   [ARTICHOKE BOTTOMS   prepared
  as above

Top with   [SALMON ROE CAVIAR
Sprinkle with   [FRESH DILL   snipped

Option   -   Mix Salmon Roe into the Egg Salad. Sprinkle with minced Parsley or Fresh Dill.

VARIATION   -   Substitute Artichokes with individual PRECOOKED TARTLETS crisped in the oven.

CAVIAR - SALMON ROE OMELET

OMELET - EGGS
see "BASIC RECIPES"

Serves 2

In a bowl, beat lightly	[4	EGGS
with	[1 TB	MILK
	[a pinch	SALT, GROUND BLACK PEPPER
Cut into small dice to obtain	[1/4-cup	BRIE CHEESE
and	[1/4-cup	AVOCADO
In an 8-inch nonstick skillet, heat	[1 TB	BUTTER

When it sizzles, cook the Omelet.
When it is almost set, but the top still runny,
spread on one half the Brie and Avocado.

Spread over it	[2 or 3 TB	SALMON ROE CAVIAR

Flip plain half of Omelet over the Filling. Finish cooking following directions in "BASIC RECIPES".

CLAM CHOWDER LEFTOVERS

WITH PASTA   If needed: thin Red or White Chowder with a little milk.

Add to 1 cup Chowder	[1 tp	PARSLEY finely chopped
Toss Chowder with	[	FETTUCCINI or LINGUINE

IN PUFF PASTRY   (see CRAB MEAT in PUFF PASTRY SHELLS)

- If the Chowder is too thin, thicken it by cooking first Butter and Flour as in a White Sauce.
- Add the Chowder. Stir until it thickens. Turn off heat, add a little grated SWISS CHEESE.
- Stir in cooked SEAFOOD or FISH. Optional, cooked Asparagus, Mushrooms or Green Peas.

WITH SAFFRON RICE   *Serves 2*

Heat in a saucepan	[1-1/3 cups	CHICKEN BROTH
Add	[1/4-tp	SAFFRON THREADS crumbled
	[to taste	SALT

The quantity of Broth needed may vary,
according to the brand of Rice you are using.

In a heavy skillet, heat	[2 tp	VEGETABLE OIL
When a light haze forms, sauté	[2 TB	ONION finely chopped
When Onion is translucent, add	[1/2-cup	LONG GRAIN WHITE RICE

- Stir the Rice to coat it with Oil.
- Add the Saffron Broth. Bring to a boil.
- Reduce heat to low, cover, simmer until
  the Rice is done.

Serve it with a Sauce of	[	WHITE CLAM CHOWDER

WITH SCRAMBLED EGGS	Beat	[2	EGGS
	with	[2 TB	MILK or LIGHT CREAM
		[	SALT and PEPPER

Scramble to a soft creamy texture.	Serve on	[	TOAST or CROUSTADE
	Top with	[	RED or WHITE CLAM CHOWDER

CLAM PESTO with LINGUINE

Serves 2 as an appetizer

Drain [6-1/2 oz-can   MINCED CLAMS reserve Liquor

Add to salted boiling water [3 oz   LINGUINE

Over low heat, in a small nonstick skillet, heat [5 TB   PESTO   ready-made
Add the MINCED CLAMS and [2 TB   CLAM LIQUOR

When the Mixture begins to bubble, turn off heat.
For a thicker Sauce add more Pesto. For a thinner Sauce add more Clam Liquor.

Drain the Linguine, transfer to a heated bowl and toss with the Clam Pesto.

NOTE   - To serve 2 as a main course, use 2 cans of Minced Clams.
        - If you are using canned Whole Clams, heat them a bit longer in the Pesto.

VARIATION   After adding Clam Liquor, add [1/2-cup   TOMATOES seeded, diced

A NOTE ON CRAB MEAT

Before using, check it thoroughly. Pick out any shell bits and cartilage.

CRAB MEAT - CRÊPES

CRÊPES see "BASIC RECIPES"

Filling yields about 2-1/4 cups

See "SAUCES". Prepare a [CREAMY BÉCHAMEL
with [3 TB   BUTTER
When it sizzles, add and sauté [2 TB   SHALLOTS finely chopped
When Shallots are soft, add [3 TB   FLOUR

When smooth remove from heat, and
gradually whisk in [1 cup   MILK   hot but not boiling
- Smooth out lumps.
- Return to heat. When the Sauce reaches
the boiling point, reduce heat, stir until it
thickens. Remove from heat.
Beat [1   EGG YOLK
with [1 TB   of the hot Sauce
- Whisk the Yolk into the Sauce.
- Return the Sauce over low heat and stir
until the Yolk is well incorporated.

Turn off heat and stir in until melted [1/3-cup   SWISS CHEESE   coarse-grated
Mix in [1-1/4 cups   CRAB MEAT   flaked with a fork
[1 TB   PARSLEY
[WHITE PEPPER, SALT if needed

Transfer Mixture to a bowl, cover the surface with plastic wrap. Let cool. Refrigerate.
Place the *filled* Crêpes in a greased or sprayed oven-proof dish, cover with foil, refrigerate.

To serve   - Preheat oven to 300°. Bake covered with foil, from 15-to-20 minutes.
           - Serve immediately. Optional: serve on the side a hot ALFREDO SAUCE.

VARIATION   - Use 3/4-cup Crab Meat and 1/2-cup cooked Asparagus sliced very thinly.
            - Substitute Crab Meat with Lobster or Salmon.

CRAB MEAT - CROQUETTES

CROQUETTES see "BASIC RECIPES"

Yields about 3-1/3 cups

Check thoroughly for shell bits and cartilage	[2 cups	CRAB MEAT finely flake it
See "SAUCES". Prepare a	[	VERY THICK BÉCHAMEL
When the Sauce begins to thicken, stir in	[1/2-tp	PREPARED YELLOW MUSTARD
Beat with 2 TB of the hot SAUCE	[1 whole	EGG + 2 EGG YOLKS

When the Sauce is very thick, reduce heat to
low. Add the EGGS.

When incorporated, add	[	SALT and WHITE PEPPER

- Add the CRAB MEAT. Stir with wooden a spoon until the Mixture separates from the skillet.
- Transfer it to a buttered dish. Spread it lightly. Cover with plastic wrap. Refrigerate.
- Shape Croquettes into the size of dates or cherry tomatoes. To fry - see "BASIC RECIPES".
- Serve with a MAYONNAISE DIP or SAUCE.
- Or shape into flat cakes and serve as an appetizer.

CRAB MEAT - POACHED EGG CROUSTADES

CROUSTADES see "SANDWICHES".   Top Croustades with Ingredients in the order listed.

ASPARAGUS TIPS

[ASPARAGUS TIPS
[CRAB MEAT
[POACHED EGG

[Top with LEMON EGG SAUCE - see "SAUCES"

FLORENTINE

[CREAMED SPINACH
[CRAB MEAT sauté in a little brown Butter

[Sprinkle   CHIVES and PAPRIKA
[Top with   POACHED EGG

BAKED BEANS

[Spread   BAKED BEANS
[Top with   BROWNED ONIONS
[CAPERS   minced
[CRAB MEAT
[POACHED EGG

HOLLANDAISE

[Spread   TOMATO   peel, seed, dice
[Sprinkle   FRESH DILL   snipped
[Top with   CRAB MEAT
[POACHED EGG
[HOLLANDAISE SAUCE

CRAB MEAT - PASTA with ASPARAGUS CREAM

Serves 2 as a main course

In a small saucepan, heat	[10 oz-can	ASPARAGUS CREAM SOUP *
with	[1/2-cup	HEAVY CREAM
Add	[1 TB	WATERCRESS or PARSLEY
		minced
In a small skillet, melt	[1 TB	BUTTER
Warm in the Butter, without browning	[1 cup	CRAB MEAT
Mix Crab Meat into	[4 oz	hot FETTUCCINI or LINGUINE

Add gradually to the Pasta as much Asparagus Cream as desired.

* Substitute Asparagus with Mushroom Cream Soup. Crab Meat with Lobster or Shrimp.

192

CRAB MEAT PASTA - BROWNED ONIONS and ARTICHOKES

Serves 2 as a main course

Drain, save Liquid from	[1 can	ARTICHOKE BOTTOMS

Use half of them.
Cut them in half and thinly slice crosswise.

In nonstick 8-inch skillet, medium heat, heat	[1 TB	EXTRA-VIRGIN OLIVE OIL
When a light haze forms, brown soft and juicy	[2 medium	ONIONS halved, thinly sliced

Transfer to a plate. Cover to keep warm.

In the skillet, over medium heat, heat	[2 TB	BUTTER

Sauté ARTICHOKES for 3 minutes and stir in	[3/4-cup	CRAB MEAT or more
	[3 TB of the	ARTICHOKE LIQUID
	[1 TB	PARSLEY minced
Stir well and add	[	SALT, GROUND BLACK PEPPER

Turn off heat. Toss into CRAB MEAT Mixture	[3 or 4 oz	COOKED FARFALLE (bow ties)
and	[	the Browned Onions

Moisten, if needed with Artichoke Liquid.

CRAB MEAT PASTA à la NEWBURG   *Serves 4 as an appetizer*

See "FISH" - SALMON à la NEWBURG	[	Follow the same recipe.
Substitute Parmesan with	[3 TB	CHEDDAR coarse-grated
Toss the SAUCE with the CRAB MEAT into	[6 oz	FETTUCCINI
Add	[2 TB	PINE NUTS toasted

CRAB MEAT with SPINACH RAVIOLI

Sauté the CRAB MEAT in	[browned	BUTTER
Serve it over	[	SPINACH RAVIOLI

CRAB MEAT in PORTOBELLO CAPS   *Egg/Crab Meat yields 1 cup*

See "VEGETABLES" - MUSHROOMS and "Prepare for cooking"	[	PORTOBELLO CAPS
Brush them with	[	EXTRA-VIRGIN OLIVE OIL
Sprinkle with	[	SALT, GROUND BLACK PEPPER

Grill or broil until tender.

Meanwhile, beat	[2	EGGS
with	[1 TB	MILK
	[to taste	SALT, GROUND BLACK PEPPER
Stir in	[1/2-cup	CRAB MEAT
In a nonstick skillet heat	[1/2-TB	BUTTER
When it sizzles, sauté	[1/4-cup	ONION finely chopped

When Onion turns golden add the EGG MIXTURE. Scramble until soft and creamy.
Serve immediately in PORTOBELLO CAPS. Amount of Filling depends on the size of Caps.

CRAB MEAT in PUFF PASTRY SHELLS   *Each Shell holds 1/3-cup*

Over medium heat, in a nonstick skillet, heat	[1 TB	BUTTER + 1 tp VEGETABLE OIL
When it sizzles, sauté	[2 TB	SHALLOT finely chopped
When Shallot begins to color, add and sauté	[1/2-cup	SLICED MUSHROOMS canned, drained
Sauté Mushrooms for 1 minute, stir in	[1-1/4 cups	CRAB MEAT split the large lumps

Turn off heat. Cover

See "SAUCES". Prepare a	[	BÉCHAMEL for PUFF PASTRY SHELL FILLINGS
When the Sauce thickens, and is smooth, turn off heat and stir in until melted	[1/4-cup	SWISS CHEESE coarse-grated

Add the CRAB MEAT/MUSHROOMS. Let cool.
Cover surface with plastic wrap. Refrigerate.

Bake following package directions	[	PUFF PASTRY SHELLS 1 pkg = 6 Shells

1.
   - A HELPFUL HINT: preheat oven to 400°, reduce heat to 350°, Shells will bake better.
   - When they turn golden, take them out. Remove the lids with a fork and set aside.
   - Scoop out with a fork inside uncooked dough, discard it. Return to oven 4 minutes.
   - Take Shells out and arrange them in an oven-proof serving dish.

2.
   - Heat well the CRAB MEAT MIXTURE. It must be hot, but not boiling.
   - With a soup spoon fill the Shells, separating Ingredients from excess Sauce.
   - Divide Filling evenly into the Shells, then add more Sauce as needed to fill them.
   - Overfill slightly, place the Shell lids on top, allowing the Filling to partially show.
   - *Filled* Shells can be kept in a warm oven 5-to-10 minutes. Longer, they'll get soggy.

CRAB MEAT and CORN QUICHE   QUICHE see "BASIC RECIPES"

Thaw in a colander and pat dry	[1/2-cup	FROZEN CORN KERNELS

Preheat oven to 375°.

In a nonstick skillet, over medium heat, heat	[1 TB	BUTTER
When it sizzles, sauté	[1/2-cup	ONION slice 1/4-inch thick, dice
When Onion begins to color add CORN and	[a pinch	SALT
Sauté the Corn just until tender then mix in	[1-1/2 cups	FRESH LUMP CRAB MEAT
In a bowl whisk	[3	EGGS
Brush with a little of the beaten Eggs a	[9-inch	FROZEN UNCOOKED PIE SHELL

Set in the oven for 2 minutes only. Let cool.

Whisk into the Eggs	[3/4-cup	LIGHT CREAM + 1/4-cup MILK
	[1/4-tp	SALT, WHITE PEPPER to taste
	[2 oz	BOURSIN PEPPER CHEESE
	[2 oz	SWISS CHEESE coarse-grated
	[1 TB	FLAT LEAF PARSLEY finely chop

To assemble and bake
   - Place the Pie Shell, in its foil pan, on a cookie sheet.
   - Spread the CRAB MEAT/CORN in it. Ladle over the CUSTARD.
   - Slide cookie sheet with Quiche into the oven. Reduce heat to 350°.
   - Bake following directions in "BASIC RECIPES".

194

CRAB MEAT SAVORY on TOAST or PANCAKES   *Serves 2*

See "SAUCES". Prepare a	[	VELOUTÉ WHITE SAUCE
When it thickens, reduce heat and stir in	[2 TB	KETCHUP or to taste
	[1 TB	CAPERS rinsed, dried, minced
	[1	HARD-COOKED EGG chopped
	[1 cup	CRAB MEAT
	[1 TB	PARSLEY minced
	[	SALT, GROUND BLACK PEPPER

Serve on Toast, Brioche, Challah, Pancakes.

CRAB MEAT - SHIRRED EGGS CARIBBEAN   EGGS see "BASIC RECIPES"

In 2 shallow oven-proof individual dishes	[spread	BLACK or RED BEANS
Over medium heat, in a nonstick skillet, heat	[2 TB	BUTTER + 1 tp VEGETABLE OIL
When it sizzles, sauté	[2 TB	ONION finely chopped
When Onion begins to color, add and sauté	[1/2-cup	CRABMEAT
	[1/2-cup	AVOCADO diced
To taste	[minced	RED PIMIENTO hot or sweet
Stir for 2 minutes and add	[1/2-tp	CAPERS rinsed, dried, minced
	[	SALT, PEPPER, TABASCO optional
Spread Crab Meat Mixture over the Beans and break on top	[1 or 2	EGGS in each dish
Sprinkle Eggs with	[	melted BUTTER, SALT, TABASCO

Bake on top rack of oven, preheated to 500°, until the Eggs are set: 4-1/2 to 5 minutes.

LOBSTER with ASPIC à la RUSSE   ASPIC see "BASIC RECIPES"
Servings for 4 (1 cup) ramekins.

Use CHICKEN BROTH to prepare	[2 cups of	ASPIC STOCK
Prepare a SALADE RUSSE with	[2/3-cup	BOILED POTATOES small dice
	[2/3-cup	COOKED BEETS small dice
	[2/3-cup	COOKED CARROTS small dice
	[2/3-cup	COOKED GREEN PEAS
	[3 or 4	RADISHES grated
	[2 TB	GREEN ONION finely chopped
	[2 TB	PARSLEY finely chopped
Mix in gradually to moisten well	[	CAPER MAYONNAISE ("SAUCES")
	[to taste	GROUND BLACK PEPPER, SALT

- Refrigerate the Salad.
- Line ramekins with 1/4-inch of ASPIC STOCK.
- Refrigerate until set.
- Split the Salad in four, spoon it into ramekins, leaving a little space around for the Stock.
- Pour the Stock around the Salad and cover it.
- Refrigerate. When set, unmold the Aspics.

To serve Surround Aspics with	[pieces of	LOBSTER
Sprinkle on the Lobster	[a few drops	LEMON JUICE, PARSLEY minced

195

LOBSTER RISOTTO

RISOTTO see "BASIC RECIPES"

Serves 2 as a main course

In a saucepan, bring to a simmer [4-1/2 cups   LOBSTER BROTH
                      see "BASIC RECIPES"

In another small saucepan, pour [1 cup of   the simmering Broth
Dissolve in it [1/4-tp   SAFFRON THREADS
                      (keep Broth simmering)

In a 7-to-8-inch heavy nonstick skillet,
over medium heat, heat [2 TB   BUTTER
[1 TB   VEGETABLE OIL
When it sizzles, sauté [2 TB   SHALLOTS   finely chopped
When the Shallots have softened, add [1 cup   ARBORIO RICE

Stir until grains are coated and glisten. Add [1/4-cup   DRY WHITE WINE

- Stir until the Wine evaporates.
- Add a 1/2-cup of the SAFFRON BROTH.
- When absorbed, continue adding the Broth,
  a 1/2-cup at a time, until 3 cups have been
  absorbed.
- Add remaining 1/2-cup of SAFFRON BROTH.
- When it has been absorbed the Rice should
  be tender but firm and creamy.
- Only use more Broth if needed.

Turn off heat and stir in bite-size pieces of a [1-to-1-1/2 lb COOKED LOBSTER
[1 TB   BUTTER   diced small
Optional [1 TB   MASCARPONE
[SALT and WHITE PEPPER

Cover. Let Risotto set for 5 minutes.

LOBSTER THERMIDOR

Serves 2 as a main course

Cut into bite-size pieces the meat from [2   COOKED LOBSTERS
                      (about 1 lb each)

Trim, wash, set Shells aside, to be filled later.

Use leftover shell bits and claws to obtain [1-1/2 cups   LOBSTER STOCK
                      see "BASIC RECIPES"
            (Unless you already have Stock)

1. In a nonstick skillet, medium heat, heat [2 TB   BUTTER
When it sizzles, sauté [1 TB   SHALLOTS   finely chopped
When Shallots have softened, add [6 oz   SLICED MUSHROOMS
Sauté for 2 minutes then sprinkle with [1/4-tp   LEMON JUICE
Stir until Mushrooms are cooked, then [sprinkle   SALT, GROUND BLACK PEPPER

Transfer Mushrooms into a bowl, set aside.

2. In a 7-to-8-inch heavy nonstick skillet,
over medium heat, heat [2-1/2 TB   BUTTER
When it sizzles, stir in [the Lobster Meat
Sauté for 1 minute then pour over [3 TB   BRANDY

Stir until the Liquid has reduced by half.
Add Lobster and Juices to the Mushrooms. Without rinsing return skillet to stove.

3.   In the skillet, over medium low heat,
prepare a BÉCHAMEL (see "SAUCES") with   [3 TB   BUTTER
                                            [2 TB   FLOUR   mixed with
                                            [1/4-tp   DRY MUSTARD
                                            [1-1/2 cups   Lobster Stock   simmering
When the Sauce is thick and smooth, remove
from heat.
                        Immediately beat [2   EGG YOLKS
                                   with   [1/4-cup   HEAVY CREAM

- Beat gradually into Yolks 3 TB of hot SAUCE.
- Whisk the Egg Mixture into the Sauce.
- Over low heat stir until the Yolks are well
  incorporated and the Sauce is smooth.
- When it begins to bubble, turn off heat.
                               Add [to taste   SALT and WHITE PEPPER
Stir in LOBSTER and MUSHROOMS.

4. Place in an oven pan the 2 Lobster Shells.
     - Fill them with the LOBSTER MIXTURE.

                   Sprinkle over each [a mixture of PARMESAN   grated
                              and   [SWISS CHEESE   coarse-grated
                   Dot each with   [1/2-TB   BUTTER   cut into tidbits

Pass under the broiler until golden brown and bubbly.

NOTE   -   If you do not have the Lobster Shells, use individual oven-proof dishes.

To serve 4 as an appetizer: use 4 oven-proof porcelain shells, or abalone shells.

MUSSELS - LINGUINE with ASPARAGUS   _Appetizer, serves 2_

Trim and steam for 3 minutes in microwave [6 medium   ASPARAGUS   then slant-cut
                                                                       into 1/2-inch pieces

In a nonstick skillet, over medium heat, heat [2 TB   EXTRA-VIRGIN OLIVE OIL
                                      Sauté   [2 TB   SHALLOTS   finely chopped
                                                [1 clove   GARLIC   mashed and minced
When Shallot softens, begins to color, stir in [the Asparagus

        Meanwhile add to salted boiling water [3 oz   LINGUINE   or more

Sauté the ASPARAGUS until tender firm. Add [1 can   MUSSELS   drained
                                             [2 TB   Mussel Liquid
When Liquid bubbles, reduce heat to low, add [1/4-cup   HEAVY CREAM

    Simmer for 5 minutes. Turn off heat. Add [1 TB   PARSLEY   finely chopped
                                                [to taste GROUND BLACK PEPPER, SALT

Drain Linguine. Toss them into skillet with the Mussels and Asparagus.
Serve immediately.

VARIATIONS   - Substitute Mussels with 1 can OYSTERS. Or use shucked Oysters.
                     With the Oysters use White Asparagus.
                  - Prepare a plain Risotto. Stir the Oyster/White Asparagus Mixture into it.
                  - Substitute the Mussels with 1 can of Clams.
                  - Or sauté with the Asparagus some sliced Scallops.

MUSSELS with SPANISH STYLE RICE   *Appetizer, serves 2*

1. In a nonstick skillet, medium heat, heat   [1 TB   EXTRA-VIRGIN OLIVE OIL
         When a light haze forms, sauté   [1/4-cup   RED ONION   finely chopped
                                          [1/4-cup   RED BELL PEPPER   diced
                                          [1/4-cup   YELLOW BELL PEPPER   diced
         When Bell Pepper begins to soften, add   [1/4-cup   GREEN PEAS   if frozen, thawed

              Stir until Peas are tender, then add   [1 cup   COOKED SHELLED MUSSELS
                                                     [1 tp   CAPERS   rinsed, dried, minced
Turn off heat.
                          Sprinkle and stir in   [1/2-tp   WHITE WINE VINEGAR
                                                 [SALT, GROUND BLACK PEPPER
                               Now stir in   [1 TB   EXTRA-VIRGIN OLIVE OIL
Cover to keep warm.

2.   In a small saucepan, heat   [1-1/2 cups   FISH BROTH
              Dissolve in the hot Broth   [1/4-tp   SAFFRON THREADS or Powder

3.   In a heavy saucepan, heat   [2 tp   EXTRA-VIRGIN OLIVE OIL
              When a light haze forms, sauté   [2 TB   ONION   finely chopped
         When the Onion is translucent, add   [1/2-cup   LONG GRAIN WHITE RICE
Stir for grains to be coated and glisten. Add   [2 TB   DRY WHITE WINE optional

- Stir until the Wine evaporates. Add the Fish Broth. (Amount as per Rice package).
- Bring to a boil, cover, reduce heat to low, simmer until the Rice is cooked.
- Stir in VEGETABLES and MUSSELS. Let set for 10 minutes. Optional, drizzle a little OLIVE OIL.

VARIATION   - Substitute Mussels with Oysters, Scallops or Shrimp. Or a combination.

MUSSELS - SPINACH AGLIO OLIO   Garlic and Oil *Serves 2 or 3*

                      Steam in microwave   [10 oz-pkg   FROZEN CHOPPED SPINACH

Over medium heat, in a nonstick skillet, heat   [2 TB   EXTRA-VIRGIN OLIVE OIL
         When a light haze forms, lightly brown   [4 cloves   GARLIC thinly sliced lengthwise
              Then add the SPINACH and   [1/4-tp   LEMON JUICE
    Sauté the Spinach for 1 minute and add   [to taste   SALT, GROUND BLACK PEPPER

    In another skillet, heat in their Liquor   [1 can   MUSSELS
              With slotted spoon add them to   [the Spinach

Moisten with their Liquor.   Serve with   [VERMICELLI PASTA
                          Drizzle with   [EXTRA-VIRGIN OLIVE OIL

MUSSELS (smoked) in MINIATURE PHYLLO SHELLS

DILL MAYONNAISE prepare and refrigerate overnight.   Crisp in the oven:

[3 TB   MAYONNAISE   ready-made   [MINIATURE PHYLLO SHELLS
[2 TB   SOUR CREAM
[3 TB   FRESH DILL   snipped   [Fill with   DILL MAYONNAISE
[1 TB   WATERCRESS   minced very finely
[1 or 2 tp   GREEN ONION   minced very finely [Top with   SMOKED MUSSELS
[1/4-tp   DIJON MUSTARD   [or   SMOKED OYSTERS
[1 tp   LEMON JUICE, SALT if needed

198

OYSTERS - BENEDICT   À la New Orleans

Split in half and toast	[	ENGLISH MUFFINS
Top each half with a slice of	[	CANADIAN BACON grilled or broiled
Top the Canadian Bacon with	[	FRIED OYSTERS
Cover with	[	HOLLANDAISE SAUCE see "SAUCES"

Serve immediately.

OYSTERS - CROSTINI

CROSTINI see "BASIC RECIPES"

Mix and refrigerate:

[3 oz	CREAM CHEESE
[2 TB	SOUR CREAM
[1 tp	HORSERADISH or more
[1 tp	GREEN ONION minced
[2 tp	WATERCRESS minced
[1/4-tp	LEMON JUICE

Drain well	[	SHUCKED OYSTERS
Sprinkle with	[	LEMON JUICE
Spread on	[	CROSTINI
	[	CREAM CHEESE MIXTURE
Top each	[	with an OYSTER

OYSTERS in MUSHROOM CAPS   Hors-d'oeuvre

Remove stems and clean	[	WHITE MUSHROOM CAPS

See "SALADS" - SPECIAL SALADS. Mix into	[	EGG SALAD
to taste	[	CHIVES
a little	[	LEMON JUICE

Fill CAPS with EGG SALAD, top with	[	SHUCKED OYSTERS

OYSTER OMELET à la ROCKEFELLER   Serves 2

THE FILLING   In a nonstick skillet, brown [3 slices   BACON   coarsely chopped

Do not crisp. Drain on paper towels.

Pour out the Fat and add to the skillet	[1 TB	BUTTER
Over medium heat, when it sizzles, sauté	[1 TB	SHALLOT finely chopped
When Shallot softens mix in	[1/4-tp	DIJON MUSTARD
and stir in	[1/2-cup	CREAMED SPINACH
	[1 TB	PARMESAN grated

When Spinach is hot add the BACON and	[8 drained	SMALL SHUCKED OYSTERS
	[to taste	SALT, GROUND BLACK PEPPER
Turn off heat, add	[optional	TABASCO a few drops

THE OMELET Beat lightly until blended	[4	EGGS
	[2 TB	MILK
	[1/4-tp	SALT and PEPPER to taste
	[1 tp	PARSLEY minced

In a 6-to 6-1/2-inch nonstick skillet, heat	[1 TB	BUTTER + 1 tp VEGETABLE OIL

When the Butter sizzles, add the EGG MIXTURE.

Cook the Omelet, add the OYSTER SPINACH FILLING as per directions in "BASIC RECIPES".

OYSTER SOUFFLÉ   *Serves 4 to 6*   SOUFFLÉ see "BASIC RECIPES"

1.   Set out at room temperature [5   EGGS you need 5 Whites, 4 Yolks

2.   Drain [1 pint   SMALL SHUCKED OYSTERS
                                                               reserve their LIQUOR

3. PERNOD MILK In a small skillet combine [1/3-cup   CHICKEN BROTH
                                                [2 TB   PERNOD
Bring to a boil, reduce by half, pour into a
measuring cup.
                                          Add [1/4-cup of the Oyster Liquor
                                          and [enough   MILK to obtain 1-1/4 cups
Option   Instead of Pernod, use:
           1/2-cup Oyster Liquor, 3/4-cup Milk.

4.   Rub a 1-1/2 quarts soufflé dish with [BUTTER
             (or use 4 ramekins) Dust it with [1-1/2 TB   FINE BREADCRUMBS refrigerate
                                                               (1-1/4 tp per ramekin)

5.   In a heavy nonstick skillet, prepare a [CREAMY BÉCHAMEL ("SAUCES")
                                   Using the [PERNOD or OYSTER MILK
                                                               hot, not boiling

- When Béchamel thickens remove from heat.
- Break 1 EGG, drop the WHITE into stainless
  steel bowl. The YOLK into the Béchamel.
- With a wire whip beat it into the Sauce.
- Repeat with 3 more Yolks, one at a time.
- Return saucepan to stove. Over low heat
  stir for 1 minute to bind the Eggs.

           Turn off heat. Stir into it, until melted [3 TB   SWISS CHEESE coarse-grated
                                                        (+ for later 1 TB, or 4 tp for ramekins)

                                                [to taste   WHITE PEPPER, SALT if needed

- Set aside to cool. Can be prepared ahead to
  this point. Cover the surface with wax paper.
- Before adding the EGG WHITES barely warm,
  it must be tepid.

6. Preheat oven to 400°. Set out soufflé dish.

                  Stir into the tepid Béchamel [1 cup of   the Small Shucked Oysters

Add to the 4 EGG WHITES 1 EGG WHITE and [1/8-tp   CREAM OF TARTAR

a) Beat the EGG WHITES until stiff and glossy, but not dry.
    - Add one ladle of WHITES to the BÉCHAMEL. Gently fold them in with a rubber spatula.
    - Then gently pour the MIXTURE into the remaining Egg Whites.
    - Fold in with the spatula, scooping from the bottom towards the top as you turn the bowl.
      Do not fold too much, it would keep the Soufflé from rising well. White spots do no harm.

b) Pour MIXTURE into soufflé dish(es). Smooth the surface with a spatula.
    - Sprinkle with the reserved 1 TB of CHEESE. Or for each ramekin 1 tp.

c) Place on middle rack of oven. Immediately reduce heat to 375°. Bake for 25-to-30 minutes.
    - Less time for the ramekins. Do not open the oven door until the Soufflé is well puffed.
    - Test by inserting a thin knife or metal skewer. If it comes out clean, the Soufflé is ready.
      If not, cook 5 minutes longer. It should have a light brown crust with a creamy center.

200

SCALLOPS and CAVIAR APPETIZER

Wash, dry on paper towels and slice thinly [SEA SCALLOPS
Arrange slices on individual plates. Sprinkle [LEMON JUICE lightly, not too much

Top each slice with a dollop of [GOLDEN WHITEFISH CAVIAR
Garnish the plates with dots of [SOUR CREAM
Sprinkle lightly with [CHIVES and PARSLEY minced

SCALLOPS - FLORENTINE

See "SAUCES". Prepare a [SHALLOT VELOUTÉ WHITE SAUCE

Cut into 1/2-inch thick slices [SCALLOPS washed and dried
Sprinkle with SALT and PEPPER. Dip lightly in [FLOUR shaking off excess

In a nonstick skillet, over medium heat, heat [BUTTER
When it sizzles brown lightly [the Scallops

Spread into individual oven-proof dishes [CREAMED SPINACH
Top the SPINACH with SCALLOPS, SAUCE and [PARMESAN grated

Pass under the Broiler to brown the top.

SCALLOPS, MUSHROOMS in CHAMPAGNE SAUCE *Serves 2*

See "SAUCES". Prepare a [CHAMPAGNE or WHITE WINE SAUCE

In heavy nonstick skillet, medium heat, heat [1 TB BUTTER
When it sizzles, sauté [2 TB ONION minced
When Onion begins to color add [4-to-6 large SEA SCALLOPS sliced 1/4-inch thick
Sauté the Scallops for 2 minutes, then add [1/2-cup sliced MUSHROOMS canned, drained
[1 TB PARSLEY minced
Stir and add, to taste [the Sauce

Serve with White Rice or Pasta. On Croustades. Or as a Filling in Puff Pastry.

SCALLOPS - OMELET *Serves 2* OMELET - EGGS see "BASIC RECIPES"

Over medium heat, in a nonstick skillet, heat [1 TB BUTTER + 1 tp VEGETABLE OIL
When it sizzles, sauté [1 TB ONION or SHALLOT minced
When Onion begins to color, add and sauté [1/2-cup SLICED MUSHROOMS
[1/4-tp DRIED TARRAGON
[to taste SALT, GROUND BLACK PEPPER
Remove Mushrooms with slotted spoon and
add to skillet [1 TB BUTTER
Turn up heat to high and sauté for 2 minutes [1/2-cup TINY BAY SCALLOPS

Turn off heat, mix in MUSHROOMS.

Beat [4 EGGS with 2 TB MILK
[1/4-tp SALT, GROUND BLACK PEPPER

In a 6-to 6-1/2-inch skillet, heat [1 TB BUTTER

When it sizzles, pour in EGG MIXTURE. Cook the Omelet, add MUSHROOM FILLING and fold.

SEAFOOD - *STEAMED MUSSELS / CLAMS à la MARINIÈRE*

In a 3-to-4-quart saucepan combine	[1-1/4 cups	DRY WHITE WINE
	[1-1/2 TB	SHALLOTS finely chopped
	[2 cloves	GARLIC
	[2 sprigs	PARSLEY
Over high heat boil for 2 minutes, then add	[2 TB	BUTTER
	[2 TB	PARSLEY finely chopped
	[to taste	GROUND BLACK PEPPER
(washed and scrubbed)	[1-1/2 quarts	MUSSELS or STEAMER CLAMS

- Bring to a boil.
- Cover tightly reduce heat to low, steam until the shells open, about 8-to-10 minutes.
- Stir twice with a wooden spoon, shaking the pan for Shellfish to cook evenly.
- Remove the opened Shellfish with a slotted spoon and serve in soup dishes.
- Steam un-opened ones a little longer. If they don't open, discard. Remove Parsley, Garlic.
- Without stirring the BROTH (to avoid any sand deposit), ladle it over the Shellfish. Or strain it through a fine sieve lined with 3 layers of cheesecloth.   *(Serves 2)*

VARIATION   - Substitute Dry White Wine with a 1/2-cup PERNOD + 3/4-cup WATER.

SEAFOOD - *RISOTTO REGINA*   *Serves 4*   RISOTTO - "BASIC RECIPE*S*"

The MUSSELS   Steam as in above recipe   [3 pints   MUSSELS in their shells
                                                            Use 1 cup DRY WHITE WINE

Remove them from shells. Cover, set aside.
Strain the BROTH through a fine sieve lined
with 3 layers of cheesecloth.

The BROTH To obtain 6 cups, combine	[strained	MUSSELS BROTH
	[1/4-cup	CLAM JUICE bottled (is salty)
and add	[	CHICKEN BROTH (reserve a
		1/2-cup more if needed)

Simmer when ready to cook the Risotto.

Heat and dissolve in 1 cup of this Broth   [1/4-tp   SAFFRON THREADS crushed, or
                                                            more to taste

The SCALLOPS and SHRIMP

In large nonstick skillet, medium heat, heat	[2 TB	BUTTER
When it sizzles, add	[16	TINY BAY SCALLOPS
Sauté Scallops for 2 minutes, then add	[12 raw	SHRIMP small, or 6 large cut into
		bite-size pieces
Sauté for 3 more minutes then add	[4 medium	ASPARAGUS *cooked firm*, and
		thinly slant-cut
Turn off heat. Add the MUSSELS	[to taste	GROUND BLACK PEPPER

The RISOTTO In 10-inch heavy skillet, heat	[3-1/2 TB	BUTTER + 1 TB VEGETABLE OIL
Over medium heat, sauté	[1/4-cup	ONION finely chopped
When Onion is translucent, add	[1-1/2 cups	ARBORIO RICE
Stir until grains are coated and glisten, add	[1/2-cup	DRY WHITE WINE

- Stir until the Wine has evaporated. Add the simmering BROTH, a ladle (1/2-cup) at a time.
- When 5 cups have been absorbed, stir in the SEAFOOD. And, in two times, SAFFRON BROTH.
- When the 6 cups of Broth have been absorbed, the Rice should be tender, but firm and creamy.
- Turn off heat.

Stir in   [2 TB   BUTTER   diced small

Cover. Let Risotto set for 5 minutes.

SEAFOOD - RISOTTO SAVOYA

Serves 4 as a main course

Drain in a colander (reserve the Liquor)	[1 pint	OYSTERS small shucked *about 16*
Also drain (reserve the Liquor)	[1 pint	LITTLENECKS shucked *about 24*

The BROTH   Combine the Shellfish LIQUOR [1 cup   DRY WHITE WINE
And to obtain 6 cups add   [CHICKEN BROTH   Reserve a
1/2-cup more

Pour this Broth into a 2-quart saucepan. Add	[2 whole	GARLIC CLOVES
	[1/4-of a	SMALL ONION
	[3 sprigs	PARSLEY, BLACK PEPPER

- Bring to a boil, reduce heat to medium low, cover, simmer for 15 minutes. Turn off heat.
- In 7-inch skillet add BROTH, 3/4-inch deep.
- Bring to a simmer over medium heat.

The SHELLFISH   Poach in the Broth the   [shucked Clams
Simmer 3 minutes, add the   [shucked Oysters

- When Oysters plump up, curl around edges, lift Shellfish with slotted spoon into a bowl.
- Add their BROTH to the rest of the BROTH.
- Pass through a sieve lined with cheesecloth.

Measure the Broth. To obtain 6 cups add   [if needed   CHICKEN BROTH and simmer

In a small skillet, over medium low heat, heat	[2 TB	BUTTER
When it sizzles, add	[1/2-tp	LEMON JUICE
Mix this Lemon Butter into	[	the Shellfish

The RISOTTO   In a 10-inch heavy nonstick
skillet, medium heat, heat	[3-1/2 TB	BUTTER + 1 TB VEGETABLE OIL
When it sizzles, sauté	[4 TB	SHALLOTS finely chopped
When translucent, add	[3 oz	MUSHROOMS chopped
Stir and add	[1-1/2 cups	ARBORIO RICE

- Stir until the grains glisten.
- Add one ladle (1/2-cup) at a time of BROTH.
- When 5-1/2 cups have been absorbed,
  stir in the SHELLFISH.   And   [2 TB   PARSLEY   finely chopped
- Add the last 1/2-cup of BROTH.
- When absorbed, the Rice should be tender, firm, creamy.

Turn off heat, stir in	[1-1/2 TB	BUTTER diced small
	[to taste	BLACK PEPPER, SALT if needed

SEAFOOD - SPAGHETTINI

Serves 2 as a main course

In a 7-inch skillet combine LIQUOR from	[1 pt shucked	OYSTERS or CHERRYSTONES
	[1/2-cup	DRY WHITE WINE
Add WATER fo fill the skillet 1/2-way, and	[1/8-tp	GARLIC SALT

Bring to a boil, reduce to a bubble 3 minutes.
Poach the Shellfish. Remove with slotted
spoon, reserve the Broth.

Melt in the skillet	[2 TB	BUTTER
When it sizzles add	[1/2-tp	LEMON JUICE and the Shellfish
Toss in	[3 or 4 oz	SPAGHETTINI
	[2 TB	PARSLEY finely chopped
Moisten if needed with BROTH. Serve with	[	GARLIC BREAD

SHRIMP - CEVICHE   Appetizer   *Also prepare with lean white Fish.*

Combine in a bowl	[8 oz	RAW SHRIMP bite-size pieces
	[8 oz	RAW SCALLOPS diced bite-size
	[cover with	LIME JUICE

Seal with plastic wrap. Refrigerate overnight.
Drain.

In a bowl, mix SHELLFISH with	[2 ripe	TOMATOES peeled, seeded, diced
	[4 oz	RED ONION diced
	[1/2-cup	AVOCADO diced
	[2 TB	LIME JUICE
	[to taste	SALT, GROUND BLACK PEPPER
	[4 TB	FRESH CILANTRO chopped
	[to taste	JALAPEÑOS finely chopped

Serve the Ceviche in chilled bowls.

SHRIMP CRÊPES with SCALLOPS   CRÊPES see "BASIC RECIPES"

Filling yields about 2-1/2 cups

THE SEAFOOD	In a nonstick skillet, heat	[1-1/2 TB	BUTTER
	When it sizzles, sauté	[2 TB	SHALLOT finely chopped
	When Shallot begins to color add	[6 oz	RAW SHRIMP diced
		[6 oz	RAW SCALLOPS diced
			Or omit Scallops, use only Shrimp
	Sauté until the Shrimp turn pink, then mix in	[1 TB	FLAT LEAF PARSLEY finely chop
	Turn off heat and	[sprinkle	SALT, GROUND BLACK PEPPER

BÉCHAMEL BASE	In a small skillet prepare a	[	CREAMY BÉCHAMEL ("SAUCES")
	using	[1-1/4 cups	SHRIMP BROTH ("BASIC RECIPES")

When it thickens remove from heat, whisk in [1   EGG YOLK beaten with 1 TB hot MILK

Over low heat whisk to incorporate the Egg.

Turn off heat and mix in, until melted	[1/4-cup	SWISS coarse-grated
	[to taste	SALT, GROUND BLACK PEPPER

- Mix the SEAFOOD into the BÉCHAMEL.
- Transfer to a bowl. Cover the surface with plastic wrap. Refrigerate.
- Heat the *filled* Crêpes, covered with foil, in oven preheated to 325°, for 15-to-20 minutes.
- Top the Crêpes with a little ALFREDO SAUCE. Serve the rest of the Sauce in a sauceboat.

SHRIMP CREOLE   *Serves 2*

In a nonstick skillet, over medium heat, heat	[2 TB	VEGETABLE OIL
When a light haze forms, sauté	[1/2-cup	ONION coarsely chopped
When it softens, add	[1 or 2	GARLIC CLOVES mashed, minced
	[1/2-cup	GREEN BELL PEPPER coarse-chop
	[1/4-cup	CELERY diced
When Vegetables soften, add	[1/2-cup	MUSHROOMS thinly sliced
Sauté for 1 minute and add	[3/4-cup	CHOPPED TOMATOES canned, drained
	[1/2-cup	Tomato Liquid
	[1 tp	CREOLE SEASONING or to taste
	[1 TB	DRY SHERRY *(continued)*

Bring to a boil, reduce heat to low, simmer for 10 minutes.

Adjust [to taste SALT, GROUND BLACK PEPPER
Add [8-to-12 oz RAW SHRIMP shelled , deveined
(small to medium size)

Add, if needed more Tomato Liquid. If you run out of it use Water.
Simmer 10 more minutes. Adjust Seasonings. If the Sauce is too thin, thicken with Arrowroot.

Serve with - White Rice, mashed Potatoes, over Croustades. Also delicious with Pasta.

SHRIMP CROQUETTES - BÉCHAMEL BASE

Yields 3 cups

See "SAUCES". Prepare a [VERY THICK BÉCHAMEL

When the Eggs are well incorporated mix in [1/4-cup   BRIE CHEESE rind removed, diced

Stir to mix the Cheese until melted.   Add [1-3/4 cups   COOKED SHRIMP   chopped in
processor

Stir until the Mixture separates from the skillet.
Transfer to a buttered dish. Spread it lightly. Cover with plastic wrap. Refrigerate.
Shape and fry Croquettes as per "BASIC RECIPES".

SHRIMP - CURRY STIR-FRY   *Serves 4*

Vegetable and Seafood amounts are flexible, use more or less, according to number of servings.

See "SAUCES". Prepare a [CURRY SAUCE or CURRY COCONUT SAUCE
Cover. Set aside.
Heat the Sauce before adding it to stir-fry.

Heat a few seconds a 10-inch nonstick skillet
then add and heat [2 TB   VEGETABLE OIL
Swirl the hot oil around and add [1 whole   GARLIC CLOVE

When the Garlic turns fragrant, discard it and
stir-fry over high heat [1 cup   ONION   coarsely chopped
When Onion is translucent, add [1 medium   GOLDEN DELICIOUS APPLE diced
Sprinkle [1/2-tp   CURRY POWDER   or to taste

Stir for 4 minutes and add [1 medium   YELLOW BELL PEPPER thin strips
[1 medium   RED BELL PEPPER thin strips
[1 cup   MUSHROOMS   thinly sliced
[1/2-cup   COOKED CARROTS   diced
[1   SCALLION   finely chopped
Stir for 3 more minutes. Reduce heat to
medium high and stir in [1-1/2 cups   RAW SHRIMP   bite-size pieces

When Shrimp turn pink, turn off heat
and sprinkle [to taste   SALT
Add to the stir-fry, amount to taste [heated   CURRY SAUCE
or   CURRY COCONUT SAUCE
Serve with [BROWNED RICE   *(next recipe)*

VARIATION - Serve over Pasta, mashed Potatoes, Muffins, Croustades.

BROWNED RICE

Serves 4

In a 2-quart saucepan, medium heat, heat [1-1/2 TB   VEGETABLE OIL
When a light haze forms, sauté [1/2-cup   ONION   finely chopped
When Onion is translucent, add [1 cup   LONG GRAIN WHITE RICE

Stir the Rice to coat it with the Oil. Continue
stirring until toasted and a light brown. Add [WATER   as per Rice pkg.
[1/4-cup   GOLDEN RAISINS
[1/4-cup   ALMONDS slivered, or PINE NUTS
[1/2-tp   SALT
[1/4-cup   COCONUT unsweetened, flaked

Bring to a boil, then reduce heat to low.
Cover tightly, simmer about 25 minutes, until the Rice is cooked and Liquid has been absorbed.

SHRIMP - DEVILED EGGS

EGGS see "BASIC RECIPES"

Slice in half lengthwise and remove Yolks from [4 large   HARD-COOKED EGGS
Finely chop in processor [2 oz   COOKED SHRIMP

"O SOLE MIO"

Mash in a bowl:

[3 TB   MAYONNAISE
[1/8-tp   SAFFRON THREADS
[the 4   Egg Yolks
Add [1 TB   GREEN ONION   finely chopped
[1 TB   SUN-DRIED TOMATOES   minced
[1 TB   FRESH BASIL   finely chopped
[1/2-tp   CAPERS   minced

- With a fork, fluff in the chopped SHRIMP.
- Add Salt and Pepper to taste.
- Pipe Mixture onto Egg Whites.
- Garnish with: FRESH BASIL   finely chopped

ROMANOFF

Mash in a bowl:

[1 TB   MAYONNAISE
[2 TB   SOUR CREAM
[the 4   Egg Yolks
[1 tp   LEMON JUICE
Add [2 TB   GOLDEN WHITEFISH CAVIAR
[1 TB   CHIVES   finely chopped
[1 TB   VODKA

- With a fork, fluff in the chopped SHRIMP.
- Season to taste. Pipe Mixture onto Egg Whites.
- Garnish with: FRESH DILL snipped

PETRUSHKA

Mash in a bowl:

[2 TB   MAYONNAISE
[2 TB   SOUR CREAM
[the 4   Egg Yolks
[1 TB   GREEN ONION   finely chop
[2 TB   DILL PICKLE   minced

Chop finely in processor:

[2 oz   COOKED SHRIMP
[1 oz   COOKED BEETS

- Fluff them into the Mayonnaise Mixture.
- Season to taste. Pipe onto Egg Whites.

VERA CRUZ

Mash in a bowl:

[3 TB   MAYONNAISE
[1/2-tp   TOMATO PASTE
[the 4   Egg Yolks
[a dash   GARLIC POWDER
[1/8-tp   GROUND CUMIN   or to taste
[1 TB   GREEN ONION   minced

- Fluff the chopped SHRIMP into Mixture.
- Season to taste. Pipe onto Egg Whites
- Garnish with: CILANTRO   finely chopped

SHRIMP JAMBALAYA

Serves 2

In heavy saucepan, over medium heat, heat [1-1/2 TB   VEGETABLE OIL
When a light haze forms, sauté [1 small   ONION   finely chopped
When Onion is translucent, add [1 clove   GARLIC   mashed and minced
[1 medium   GREEN BELL PEPPER   diced
[1/4-cup   CELERY   trimmed and diced
[1/4-tp   DRIED THYME   or more to taste

Stir. When Bell Pepper softens, add [1/2-cup   LONG GRAIN WHITE RICE
Stir the Rice to coat grains with the Oil, add [2 medium   TOMATOES peeled, seeded, diced

Add, according to directions on Rice package [WATER or BROTH salted to taste
Or add to the boiling Water [1 cube   BOUILLON Vegetable or Chicken

When the Rice is cooked, stir in [1 cup   BOILED SHRIMP bite-size pieces
[2 TB   PARSLEY   minced
[a dash   TABASCO

Cover. Wait about 5 minutes before serving.

SHRIMP PASTA - ASIAN STYLE   *Serves 2 as a main course*

In a nonstick skillet, medium high heat, heat [2 TB   VEGETABLE OIL
When a light haze forms, sauté [1/4-cup   ONION   finely chopped
When Onion is translucent, add [2 cloves   GARLIC   mashed and minced
[1 medium   GREEN BELL PEPPER   diced
When Bell Pepper is soft yet crisp, stir in [1 cup   SLICED MUSHROOMS
Stir-fry for 1 minute and add [1 cup   RAW SHRIMP   bite-size pieces
[1   SCALLION   thinly sliced
When the Shrimp turn pink, turn off heat
and add [to taste   CILANTRO finely chopped
[to taste   OYSTER SAUCE, BLACK PEPPER

Serve hot over [3 or 4 oz   ANGEL HAIR PASTA

SHRIMP PASTA - PIRAEUS   *Serves 2 as a main course*

In a heavy nonstick skillet, heat [2 TB   EXTRA-VIRGIN OLIVE OIL
When a light haze forms, sauté [1/2-cup   ONION   coarsely chopped
When Onion turns golden brown, stir in [3/4-cup   TOMATO or MARINARA SAUCE
[1/2-tp   DRIED OREGANO   crumbled
[a dash   ALLSPICE   to taste

Bring the Sauce to a boil, reduce heat to
medium low, simmer for 1 minute, add [1 cup   RAW SHRIMP   bite-size pieces
Stir until the Shrimp turn pink, add [1 TB   PARSLEY   minced
[2 TB   KALAMATA OLIVES   chopped
Turn off heat and add [1/4-cup   FETA CHEESE crumbled, or more

Toss into [3 or 4 oz   PASTA of your choice

SHRIMP PASTA - RED ONIONS and ARUGULA   *Serves 2*

In an 8-inch skillet, medium high heat, heat [4 TB   EXTRA-VIRGIN OLIVE OIL
When a light haze forms, sauté [2 medium   RED ONIONS   thinly sliced
When Onions soften, add [1 clove   GARLIC   mashed and minced
When they begin to color, add [1 cup   ARUGULA   leaves only
Stir until the Arugula is wilted, then stir in [1 cup   COOKED SHRIMP bite-size pieces
[2 TB   PINE NUTS   toasted
[SALT, GROUND BLACK PEPPER

Stir to heat through the Shrimp.
Turn off heat.
Toss into the skillet [3 or 4 oz   SPAGHETTINI   hot

207

SHRIMP PASTA - ZUCCHINI MUSHROOMS   Serves 2

In 8-inch skillet, medium high heat, heat	[2 TB	EXTRA-VIRGIN OLIVE OIL
When it sizzles, sauté	[1/4-cup	ONION finely chopped
When Onion softens, add	[1 clove	GARLIC mashed and minced
When Onion is translucent, add	[2 medium	ZUCCHINI quarter longwise, dice
Sauté Zucchini until tender crunchy then add	[4 oz	SLICED MUSHROOMS
Sauté until Zucchini/Mushrooms turn golden, reduce heat to medium low and add	[1 cup	COOKED SHRIMP bite-size pieces
	[1/3-cup	HEAVY CREAM
	[2 TB	PARMESAN grated
	[1 TB	FRESH BASIL finely chopped
	[	SALT, GROUND BLACK PEPPER
Do not let the Sauce boil.		
Toss into the skillet	[4 oz	PASTA SHELLS medium size
Serve immediately with on the side	[	PARMESAN grated

SHRIMP in PHYLLO NESTS   PHYLLO NESTS see "BASIC RECIPES"

Just before serving, fill the Nests with Ingredients in the order they are listed:

Version I	Version II	Version III
[GUACAMOLE	[GUACAMOLE	[SOUR CREAM
[BOILED SHRIMP small size with Oil and Lemon Dressing	[BOILED SHRIMP	[SALMON ROE CAVIAR
	[SALMON ROE CAVIAR	[SHRIMP and AVOCADO diced
[CILANTRO finely chopped	[PARSLEY finely chopped	with Oil and Lemon Dressing
		[FRESH DILL snipped

SHRIMP RICE - SURF AND TURF   Serves 3 or 4 as a main course

In a nonstick skillet, over medium heat, heat	[1-1/2 tp	VEGETABLE OIL
When a light haze forms, fry	[6 oz	CHORIZO diced

- When lightly browned and cooked, lift out with slotted spoon. Drain on paper towels.
- Pour out the Fat from skillet, do not rinse.

In heavy saucepan, over medium heat, heat	[1-1/2 TB	VEGETABLE OIL
When a light haze forms, add and sauté	[1/3-cup	YELLOW ONION finely chopped
When the Onion is translucent, add and sauté	[1/2-cup	RED BELL PEPPER diced
	[1/2-cup	GREEN BELL PEPPER diced
When Bell Peppers soften and begin to color, sprinkle	[	SALT, GROUND BLACK PEPPER
Stir in	[1 cup	LONG GRAIN WHITE RICE
Stir to coat the Rice with Oil and add	[	CHICKEN BROTH as per Rice pkg

Bring to a boil, add the CHORIZO. Reduce heat
to low, cover, simmer until the Rice is cooked.

Meanwhile, return to stove the skillet in which Chorizo was cooked. Over medium heat, heat	[1 TB	EXTRA-VIRGIN OLIVE OIL
When a light haze forms, sauté	[1-1/4 cups	RAW SHRIMP bite-size pieces
When the Shrimp turn pink, turn off heat, add	[lightly	SALT, GROUND BLACK PEPPER

Stir the Shrimp with its Oil into the Rice. Cover, let the Rice set for 5-to-10 minutes.

208

SHRIMP - SALONIKI

Serves 2 as an appetizer

In nonstick 8-inch skillet, medium heat, heat	[3 TB	EXTRA-VIRGIN OLIVE OIL
When a light haze forms, sauté	[1 large	RED ONION halved, thinly sliced
When the Onion softens, add	[2-to-4	GARLIC CLOVES mashed, minced

Stir. When Onion turns golden brown, add	[12	COOKED SHRIMP medium size
	[	SALT, GROUND BLACK PEPPER

Reduce heat to low, stir the Shrimp to heat it
and add   [1 or 2 TB   OUZO

Stir until the Ouzo evaporates.

Turn up heat to medium low and add a	[1/2-cup	CRUSHED TOMATOES canned drained
	[1 tp	LEMON JUICE
	[1/4-cup	BLACK OLIVES chopped
	[2 TB	FRESH PARSLEY finely chopped

Stir for 2 minutes and turn off heat.

Spread into 2 individual oven-proof dishes   [thinly sliced   BAGUETTE   fried in a little
EXTRA-VIRGIN OLIVE OIL

Cover it with the SHRIMP MIXTURE. Top with   [plenty of   FETA CHEESE   crumbled

Pass under the broiler until the Feta melts.

SHRIMP - SOUTHAMPTON GRATINÉE

Yields about 3 cups

BUTTER individual oven-proof porcelain shells, or large abalone shells.

Sauté in	[1/2-TB	BUTTER
	[1/2-cup	SLICED MUSHROOMS canned, drained

See "SAUCES". Prepare   [1 cup   SHALLOT MEDIUM WHITE SAUCE

When it thickens and is smooth, turn off heat.

Stir in until melted	[4 TB	CHEDDAR coarse-grated
	[2 TB	PARMESAN grated

Then add the MUSHROOMS and	[1-1/2 cups	COOKED SHRIMP bite-size pieces
	[2 tp	PARSLEY finely chopped
A few drops	[to taste	WORCESTERSHIRE SAUCE
	[	WHITE PEPPER, SALT if needed

Spoon Mixture into the shells.
Can be prepared ahead and refrigerated.

To serve   Bring to room temperature and

sprinkle generously with	[	BREADCRUMBS
Dot with	[	BUTTER tidbits

Pass under the broiler until golden brown.
Serve Immediately.

VARIATIONS   Substitute Shrimp with   [CRAB MEAT, LOBSTER or other SEAFOOD

Substitute Cheddar with   [SWISS CHEESE

SHRIMP STIR-FRY - SORRENTO

Serves 4

In a 10-to-12-inch nonstick skillet,
over medium high heat, heat [1/4-cup   EXTRA-VIRGIN OLIVE OIL
When a light haze forms, sauté [1 cup   ONION   halved and thinly sliced
When it softens, add [1 TB   GARLIC   mashed and minced

When Garlic is fragrant, add [3 or 4   ANCHOVY FILLETS canned, drain

Mash to dissolve the Anchovies. Add [1 cup red   BELL PEPPER   short thin strips
[1 cup yellow   BELL PEPPER   same cut

Sauté Bell Peppers for 1 minute, then add [1 cup sliced   BROCCOLI FLORETS   *al dente*
[1 cup sliced   CAULIFLOWER FLORETS   *al dente*
[1 TB   TINY CAPERS   rinsed, drained
[1/4-cup   CHICKEN BROTH   lightly salted
[1 tp   LEMON JUICE
[1 tp   BALSAMIC VINEGAR
[sprinkle   SALT, GROUND BLACK PEPPER
Stir-fry for 2 minutes.
Add [2 cups   RAW SHRIMP   bite-size pieces
Stir-fry until the Shrimp turn pink.

Turn off heat and mix in [1/4-cup   BLACK OLIVES halved or chopped
[3 TB   FRESH BASIL finely chopped
[to taste   SALT, GROUND BLACK PEPPER
If needed, add a little more Lemon Juice or
Balsamic Vinegar.
Serve immediately with [crunchy   GARLIC BREAD

SHRIMP TACOS - TEX-MEX

Yields about 2 cups

In a skillet, medium high heat, heat [1 TB   EXTRA-VIRGIN OLIVE OIL
When a light haze forms, sauté [1 medium   RED ONION   halved, thinly sliced
[1/2-cup   SHREDDED CARROTS

When the Carrots begin to soften, add [1/2-cup   GREEN BELL PEPPER thin strips
[to taste   JALAPEÑO   minced
[1/8-tp   GROUND CUMIN   or more
[SALT, GROUND BLACK PEPPER
When the Vegetables are tender, yet crunchy,
add [1 cup   COOKED SHRIMP bite-size pieces
Stir to heat the Shrimp. Turn off heat.

Place some VEGETABLE/SHRIMP MIXTURE in [TACO SHELLS
Top with [TOMATO   seeded and diced
[shredded   CHEDDAR or MONTEREY JACK
Sprinkle with [FRESH CILANTRO   finely chopped

VARIATION   Spoon into [TACO SHELLS
[MASHED BEANS
[RED ONION   minced
[COOKED SHRIMP   chopped
[a little   RED SALSA CRUDA
[AVOCADO   diced
[a touch of   SOUR CREAM
Sprinkle with [CHEDDAR   grated

XI

POULTRY

HELPFUL HINTS

Chicken is cooked when internal doneness reaches 185°.

Always add cooked Chicken at the end of a hot preparation.
Do not re-cook Chicken.

To store cooked Chicken:

Wrap it in wax paper or foil. Refrigerate.

Or remove skin and bones. Keep pieces moist in Chicken Broth.

Refrigerate or freeze.

Using a food processor:

Cut cooked Chicken into small pieces.

Process with short pulses until a flaky texture is obtained.

Do not over-process into a paste.

"Poultry is for the cook what canvas is for the painter."

Brillat-Savarin

POULTRY

CHICKEN

DUCK, CHICKEN or TURKEY

TURKEY

CHICKEN

PRE-COOKING PREPARATION   For broiled, grilled or roasted.

In a baking-pan or dish, lay the Chicken, whole or pieces.
Brush it lightly with Vegetable Oil. Sprinkle with Salt, Pepper, any of: Garlic Powder, Spices.
Scrub it all over with wedges of a quartered LEMON. Cooked, it won't have a lemony taste.
Lemon will render the skin crispier.

Wrap the dish in foil. Refrigerate for an hour, longer, or overnight.
Roast in oven preheated to 400°. For Breasts or Thighs with bones, 50 minutes to 1 hour.

Option:	To avoid cooking the Chicken it its Fat, place a grilling rack over the pan. Lay on it the Chicken. Broil or roast. The Fat will run out into the pan.
LEMON CHICKEN	- For a medium size Chicken, prepare a Marinade with 2 TB LEMON JUICE and 2 tp EXTRA-VIRGIN OLIVE OIL. Add Seasonings to taste. - Rub the inside of the Chicken with Lemon. Leave in it 4 Lemon quarters. - Brush the whole Chicken or pieces with the Marinade. Cover, refrigerate.
YOGURT	- Beat in a bowl Plain Yogurt. Add to taste: Salt, Pepper, Spices, Garlic powder or finely chopped Parsley, Basil, Cilantro, or other. - Dip skinned Chicken Breasts into a seasoned Yogurt. Refrigerate for at least 3 hours. Pan-fry in Butter and Vegetable Oil: equal parts.
OTHER	Brush the Chicken with a Creamy Salad Dressing like Honey Mustard. Or mix Honey, Mustard or Lemon, Spices, Curry. Brush the Chicken with it.

CHICKEN in ASPIC   ASPIC see "BASIC RECIPES"

Spread in the mold(s) a first 1/4-inch layer of [ASPIC STOCK made with CHICKEN STOCK

Refrigerate until set.   Arrange on top [slices of STUFFED MANZANILLA OLIVES

Then alternate the STOCK with layers of [ARTICHOKE BOTTOMS   thinly sliced

and [chopped CHICKEN SALAD made with
[MAYONNAISE, CHIVES or ONION,
[PIMIENTOS, PICKLES, seasoned to taste

Leave around the Chicken Salad a little space.
Fill with the Aspic Stock. Finish with a layer of sliced Artichoke Bottoms.

BONELESS BREASTS - SKINNED   Also called SUPRÊMES

POACHED   In a skillet bring to a boil just [enough   WATER   to cover the Suprêmes
Add [1/2-of a   CHICKEN BOUILLON CUBE
(it is salty)

Optional: add [1/4-cup   WHITE WINE
[1 slice   ONION
[a sprig of   PARSLEY, TARRAGON or THYME

Bring to a boil. Add the SUPRÊMES.
Cover, reduce heat to medium low, simmer from 8-to-10 minutes, until tender. Cooking time
depends on thickness. If very thin, less time. Serve cold, with Salads, chopped Chicken Salad.

SAUTÉED   Melt BUTTER in a skillet. Sauté the Suprêmes on both sides until golden brown.
About 6-to-8 minutes until springy to the touch, and the juice is clear.

214

CHICKEN alla CACCIATORA   Hunter Style   (Italy)   _Serves 4_

Dust with FLOUR a	[3 lb	CHICKEN cut into pieces
In a large skillet, brown it on all sides in	[	EXTRA-VIRGIN OLIVE OIL

Remove from skillet. Pour out Fat leaving a
thin film, return to stove, medium heat, add

	[1/3-cup	ONION finely chopped
	[1 tp	GARLIC finely chopped
When it begins to color add	[1 large	GREEN BELL PEPPER diced
	[8 oz	SMALL MUSHROOMS
Stir until lightly browned and add	[1/2-cup	DRY WHITE WINE

Deglaze the skillet, stirring the Wine until

it has reduced by half, then add a	[28 oz-can	CHOPPED TOMATOES with Liquid
	[1/2-tp	DRIED OREGANO + 1 BAY LEAF
	[to taste	SALT, GROUND BLACK PEPPER

- Boil for 2 minutes. Add the CHICKEN, baste.
- Reduce heat to low, cover, simmer until the
  Chicken is done and juice runs clear when
  pierced with a skewer. 30-to-40 minutes.
- Baste occasionally.

Stir in	[2 TB	BLACK OLIVES slivered
	[3 flat	ANCHOVY FILLETS finely chopped

SPEEDY RECIPE   _Serves 2 or 3_

In a nonstick skillet,

medium high heat, heat	[3 TB	EXTRA-VIRGIN OIL
When a light haze forms, add	[1/2-cup	ONION halved and thinly sliced
When Onion softens add	[2 cloves	GARLIC mashed and minced
Mash in	[3 flat	ANCHOVY FILLETS optional
Add	[2 medium	GREEN BELL PEPPERS thin strips
When the Bell Peppers begin to soften, add	[8 oz	SLICED MUSHROOMS
When the Mushrooms begin to brown, add	[1/4--cup	DRY WHITE WINE

Stir until the Wine evaporates by half. Add	[14.5 oz-can	CHOPPED TOMATOES with Liquid
	[1/4-tp	DRIED OREGANO or to taste
	[	SALT, GROUND BLACK PEPPER

Bring to a boil. Cover, reduce heat to low.
Simmer until the Sauce thickens. About
15-to-20 minutes.

Lay in a heated oven dish [the pieces of a cooked ROTISSERIE CHICKEN

Top with the Vegetables and Sauce. Cover with foil. Keep warm in oven until ready to serve.

CHICKEN CREOLE   _Serves 2_

In a nonstick skillet, over medium heat, heat	[2 TB	VEGETABLE OIL
When a light haze forms, sauté	[1/3-cup	ONION chop into small pieces
When it softens, add	[2 cloves	GARLIC mashed and minced
When Onion is translucent, add	[1/3-cup	CELERY sliced 1/4-inch thick
When Celery begins to soften, add	[1/2-cup	GREEN BELL PEPPER large dice
Stir for 2 minutes and add	[1 cup	CHOPPED TOMATOES canned with liquid
	[1 TB	PARSLEY finely chopped
	[1/4-tp	CREOLE SEASONING or to taste
	[to taste	SALT, GROUND BLACK PEPPER

Bring to a boil, reduce heat to low.
Cover, simmer 20 minutes until the Sauce thickens. Serve over pieces of roasted CHICKEN.

CHICKEN CRÊPES

EXCELSIOR

Filling yields about 2-1/4 cups   CRÊPES see "BASIC RECIPES"

In a nonstick skillet, medium high heat, heat	[1 TB	BUTTER
Brown	[8 oz	ONION chopped not too finely
Turn off heat and mix in	[1/4-cup	GOLDEN RAISINS
	[2 TB	PECANS chopped
	[1 TB	FRESH GINGER grated
	[1 TB	PLUM SAUCE
	[1-1/4 cups	COOKED CHICKEN coarsely chopped in processor
In a bowl, mash	[4 TB	MASCARPONE room temperature
with	[3 oz	CREAM CHEESE
Stir in the CHICKEN MIXTURE and add	[	SALT, GROUND BLACK PEPPER

Cover the surface with plastic wrap. Refrigerate. Fill the Crêpes. Cover the dish with foil.
Refrigerate. Bring to room temperature. Warm in oven preheated to 300° for 15 minutes.

NAPOLI

Filling yields about 2-1/4 cups

In a nonstick skillet, medium high heat, heat	[1 TB	EXTRA-VIRGIN OLIVE OIL
Sauté	[1/4-cup	ONION finely chopped
When Onion is translucent, add	[1/2-cup	GREEN BELL PEPPER diced
When Bell Pepper softens, add	[4 oz raw	ITALIAN SAUSAGE remove from casing

Stir to crumble meat lumps. When browned,
tilt the skillet to remove the Fat. Soak up
remaining Fat with a paper towel.

Add	[1/4-cup	TOMATO or MARINARA SAUCE
	[1 TB	PARSLEY finely chopped
Stir to heat the Sauce. Turn off heat, add	[3/4-cup	COOKED CHICKEN coarsely chopped in processor
In a bowl mix CHICKEN SAUSAGE with	[2 TB	MASCARPONE
	[1/4-cup	PARMESAN grated
	[1/4-cup	MOZZARELLA coarse-grated
	[to taste	GROUND BLACK PEPPER

Cover the surface with plastic wrap.
Refrigerate. Warm the Crêpes as above.

To serve Spoon over the Crêpes	[	TOMATO or MARINARA SAUCE
Sprinkle with	[	PARMESAN grated

PEKING STYLE

Use ready-made PANCAKE CRÊPES found in Asian markets. Heat according to package directions.

Arrange in separate dishes [	SCALLIONS cut longwise into thin strips
[	PERSIAN CUCUMBER long thin strips
[	CRISPY BACON STRIPS
[	CHICKEN strips, wrap in foil, warm in oven
[	PLUM SAUCE

Place Ingredients horizontally on Crêpes.
Fold in left flap. Fold over bottom flap, roll up. Pick up with fingers, and enjoy.

216

CHICKEN CROQUETTES - BÉCHAMEL BASE   *Yields about 3-1/4 cups*

See "SAUCES". Prepare a	[	VERY THICK BÉCHAMEL
with	[4 TB	BUTTER
	[4 TB	FLOUR mixed with
	[1/4-tp	DRY MUSTARD
	[1-1/4 cups	MILK
	[to taste	SALT, GROUND BLACK PEPPER

Stir until the Sauce becomes very thick.

Beat	[1 whole	EGG + 2 EGG YOLKS
Add and beat in	[2 TB of	the hot Sauce

Reduce heat to low.
Whisk the Eggs into the Sauce until blended.

Add	[4 TB	PARMESAN grated
Stir until melted. Add	[1/8-tp	GROUND NUTMEG
	[1-3/4 cups	COOKED CHICKEN finely chopped in processor

Stir until the Mixture separates from the skillet, like dough.
Transfer to a buttered dish. Spread lightly. Cover with plastic wrap to prevent skin from forming.
Refrigerate. Shape and fry Croquettes following directions in "BASIC RECIPES".

Serve hot as hors-d'oeuvre   -   Sprinkle with grated PARMESAN.
As an appetizer or light lunch   -   Form larger Croquettes, or flat cakes. Serve with a Salad.

CHICKEN - CROUSTADES BARBECUE BÉCHAMEL

See "SAUCES". Prepare a	[	CHEESE VELOUTÉ WHITE SAUCE
with	[	CHEDDAR
Stir in to taste	[	BARBECUE SAUCE
Place in individual oven-proof dishes	[	CROUSTADES (see "SANDWICHES)
Top with	[	CHICKEN or TURKEY
Cover with the SAUCE and	[	CHEDDAR shredded

Pass under the broiler until the Cheddar melts and turns golden.

CHICKEN - CURRIED with POTATOES   *Serves 2*

In a nonstick skillet, over medium heat, heat	[2 TB	VEGETABLE OIL
When a light haze forms, sauté	[1/2-cup	ONION coarsely chopped
Sprinkle	[1 tp	CURRY POWDER or to taste

When Onion turns golden brown, reduce heat
to low and stir in

	[1 cup	COOKED CHICKEN bite-size
	[1 TB	PINE NUTS toasted
	[a dash	GROUND CINNAMON
	[2 TB	RAISINS

Stir to heat the Chicken. Turn off heat.

Add	[1/3-cup	PLAIN YOGURT optional
Serve over	[sliced	BOILED POTATOES or PANCAKES
Condiments	[	shredded COCONUT, CHUTNEY, BANANAS

CHICKEN CURRY with VEGETABLES   *Yields about 6 cups*

In a nonstick skillet, medium high heat, heat	[2 TB	VEGETABLE OIL
Sauté	[1/2-cup	ONION (Garlic to taste)
When Onion is translucent, add any of	[2 cups	blanched CARROTS, BROCCOLI, CAULIFLOWER, other
When the Vegetables are cooked, stir in	[2 cups	COOKED CHICKEN bite-size
Add	[2 cups of	CURRY SAUCE (see "SAUCES")
Stir to heat through.		
Serve with	[	BROWN RICE and CONDIMENTS

CHICKEN HASH with LETTUCE   *Yields about 1-1/2 cups*

In a nonstick skillet, over medium heat, heat	[1 TB	VEGETABLE OIL
When a light haze forms, sauté	[1/3-cup	ONION finely chopped
When Onion is translucent, add	[1/3-cup	GREEN BELL PEPPER finely diced
Cook Bell Pepper "al dente". Stir in to warm	[1 cup	CHICKEN finely diced or chopped
	[to taste	GINGER grated
	[	GROUND BLACK PEPPER, SALT
Serve in separate dishes the CHICKEN HASH	[	ICEBERG LETTUCE LEAVES
	[	FRESH MINT LEAVES
	[	PLUM SAUCE

Spoon the Hash on a Lettuce Leaf.
Add the Mint, Plum Sauce, roll, pick up with your fingers, enjoy.

CHICKEN - LEMON MAYONNAISE

Mix	[4 TB	MAYONNAISE ready-made	Spread	[	CHICKEN BREASTS skinned
	[1 tp	EXTRA-VIRGIN OLIVE OIL	with	[	the MAYONNAISE
	[1 TB	LEMON JUICE	Garnish with	[	HARD-COOKED EGGS
	[2 tp	FRESH DILL snipped		[	BLACK OLIVES

CHICKEN - MATADOR   *Sauce yields about 2-1/2 cups*

In a nonstick skillet, medium high heat, heat	[3 TB	EXTRA-VIRGIN OLIVE OIL
When a light haze forms sauté	[1 cup	ONION slice 1/4-inch thick, chop
When the Onion softens, add	[3 cloves	GARLIC minced
When the Garlic is fragrant, stir in	[to taste	HOT CHILI seeded, minced, or DRIED CHILI
When the Onion begins to color add	[1/2-cup	DRY WHITE WINE
Stir until the Wine has reduced by half. Add	[12-to-16 oz	DICED TOMATOES canned, with their Liquid
Reduce heat to medium low, simmer until the Tomatoes melt into a thick Sauce. Add	[1/4-tp	GROUND CUMIN or to taste
Adjust SEASONINGS, add	[3 TB	FLAT LEAF PARSLEY finely chop
See "VEGETABLES" - BELL PEPPERS. Stir in	[1/2-cup	RED ROASTED BELL PEPPERS coarsely chopped
Add	[cut up pieces of a ROASTED CHICKEN (warm)	

Turn off heat. Cover, let flavors blend.

218

CHICKEN in PUFF PASTRY SHELLS   *Filling about 1/3-cup per Shell*

In a nonstick skillet, over medium heat, heat	[1 TB	BUTTER + 1 tp VEGETABLE OIL
When it sizzles, sauté	[2 TB	ONION finely chopped
When the Onion is translucent add and sauté	[1/2-cup	SLICED MUSHROOMS canned, drained
Sauté the Mushrooms for 1 minute and add	[1-1/4 cups	COOKED CHICKEN diced
	[a dash	NUTMEG grated

Set aside, cover.

See "SAUCES". Prepare a	[	BÉCHAMEL for PUFF PASTRY SHELL FILLINGS

When the Sauce thickens and is smooth, turn off heat and stir in until melted	[3 TB	SWISS CHEESE coarse-grated
	[2 TB	PARMESAN, WHITE PEPPER

Turn off heat. Add CHICKEN / MUSHROOMS.
Adjust Seasonings. Let cool.
Cover the surface with plastic wrap, refrigerate.

Bake according to package directions	[1 pkg	PUFF PASTRY SHELLS 6 Shells

1.   - A HELPFUL HINT: preheat oven to 400°, reduce heat to 350°, Shells will bake better.
     - When they turn golden, take them out. Remove the lids with a fork and set aside.
     - Scoop out with a fork the inside uncooked dough, discard it. Return to oven 4 minutes.
     - Take Shells out and arrange them in an oven-proof serving dish.

2.   - Heat well the CHICKEN MIXTURE. It must be hot, but not boiling.
     - With a soup spoon fill the Shells, separating Chicken / Mushrooms from excess Sauce.
     - Divide the Filling evenly into the Shells, then add more Sauce, as needed to fill them.
     - Overfill slightly, place the lids on top, allowing the Filling to partially show.
     - Filled Shells can be kept in a <u>warm</u> oven 5-to-10 minutes. If longer, they'll get soggy.

VARIATION - Substitute Chicken with Ham, Turkey, a mixture of both. Add Bacon or Prosciutto.

CHICKEN RISOTTO alla CARBONARA   *Serves 2*

In a small saucepan, moisten with Broth	[1 cup	COOKED CHICKEN small pieces
Fry soft	[3 strips	BACON chopped into small pieces

Drain on a paper towel.

Simmer	[3 cups	CHICKEN BROTH lightly salted (+ 1/4-cup if needed)

In an 8-inch heavy skillet, medium heat, heat	[1-1/2 TB	BUTTER + 2 tp VEGETABLE OIL
When it sizzles, sauté	[1/4-cup	ONION minced
When Onion begins to color, add	[3/4-cup	ARBORIO RICE

- Stir until the grains are coated and glisten.
- Add <u>one ladle</u> (1/2-cup) at a time of BROTH.

- When 3 cups have been absorbed, the Rice
  should be tender but firm and creamy.

Turn off heat and mix in	[1	EGG beaten with 1-1/2 TB LIGHT CREAM

With slotted spoon lift CHICKEN from Broth.

Stir it into the Risotto with the BACON. Mix in	[1 TB	BUTTER diced small
	[2 TB	PARMESAN, adjust Seasonings

CHICKEN SCALOPPINE

VEAL SCALOPPINE see "MEATS"

SKINNED CHICKEN BREASTS - Pound flat and cook as in Veal Scaloppine. Use the same Sauces.

CHICKEN PAILLARD (páh-yáhr) is simply grilled Chicken Scaloppine.
They can be first brushed with a Marinade, then grilled, or left to marinate for a while.

CHICKEN SCALOPPINE - VIA VENETO   *Serves 2*

Drench in	[	FLOUR	
	[2 or 4	SCALOPPINE depending on size	

Shake off excess, set aside.

Brown in	[1 TB	BUTTER
	[1 cup	ONION

Set Onions on a plate.

Add to the skillet	[1 TB	BUTTER

When it sizzles, sauté the Scaloppine until
done and still juicy.
Place them in a sprayed oven dish and top
with the ONIONS.

Cover with	[chopped	PROSCIUTTO
Top Prosciutto with	[shredded	MOZZARELLA

Pass under the broiler until the Cheese melts, do not brown it. Serve with a Salad or Pasta.

CHICKEN - AVGOLEMONO SOUP   Egg Lemon (Greece)   *Serves 4*

Bring to a boil	[4 cups	CHICKEN BROTH
When the Broth begins to boil add	[1/2-cup	UNCOOKED WHITE RICE

Reduce heat to low. Cover, simmer until the
Rice is cooked. Can be prepared ahead.

To serve   Heat well the Soup. Remove from
heat.

In a bowl beat with a fork	[2	EGG YOLKS
with	[1 TB	WATER
When frothy, add	[2 TB	LEMON JUICE

Beat for 1 minute.
Add 1 TB of hot BROTH. Continue beating, add 2 TB of Broth, then gradually a 1/2-cup.
Pour gradually beaten Yolks into the SOUP, stirring with a wooden spoon, until it thickens.
Return to very low heat and stir for 2 minutes. Do not let the Soup boil.

Adjust Seasonings. Add	[	COOKED CHICKEN bite-size pieces

Serve immediately.

CHICKEN in ONION SOUP GRATINÉE

See "VEGETABLES" - ONION	[	ONION SOUP GRATINÉE

Place on the bottom of the oven-proof soup
bowls the toasted BAGUETTE slices.

Top with	[	CHICKEN or TURKEY bite-size pieces

Add the ONION SOUP.
Top with the Baguette slices and Cheese. Pass under the broiler.

220

CHICKEN SOUP with VEGETABLES and TORTELLINI

One of my favorite soups for a casual cold winter evening. It can serve a wide number of guests.

QUANTITIES   Measure the capacity of your soup bowls and multiply it by the number of people you plan to serve. Doubling for seconds. This is a meal.

Per serving   1/2-cup BROTH + 3/4-to 1 cup VEGETABLES + PASTA + CHICKEN.

BROTH   Plan EXTRA BROTH to add more, if needed, when the Soup is ready.
Prepare it one or two days ahead. See "BASIC RECIPES".
It must be strained. Then refrigerated, and de-greased when cold.

The Broth needs a light garlicky taste. GARLIC CLOVES can be added when making the Broth, and removed when the Broth is strained. Or use GARLIC POWDER to taste. Use it with ready-made Chicken Broth.

VEGETABLES   It isn't necessary to use all the Vegetables in this recipe, but the more variety the better. Nor is it necessary to use equal amounts.
What's essential is that there should be more INGREDIENTS than Broth.
Cut the Vegetables into bite-size, keep in mind that some will reduce when cooked. Do not overcook. THEY MUST REMAIN CRUNCHY.
Pare, wash, string, slice, all Vegetables. Refrigerate until ready to cook.

PASTA   Cook it separately. Add it to the Soup before serving.

Serves 6

THE SOUP   Add 1-1/2 extra cups of Broth to allow for evaporation during the cooking.

In a stockpot, bring to a boil	[8-1/2 cups	CHICKEN BROTH seasoned
When the Broth begins to boil, add	[1 cup	CARROTS sliced 1/4-inch thick
	[1 cup	CELERY 1/2-inch slices
	[1-1/2 cups	LEEKS cut into 1/2-inch slices
Bring to a boil for 4 minutes.		
Add	[1-1/2 cups	BROCCOLI FLORETS sliced or bite-size
	[1-1/2 cups	CAULIFLOWER FLORETS cut the same
Bring to a boil for 3 minutes then add	[1-1/2 cups	SNOW PEAS
Boil for 2 minutes then add	[1-1/2 cups	SLICED MUSHROOMS
	[1 cup	BEAN SPROUTS
Boil for 1 minute. Turn off heat, add	[3 cups	COOKED CHICKEN cut into small pieces
	[adjust	SALT and GROUND BLACK PEPPER
Meanwhile, time and cook *al dente*	[	CHEESE TORTELLINI 6 per serving
		(or more)

Add TORTELLINI. If the Soup needs
more BROTH, have some simmering.
Serve in a tureen.

On the side   [GARLIC BREAD

VARIATIONS - It can just be a Vegetable and Tortellini Soup without Chicken.
          - For a VEGETABLE/SEAFOOD SOUP combine CHICKEN and FISH BROTH.

When Vegetables are ready add [any of   raw SHRIMP, SCALLOPS, shucked CLAMS, shucked OYSTERS, MUSSELS
They will cook fast in the simmering Soup.
Serve with crusty BAGUETTE and AÏOLI ("SAUCES") or ROUILLE (see FISH - BOUILLABAISSE).

221

CHICKEN STIR-FRY in PHYLLO NESTS

PHYLLO see
"BASIC RECIPES"

Stir-fry yields about 4-1/2 cups.

In a skillet or wok, medium high heat, heat	[2 TB	VEGETABLE OIL
Stir-fry to light golden	[1 or 2	GARLIC CLOVES mashed
Discard Garlic. Add and stir-fry	[1/2-cup	ONION slice 1/4-inch thick, dice
When Onion is translucent add	[1 cup	FRESH SNOW PEAS
	[1/4-cup	CELERY diced
	[1 cup	RED BELL PEPPER thin strips
When Vegetables are cooked "crunchy", add	[1 cup	BEAN SPROUTS
	[1 cup	SLICED MUSHROOMS
Stir-fry for 3 minutes. Turn off heat and add	[1-1/2 cups	COOKED CHICKEN bite-size
Stir to heat the Chicken, add a Sauce	[any of	SOY, DUCK, PLUM, SWEET/SOUR
	[to taste	FRESH GINGER grated
To serve	Spoon the stir-fry into [	PHYLLO NESTS

CHICKEN with TARTARE BÉCHAMEL

Yields about 1-1/4 cups
Also serve with Fish.

Combine in a bowl	[4 flat TB	MAYONNAISE
	[1 tp	CAPERS rinsed, drained, minced
	[1/4-tp	DRIED TARRAGON crumbled
	[1 tp	PARSLEY finely chopped
	[1 tp	ONION grated
	[1 tp	CORNICHONS minced
See "SAUCES". Prepare	[1 cup	THIN WHITE SAUCE

When ready, over low heat, mix in MAYONNAISE MIXTURE. Stir until hot. Turn off heat.
Adjust Seasonings. Serve immediately over CHICKEN BREASTS and STEAMED VEGETABLES.

CHICKEN TEX-MEX - QUESADILLAS Toasted Tortilla Sandwiches

Mix in equal amounts	[	MONTEREY JACK shredded
and	[	CHEDDAR (mild or sharp) shredded
		Use 4 TB of Cheese Mixture per Tortilla.
Leaving a 1/2-inch around the edge, with a pastry brush spread thinly over	[	FLOUR or CORN TORTILLAS
	[	TOMATO SAUCE with a dash of TABASCO
	or HOT SALSA	
Spread over one half of the Tortilla the CHEESE MIXTURE and top with	[	CHICKEN tidbits
	[	PICKLED JALAPEÑO minced, optional

Fold the Tortilla, press the edges to seal it.
Heat, over medium heat, a greased nonstick skillet. Or use a griddle.
Toast the Quesadillas for 1 minute on each side. Serve immediately, with Salsa.

As an Hors-d'oeuvre   -   Cut Quesadillas in half, or in wedges. Serve with SALSA.

VARIATION   -   Substitute Chicken with TURKEY, HAM or SHRIMP.

222

CHICKEN with TURNIP GREENS   Middle Eastern Style   *Serves 2*

Simmer	[1/2-cup	CHICKEN BROTH
In a 7-inch skillet, medium heat, heat	[1/2-TB	BUTTER
	[1/2-TB	MARGARINE it prevents Butter from burning
When it sizzles, sauté	[1-1/2 tp	GARLIC minced

Stir with a wooden spoon. Do not brown.

After 3 minutes, stir in with the Garlic	[1-1/2 tp	GROUND CORIANDER

Keep stirring and sauté for 2 more minutes.
Carefully pour into the skillet the 1/2-cup of
Chicken Broth. Stand back, it will splatter.
Keep stirring.

As soon as the Broth comes to a boil, add a	[10 oz-can	TURNIP or MUSTARD GREENS with their Liquid

Stir, bring the Greens to a boil. Cover.
Reduce heat to low, simmer for 10 minutes.

Add	[to taste	SALT, GROUND BLACK PEPPER
To serve Over low heat, add to Greens	[1 cup	COOKED CHICKEN bite-size (or more)
Stir to heat the Chicken. Turn off heat, add	[1/4-tp	LEMON JUICE or more to taste
Serve over	[	WHITE RICE
On the side	[minced	RED ONION sprinkle some over individual servings

NOTE   - Greens can be prepared ahead of time, warmed before serving.
         - A Middle Eastern soup "Molokhia" is prepared with this flavor. See "VEGETABLES".

CHICKEN in WHITE WINE CREAM SAUCE   *Serves 2*

In a nonstick skillet, over medium heat, heat	[1-1/2 TB	BUTTER
When it sizzles, sauté	[1 TB	SHALLOTS finely chopped
When Shallots turn golden, add	[4 oz	SLICED MUSHROOMS
		or MORELS (see "MUSHROOMS")

Sauté the Mushrooms until tender browned and stir in	[1 cup	COOKED CHICKEN bite-size
Turn off heat, add	[to taste	SALT, GROUND BLACK PEPPER

Cover to keep warm

See "SAUCES". Prepare a	[	WHITE WINE CREAM SAUCE

When it thickens mix in the Mushrooms and
Chicken.

Serve over	[	WHITE RICE

VARIATION I   - Omit adding the Chicken to the Sauce.

Serve the Sauce with Mushrooms over	[	WHITE RICE and SUPRÊMES sautéed or poached

VARIATION II   - Omit Mushrooms. Serve the SAUCE over White Rice and Suprêmes.

223

DUCK on PANCAKES

Duck can be substituted with CHICKEN or TURKEY.

APPLE SAUCE

Heat	[1 TB	BUTTER + 1 tp VEGETABLE OIL
When it sizzles, sauté	[2 TB	ONION finely chopped
When Onion is translucent, stir in	[1/2-cup	APPLES diced
When Apples soften and begin to brown, add	[1/2-cup	APPLE SAUCE
	[to taste	GROUND CINNAMON

Stir to heat the Sauce through.

Top	[	PANCAKES
with	[	DUCK thinly sliced
Sprinkle with	[	CHEDDAR coarse-grated
Top with	[	hot Apple Sauce

CRANBERRY JALAPEÑO

Heat	[	VEGETABLE OIL
Brown	[	YELLOW ONIONS thinly sliced
Sprinkle with	[	SALT, PEPPER, GROUND CUMIN

Spread browned Onions over	[	PANCAKES
Top with	[	DUCK thinly sliced
And	[	CRANBERRY JALAPEÑO SAUCE *

CRANBERRY ORANGE

Top	[	PANCAKES
with	[	BRIE or CAMEMBERT thinly sliced pieces

Place in oven preheated to 350° until the Cheese melts.

Top with	[	DUCK thinly sliced
And	[	CRANBERRY ORANGE SAUCE *

CRANBERRY TARRAGON

Heat	[	BUTTER
Sauté	[	SHALLOT finely chopped
When it softens, add	[	FROZEN FRENCH CUT GREEN BEANS
	[	SLIVERED ALMONDS
Sauté until Beans are tender crunchy. Add	[	SALT and GROUND BLACK PEPPER

Spread GREEN BEANS over	[	PANCAKES or TOAST
Top them with	[	DUCK thinly sliced
Spread lightly over it	[	CRANBERRY TARRAGON SAUCE *

* See "SAUCES" - SWEET SAUCES)

SWEET and SOUR SAUCE

Version I

Heat	[	SWEET and SOUR SAUCE
Mix in	[	GOLDEN RAISINS
	[	PECANS or WALNUTS chopped

Top	[	PANCAKES
with	[	AVOCADO
	[	GINGER grated
	[	DUCK thinly sliced
	[	hot SWEET and SOUR SAUCE

Version II

In	[	BUTTER
Brown until tender	[	APPLE thin wedges

Heat	[	SWEET and SOUR SAUCE
Add	[	SCALLIONS minced
	[	SESAME SEEDS toasted

Top	[	PANCAKES with Apples
	[	DUCK thinly sliced
	[	SWEET and SOUR SAUCE

DUCK, CHICKEN or TURKEY

SAUERKRAUT   *Serves 2 as a main course, amounts are flexible*

Soak in water	[10	DRIED APRICOTS

Pat dry, cut in half or quarters.

Heat, following package directions	[1 cup	SAUERKRAUT pre-cooked
Substitute Sauerkraut Liquid with any of	[optional	BEER, CHAMPAGNE, WHITE WINE
Add	[to taste	BLACK PEPPERCORNS
	[	Soaked Apricots
	[2 TB	GOLDEN RAISINS
When Sauerkraut is ready, stir in	[2 oz	COOKED SAUSAGE sliced
	[1 cup	DUCK or TURKEY bite-size pieces
	[optional	GROUND BLACK PEPPER

Simmer for 3 minutes.

Serve with	[boiled	NEW POTATOES

STIR-FRY - ASIAN   *Serves 2*

Heat a wok or skillet and swirl in it	[2 TB	VEGETABLE OIL
Over high heat stir-fry for 1 minute	[1 medium	ONION coarsely chopped
Add	[1 medium	RED BELL PEPPER thin strips
	[4	WATER CHESTNUTS sliced
Stir-fry for 2 minutes and add	[1-1/4 cups	BEAN SPROUTS
Optional	[	HOT RED or GREEN CHILI minced

Stir-fry for 2 minutes.

Mix in	[to taste	CASHEWS or PEANUTS
Add bite-size pieces of	[	DUCK, CHICKEN or TURKEY
Stir to heat. Season with	[any of	SOY, PLUM or DUCK SAUCE

Serve with Cellophane Noodles, Rice, Angel Hair Pasta.

STIR-FRY - COLE SLAW   *Yields about 5 cups, amounts are flexible*

Heat a wok or skillet and swirl in it	[3 TB	VEGETABLE OIL
Stir-fry	[1 medium	ONION halved, thinly sliced
When Onion is translucent, add	[1-1/2 cups	COLE SLAW
	[1 medium	GREEN BELL PEPPER thin strips
	[1 medium	RED BELL PEPPER thin strips
	[1 medium	RED APPLE diced
	[1/2-cup	CELERY thinly sliced
Sprinkle	[1 TB	RED WINE VINEGAR
		or RICE WINE VINEGAR

Stir-fry Vegetables *al dente*.

Sprinkle	[	SALT, GROUND BLACK PEPPER
Mix in	[1-1/2 cups	DUCK, CHICKEN or TURKEY
	[3 TB	RAISINS
	[1/4-cup	SPICY PECANS
	[to taste	GINGER grated
	[	SOY SAUCE
Serve with	[	WILD RICE

TURKEY

Also substitute Turkey with CHICKEN in the following recipes.

TURKEY - ALFREDO
Serves 2

Heat and add to [2/3-cup   ALFREDO SAUCE   ready-made
[1 cup   TURKEY   cut into small pieces
[2 TB   PINE NUTS   toasted

Toss into [3 or 4 oz   FETTUCCINI

TURKEY - ARTICHOKE HEARTS
Serves 2

See "FISH" - ARTICHOKE HEARTS.   Prepare [ARTICHOKE HEARTS the same way

When Artichokes are ready, stir in [SLICED MUSHROOMS small can, drained

Serve over [sliced TURKEY and WHITE RICE

TURKEY - CHILI CREAM SAUCE
Serves 3 or 4

See "SAUCES".   Prepare [1 cup   VELOUTÉ WHITE SAUCE
Add [to taste   CHILI SAUCE
[GROUND CUMIN
[2 TB   GOLDEN RAISINS
[1 tp   PARSLEY minced

Serve [TURKEY or SMOKED TURKEY
over [MASHED POTATOES
Top with [CHILI CREAM SAUCE

TURKEY - ENCHILADAS
Filling yields about 2-1/2 cups

In a nonstick skillet, over medium heat, heat [2 TB   VEGETABLE OIL
When a light haze forms, sauté [1 clove   GARLIC   mashed
When fragrant, discard Garlic and add [1/2-cup   ONION finely chopped
When Onion turns golden, add [3/4-cup   TOMATO SAUCE
When it bubbles, add [to taste   HOT CHILI PASTE   optional

Stir for 2 minutes and add [1-1/2 cups   TURKEY shredded
[to taste   GROUND CUMIN, SALT if needed

Stir to heat through. Turn off heat.

In a skillet, one at a time, soften [TORTILLAS   for 10 seconds on
each side

Spoon Turkey Mixture on Tortillas.   Sprinkle [a little   CHEDDAR   shredded
[diced   AVOCADO

Roll Tortillas into cylinders.
Place them in a sprayed oven-proof dish,
seam side down, side-by-side.

Top them with a [CHEDDAR VELOUTÉ WHITE SAUCE
(See "SAUCES")

Warm in oven preheated to 350°.

226

TURKEY - FLORENTINE

Arrange in a sprayed oven-proof dish	[	sliced	BOILED or BAKED YAMS
Sprinkle with	[		CAYENNE PEPPER
Top with	[	sliced	TURKEY
Top with plenty of	[	shredded	CHEDDAR
Cover with hot	[		CREAMED SPINACH

Cover with foil.
Warm in 300° oven for 10 minutes.

Top with	[	sliced	HARD-COOKED EGGS

TURKEY and GREEN LENTILS with MINT

See "VEGETABLES" - LENTILS.

Sprinkle	[		GREEN LENTILS
with	[		FRESH MINT finely chopped
and	[	crumbled	FETA CHEESE
Top with	[	sliced	TURKEY
	[		TOMATOES seeded and diced

TURKEY HASH - PARMENTIER   *Serves 2*

Mix	[	2 cups	MASHED POTATOES
	[	2 TB	MELTED BUTTER
	[	to taste	HORSERADISH prepared
In a nonstick skillet, over medium heat, heat	[	1 TB	VEGETABLE OIL
Sauté	[	4 TB	ONION minced
When Onion is translucent, add	[	8 oz	SAUSAGE MEAT casing removed

Break up lumps and stir until the Meat is
cooked and slightly browned.

Mix in	[	1-1/2 cups	COOKED TURKEY chopped

Spread MIXTURE in sprayed baking dish and

top with	[		the Mashed Potatoes
Cover with	[		BREADCRUMBS
Sprinkle with	[		PARMESAN grated
Dot with	[		BUTTER bits

Bake for 15 minutes in oven preheated to 350°. Pass under the broiler.
Optional, top with Fried or Poached Eggs, for a hearty brunch.

TURKEY and MUSHROOMS in CREAM SAUCE   *Serves 2*

In a nonstick skillet, over medium heat, heat	[	1-1/2 TB	BUTTER
When it sizzles, sauté	[	1 TB	SHALLOT finely chopped
When Shallot softens, add and sauté	[	4 oz	SLICED MUSHROOMS
Then sprinkle	[		SALT, GROUND BLACK PEPPER
See "SAUCES". Prepare a	[		VELOUTÉ WHITE SAUCE
using	[	1/2-cup	HEAVY CREAM + 1/2-cup MILK
Stir in	[	1/4-cup	PARMESAN grated
Add the MUSHROOMS to the Sauce and	[	1-1/4 cups	TURKEY bite-size pieces
	[		GROUND BLACK PEPPER, SALT

Toss into PASTA or serve over MASHED POTATOES.

TURKEY on PANCAKES, TOAST or ENGLISH MUFFINS

Place Ingredients in the order listed.

APPLES

[APPLE slices, sauté in BUTTER
[GROUND CINNAMON
[TURKEY
[APPLE SAUCE ready-made

CREAMED CORN

[AVOCADO thinly sliced
[TURKEY
[CRISPY BACON strips
[CREAMED CORN

CREAMED PEARL ONIONS

[PROSCIUTTO
[TURKEY
[CREAMED PEARL ONIONS
[CHIVES

CREOLE SAUCE *

[TURKEY
[CRISPY BACON STRIPS
[FRIED EGG
[CREOLE SAUCE

* See "SAUCES" - Serve Sauces hot.

HORSERADISH VELOUTÉ

[ONIONS caramelized
[TURKEY
[Add HORSERADISH to VELOUTÉ BÉCHAMEL*
[CHIVES

MASCARPONE VELOUTÉ

[TURKEY
[ASPARAGUS TIPS
[HARD-COOKED EGGS ,chopped
[MASCARPONE VELOUTÉ BÉCHAMEL *

MUSHROOMS - CHEDDAR

[MUSHROOMS sautéed with ONIONS
[TURKEY
[PICKLED JALAPEÑOS minced
[Add CHEDDAR to VELOUTÉ BÉCHAMEL *

SOUR CREAM - CRANBERRY

[AVOCADO thinly sliced
[TURKEY
[CRANBERRY SAUCE heat and mix with
[SOUR CREAM

TURKEY - PASTA alla PARMIGIANA   *Serves 4 as a main course*

Cook *al dente*	[5 oz	ELBOW PASTA drain, let cool in a colander
In a nonstick skillet, over medium heat, heat	[1 TB	BUTTER
When it sizzles, sauté	[2 TB	ONION finely chopped
When translucent, add and sauté until tender	[4 oz sliced	CREMINI MUSHROOMS or other
Mix in a bowl the PASTA, MUSHROOMS, and	[1-1/2 cups	TURKEY cut into small pieces

Spread MIXTURE in a sprayed 8 x 8 oven-dish.

See "SAUCES". Prepare	[1-1/2 cups	MEDIUM WHITE SAUCE
When it thickens, turn off heat and stir in	[2 TB	SWISS CHEESE coarse-grated
	[1/4-cup	PARMESAN grated
	[to taste	SALT and WHITE PEPPER
	[a dash	NUTMEG grated

Pour evenly 3/4-of the Sauce over PASTA.
Let it seep through and set for 10 minutes.
Cover with the remaining Sauce.

Mix	[3 TB	BREADCRUMBS
	[4 TB	PARMESAN grated
	[2 tp	MELTED BUTTER

Spread Breadcrumb Mixture over the Pasta.
Bake in oven preheated to 375° for 15 minutes. Pass under the broiler to brown the top.

TURKEY RISOTTO - PRIMAVERA   RISOTTO see "BASIC RECIPES"

Serves 2 as a main course. For larger Rice portions use the 1 cup amounts. Increase Vegetables.

In a saucepan, simmer	[3 cups	CHICKEN BROTH lightly salted (+ 1/4-cup if needed)
In a 10-inch nonstick heavy skillet, over medium heat, heat	[2 TB	BUTTER + 1 TB VEGETABLE OIL
When it sizzles, sauté	[1/4-cup	ONION finely chopped
When Onion is soft and translucent, add	[1/2-cup	ZUCCHINI quartered lengthwise and diced
Sauté the Zucchini for 3 minutes then stir in	[1/2-cup	ASPARAGUS *al dente,* slant-cut into 1/2-inch pieces
Stir for 3 minutes. Sprinkle with	[	SALT, GROUND BLACK -PEPPER
Add	[3/4-cup	ARBORIO RICE
Stir until grains are coated and glisten. Add	[1/4-cup	DRY WHITE WINE

Stir until the Wine evaporates.
Add one ladle (1/2-cup) at a time of BROTH.

When 2 cups have been absorbed, stir in	[1/2-cup	FROZEN GREEN PEAS thawed

When 3 cups of Broth have been absorbed,
the Rice should be tender but firm, creamy.
Turn off heat.

Stir in	[1 TB	BUTTER diced small
	[1 cup	TURKEY cut into small pieces
	[1 TB	MASCARPONE optional
	[2 TB	PARMESAN grated, or more
	[to taste	GROUND BLACK PEPPER, SALT

Cover, let set 5 minutes.

Serve on the side	[	PARMESAN grated

TURKEY RISOTTO al PESTO   RISOTTO see "BASIC RECIPES"

Serves 2 as a main course. For larger Rice portions use the 1 cup amounts.

In a saucepan, simmer	[3 cups	CHICKEN BROTH lightly salted (+ 1/4-cup if needed)
In an 8-inch nonstick heavy skillet, over medium heat, heat	[1-1/2 TB	BUTTER + 2 tp VEGETABLE OIL
When it sizzles, sauté	[2 TB	SHALLOTS finely chopped
When Shallots begin to color, add	[3/4-cup	ARBORIO RICE

- Stir until grains are coated and glisten.
- Add one ladle (1/2-cup) at a time of BROTH.

When 2 cups have been absorbed, stir in	[4 TB	PESTO SAUCE ready-made, or more to taste

When 3 cups have been absorbed, the Rice
should be tender but firm, creamy.

Mix in	[1 cup	TURKEY cut into small pieces
Turn off heat and stir in	[2 TB	PARMESAN grated
	[to taste	GROUND BLACK PEPPER, SALT

Cover, let the Risotto set for 5 minutes.

229

TURKEY - SOUTH SEAS

Mix	[	PINEAPPLE and ORANGE bite-size pieces
with	[	UNSWEETENED COCONUT flaked
	[	SALTED PEANUTS or CASHEWS chopped
	[	TURKEY cut into small pieces
Mix to taste with	[	MAYONNAISE, a few drops LEMON JUICE
Serve on	[	SALAD GREENS Vinaigrette Seasoning
Sprinkle with	[	HERB CROUTONS

TURKEY STUFFING with SHIRRED EGGS   EGGS - "BASIC RECIPES"

Spread into individual oven-proof dishes	[	COOKED TURKEY STUFFING leftovers
Drizzle the Stuffing with	[	GRAVY
Poke with a fork for it to seep in. Sprinkle	[	CHEDDAR shredded
Break on top of Stuffing	[	EGG(S)
Sprinkle the Eggs with	[	melted BUTTER, SALT, PEPPER

Bake on top rack of oven, preheated to 500°, until the Eggs are set: 4-1/2 to 5 minutes.

<u>WITH FRIED EGGS</u>   - Spread in nonstick skillet the Stuffing. Drizzle with Gravy and heat it.
                           - Make a well in the center, melt in it Butter, and break the Eggs into it.
                           - Poke the Stuffing to spread the Egg White into it. Fry the Eggs.

TURKEY - TORTILLAS RANCHERAS

In a nonstick skillet, over medium heat, heat	[	1 TB	VEGETABLE OIL
When a light haze forms, sauté	[	1/3-cup	ONION sliced a 1/4-thick, diced
When Onion softens, add	[	1 or 2	GARLIC CLOVES mashed, minced
When Onion turns golden, add (canned)	[	1 cup	CHOPPED TOMATOES drained
To taste	[	1	SERRANO CHILE canned, minced
	[	a pinch	SUGAR, SALT

Bring to a boil, cover, reduce heat to low
and simmer until the Sauce thickens.

Add	[	2 tp	CILANTRO finely chopped
Warm or fry	[		TORTILLAS
Top Tortillas with	[		TURKEY
Cover with the SAUCE and top with	[		FRIED EGGS

TURKEY - WELSH RAREBIT

	Prepare a	[WELSH RAREBIT see "BASIC RECIPES" - FONDUES
The "DUNKS"	<u>Poultry and Meats</u>	[TURKEY, CHORIZO, HAM, SPICY SAUSAGE
<u>Vegetables</u>	Steamed or boiled	[BROCCOLI, CAULIFLOWER, BRUSSELS SPROUTS
	Roasted or boiled	[CHESTNUTS, POTATOES, YAMS, MUSHROOMS sautéed
	<u>Fruit</u>	[APPLE, AVOCADO, soaked DRIED APRICOTS and FIGS,
		[GRAPES, KIWI, PAPAYA, PEACH, PEAR, PINEAPPLE
	<u>Breads and Other</u>	[BAGUETTE, RYE, SOURDOUGH

230

XII

CURED MEATS

HORS-D'OEUVRE

Wrap thinly sliced PROSCIUTTO, HAM or SALAMI around any of the following.

Skewer them on toothpicks.

ARTICHOKE BOTTOMS	-	Cut into cubes. Spread with a little Mayonnaise.
ASPARAGUS TIPS	-	Raw thin Asparagus. About 3-inches long.
AVOCADO	-	Chunks. Sprinkle with Lemon Juice. Stir to coat them with the Juice.

BRIE or CAMEMBERT	-	Small cubes. Sprinkle with Paprika.
BRUSSELS SPROUTS	-	Cook *al dente*. Split in half if too big. Dab a touch of Horseradish.
DRIED APRICOTS	-	Soak in Apple Juice or Cider. Add Brandy or Rum to taste. Pat dry.
DRIED FIGS	-	Stuff with Gorgonzola, Stilton or Blue Cheese.
FRESH FIGS	-	Cut into wedges.
MELON	-	Bite-size chunks. Sprinkle with a little Ground Black Pepper.

MOZZARELLA BALLS	-	Bite-size Bocconcini or chunks. Add a fresh Basil leaf.
MUSHROOMS	-	Raw or pickled. Dab with a touch of Sour Cream.
PALM HEARTS	-	Canned. Pat dry. Cut into 3/4-inch pieces. Add minced Capers.
PARMESAN	-	Bite-size chunks. Add Olive or Cornichon slivers.
PINEAPPLE	-	Bite-size chunks. Sprinkle with a little Ground Ginger.
YAMS	-	Boiled or baked. Bite-size cubes.

PHYLLO SHELLS - MINIATURE size. *Available frozen*

       Mix - 1/4-cup chopped Prosciutto or Ham
            - 1 flat TB Mascarpone
            - 1 TB grated Parmesan.

- Then add to taste more of each, according to amount needed.
- Fill Shells before serving.

"I begin with an idea and then it becomes something else."

Pablo Picasso

232

CURED MEATS

HAM in ASPIC

ASPIC see "BASIC RECIPES"

Use 4 (1 cup) ramekins or a 4-cup ring mold.

Use CHICKEN STOCK to prepare [	2 cups	ASPIC STOCK add to taste
		DRY SHERRY
Chop in processor, not too finely, to obtain [	1-3/4 cups	HAM
Then mix in [	to taste	CORNICHONS finely chopped
[		SWEET PIMIENTOS minced
[		TARRAGON finely chopped
[	just enough	MAYONNAISE to bind

Refrigerate.

Line ramekins with [	a layer of	ASPIC STOCK 1/4-inch deep

Refrigerate until set.

Decorate with [	slices of	PIMIENTO OLIVES
Add, just to cover [		ASPIC STOCK

Refrigerate until set.
Divide the Ham Mixture in four. Spoon it
into the ramekins, leaving a little space
around for the Stock.

Fill and cover with [		ASPIC STOCK

Refrigerate until set.

HAM - CRÊPES with ASPARAGUS

CRÊPES see "BASIC RECIPES"

Leaving 1-inch around the edge, spread on [	CRÊPES
a thin coat of [	ALFREDO SAUCE available read-made
Top with sliced [	HAM or PROSCIUTTO
Spread on the Ham a thin coat of [	ALFREDO SAUCE

Place at 1-1/2-inches from the bottom [	2	COOKED ASPARAGUS TIPS 3 inches long

Fold in the Crêpe sides. Fold over the bottom, roll. Place them in a sprayed oven-proof dish.
Cover with foil. Refrigerate. Warm in a 325° oven for 15 minutes. Serve with ALFREDO SAUCE.

HAM - CRÊPES with MUSHROOMS

Filling yields about 2-1/4 cups

Drain a [	6 oz-can	SLICED MUSHROOMS
Add to their Liquid [	enough	MILK to obtain 2/3-cup
Prepare a CREAMY BÉCHAMEL with [	1-1/2 TB	BUTTER (See "SAUCES")
[	1-1/2 TB	FLOUR
[	2/3-cup	MUSHROOM / MILK
When it thickens, add [	4 TB	PARMESAN
In a nonstick skillet, over medium heat, heat [	1 TB	BUTTER
When it sizzles, sauté [	1/2-cup	ONION finely chopped
When Onion is translucent, add [		the Mushrooms
Sauté and add [	1 TB	PARSLEY minced
[	1 cup	HAM coarsely chop in processor
[	a dash	NUTMEG grated, PEPPER
Transfer to a bowl, mix in the BÉCHAMEL and [	1/4-cup	SWISS CHEESE coarse-grated

Cover the surface with plastic wrap, refrigerate until ready to fill the Crêpes.

234

HAM CROQUETTES - BÉCHAMEL BASE   *Yields about 3 cups*

Finely chop in processor (do not purée)   [1-3/4 cups   HAM

Then mix in   [1 TB   FRESH BASIL   finely chopped

See "SAUCES".   Prepare a   [VERY THICK BÉCHAMEL
with   [4 TB   BUTTER
[4 TB   FLOUR   mixed with
[1/2-tp   DRY MUSTARD
[1-1/4 cups   MILK

Stir until the Sauce becomes very thick. Add   [4 TB   PARMESAN   grated
[to taste   NUTMEG   grated
Reduce heat to low.
Immediately beat   [1 whole   EGG + 2 EGG YOLKS
with   [1 TB   hot MILK

Gradually whisk the EGGS into the Sauce.
When well incorporated, mix in the HAM. Adjust Seasonings.

Stir until the Mixture separates from the skillet, like dough. Transfer it to a buttered dish.
Spread it lightly. Cover with plastic wrap to prevent skin from forming. Refrigerate.

Shape and fry Croquettes following directions in "BASIC RECIPES".

To serve sprinkle with grated PARMESAN.

VARIATION   - Use 1-1/4 cups HAM and 1/2-cup PROSCIUTTO.

HAM CROQUETTES - POTATO BASE   *Yields about 4 cups*

Finely chop in processor to obtain   [2 cups   HAM *

See "VEGETABLES" - POTATOES.   Prepare   [the CROQUETTE BASE
with   [1/4-cup   PARMESAN   grated
Add to the beaten EGGS   [1/8-tp   NUTMEG   grated or ground

Transfer Mixture to a bowl.

In a nonstick skillet, over medium heat, heat   [1 TB   BUTTER + 1 tp VEGETABLE OIL
When it sizzles, sauté   [2 TB   SHALLOT   finely chopped
When the Shallot turns golden, stir in   [the Ham
[1 TB   PARSLEY   finely chopped
[2 TB   PARMESAN   grated
[WHITE or BLACK PEPPER
Turn off heat. Set aside to cool.
Mix well the HAM and CROQUETTE BASE.
Transfer Mixture to a buttered dish. Spread it lightly. Cover with plastic wrap. Refrigerate.

Croquettes can be frozen between layers of wax paper.

Shape and fry Croquettes following directions in "BASIC RECIPES".

Serve as an hors-d'oeuvre or appetizer. Sprinkle with grated Parmesan.

*   For 1 cup of HAM use half of Ingredients in the Ham Mixture. Mix with 1 cup of Croquette Base.
    - Remaining Croquette Base can be wrapped and frozen. Thaw, purée again before using.

HAM and EGGS with ARTICHOKES

Cook in their Liquid until tender [ARTICHOKE BOTTOMS canned

Dry on paper towels, wrap in foil, keep warm
in the oven.
See "SAUCES". Prepare a [LEMON EGG or HOLLANDAISE SAUCE

Keep it warm in a double boiler.
Toast [CROISSANTS split in half horizontally
Poach or fry [EGGS
Set Artichokes on plates.

Surround with Croissant halves topped with [SLICED HAM   plain, grilled or broiled

Fill each Artichoke Bottom with a poached or fried Egg. Top the whole with the SAUCE.

HAM and EGGS - DEVILED

Slice in half lengthwise, remove Yolks from [4   HARD-COOKED EGGS

Mash in a bowl [the 4   Egg Yolks
with [2 TB   MAYONNAISE
[1/2-tp   DIJON MUSTARD
[1 oz   HAM   finely chopped in processor
[1 tp   CHIVES
[1 TB   PICKLES or CORNICHONS minced
Pipe Mixture into Egg Whites. Sprinkle with [PARSLEY   minced

HAM and SHIRRED EGGS - CREAM OF CORN   *Serves 2*

In a nonstick skillet, over medium heat, heat [2 tp   BUTTER + 1 tp VEGETABLE OIL
When it sizzles, sauté [2 TB   ONION   minced
with [1/2-cup   RED BELL PEPPER   finely diced
Optional [to taste   JALAPEÑO   seeded, minced

When Bell Pepper softens, stir in [1 cup   CREAM OF CORN
Stir the Corn to heat through and add [3/4-cup   HAM   cut into small pieces
[to taste   GROUND BLACK PEPPER, SALT
Spread Corn Mixture into 2 shallow
oven-proof individual dishes. Sprinkle with [AVOCADO   diced
Break on top of each [1 or 2   EGGS
Drizzle over the Eggs [a little   melted BUTTER, SALT, PEPPER

Bake on top rack of oven, preheated to 500° until the Eggs are set: 4-1/2 to 5 minutes.

HAM and SHIRRED EGGS - YAMS   EGGS see "BASIC RECIPES"

Into shallow individual oven-proof dishes,
spread [warm   MASHED YAMS
Top with [CARAMELIZED ONIONS
[HAM   bite-size pieces
Break on top [1 or 2   EGGS
Drizzle over the Eggs [a little   melted BUTTER, SALT, PEPPER

Bake on top rack of oven, preheated to 500°, until the Eggs are set: 4-1/2 to 5 minutes.

HAM - FRITTATA   _Serves 2 or 3_   FRITTATA see "BASIC RECIPES"

Sauté to a golden brown in	[1/2-TB	BUTTER
	[1 cup	ONION halved, thinly sliced
In a bowl whisk	[3 large	EGGS
	[a pinch	SALT, GROUND BLACK PEPPER
When blended, whisk in	[1/4-cup	PARMESAN grated
Add	[	the Browned Onions
	[3/4-cup	HAM coarsely chop in processor
In a 7-to-8-inch skillet than can go under the broiler, over medium heat, heat	[1 TB	BUTTER + 1 TB VEGETABLE OIL

When it sizzles add the EGG MIXTURE. Spread it evenly with a spatula. Reduce heat to low.
Cook and pass the Frittata under preheated broiler as per "BASIC RECIPES".

HAM FRITTATA with BRUSSELS SPROUTS   _Serves 4_

In a nonstick skillet, medium heat, heat	[1 TB	BUTTER + 1 tp VEGETABLE OIL
When it sizzles, sauté	[1/2-cup	ONION slice 1/4-inch thick, dice
When the Onion turns golden, stir in	[1 cup	BRUSSELS SPROUTS cooked, coarsely chopped
Sauté for 1 minute. Remove from heat and	[sprinkle	SALT, GROUND BLACK PEPPER
In a bowl whisk	[5 large	EGGS
When well blended, whisk in	[1/4-cup	PARMESAN grated
	[1/4-cup	SWISS CHEESE coarse-grated
Stir in the BRUSSELS SPROUTS and	[1-1/4 cups	HAM coarsely chop in processor
	[	GROUND BLACK PEPPER
In a 10-inch skillet that can go under the broiler, over medium heat, heat	[2 TB	BUTTER + 1 TB VEGETABLE OIL

When it sizzles, pour into skillet the EGG MIXTURE and proceed as in above recipe.

HAM FRITTATA with POTATOES   _Serves 4 to 6_

Peel, wash, dry, shred in processor to obtain	[1-1/4 cups	YUKON GOLD POTATOES then dry in a towel
In a nonstick skillet, over medium heat, heat	[1-1/2 TB	VEGETABLE OIL
When hot, sauté until golden brown	[3/4-cup	ONION halved and thinly sliced
Drain Onions in a sieve.		
In a bowl whisk	[5 large	EGGS
When well blended, whisk in	[1/2-cup	PARMESAN grated
Stir in the BROWNED ONIONS and	[1-1/4 cups	HAM coarsely chop in processor
	[a pinch	SALT, GROUND BLACK PEPPER
In a 10-inch skillet than can go under the broiler, over medium heat, heat	[3-1/2 TB	BUTTER
	[1-1/2 TB	VEGETABLE OIL
When it sizzles, stir in	[	the Potatoes
Cook the Potatoes until tender and golden	[sprinkle	SALT, GROUND BLACK PEPPER

Spread the Potatoes evenly in the skillet. Pour over them the EGG MIXTURE.
Spread it evenly with a spatula. Reduce heat to low. Proceed as in top recipe.

HAM MOUSSE for CANAPÉS and DIPS

About 1 cup
before adding Cream

Pulse in processor until finely chopped	[6 oz	HAM
Then add and pulse	[2 oz	RICOTTA
	[1 TB	MAYONNAISE
	[3 TB	PARMESAN grated
	[1/4- tp	DIJON MUSTARD or to taste
Taste the Mixture and add	[	GROUND BLACK PEPPER, SALT
Optional, to taste	[1 or 2 tp	DRY SHERRY or COGNAC

FOR CANAPÉS   - Transfer to a crock or bowl. Cover with plastic wrap. Refrigerate.

FOR DIPS   - With electric beater or blender, whip 1/4-cup HEAVY CREAM
                  - Fold it gradually into the MOUSSE. You may not need it all. Adjust Seasonings.

Optional: add to the Mousse any of the following: (Salt and Pepper after adding all Ingredients).

CAPERS minced	CHIVES	DILL snipped	JALAPEÑO minced
CELERY finely chopped	CORNICHONS minced	GREEN OLIVES minced	RELISH
CHILIES	CRISPY BACON crumbled	HORSERADISH	SWEET PIMIENTOS

HAM MOUSSE in ARTICHOKE BOTTOMS   *Appetizer or buffet*

Spread into	[canned	ARTICHOKE BOTTOMS
A layer of	[	PROSCIUTTO coarsely chopped
Top with a heap of	[	HAM MOUSSE
Garnish with	[	PARSLEY finely chopped
Serve on a bed of	[	GREENS
	[tossed with	OIL and LEMON DRESSING

HAM MOUSSE in a MOLD   *Yields about 4-1/2 cups*

Cut into small pieces to obtain	[2 cups	HAM (well stacked)
Pour into processor	[1/2-cup cold	CHICKEN BROTH degreased
Sprinkle over it	[2 TB	POWDERED GELATINE

Let it set for 10 minutes.

Heat	[1/2-cup	CHICKEN BROTH degreased

Add it to Gelatine, process to mix.

Then add	[	the Ham
	[2 TB	MAYONNAISE
	[1 tp	DIJON MUSTARD
	[2 TB	CHIVES
	[2 TB	WATERCRESS finely chopped
Optional	[1 TB	DRY SHERRY or more to taste
	[	GROUND BLACK PEPPER

Process with quick pulses until smooth.
Adjust seasonings. Pulse again. Transfer
to a bowl. Let it cool.

Whip in blender	[1/2-cup	HEAVY CREAM

Fold WHIPPED CREAM into the Ham Mixture. Pour it into a ring mold. Refrigerate until firm.
To unmold: dip the mold a few seconds in hot water. Top it with a platter, overturn.

Garnish with any of   - Asparagus Tips, sliced Cucumbers, Palm Hearts, Pineapple.
                                  - Olives, Pickles, marinated Mushrooms or Artichoke Hearts.

238

HAM - PASTA and ARTICHOKES alla CARBONARA

Serves 2

In a nonstick skillet, over medium heat, heat	[2 TB	BUTTER + 1 tp VEGETABLE OIL
When it sizzles, sauté	[1 clove	GARLIC mashed
When fragrant discard the Garlic and add	[2 TB	SHALLOTS finely chopped
When Shallots soften, add	[1/2-cup	ARTICHOKE BOTTOMS canned, drained, diced
Sauté until the Shallots turn golden, mix in	[1/2-cup	HAM diced or chopped
	[	GROUND BLACK PEPPER
Stir, turn off heat.		
Add to salted boiling water	[3 oz	FETTUCCINI
Beat in a small bowl	[1	EGG
	[1/4-cup	LIGHT CREAM
	[1/4-cup	PARMESAN grated

Drain FETTUCCINI. Transfer to a heated bowl
Toss in the EGG MIXTURE. Stir well, add ARTICHOKES and HAM. Serve with grated PARMESAN.

HAM - PASTA with BLUE CHEESE SAUCE   *Appetizer, serves 4*

See "SAUCES". Prepare	[1 cup	VELOUTÉ WHITE SAUCE
Add	[2-to-3 TB	BLUE CHEESE to taste
Toss the hot Sauce into	[6 oz	LINGUINE or FETTUCCINI
And stir in	[1-1/2 cups	HAM diced or chopped
	[3 TB	PINE NUTS toasted

HAM - PASTA CHAMPAGNE or WHITE WINE SAUCE

Serves 4 as an appetizer

See "SAUCES". Prepare a	[	CHAMPAGNE or WHITE WINE CREAM SAUCE
In a 6-inch skillet, medium heat, heat	[1-1/2 TB	BUTTER
When it sizzles, sauté	[1 cup	ASPARAGUS *al dente,* slant-cut into 3/4-inch pieces
Sauté for 1 minute and mix in	[1-1/2 cups	HAM coarsely chopped
	[2 TB	PINE NUTS toasted

Add Asparagus and Ham to the SAUCE.

Meanwhile cook and transfer to a heated bowl	[6 oz	LINGUINE or FETTUCCINI
Toss in the SAUCE MIXTURE. Serve	[on the side	PARMESAN grated

VARIATION   - Substitute the Asparagus with sliced MUSHROOMS.

HAM - PASTA with PESTO   *Serves 1 as a main course*

Heat in a small skillet	[3 TB	PESTO SAUCE ready-made
	[2 TB	ALFREDO SAUCE
Toss the Sauce into	[2 oz	COOKED PASTA
Add	[to taste	HAM chopped or diced

HAM - QUICHE with BROCCOLI   QUICHE see "BASIC RECIPES"

Thaw in a colander	[10 oz-pkg	FROZEN CHOPPED BROCCOLI

Press down to remove excess moisture.

In a nonstick skillet, heat	[1 TB	VEGETABLE OIL
When a light haze forms, sauté	[1/2-cup	ONION finely chopped

When translucent, add the BROCCOLI. Stir
until cooked and all Liquid has evaporated.

Sprinkle with	[	SALT, GROUND BLACK PEPPER
Stir in	[1-1/4 cups	HAM coarsely chop in processor
	[to taste	NUTMEG grated

Turn off heat and let cool.
Preheat oven to 375°.

In a large bowl, beat	[3	EGGS
Brush with a little of the beaten EGGS a	[9-inch	FROZEN UNCOOKED PIE SHELL

Set in the oven for 2 minutes only. Let cool

Whisk into the Eggs	[2/3-cup	HEAVY CREAM + 1/3-cup MILK
	[2 oz	SWISS CHEESE coarse-grated
	[1/4-cup	PARMESAN grated
	[1/4-tp	SALT
	[1/4-tp	GROUND BLACK PEPPER

To assemble   - Place the Pie Shell, in its foil pan, on a cookie sheet.
                 - Spread the BROCCOLI HAM MIXTURE into it.
                 - Pour over slowly the CUSTARD. Smooth the surface with the back of a spoon.

To bake   - Slide cookie sheet with Quiche into the oven. Reduce heat to 350°.
                 - Follow directions in "BASIC RECIPES".

HAM - QUICHE with CARAMELIZED ONIONS

In a nonstick skillet, medium high heat, heat	[1 TB	VEGETABLE OIL
Sauté until caramelized	[14 oz	ONIONS coarsely chopped
Then sprinkle with a little	[	SALT, GROUND BLACK PEPPER

Set aside.
Preheat oven to 375°.

In a large bowl beat	[3	EGGS
Brush with a little of the beaten EGGS a	[9-inch	FROZEN UNCOOKED PIE SHELL

Set in the oven for 2 minutes only. Let cool.

Whisk into the Eggs	[3/4-cup	HEAVY CREAM + 1/4-cup MILK
	[1 cup	HAM coarsely chop in processor
	[2 oz	SWISS CHEESE coarse-grated
Crumbled	[2 oz	GARLIC HERB BOURSIN CHEESE
		(comes in a 5-oz package)
	[1/4-tp	SALT, GROUND BLACK PEPPER
	[to taste	NUTMEG grated

To assemble   - Place the Pie Shell, in its foil pan, on a cookie sheet. Spread the ONIONS in it.
                 - Pour over slowly the HAM CUSTARD. Smooth surface with the back of a spoon.

To bake   - Follow directions as in previous recipe.

HAM - QUICHE LORRAINE

QUICHE see "BASIC RECIPES"

In a nonstick skillet, fry soft (not crisp)	[6 strips	BACON chopped into small pieces.
		Drain on paper towel.
Keep 1 tp of BACON FAT in the skillet and add	[2 tp	VEGETABLE OIL
Sauté until golden	[3/4-cup	ONION slice 1/4-inch thick, chop
Preheat oven to 375°.		
In a large bowl beat	[3	EGGS
Brush with a little of the beaten EGGS a	[9-inch	FROZEN UNCOOKED PIE SHELL

Set in the oven for 2 minutes only. Let cool.

Whisk into the Eggs	[3/4-cup	HEAVY CREAM + 1/4-cup MILK
	[1/4-tp	SALT, 1/4-tp PEPPER
	[to taste	NUTMEG grated
	[4 oz	SWISS CHEESE coarse-grated
Add BACON and ONIONS and	[1 cup	HAM coarsely chop in processor

To assemble and bake - Place the Pie Shell in its foil pan, on a cookie sheet.
                - Ladle the CUSTARD into it. Slide into oven. Reduce heat to 350°.
                - Bake following directions in "BASIC RECIPES".

HAM - QUICHE with SPINACH

Preheat oven to 375°. Thaw in a colander	[10 oz-pkg	FROZEN CHOPPED SPINACH
		Squeeze out remaining water.
In a nonstick skillet, over medium heat, heat	[1 TB	VEGETABLE OIL
When a light haze forms, sauté	[1/2-cup	ONION thinly slice, coarsely chop
When Onion softens, add, optional	[1 or 2	GARLIC CLOVES mashed, minced
When Onion is translucent add SPINACH and	[1/4-tp	DRIED THYME or ROSEMARY

Stir until the Spinach is cooked and all liquid
   has evaporated. Turn off heat and sprinkle [SALT, GROUND BLACK PEPPER

In a bowl beat	[3	EGGS
Brush with a little of the beaten EGGS a	[9-inch	FROZEN UNCOOKED PIE SHELL

Set in the oven for 2 minutes only. Let cool.

Whisk into the Eggs	[3/4-cup	HEAVY CREAM + 1/4-cup MILK
	[2 oz	SWISS CHEESE coarse-grated
Crumbled	[2 oz	GARLIC HERB BOURSIN CHEESE
Mix well and add	[2/3-cup	HAM coarsely chop in processor
	[	the Cooked Spinach

Assemble and bake as above.

HAM - MINI QUICHES

MINI QUICHES see "BASIC RECIPES"

Spray a tray of 12 small muffin cups (1/4-cup size) with Cooking Spray. Preheat oven to 375°.

In a bowl whisk	[4	EGGS
	[1/4-cup	HEAVY CREAM
	[4 TB	PARMESAN grated
	[2 TB	PARSLEY finely chopped
	[1/4-tp	SALT, PEPPER, NUTMEG

Spread into each muffing cup:

[1 TB + 1 tp HAM chopped

Assemble, bake as per "BASIC RECIPES".

HAM - RISOTTO with ASPARAGUS

RISOTTO see "BASIC RECIPES"
Serves 4 as an appetizer

Cut off hard ends, trim, wash, dry and steam in microwave for 3 minutes	[12 medium	ASPARAGUS

- Slant-cut 8 Asparagus into 1/2-inch pieces, and the Tips of the 4 remaining Asparagus.
- In processor chop finely the stems of the 4 remaining Asparagus.

Simmer	[6 cups	CHICKEN BROTH lightly salted (+ 1/2-cup more if needed)
In a 10-inch heavy nonstick skillet, over medium heat, heat	[3-1/2 TB	BUTTER + 1 TB VEGETABLE OIL
When it sizzles, sauté	[2 TB	ONION finely chopped
When Onion is translucent add	[	chopped Asparagus and all the cut pieces
Sauté, for 2 minutes and add	[1-1/2 cups	ARBORIO RICE
Stir until grains are coated and glisten, add	[1/4-cup	DRY WHITE WINE

Stir until the Wine evaporates.
Add one ladle (1/2-cup) at a time of BROTH.

When 5 cups have been absorbed, add	[1-1/4 cups	HAM cut into small pieces

When 6 cups of Broth have been absorbed,
the Rice should be tender but firm, creamy.

Turn off heat and stir in	[1-1/2 TB	BUTTER diced small
	[4 TB	PARMESAN grated
	[to taste	SALT, GROUND BLACK PEPPER

Cover, let Risotto set for 5 minutes. Serve	[on the side	PARMESAN grated

HAM - RISOTTO PRIMAVERA

Serves 2

Dice small and combine in a strainer	[1/3-cup	CARROTS
	[1/3-cup	CELERY
	[1/3-cup	ZUCCHINI

Plunge the strainer into boiling water, blanch
2 minutes. Set strainer over a bowl, drain.

In a saucepan, simmer	[3 cups	CHICKEN BROTH lightly salted (+ 1/2-cup more if needed)
In nonstick 8-inch skillet, medium heat, heat	[1-1/2 TB	BUTTER
	[1 TB	EXTRA-VIRGIN OLIVE OIL
When it sizzles, sauté	[1/4-cup	ONION finely chopped
When translucent, add	[	the diced Vegetables
Sauté the Vegetables for 2 minutes and	[sprinkle	SALT, GROUND BLACK PEPPER
Add	[3/4-cup	ARBORIO RICE

Stir until grains are coated and glisten.
Add one ladle (1/2-cup) at a time of BROTH.

When 2 cups have been absorbed, mix in	[1/3-cup	FROZEN GREEN PEAS thawed
Add 1/2-cup of BROTH. When absorbed, add	[1 cup	HAM cut into small pieces

(continued)

242

When the 3 cups of Broth have been absorbed the Rice should be tender, firm, creamy.

	Add	[2 TB	FRESH BASIL finely chopped
	Turn off heat and stir in	[1 TB	BUTTER diced small
		[2 TB	PARMESAN grated
		[to taste	SALT, GROUND BLACK PEPPER

Cover, let Risotto set for 5 minutes.   Serve [on the side   PARMESAN grated

HAM and CHEESE SOUFFLÉ

SOUFFLÉ - "BASIC RECIPES"
Serves 4 to 6

1.   Rub a 1-1/2 quarts soufflé dish with   [BUTTER
        (or use 4 soufflé ramekins)   Dust with [1-1/2 TB   PARMESAN   refrigerate the dish
                                                                  (1-1/4 tp per ramekin)

2.   Set out at room temperature [5   EGGS you need 5 Whites, 4 Yolks

3.   In a heavy nonstick skillet, prepare a   [CREAMY BÉCHAMEL ("SAUCES")
                        mixing into the FLOUR   [1/2-tp   DRY MUSTARD
                                                 [1/8-tp   ONION POWDER

- When Béchamel thickens remove from heat.
- Break 1 EGG, drop the WHITE into stainless
  steel bowl. The YOLK into the Béchamel.
- With a wire whip beat it into the Sauce.
- Repeat with 3 more Yolks, one at a time.
- Return saucepan to stove. Over <u>low heat</u>
  stir for 1 minute to bind the Eggs.

            Turn off heat. Stir into it, until melted   [1/2-cup   SWISS CHEESE coarse-grated
                                                                      (+ for later 1 TB, or 4 tp for ramekins)

                                        Then add   [3/4-cup   HAM finely chopped in processor
                                                   [to taste   WHITE PEPPER, SALT if needed
                                                   [to taste   NUTMEG   grated

- Set aside to cool. Can be prepared ahead to
  this point. Cover the surface with wax paper.
- Warm barely before adding the EGG WHITES.

4. Preheat oven to 400°. Set out soufflé dish(es).

Add to the 4 EGG WHITES 1 EGG WHITE and   [1/8-tp   CREAM OF TARTAR

a) Beat the EGG WHITES until stiff and glossy, but not dry.
      - Add one ladle of WHITES to the BÉCHAMEL. Gently fold them in with a rubber spatula.
      - Then gently pour the BÉCHAMEL into the remaining Egg Whites.
      - Fold in with the spatula, scooping from the bottom towards the top as you turn the bowl.
        Do not fold too much, it would keep the Soufflé from rising well. White spots do no harm.

b) Pour MIXTURE into the soufflé dish. Smooth the surface with a spatula or flat side of a knife.
      - Sprinkle with the reserved 1 TB of CHEESE. Or for each ramekin 1 tp.

c) Place on middle rack of oven. Immediately reduce heat to 375°. Bake for 25-to-30 minutes.
      - Less time for the ramekins. Do not open the oven door until the Soufflé is well puffed.
      - Test by inserting a thin knife or metal skewer. If it comes out clean, the Soufflé is ready.
        If not, cook 5 minutes longer. It should have a light brown crust with a creamy center.

PROSCIUTTO

Cooked, Prosciutto turns to a lighter color. Thinly sliced, it will curl, to look like fatless Bacon.
To maintain its original texture, add it to Sauces or other Ingredients after they've been cooked.

PROSCIUTTO CRÊPES with ASPARAGUS

CRÊPES
see "BASIC RECIPES"

Filling yields about 2-1/4 cups

Trim off any excess Fat bordering the slices of [12 oz   PROSCIUTTO   then chop it in
processor, not too finely

In a bowl, mix chopped PROSCIUTTO with

[	6 TB	ALFREDO SAUCE ready-made
[	1 oz	SWISS CHEESE coarse-grated
[	3 oz	CREAM CHEESE soft, tidbits
[	to taste	NUTMEG grated, BLACK PEPPER

Cover Mixture with Plastic wrap. Refrigerate.

THE CRÊPES   Place some Prosciutto Mixture
on each one and top with   [1 or 2   ASPARAGUS TIPS cooked, 3 " long
(1 or 2: depending on thickness)

- Roll Crêpes, lay them in a sprayed oven dish.
- Cover with foil, refrigerate.
- Warm 15 minutes in oven preheated to 350°.

Serve with [ALFREDO SAUCE   thin with a little Milk

PROSCIUTTO CRÊPES à la SUZETTE

Use a pastry brush to brush each Crêpe with   [ALFREDO SAUCE
Spread over the Sauce   [sliced   PROSCIUTTO
Sprinkle lightly one half of Crêpe with   [MOZZARELLA   shredded

- Fold over the other half. Fold again to form a triangle. Overlap Crêpes in a sprayed oven dish.
- Cover with foil. Warm in a 325° oven for about 10 minutes. Serve with ALFREDO SAUCE.

PROSCIUTTO DEVILED EGGS

Slice lengthwise and remove Yolks from [4   HARD-COOKED EGGS

WITH MAYONNAISE	WITH SOUR CREAM
Purée in processor:	Purée in processor:
[1 oz PROSCIUTTO [the 4 Egg Yolks [1 TB MAYONNAISE [1/2-tp DIJON MUSTARD [1 tp GREEN ONION minced	[1 oz PROSCIUTTO [the 4 Egg Yolks [1 TB SOUR CREAM [1/2-tp DIJON MUSTARD [1 TB PARMESAN grated
Transfer to a bowl, stir in:	Transfer to a bowl, stir in:
[2 tp BLACK OLIVES minced [GROUND BLACK PEPPER	[2 tp CORNICHONS minced [GROUND BLACK PEPPER
[Fill EGG WHITES [garnish WATERCRESS minced	[Fill EGG WHITES [garnish FRESH BASIL minced

PROSCIUTTO FRITTATA with SPAGHETTI

FRITTATA see "BASIC RECIPES"

Serves 4 to 6

In a large bowl, whisk	[5 large	EGGS
	[1/4-tp	SALT, GROUND BLACK PEPPER
When well blended, whisk in	[1/2-cup	PARMESAN grated
	[6 oz	PROSCIUTTO coarsely chopped in processor
	[1-1/2 cups	COOKED SPAGHETTI cut up
In a 10-inch skillet than can go under the broiler, over medium heat, heat	[2 TB	BUTTER
	[1 TB	EXTRA-VIRGIN OLIVE OIL
Sauté in it until golden	[1/2-cup	ONION finely chopped

- Pour the EGG MIXTURE into the skillet. Spread it evenly with a spatula. Reduce heat to low.
- Cook the Frittata until the bottom gets crusty and browned.
- With the top set but still creamy, sprinkle it with grated Parmesan.
- Place the skillet under preheated broiler until the top gets crusty browned.

Slide the Frittata onto a platter. Serve hot as an appetizer or light lunch with a Salad.

VARIATION   - Substitute the Prosciutto with 3/4-cup chopped cooked SAUSAGE or SALAMI.

PROSCIUTTO FRITTATA with ZUCCHINI

Serves 4

Scrape any blemishes, wash, dry, cut ends of	[3 medium	LIGHT GREEN ZUCCHINI slice thinly
In a nonstick skillet, heat	[3 TB	VEGETABLE OIL
When hot, sauté until it begins to color	[1/2-cup	ONION halved and thinly sliced
Add and sauté to a light golden brown	[	the Zucchini
Then sprinkle with	[	SALT, GROUND BLACK PEPPER
Spread in a sieve to cool.		
In a bowl, whisk	[5 large	EGGS
	[1/8-tp	SALT, GROUND BLACK PEPPER
When well blended, whisk in	[1/3-cup	PARMESAN grated
	[2 TB	SWISS CHEESE coarse-grated
	[2 TB	PARSLEY finely chopped
Stir in the ZUCCHINI and	[5 oz	PROSCIUTTO coarsely chopped in processor
In a 10-inch skillet that can go under the broiler, over medium heat, heat	[2 TB	BUTTER + 1 TB VEGETABLE OIL

When it sizzles, pour the EGG MIXTURE. Spread it evenly with a spatula. Reduce heat to low.
Cook and pass the Frittata under preheated broiler following directions in "BASIC RECIPES".

PROSCIUTTO - PASTA with CREAM of MUSHROOMS

In a small saucepan heat	[1 can	CREAM of MUSHROOM SOUP
Add to taste	[a little	MILK or LIGHT CREAM
Toss	[	PROSCIUTTO coarsely chopped
into	[	FETTUCCINI or other kind
Add, to taste the CREAM of MUSHROOMS and	[	PARMESAN grated
Optional	[toasted	PINE NUTS

PROSCIUTTO - PASTA, GARLIC and OIL   AGLIO OLIO   *Serves 2*

Over medium heat, heat in a skillet	[1/3-cup	EXTRA-VIRGIN OLIVE OIL
When hot, sauté to golden brown	[6 cloves	GARLIC finely sliced lengthwise, or more
Drain and toss into skillet	[3 oz	SPAGHETTINI
And	[3 oz	PROSCIUTTO coarsely chopped
	[1 TB	PARSLEY minced
	[	SALT, GROUND BLACK PEPPER

Serve with GARLIC BREAD.

PROSCIUTTO - PASTA, GORGONZOLA, ARTICHOKES

Serves 2

In nonstick 8-inch skillet, medium heat, heat	[1 TB	BUTTER + 1 tp VEGETABLE OIL
When it sizzles, sauté	[2 medium	ONIONS coarsely chopped

Stir Onions often.
When caramelized, set aside.

Add to salted boiling water	[3 or 4 oz	SPAGHETTINI
In nonstick 7-inch skillet, medium heat, heat	[1 TB	BUTTER
When it sizzles, add	[1/2-cup	ARTICHOKE BOTTOMS canned, diced
Sauté the ARTICHOKES for 1 minute. Add	[1/2-cup	LIGHT CREAM
When the CREAM is hot (do not boil), add	[3 oz	PROSCIUTTO coarsely chopped
Turn off heat and mix in, crumbled	[3 TB	GORGONZOLA or BLUE CHEESE

Toss SPAGHETTINI into PROSCIUTTO Mixture. Add CARAMELIZED ONIONS. Serve immediately.

PROSCIUTTO - PASTA with MUSHROOMS   *Serves 2*

In a nonstick skillet, over medium heat, heat	[2 TB	EXTRA-VIRGIN OLIVE OIL
When a light haze forms, sauté	[1 clove	GARLIC mashed and minced
When Garlic begins to color, add	[4 oz	SLICED MUSHROOMS
Sauté them for 1 minute, and add	[6 TB	BROTH hot, lightly salted
	[2 TB	DRY WHITE WINE optional

Cook Mushrooms until tender.

Add	[3-to-4 oz	PROSCIUTTO coarsely chopped

Stir a few seconds. Season to taste.

Toss into	[3 or 4 oz	PASTA of your choice

PROSCIUTTO - RAVIOLI and ZUCCHINI   *Serves 2*

Scrape off dark skin, wash and cut off ends of	[10 oz	ZUCCHINI and slice them thinly
In a nonstick skillet, over medium heat, heat	[3 TB	EXTRA-VIRGIN OLIVE OIL
When a light haze forms, sauté until golden	[1 clove	GARLIC cut in half
Discard Garlic. Add and sauté	[	the Zucchini
When they turn golden, sprinkle with	[2 TB	PARMESAN grated
Add	[3-to-4 oz	PROSCIUTTO finely chopped
	[1/4-cup	HEAVY CREAM
Stir to heat through and add	[to taste	GROUND BLACK PEPPER
Serve ZUCCHINI PROSCIUTTO MIXTURE over	[	CHEESE RAVIOLI

PROSCIUTTO - QUICHE VIA VENETO   QUICHE - "BASIC RECIPES"

In a nonstick skillet, over medium heat, heat [1 TB   BUTTER
When it sizzles, sauté until golden [1/2-cup   ONION   slice 1/4-inch thick, dice
[3 oz   PANCETTA   diced

Transfer Onion/Pancetta to a sieve to drain.
Preheat oven to 375°.
In a large bowl whisk [3   EGGS
Brush with a little of the beaten EGGS a [9 -inch   FROZEN UNCOOKED PIE SHELL

Set in the oven for 2 minutes only. Let cool.

Whisk into the Eggs [3/4-cup   HEAVY CREAM + 1/4-cup MILK
[2 oz   PARMESAN   grated
[2 oz   SWISS CHEESE   coarse-grated
[1/4-tp   SALT, GROUND BLACK PEPPER
[6 oz   PROSCIUTTO   coarsely chopped
Add the PANCETTA ONION MIXTURE and [1 TB   FRESH BASIL   finely chopped
[1 TB   CAPERS drained, rinsed, minced

To assemble   - Place the Pie Shell, in its foil pan, on a cookie sheet.
              - Spoon the CUSTARD into it. Smooth the surface with the back of a spoon.
To bake   - Slide cookie sheet with Quiche into the oven. Reduce heat to 350°.
              - Follow directions in "BASIC RECIPES". Serve at room temperature.

PROSCIUTTO - RISOTTO au GRATIN   Appetizer, serves 4 to 5

1.   In an 8-inch skillet, medium heat, heat [2 TB   BUTTER
When it sizzles, sauté [2 TB   ONION   finely chopped
When Onion begins to color, add [6 oz   SLICED MUSHROOMS   Cremini
                                                                or other
Sauté until browned, turn off heat and mix in [6 oz   PROSCIUTTO   coarsely chopped

2.   See "SAUCES". Prepare [1 cup   THIN WHITE SAUCE
When it thickens, stir in until melted [4 TB   SWISS CHEESE coarse-grated
[4 TB   PARMESAN grated (You will need
                                                                more later)
Mix the Sauce into Prosciutto Mixture, add [to taste   GROUND BLACK PEPPER

3. THE RISOTTO   Bring to a simmer [6 cups   CHICKEN BROTH   lightly salted

In a 10-inch skillet, over medium heat, heat [3-1/2 TB   BUTTER + 1 TB VEGETABLE OIL
When it sizzles, sauté [2 TB   SHALLOTS   finely chopped
When the Shallots have softened, add [1-1/2 cups   ARBORIO RICE
Stir until grains are coated and glisten. Add [1/3-cup   DRY WHITE WINE

- Stir until the Wine evaporates.
- Add one ladle (1/2-cup) at a time of BROTH.
- When 6 cups of Broth have been absorbed
  turn off heat.
Stir in   [the PROSCIUTTO MIXTURE

4. Spray a 1-1/2 quarts oven-proof dish,
   1-3/4 inches deep, with COOKING SPRAY.

Spread the RISOTTO in it.   Sprinkle with [plenty of   SWISS and PARMESAN

Bake in oven preheated to 350° for 20 minutes. Let Gratin set for 5-to-10 minutes before serving.

SALAMI

To use in cooking, avoid Salamis with a tough skin. Unless you remove it.

SALAMI FRITTATA with BELL PEPPERS   Serves 4

In a nonstick skillet, over medium heat, heat	[1-1/2 TB	EXTRA-VIRGIN OLIVE OIL
When a light haze forms, sauté	[1/2-cup	ONION halved and thinly sliced
	[1-1/4 cups	GREEN BELL PEPPERS thin strips

When Onion turns golden and Bell Peppers
are tender, spread them in a sieve to cool.

In a bowl whisk	[4 large	EGGS
	[1/8-tp	SALT, GROUND BLACK PEPPER
When well blended, whisk in	[1/4-cup	MOZZARELLA coarse-grated
	[1/4-cup	PARMESAN grated
	[1 TB	FRESH BASIL finely chopped
Stir in the BELL PEPPERS/ONIONS and	[4 oz	SALAMI thinly sliced, coarsely chopped in processor
In a 10-inch skillet than can go under the broiler, over medium heat, heat	[2 TB	BUTTER
	[1 TB	EXTRA-VIRGIN OLIVE OIL

When it sizzles, pour into skillet the EGGS.
Spread evenly. Reduce heat to low. Cook and pass under the broiler as per "BASIC RECIPES".

SALAMI with PASTA

AEGEAN   -   Toss Pasta with Extra-Virgin Olive Oil, Feta Cheese, diced Tomatoes,
                     chopped Black Olives, finely chopped Parsley, Salami chopped in processor.

ALFREDO   -   Toss Pasta with Alfredo Sauce and finely chopped Salami.

CAPRESE   -   Toss Pasta with diced Mozzarella, Tomatoes, chopped Basil, chopped Salami.

PARMESAN   -   Mix grated Parmesan with finely chopped Salami and toss into the Pasta.

PRIMAVERA   -   See "VEGETABLES" - VEGETABLES MISCELLANEOUS. Add Capers, Salami.

RAVIOLI   -   Drizzle hot melted Butter over Cheese Ravioli. Sprinkle finely chopped Salami.

SALAMI - MINI QUICHES   MINI QUICHES see "BASIC RECIPES"

Spray a tray of 12 small muffin cups (1/4-cup size) with Cooking Spray. Preheat oven to 375°.

Spread into each muffin cup	[1 TB + 1 tp	SALAMI thinly sliced and chopped
A few bits of	[	DILL PICKLE chopped
In a bowl whisk	[4	EGGS
Whisk into the Eggs	[1/4-cup	LIGHT CREAM
	[1 oz	SWISS CHEESE coarse-grated
	[2 TB	PARMESAN grated
	[1/2-tp	DRIED SWEET BASIL, PEPPER

Pour 1/8-cup of Mixture into each cup.
Stir to even Ingredients. Bake 10-to-12 minutes until golden, as per "BASIC RECIPES".

248

SALAMI - QUICHE with ROASTED BELL PEPPERS

See "VEGETABLES" - BELL PEPPERS.   Roast [3 large   BELL PEPPERS   orange
                                                            (Prepare ahead, refrigerate)

Cut Roasted Peppers into 2-inch wide strips.

In a nonstick skillet, over medium heat, heat [1 TB   VEGETABLE OIL
              When a light haze forms, sauté [1 cup   ONION   quartered, thinly sliced
        When golden brown, turn off heat [sprinkle   a little SALT

Preheat oven to 375°.
                        In a large bowl beat [3   EGGS
        Brush with a little of the beaten Eggs a [9-inch   FROZEN UNCOOKED PIE SHELL

Set in the oven for 2 minutes only. Let cool.

                      Whisk into the Eggs [3/4-cup   LIGHT CREAM + 1/4-cup MILK
                                             [2 TB   FLAT LEAF PARSLEY   finely chop
                                             [2 oz   SWISS CHEESE   coarse-grated
                                             [1/4-cup   PARMESAN   grated
                                             [a pinch   SALT, GROUND BLACK PEPPER
            Add the BROWNED ONIONS and [4 oz   SALAMI   coarsely chopped in
                                                                                      processor

To assemble   - Place the Pie Shell, in its foil pan, on a cookie sheet.
               - Spread in it half of the BELL PEPPERS. Cover with half of the CUSTARD.
               - Spread the remaining Bell Peppers. Top with the remaining CUSTARD.
To bake   - Slide Quiche into oven. Reduce heat to 350°. Bake as per "BASIC RECIPES".

SALAMI - RISOTTO alla PUTTANESCA   *Appetizer, serves 2*

In a small nonstick skillet, medium heat, heat [1-1/2 TB   EXTRA-VIRGIN OLIVE OIL
          When a light haze forms, sauté until soft [2 cloves   GARLIC   mashed
With a wooden spoon, mash the Cloves with [3   ANCHOVY FILLETS   chopped
      When they are dissolved in the Oil stir in [1/2-cup   DICED TOMATOES canned, drain

Stir until moisture evaporates and Tomatoes
turn into a Purée.
                        Bring to a simmer [3 cups   CHICKEN BROTH   lightly salted
                                                               (+ 1/4-cup if needed)
In an 8-inch skillet, over medium heat, heat [1-1/2 TB   BUTTER
                                             [2 tp   EXTRA-VIRGIN OLIVE OIL
                  When it sizzles, sauté [2 TB   ONION   finely chopped
          When Onion begins to color, add [3/4-cup   ARBORIO RICE
  Stir until grains are coated and glisten, add [2 TB   DRY VERMOUTH

Stir until the Vermouth evaporates.   Mix in [the Anchovy/Tomato mixture

Add one ladle (1/2-cup) at a time of BROTH.

      When 2 cups have been absorbed, mix in [3 oz   SALAMI   slices coarsely chopped
                                             [1 tp   TINY CAPERS   rinsed, drained
When 3 cups have been absorbed, the Rice
should be tender, firm, creamy.   Stir in [2 TB   BLACK OLIVES   chopped
                                             [1 TB   FRESH BASIL   finely chopped
              Turn off heat and mix in [2 TB   PARMESAN   grated
                                             [to taste   SALT, GROUND BLACK PEPPER
Cover. Let Risotto set for 5 minutes.

SAUSAGE - CASSOULET THE SIMPLE WAY   (France)

Cassoulet is a French Bean Casserole requiring a long preparation. The original dish consists of White Beans, Meats and Sausage cooked in Goose Fat. As well as other Meats, Goose or Duck, cooked separately. Then everything assembled and baked.

Here is my version. Prepare the Cassoulet a day ahead to allow flavors to blend. Refrigerate.

Serves 4 to 6

THE BEANS See "VEGETABLES" - BEANS [		"Pre-cooking Preparation".
Prepare for cooking [	1-1/2 cups	NAVY BEANS
In a 2-quart heavy saucepan, medium heat, cook soft [	6 strips	BACON cut into small pieces. Drain on paper towels.
Pour FAT out of saucepan except for 1 TB and add to it [	2 TB	VEGETABLE OIL
When a light haze forms, medium heat, add [	1 large	ONION finely chopped
When Onion begins to soften, add [	3 cloves	GARLIC mashed and minced
When Onion is translucent, stir in [		the Navy Beans
[	2 TB	TOMATO PURÉE
[	1 TB	TOMATO PASTE
[	1/4-tp	DRIED THYME crumbled
[	1/8-tp	GROUND CLOVES
[	to taste	GROUND BLACK PEPPER
[	2 TB	WHITE WINE or BRANDY

Stir until the Liquor evaporates.

Add a [	10.5 oz-can	BEEF BOUILLON
[	3-1/4 cups	WATER

Bring to a rapid boil. Reduce heat to low, cover and simmer.

After 30 minutes stir in [	1-1/2 lbs	RAW SAUSAGE 3/4-inch chunks It can be a variety of Sausage.

- Bring rapidly to a boil, reduce heat to low, cover, simmer, stir once in a while.
- Cook 1 hour, or until the Beans are tender.
- Add the cooked BACON. SALT and PEPPER. *

THE CASSOULET

Cooked

Transfer the hot Beans and Sausage to an oven-proof casserole, layering in-between [	any of	PORC, FRANKFURTERS,
[		HAM, DUCK, TURKEY
[		Also use Leftovers

- Cover with foil. Refrigerate overnight.
- Before baking, bring to room temperature.
- Preheat oven to 350°.

Pour over the Beans [	1/3-cup	CHICKEN or MEAT BROTH
Poke with a fork to let Broth sink in, sprinkle [		COARSE BREADCRUMBS
Dot with [	3 TB	BUTTER cut into tidbits

Cover with foil. Bake 30 minutes.
Uncover, bake for 15 minutes longer. Pass under the broiler to crust the top.

*   At this point, without continuing the recipe, the Beans can be covered, cooled, refrigerated and served the next day as is.

SAUSAGE - CRÊPE FILLING

CRÊPES see "BASIC RECIPES"

Filling yields about 2-1/4 cups

In a nonstick skillet, over medium heat, heat	[2 tp	VEGETABLE OIL
When a light haze forms, sauté	[1/2-cup	ONION finely chopped
	[1/2-cup	GREEN BELL PEPPER finely chop
When Onion is translucent add	[10 oz	RAW SAUSAGE casing removed

Stir to break up lumps and cook the Sausage
until done and lightly browned.
Place in a sieve to drain.

Mix in a bowl	[1/3-cup	RICOTTA CHEESE
	[1/4-cup	PARMESAN grated
	[1/4-cup	MOZZARELLA coarse-grated
	[2 TB	PARSLEY finely chopped

Mix in the SAUSAGE. Cover the surface with
plastic wrap. Refrigerate.
Fill and roll the Crêpes.

Heat, serve with	[	ALFREDO SAUCE on the side
	[or	TOMATO SAUCE for Pasta

SAUSAGE - BAKED OMELET FLAMENCO

Appetizer
Serves 4 to 6

In a nonstick skillet, heat	[1 tp	VEGETABLE OIL
Swirl it in the skillet. Cook	[10 oz	CHORIZO casing removed

Stir until well cooked, breaking up lumps.
Drain in a sieve.

Peel, wash, dry, dice	[10 oz	BAKING POTATOES

In an 8-inch oven-proof skillet,

over medium high heat, heat	[4 TB	EXTRA-VIRGIN OLIVE OIL

When a light haze forms, add and sauté the
POTATOES until they begin to soften.

Add	[1/2-cup	ONION finely chopped
When Onion softens add	[2 cloves	GARLIC mashed and minced
When Onion is translucent, add	[1 medium	GREEN BELL PEPPER diced

Stir until the Potatoes are cooked. Sprinkle	[	SALT, GROUND BLACK PEPPER
Optional	[crushed	DRIED HOT RED PEPPER or flakes

Turn off heat. Add the CHORIZO.
Spread the Mixture evenly in the skillet.

Preheat oven to 425°. Beat with a whisk	[6 large	EGGS
	[1/4-tp	SALT, GROUND BLACK PEPPER
	[1/4-tp	SAFFRON THREADS crushed
Then mix in	[4 TB	FLAT LEAF PARSLEY finely chop
	[1/3-cup	MANCHEGO CHEESE coarse-grate

- Pour EGGS into skillet, over Potato Mixture.
- Spread evenly with a spatula, poking at random for the EGGS to run to the bottom.

- Place the skillet on middle rack of oven. Reduce heat to 400°. Bake for 15 minutes.
- Insert a skewer in the center, if it comes out clean, the Omelet is ready. If sticky, cook longer.
- Slide Omelet onto a serving platter. Or let it cool a few minutes and overturn onto a platter.
- <u>Serve</u> warm or at room temperature, with a Salad.

SAUSAGE - MACARONI PASTITSIO   Greek style   *Serves 4 to 6*

1. Cook in salted boiling water for 6 minutes [4 oz   ELBOW PASTA   drain, let cool
When cooled, transfer to a bowl and mix in [1 TB   MELTED BUTTER
                                            [2 oz   PARMESAN   grated

In a nonstick skillet, over medium heat, heat [2 tp   VEGETABLE OIL
When a light haze forms, sauté [1/2-cup   ONION   finely chopped
When Onion is translucent, stir in [3/4-lb   RAW SAUSAGE   casing removed
Sprinkle [1/4-tp   ALLSPICE
          [1/8-tp   GROUND CINNAMON
Cook Sausage. When lightly browned, mix in [1 oz   PARMESAN   grated

2. Spray an 8 x 8 baking dish.
Spread in it half of the Pasta. Cover with
the Sausage. Top with remaining Pasta.

3.   See "SAUCES". Prepare [2 cups   VELOUTÉ WHITE SAUCE
Turn off heat.
                              In a bowl, beat [2   EGGS + 1 EGG YOLK
                      Add one at a time, beating [4 TB   of the hot Sauce

Over <u>low</u> heat gradually whisk the EGGS into
the Sauce until well incorporated.

Turn off heat and stir in until melted [2 oz   SWISS CHEESE coarse-grated
                                        [1 oz   PARMESAN   grated
Pour 3/4-of the Sauce over the Pasta.
Let it set for 10 minutes. Cover with the
remaining Sauce. Smooth the surface. *

Before baking sprinkle with [2 oz   PARMESAN/SWISS   mixed in
                                                      equal amounts
Bake in oven preheated to 350° for 30-to-40 minutes.

* To bake later, cover with plastic wrap, refrigerate. Bring to room temperature before baking.

SAUSAGE - PASTA DIVA   *Serves 2 as a main course*

In an 8-inch skillet, medium heat, heat [2 tp   VEGETABLE OIL
When a light haze forms, sauté [2 TB   ONION   finely chopped
When Onion is translucent, add [8 oz   SAUSAGE   removed from casing
When Meat is done and lightly browned, add [1 TB   TINY CAPERS rinsed, drained

Remove the Meat with a slotted spoon into a
bowl and set aside. Pour out skillet grease.

In the skillet, over medium heat, heat [2 TB   EXTRA-VIRGIN OLIVE OIL
When a light haze forms, sauté [2 TB   ONION   finely chopped
When Onion is translucent, add [3 oz   SLICED MUSHROOMS
Sauté Mushrooms for 2 minutes and add [3 small   ARTICHOKE HEARTS canned, pat
                                                      dry, cut longwise into wedges

Stir to heat well the Artichokes. Add [to taste   SALT, GROUND BLACK PEPPER

Mix in [the Cooked Sausage Meat
Turn off heat.
Toss Sausage Mixture into [3 oz   hot PENNE
Serve [on the side PARMESAN   grated

252

SAUSAGE - PASTA FAGIOLI

Serves 4 as a main course

In a nonstick skillet, over medium heat, heat	[2 TB	EXTRA-VIRGIN OLIVE OIL
When a light haze forms, sauté	[2 cloves	GARLIC mashed and minced
When Garlic is fragrant, stir in	[7-to-10 oz-can	FAVA BEANS rinsed, drained
Sauté the Beans for 4 minutes, then add	[12 oz	COOKED SAUSAGE diced
Stir to heat the Sausage and add	[2 TB	FRESH BASIL finely chopped
Toss the SAUSAGE MIXTURE into	[6 oz	hot PASTA SHELLS
	[drizzle with	EXTRA-VIRGIN OLIVE OIL

SAUSAGE - PASTA PRIMA DONNA

Serves 4 as a main course

Steam in microwave for 6 minutes a	[10 oz-pkg	FROZEN CHOPPED SPINACH
In a nonstick skillet, over medium heat, heat	[1 TB	EXTRA-VIRGIN OLIVE OIL
When a light haze forms, sauté	[1/4-cup	ONION finely chopped
When it begins to color, cook	[10 oz	SAUSAGE MEAT casing removed

Drain in a sieve.

Heat in the skillet	[2 TB	EXTRA-VIRGIN OLIVE OIL
When a light haze forms, sauté	[2 cloves	GARLIC mashed and minced
When Garlic begins to color, add the	[	the Spinach
Stir for 2 minutes and add	[	the Sausage Meat
Stir to heat through, mix in	[1/4-cup	PARMESAN grated
	[3 TB	PINE NUTS toasted

Turn off heat, add PEPPER to taste.

Toss into	[6 oz	hot PENNE or RIGATONI
Serve with	[grated	PARMESAN on the side

SAUSAGE - QUICHE with SAUERKRAUT

Measure	[1-1/4 cups	PRE-COOKED SAUERKRAUT
		(Drained, rinse if needed)
In a nonstick skillet, over medium heat, heat	[1 TB	BUTTER + 1 tp VEGETABLE OIL
When it sizzles, sauté	[1 cup	ONION sliced, coarsely chopped
When the Onion turns golden, add	[	the Sauerkraut
Stir for 1 minute and add	[4 TB	WHITE WINE
Stir and sprinkle	[to taste	NUTMEG grated, GROUND CUMIN
	[	CRACKED BLACK PEPPER

Reduce heat to medium low. Cook until very
tender and all Liquid has evaporated.
Cool in a sieve.

Mix into SAUERKRAUT	[5 oz	COOKED KIELBASA SAUSAGE
		Chopped coarsely in processor

Preheat oven to 375°.

In a bowl beat	[3	EGGS
Brush with a little of the beaten EGGS a	[9-inch	FROZEN UNCOOKED PIE SHELL

Set in the oven for 2 minutes only. Let cool.

Whisk into the Eggs	[1 cup	HALF-AND-HALF
	[1 cup	CHEDDAR coarse-grated

- Lay the Pie Shell on a cookie sheet.
- Spread in it the SAUERKRAUT. Ladle the CUSTARD over it.
- Slide Quiche into the oven. Reduce heat to 350°. Bake as per "BASIC RECIPES".

SAUSAGE and RICE a la CUBANA

Serves 2 as a main course

In a nonstick skillet, medium heat, heat [2 TB   EXTRA-VIRGIN OLIVE OIL
When a light haze forms, sauté [1/2-cup   ONION   finely chopped
When Onion softens, add [1/2-tp   GARLIC   minced
[1 cup   GREEN BELL PEPPER diced
When Bell Pepper softens, add [1 cup   BLACK BEANS   canned, rinse,
drain
Stir, cook the Beans for 5 minutes and add [to taste   GROUND BLACK PEPPER, SALT
Mix in [4-to-6 oz   COOKED SAUSAGE   diced
[1/2-cup   PINEAPPLE   canned, drain, dice
Cover, simmer for 5 minutes.
Mix into Beans [1 cup   COOKED WHITE RICE
[1/4-cup   CHICKEN BROTH
Cover, simmer for 5 minutes. Serve hot.

SAUSAGE and RICE a la TURCA

Serves 4   LENTILS - "VEGETABLES"

In heavy saucepan, over medium heat, heat [1 TB   VEGETABLE OIL
When a light haze forms sauté [1/2-cup   ONION   finely chopped
When translucent, stir in [1/2-cup   BROWN LENTILS "prepared"
[1/4-tp   GROUND CUMIN
Add [WATER   as per Lentil package
Also add [WATER for the Rice, as per pkg.
directions
Bring Water to a boil and dissolve in it [1 cube   BOUILLON   crumbled

Cook Lentils for 20 minutes and add [1/2-cup   UNCOOKED WHITE RICE

Bring to a boil, reduce heat to low, simmer until
the Rice is done.
Meanwhile, in a skillet, heat [2 TB   BUTTER
When it sizzles, toast in it [3 TB   PINE NUTS
When the Nuts turn light golden brown, stir in [1/4-cup   GOLDEN RAISINS
[3 TB   PISTACHIOS peeled
[6 oz   COOKED SAUSAGE diced
Stir to heat well the Sausage.
Pour the SAUSAGE MIXTURE into the cooked Rice and Lentils. Mix well and serve.

SAUSAGE and RICE - BALALAIKA

Serves 4

Blanch for 5 minutes in salted boiling Water [3 cups   RED CABBAGE shredded. Drain.

In a 10-inch skillet, medium heat, heat [1 TB   BUTTER + 1 tp VEGETABLE OIL
When it sizzles, sauté [1 cup   ONION sliced 1/4-inch thick, diced
When it softens add [1/2-tp   GARLIC   mashed and minced
When Onion turns golden add the CABBAGE [1/4-cup   BLACK CURRANTS
Stir in [1/3-cup   DRY WHITE WINE
[1/3-cup   BROTH   (more as needed)
- Bring to a boil, cover, reduce heat to low.
- Cook the Cabbage until tender, adding more
if needed, to keep it moist.
Then stir in [6 oz   COOKED SAUSAGE   diced
[1 cup   COOKED WHITE RICE   or more
Leave for 3 minutes over low heat. Serve.

SAUSAGE and RICE - JAMBALAYA   *Serves 2*

In heavy saucepan, over medium heat, heat	[2 TB + 1 tp	VEGETABLE OIL
When a light haze forms, add	[1 clove	GARLIC mashed
Stir until Garlic is fragrant. Discard it. Add	[1/2-cup	ONION finely chopped
When translucent, stir in	[1/4-cup	CELERY finely diced
	[1/2-cup	GREEN BELL PEPPER diced
	[1/2-cup	RED BELL PEPPER diced
Stir for 1 minute and add	[1/2-cup	UNCOOKED WHITE RICE
Stir to coat the grains with the Oil and mix in	[4 oz	COOKED SAUSAGE diced
As per Rice package directions, add	[	needed amount of WATER
	[to taste	SALT

Bring to a boil.
Reduce heat to low, cover, simmer until the Rice is done. Fluff it with a fork before serving.

SAUSAGE and RICE - MEXICANA   *Serves 2*

In a nonstick skillet, medium heat, heat	[2 TB	EXTRA-VIRGIN OLIVE OIL
When a light haze forms, sauté	[1/2-cup	RED ONION finely chopped
When Onion softens add	[1/2-tp	GARLIC minced
	[1/2-cup	RED BELL PEPPER diced
When Bell Pepper softens, add	[1/2-cup	GARBANZOS canned, drain, rinse
Sprinkle with	[1/4-tp	GROUND CUMIN
	[1/4-cup	BROTH
Stir, cook Garbanzos for 4 or 5 minutes,		
until they have softened, and add	[1 cup	COOKED CHORIZO diced
	[1 cup	COOKED WHITE RICE
	[to taste	PICKLED JALAPEÑO chopped
Stir to heat the Chorizo and Rice.		
Mix in	[1/2-cup	TOMATOES peeled, seeded, diced
	[2 TB	CILANTRO finely chopped

Turn off heat and let set for 5 minutes.

SAUSAGE and RICE - SEVILLANA   *Serves 3 or 4*

Heat a nonstick skillet, and swirl in it	[1 TB	VEGETABLE OIL
When hot, fry until well cooked, lightly brown	[8 oz	CHORIZO sliced 1/4-inch thick
		Or other raw Sausage
Drain on paper towels.		
Dissolve	[1/4-tp	SAFFRON THREADS pulverized
in	[hot	CHICKEN BROTH as needed to
		cook 1 cup Rice
In a heavy saucepan, over medium heat, heat	[2 TB	OLIVE OIL for cooking
When a light haze forms, sauté	[1/2-cup	ONION finely chopped
When Onion softens add	[1/2-tp	GARLIC finely chopped
	[1 cup	RED BELL PEPPER finely diced
When Bell Pepper has softened, stir in	[1/2-cup	FROZEN GREEN PEAS thaw, drain
	[to taste	GROUND BLACK PEPPER
Stir the Peas for 1 minute and add	[1 cup	UNCOOKED WHITE RICE
Stir the Rice to coat it with Oil, add	[	the Chorizo cut into bite-size
	[2 TB	PIMIENTO chopped

Add the CHICKEN BROTH. Bring to a boil.
Reduce heat to low, cover, simmer until the Rice is done. Fluff with a fork before serving.

SAUSAGE - RISOTTO TAJ MAHAL   RISOTTO see "BASIC RECIPES"

Serves 2 as a main course

Bring to a simmer	[3 cups	CHICKEN BROTH lightly salted
		(+ 1/4-cup more if needed)
Put in a small saucepan	[1 TB mild	CURRY POWDER (or 1/2-TB hot)
To dissolve Curry Powder, stir in gradually	[1 cup	of the simmering Chicken Broth
Keep simmering and add	[a sprinkle	GARLIC POWDER
In a heavy 8-inch nonstick skillet,		
over medium heat, heat	[1-1/2 TB	BUTTER + 1 TB VEGETABLE OIL
When it sizzles, sauté	[1/3-cup	ONION finely chopped
When Onion is translucent, add	[1/2-cup	BOILED BABY CARROTS
		thinly sliced
When the Carrots start browning, add	[3/4-cup	ARBORIO RICE
Stir until grains are coated and glisten. Add	[1/4-cup	DRY WHITE WINE

Stir until the Wine evaporates.
Add, a 1/2-cup of the CURRY BROTH.
Continue with 2 cups of the BROTH.

When it has been absorbed, stir in	[4 oz	COOKED SAUSAGE diced
	[3 TB	GOLDEN RAISINS

Add the last 1/2-cup of CURRY BROTH.
When absorbed, the Rice should be tender,
firm, creamy.

Turn off heat and stir in	[2 TB	PINE NUTS toasted
	[1 TB	BUTTER diced small
	[to taste	SALT, GROUND BLACK PEPPER

Cover. Let the Risotto set for 5 minutes.

SAUSAGE with SOUPS   Add SAUSAGE to Soups and make it a meal.

SOUPS	CAULIFLOWER CREAM	[with	CHEESE CROUTONS, grated PARMESAN
	LENTIL	[	HERB CROUTONS, ONIONS fried, canned
	NAVY BEAN	[	crumbled TORTILLA CHIPS and TABASCO
	ONION	[	with two or three kinds of Sausage
	SPLIT PEA	[	TOASTED GARLIC BREAD dunks
	VEGETABLE	[	CORNBREAD

SAUSAGE with SPEEDY BEAN WELSH RAREBIT

In a nonstick skillet, heat	[1 can	BAKED or BARBECUED BEANS
To thin the Beans add	[2 or 3 TB	BEER or BROTH
When the Beans are hot, mix in	[1/2-cup	CHEDDAR shredded

When Cheddar has melted into the Beans,
add more, according to taste.

Add	[to taste	WORCESTERSHIRE SAUCE

Serve the Beans hot, with grilled or fried SAUSAGE.
To make a Welsh Rarebit see "BASIC RECIPES" - FONDUES

256

XIII

MEATS

HELPFUL HINTS

Damp meat will not brown well.
Pat dry it with paper towels before seasoning and cooking.

To obtain an even cooking, bring first to room temperature.

Long cooking reduces meat by almost a quarter of its size.

COOKING TEMPERATURES FOR MEATS

Boneless cuts need a longer cooking time.
Allow 8-to-10 minutes more per pound.

To determine the correct internal doneness you must use
a meat thermometer inserted in the center of the cut.

ROASTING

			Oven Temperature	Internal Temperature	Minutes Per Pound
BEEF	Whole Tenderloin	*Rare*	300°	140°	18 - 20
		Medium	300°	160°	22 - 25
LAMB	Crown Roast	*Medium to well*	350°	175° - 180°	30 - 35
	Shoulder	*Well done*	350°	175° - 180°	30 - 35
	Leg of Lamb	*Medium*	350°	170° - 175°	25 - 30
		Well done	350°	180°	30 - 35
PORK	Tenderloin	*Well done*	350°	185°	30 - 40
	Shoulder	*Well done*	350°	185°	40 - 45
VEAL	Loin	*Well done*	325°	170°	30 - 35
	Shoulder/Rack	*Well done*	325°	170°	25 - 35

BROILING

				Rare		*Medium*
BEEF	Filet Mignon	1" thick	500°	5	*minutes*	6 - 7
		1-1/2-to-2"		9 - 14		12 - 18
	Sirloin	1"	500°	9 - 12		14 - 16
		1-1/2-to-2"	500°	15 - 25		20 - 30
LAMB	Chops	1"- thick	500°	10		12
		1-1/2-to-2"	500°	15 - 18		18 - 22

BRAISING

BEEF	Pot Roast	3 - 5 pounds	3 to 4 hours
PORK	Chops	3/4-to-1-1/4 inch thick	45 - 60 minutes
LAMB and VEAL	Stew Meat	1-1/2 inch cubes	1-1/4 to 1-1/2 hours
VEAL	Chops	3/4-to-1 inch thick	40 - 60 minutes

258

MEATS

BEEF

SEASONED BUTTERS for FILLETS and STEAKS

Use Ingredients at room temperature. Mash in processor until smooth.

HERBS

[4 oz	UNSALTED BUTTER	
[2 tp	DRIED GREEN ONION	
[2 tp	DRIED PARSLEY	
[2 tp	DRIED TARRAGON	
[1/2-tp	SALT or to taste	
[to taste	BLACK PEPPER	

HORSERADISH

[4 oz	UNSALTED BUTTER	
[2 TB	PREPARED HORSERADISH	
[		or to taste
[1 tp	DRIED THYME	
[1/2-tp	SALT or to taste	
[1/4-tp	SWEET PAPRIKA	

MUSTARD

[4 oz	UNSALTED BUTTER	
[1 TB	DIJON MUSTARD	
[1 TB	COARSE-GRAIN	
[		MUSTARD
[1 tp	GREEN ONION	
[2 tp	SWEET BASIL	

BLUE CHEESE

[4 oz	UNSALTED BUTTER	
[3 oz	BLUE CHEESE	
[2 tp	DRIED GREEN ONION	
[2 tp	DRIED PARSLEY	
[1/4-tp	WHITE PEPPER	

Optional
[1/8-tp GARLIC POWDER

PARMESAN

[4 oz	UNSALTED BUTTER	
[3 oz	PARMESAN grated	
[1 tp	DRIED GREEN ONION	
[2 tp	DRIED BASIL	
[to taste	GROUND BLACK PEPPER	

Optional
[1/4-tp   RED PEPPER FLAKES crushed

FETA CHEESE

[4 oz	UNSALTED BUTTER	
[3 oz	FETA CHEESE	
[1/8-tp	GARLIC POWDER	
[1 tp	DRIED PARSLEY	
[1 tp	DRIED OREGANO	
	or	DRIED MINT
[	GROUND BLACK PEPPER	
[	BLACK CARAWAY SEEDS	

- After mixing, taste, adjust by adding Seasonings. Process once more.
- Put Mixture on a piece of wax paper. Wrap tightly. Twist ends. Roll into a sausage. Refrigerate.
- Serve a 1/4-inch thick slice of the Seasoned Butter on top of a hot Fillet or Steak.

FILET MIGNON with BLUE CHEESE DRESSING

Place in a plastic bag	[2	FILETS MIGNON
To coat them well, pour gradually in enough	[ready-made	BLUE CHEESE DRESSING
Optional	[1 TB	ONION finely chopped

- Seal, toss well, refrigerate, marinate for 2 or 3 hours, toss and turn the bag once in a while.
- Pat dry the Filets and grill them. Top with a slice of BLUE CHEESE SEASONED BUTTER.

VARIATION - Marinate with an Italian Dressing. Top with Parmesan Seasoned Butter.
         - Or with a Herb and Garlic Dressing and top with Feta Cheese Seasoned Butter.

BOLLITO MISTO   Boiled Mixture (of Meats)   (Italy)   *The simple version.*

Consists of Meats and Vegetables boiled together, Poultry and Sausage cooked separately. Then everything combined and served hot, warm or cold with the Italian GREEN SAUCE (SALSA VERDE).

See "SAUCES" - COLD SAUCES.   Prepare [the GREEN SAUCE refrigerate, bring to room
                                                     temperature before serving.

Arrange in an oven-proof dish cooked Meats,
                   any of [BRISKET or other boiled Meats,
                             [CHICKEN skinned and boned, LAMB, VEAL,
                             [SAUSAGE, BEEF TONGUE

Surround with steamed or boiled, any of [BROCCOLI, BRUSSELS SPROUTS, CABBAGE,
                                       [CARROTS, CAULIFLOWER, GREEN BEANS,
                                       [POTATOES, PEARL ONIONS, ZUCCHINI

Cover with foil.
Heat or keep warm in oven preheated to 200°. Serve the SALSA VERDE on the side.

BRISKET with VEGETABLES

Serves 6

Use a stockpot in which the Brisket and Vegetables can fit snugly. If too large, you will have to use too much cooking Liquid, thus diluting the flavor.

Heat the stockpot and smear over the bottom	[1 TB	MARGARINE
Sear on all sides a	[3 lb	BRISKET trussed
Then add to the stockpot	[2 cans	BEEF BROTH 10.5 oz each
	[1 medium	ONION whole
	[2 ribs	CELERY cut in half
	[1 large	CARROT quartered
A BOUQUET GARNI tied in cheesecloth with	[2 sprigs	PARSLEY + 1 sprig THYME
	[1	BAY LEAF and 4 PEPPERCORNS
Add	[enough	WATER to cover the Brisket
		by 2-inches

Bring to a boil over high heat.
Then reduce to medium heat. Skim as the
scum rises to the surface.

When the Broth is about clear, add	[1 can	BEEF BROTH and more WATER
		to cover by 2-inches

- Bring to a boil. Reduce heat to medium low.
  Cover and simmer. Skim occasionally.
- 2 hours later, with slotted spoon remove and
  discard Vegetables and Herb Bouquet.

Add	[6 medium	CARROTS cut into 1-inch pieces
	[2 lbs	YUKON GOLD POTATOES cubed
Add more Broth or Water to cover and	[to taste	SALT, GROUND BLACK PEPPER

Bring to a boil, cover, reduce heat to low, simmer for 1-1/2 hours or until the Meat is tender.
Arrange Meat and Vegetables in a baking-dish. Moisten with Broth. Cover with foil.
Keep warm in the oven until ready to serve.

BRISKET SALAD

Prepare a VINAIGRETTE - see "DRESSINGS"

[LEFTOVER BRISKET cut into bite-size pieces		
[BOILED POTATOES bite-size cubes	Use [	RED WINE VINEGAR or TARRAGON VINEGAR
[CELERY HEART RIBS thinly sliced	Add [	CAPERS rinsed, drained, dried, chopped
[RAW MUSHROOMS thinly sliced	[	PARSLEY or WATERCRESS finely chopped
[GREEN ONION finely chopped	Garnish with [	HARD-COOKED EGGS wedges

BROTH - FATTA (Fáht-táh) Pita Bread Soup (Middle East) *Serves 2*

See "SANDWICHES". Quarter and toast	[	PLAIN WHITE PITA BREAD
		Other Bread can be used.
Heat in a small saucepan	[2 cups	BEEF BROTH do not use canned
Adjust Seasonings and add	[1 tp	RED WINE VINEGAR

Taste.
Add gradually drops of Vinegar until it reaches
a vinegary flavor pleasant to your taste.

Break toasted PITA into 2 soup plates, add	[	BOILED BEEF
	[	the Broth
Top with	[scoops of	PLAIN YOGURT
Sprinkle with	[	PARSLEY finely chopped

261

ROAST BEEF - CARPACCIO

To obtain very thin slices of cooked Roast Beef, place it in the freezer for 30-to-45 minutes. Use an electric knife to slice it. Arrange the slices on individual plates or on a serving platter:

1.   Drizzle over the ROAST BEEF [TRUFFLE OIL
                        Sprinkle with [PARSLEY   minced
                           Top with [PARMESAN shavings

2.   Thin with EXTRA-VIRGIN OLIVE OIL [PESTO SAUCE   ready-made
                 Spread on plates or platter [ARUGULA
     Top with ROAST BEEF, PESTO SAUCE and [PARMESAN   shavings

3.   Spread on plates or platter [SLICED RAW MUSHROOMS
         Top with ROAST BEEF. Spoon over [HORSERADISH CREAM see "SAUCES"
                                and [WATERCRESS   finely chopped

STEAK à la STROGANOFF   (Russia)   *Serves 2*

There are many fancy recipes for this dish. Here is the simple Russian way.

              In a 7-to-8 inch nonstick skillet, heat [1 TB   BUTTER + 1 TB VEGETABLE OIL
     Over medium high heat, when it sizzles, sauté [8 oz   * TENDERLOIN STEAK   cut into
                                                           strips 2" long x 1/2-inch thick.

Stir for 2 or 3 minutes, until lightly browned.
Remove with slotted spoon, set on a plate.
Sprinkle with SALT and PEPPER. Cover.

                 Over medium heat, add to the skillet [1 TB   BUTTER + 1 tp VEGETABLE OIL

When it melts, deglaze the skillet, scraping it
   with a wooden spoon. When it sizzles, add [1 cup   ONIONS thinly sliced (use small
                                                           Onions to obtain small rings)
     Sauté until the Onions begin to color, add [4 oz   SLICED MUSHROOMS

Sauté for 1 minute. Reduce heat to low, cover.
Simmer for 15 minutes.
                        Meanwhile, mix [1/2-cup   SOUR CREAM
                                        [2 TB   CHICKEN BROTH   cold
                                        [1/2-tp   YELLOW MUSTARD

- Sprinkle the MUSHROOMS with SALT, GROUND BLACK PEPPER. Add the STEAK, stir 1 minute.
- Then gradually, still over low heat, spoon in the SOUR CREAM. Mix it well before adding more.

Seve with   Kasha, Noodles, Spätzle Noodles, small Pasta, sautéed Potatoes, Croustades.

* If the strips are cut thinner, the sautéed Meat will be immediately well done.
   If you like the Meat very rare, brown the tenderloin fillets whole, then cut them into thin strips.

KASHA   In a 1-qt saucepan, medium heat,
           stir (2-to-3 minutes) until toasted [1/2-cup   KASHA (Buckwheat Groats)
                                Add [1 tp   VEGETABLE OIL
        Stir the Oil into the Kasha and add [1/3-cup   ONION   finely chopped
         When Onion is translucent, add [1 cup hot   CHICKEN BROTH   salted to taste
                                        [1 TB   BUTTER
                        Optional [3 TB   GOLDEN RAISINS, PEPPER
Bring to a boil.
Cover. Reduce heat to low, simmer for 12-to-15 minutes, until Kasha is cooked. *Serves 2.*

STEAK TARTARE   *Recipe per 4 oz of Meat*

The raw Egg Yolk in the classic recipe is substituted here with Mayonnaise.

THE DRESSING   With a fork, mix in a bowl [1 tp   MAYONNAISE
                                                  [1/4-tp   DIJON MUSTARD
                                                  [1 tp   CAPERS   rinsed, drained, minced
                                                  [1 TB   ONION minced, or more to taste
                                                  [2 tp   PARSLEY   finely chopped
                                                  [to taste WORCESTERSHIRE SAUCE
                                                  [1   ANCHOVY FILLET   mashed
                          Optional [1 or 2 TB   VODKA adds pizzazz

          With a wooden spoon, mix into the Dressing [4 oz   SIRLOIN or TENDERLOIN
                                                                      ground 3 times

Adjust Seasonings to taste. Refrigerate until
ready to serve.
                          Serve with thinly sliced [RYE, PUMPERNICKEL, SOURDOUGH

BEEF STEW   *Stews prepared a day ahead allow flavors to blend.*   *Serves 4 to 6*

     In a stewpan, over medium high heat, heat [2 TB   BUTTER + 1 tp VEGETABLE OIL
              When it sizzles, brown rapidly [16 small PEARL or CIPOLLINI ONIONS
                                                             (Peeled - see "VEGETABLES")
Remove Onions with slotted spoon, set aside.

                    In the stewpan, over high heat,
                    sear on all sides, in 2 batches [2 lbs lean   BEEF CHUCK 1-1/2 inch cubes

          Combine the Beef in the stewpan and [sprinkle   SALT, GROUND BLACK PEPPER
                    Stir, then sprinkle with [3 TB   FLOUR

          Stir the Meat to brown the Flour. Add [10.5 oz-can BEEF BROTH
                                                  [2 ribs   CELERY   cut in half
                                                  [1 medium   CARROT   pared and quartered
                                                  [1 small   ONION   whole
And a BOUQUET GATNI tied in cheesecloth of [1 sprig   THYME   +   2 sprigs PARSLEY
                                                  [2 cloves   GARLIC   +   1 BAY LEAF
                                                  [enough   WATER to cover by 2-inches

- Bring to a boil. Reduce heat to medium low.
- Cover, simmer. Skim the scum as needed.
- 1-1/4 hours later, with slotted spoon remove
  and discard Vegetables/Herb Bouquet.
                                      Add [1 can   BEEF BROTH
                                                  [4 medium   CARROTS   sliced a 1/4-inch thick
                                                  [1-1/2 lbs FINGERLING POTATOES
                                                  [enough   WATER to cover
                          Gradually mix in [to taste   BROWNING & SEASONING SAUCE
- Bring to a boil.
- Reduce heat to low, simmer 45 minutes.
- Add the browned ONIONS.
- Cook Meat/Vegetables until fork tender.
- Remove them with a slotted spoon into an
  oven-proof casserole.
                    Add to Cooking Juices [1 TB   ARROWROOT dissolved in 3 TB WATER

Over medium heat, stir until the Sauce thickens. Adjust Seasonings.
Pour over the Meat and Vegetables. Let cool, cover, refrigerate overnight. Warm in oven.

BEEF STEW - BOEUF BOURGUIGNON   Red Wine Stew (France)
Serves 4 to 6

In a stewpan, over medium high heat, heat	[2 TB	BUTTER + 1 tp VEGETABLE OIL
When it sizzles, brown lightly and rapidly	[16 small	PEARL or CIPOLLINI ONIONS
		(Peeled - see "VEGETABLES")

Remove Onions with slotted spoon. Set aside.

Fry in the stewpan	[2 oz	BACON SLAB diced (optional)

Drain on paper towels.

In the stewpan, over high heat, in 2 batches, sear on all sides	[2 lbs lean	BEEF CHUCK 1-1/2 inch cubes

Combine them in the stewpan	[sprinkle	SALT, GROUND BLACK PEPPER
If using, add the fried BACON, sprinkle with	[3 TB	FLOUR
Stir the Meat to brown the Flour. Then add	[1-1/2 cups	DRY RED WINE
Bring to a boil. Stir 2 or 3 times, then add	[2 cups	BEEF BROTH canned
	[1/4-tp	BROWN SUGAR
	[3 medium	CARROTS sliced a 1/4-inch thick
	[	BOUQUET GARNI previous recipe

- Bring to a boil. Cover, reduce heat to low,
  simmer for 1-3/4 hours. Add the ONIONS.
- Bring to a rapid boil, reduce heat to low and
  simmer until the Meat is fork tender.
- With slotted spoon transfer Meat/Vegetables
  to an oven casserole.

Add to Cooking Juices	[1 TB	ARROWROOT dissolved in 3 TB WATER

Over medium heat, stir until Sauce thickens. Adjust Seasonings. Pour it over the Meat. Cover.
Cool. Refrigerate overnight. Warm in oven. Serve with mashed, boiled or steamed Potatoes.

BEEF STEW - GOULASH   (Hungary)   *Serves 4 to 6*

In a stewpan brown lightly	[6 strips	BACON Remove with slotted spoon, drain on paper towels.

In the BACON FAT, over high heat, sear on all sides (in 2 batches)	[2 lbs lean	BEEF CHUCK 1-1/2 inch cubes

Set the cubes aside in a bowl.

If there is Fat in the stewpan, sauté in it	[1-1/2 cups	ONION finely chopped

NOTE - If the pan is dry, add 1 TB Margarine.

When Onion is translucent, stir in the Beef and dust the cubes lightly with	[	FLOUR

Stir, brown on all sides. Sprinkle with	[1 TB	SWEET HUNGARIAN PAPRIKA
Stir and add	[to taste	SALT, GROUND BLACK PEPPER
	[1/2-cup	GREEN BELL PEPPER finely chop
Add cooked BACON, coarsely chopped and	[2/3-cup	DRY RED WINE
	[10.5 oz-can	BEEF BROTH + 1 can WATER
or	[2-1/2 cups	Home-made Beef Broth

Stir, bring to a boil. Reduce heat to low.
Cover. Stir occasionally. Adjust Seasonings. Simmer 2-1/2 hours, or until the Meat is fork tender.

Serve with Spätzle, small Pasta, mashed, steamed or boiled Potatoes, Carrots, Sauerkraut.

STEW LEFTOVERS

À LA PARMENTIER

Fill 2/3 of ramekins or oven-proof dishes	[with	BEEF STEW or BEEF BOURGUIGNON
Top with	[	MASHED POTATOES seasoned to taste
Sprinkle with	[	CHEDDAR, SWISS or PARMESAN

Pass under the broiler until golden brown.

CROUSTADES

Prepare	[	CROUSTADES see "SANDWICHES"
Serve over them	[	BEEF STEW or BOEUF BOURGUIGNON

FAJITAS

Drain Gravy from the	[	STEW then cut up Meat and Vegetables
Spread	[	TORTILLAS
with	[	SOUR CREAM
Sprinkle lightly with	[	GREEN ONION minced
Top with MEAT / VEGETABLES Sprinkle with	[	CHEDDAR or MONTEREY JACK shredded

Roll and place Fajitas in a greased oven-dish.
Cover with foil. Warm them in the oven.
Serve with the STEW GRAVY or SALSA.

With PASTA

Toss STEW into	[	BOW TIES, ORECCHIETTE, PENNE,
	[	RIGATONI, SHELLS, CHEESE TORTELLINI

With RICE

In a saucepan heat	[1 TB	VEGETABLE OIL
Sauté until limp	[4 TB	ONION finely chopped
Add	[	RICE amount for 2 servings

Stir the Rice until lightly toasted.

Add	[	BEEF BROTH amount to cook the Rice

Bring to a boil. Cover.
Reduce heat to low, simmer until the Rice
is almost done.

Stir in to taste	[	FROZEN GREEN PEAS thawed

Cover, finish cooking the Rice.

Serve with	[hot	BEEF STEW or BOEUF BOURGUIGNON

RISOTTO CASSEROLE

Prepare a	[	PLAIN RISOTTO see "BASIC RECIPES"
Add	[	FONTINA or PECORINO ROMANO

BUTTER an oven-proof dish. Sprinkle all over   [BREADCRUMBS

Spread half of RISOTTO in the dish. Top with   [BEEF STEW

Top with remaining RISOTTO.

Smooth the surface and sprinkle with	[any of grated PARMESAN, PECORINO ROMANO
and	[BREADCRUMBS
Dot with	[BUTTER tidbits

Bake in oven preheated to 350° for 15 minutes. Pass under the broiler for a light golden brown.

GROUND BEEF

ETHNIC BURGERS

Omit the ONION for "rare" burgers unless you like the taste of raw Onion.
Or blanch Onion segments for 1 minute. Pat dry, let cool. Chop finely.
First mix the following combinations. Knead into 1 lb SIRLOIN or CHUCK.
After kneading, taste, then adjust Seasonings adding more if needed.

AFRICAN

[1/4-cup   ONION   grated
[1/4-tp   HOT CHILI PASTE   or to taste
[2 TB   COCONUT MILK
[2 TB   DRIED MINT   crumbled
[2 TB   SALTED PEANUTS   pulverized
[1/2-tp   ALLSPICE   or to taste
[1/8-tp   GARLIC POWDER or to taste
[1/2-tp   SALT

ASIAN

[1/4-cup   ONION grated
[2 TB   FRESH GINGER   grated
[1 TB   SOY SAUCE
[3 TB   FRESH CILANTRO   chopped
[1/4-tp   HOT MUSTARD   or to taste
[1/2-tp   GROUND CUMIN
[1/8-tp   GARLIC POWDER   or more
[1/2-tp   SALT, PEPPER   to taste

CARIBBEAN

[1/4-cup   ONION   grated
[2 TB   SWEET PIMIENTOS chopped
[2 TB   DARK RUM
[3 TB   FRESH CILANTRO   chopped
[2 TB   GREEN OLIVES chopped
[1/2-tp   GROUND CUMIN
[1/8-tp   GARLIC POWDER or more to taste
[1 tp   SALT
[to taste   GROUND BLACK PEPPER
[optional   TABASCO

GREEK

[1/4-cup   ONION   grated
[1 TB   OUZO
[1 TB   DRIED OREGANO crumbled
[2 TB   FRESH PARSLEY   chopped
[1/4-tp   GROUND CINNAMON
[1/8-tp   GARLIC POWDER
[1/2-tp   SALT, PEPPER   to taste

    Knead the Mixture then add:
[1/4-cup   FETA CHEESE   crumbled

INDIAN

[1/4-cup   ONION   grated
[1 TB   PLAIN YOGURT
[2 TB   CHUTNEY   of your choice
[2 TB   FRESH CILANTRO   chopped
[1 tp   GARAM MASALA (Indian spice)
[1/4-tp   DRY MUSTARD
[1/8-tp   GARLIC POWDER or to taste
[1 tp   SALT, GROUND BLACK PEPPER

ITALIAN

[1/4-cup   ONION   grated
[1 TB   TOMATO PASTE
[3 TB   FRESH BASIL chopped
[1/8-tp   GARLIC POWDER   or more

    Knead the Mixture then add:
[4 TB   PARMESAN   grated
[2 TB   TINY CAPERS

MEXICAN

[1/4-cup   RED ONION   grated
[2 TB   MAYONNAISE
[2 TB   TORTILLA CHIPS pulverized
[1 or 2 TB PICKLED JALAPEÑOS chopped
[1/2-tp   GROUND CUMIN
[1/8-tp   GARLIC POWDER or more to taste
[to taste   HOT CHILI or GROUND BLACK PEPPER

MIDDLE EASTERN

[1/4-cup   ONION   grated
[2 TB   TAHINI SAUCE   prepared
[1/2-tp   GROUND CORIANDER
[1/4-tp   ALLSPICE
[2 TB   DRIED MINT   crumbled
[1/8-tp   GARLIC POWDER
[1/2-tp   SALT, BLACK PEPPER

MOROCCAN

[1/4-cup ONION grated
[1/4-tp   GROUND CUMIN
[1/2-tp   GROUND CORIANDER

[1/2-tp   DRIED MINT   crumbled
[3 TB   CILANTRO   finely chopped
[1 tp   SALT, CAYENNE   to taste

BOLOGNESE SAUCE   *Yields 3-to-3-1/2 cups*   Speedy Bolognese see "SAUCES

In a heavy saucepan, over medium heat, heat	[2 TB	EXTRA-VIRGIN OLIVE OIL
	[1 TB	BUTTER
When it sizzles, sauté	[1/2-cup	ONION finely chopped
When Onion is translucent, stir in	[3 TB	CARROT finely chopped
	[3 TB	CELERY finely chopped
Stir for a couple of minutes and add	[1 lb	LEAN GROUND ROUND
	[to taste	NUTMEG grated

With wooden spoon break up lumps, stir until
the meat is cooked. Before it browns add   [1/2-cup   DRY WHITE WINE
                                             [sprinkle   SALT, GROUND BLACK PEPPER

Stir until the Wine has evaporated. Then add   [2 TB   TOMATO PASTE
Stir blending Paste into the Meat, then add   [28 oz-can   CHOPPED TOMATOES   with juice
                                                 [1   BAY LEAF

Bring to a quick boil. Reduce heat to low.
Cover, simmer for 1 hour. Adjust Seasonings and simmer for 30 minutes. Turn off heat.
Remove the Bay Leaf. Let the Sauce cool uncovered. Refrigerate overnight.

WITH FRIED EGGS   -   Spread the Sauce into a skillet. Heat it. Break into it the Eggs.
                       Let the Whites run into the Meat Sauce. Fry the Eggs.

CHILI con CARNE   *Yields 6-1/2 to 7 cups*

In large heavy saucepan, medium heat, heat   [1-1/2 TB   VEGETABLE OIL
            When a light haze forms, sauté   [1 large   ONION   finely chopped
When Onion is translucent, add and sauté   [2 lbs   LEAN ROUND or CHUCK
                                                                         coarsely ground

Use a wooden spoon to break up the lumps.

When the Meat has browned, stir in   [1 kit   CHILI MIX like "2 Alarm Chili Kit"
                            Add   [10.5 oz-can   BEEF BOUILLON
                                      [1 can   WATER
                            and   [10.5 oz-can   ROTEL TOMATOES and CHILIES

Bring slowly to a boil.
Cover, reduce heat to low and simmer for 30-to-40 minutes. Then add SALT to taste.
Cool and refrigerate to let the flavors blend. It tastes best the next day. It can also be frozen.

CHILI - PASTA au GRATIN   *Serves 4*

Mix in a bowl   [5 oz   PENNE   cooked *al dente*
                 [1-1/2 cups   CHILI con CARNE   drained
                 [1/4-cup of   drained Chili Sauce
                 [1/2-cup   CHEDDAR   coarse-grated

See "SAUCES". Prepare   [1 cup   MEDIUM WHITE SAUCE
When it thickens, turn off heat and stir in   [1/4-cup   PARMESAN   grated
                                       [SALT if needed

Mix the SAUCE into the PENNE. Spread them
into sprayed 8 x 8 oven-dish.
                Sprinkle   [2 TB each   CHEDDAR and PARMESAN mixed

Bake in oven preheated to 350° for 20 minutes. Pass under the broiler to brown the top.

CHILI - WELSH RAREBIT

See "BASIC RECIPES" - FONDUES

As an hors-d'oeuvre, serve hot in chafing dish [with   TORTILLA CHIPS

Version 1	Mix	[1/2-tp	CORNSTARCH or FLOUR
	with	[1/8-tp	DRY MUSTARD or more to taste
	Mix the Flour with	[4 oz	SHREDDED CHEDDAR (1 cup)
	Pour into a heavy saucepan	[1/4-cup	BEER or ALE room temperature

Over medium heat bring to a simmer, reduce
heat to low. With a wooden spoon gradually
stir in the Cheddar.

	When smooth add	[to taste	WORCESTERSHIRE SAUCE
	Stir in	[3/4-cup	CHILI con CARNE or more
Version 2	In a heavy saucepan heat	[3/4-cup	CHILI con CARNE
	When hot, gradually stir in	[4 oz	SHREDDED CHEDDAR (1 cup)

Start with 3 parts Chili to 4 parts Cheese. Then add more to taste. If needed thin with Beer.

CRÊPES BOLOGNESE

Filling yields 2-1/4 cups   CRÊPES - "BASIC RECIPES"

In a nonstick skillet, heat	[1 TB	VEGETABLE OIL
Sauté	[2 TB	ONION finely chopped
When Onion turns golden add	[1-1/4 cups	BOLOGNESE SAUCE drained
	[2 TB	of the drained Sauce
	[to taste	ALLSPICE or NUTMEG

Let cool completely.

In a large bowl mix	[1/2-cup	RICOTTA CHEESE
	[1/4-cup	MOZZARELLA coarse-grated
	[1/4-cup	PARMESAN grated
	[	GROUND BLACK PEPPER
Add	[	the Meat Mixture
	[adjust	Seasonings

Cover the surface with plastic wrap.
Refrigerate until ready to fill the Crêpes.
Heat Crêpes in 350° oven for 15 minutes.

To serve	Sprinkle the Crêpes with [a little	PARMESAN grated

CRÊPES with CHILI con CARNE

Yields 2-1/4 cups

In the above recipe, substitute the Bolognese

with	[1-1/4 cups	CHILI con CARNE drained
	[2 TB	of the drained Sauce

Omit Allspice and Nutmeg.

Substitute Mozzarella and Parmesan with	[1/2-cup	CHEDDAR coarse-grated

To serve	Spread over each filled Crêpe [a little	ALFREDO SAUCE ready-made
	Sprinkle with [	CHEDDAR coarse-grated

Cover the dish with foil.
Bake in oven preheated to 350° for 15 minutes. Uncover. Bake for 5 more minutes.

268

MACARONI and CHILI   Western style Pastitsio   *Serves 4 to 6*

1.   Cook for 6 minutes only   [4 oz   ELBOW PASTA drain, let cool
        Transfer to a large bowl and mix in   [1 TB   MELTED BUTTER
                                               [1-1/2 cups CHILI con CARNE drained
                                               [1/4-cup   of the drained Sauce
                                               [2 oz   SHARP CHEDDAR coarse-grated

2.   See "SAUCES". Prepare   [1-1/2 cups VELOUTÉ WHITE SAUCE

Remove from heat.   Beat   [2   EGGS + 1 EGG YOLK
                                     with   [4 TB of the hot Sauce, add it gradually
Slowly whisk EGGS into the SAUCE.
Over low heat, stir until well incorporated.
Turn off heat.
                    Stir in until melted   [2 oz   SHARP CHEDDAR coarse-grated
                                            [1 oz   PARMESAN grated
                                     Add   [a pinch   GROUND CUMIN, PEPPER
Mix the SAUCE into the PASTA mixture.

3. Spray an 8 x 8 oven-dish. Pour the Pasta
        into it, smooth the surface. Sprinkle with   [2 oz   SHARP CHEDDAR (in all 6 oz)
                                        Dot with   [1 TB   BUTTER halved, cut into tidbits
Preheat oven to 350°.
Bake for 30-to-40 minutes. Let Macaroni stand a few minutes before serving.

MACARONI PASTITSIO   Baked Macaroni (Greece)   *Serves 4 to 6*

1.   Cook for 6 minutes only   [4 oz   ELBOW PASTA drain and let cool
            Transfer to a bowl and mix in   [1 TB   MELTED BUTTER
                                             [2 oz   PARMESAN grated

2.   In nonstick skillet, medium heat, heat   [1 TB   BUTTER + 1 tp VEGETABLE OIL
                    When it sizzles, sauté   [1/2-cup   ONION finely chopped
                    When translucent, add   [1 lb   LEAN GROUND ROUND or CHUCK
        Stir, break up lumps, brown the Meat. Add   [1 TB   TOMATO PASTE
                                             [3/4-cup   TOMATO or MARINARA SAUCE
                                             [1/8-tp   GROUND CINNAMON or to taste

            Reduce heat to low, cover, simmer for
        40 minutes, then turn off heat and mix in   [1 oz grated PARMESAN, SALT and PEPPER

3.   See "SAUCES". Prepare   [1-1/2 cups VELOUTÉ WHITE SAUCE

Remove from heat.   Beat   [2   EGGS + 1 EGG YOLK
                                     with   [4 TB of the hot Sauce, add it gradually
Slowly whisk the EGGS into the SAUCE.
Over low heat, stir until well incorporated.
Turn off heat.
                    Stir in until melted   [1 oz   SWISS CHEESE coarse-grated
                                            [2 oz   PARMESAN grated
                                            [to taste   NUTMEG grated

4. In sprayed 8 x 8 oven-dish spread half of
    the Pasta. Cover with the Meat. Top with
    remaining Pasta. Pour evenly the SAUCE.

                    Sprinkle with   [2 oz   PARMESAN/SWISS mixed equally
                         Dot with   [1 TB   BUTTER halved, cut into tidbits
Bake as in above recipe.

MEATBALLS - PREPARATION

(For 1 lb Meat)

SOAKED BREAD   Soak in shallow dish [2 slices firm WHITE BREAD crust removed
with [1/2-cup   MILK

Mash with a fork.
When well soaked, squeeze down with your hand or a spatula and pour out excess Milk.

     NOTE   - 3 or 4 TB of Breadcrumbs can substitute for Bread, but the Mixture will be drier.
Add 2 TB of Milk or Water. Breadcrumbs work best with Meatloaf.

MEATBALLS   - Use coarsely ground Meat, not too lean. With wet hands or a wooden spoon
knead the Meat.   Refrigerate for 1 hour. The Meatballs will be easier to form.
  - Lay them on a tray, cover with plastic wrap, refrigerate 1 hour before cooking.

Cocktail size   - Like a cherry tomato. <u>Regular</u> - 1-inch in diameter, the size of a walnut.
Larger size   - Cannot be pan-fried. Poach or bake them. Patties of any size can be fried.

PAN-FRIED   - Use a 10-inch heavy skillet. Heat Vegetable Oil - 1/4-inch deep.
  - When a light haze forms, fry the Meatballs without overcrowding the skillet.
  - Brown all sides. Cook 8-to-10 minutes. The inside should be soft, well done,
not pink. Drain on paper towels.
  - Add more Oil if needed, heat until a light haze forms, then add more Meatballs.
  - *Optional*: the Meatballs can be rolled in Flour before frying.

DEEP-FRIED   - Small, up to 1-inch in diameter can be deep-fried. Large ones will fall apart.

POACHED   - First bake the Meatballs in oven preheated to 350° until browned.
  - Bring to slow boil, over medium heat, a Sauce or Broth. Lay in it the Meatballs.
  - Cover, reduce heat to low, simmer for 20-to-30 minutes, according to their size.

THE ONION   - Must be finely chopped. I prefer puréeing it in a blender, with Seasonings and
the Egg, then knead it into the Meat. It is faster and easier.

CARIBBEAN ALBÓNDIGAS

Place in a large bowl:

Purée in blender:

[1   EGG
[4 oz   ONION
[1/8-tp   GARLIC POWDER
[1/2-tp   GROUND NUTMEG
[1 tp   SALT
[1/4-tp   BLACK PEPPER

[1 lb   GROUND BEEF round or chuck

Knead in gradually the blender MIXTURE and

[2 slices BREAD soaked in MILK
[3 TB   CILANTRO finely chopped

Fry.
Serve with [AVOCADO DIP - see "DIPS and SPREADS"

CHINESE TREATS

Place in a large bowl:

Purée in blender:

[1 lb   GROUND BEEF or PORK or mixed

[1   EGG
[1-1/2 oz ONION
[2   SCALLIONS
[2 TB   SOY SAUCE
[1 TB   FRESH GINGER grated
[1/8-tp   GARLIC POWDER or to taste
[1/4-tp   SALT, BLACK PEPPER to taste

Knead in gradually the blender MIXTURE and

[2 slices BREAD soaked in CHICKEN BROTH
[2 TB   CILANTRO finely chopped

Fry in VEGETABLE OIL.

- Sprinkle with finely chopped Cilantro, serve with Soy Sauce Mayonnaise (see "SAUCES").
- Or serve with Chinese Vegetables. Or poach in Chicken Broth, serve in a Vegetable Soup.

270

GREEK KEFTEDES

Purée in blender:

Place in a large bowl:

[1   EGG
[4 oz   ONION
[1 TB   DRIED OREGANO   crumbled
[1/4-tp   GROUND CINNAMON
[1 tp   SALT
[1/4-tp   BLACK PEPPER

[1 lb   GROUND BEEF or LAMB or mixed

Knead in gradually the blender MIXTURE and

[2 slices BREAD soaked in MILK
[3 TB   PARSLEY   finely chopped

Fry in [VEGETABLE / OLIVE OIL   equal amounts
Sprinkle with [PARSLEY   finely chopped
Serve as a Dip [TOMATO or MARINARA SAUCE

VARIATION   Heat the Tomato Sauce, add fried Meatballs. Simmer 5-to-10 minutes. Serve in chafing dish.

GREEK KEFTEDES with OUZO

Soak   [2 slices FIRM WHITE BREAD no crust
in   [2 TB   OUZO + 2 TB MILK

Purée in blender

[1   EGG
[4 oz   ONION
[1/8-tp   GARLIC POWDER
[1/4-tp   GROUND CUMIN
[1 tp   SALT
[1/4-tp   BLACK PEPPER

Place in a large bowl:

[1 lb   GROUND BEEF or LAMB or mixed

Knead in gradually the blender MIXTURE and

[2 slices BREAD soaked in OUZO and MILK
[4 TB   PARSLEY   finely chopped

Fry in [VEGETABLE/OLIVE OIL   equal amounts

Serve with [CUCUMBER TZAZIKI   (YOGURT SAUCE)

INDIAN KOFTA

Purée in blender:

Place in a large bowl:

[1   EGG
[4 oz   ONION
[1 TB   FRESH GINGER   grated
[1/4-tp   GARLIC POWDER
[1 TB   GARAM MASALA Indian Spice
[1 tp   SALT, GROUND BLACK PEPPER
[or to taste   HOT RED PEPPER

[1 lb   GROUND BEEF or LAMB or mixed

Knead in gradually the blender MIXTURE and

[2 slices BREAD soaked in MILK
[2 TB   CILANTRO   finely chopped

Roll Meatballs in [FLOUR
Fry and brown in [VEGETABLE OIL
Serve as a Dip [DILL CURRY YOGURT SAUCE ("SAUCES")

VARIATION   Simmer the cooked Koftas for 10 minutes in a CURRY SAUCE - see"SAUCES".

ITALIAN POLPETTINE

Purée in blender:

Place in a large bowl:

[1   EGG
[3 oz   ONION
[1/2-tp   SALT
[1/4-tp   GROUND BLACK PEPPER

[1 lb   GROUND BEEF   round or chuck

Knead in gradually the blender MIXTURE and

[2 slices BREAD soaked in MILK
[2 TB   FRESH BASIL   finely chopped
[4 TB   PARMESAN grated

Fry in [VEGETABLE / OLIVE OIL   equal amounts
Sprinkle with [PARMESAN or PECORINO
Serve as a Dip [MARINARA SAUCE
Or a [ROASTED GARLIC PASTA SAUCE

271

ITALIAN SAUSAGE and BEEF

Purée in blender:

[1   EGG
[2 oz   ONION
[1/4-tp   SALT
[1/4-tp   BLACK PEPPER

Place in a large bowl:

[3/4-lb   GROUND BEEF round or chuck
[1/4-lb   RAW ITALIAN SAUSAGE MEAT

Knead in gradually the blender MIXTURE and

Then add [2 slices   BREAD soaked in MILK
         [3 TB   PARSLEY finely chopped
         [4 TB   PARMESAN grated

Fry in [VEGETABLE / OLIVE OIL   equal amounts
Sprinkle [PARMESAN grated

MIDDLE EASTERN KAFTA

Have the butcher coarsely grind together:

[1/2-lb   BEEF round or chuck
[1/2-lb   LEAN LAMB or use only Lamb or Beef

Purée in blender:

[1   EGG
[4 oz   ONION
[1/8-tp   GARLIC POWDER
[1 TB   DRIED MINT crumbled
[1 tp   SALT , 1/4-tp BLACK PEPPER

VARIATION add   1/2-tp   ALLSPICE
                  1/2-tp   GROUND CORIANDER

Place in a large bowl:

[the Ground Meat

Knead in gradually the blender MIXTURE and

[2 slices   BREAD soaked in MILK
[2 TB   PARSLEY finely chopped

[Fry in   VEGETABLE OIL

[Serve with   TAHINI or HUMMUS DIP

Or shape into patties, grill in a cast iron skillet.
Serve in a Pita Bread Sandw

MIDDLE EASTERN DILL KAFTA   Kafta Shabat   A *main course*

Crush in processor [8 oz   UNCOOKED WHITE RICE
Set aside.

Chop finely in processor [4 oz   ONION
                with [1/2-cup   FRESH DILL
                     [1 tp   SALT and 1/4-tp WHITE PEPPER

In a large bowl knead the ONION MIXTURE
                with [8 oz   GROUND BEEF round or chuck
- Then knead in gradually the RICE.
- Split the Mixture in half. Quick pulse each
  piece in processor 4 or 5 times.
- Knead all the Meat together. Refrigerate.
- Shape into balls the size of cherry tomatoes.
- Refrigerate.

In a heavy skillet, heat [VEGETABLE OIL   1/4-inch deep

Over high heat brown the Meatballs, do not
cook them. Place them in a saucepan.

Just cover with [CHICKEN BROTH   lightly salted
- Bring to a slow boil.
- Cover, reduce heat to medium low,
  simmer until the Meatballs are cooked.
- About 30 minutes. Turn off heat.

Beat [2   EGGS
with [3 TB   LEMON JUICE + 1/4-tp SALT

272

- Beat into the Eggs 2 or 3 TB of the hot BROTH.
- Pour the Eggs into the Broth with Meatballs. Stir with a wooden spoon.
- Reduce heat to low, simmer. When it reaches a slow boil, turn off heat. Do not let it boil.

<u>Serve</u> with sliced boiled Potatoes or White Rice.

MOROCCAN KEFTA

Place in a large bowl:

Purée in blender:

[1   EGG
[4 oz   ONION
[1 tp   DRIED MINT   crumbled
[1/4-tp   GROUND CORIANDER
[1/4-tp   GROUND CUMIN
[1tp   SALT
[1/4-tp   PEPPER
[a pinch   PAPRIKA

[1 lb   GROUND BEEF or LAMB or mixed

Knead in gradually the blender MIXTURE and

[2 slices   BREAD soaked in MILK
[2 TB   PARSLEY   finely chopped

Fry in   [VEGETABLE OIL
Serve with a Dip [TOMATO SAUCE, add CINNAMON

VARIATION   Shape into patties, grill in a cast iron skillet.

SWEDISH KÖTTBULLAR

Place in a large bowl:

Purée in blender:

[1   EGG
[2 oz   ONION
[1 tp   WHITE WINE VINEGAR
[1/2-tp   HORSERADISH   prepared
[1 tp   SALT
[1 TB   CAPERS   rinsed, dried

[1 lb   GROUND BEEF   round or chuck

Knead in gradually the blender MIXTURE and

[3 TB   FRESH DILL   snipped
[1/2-cup   MASHED BOILED POTATOES

Fry in   [BUTTER / VEGETABLE OIL   equal amounts

Optional: Serve in a chafing dish with [LEMON EGG SAUCE - see "SAUCES"

MEATBALLS and PASTA

Purée in blender	[1	EGG
	[2 oz	ONION
	[1/8-tp	GARLIC POWDER
	[1/2-tp	SALT, 1/4-tp BLACK PEPPER
Optional	[1/2-tp	ALLSPICE
Place in a large bowl	[1 lb	GROUND ROUND or CHUCK
Knead the Meat, <u>adding gradually</u> into it	[	the Blender Mixture
	[4 TB	PLAIN BREAD CRUMBS
	[4 TB	PARMESAN or PECORINO
	[2 TB	FRESH PARSLEY finely chopped
Optional	[1/2-tp	DRIED OREGANO
Or	[2 TB	FRESH BASIL finely chopped

Shape Meatballs the size of ping-pong balls
and stuff into the center of each [MOZZARELLA a small piece

Bake in oven preheated to 350° until browned.

Place Meatballs in a saucepan, cover with   [PASTA SAUCE of your choice

Bring to a boil, simmer for 10-to-15 minutes. Serve with Spaghetti or other Pasta.

MEATLOAF

- Use any of the MEATBALL recipes. Substitute the soaked Bread with 4 TB BREADCRUMBS.

- Spray a loaf pan, put the Meat Mixture in it. Melt a 1/2-TB BUTTER in 4 TB hot Water.
- Baste the Loaf with half of it. Bake 1 hour in oven preheated to 350°. Half-way, baste again.

- The loaf will separate from the pan. Insert a skewer to test doneness. If it comes out clean,
  the Meatloaf is done. If sticky, cook a little longer. Juices should run white and clear.
- Lift Meatloaf out of pan, wrap in foil to seal in juices. Refrigerate.

MIDDLE EAST - KIBBEE - BASIC RECIPE   Kibbee Nayyeh (raw)

KIBBEE NAYYEH is the Middle Eastern version of "Steak Tartare", served as an hors-d'oeuvre.

- To serve 4 to 6 as an hors-d'oeuvre, half of this recipe amount is plenty.

- To serve raw, use BEEF TENDERLOIN. To cook: lean ground ROUND, CHUCK or LAMB, or mixed.

The BULGUR - Cracked Wheat. Put it in a measuring cup, cover with Water. Soak 10 minutes.
- Impurities will rise to the surface. Drain by pouring the Bulgur into a fine sieve.
- Rinse 4 or 5 times under running cold Water, stirring it with your hand.
- Return to a bowl, cover with Water. Soak for 15 minutes, not longer. Drain in
  the sieve. Press to squeeze out liquid. Sprinkle with a little SALT. Stir.

For this recipe use	[3/4-cup	BULGUR	very fine #1 grade

The SEASONING	Purée in blender	[4 oz	ONION coarsely chopped
	with	[1/2-tp	ALLSPICE
		[1/2-tp	GROUND CORIANDER
		[1 tp	SALT
		[1/4-tp	GROUND BLACK PEPPER

The KIBBEE	Wet your hands in cold Water		
	as you knead, in a large bowl	[1 lb	BEEF TENDERLOIN ground 3 times
	with the	[	Blended Onion Mixture
	When well mixed, knead in gradually	[	the Soaked Bulgur

- When the Mixture is smooth, taste it, add, if needed, Salt and Pepper.
- Spread the Kibbee neatly on a serving platter. Cover with plastic wrap. Refrigerate.
- When cold, with a knife draw a diamond design on the surface.
- Garnish with toasted PINE NUTS. Serve on the side, soft Pita Bread, toasted Pita Bread chips.

KIBBEE - PATTIES

- Line a skillet with 1/8-inch deep of Vegetable Oil. Heat the Oil over medium high heat.
- Fry the patties in it. Or cook them on the grill. Or grill them in a greased grilling pan.
- Or brush them lightly with melted Butter and place them in a greased pan.
- Bake in oven preheated to 350° for 25 minutes, until browned. Turn once to brown other side.

HORS-D'OEUVRE - Serve patties on Mini Buns spread with Hummus or Tahini. See "SAUCES".

APPETIZER - With Middle Eastern Mezzés.   See "SALADS" - ETHNIC HORS D'OEUVRES.

ENTRÉE - With white or brown Rice and Cucumber Yogurt Sauce. See "SAUCES".
- With a mixed Salad or Tabbouleh. See "SALADS" - SPECIAL SALADS.

KIBBEE - THE STUFFING
For Kibbee Balls and Pan Baked Kibbee

In a nonstick skillet, heat	[2 TB	BUTTER + 1 tp VEGETABLE OIL
When it sizzles, sauté	[6 oz	ONION finely chopped
When Onion is translucent, add	[1/2-lb	LEAN GROUND ROUND or LAMB, or a Mixture

Crumble and brown the Meat.   Then stir in
	[1/2-tp	SALT
	[1/2-tp	ALLSPICE
	[1/4-tp	GROUND CINNAMON
	[to taste	GROUND BLACK PEPPER

When the Meat is cooked turn off heat. Tilt
the skillet, soak up grease with a paper towel.

Mix in   [1/4-cup   PINE NUTS (toasted in a little melted Butter)

NOTE - Refrigerate the Stuffing. It will hold better and be easier to use.

KIBBEE BALLS - *Baked*

THE KIBBEE   Follow the BASIC RECIPE using   [1 lb   LEAN GROUND ROUND or LAMB, or a mixture

[3/4-cup   BULGUR very fine #1 grade

THE STUFFING - Prepared as in above recipe. Leftover Stuffing can be frozen.

PREPARATION - HORS-D'OEUVRE size: use a chunk of Kibbee a little larger than a walnut.

- APPETIZER: a chunk about the size of a ping-pong ball.

- ENTRÉE: divide Kibbee into 8 pieces. Form them into the shape of footballs about 3-1/2 inches long.

1.   - Wet hands in cold water. Place a chunk of KIBBEE in the palm of your hand.

2.   - Flatten and press down, creating a cavity. Continue, widening the cavity.

3.   - Place in the cavity the STUFFING:
Hors-d'oeuvre 1 teaspoon. Appetizer 1-1/2 teaspoons . Entrée 1 tablespoon.

4.   - Seal around the Stuffing and roll into a football shape. External thickness of the Kibbee around the stuffing should be about 1/4-inch. If less, it will tear.

TO BAKE   - Place stuffed Kibbee Balls in a greased pan.
- Brush lightly each ball with a little melted Butter.
- Bake in oven preheated to 350° for 25-to-30 minutes.
- The Kibbee Balls must be well browned, but not dry.
- Turn them once to brown evenly.

Serve   - As an hors-d'oeuvre with a Hummus, Tahini or Yogurt Dip. See "SAUCES".
- As an entrée: White or Brown Rice with Pine Nuts, Raisins, and Plain Yogurt.

TO OMIT THE STUFFING   -   Cut 1 TB BUTTER into 4 dice.

- Shape the footballs. Drive your finger through one end to form a cavity.
- According to the size of football, place one, two, or three Butter dice in it. Seal the cavity.
- The cavity allows the Kibbee to cook evenly.

KIBBEE BALLS in YOGURT SOUP   Kibbee Labanniyeh   *Serves 4*

The STUFFING   Follow the STUFFING recipe. Leftover Stuffing can be frozen.

The KIBBEE   Follow the BASIC RECIPE using

[	1 lb	LAMB, BEEF, or a Mixture
[	3/4-cup	BULGUR very fine #1 grade

Divide in half, make out of each half 4 stuffed
footballs 3-1/2 inches long (previous recipe).

In a heavy saucepan, in which Kibbee Balls
can fit in one layer, bring to a boil   [4 cups   CHICKEN BROTH lightly salted
(Have at hand 2 more cups)

- With a mesh spoon lower into the Broth the
  8 KIBBEE BALLS.   If the Broth doesn't cover
  them, add more Broth to cover.
- Bring to a boil and cook for 3 minutes.
- Remove with a mesh spoon. Set on a plate.
- Reserve the BROTH in a bowl.

The SOUP

Cook	[1/2-cup	WHITE RICE
using some of the	[	Broth in which the Kibbee cooked
In a medium-size bowl, beat with a fork	[1 cup	PLAIN YOGURT
	[1 TB	CORNSTARCH
In a large heavy saucepan, whisk	[4 cups	YOGURT
Add	[	the Yogurt with Cornstarch
	[1 cup of	Broth in which the Kibbee cooked
	[1/8-tp	GARLIC POWDER or to taste
	[to taste	SALT

- Over low heat bring to a boil.
- Stir in the COOKED RICE. Reduce heat to low. Simmer for 3 minutes.
- Add the KIBBEE BALLS and simmer for another 5 minutes. Turn off heat.
- Pour into a tureen. Serve immediately in soup dishes. Also delicious served cold.

KIBBEE - PAN-BAKED   Kibbee Bil Saneeyeh   (in a tray)

THE STUFFING   Double recipe amounts using   [1 lb   GROUND BEEF or LAMB, or mixed

THE KIBBEE   Double BASIC RECIPE using

[	2 lbs	GROUND BEEF or LAMB or mixed
[	1-1/2 cups	BULGUR very fine #1 grade

In a small skillet, over low heat, melt   [4 oz   BUTTER

Clarify the BUTTER. See "HELPFUL HINTS". Brush with it an 8 x 12 x 2 baking dish or pan.

1.   - Divide the KIBBEE in half. Cut first half into four equal pieces.
     - Spread and flatten each piece into a 1/2-inch thick. Lay each in a corner of the dish.
     - Piece them together to form a smooth surface.

2.   - Spread evenly over the Kibbee all of the STUFFING.

3.   - For remaining half, repeat as in step 1. Lay over the Stuffing, smooth the surface.

4.   - Use a ruler to draw with a knife, two diagonals from corner to corner, obtaining an X.
     - Follow diagonal lines to draw 2-inch diamonds. Or squares, if easier. (Like Baklava)
     - Cut down, along the lines, into the top layer only.
5.   - Run a knife around the edges to loosen the Kibbee from the sides.   *(continued)*

6.   - Heat the CLARIFIED BUTTER and pour it all over and around the Kibbee.

7.   - Bake in oven preheated to 350° for 30-to-40 minutes, until done and browned on top.
        - Insert a knife in the center. If it comes out clean, the Kibbee is ready.
        - Cover loosely with foil. Serve warm or at room temperature.

MIDDLE EAST - MEAT PIES   *Meat Mixture yields about 1-1/2 cups*

Mix [	1/2-cup	ONION finely chopped
with [	1/2-tp	SALT

Put it in a sieve to drain for 30 minutes.

In a small skillet, over medium heat, heat [	1/2-tp	BUTTER
[	1/2-tp	EXTRA-VIRGIN OLIVE OIL
When it sizzles, stir until lightly toasted [	2 TB	PINE NUTS drain on paper towel
Mix in a small bowl [	2 TB	LEMON JUICE
[	1 TB	RED WINE VINEGAR
[	1 tp	TOMATO PASTE
[	1/4-tp	ALLSPICE
[	2 TB	PARSLEY finely chopped
[	1/2-tp	SALT, 1/4-tp BLACK PEPPER
Press to squeeze out excess liquid and add [		the Onions
Wet hands and knead in a larger bowl [	8 oz	BEEF or LAMB coarsely ground
with [		the Onion Mixture
When smooth, mix in [		the Pine Nuts
Spray a cookie sheet with [	a mist of	COOKING SPRAY
Sprinkle a pastry board with [		FLOUR
With a rolling pin, roll out [		PIZZA DOUGH 1/8-inch thick

- With a glass or cookie cutter, cut rounds of Dough 3 or 4 inches in diameter.
- Put them on cookie sheet. Spread with Meat Mixture, leave 1/2-inch of space around the edge.
- Preheat oven as per Pizza Dough directions. Bake until Pies are a light golden color.
- Do not dry the Meat. Serve hot or at room temperature. Also make hors-d'oeuvre sizes.

MIDDLE EAST - PHYLLO TRIANGLES   *Yields about 18 TB ***

THE FILLING In a skillet, medium heat, heat [	1 TB	BUTTER + 1 tp VEGETABLE OIL
When it sizzles, sauté [	1/2-cup	ONION finely chopped
When Onion is translucent, add [	8 oz	LEAN GROUND ROUND or CHUCK
Stir. When the Meat begins to brown, add [	to taste	SALT, GROUND BLACK PEPPER
[	1/4-tp	ALLSPICE or more to taste
When the Meat is cooked and moist		
(do not dry it), turn off heat and mix in [	1/2-TB	BUTTER
[	3 TB	PINE NUTS toasted

Transfer to a bowl.
Cover the surface with wax paper and refrigerate. The Filling is easier to use when cold.

* Filling amounts per Triangle, and to make and bake Triangles, see "BASIC RECIPES" - PHYLLO.

GREEK VARIATION Follow above recipe. Use [	1/4-tp	ALLSPICE + 1/4-tp CINNAMON
Mix in [	4 TB	FETA CHEESE crumbled

MOUSSAKA   Baked Eggplant   (Greece)

Serves 8 to 10. For less servings reduce amounts by half.

The EGGPLANT   Follow "Preparation for cooking" and "Cooking" - see "VEGETABLES".

Do not peel, slice into rounds 1/4-inch thick	[2	EGGPLANTS total: about 2 lbs Use the elongated shape.
Skillet-fry the Eggplant after dusting it with	[	FLOUR
Or broil it after brushing with	[	EXTRA-VIRGIN OLIVE OIL

Set it on paper towels to drain.

The MEAT   In an 8-inch nonstick skillet,

over medium heat, heat	[1/2-TB	BUTTER + 2 tp VEGETABLE OIL
When it sizzles, sauté	[1 cup	ONION slice 1/4-inch thick, dice
When Onion softens add	[2 cloves	GARLIC mashed and minced
When Onion is translucent, add	[1 lb	LEAN GROUND BEEF

Stir with a wooden spoon, breaking up lumps
and brown the Meat.

Add	[1/4-cup	DRY WHITE WINE
	[1 cup	CHOPPED TOMATOES canned, drained
	[1 TB	TOMATO PASTE
	[1/8-tp	GROUND CINNAMON or to taste
	[1/8-tp	ALLSPICE or to taste
	[1/2-tp	SUGAR
	[to taste	SALT, GROUND BLACK PEPPER

Simmer over low heat. Stir occasionally, until
the Meat is cooked and moist.

Stir in	[2 TB	PARSLEY finely chopped
Turn off heat and add	[1/4-cup	PARMESAN grated (total needed 1-1/4 cups = 5 oz)

The SAUCE   See "SAUCES". Prepare

	[2 cups	MEDIUM WHITE SAUCE
using	[1 cup	MILK
	[1 cup	LIGHT CREAM

Remove from heat.

Beat in a small bowl	[2	EGGS
Add one at a time, beating	[4 TB	of the hot Sauce

Gradually whisk the EGGS into the Sauce.
Over low heat stir until well incorporated.
Turn off heat.

Stir in until melted	[1/2-cup	PARMESAN grated
	[to taste	NUTMEG grated
	[	SALT, WHITE or BLACK PEPPER

To ASSEMBLE

Spray 8 x 12 oven-dish with	[a mist of	COOKING SPRAY
Sprinkle the bottom with	[3 TB	PLAIN BREAD CRUMBS

Overlap in it half of EGGPLANT slices.
Spread evenly over it the MEAT MIXTURE.
Top with the remaining EGGPLANT.

Pour over the WHITE SAUCE, sprinkle with	[1/2-cup	PARMESAN grated
and	[1/4-cup	PLAIN BREAD CRUMBS

Bake in oven preheated to 350° for 45 minutes to 1 hour, or until the top is light golden brown.
Let cool for 15 minutes. Cut into squares and serve. Cover with foil, reheat in warm oven.

STUFFED BELL PEPPERS and TOMATOES   *12 pieces*

Prepare 6 GREEN BELL PEPPERS   Of a rather medium size. Shaped to sit upright.
If larger, you will need to increase the Filling recipe.

1. Wash, pat dry. Cut a circle at a 1/2-inch around the cap. Pull out the Cap, cut off the stem.
2. Cut away inside core of the caps, so they can sit flat on the Stuffing. Set them aside.
3. Remove all seeds. Use a grapefruit spoon to de-rib the Bell Peppers.
4. Rinse the inside under running cold water. Turn them upside down on paper towels to drain.

Prepare 6 TOMATOES   Ripe but not soft, medium to medium large, matching approximately
the Bell Pepper size. Use the regular kind, their skin is more resistant
and matches the Bell Pepper cooking time when baked together.

1. Remove stems and leaves. Wash and dry the Tomatoes.
2. Cut a circle around the tops, about 2-inches in diameter. Remove the caps and set aside.
3. With a grapefruit spoon scoop out pulp, seeds, membranes and drop them into a blender.
4. Place Tomatoes upside down on paper towels to drain.

BLENDER LIQUID   Liquefy Tomato pulp and

[	1 cup	CHICKEN BROTH
[	2 TB	MELTED BUTTER
[	2 TB	MELTED MARGARINE
[	1/2-tp	GROUND CINNAMON
[	1/2-tp	ALLSPICE
[	1 tp	SALT, BLACK PEPPER to taste
[	1/2-tp	GRANULATED SUGAR

BAKING DISH

Spray a 9 x 13 with	[a mist of	COOKING SPRAY
Arrange in it	[	TOMATOES and BELL PEPPERS
Put into each Tomato	[1/4-tp of	GRANULATED SUGAR
You will need	[	PLAIN BREADCRUMBS to sprinkle over the stuffed Vegetables

The STUFFING

In a nonstick skillet, over medium heat, heat	[3 TB	VEGETABLE OIL
and	[3 TB	MARGARINE
When it sizzles, sauté	[1-1/2 cups	ONION finely chopped
When Onion is translucent, add	[1-1/4 lbs	GROUND CHUCK

Use a wooden spoon to break up the lumps.

Sauté until the Meat loses its raw color. Add	[1 tp	GROUND CINNAMON to taste
	[1 tp	ALLSPICE
Sift over the Meat	[2-1/2 TB	FLOUR
Stir and add	[1/2-cup	PARMESAN grated
Turn off heat and add	[1 tp	SALT, BLACK PEPPER to taste
	[6 TB	PINE NUTS
When well blended, add and mix well	[1/2-cup	LONG GRAIN WHITE RICE Use "Converted" for this recipe.
Mix well into the Meat Mixture	[1-1/2 cups	BLENDER LIQUID

Spread Meat Mixture evenly in the skillet. Let it cool.
Use a knife to split it evenly into quarters. Use each quarter of Mixture to fill 3 pieces.

To ASSEMBLE - Fill Vegetables 3/4-full with the STUFFING, leaving space for the Rice to swell.
- Place Caps over the Tomatoes and Bell Peppers.
- Blend the LIQUID once more, then pour it over the Vegetables.
- Sprinkle BREADCRUMBS over the Vegetables.

- Bake in oven preheated to 350° for 1-1/2 hours, or until tender and lightly browned.
- Baste every 20-to-25 minutes. Can be baked ahead of time, covered with foil, refrigerated.
- Heat in a warm oven, covered with foil. This is a lovely buffet dish. Serve with PLAIN YOGURT.

STUFFED CABBAGE ROLLS (Greece and Middle East)   *Serves 6 to 8*

- *Less servings*: use a 2-1/2 lb Cabbage. Make the rolls needed. Freeze leftover Stuffing.
- Or use half of Stuffing recipe amounts. To use the rest of the Cabbage, see - "VEGETABLES".

The STUFFING   Mix in processor   [8 oz   ONION   coarsely chopped
                                             [2 TB   MELTED BUTTER
                                             [1 tp   SALT
                                             [1/4-tp   GROUND BLACK PEPPER
                                             [1-1/2 tp GROUND CUMIN

In a large bowl, knead with ONION MIXTURE   [1 lb   LEAN GROUND ROUND or LAMB
       When well blended, gradually knead in [4 oz   LONG GRAIN WHITE RICE
                                                          Use "Converted" for this recipe.

Refrigerate until ready to use.

CLARIFIED BUTTER   Clarify in a skillet [3 oz   BUTTER - see "HELPFUL HINTS"

The CABBAGE   A   [3-1/2 lb   CABBAGE   makes 45-to-50 Rolls

   - The Cabbage Leaves have to be blanched, to soften them for rolling.
   - Bring to a boil a large pot of WATER and add 1/2-tp of Salt per quart

   - Core the Cabbage. Plunge entirely into the boiling Water, cored side down.
   - Boil 3 minutes. Remove and place it in a colander to drain. Cool enough to handle.
   - Peel off outer large leaves. Set aside rough ones, too tough to roll. Use as lining.
   - Remove the leaves that are tender and pliable. Pat dry and stack them on a towel.
   - When you reach the leaves still difficult to remove, return the Cabbage to boiling
     water for 3 minutes. Repeat all leaves are separated. Save the little pieces.

NOTE - If you can remove some leaves without breaking, blanch them separately.

A HEAVY SAUCEPAN   presentable at the table.
                    Inside W 9-1/2 x 3-1/2 D   Melt in it [1 TB   BUTTER

        Line the bottom of the saucepan with 2 layers of large tough blanched leaves.

SET UP A WORK AREA at which you can sit comfortably. Place on it:

1.   - The stacks of CABBAGE LEAVES. The STUFFING. A measuring tablespoon.
2.   - The saucepan lined with the Cabbage Leaves.
3.   - A small cutting board on which to prepare the rolls.
4.   - A small sharp pointed knife to cut out the veins from tough Leaves.

STUFFING the LEAVES   - Veins are tender and pliable in the small and medium size Leaves.
                          - Tough in the large Leaves. Cut them away, splitting the leaf in two.
                          - For uniform rolls, trim Leaves as you work, to approximately 4 x 5".
                            Do some patching with small ones. Use veins and bits for top lining.

1.   - Spread a Leaf on the cutting board. Inner surface up, narrower side towards you.
2.   - Roll into a sausage 2-inches long: 1 HEAPED TB of STUFFING.
3.   - Place it along the narrow end of Leaf, at 3/4-inch from the edge. Roll up 2 turns.
4.   - Fold in the sides, roll up (size of a short fat cigar). Squeeze gently in your hand.

Layer 1 Set Rolls side-by-side in saucepan, seam side down, in concentric circles. Start with
         outer circle. Sprinkle them with 2 TB CLARIFIED BUTTER. Warm the Butter if cold.

2   - Place first Roll between two bottom ones, continue same pattern, sprinkle 2 TB Butter.

3   - Repeat as in Layer 2, sprinkle 2 TB Butter. For even cooking do not add more layers.

- Cover the Rolls with a layer of tough blanched leaves, or leftover trimmings.
- Top with an inverted flat dinner plate. It helps the cooking and keeps the Rolls in place.
- Can be covered and refrigerated. To cook the next day, bring to room temperature.

COOKING the CABBAGE ROLLS   -   Place the saucepan on the stove, remove the lid.

Heat until hot but not boiling   [3 cups WATER + 1/4-tp SALT, you may not need all the Water.

- Pour around the inverted plate 1 cup of the HOT WATER.
- Wait until it levels, pour some more. Wait until it levels. Continue until the Water reaches the rim of the inverted plate. Do not add more.
- Cover the saucepan. Cook over medium heat for 20 minutes.

- Check Liquid level. If lowered, add more Hot Water, up to the plate level. That's it.
- Reduce heat to medium low. Keep the saucepan covered with its lid at all times.
- Cook until the Cabbage leaves are fork tender. In total 1-1/4 to 1-1/2 hours.
- Only if you think a little more water is needed, add some. Do not let it dry.
- There should be about a 1/4-cup of Liquid left at the bottom of the saucepan.

- Best the next day. Let cool, refrigerate. It is helpful to have them ready a day ahead.
- If cold, bring to room temperature for 3 hours. Add a 1/4-cup of Water around the inverted plate, cover the saucepan. Heat over low heat, for 30 minutes or longer.

To serve   Remove inverted plate and top lining. Bring the saucepan to the table or buffet table.

THE SAUCE   Serve with AVGOLEMONO SAUCE - see "SAUCES".

To unmold - Refrigerate overnight. Before unmolding remove inverted plate. Be aware that the saucepan is heavy and that some liquid may run out when unmolding.
- Place over the saucepan an oven-proof platter. Hold platter and saucepan firmly, invert. Cover Rolls with foil. Heat in oven preheated to 225° for 30 minutes.

STUFFED CABBAGE ROLLS in TOMATO SAUCE

The STUFFING   Mix in processor:

[8 oz   ONION   coarsely chopped
[2 TB   MELTED BUTTER
[1 TB   TOMATO PURÉE
[1/4-tp   ALLSPICE
[1/4-tp   GROUND CINNAMON
[1 tp   SALT, BLACK PEPPER   to taste

The SAUCE   Heat:

[1-1/2-cups TOMATO SAUCE
[1 tp   LEMON JUICE
[to taste   SALT, PEPPER,
[ALLSPICE, CINNAMON

In a large bowl knead:

[1 lb   Lean GROUND ROUND or LAMB
[with   ONION MIXTURE

When blended, gradually knead in:

[4 oz   UNCOOKED LONG GRAIN WHITE RICE
                          Use "Converted"

The BUTTER

Melt in a skillet:

[3 oz   BUTTER do not clarify

The ROLLS   -   Follow the previous recipe.
-   Sprinkle over each layer 2 TB of BUTTER and 1/2-cup of the SAUCE.
-   Cover with blanched leaves and inverted plate.

Heat until hot but not boiling   [2 cups WATER + 1/2-tp LEMON JUICE.

- Pour some Water around the inverted plate. Wait until it levels. Continue until it reaches the plate rim. Cook for 20 minutes. Add more hot Water up to the plate level. And that's it.
- Cook and serve as in previous recipe. Serve on the side PLAIN YOGURT.
- For LARGE ROLLS, line the saucepan, fit them snugly in one layer, cover with lining and plate.

LAMB

PRE-COOKING PREPARATION

- Lay the piece of Lamb in a pan. If you are going to roast it, place it in its roasting pan.
- Rub it lightly with VEGETABLE OIL. Sprinkle SALT, PEPPER. Optional: Garlic Powder, Spices.
- Quarter lengthwise a LEMON. Or more, depending on the size or amount of the Lamb.
- Rub well the Lamb with the Lemon. Sprinkle again with Salt, Pepper, Garlic Powder, Spices.
- Wrap foil tightly around the pan and refrigerate overnight.
- For cubed Lamb use a Marinade. See recipes.

- The Lemon tenderizes the Meat and crisps the skin during the cooking.
- It won't affect other Seasonings. It also tones down that light odor akin to Lamb.

LAMB - BRAISED   *Serves 3*

The MARINADE: mix in a cup	[2-1/2 TB	LEMON JUICE
	[1-1/2 TB	VEGETABLE OIL
	[1/2-tp	SALT, 1/4-tp BLACK PEPPER
Place in a bowl	[1-1/4 lb lean	BONELESS LAMB SHOULDER
		cut into 1-1/2 inch cubes

- Pour over the Marinade and rub the cubes
  with it. (Wearing latex gloves is helpful).
- Cover with a plate. Let rest about an hour.
- Transfer to a sieve and drain. Pat dry.

In a heavy saucepan, over high heat, heat	[1 TB	VEGETABLE OIL spread it with
		a wooden spoon

When it sizzles, sear the LAMB cubes on all
sides. Turn off heat.

Sprinkle with	[a pinch	SALT, GROUND BLACK PEPPER

Remove with slotted spoon.
Set aside.

Add to the saucepan	[2 TB	BUTTER

Over medium heat, as it melts, scrape tidbits.

When it sizzles, add	[1 TB + 1 tp	SHALLOTS finely chopped
	[3 TB	ONION finely chopped
	[1 clove	GARLIC mashed and minced
When Onion is translucent, add	[2 medium	CARROTS pared, 1/4-inch slices
Stir until the Carrots are lightly browned, add	[1/3-cup	DRY WHITE WINE

Deglaze the saucepan, stir until the Wine is
reduced by half. Add the Lamb.

Dissolve in	[1 cup	HOT WATER
	[1/2-cube	CHICKEN BOUILLON

- Pour it over the Lamb.
- Bring to a boil. Cover tightly, reduce heat to low, simmer for about 1-1/2 hours, or until
  the Lamb is tender and shows no resistance when pierced with a fork. Stir a couple of times.
- With a slotted spoon transfer the Lamb and Carrots into an oven-proof serving casserole.

In a small cup dissolve	[2 tp	ARROWROOT in 2 TB WATER

- Simmer the Sauce in the saucepan. Add the Arrowroot. Stir until the Sauce thickens.
- Add it to the Lamb. To serve later, heat in a warm oven, in the covered oven-proof casserole.
- <u>Serve with</u> Browned Rice or Saffron Rice.

LAMB - BURGERS in PITA BREAD with FETA SAUCE

SEASONINGS   Mix in a bowl:

[1/4-cup   ONION   grated
[1/2-tp   LEMON JUICE
[1 tp   TOMATO PASTE
[1/2-tp   ALLSPICE
[2 tp   DRIED MINT   crushed
[1/8-tp   GARLIC POWDER
[1 tp   SALT, GROUND BLACK PEPPER

After blending mix in 2 TB PARSLEY finely chopped.

FETA SAUCE: Mix in processor:

[1-1/2 oz   FETA CHEESE
[2 flat TB   SOUR CREAM
[2 TB   MILK
[3 TB   CHIVES
[1 TB   DRIED MINT   crushed
[1 TB   EXTRA-VIRGIN OLIVE OIL

Refrigerate. Use at room temperature.

In a large bowl knead SEASONINGS with   [1 lb   LEAN LAMB   coarsely ground

- Shape into Patties 1/2-inch thick by 2-to-2-1/2-inches in diameter.
- Place them on a tray, cover with plastic wrap or foil and refrigerate for at least 1 hour.

- Rub a cast iron grill with Extra-Virgin Olive Oil. Grill Burger patties. Or use a charcoal grill.
- Spread some Feta Sauce into the Pita pockets. Fill with Burgers. Spread the Sauce over them.
- Add a little shredded LETTUCE. Wrap half of the Sandwich in foil. Prevents drippings.

LAMB - BURGERS in PITA BREAD with HUMMUS

Mix in blender:

[4 oz   ONION   chopped coarsely
[1 tp   LEMON JUICE
[1/4-tp   GROUND CUMIN
[1/4-tp   GROUND CORIANDER
[1/8-tp   GARLIC POWDER
[1 tp   SALT, BLACK PEPPER to taste

After blending mix in 2 TB PARSLEY finely chopped.

Place in a large bowl:

[1 lb   LEAN LAMB   coarsely ground

Knead in gradually the blender MIXTURE.

Cook the Patties as in above recipe.

Spread [PITA POCKETS with HUMMUS.
Add   [LETTUCE and sliced TOMATOES

LAMB - CHOPS and SHISH KEBAB

SHISH KEBAB MARINADE

CHOPS   Mix in a cup

[2 TB   LEMON JUICE
[1 TB   VEGETABLE OIL
[1/2-tp   SALT, BLACK PEPPER   to taste
[to taste   GARLIC POWDER

Mix in blender [1 TB   EXTRA-VIRGIN OLIVE OIL
                [1-1/2 TB   LEMON JUICE
                [1 TB   RED WINE VINEGAR
                [1   GARLIC CLOVE   mashed
                [1/2-tp   SALT, BLACK PEPPER
                [1/4-tp   ALLSPICE *

THE CHOPS   - Place in a pan 1 lb LAMB CHOPS. Brush with the Marinade.
             - Refrigerate for 1 hour. Grill over charcoal or in a cast-iron grill skillet.

KEBAB   - Rub Marinade into 1 lb LEAN LAMB 1-1/2 inch cubes. Refrigerate overnight.
             - Brush metal skewers with Oil. Pat dry the cubes. Thread them on skewers.
             - Optional, thread in between PEARL ONIONS, BELL PEPPER chunks.
             - Cook over a charcoal grill or in a cast-iron grill skillet.

             - To Broil: align the skewers over a pan with their ends resting on the pan rim.
             - Brush with Marinade left in the bowl. Set under broiler at 6 inches from heat.
             - Turn to broil evenly. Cook for 40-to-45 minutes, until tender and browned.

* Shish Kebab Seasoning is available in Middle Eastern stores. If you use it, omit the Allspice.

LEG OF LAMB - ROASTED   Greek Style   VERSION I - *4 day preparation*

The pressure is off the day your guests arrive. All you will need to do is heat this lovely dish. It can preside at buffet parties and on Holidays. *NOTE*: the Greeks like their Leg of Lamb well done.

If the Leg has a meatless protruding bone, have your butcher saw it off. This will allow the Leg to fit comfortably in the roasting pan. I use a large oval aluminum disposable roasting pan. Trim off excess Fat. Do not remove the skin. Save the BONE to make the Broth.

DAY 1 - MARINATE Place in roasting pan the [LEG OF LAMB (4 to 5 lbs) *serves 8 to 10*
Sprinkle with [OLIVE OIL   massage it all over the Lamb

Then sprinkle all over with [SALT and GROUND BLACK PEPPER
Scrub the Lamb with [2   LEMONS split lengthwise into quarters
Keep in the pan 4 used quarters.

With a small sharp knife, make 10 incisions, about a 1/2-inch each, all around and under the skin, and insert into each one a [GARLIC CLOVE (you will need 10 cloves)
Sprinkle all over (optional) [DRIED THYME or DRIED ROSEMARY

Lay the Lamb in the pan skin side up. Wrap the pan tightly with heavy foil. Refrigerate overnight.

DAY 2 - ROAST   Bring to room temperature for 3-to-4 hours. Discard foil.
Pour WATER into the pan, about 3/4-inch deep.

- Place in oven preheated to 450°. When the skin is seared, reduce heat to 350°.
- After 15 minutes add Water to keep it at 3/4-inch level. Baste every 25 minutes.
- Allow 30-to-35 minutes per pound.   Test by inserting a meat thermometer into the fleshiest part. When it reaches 180° it is well done and tender.

- Remove the pan from oven. Spread a large sheet of heavy foil on your counter.
- With 2 big forks lift the Lamb onto the foil, wrap tightly, refrigerate overnight.

DEGLAZING   - Place the pan over low heat. Add 1/4-inch of Hot Water. Bring to boiling point.
- Scrape with wooden spoon. Pour into a bowl with Lemon quarters, refrigerate.

DAY 3   - If the FAT topping the GRAVY is not solidified, place in the freezer for 1 hour.

THE GRAVY   - With slotted spoon remove the FAT, wrap in foil, freeze (for roasting Potatoes).
- Pour the Gravy into a measuring pitcher, measure the quantity you have.
- Add 2 of the roasted Lemon quarters (save the 2 others). Cover, set aside.

THE LAMB   - Unwrap, place it on a carving board. Add any Juices (in the foil) to the Gravy.
- With a large sharp knife, or electric knife, slice the Lamb. Save the BONE.
- Stack the slices on the foil. When you are through slicing the Lamb, arrange the slices by size, wrap them in the foil. Leave them at room temperature.
- Gather Meat tidbits and Garlic cloves on the board, set aside.

THE BROTH   In a heavy saucepan heat [2 tp   VEGETABLE OIL spread it with a spatula
Sear until well browned [The BONE sawed off from the Leg
[The BONE left from the Meat: disjoint it.

Then stir in until browned [5   GARLIC CLOVES
Add [1   SMALL ONION   quartered
Add all tidbits and Garlic from carving and [2 saved roasted Lemon quarters
[1/2-tp   DRIED THYME or ROSEMARY
Add enough WATER to cover by 1-inch and [1/2-tp   SALT, GROUND BLACK PEPPER

- Bring to a boil. Cover, reduce heat to medium low and simmer for 2 hours.
- Discard the Bones. Pass the Broth through a fine sieve lined with Cheese Cloth. Discard solids.

THE GRAVY   Add to it [enough   LAMB BROTH to obtain 2-1/2 cups
                                                            Save any remaining Broth.
                                                            Freeze for some other time.

                     Dissolve in 4 TB COLD BROTH [1 TB + 2 tp ARROWROOT POWDER

                 -   In a saucepan bring GRAVY to a boil. Reduce heat to medium low, simmer,
                     add ARROWROOT, stir until thickened. Turn off heat. Season to taste.

THE DISH   -   Dab a little of the hot Gravy over the bottom of a rectangular oven-proof dish.
                 -   Starting with the small pieces, overlap the Lamb slices in two rows, dabbing
                     them with a little Gravy. Then pour the rest of the Gravy all over them.
                 -   Wrap tightly with foil. Refrigerate overnight.

DAY 4   -   Bring to room temperature for 3 hours. Heat, wrapped in foil, in warm oven.

LEG OF LAMB - ROASTED   VERSION II - *2 day preparation*

DAY 1   -   Prepare the Lamb: VERSION I. Wrap the pan with foil, refrigerate overnight.

DAY 2   -   Roast the Lamb as in VERSION I. Wrap in foil. Keep at room temperature.

THE GRAVY   -   Deglaze the pan as in VERSION I. Place the Gravy in the freezer for 1 hour.
                 -   Skim off the solidified Fat, set aside in a cup. Use some to roast the Potatoes.
                 -   Pass the Gravy through a fine sieve and measure it in a measuring pitcher.
                 -   Pour it into a saucepan. Bring to a boil, then simmer for a few minutes.

Option 1   Add per 1 cup of Gravy [2 tp   ARROWROOT dissolved in 2 TB WATER
                     When it thickens, add to taste [BROWNING & SEASONING SAUCE

Option 2   Add to the GRAVY [enough   WATER to obtain 2-1/2 cups
                       Bring to a slow boil, add [1 cube   BEEF BOUILLON   crumbled
                                            [2 cloves   GARLIC   mashed

Simmer uncovered for 10 minutes. Thicken with ARROWROOT. Discard Garlic. Adjust Seasonings.

TO SERVE THE LEG OF LAMB WHOLE   -   Warm it wrapped in foil, in oven preheated to 250°.
                                  -   Serve the Gravy in a sauceboat.

ROASTED POTATOES   *Serves 8*

-   Wash and use the roasting pan in which the Lamb cooked. Or an oven to table baking dish.
-   The POTATOES should begin roasting an hour and a half before the meal is served.

                 Peel, cut into 1-inch cubes, rinse, dry [12 large   YUKON GOLD POTATOES
                                                                      includes second servings
Wrap in a dry towel.
Preheat oven to 375°.
                              Combine in the pan [2-1/2 TB   LAMB FAT   (from the Gravy)
                                              [2 TB   EXTRA-VIRGIN OLIVE OIL
                                              [2 TB   MARGARINE
                                              [1-1/2 TB   LEMON JUICE
Slide the pan into the oven until Fats have
melted.
                         Spread the POTATOES in the pan [sprinkle   SALT, GROUND BLACK PEPPER
                                              Add [3 medium   ONIONS   quartered
-   Stir to separate roughly Onion layers.
-   Stir to coat Potatoes/Onions with the Fat. Place the pan in the oven. Stir a couple of times.
-   When the Potatoes turn golden brown, reduce heat to 350°. Continue cooking until tender.

LEG OF LAMB with ORZO   *Serves 8   (4 servings reduce amounts by half)*

In a 2-quart heavy saucepan, heat	[2 TB	LAMB FAT (from Gravy)
When it sizzles, sauté in the Fat	[1 cup	ONION finely chopped
When Onion softens, add	[2 cloves	GARLIC mashed and minced
When Onion begins to color, add	[1/4-cup	TOMATO SAUCE
	[1 TB	TOMATO PASTE
	[1 TB	DRIED OREGANO crumbled
	[1/2-tp	GROUND ALLSPICE
	[to taste	NUTMEG grated
Stir until the Mixture is hot, then add	[enough	WATER for 1 lb Orzo *as per pkg.*
Add to the Water	[to taste	SALT
When the Water comes to a boil, add	[1 lb	ORZO

Cooking time as per package directions. Turn off heat. Adjust Seasonings.
NOTE - Prepare the Tomato Mixture ahead of time. Cook Orzo before serving.

LEG OF LAMB LEFTOVERS - Cook Orzo as above. Stir into it Leftovers cut into bite-size pieces.

LEG OF LAMB LEFTOVERS in ORZO SALAD

Mix	[ORZO cooked in CHICKEN BROTH	THE DRESSING
with	[ROASTED BELL PEPPERS coarsely chopped	
	[CELERY HEART RIBS thinly sliced	Mix [OIL and LEMON DRESSING
	[SMALL RAW MUSHROOMS sliced	with [a sprinkle GARLIC POWDER
	[GREEN ONIONS very thinly sliced	
	[FETA CHEESE crumbled	Garnish with:
	[PINE NUTS toasted	
	[FRESH BASIL finely chopped	[HARD-COOKED EGGS wedges
	[LEG OF LAMB LEFTOVERS bite-size pieces	[BLACK OLIVES

LEG OF LAMB LEFTOVERS

HORS-D'OEUVRE   Cut the Lamb into bite-size cubes. Stick with toothpicks.

See "DIPS and SPREADS" - serve with DIPS	[[	BLACK BEANS, CURRY MAYONNAISE, BABAGHANOUSH, HUMMUS
See "SAUCES". Use as Dips	[	AÏOLI, GINGER MAYONNAISE, SKORDALIA, TAHINI
See "SAUCES". Use as Dips	[	YOGURT SAUCES
SALADS Toss Lamb bite-size pieces with	[[	BOILED POTATO diced, CAPERS, TARRAGON VINAIGRETTE ("DRESSINGS")
Or Toss Lamb with	[	NAVY BEAN SALAD see "VEGETABLES"
Or Arrange on a platter sliced Lamb with	[[	sliced TOMATOES, RED ONIONS, FETA, MINT leaves, OIL and LEMON DRESSING
See "VEGETABLES" Add Lamb to	[[	Beans, Caponata, Ratatouille, Patatouille, Bell Peppers with Pasta
Serve Lamb with	[	sliced fried EGGPLANT
and PLAIN YOGURT	[	beaten with hot BROTH to taste

LEG OF LAMB LEFTOVERS with CAULIFLOWER

Spread in a pan	[		RAW CAULIFLOWER FLORETS
Sprinkle with	[	to taste	CURRY POWDER
	[	a pinch	GARLIC POWDER
	[		SALT, GROUND BLACK PEPPER
Put Florets in a plastic bag and drizzle with	[		EXTRA-VIRGIN OLIVE OIL

- Seal and toss to coat them well. Let stand for 2 or 3 hours. Put them in a sprayed baking dish.
- Bake at 375° until tender and golden brown. About 45 minutes.

- Prepare a BROWN RICE, adding to taste, from the start GOLDEN RAISINS and PINE NUTS.
- Whip in a bowl PLAIN YOGURT with 1/3-of its amount in hot CHICKEN BROTH.
- Serve the Rice topped with the Cauliflower. Surround with the LAMB. Spoon over the Yogurt.

LEG OF LAMB LEFTOVERS with MINT SAUCE   *Omit the Anchovies*

See "SAUCES" - GREEN SAUCE.	Use	[1/2-cup	FLAT LEAF PARSLEY leaves
	and	[1/2-cup	MINT leaves

LEG OF LAMB LEFTOVERS - SPEEDY COUSCOUS   *Serves 2 or 3*

In a heavy saucepan, heat	[1 TB		EXTRA-VIRGIN OLIVE OIL
When a light haze forms, sauté	[1/2-cup		ONION finely chopped
When Onion begins to color, stir in	[3 medium		CARROTS pared, 1/2-inch slices
	[2		YUKON GOLD POTATOES cubed
Sauté for 2 minutes and sprinkle with	[1/4-tp		GROUND CUMIN
Stir and add	[2 cups		CHICKEN BROTH
		or	1 cup Lamb Broth, 1 cup Chicken
	[1/3-cup		TOMATO SAUCE
	[to taste		SALT, GROUND BLACK PEPPER
Bring to a boil. Cover, reduce heat to low, simmer for 20 minutes. Then add	[3 medium		ZUCCHINI 3/4-inch pieces

If Liquid doesn't cover add more Broth. Bring to a boil, reduce heat to low, simmer until the Vegetables are tender, but still firm.

Add	[1/2-cup		CHICK PEAS canned, drain, rinse
	[3 TB		GOLDEN RAISINS
Simmer for 5-to-10 minutes. Adjust	[		Seasonings
Prepare following package directions	[		COUSCOUS *as per servings*
When Couscous is cooked, fluff it adding	[a patty of		BUTTER
Serve Couscous and Vegetables with	[		LEG OF LAMB Leftovers
On the side	[		HARISSA hot red Moroccan paste

LEG OF LAMB - SEASONINGS   (Before roasting)

- Rub Leg of Lamb with Olive Oil. Sprinkle with Salt, Ground Black Pepper. Rub with Lemon.
- In processor purée Onion and Garlic. Drain in a sieve to rid of Fluid. Mix in Ingredients below.
- Rub Paste all over the Lamb. Wrap tightly in plastic wrap, then in foil. Refrigerate overnight.

INDIAN			MEDITERRANEAN		
[1 large	ONION		[1 LARGE	ONION	
[4	GARLIC CLOVES		[3	GARLIC CLOVES	
[1 TB	CURRY POWDER		[1 tp	DRIED THYME	
[1/2-tp	GROUND GINGER		[1 tp	dried ROSEMARY or OREGANO	

287

LAMB STEW - CURRY

Serves 4 to 5

<u>THE MARINADE</u>   Mix in a cup [3 TB   LEMON JUICE
                                    [3 TB   VEGETABLE OIL
                                    [1/2-tp   SALT
                                    [1 tp mild   CURRY POWDER (or 1/2-tp hot)
                                    [1/8-tp   GARLIC POWDER or more to taste

Mix in a bowl the MARINADE with [2 lbs   LEAN BONELESS LAMB
                                            Leg or shoulder 1-1/2 inch cubes

- Rub Marinade into the cubes. (Wearing latex
  gloves is helpful). Cover, let stand 2 hours.
- Or refrigerate overnight. Drain, pat dry.

In a heavy stewpan over high heat, heat [1 TB   VEGETABLE OIL   spread it with
                                                          a wooden spoon

Sear on all sides, in 2 batches, the cubes.
Remove with slotted spoon, set aside.
Return stewpan to stove.
                     Heat in it [1 TB   BUTTER + 1 TB MARGARINE
Over medium heat, when it sizzles, add [3/4-cup   ONION   finely chopped

With a wooden spoon scrape to loosen tidbits.

When Onion is translucent, add [2 cloves   GARLIC   mashed and minced
Stir until Garlic softens, then add [2 TB   FLOUR   mixed with
                                     [3 TB mild   CURRY POWDER or 1-1/2 TB hot
Stir until Flour/Curry is smooth, then add [1 TB + 2 tp   RED WINE VINEGAR
                     Gradually add [3 cups   CHICKEN BROTH   lightly salted
Smooth out lumps.
                At boiling point adjust [SALT, GROUND BLACK PEPPER
                              Add [the Lamb

Stir, bring to a boil. Cover, reduce heat to low,
simmer for about 1-1/2 hours or until the Meat
is tender when pierced with a fork.
                        Mix in [2 tp   LEMON JUICE   or more to taste
Turn off heat.
Pour into an oven-proof casserole, refrigerate overnight. Heat in a warm oven.

<u>Serve with</u> COCONUT RAISIN BROWNED RICE, and CONDIMENTS - see "SAUCES" - CURRY.

COCONUT RAISIN BROWNED RICE

Serves 4

In a heavy saucepan, over medium heat, heat [2 TB   VEGETABLE OIL
            When a light haze forms, sauté [1/4-cup   ONION   finely chopped
            When Onion is translucent, add [1 cup   UNCOOKED WHITE RICE

Toast the Rice to a golden brown, then add [WATER   as per Rice package
                                            [+ 3 TB   WATER for Coconut, Raisins, Nuts
                                            [1/4-tp   SALT
                     Bring to a boil and add [1/4-cup   UNSWEETENED COCONUT flaked
                                            [1   CINNAMON STICK
                                            [3 TB   GOLDEN RAISINS
                                            [3 TB   ALMONDS slivered, or PINE NUTS

Cover and simmer until the Rice is cooked.

WHITE RICE   -   Do not toast. Add to 1/2-cup COCONUT MILK amount of Water needed.

LAMB STEW - CURRY with VEGETABLES   *Serves 4 to 5*

Marinate and sear as in previous recipe	[2 lbs	LEAN BONELESS LAMB
		1-1/2 inch cubes
Mix in a bowl	[3 TB	FLOUR
with	[3 TB mild	CURRY POWDER or 1-1/2 TB hot
In the stewpan where the Lamb was seared, over medium heat, heat	[2 TB	BUTTER + 1 TB MARGARINE
When it sizzles, sauté	[3/4-cup	ONION finely chopped
When Onion softens, add	[2 cloves	GARLIC mashed and minced
	[	the Flour/Curry Mixture
Stir until the Garlic is fragrant, add	[3 medium	CARROTS pared, 1/2-inch slices
	[4 stalks	CELERY HEART 3/4-inch pieces
	[1 medium	PARSNIP 1/2-inch dices
Sauté the Vegetables for 3 minutes, sprinkle	[a little	SALT
Add	[2 TB	RED WINE VINEGAR
	[3 cups	CHICKEN BROTH
At boiling point add	[	the seared Lamb

Bring to a boil. Cover.
Reduce heat to low, simmer until the Lamb
is tender. About 1-1/2 hours.

Add	[2 tp	LEMON JUICE or more to taste
Stir and turn off heat. Adjust	[if needed	Seasonings

Allow 1 or 2 hours for flavors to blend. Or refrigerate overnight. Serve with Brown or White RICE.

LAMB STEW - CURRY LEFTOVERS

Halve crosswise, lay cut side up in oven dish	[	CINNAMON ROLLS
Top each with	[overlapping	APPLE wedges, thinly sliced
	[sprinkle	GRANULATED SUGAR

Pass under the broiler to brown.
Spoon over the hot Lamb Curry. Serve immediately. Also with Croustades, Pancakes, Pasta.

LAMB STEW - DRIED APRICOTS and TOMATOES

Marinate and sear as in Lamb Stew - Curry *(Omitting in the Marinade Garlic and Curry)*	[2 lbs	LEAN BONELESS LAMB
		1-1/2inch cubes
Meanwhile soak in Water and drain	[3/4-cup	DRIED APRICOTS not plump ones
		Then cut them in half.
In the stewpan where Lamb was seared, over medium heat, heat	[2 TB	COOKING OLIVE OIL
Scrape the Lamb tidbits. When hot, sauté	[10 oz	ONION quartered, thinly sliced
When the Onion begins to color add	[28 oz-can	DICED TOMATOES with Liquid
	[to taste	SALT, GROUND BLACK PEPPER
Stir with a wooden spoon until the Tomatoes melt into the Onions. Then add	[	the Apricots and the Lamb
	[just enough	WATER to cover

Bring to a boil. Cover. Reduce heat to low,
simmer until the Lamb is tender.

Mix in	[1/4-cup	PINE NUTS toasted
Serve with	[	COUSCOUS

LAMB STEW - DRIED FRUIT
Serves 4 or 5

The FRUIT   Soak, until plumped up   [1-1/2 cups   DRIED FRUIT MIX (or your own)
                                   in   [APPLE CIDER   cover by 2-inches
Drain. Reserve the SOAKING LIQUID.
Cut large pieces into bite-size.

The MARINADE   Mix in a cup   [3 TB   LEMON JUICE
                                           [3 TB   EXTRA-VIRGIN OLIVE OIL
                                           [1/2-tp   SALT
                                           [1/2-tp   ALLSPICE

In a large bowl, pour the MARINADE over   [2 lbs   LEAN BONELESS LAMB
                                                         Leg or shoulder 1-1/2 inch cubes

- Rub Marinade into the cubes. (Wearing latex
  gloves is helpful). Cover, let stand 2 hours.
- Or refrigerate overnight. Drain, pat dry.

The LAMB   In stewpan, over high heat, heat   [1 TB   VEGETABLE OIL   spread it with
                                                                 a wooden spoon

When a light haze forms, add <u>half</u> the Lamb,
                       sprinkle it with   [1 flat TB   FLOUR
Sear it on all sides.
Remove and set aside in a bowl. Repeat
with other half.
                    Combine all the Lamb   [sprinkle   SALT, GROUND BLACK PEPPER
Preheat oven to 350°.

The STEW   In the same stewpan,
                  over medium heat, heat   [1 TB   BUTTER + 1 TB MARGARINE

With a wooden spoon scrape the Lamb tidbits.
           When the Butter sizzles, sauté   [1 cup   ONION finely chopped

When Onion lightly browns, add the LAMB
                  and sprinkle with   [1/4-tp   ALLSPICE
                                      [1/4-tp   GROUND CINNAMON
Mix well and stir in the FRUIT with its
         SOAKING LIQUID then add   [just enough   APPLE CIDER   to cover
                                      [1 TB   LEMON JUICE
Stir as you bring to a boil.
                     Taste and add   [to taste   SALT, GROUND BLACK PEPPER
                            Stir in   [1/4-cup   BLANCHED WHOLE ALMONDS
Place the lid tightly on the saucepan.
Bake from 45 minutes to 1 hour, or until the Lamb is fork tender.
<u>Serve with</u>   Saffron Rice, or Wild Rice. Or a Saffron Risotto.

LAMB STEW - IRISH
Serves 4 or 5

             See "VEGETABLES" - ONIONS, peel   [16-to-20   PEARL ONIONS
            Pare, wash, cut into 1-inch chunks   [4-to-5   CARROTS   medium size
                     Peel, wash and quarter   [4-to-5   YUKON GOLD POTATOES

                            Put in a bowl   [2 lbs lean   BONELESS LAMB SHOULDER
                                                       cut into 1-1/2 inch cubes
                          Sprinkle with   [2 TB   LEMON JUICE
                                         [lightly   SALT, GROUND BLACK PEPPER
                                         [1/4-tp   DRIED THYME   crumbled

Rub the Lamb cubes to coat them with Seasonings.

In a stewpan or Dutch oven, place [half of   the Lamb cubes

Top with half of POTATOES, CARROTS and
    ONIONS mixed together. Sprinkle with [SALT, GROUND BLACK PEPPER

- Repeat, with the rest of the LAMB.
- Top with the rest of Potatoes, Carrots and
  Onions. Sprinkle with Salt and Pepper.

Dissolve in [1 cup   BOILING WATER
            [2 cubes   CHICKEN BOUILLON
Pour it into the stewpan and add [enough   WATER to cover the Vegetables

- Do not stir. Bring to a boil, cover tightly. Reduce heat to low, simmer for 1-1/2 hours, or until
  Meat and Vegetables are fork tender. Check occasionally. Add boiling Water as it evaporates.
- Optional: when the Stew is ready, add 1 cup of boiled GREEN PEAS. Serve from the stewpan.

LAMB STEW - PRIMAVERA   *Serves 4 or 5*

The MARINADE   Mix in a cup [2 TB   LEMON JUICE
                                         [2 TB   EXTRA-VIRGIN OLIVE OIL
                                         [1/2-tp   SALT, GROUND BLACK PEPPER

                      Rub the Marinade into [2 lbs   LEAN BONELESS LAMB
                                                         Leg or shoulder 1-1/2 inch cubes
Marinate for 2 hours, or refrigerate overnight.
Drain. Pat dry before searing.

BOUQUET GARNI   Tie into cheesecloth [3 sprigs   PARSLEY + 1 sprig THYME
                                          [3 cloves   GARLIC   + 1 BAY LEAF

The BROTH   In a saucepan, bring to a boil [3-1/4 cups   CHICKEN BROTH
                            Dissolve in it [4 flat TB   TOMATO PURÉE
                         Turn off heat and add [to taste   SALT, GROUND BLACK PEPPER

The LAMB   In a stewpan heat [1 TB   VEGETABLE OIL
                      Over high heat add [half of   the Lamb cubes
                             Sprinkle [1 flat TB   FLOUR
Brown on all sides.
Remove to a bowl. Repeat with other half.
Combine the Lamb in the stewpan.
                                    Use [some of   the Broth to cover the Lamb
                                    Add [the Herb Bunch
Bring to a boil. Cover tightly.
Reduce heat to low, simmer for 1 hour.
Skim if needed.
                          Then stir in [24   BABY CARROTS   ready-to-eat
                                       [16-to-20   SMALL PEARL ONIONS   blanched
                                                                  and peeled
                                       [12   NEW POTATOES or more,
                                                            depending on size
              Add to cover the Vegetables [remaining   Broth Mixture + more if needed

- Bring to a boil, cover tightly, reduce heat to low, simmer for about 1-1/2 hours or until Meat
  and Vegetables are fork tender. Stir occasionally. Add Broth if needed. Adjust Seasonings.
- When done, remove the Herb Bouquet. Stir in 1 cup boiled GREEN PEAS.

LAMB STEW - TAVERNA

Serves 4 or 5

The MARINADE   Mix in a cup   [3 TB   LEMON JUICE
   [2 TB   EXTRA-VIRGIN OLIVE OIL
   [1/2-tp   SALT, GROUND BLACK PEPPER
   [1/8-tp   GARLIC POWDER   or more

Mix in a large bowl the MARINADE with   [2 lbs lean   BONELESS LAMB SHOULDER
         cut into 1-1/2 inch cubes

- Rub the Marinade into the Lamb. Let it sit
  2 hours or longer. Or refrigerate overnight.
- Drain. Pat dry. Reserve Marinade Juices.

The ONION   In a nonstick skillet,
over medium heat, heat   [1/2-TB   BUTTER   +   1/2-TB   OLIVE OIL
When it sizzles, sauté until golden brown   [1 cup   ONION   1/2-inch slices coarsely
         chopped

Set aside.

The LAMB   In a stewpan,
over high heat, heat   [1 TB   COOKING OLIVE OIL
When a light haze forms, add   [half of   the Lamb

Brown it on all sides. Transfer to a bowl.
Repeat. Combine all the Lamb in stewpan.

Sprinkle with   [SALT, GROUND BLACK PEPPER
Add the sautéed ONIONS and   [Marinade Juices
Sprinkle with   [1/4-tp   DRIED ROSEMARY
Add   [1/2-cup   DRY WHITE WINE

Stir, reduce heat to low.
Simmer until half the Wine has evaporated.

Add   [2 cups   TOMATO SAUCE
   [enough   WATER   to cover by 1/2-inch

- Turn up heat, bring to a boil. Cover, reduce
  heat to low, simmer until the Meat is tender.
- About 1-1/2 hours.

Meanwhile, thaw, drain   [2 pkg   FROZEN FRENCH CUT GREEN BEANS
         (10 oz each)

When the Meat is tender, add the GREEN BEANS. Cover, simmer for 10 minutes.
Adjust Seasonings. Prepare ahead. Best the next day. Serve with RICE PILAFF.

RICE PILAFF

Serves 4

Bring to a boil   [enough   WATER to cook 1 cup RICE
Dissolve in it   [1 cube   CHICKEN BOUILLON

In a small saucepan, dissolve in   [1 cup   of the simmering Broth
   [1/4-tp   SAFFRON THREADS

In a heavy saucepan, over medium heat, heat   [1 TB   VEGETABLE OIL
When a light haze forms, sauté   [1/2-cup   ONION   finely chopped
When it begins to color, add   [1 cup   UNCOOKED WHITE RICE

- Stir to coat the Rice until the grains glisten, then add the SAFFRON BROTH.
- When it comes to a boil, add the rest of the BROTH and bring to a boil.
- Optional, add 1/4-cup PINE NUTS. Cover, reduce heat to low, simmer until the Rice is cooked.

LAMB STEW - YOGURT DELIGHT

Serves 4

The MARINADE   Purée in blender [2 oz   ONION
                                         [3 cloves   GARLIC
                                         [2 TB   LEMON JUICE
                                         [2 tp   EXTRA-VIRGIN OLIVE OIL
                                         [1/2-tp   SALT
                                         [1/4-tp   GROUND BLACK PEPPER
                                         [1 tp   GROUND CORIANDER
                                         [1/4-tp   GROUND CINNAMON

                          Place in a bowl [2 lbs lean   BONELESS LAMB SHOULDER
                                                              cut into 1-1/2 inch cubes

Rub the MARINADE into the Lamb cubes.
Cover, refrigerate for 3 hours or overnight.
Drain. Reserve the MARINADE JUICES.

The STEW   In a stewpan, over medium heat,
                                    heat [2 TB   BUTTER + 1 TB OLIVE OIL
       When it sizzles, sauté until golden brown [3 cups   ONIONS halved and thinly sliced

Remove them with a slotted spoon, set aside.

                          Add to the saucepan [1 TB   VEGETABLE OIL

Over high heat, in two batches, sear
the LAMB on all sides.
Combine all the Lamb in the saucepan.
                                   Add [browned Onions
                                       [Marinade Juices
                                       [1 cup   CHICKEN BROTH

Reduce heat to medium. Cover.
Cook the Lamb for 20 minutes.

           Meanwhile, in a saucepan, mix [2 cups   PLAIN THICK YOGURT not low fat
                                   with [1 TB   CORNSTARCH
                                    Add [1 cup   CHICKEN BROTH
           Bring to a slow boil, add [to taste   SALT
Turn off heat.

- After the Lamb has cooked for 20 minutes, add the YOGURT MIXTURE.
- Over medium heat, bring to a simmer, then reduce heat to low, cover and simmer until the
  Lamb is fork tender. About 1-1/2 hours, or until the Lamb is done. Stir once in a while.

Serve with   RAISIN RICE.

RAISIN RICE

Serves 4

In a heavy saucepan, over medium heat, heat [1 TB   VEGETABLE OIL
           When a light haze forms add [1 cup   UNCOOKED BASMATI RICE, or
                                                              other of your choice

   With a wooden spoon stir the Rice until well
      coated with the Oil. Do not brown it. Add [WATER   as per Rice package
                                       [to taste   SALT
           When the Water begins to boil, add [1/3-cup   GOLDEN RAISINS
                                       [1 stick   CINNAMON

Cover, reduce heat to low and simmer until the Rice is done. Remove Cinnamon stick.

LAMB - STUFFED BABY EGGPLANT   *Serves 4*

The EGGPLANTS   Wash, dry, cut stems of [8   BABY EGGPLANTS   of equal size

- With a serrated corer remove some of the
  Pulp, leaving at least a 1/4-inch wall.
- Rinse the inside under running cold Water.
- Drain upside down on paper towels.
- Mash the Pulp. Reserve a 1/2-cup of it.

The STUFFING   In an 8-inch nonstick skillet,
over medium heat, heat	[1 TB	VEGETABLE OIL + 1/2-TB BUTTER
When it sizzles, sauté	[1 cup	ONION finely chopped
When Onion is translucent, add	[12 oz	LEAN GROUND LAMB or BEEF
		or mixed
Stir in	[1/2-tp	LEMON JUICE (omit if using Beef)

With a wooden spoon break up lumps, stir
until the Meat has lost its raw color. Add   [1/4-tp   GROUND ALLSPICE   or to taste
                                              [1/8-tp   GROUND CINNAMON

When the Meat is cooked, mix in	[1/2-cup	Eggplant Pulp
and	[1/2-cup	TOMATO or MARINARA SAUCE
Stir for 3 minutes then turn off heat, mix in	[1/4-cup	PARMESAN grated
	[to taste	SALT, GROUND BLACK PEPPER
Then stir in	[4 flat TB	LONG GRAIN WHITE RICE
		Use "Converted" for this recipe.

Flatten the Mixture, let cool.

The SAUCE   Mix with [2 cups   TOMATO or MARINARA SAUCE
                                          [1/2-cup   WATER
                      Taste, add [if needed   SALT, GROUND BLACK PEPPER

The OVEN-PROOF DISH

Select a dish in which the Eggplants can fit
     snugly in one layer, and spray it with [a mist of   COOKING SPRAY

STUFFING the EGGPLANTS

- With a knife divide the STUFFING into quarters. Use each quarter for 2 Eggplants.
- With an ice-tea spoon stuff the Eggplants. With the handle of a wooden spoon push
  it down. Do not pack too tight, allow a 1/2-inch at the top, for the Rice to expand.

ASSEMBLING the DISH   -   Arrange the stuffed Eggplants in the sprayed oven-proof dish.

- Pour over the SAUCE. The Eggplants should only be one-third immersed in the Sauce.
- If there isn't enough Sauce, mix a little more of the Marinara and Water.
- Cover tightly with foil. Pierce the foil once in each corner with a fork.

BAKE - In oven preheated to 375°. Lift the foil to baste every 30 minutes.
- After 1 hour and 20 minutes, check doneness by inserting a skewer into an Eggplant.
  It should present little resistance when done. Do not overbake to mushy.
- When done, remove foil, bake uncovered for 5 minutes.

SERVE - With additional MARINARA SAUCE on the side. Or PLAIN YOGURT.
- This dish can be prepared a day ahead. Cover it with foil, cool, refrigerate.
  It tastes best the next day. To heat, bring to room temperature.
  Add more Sauce if needed. Cover with foil, heat in warm oven.

294

LAMB - STUFFED GRAPEVINE LEAVES *Worth the time they take!*

CLARIFIED BUTTER   Clarify in a skillet [4 oz (1 stick) BUTTER see "HELPFUL HINTS"

The STUFFING   Chop finely in processor [6 oz   ONION   do not purée
                          Mix into it [1/2-tp   SALT, 1/4-tp BLACK PEPPER

                In a bowl, knead the ONION with [1 lb   LEAN GROUND LAMB or BEEF
                        Then gradually knead in [1/2-cup   LONG GRAIN WHITE RICE
           When well blended, gradually knead in [all the CLARIFIED BUTTER
                                                               Butter keeps the Leaves from drying.

Refrigerate. It will be easier to use.

The GRAPEVINE LEAVES   Drain in colander a 1 lb jar (55-65) GRAPEVINE LEAVES brine-packed.

1. Wear latex gloves, the Leaves will stain your fingers. Handle them gently to avoid tearing.

2. Scatter the Leaves in a colander. Rinse them under a thin stream of cold Water.

3. Boil Water in medium-size saucepan. Pick up the Leaves, plunge them in it. Turn off heat.
   - Keep them in the Water for 5 minutes.

4. Remove the Leaves with a flat slotted spoon and plunge them in a large bowl of cold Water.

5. Pick them up. Let Water drip, return them to clean and dry colander. Let drip for 15 minutes.

6. Set aside damaged Leaves for lining and covering Rolls. If there aren't enough damaged leaves, save a few of the thick ones.

A HEAVY SAUCEPAN   Inside W 9-1/2 x 3-1/2 D   Melt in it [1 TB   BUTTER

        - Line the bottom with damaged or thick Leaves.
        - To avoid unmolding the Rolls, use a saucepan presentable at the table.

SET UP A WORK AREA at which you can sit comfortably. Place on it:

1.   - The colander with the LEAVES. The STUFFING. A measuring teaspoon.
2.   - The SAUCEPAN lined with the Leaves. A small sharp knife to cut off stems, if any.
3.   - An upside-down dinner plate on which to prepare the rolls. Or a small cutting board.

STUFFING the LEAVES   - Spread the Leaf out. Its shiny side against the surface of the plate.
                          - Rough side up, <u>wide end</u> facing you. Cut off the stem if it has one.

- Roll into a sausage <u>1 heaped teaspoon of Stuffing</u>. Place it on wide end at 3/4-inch from edge.
- Roll one turn. Fold in sides, roll up. Try to obtain uniform rolls the thickness of a pinky.

Layer 1 - Start with outer circle, placing the Rolls in the saucepan, tightly side-by-side, seam side down. Lay them in concentric circles all the way to the center.
2   - Alternate by placing Rolls end to end around the saucepan, all the way to center.
3   - Repeat Layer 1 pattern. To obtain even cooking, do not add more layers.

Top the Rolls with a layer of damaged Leaves or scraps. Cover with an inverted dinner plate.

COOKING the ROLLS   Cooking Liquid: heat [2 cups   WATER + 1/2-tp SALT
                                                    [4 TB   LIME JUICE
- Place the saucepan over medium heat, uncovered.
- As soon as you hear the Butter sizzle, pour around the plate 3/4-cup of the Cooking Liquid.
- Cover the saucepan, keep covered. After 15 minutes add a little more of the Cooking Liquid.
- 10 minutes later add the rest. Reduce heat to medium low. Cook the Rolls 50-to-60 minutes or until the Leaves are very tender. Taste for doneness. To serve later, warm over low heat.
- Serve with beaten PLAIN YOGURT or AVGOLEMONO SAUCE (see "SAUCES").

LAMB - STUFFED ZUCCHINI, AVGOLEMONO SAUCE

8 ZUCCHINI   Of medium length. Fairly thick. Of a bright green color with no blemishes.
- Scrape away any grit. Wash, cut off stem end.
- With a serrated corer remove the Pulp, leaving a 1/4-inch wall all around.
- Under running water rinse the inside. Turn upside down on paper towels.
- Purée the PULP in processor.

The STUFFING   In an 8-inch nonstick skillet,

over medium heat, heat	[1 TB	VEGETABLE OIL
When it sizzles, sauté	[1 cup	ONION finely chopped
When Onion is translucent, add	[8 oz	LEAN GROUND LAMB or BEEF
Stir in	[1/2-tp	LEMON JUICE (omit if using Beef)

When the Meat has lost its raw color, mix in	[1/4-cup of	Zucchini Pulp
and	[to taste	NUTMEG grated
When the Meat is cooked, add	[1/2-cup	CHICKEN BROTH
Stir for 1 minute, turn off heat and mix in	[4 TB	SWISS CHEESE coarse-grated
	[2 TB	FRESH DILL finely chopped
	[to taste	SALT, GROUND BLACK PEPPER
Then stir in	[4 flat TB	LONG GRAIN WHITE RICE
		Use "Converted" for this recipe.

Flatten the Stuffing, let it cool.

The COOKING LIQUID   In nonstick skillet,

over medium heat, heat	[3 TB	BUTTER
When it sizzles, sauté	[1/3-cup	ONION finely chopped
When Onion is translucent, add	[1/2-cup	Zucchini Pulp puréed

Stir for 2 minutes, do not brown, and add	[2 cups	CHICKEN BROTH
	[1/2-tp	LEMON JUICE
	[1 TB	FRESH DILL finely chopped
Bring to a boil, then simmer 5 minutes. Add	[to taste	SALT, BLACK or WHITE PEPPER

Liquefy in blender.

An OVEN-PROOF DISH   - In which the Zucchini can fit snugly in one layer.
- Spray it with COOKING SPRAY.

STUFFING the ZUCCHINI   Quarter the STUFFING like a pie. Each quarter to fill 2 Zucchini.

With an ice-tea spoon stuff the Zucchini, leaving 1-inch at the top, to allow the Rice
to expand. With the handle of a wooden spoon push down the Stuffing, not too tight.

ASSEMBLING the DISH   Arrange the stuffed Zucchini in the sprayed oven-proof dish.

- Pour over the COOKING LIQUID. Immerse only to level where the Stuffing begins.
- Avoid the Liquid running into the Stuffing, it will draw it out. Save the rest of the
  LIQUID. During the cooking, the Zucchini will give off some liquid.
- Cover tightly with foil. Pierce the foil once in each corner with a fork.

BAKE - In oven preheated to 375° for 1 hour and 30 minutes or until Zucchini are fork tender.
- 45 minutes into the cooking, baste the Zucchini. If needed, add Cooking Liquid.
  Cover with foil. When Zucchini are ready, remove foil. Bake uncovered 5 minutes.

Prepare before serving, and serve on the side [AVGOLEMONO SAUCE - see "SAUCES".

LAMB - STUFFED ZUCCHINI with CURRY SAUCE

Prepare and stuff as on page 296	[8	ZUCCHINI

The CURRY SAUCE See "SAUCES". Prepare	[2 cups	CURRY SAUCE
Using	[3 TB mild	CURRY or 1-1/2 TB hot
Thin the Sauce with	[3/4-cup	CHICKEN BROTH

The STUFFING In an 8-inch nonstick skillet,		
over medium heat, heat	[1 TB	VEGETABLE OIL
When it sizzles, sauté	[1 cup	ONION finely chopped
When Onion softens, add	[2 cloves	GARLIC mashed and minced
When Onion is translucent, add	[8 oz	LEAN GROUND LAMB or BEEF
Stir in	[1/2-tp	LEMON JUICE (also with Beef)

When the Meat has lost its raw color, stir in a	[1/4-cup	Zucchini Pulp puréed
	[1 tp mild	CURRY POWDER or 1/2-tp hot
	[1/4-tp	GROUND CINNAMON
Stir for 2 minutes and add	[1/2-cup	CHICKEN BROTH
Stir for 1 minute, add to taste	[	SALT, PEPPER if needed
Turn off heat and mix in	[3 TB	GOLDEN RAISINS minced
	[3 TB	FRESH CILANTRO finely chopped
	[4 flat TB	LONG GRAIN WHITE RICE
		Use "Converted"

Lay the Zucchini in a sprayed baking dish. Pour over the CURRY SAUCE.
Cover tightly with foil, bake and baste. Before serving, heat and top with remaining CURRY SAUCE.

LAMB - STUFFED ZUCCHINI with MARINARA SAUCE

Prepare as on page 296	[8 medium	ZUCCHINI

The STUFFING In an 8-inch nonstick skillet,		
over medium heat, heat	[1 TB	VEGETABLE OIL
When it sizzles, sauté	[1 cup	ONION finely chopped
When Onion is translucent, add	[8 oz	LEAN GROUND LAMB or BEEF
Stir in	[1/2-tp	LEMON JUICE (omit if using Beef)

Stir until the Meat has lost its raw color. Add	[1/2-tp	DRIED OREGANO crushed
	[a dash	NUTMEG grated
When the Meat is cooked, add	[3/4-cup	MARINARA SAUCE ready-made
	[1/4-cup	Zucchini Pulp puréed or mashed
Stir for 2 minutes then turn off heat, mix in	[4 TB	PARMESAN grated
	[to taste	SALT, PEPPER, PEPERONCINI
Stir in	[3 TB	BASIL or PARSLEY finely chopped
	[4 flat TB	WHITE RICE use "Converted"

Flatten the Stuffing, let it cool in the skillet.

The SAUCE	Mix with	[2-1/4 cups	MARINARA SAUCE ready-made
		[1/4-cup	WATER
		[to taste	SALT if needed, and ALLSPICE

- As on page 296, stuff the Zucchini.
- The same way, assemble the dish, pour over some of the Marinara Sauce, cover and bake.
- Can be refrigerated, heated and served the next day. Serve MARINARA SAUCE on the side.

PORK

PORK CHOPS - BRAISED with SAUCES

Use bottled Sauces and Dressings like Apricot Mustard, Honey Mustard, Sweet and Sour.

- Pat dry the Chops. Dust with FLOUR. Heat a cast iron skillet, add a little Vegetable Oil.
- Over high heat sear the Chops on both sides. Spread over each, a Tablespoon of Sauce, on each side. Cover the skillet, reduce heat to medium low. Cook until tender, 40-to-60 minutes, depending on thickness. Turn twice. Moisten with a little more Sauce.

PORK CHOPS - BREADED   *Wiener Schnitzel*   See VEAL CHOPS - MILANESE

- 3/8-inch thick Chops are pounded flat to a 1/4-inch. The bone usually remains attached.
- They are first dipped in FLOUR. Then in EGG WASH. And last in BREADCRUMBS.
- Mostly, the Pork Wiener Schnitzel is cooked in LARD. You may prefer it *"alla Milanese"*.

PORK CHOPS - HABANERA   *Serves 4*

Trim, dry with paper towels, place in a pan	[4	PORK CHOPS 1-to-1-1/4-inch thick

The MARINADE	Mix in a bowl	[3 TB	EXTRA-VIRGIN OLIVE OIL
		[2 TB	LEMON JUICE
		[2 TB	ONION finely chopped
		[1 clove	GARLIC mashed and minced
		[1/2-tp	GROUND CUMIN
		[1/4-tp	SALT, CAYENNE, HOT PEPPER

Brush the Chops with all the Marinade. Stack them in 2 pairs. Cover. Refrigerate overnight.

The CHOPS	In a large nonstick skillet, over high heat, heat	[1 TB	BUTTER
		[1 TB	EXTRA-VIRGIN OLIVE OIL

- When sizzling, add the Chops, pat dried.
- Brown them on both sides.
- Reduce heat to medium, cover the skillet, cook them for 30 minutes, turn once.
- With tongs remove them onto a plate.

Deglaze the skillet, medium heat, by adding	[2 TB	LIGHT RUM
Scrape meat tidbits, then add and sauté	[1/2-cup	ONION finely chopped
When the Onion begins to color, add	[1-1/2 cups	FRESH PINEAPPLE small cubes
	[1 medium	GREEN BELL PEPPER diced
	[1/4-tp	GROUND CINNAMON
	[1/4-tp	GROUND CUMIN
Sauté for 3 minutes and add	[1 TB	CAPERS drained, rinsed, drained
	[1/4-cup	WATER

Add the CHOPS. Spoon over the Mixture.
Cover, cook over medium low heat until the Chops are tender. Stir occasionally, turn the Chops.
Serve with   BLACK BEANS.

298

PORK CHOPS - LITTLE ITALY   *Serves 4*

| Trim off excess Fat, pat dry, place in a pan | [4 | PORK CHOPS 1-to-1-1/4-inch thick |

The MARINADE   Mix

	[3 TB	EXTRA-VIRGIN OLIVE OIL
	[2 TB	BALSAMIC VINEGAR
	[1 clove	GARLIC mashed and minced
	[1 tp	DRIED OREGANO crumbled
	[1/4-tp	SALT, GROUND BLACK PEPPER

Brush the Chops with all the Marinade. Stack
them in 2 pairs. Cover. Refrigerate overnight.

The CHOPS Heat a 10-inch skillet, high heat,

| swirl in it | [1-1/2 TB | EXTRA-VIRGIN OLIVE OIL |

Pat dry. Brown the Chops on both
sides. Remove to a plate.

Add to the skillet	[1 TB	EXTRA-VIRGIN OLIVE OIL
Deglaze, medium heat, scraping tidbits, add	[1/2-cup	ONION finely chopped
When the Onion softens, add	[2 cloves	GARLIC mashed and minced
When Onion is translucent add	[26-28 oz-can	PEELED TOMATOES drained
	[1 TB	CAPERS rinsed, drained
	[1 TB	DRIED OREGANO crumbled
	[	SALT, GROUND BLACK PEPPER

Mash, stir the Tomatoes with wooden spoon.
When they begin to bubble, add the CHOPS. Spoon the Tomatoes over them. Cover the skillet
tightly, reduce heat to medium low. 20 minutes later turn the Chops. Cook until they are done.

VARIATION   - After cooking, lay the Chops in a sprayed baking dish, cover with the Tomatoes.
              - Top with shredded MOZZARELLA. Melt under the broiler. Serve with Pasta.

PORK CHOPS - MANDARIN   *Serves 4*

The MARINADE   Mix

	[2 TB	SESAME SEED OIL
	[3 TB	SOY SAUCE
	[1-1/2 TB	FRESH GINGER grated
	[1 clove	GARLIC mashed and minced
	[	GROUND BLACK PEPPER
	[1/4-tp	BROWN SUGAR

As in above recipe, brush with this Marinade

| and refrigerate overnight | [4 | PORK CHOPS 1-to-1-1/4-inch thick |

The CHOPS   As above, brown the Chops in   [1-1/2 TB   VEGETABLE OIL
              (reserve the Marinade Juices)
Set Chops aside.

Add to the skillet	[1 tp	VEGETABLE OIL
Over medium heat, deglaze the skillet, add	[2 cups	ONIONS halved, thinly sliced
	[1 medium	GREEN BELL PEPPER thin strips
	[1 medium	RED BELL PEPPER thin strips
Stir-fry. When Onion is translucent, sprinkle	[a little	SALT, GROUND BLACK PEPPER

- Place the browned CHOPS on top of the Vegetables. Drizzle with the MARINADE JUICES.
- Cover the skillet tightly, reduce heat to medium low. After 20 minutes turn the Chops.
- Cover, cook until the Chops are done. Serve with Chinese Noodles, or an Egg Noodle Pasta.

PORK CHOPS with SAUERKRAUT   *Serves 4*

1.   Trim the Fat. Pat dry with paper towels   [4   PORK CHOPS 1-1/4 to 1-1/2-inch thick
                              Optional, rub with   [GARLIC CLOVES split in half lengthwise

2.   In a nonstick skillet, medium heat, fry   [3 strips   SMOKED BACON cut into 1-inch
                                                                                            pieces

When light golden brown and soft, drain on
paper towel.
                                    Add to skillet   [1-1/2 TB   BUTTER + 1 tp VEGETABLE OIL
         Over medium heat, when it sizzles, sauté   [1/2-cup   ONION   finely chopped
                         When translucent, add   [1 lb-pkg   PRECOOKED SAUERKRAUT drain
                                                                    (rinse if indicated on package)
     Stir for 2 minutes separating strands. Add   [1/2-cup   DRY WHITE WINE
          Stir 1 minute, as Wine evaporates, add   [1/4-cup   CHICKEN BROTH
                                                   [6   BLACK PEPPERCORNS
                                                   [1/8-tp   GROUND CLOVES
                                                   [the fried Bacon pieces

Bring to a boil, reduce heat to medium low,
cover, simmer for 15 minutes, turn off heat.

3.   In a 10-inch heavy skillet, with a lid,
               over high heat, heat until it sizzles   [1 TB   VEGETABLE OIL
     Add the CHOPS, sear golden brown, sprinkle   [a little   SALT, GROUND BLACK PEPPER

Set aside. Pour out Fat.   In the skillet add   [1 TB   BUTTER
         Over medium heat, when it sizzles, add   [1-1/2 cups ONION   halved, thinly sliced

Stir Onion, scrape the skillet to loosen tidbits.
     When Onion turns a light golden brown, add   [3 TB   DRY WHITE WINE

       - Stir for 1 minute. Add the Chops, cover with the Onions. Place lid tightly over skillet.
       - Reduce heat to medium low. Cook 20 minutes. Turn the Chops, baste with Juices.

4.   - Pour the SAUERKRAUT over the CHOPS. Cover, cook over medium low heat until the
           Chops are done. Poke with a pointed knife, if Juice is white and clear, they're ready.
         - Transfer to a platter, or oven-proof dish. Cover with foil and keep warm in the oven.

Serve with steamed or boiled POTATOES.

PORK CHOPS with SAUERKRAUT and PINEAPPLE

In a nonstick skillet, over medium heat, heat   [1-1/2 TB   BUTTER + 1 tp VEGETABLE OIL
                         When it sizzles, sauté   [1/2-cup   ONION   finely chopped
           When Onion is translucent, add   [1 lb-pkg   PRECOOKED SAUERKRAUT drain
                                                                    (rinse if indicated on package)
                               1 can   [8-to-10 oz PINEAPPLE CHUNKS with Juice
                                       [6   BLACK PEPPERCORNS
                                       [1/8-tp   GROUND CINNAMON
- Bring to a boil, reduce heat to medium low.
- Simmer for 15 minutes. Turn off heat.
- Cook the 4 PORK CHOPS as in above recipe: step 3.
- Pour the SAUERKRAUT over the PORK CHOPS and continue as in above recipe.

SMOKED PORK CHOPS - BAKED with SAUERKRAUT

Serves 4

In a sprayed oven-proof dish place	[4	SMOKED PORK CHOPS
In an 8-inch heavy skillet, medium heat, heat	[1 TB	BUTTER + 1 tp VEGETABLE OIL
When it sizzles, fry	[3 strips	SMOKED BACON coarsely chop
When the Bacon begins to brown, sauté	[1 cup	RED ONION 1/4-inch slices diced
	[2 cloves	GARLIC mashed and minced
When Onion is translucent, stir in	[1 lb-pkg	PRECOOKED SAUERKRAUT drain (rinse if indicated on package)
	[1/2-cup	DRY WHITE WINE
	[1/4- cup	CHICKEN BROTH
	[3 TB	DRIED BLACK or RED CURRANTS
	[6	BLACK PEPPERCORNS

- Slowly bring to a boil and stir for 2 minutes.
- Cover the CHOPS with the SAUERKRAUT. Cover the dish with foil.
- Poke the four corners of the foil with a fork.
- Bake in oven preheated to 350° for 30-to-45 minutes, until the Chops are done.

Serve with CRUSTY BAGUETTE and MUSTARD on the side

PORK LOIN MEDALLIONS - SOUR CREAM MUSHROOMS

Serves 2

Trim off Fat. Pat dry with paper towels	[4	PORK LOIN MEDALLIONS 1-to-1-1/4-inch thick
In a heavy nonstick skillet, high heat, heat	[1 TB	VEGETABLE OIL

- When hot, brown MEDALLIONS on both sides.
- Cook 4-to-5 minutes on each side or longer, until done.

Sprinkle	[	SALT, GROUND BLACK PEPPER

Wrap in foil. Keep in warm oven.
Pour Fat out of skillet.

In the skillet, over medium heat, heat	[1-1/2 TB	BUTTER + 1 tp VEGETABLE OIL
When it sizzles, sauté until golden	[3/4-cup	ONIONS quartered, thinly sliced
Then add	[3 oz	SLICED MUSHROOMS
	[to taste	NUTMEG grated
When Mushrooms are tender and browned	[sprinkle	SALT, GROUND BLACK PEPPER
Meanwhile beat	[1/2-cup	SOUR CREAM
	[3 TB	hot BROTH

When Mushrooms have browned, gradually
add the SOUR CREAM, stir until hot.

Adjust	[if needed	SALT and PEPPER

Turn off heat.
Set the Pork Medallions on a platter. Spoon over the Mushroom Sauce. Serve immediately.

301

PORK - ROASTED TENDERLOIN   *Serves 4*

The MARINADE		Version I	Version II	[2 TB	VEGETABLE OIL
				[1 tp	LEMON JUICE
Mix	[2 TB	VEGETABLE OIL		[2 TB	BALSAMIC VINEGAR or SOY SAUCE
	[2 TB	LEMON JUICE		[1	GARLIC CLOVE minced
	[1	GARLIC CLOVE minced		[1/4-tp	BROWN SUGAR
	[1/2-tp	SALT		[1/2-tp	SALT (none if using Soy Sauce)
	[1/4-tp	GROUND BLACK PEPPER		[1/4-tp	GROUND BLACK PEPPER or to taste
	[1/2-tp	DIJON MUSTARD		[1/4-tp	GROUND GINGER

The LOIN   Pat dry with paper towels a   [2 lb trussed   BONELESS TENDERLOIN or LOIN
Will shrink sizeably when cooked.

- Place it on heavy foil. Rub with MARINADE.
- Wrap it in the foil. Refrigerate overnight.
- Use an oven-proof saucepan with a lid, to fit
  snugly the Loin (prevents juices from drying).
- Preheat oven to 350°.

In the saucepan, over medium heat, heat   [2 tp   VEGETABLE OIL   spread it with
                                                                                              a wooden spoon

When hot, brown on all sides the LOIN.
Remove and set aside on a plate.

Add to the saucepan   [1 cup   BEEF BROTH canned
                                     [2 TB   WATER
Bring to a slow boil, scraping tidbits with a
wooden spoon and deglazing the saucepan,
                        then stir in and dissolve   [2 tp   BROWNING & SEASONING SAUCE

- Add to taste BLACK PEPPER. Turn off heat.
- Set LOIN in the saucepan, baste with Broth.
- Cover tightly with the lid, place in the oven.
- Baste every 25 minutes.
- The Loin is done when internal temperature
  reaches 185° (30-to-35 minutes per pound).
- Remove and wrap it immediately in foil.
- Refrigerate, if it is to be served the next day.
- Return saucepan with Juices to the stove.

The GRAVY   Dissolve in a   [1/4-cup of   cold BEEF BROTH   canned
                                              [2 tp   ARROWROOT
- Over low heat bring Juices to a simmer.
- Scrape with wooden spoon, deglaze the saucepan. Add Arrowroot, stir until the Sauce thickens.
- Use more Broth, Seasoning Sauce and Arrowroot for a larger amount of Gravy.
- Serve the sliced Loin, on a platter, with Gravy on the side.

Serve with   [POLENTA, roasted or mashed POTATOES,
                      [ORZO cooked in Chicken Broth, PASTA

<u>To serve the next day</u>   -   Slice the LOIN. Overlap slices in an oven-proof dish. Heat the GRAVY.
                              -   Pour it over the Loin, cover with foil. Heat in warm oven.

VARIATION   Before roasting, surround with   [3 medium   CARROTS cut into 1/2-inch chunks
                                                 [16 small   PEARL ONIONS   peeled
Use a larger saucepan and 2 cups of BROTH.

PORK - ROASTED TENDERLOIN with RED CABBAGE

Serves 6

The MARINADE   Mix in a small bowl   [2 TB   EXTRA-VIRGIN OLIVE OIL
                                                        [2 TB   LEMON JUICE
                                                        [1 tp   DIJON MUSTARD
                                                        [1/8-tp   GROUND CLOVES
                                                        [1 clove   GARLIC   mashed and minced

Pat dry and place on heavy foil a   [3 lb trussed   LEAN BONELESS TENDERLOIN
This cut will shrink sizeably.

Drizzle and rub it with the MARINADE.
Wrap in the foil. Refrigerate overnight.

The CABBAGE   See "VEGETABLES"
                       "Preparation for Cooking"

Julienne into 1/2-inch wide ribbons a   [2 lb   HEAD of RED CABBAGE   7-to-8 cups

The TENDERLOIN   In a large oven-proof
                         saucepan or Dutch oven,
                      over high heat, heat   [1 TB   VEGETABLE OIL   spread it with
                                                                    a wooden spoon

- Pat dry the TENDERLOIN. Brown on all sides.
- If too long to fit in the saucepan, cut it in
  half and brown the halves separately.
- Set them aside. Pour the Fat out of the
  saucepan. Do not rinse it.

The CABBAGE   Preheat oven to 350°.

In the same saucepan, medium heat, heat   [4 TB   BUTTER
                        When it sizzles, sauté   [1 cup   ONION   halved, thinly sliced
When Onion is translucent, mix in gradually   [the Cabbage

Cover, reduce heat to medium low, simmer for
10 minutes, or until limp.
                         Meanwhile, mix a   [10.5 oz-can   CHICKEN BROTH with 1 can Water

Stir into the Cabbage   [2 TB   RED WINE VINEGAR
                                            [1/2-cup   of the Chicken Broth
                                            [1/8-tp   SALT, GROUND BLACK PEPPER
                                            [1/8-tp   GROUND CLOVES
Bring to a simmer. Cover tightly.
Bake on middle rack of oven for 45 minutes.

The TENDERLOIN   Then stir into Cabbage   [1/2-cup   BLUEBERRIES or TART APPLES
                                                                    diced

                                                 [1 cup   CHICKEN BROTH
- Place on top the TENDERLOIN. Baste it.
- Cover tightly the saucepan. Continue the oven-cooking. Baste every 25 minutes.
- Add more BROTH if needed, do not allow to dry. Bake about 1 hour and 45 minutes. The
  Roast is done when internal temperature reaches 185°. The Cabbage will have almost melted.

Serve with any of   BOILED or MASHED POTATOES, small PASTA, SPÄETZLE.

PORK - ROASTED TENDERLOIN *with* DRIED FRUIT

Serves 6. Prepare this delicious dish a day ahead and refrigerate. It allows flavors to blend.

SOAK the DRIED FRUIT   Cut in half   [4 oz   DRIED APRICOTS not plump ones
                                      and   [4 oz small   DRIED FIGS or use 8 oz Apricots
          Place them in a bowl and cover with   [APPLE JUICE + 1 TB Brandy

                      Place in another bowl   [3 oz   DRIED CRANBERRIES
                              Cover with   [APPLE JUICE

The COOKING BROTH   In a saucepan, heat   [2 cups   CHICKEN BROTH   lightly salted
                                      and   [2 cups   APPLE JUICE

                              Mix in a bowl   [1/2-cup   APRICOT PRESERVES
                                            [4 TB   GRAINY DIJON MUSTARD
                                            [1/4-cup   CIDER VINEGAR
                                            [1/2-tp   GROUND CINNAMON
                                            [1/4-tp   ALLSPICE
                                            [1/4-tp   SALT
                                            [1/4-tp   GROUND BLACK PEPPER
               Dilute by adding gradually   [a little   of the hot Broth/Juice

- When diluted, add it to the Broth.
- Stir, bring to a boil. Boil for only 5 minutes.
- Taste the Broth. You may want to add, to
  taste any of: Salt, Mustard, Vinegar, Spices.

The LOIN   Pat dry with paper towels a   [3 lb trussed LEAN BONELESS TENDERLOIN
                                                    This cut will shrink sizeably.
                              Sprinkle with   [SALT, GROUND BLACK PEPPER
                              Rub with   [1   LEMON   cut into 4 wedges

Select an oven-proof large saucepan with a lid,
or a Dutch oven. If the Tenderloin is too long
to fit in it, cut it in half.

                  Over high heat, heat in the saucepan   [1 TB   VEGETABLE OIL   spread it

- Brown the Tenderloin on all sides. If halved,
  brown each half separately. Set aside.
- Preheat oven to 350°.

      Pour Fat out of Saucepan, keep 1 tp, add   [1/2-TB   BUTTER
      Return to stove. Over medium heat, sauté   [1/2-cup   ONION   finely chopped

      - When Onion begins to brown, pour into the Saucepan 1 cup of COOKING BROTH.
      - Over medium heat, bring to a boil, deglaze with a wooden spoon.

      - Place in it the Tenderloin. Add more Broth to immerse it 1/3-way up. Baste it.
      - Cover, place in oven. Baste every 25 minutes. The Loin is done when internal
        temperature reaches 185° (30-35 minutes per pound) and the Loin is tender.

      - Wrap the Loin in foil and refrigerate. Wrap halves separately.
      - Let the saucepan cool. Refrigerate until the surface Fat of Cooking Juices
        solidifies, skim it off. *(continued)*

COOKING the FRUIT   Add to Cooking Juices [Soaked Fruit with Soaking Juices
                                                    [the rest of the Cooking Broth
                                                    [1/2-cup   SLIVERED ALMONDS
Bring to a boil. Reduce heat to low.
Simmer for 1 hour, or until the Juice thickens into a Sauce. Do not overcook. The Fruit pieces
must remain whole. Cool a few minutes. Transfer to a bowl. When cold, cover, refrigerate.

NEXT DAY   - Place the Fruit in a saucepan over low heat, until hot enough to test the Sauce
                        thickness. If too thick, add APPLE JUICE until desired consistency is obtained.

To serve   - Spread some of the Fruit Sauce in an oven-proof serving dish.
                    - Slice the Tenderloin and overlap the slices lengthwise in the center of the dish.
                    - With a slotted spoon remove the Fruit, spread it on both sides of the Tenderloin.
                    - Stir the remaining Sauce and pour it over the Tenderloin and Fruit.

                    - Cover the dish with heavy foil. It can be left out and heated later in a warm
                        oven. Or it can be refrigerated.
                    - Bring to room temperature before heating.
                    - Heat in oven preheated to 200° for 20-to-25 minutes.

Serve with SAFFRON RICE or SAFFRON RISOTTO (see "BASIC RECIPES" - RISOTTO MILANESE).

SAFFRON RICE   *Serves 6*

                    Add enough WATER to [1 can   CHICKEN BROTH to cook 2 cups
                                                                                                            Rice
        In a small saucepan, simmer [1 cup of   the Broth
                        and dissolve in it [1/4-tp   SAFFRON THREADS   pulverized
                                                                                    or more to taste
Bring to a simmer the rest of the Broth.

In a heavy saucepan, over medium heat, heat [2 TB   VEGETABLE OIL
            When a light haze forms, sauté [1/2-cup   ONION   finely chopped
            When Onion is translucent, add [2 cups   LONG GRAIN WHITE RICE

- Stir to coat the Rice with the Oil until the grains glisten, but remain white. (Do not toast)
- Add the 1 cup of SAFFRON BROTH. Bring to a boil, stir for 1 minute. Add remaining BROTH.
- Bring the Broth to a boil, cover the saucepan, reduce heat to low, simmer until the Rice is done.
- Do not stir it during the cooking. Optional: mix into cooked Rice 2 TB of softened BUTTER.

ROAST PORK LEFTOVERS - BRUSSELS SPROUTS and PASTA

                        Microwave until tender [10 oz-pkg   FROZEN BRUSSELS SPROUTS

    In a nonstick skillet, sauté the Sprouts in [2 TB   BUTTER
                                                        [to taste   SALT, PEPPER, NUTMEG
                                Stir in [ROAST PORK bite-size pieces
                                                        [3 TB   PECANS   chopped

                        Dissolve in [1/3-cup   hot CHICKEN BROTH
                                                    [1/4-tp   MUSTARD
Moisten with the Broth the Sprouts and Broth.

                        Toss them into [hot small PASTA

PORK STEW - DRIED FRUIT CURRY SAUCE   *Serves 4*

The FRUIT   Soak in a bowl until plump   [4 oz   DRIED APPLES break into bite-size
                                                    [2 oz   GOLDEN RAISINS (1/2-cup)
                                     Cover with   [APPLE CIDER or APPLE JUICE

              Cut in half lengthwise, place in another bowl   [4 oz   DRIED PITTED PRUNES
                                     Cover with   [APPLE CIDER or APPLE JUICE

The PORK   Mix in a cup   [2 TB   LEMON JUICE
                                                    [2 TB   VEGETABLE OIL
                                                    [1 tp mild   CURRY POWDER   or 1/2-tp hot

                          Pat dry with paper towels [2 lbs   PORK SIRLOIN   1-1/2 inch cubes

In a large bowl, rub cubes with Lemon Mixture.
Marinate for 2 hours. Drain. Pat dry.

                   In a stewpan, over high heat, heat [1 TB   VEGETABLE OIL
                             Brown on all sides   [half of   the Pork cubes
Transfer to a bowl.
Repeat. Combine all the Pork.   Sprinkle   [to taste   SALT, GROUND BLACK PEPPER

The CURRY   Mix   [2 TB   FLOUR
                                       with   [2 TB mild   CURRY POWDER   or 1 TB hot
                                                    [1/4-tp   GROUND CINNAMON
                                                    [1/4-tp   GROUND GINGER

Pour Fat out of stewpan, return to stove, add   [1 TB   BUTTER + 1 TB MARGARINE
       When it sizzles, over medium heat, sauté   [1 cup   ONION   finely chopped
Scrape to deglaze. When Onion softens add   [Flour / Curry
                             Stir to blend, add   [1 TB   RED WINE VINEGAR
Stir in the PORK cubes.
                                          Add   [1 cup   CHICKEN BROTH   lightly salted
                                                    [enough   APPLE CIDER   to cover

- Bring to a boil, cover, reduce heat to low,
  simmer for 45 minutes.
- Add APPLES, RAISINS, with Soaking Liquid.
- Add the PRUNES drained. Discard Soaking
  Liquid (too heavy and sweet).
                                          Add   [enough   APPLE CIDER   to cover
Bring to a boil, cover, reduce heat to low,
simmer for 45 minutes or until the Pork is
fork tender. Stir occasionally.
                                       Mix in   [1 TB   LEMON JUICE   or more to taste
                                                    [adjust   Seasonings

- Transfer to oven-proof casserole, cover.
- Refrigerate overnight. Allows flavors to blend.
- Bring to room temperature before heating.
- Heat, covered, in a warm oven.

To serve   Sprinkle with   [SHREDDED COCONUT
                               Accompany with   [WILD RICE or a SAFFRON RICE
                                        and   [CONDIMENTS see "SAUCES" - CURRY

VARIATION   - substitute Prunes with DRIED PINEAPPLE bite-size chunks. Add Soaking Liquid.

306

VEAL

CHOPS - SAUTÉED

Pat dry and dip lightly in FLOUR	[	4	VEAL CHOPS 1-inch thick
In heavy nonstick skillet, medium heat, heat	[	3 TB	BUTTER + 1 tp VEGETABLE OIL
When it sizzles, brown CHOPS on both sides	[	sprinkle	SALT, GROUND BLACK PEPPER

- Cover the skillet, reduce heat to medium low.
- Cook 20-to-25 minutes, turning them once.
- When done, juices will run clear when the
  Chops are pierced with a fork. Set aside.

<u>Deglaze the skillet</u>	Add to pan Juices [	1/4-cup	BEEF BROTH
	[		or 3 TB Broth + 1 TB Dry White Wine

Over medium heat, bring to a quick boil.
Scrape tidbits with wooden spoon. Let Juices thicken, adjust Seasonings, serve over the Chops.

CHOPS - MUSHROOMS WHITE WINE CREAM SAUCE

Sauté as above	[	4	VEAL CHOPS
Whilst Veal Chops are cooking, prepare a	[		CHAMPAGNE or WHITE WINE SAUCE see "SAUCES"

Lay the Chops in an oven-dish, cover with foil,
keep in warm oven.

Add to pan juices	[	1 TB	BUTTER
When it sizzles, over medium heat, sauté	[	1 TB	SHALLOTS finely chopped
When Shallots soften and begin to color, add	[	6 oz	MUSHROOMS thinly sliced
When Mushrooms are tender, sprinkle	[	to taste	SALT, GROUND BLACK PEPPER

Stir MUSHROOMS into the SAUCE. Warm over low heat. Pour over the CHOPS. Serve immediately.

CHOPS - NAPOLITANA   *For 4 Veal Chops*

In a nonstick skillet, over medium heat, heat	[	2 TB	EXTRA-VIRGIN OLIVE OIL
When a light haze forms, sauté	[	1 cup	ONION slice 1/4-inch thick, dice
When translucent add	[	1 clove	GARLIC mashed and minced
When fragrant, add	[	2 medium	GREEN BELL PEPPERS diced
	[	1 medium	ZUCCHINI quarter longwise, dice
When the Vegetables soften, sprinkle with	[		SALT, GROUND BLACK PEPPER
Add	[	1 cup	TOMATOES peeled, seeded, diced
	[	1/2-cup	TOMATO or MARINARA SAUCE
	[	2 tp	TINY CAPERS rinsed, drained

Reduce heat to medium low, bring to a boil,
cover and simmer for 20 minutes.

Add	[	1/4-cup	BLACK OLIVES sliced or chopped
	[	2 TB	FRESH BASIL finely chopped

Adjust Seasonings.

Serve with	[	sautéed	VEAL CHOPS, PASTA or GNOCCHI

VEAL CHOPS alla MILANESE   (Wiener Schnitzel)*   Serves 2

Have your butcher cut 3/8-inch thick VEAL CHOPS, with or without the bone, and pound them flat to a 1/4-inch. They will spread out and be very large. Just one will fit in a frying pan.

For 2 CHOPS   In a shallow dish beat   [1   EGG + 1 TB WATER
                                               [1/4-tp   SALT, GROUND BLACK PEPPER

                     Put in another shallow dish [FINE BREAD CRUMBS
                                                                  plain or seasoned

Dip the Chops into the beaten Egg. Then into
the Bread Crumbs. Pat them into Egg coating.
Set Chops on a tray. Refrigerate 30 minutes.

          In a frying pan, over medium heat, heat [enough   BUTTER to cover the base of pan
                                          Add   [1 tp   VEGETABLE OIL
When it sizzles, add the Chop.
Brown for 15 seconds on each side, reduce heat to medium low, cook for 5 minutes on each side.

VARIATION   Add to beaten Egg [1 TB   PARMESAN grated
                                    and [1 tp   PARSLEY   finely chopped

* The WIENER SCHNITZEL is the Austrian version. See PORK CHOPS - BREADED.

VEAL - COLD ROAST - "VITELLO TONNATO"   (Italy)

A delicious dish than can be served as an appetizer, a light lunch with a Salad, or on a buffet.
It can also be prepared with sliced BONELESS TURKEY BREAST.

See "SAUCES" - COLD.   Prepare a [TUNA MAYONNAISE   recipe yields 2-1/4 cups

For more than a 2-1/2 lb Roast, double the
SAUCE recipe, or add a half of it. Refrigerate.
To spread it, first bring to room temperature.

Spread thinly the TUNA SAUCE over the base
of a serving dish.
                  Overlap barely, a layer of [thinly sliced   ROASTED BONELESS VEAL LOIN
                                                                   (see recipe *)

- Spread with a spatula the SAUCE over the
  slices. Repeat the layers of Veal and Sauce.
- Top the last layer with the Sauce. Cover
  with plastic wrap. Refrigerate overnight.

To serve   Garnish with [TINY CAPERS   rinsed, drained, dried
                                     [OLIVES   sliced or halved
                                     [CORNICHONS   shaped into fans**
                                     [FLAT LEAF PARSLEY   finely chopped

* You don't need a Gravy. Wrap the Roast in foil, refrigerate overnight. Cold, it is easily sliced.

** Make 2 lengthwise cuts, dividing small Cornichons in 3 sections attached at one end. Spread
   out the sections in the shape of a fan.

308

VEAL MEDALLIONS with MUSHROOMS   *Serves 2 or 4*

Dust with FLOUR	[4	LOIN MEDALLIONS 3/4-inch thick
In a nonstick skillet, over medium heat, heat	[1-1/2 TB	BUTTER + 1 tp VEGETABLE OIL
Brown Medallions on both sides.	[sprinkle	SALT, GROUND BLACK PEPPER

- Cover the skillet, reduce heat to medium low,
  cook Medallions for 3 minutes on each side.
- Remove to a plate and cover with foil.
- Return skillet to stove.

Over medium heat, add to pan Juices	[1 TB	BUTTER
When it sizzles add and sauté	[1 TB	SHALLOTS finely chopped
When Shallots have softened add	[6 oz	SLICED MUSHROOMS

Sauté the Mushrooms until tender. Sprinkle	[	SALT, GROUND BLACK PEPPER
Then add	[2 TB	DRY VERMOUTH or SHERRY

Stir until Vermouth boils.
Keep stirring until it almost evaporates.

Reduce heat to medium low, add	[1/2-cup	HEAVY CREAM

Stir until it thickens into a smooth Sauce. Warm Medallions in the Sauce, serve immediately.

VEAL MEDALLION STRIPS with MIXED MUSHROOMS

Serves 2

Freeze for 30 minutes	[2	LOIN MEDALLIONS 1/2-inch thick

Lay them flat.
Slice them into strips 1/4-inch thick.

In nonstick skillet, over medium heat, heat	[1 TB	BUTTER + 1/2-tp VEGETABLE OIL
When it sizzles, sauté	[	the Veal Strips
When they are cooked, tender, browned	[sprinkle	SALT, GROUND BLACK PEPPER

Remove with a slotted spoon, set on a plate.

Return skillet to stove and over medium heat,

add to pan Juices	[1 TB	BUTTER
Deglaze the skillet, when Butter sizzles sauté	[2 TB	SHALLOTS finely chopped
When Shallots have softened, add	[3 oz	MORELS cleaned ("VEGETABLES")
When they begin to soften, stir in	[3 oz	SLICED CREMINI
Sauté for 2 minutes. Sprinkle	[to taste	SALT, GROUND BLACK PEPPER
and add	[1/4-cup	DRY WHITE WINE
When the Wine reduces by half, add	[1/4-cup	CHICKEN BROTH
When it comes to a boil, reduce heat and add	[1/4-cup	HEAVY CREAM

When thick and smooth add	[	the Medallion Strips
Stir for 1 minute, adjust Seasonings, add	[1 tp	FLAT LEAF PARSLEY finely chop
Serve immediately with	[	EGG NOODLES or TAGLIATELLE

309

VEAL - POT ROAST   *Serves 6*

The LOIN   Sprinkle a   [3 lb   BONELESS LOIN   trussed
                                               with   [SALT, GROUND BLACK PEPPER
                                          Rub it with   [LEMON quartered wedges 2 or 3

In a heavy saucepan, over high heat, heat [1 TB   VEGETABLE OIL   spread it with
                                                                               a wooden spoon

- When it sizzles, brown the LOIN on all sides.
  If too long to fit in saucepan, cut it in half.
- Brown halves separately. Set them aside.

                Over medium heat, heat in the saucepan [1 TB   BUTTER + 1 tp MARGARINE
            With wooden spoon scrape tidbits and sauté [3 TB   SHALLOTS   finely chopped
                       When Shallots begin to color, add [1 cup   DRY WHITE WINE
                      Bring to a boil, stir 30 seconds, add [3/4-cup   BEEF BROTH   canned
                   Bring to a boil, dissolve in it, to taste [2 tp   BROWNING & SEASONING SAUCE
                                                          [to taste   GROUND BLACK PEPPER, SALT

- Add the LOIN and baste it with the BROTH.
- Bring slowly to a boil. Cover the saucepan
  and reduce heat to medium low.
- Turn a few times during the cooking.

- About 1-1/2 to 2 hours. It is done when
  internal temperature reaches 170°.
- Test with a meat thermometer. Pierce with
  a skewer: the juice must be white and clear.

- Remove from saucepan, wrap immediately in
  foil and place in warm oven.
- Strain the Cooking Juices through a fine sieve.

The GRAVY   Measure Cooking Juices. Add [enough   BEEF BROTH to obtain 1-1/2 cups

             If the BROTH is canned, mix it with [WATER in equal amounts

Pour it into a small saucepan, heat and add [if needed   BROWNING & SEASONING SAUCE

                                      Dissolve [2-1/2 tp   ARROWROOT POWDER
                                          with [1/4-cup   WATER
Pour Arrowroot into the Gravy.
Stir until it thickens. Turn off heat. Adjust Seasonings. Cover.
Warm the Gravy over low heat. Serve the Roast on a platter. The Gravy in a sauceboat.

VARIATION - POT ROAST with VEGETABLES   Use a larger saucepan.

                       Increase to [1-1/4 cups   the Broth to cook the Loin
                  Cook the Loin with [4 medium   CARROTS pared, 3/4-inch chunks

About 45 minutes into the cooking add [5 medium   YUKON GOLD POTATOES
                                                                         3/4-inch cubes

                                      [24   PEARL ONIONS
               To cover the Vegetables, add [BEEF BROTH

- When done, with a slotted spoon, remove Roast and Vegetables to a platter. Cover with foil.
- Prepare the Gravy in the saucepan, use: 1-1/2 tp Arrowroot per cup of Gravy.

310

VEAL ROAST - BAKED   Serves 6   *Can be prepared a day ahead.*

The LOIN   Sprinkle a   [3 lb   BONELESS LOIN *   trussed
                                          with   [SALT, GROUND BLACK PEPPER
                                  and rub it with   [1   LEMON quartered wedges 2 or 3
Preheat oven to 350°.

      In an oven-proof saucepan, high heat, heat   [1 TB   VEGETABLE OIL   spread it with
                                                                                      a wooden spoon

- Brown on all sides the LOIN. Set it aside.
  If too long to fit in saucepan, cut it in half.
- Brown halves separately.
                                  Add to saucepan   [1 can   BEEF JELLY CONSOMMÉ
                                                        [1 can   WATER
Over low heat, with a wooden spoon, scrape
the saucepan to loosen meat tidbits.

      When liquid comes to a boil, dissolve in it   [1 TB   BROWNING & SEASONING SAUCE
                                                   or   BEEF BROTH CONCENTRATE
                                                   or   BEEF or VEAL DEMI-GLACE
                                      Then stir in   [1 TB   ONION SOUP MIX
- Boil for 1 minute, turn off heat.
- Place the LOIN in the saucepan.
- The Broth should come up to 1/3 of it.
- If it is more, remove excess BROTH, set
  aside to use later.
                              Place around the Loin   [2 large   CARROTS pared, 1/2-inch chunks
- Cover the saucepan.
- Bake for 1-1/2 hours or longer. It is done
  when internal temperature reaches 170°.
  The Juice must run out white and clear.
- Baste every 20-to-25 minutes.
- Wrap the Loin in heavy foil. Refrigerate to
  seal in Juices. Cold, it will be easier to slice.
- Remove Carrots with slotted spoon. Cover,
  set aside. Use them to garnish the Roast.

The GRAVY   Return saucepan to stove, add   [to Juices any BROTH set aside
                                          plus   [1 can   BEEF BROTH

              Dissolve with a 1/4-cup WATER   [2 TB   ARROWROOT POWDER

Bring the Broth to a slow boil, then add the Arrowroot and stir until the Gravy thickens.
Turn off heat, keep covered. Refrigerate if it is to be served the next day.

Method 1   - Slice the cold Roast. Wrap it in foil. Heat in a warm oven for 30 minutes.
           - Lay the Roast on a platter. Serve the Gravy on the side in a sauceboat.

Method 2   - (Preferred) Warm the Gravy. Spread a little of it in an oven-proof dish.
           - Overlap the Roast slices in the dish, 2 or 3 rows in a single layer. Pour over
             them the Gravy. Cover tightly with foil. If prepared a day ahead, refrigerate.
           - Bring to room temperature before warming for 25 minutes in a 250° oven.

Serve with   Risotto, roasted or mashed Potatoes.

*   For a 2-to 2-1/2 lb Loin use same amounts. Per cup of Gravy: 1-1/2 tp of Arrowroot.

VEAL SCALOPPINE - SAUTÉED   *Serves 2*

- Scaloppine are boneless Veal Cutlets taken from the tenderloin or the loin.
- They are cut 3/4-inch thick and pounded flat into a 1/4-inch. Can be done by your butcher.
  To do it yourself, place each piece between plastic wrap. Pound flat with a heavy skillet.

Pat dry with paper towels	[8 oz (4)	VEAL SCALOPPINE
Just before cooking, dip them in	[	FLOUR shake off excess
In an 8-inch skillet, medium high heat, heat	[1-1/2 TB	BUTTER + 1 tp VEGETABLE OIL

When it sizzles, golden brown the Scaloppine.

Cook them for 2-to-3 minutes on each side	[sprinkle	SALT, GROUND BLACK PEPPER

- Wrap them in foil and keep warm in a 200° oven.   Save the PAN JUICES to prepare a Sauce.
- To deglaze the skillet use a wooden spoon to scrape and loosen tidbits.

SERVE THE SAUTÉED SCALOPPINE WITH ANY OF THE FOLLOWING

Recipes yield servings for 4 Scaloppine (8 oz)

ARTICHOKE HEARTS

Pour into a measuring pitcher the Liquid from	[14 oz-can	SMALL ARTICHOKE HEARTS
Add to this LIQUID	[enough	COLD WATER to obtain 1 cup
Dissolve	[2 tp	FLOUR
with	[1/4-cup	of the LIQUID
Melt into PAN JUICES	[1/2-TB	BUTTER
Scrape to loosen tidbits and sauté	[2 TB	SHALLOTS finely chopped
When they soften and begin to color, add	[	Artichoke Liquid, Liquid / Flour
	[1/4-tp	LEMON JUICE

Stir until the Liquid thickens.
Add the Artichokes. Cover, reduce heat to low, simmer 10 minutes. Adjust Seasonings.

CREMINI MUSHROOMS

Add to PAN JUICES	[2 TB	BUTTER

Over medium heat, when it sizzles, deglaze and sauté	[2 TB	SHALLOTS finely chopped
When they begin to color, add	[6 oz	CREMINI MUSHROOMS sliced
When Mushrooms are tender, golden brown	[sprinkle	SALT, GROUND BLACK PEPPER
	[to taste	NUTMEG grated

Turn off heat.
Set the Scaloppine on two individual plates.

Rest a ladle on the skillet edge, pour into it	[1 TB	BRANDY

Ignite the Brandy and pour it over the Mushrooms. Stir with a long spoon.
When the flames die down, serve the Mushrooms over the Scaloppine.

312

LEMON SAUCE

Add to PAN JUICES	[1-1/2 TB	BUTTER
	[1 TB	LEMON JUICE
Over medium low heat, scrape tidbits, add	[1 TB	PARSLEY finely chopped
	[1/2-tp	TINY CAPERS rinsed, drained

Add Scaloppine to skillet, coat with the Sauce.

MARSALA SAUCE

Add to JUICES	[1/4-cup	DRY MARSALA WINE
	[2 TB	CHICKEN BROTH

- Bring to a quick boil, scraping tidbits.
- Add the sautéed Scaloppine. Reduce heat to low, cover, simmer for 10 minutes. Baste twice.
- Transfer Scaloppine to a platter. Over medium heat stir reducing Sauce to a syrupy texture.
- Turn off heat, melt in it 1-1/2 TB soft BUTTER. Adjust Seasonings. Pour over the Scaloppine.

PIZZAIOLA

Put in sprayed baking dish	[	the Scaloppine
Sprinkle with	[	PARMESAN grated
Top with	[sliced	MOZZARELLA
Pour over	[ready-made	PIZZAIOLA SAUCE heated
Sprinkle with plenty of	[	PARMESAN grated

Pass under the broiler until the Mozzarella has melted.

PROSCIUTTO and MOZZARELLA

Put in a sprayed oven-dish	[	the Sautéed Scaloppine
Top each with	[2 or 3 slices	PROSCIUTTO folded
Sprinkle with a little	[	PARMESAN grated
Top the Prosciutto with	[sliced	GRUYÈRE or MOZZARELLA

Pass under the broiler until the Cheese has melted to a golden color.

SAUTÉED ONIONS

Heat	[1 TB	BUTTER + 1 tp OLIVE OIL
Sauté	[2 cups	ONIONS thin rings (small size)

When golden brown remove with a
slotted spoon and set aside.

Add to skillet	[1 TB	BUTTER
Sauté in it	[4	SCALOPPINE

Set Scaloppine aside.

Add to the Pan Juices	[3 TB	DRY SHERRY
When it has evaporated by half, add	[	the Onions, SALT and PEPPER

Serve the Onions over the Scaloppine.

WHITE WINE

Add to PAN JUICES	[1/2-TB	BUTTER
When it sizzles, sauté	[2 TB	SHALLOTS finely chopped
When the Shallots turn golden, add	[2 TB	DRY WHITE WINE
Stir until the Wine reduces by half, then add	[1/2-cup	HEAVY CREAM
	[to taste	SALT and WHITE PEPPER

When the Cream bubbles and thickens, stir in the Scaloppine. Serve immediately.

313

VEAL SCALOPPINE - ROLLS   *Serves 2*

HAM and MOZZARELLA   Lay flat   [4 (8 oz)   VEAL SCALOPPINE   1/4-inch thick
                                                                                about 4 x 5 inches

Spread the Scaloppine with a slight touch of [MUSTARD

                     Cut to the size of Scaloppine [4 slices   HAM or SMOKED HAM

                          Cut into 3 X 3-1/2 inches [4 slices   MOZZARELLA   thinly sliced

- Place on each Scaloppine a slice of Ham.
- Center the Mozzarella on the Ham.
- Roll the Scaloppine tightly and truss them
  around the center. Tuck in the ends and
  truss them tightly.
                          Dip the Rolls in   [FLOUR   shake off excess

 In a nonstick skillet, just big enough for the
4 Rolls to fit in, over medium high heat, heat   [2 TB   BUTTER

   When it sizzles brown the Rolls on all sides.
     Remove with slotted spoon, set on a plate. [sprinkle   SALT, GROUND BLACK PEPPER

                         Add to Pan Juices [1/4-cup   DRY WHITE WINE or MARSALA
Reduce heat to medium.
Bring to a boil. Deglaze the skillet.

 When the Wine has evaporated by half, add   [1/4-cup   CHICKEN BROTH
                                             [to taste   SALT if needed
- Bring to a boil. Raise heat to medium high.
- Add the Veal Rolls. Cook from 4-to-6 minutes, turning the Rolls with tongs.
- Set the Rolls on a platter. Bring to a bubble , reduce Pan Juices. Serve with MASHED POTATOES.

PROSCIUTTO and MUSHROOMS

THE FILLING In a skillet, medium heat, heat [1-1/2 TB   BUTTER + 1 tp VEGETABLE OIL
                      When it sizzles, sauté [1/2-cup   ONION   finely chopped
       When Onion begins to brown, stir in [2 oz   MUSHROOMS chop into tidbits

       When browned turn off heat, stir in [2-1/2 oz   PROSCIUTTO chop into tidbits
                                             [1 TB   PARMESAN   grated
                                             [1 TB   MASCARPONE
                                             [1 tp   PARSLEY   finely chopped
                                             [to taste   GROUND BLACK PEPPER
    Divide the Filling into 4 equal parts. Spoon
  each part at 1-inch from the bottom edge of [4   SCALOPPINE   1/4-inch thick
                                                                                about 4 x 5 inches
Leave a 1/2-inch of empty space around. Roll,
truss and cook as above.
                      Serve with [PARMESAN RISOTTO

VARIATION Over low heat, add to Pan Juices [1/3-cup   HEAVY CREAM
              Stir until it thickens and add [1 tp   PARSLEY finely chopped
                                             [adjust   Seasonings
Pour over the Rolls. Serve with PASTA.

314

VEAL SHANKS - OSSOBUCO "osso: bone, buco: hole" (Italy) *Serves 4*

The SHANKS Pat dry, lay flat on a board [4   SHANKS 2-inches thick, trussed
                                                              around their thickness.

Before searing sprinkle the Shanks with [SALT, GROUND BLACK PEPPER
                        Dredge them in [FLOUR   shake of excess

In a heavy skillet where all the Shanks fit flat,
                over medium high heat, heat [3 TB   VEGETABLE OIL + 1 TB OLIVE OIL

- Sear the Shanks on all sides. Lift them with
  a slotted spoon, set them on a plate.
- Pour out skillet Fat, do not rinse the skillet.

The VEGETABLES   Preheat oven to 350°.

In an oven-proof heavy saucepan with a lid,
  or in a Dutch oven, over medium heat, heat [2 TB   BUTTER + 1 tp VEGETABLE OIL
                When it sizzles, sauté [3/4-cup   ONION   finely chopped
                                        [1/2-cup   CELERY   finely chopped
                                        [1/2-cup   CARROT   finely chopped
                                        [1/2-tp   GARLIC   mashed and minced

- Stir and cook for about 10 minutes, until
  Vegetables have softened. Turn off heat.
- Stand the SHANKS vertically, side-by-side,
  on top of the Vegetables.

The BROTH   Pour into the searing skillet [1/2-cup   DRY WHITE WINE or MARSALA

Over medium heat bring the WINE to a boil.
With a wooden spoon deglaze the skillet.

When the Wine has reduced by half, add [1 cup   BEEF BROTH canned can be used
                                        [1-1/2 cups   WHOLE TOMATOES canned, drain
                                                                       and chop
                                        [1/4-tp   GRANULATED SUGAR
                                        [1/4-tp   DRIED THYME
                                        [1/4-tp   DRIED SWEET BASIL
                                        [2 sprigs   PARSLEY + 1 BAY LEAF
Bring Broth Mixture to a boil, stir, taste, add [to taste   SALT, GROUND BLACK PEPPER

The SHANKS - Pour it, boiling over the SHANKS. If it doesn't barely cover, add more BROTH.
                - Bring to a boil. Cover the saucepan tightly. Bake in lower third of oven, for
                  80-to-90 minutes or until fork tender. Baste every 25 minutes.
                - Add more Broth if the Sauce has reduced too much and is too thick.

                - To prevent the Marrow from sliding out, lift the Shanks carefully with tongs and
                  a slotted spoon. Lay them flat in an oven-proof dish, cut off trussing string.

The SAUCE   - Remove Bay Leaf and Parsley. Place a fine sieve over a bowl.
                - Pass the Sauce. Mash with the back of a wooden spoon to extract Juices.
                - Return to saucepan. Bring to a boil. If too thin, use 2 tp Arrowroot dissolved
                  in 2 TB Water. Stir until it thickens. If needed, add more Arrowroot. Pour it
                  over the Shanks. Cover. Refrigerate overnight. Warm in oven.

            Serve with   RISOTTO MILANESE - see "BASIC RECIPES".

VEAL STEW - *Blanquette de Veau "Old Style"* (France) *Serves 4 or 5*

The VEAL   In a heavy stockpot place   [2 lbs   VEAL SHOULDER 1-1/2-inch cubes
                                             [cover with   COLD WATER

- Over high heat bring to a boil for 2 minutes.
- Drain the Meat in a colander.
- Rinse under running cold water to rid of scum.

Wash the stockpot, return the Veal to it, add   [2 cans   CHICKEN BROTH 10.5 oz each
                                                 [enough   COLD WATER to cover

Bring to a boil, reduce heat to low, simmer
for 20 minutes, removing the scum.
                                        Add   [1 medium   ONION   whole
                                               [1 medium   CARROT   pared, cut in 4
                                               [1 stalk   CELERY   cut in 4
        A BOUQUET GARNI tied in cheesecloth   [1 sprig   THYME + 2 sprigs PARSLEY
                                               [1   BAY LEAF + 4 PEPPERCORNS
                    If needed, to cover, add   [more   WATER

- Bring to a boil.
- Cover, reduce heat to low, simmer for
  1-1/2 hours or until the Veal is fork tender.

- In a sieve lined with cheesecloth over a bowl,
  transfer the Vegetables with a slotted spoon.
- Then with slotted spoon transfer the Veal to
  a presentable from stove to table stewpot.
  *(Otherwise, cook in a regular saucepan, then
  serve in a tureen or oven-proof casserole).*

- Add the BROTH to the sieve with Vegetables.
- Strain, mashing all solids with wooden spoon.

The ONIONS   In a nonstick skillet, heat   [2 TB   BUTTER
                     When it sizzles, add   [16 small   ONIONS (like Cipollini) peeled
   They have to fit in one layer. Stir and add   [1/2-cup   of the strained BROTH
                                               [sprinkle   SALT, GROUND BLACK PEPPER

Reduce heat to low, cover the skillet, simmer
25-to-30 minutes or until Onions are tender.
With slotted spoon add ONIONS to the Veal.

The MUSHROOMS   Add to ONION JUICES   [1/4-cup of   the BROTH
                                            [1 tp   LEMON JUICE
                                            [12 oz small   MUSHROOMS if large, quartered

Bring to a boil, cover, simmer for 6 minutes.
With slotted spoon add Mushrooms to the Veal.

Pour the Juices into a measuring pitcher, add   [enough of   strained BROTH to obtain 2 cups
                                        Add   [2 tp   LEMON JUICE

The SAUCE   With this BROTH prepare   [2 cups   VELOUTÉ WHITE SAUCE ("SAUCES")
                                            [adjust   SEASONINGS

Stir it into the Veal, cover until ready to serve.

To serve   Heat the Veal, turn off heat.   Beat   [2   EGG YOLKS
                                     with   [3 TB   HEAVY CREAM
                      Beat in, <u>gradually</u>   [1/2-cup of   hot Veal Sauce   *(continued)*

316

- Stir the Yolks into the Stew. Over medium low heat, mix well, until the Sauce thickens, do not let it boil. Cover, keep in warm oven until ready to serve.
- Or transfer to an oven-proof casserole, keep in warm oven.
- <u>Serve with</u> White Rice, Egg Noodles, small Pasta, Fettuccini, boiled/steamed/mashed Potatoes.

<u>*VEAL STEW*</u> - *Blanquette de Veau*   A simpler version   *Serves 4 or 5 **

The VEAL	Pat dry	[2 lbs	VEAL SHOULDER 1-1/2" cubes

In a stewpan**, over high heat, heat	[1 TB	VEGETABLE OIL
When a light haze forms, sear on all sides	[half of	the Veal cubes

Transfer to a bowl. Repeat.
Combine all the Veal in the bowl.
Pour out grease, return stewpan to stove.

The BROTH   Heat in the stewpan   [2 TB   BUTTER

Over medium low heat deglaze the stewpan,
loosening the browned tidbits. Turn up to
medium heat.

When the Butter sizzles add	[3	SHALLOTS cut into thin wedges
Sauté until the Shallots are limp then add	[2 TB	FLOUR

Stir until Butter/Flour turn pale yellow. Add	[10.5 oz-can	CHICKEN BROTH
Stir, keep deglazing as Broth thickens, add	[2 cups	WATER

The STEW   Stir until the Broth begins to boil
          and thicken. Add the VEAL and   [16 small   ONIONS (Cipollini) peeled ***
                    [4 medium   CARROTS pared, 3/4-inch pieces
                    [3 stalks   CELERY HEARTS 1/2-inch pieces
                    [1 sprig   THYME + 1 BAY LEAF
                    [2 TB   LEMON JUICE
   If the Veal and Vegetables are not covered,
                    add just until covered [WATER
                    Stir well, add [to taste   SALT, GROUND BLACK PEPPER
- Bring to a boil.
- Cover, reduce heat to low, simmer for
  1-1/2 to 2 hours until the Veal is fork tender.
  Stir occasionally. (Can be prepared ahead)

<u>To serve</u>   Heat the Veal, turn off heat. Beat   [2   EGG YOLKS
                    with [3 TB   HEAVY CREAM
                    Beat in, <u>gradually</u> [1/2-cup of   the hot Veal Sauce
- Add Yolks to the Stew.
- Over medium low heat stir until the Sauce thickens, do not let it boil. Cover, keep warm in oven.

*   *To serve 6:* 3 lbs Veal, 3 TB Butter, 3 Shallots, 3 TB Flour, 20 onions, 6 Carrots, 4 stalks
     Celery, 3 Egg Yolks, 6 TB Heavy Cream.

**   If you have a "from-stove-to-table" stewpan, use it. Some come in heavy enameled metal,
     or with an earthenware appearance. Or transfer the stew to an oven casserole, or tureen.

*** To peel small Onions see "VEGETABLES" - ONIONS.

VEAL STEW - PORTOFINO   *Serves 4*

The VEAL   Preheat oven to 375°.   Pat dry   [2 lbs   VEAL STEW MEAT 1-1/2" cubes

In an oven-proof saucepan, high heat, heat   [1 TB   EXTRA-VIRGIN OLIVE OIL
When a light haze forms, sear on all sides   [half of   the Veal cubes

Transfer to a bowl. Repeat. Combine all the
Veal, sprinkle with   [SALT, GROUND BLACK PEPPER

Return saucepan to stove and add   [1 TB   EXTRA-VIRGIN OLIVE OIL

Over medium heat, heat the Oil, scrape with
a wooden spoon to loosen tidbits, and sauté   [1/2-cup   ONION   finely chopped
When the Onion softens, add   [2 cloves   GARLIC   mashed and minced
When Garlic is fragrant, add   [1/2-cup   DRY WHITE WINE

Continue deglazing whilst the Wine is boiling.

When half of the Wine has evaporated, add   [28 oz-can   WHOLE TOMATOES   with Liquid
[1 tp   DRIED BASIL   crushed
[1/4-tp   SALT, GROUND BLACK PEPPER
[1/4-tp   GRANULATED SUGAR

- Break the Tomatoes with a wooden spoon.
- When bubbly, mix in the VEAL. Cover and
  place in the oven. Reduce heat to 350°.
- Bake for 1-1/2 hours, or until the Veal is
  fork tender. Stir once in a while.
- About 1-1/4 hours into the Veal cooking
  begin cooking the Vegetables.

The VEGETABLES   In a large skillet, over
high heat, heat   [2 TB   BUTTER
[1 TB   EXTRA-VIRGIN OLIVE OIL
When a light haze forms, sauté   [2 TB   SHALLOTS   finely chopped
When the Shallots soften, add   [8 oz   SLICED MUSHROOMS

Sauté the Mushrooms for 2 minutes, add   [2 pkg frozen   FRENCH CUT GREEN BEANS
(10-oz each) thawed and drained
Sauté the Vegetables until tender and stir in   [2 TB   FRESH BASIL   finely chopped
[to taste   SALT, GROUND BLACK PEPPER
Turn off heat and cover to keep warm.

The STEW   - When the Veal is done, remove from oven. Stir in the VEGETABLES.
- Cover the saucepan and let cool, allowing flavors to blend.

To serve the same day - Heat in a warm oven, or on the stove over low heat.

To serve the next day - Transfer to an oven-proof casserole, cover with lid or foil. Refrigerate.
- Bring to room temperature before heating, covered, in a warm oven.

Optional - Before serving, mix in a 1/4-cup sliced BLACK or GREEN OLIVES.

Serve with - PASTA and grated PARMESAN on the side.

VARIATION - Omit Vegetables. Serve the Stew with Pasta and grated Parmesan.

318

XIV

VEGETABLES

VEGETABLES

"Let us be grateful to people who make us happy;
they are the charming gardeners who make our souls blossom."

Marcel Proust

BLANCHING VEGETABLES (Parboiling)

Use a pasta cooker with a strainer, or a wire basket that fits into your stockpot.
Measure as you fill the pot, the amount of Water, enough to cover the Vegetables
by 2-inches. Add 1/2-tp SALT per quart of Water.
- Large pieces like, Endives, whole Onions, can be removed with a slotted spoon.

Bring the Water rapidly to a boil, uncovered. Plunge the Vegetables from 3-to-5 minutes
or longer, depending on the Vegetables and desired doneness.

Lift out the wire basket, run cold water over the Vegetables to stop the cooking. Drain.
- Pat dry if needed. To remove excess moisture toss them in a skillet over medium heat.

BOILING

Plunge the Vegetables into a large pot of salted rapidly boiling Water: SALT - 1/2-tp per
quart. Add 1 teaspoon of Lemon Juice for every quart, to maintain their color.
- Boil uncovered until the Vegetables have cooked to the desired doneness.

Drain. Run cold Water over the Vegetables, if you are not using them right away.
Some Vegetables should be steamed, not boiled, to maintain a better flavor.

BRAISING

Unless otherwise indicated, blanch first Vegetables that take long to cook.
- In a skillet, medium low heat, melt Butter. Sauté Vegetables until lightly browned.

Add a little Broth, Seasonings, White Wine. Cover, reduce heat to low, simmer until
cooked and a little juice is left in the pan. Add Broth if needed to prevent from drying.

Or, simmer 5 minutes, transfer Vegetables with juices to a baking dish, add a little more
Broth, cover with foil. Bake in oven preheated to 350° until tender. Baste occasionally.

GLAZING

For 1 lb Vegetables like Bell Peppers, Mushrooms, Snow Peas. In a skillet, bring to a boil:

1/4-cup BROTH or WATER,   2 tp BROWN SUGAR or HONEY,   1 TB BUTTER,   1/4-tp SALT

Add Vegetables, coat with the Syrup, stir until the Vegetables are tender, 4-to-6 minutes.
- Vegetables that take long to cook, like Carrots, Pearl Onions, should be blanched first.

WATERLESS COOKING

Cook together in a saucepan with a *tight-fitting lid* Vegetables than take the same time to
cook. The moisture produced is turned into steam, and the Vegetables cook in their steam.

Place Vegetables in the saucepan: whole, sliced, cubed, diced, julienne. Sprinkle Salt and
Pepper. You can also add a little Butter, which will spread over the bottom of the pan.

Cover tightly. Cook over <u>very low</u> heat. They won't take long to cook.
- The Vegetables are cooked when all moisture has evaporated, and they remain crunchy.

À LA GRECQUE   (Greek Style)

Vegetables are stewed in Water or Broth, Olive Oil, Seasonings. (Recipes in this chapter)

BASIC PURÉES, SAUCES and CREAM SOUPS

The PURÉE

- Save the Cooking Liquid from boiled Vegetables. Purée the Cooked Vegetables in a processor. Transfer to a saucepan. With a wooden spoon, stir over low heat to rid of any liquid.

- Add for every cup of Purée: 1 TB of LIGHT or HEAVY CREAM, or a 1/2-TB of BUTTER.

- Then gradually add Cooking Liquid, Broth, Milk, or Cream, until desired consistency is obtained.

- By adding more or less Liquid and/or Cream to the Purée, it will become a Sauce or a Soup.

  NOTE - Non-starchy Vegetables make a thin Purée. A quarter of their volume in starch should be added. The Potato creates the right balance..

BLENDER SAUCE and SOUP

- With a slotted spoon remove the boiled Vegetables from the Cooking Liquid.

- Transfer them to a blender and add 1/3-of their volume in Cooking Liquid. Blend.
- With the blender on, gradually add Cooking Liquid, Broth, hot Milk, Cream, or a combination of any, until the desired consistency is obtained. Add Seasonings.

FROZEN VEGETABLE SOUP

- Place Frozen Vegetables in a Saucepan. Add Water or Broth to cover. Boil until tender.
- Remove with a slotted spoon, transfer to a blender. Blend, adding gradually Cooking Liquid until the desired consistency is obtained. Season to taste. Serve hot or cold.

VELOUTÉ SOUP or SAUCE   Béchamel base made with Broth from cooked Vegetables.

Soup	1/4-of	PURÉED VEGETABLES	Example:	1/2-cup	Vegetables
	1/2-of	VELOUTÉ WHITE SAUCE		1 cup	Sauce
	1/4-of	BROTH or amount to taste		1/2-cup	Broth

2	EGG YOLKS per 2 cups of Soup, beaten with
2 TB	LIGHT CREAM + 2 TB BROTH

- Stir the PURÉED VEGETABLES into the hot VELOUTÉ WHITE SAUCE - see "SAUCES".
- Gradually add the BROTH, giving the Soup or Sauce the desired consistency.
- Beat the EGG YOLKS in a bowl with the LIGHT CREAM and warm BROTH.

- Gradually whisk in the beaten YOLKS to tie the Velouté. Bring to a slow boil.
- Whisk until the texture is smooth and creamy. Add Seasonings. Serve immediately.

VICHYSSOISE   - Preparation: see "BASIC RECIPES" and AVOCADO VICHYSSOISE.
- Put the Vichyssoise in a blender, add cooked Vegetables and blend.

For recipes see ARTICHOKES, BEETS (COLD BORSCHT), CAULIFLOWER.

ARTICHOKES - *Preparation for Cooking*

1. - Add to a bowl of Water, to cover the Artichokes, 1-1/2 TB LEMON JUICE per 2 cups Water.

2. - Remove the dark tough leaves and blades. Slice off evenly the top points. Cut the
     lower leaf points with scissors. Trim the stem, or cut it off for Artichoke to sit flat.
   - If the Artichoke is large, peel off the tough skin covering the Artichoke bottom.
   - Place the Artichoke in the lemony Water. Then proceed to trim the next one.
   - Keep them in the lemony water until you are ready to use them.

3. - Drain. Do not rinse them. If whole, place upside down on paper towels.
   - To boil, no need to dry them. Boil in salted Water.

     TO STUFF ARTICHOKES   Prepare them for cooking. Cut off the stem, level the base.

   - Remove the center leaves and heart. With a grapefruit spoon, scrape out the choke.
   - Rinse out the center, put Artichokes in Lemony Water until ready to use.
   - Drain them upside down on paper towels before stuffing.

     CANNED ARTICHOKES - HEARTS AND BOTTOMS   To tenderize, simmer in their Liquid.

ARTICHOKES à la GRECQUE   *Serve cold or at room temperature.*

Thaw, drain, pat dry	[10 oz-pkg	FROZEN ARTICHOKE HEARTS
		Whole or cut in half.
In a 5-1/2 inch heavy saucepan combine	[1 cup	WATER
	[4 TB	EXTRA-VIRGIN OLIVE OIL
	[1/2-tp	LEMON JUICE
	[1	GREEN ONION cut in half
	[1/2-tp	DRIED SWEET BASIL
	[1/4-tp	SALT, GROUND BLACK PEPPER

- Bring to a boil, cover, reduce heat to low.
- Simmer for 10 minutes. Turn off heat. If needed, add Salt and Pepper. Add the Artichokes.
- Bring to a boil. Cover, reduce heat to low, simmer until fork tender: about 10 minutes.
- Remove the Artichokes with a slotted spoon and place them in a serving bowl or dish.

- Bring the Cooking Liquid to a boil and continue boiling, uncovered, until it is reduced to 1/4-cup.
- Measure it. If too much, boil longer. Pour it through a sieve over the Artichokes. Let cool.
- Cover and refrigerate overnight. Serve with Hors-d'oeuvres, Meats, Fish, Seafood, Poultry.

SMALL FRESH ARTICHOKES   First simmer for 30-to-40 minutes. Then prepare à la Grecque.

ARTICHOKES - BOILED

In a saucepan filled with plenty of Water place	[whole raw	ARTICHOKES prepared
Add per quart of Water	[1 tp	SALT + 1 tp LEMON JUICE
	[a sprinkle	GARLIC POWDER optional

- Bring to a boil. Reduce heat to medium low.
- Cook from 40-to-50 minutes, or until tender. Test by pulling a leaf, it should come off easily.
- Remove Artichokes with slotted spoon. Turn upside-down on paper towels to drain. Pat dry.
- Serve on the side, for dipping: DRAWN BUTTER + LEMON JUICE to taste. Or a VINAIGRETTE.

ARTICHOKE BOTTOMS - STUFFED

With EGG SALAD   Cold appetizer   EGG SALAD see "SALADS" - SPECIAL SALADS

1.   Fill Artichoke Bottoms with the [EGG SALAD
                        Optional, top with [SMALL BOILED WHOLE SHRIMP
                    Sprinkle the Shrimp with [LEMON JUICE, PARSLEY   finely chopped

2.   Mix into the Egg Salad any of [FISH, SEAFOOD, SMOKED SALMON,
                                           [SALMON CAVIAR, HAM, PROSCIUTTO

With EGGS - SARDOU   (New Orleans)

            Heat and serve on individual plates [CREAMED SPINACH
                        Top the Spinach with [ARTICHOKE BOTTOMS
            Place in each Artichoke Bottom a [POACHED EGG
                                Top with [HOLLANDAISE SAUCE ("SAUCES")
                              Sprinkle with [CHIVES

With MUSHROOMS   *Mushrooms yield about 2 cups*

In a large nonstick skillet, medium heat, heat [2 TB   BUTTER
                                             [1 TB   EXTRA-VIRGIN OLIVE OIL
                    When it sizzles, sauté [1 clove GARLIC   mashed
    When fragrant, discard the Garlic and sauté [3 TB   SHALLOTS   finely chopped
        When the Shallots begin to color, add [12 oz   SLICED MUSHROOMS

Sauté until tender, lightly browned, then add [to taste SALT, GROUND BLACK PEPPER
                              Sprinkle with [1 or 2 TB BRANDY or DRY SHERRY optional
Stir until Liquor evaporates.
                                Toss with [1 tp   DRIED TARRAGON or to taste
                                    Fill [ARTICHOKE BOTTOMS
VARIATION   Omit Tarragon.
                                 Prepare [1 cup   VELOUTÉ WHITE SAUCE
        When it thickens turn off heat and stir in [3 TB   SWISS CHEESE   coarse-grated
                                             [1 TB   PARMESAN   grated
        When melted mix in the MUSHROOMS, add [to taste NUTMEG grated, PEPPER

Fill the ARTICHOKE BOTTOMS.   Top with [plenty of PARMESAN and SWISS   mixed

Pass under the broiler until golden.
Optional: mix into Mushrooms and Sauce cooked FISH, SEAFOOD, HAM, PROSCIUTTO.

With SALADE RUSSE   Cold appetizer or buffet servings.

                                    Fill [ARTICHOKE BOTTOMS
                                    with [SALADE RUSSE (see page 136)
                                  Sprinkle [PARSLEY   finely chopped
Refrigerate until ready to serve.
                              Serve with [POACHED SALMON
                                         [CHICKEN, cold VEAL ROAST

VARIATION - Mix into the Salad SALMON ROE CAVIAR, FISH, SEAFOOD, SMOKED SALMON.

ARTICHOKE CASSEROLE - LIMAS / BLACKEYED PEAS

Amounts in this recipe are for a buffet dish. For less servings, reduce amounts according to taste.
In the South, Blackeyed Peas are served on New Year's Day for good luck!

Thaw in a large colander	[(3) 10 oz-pkg	FROZEN BLACKEYED PEAS
In another colander	[(2) 10 oz-pkg	FROZEN BABY LIMA BEANS
Drain	[24 canned	ARTICHOKE BOTTOMS small to medium, or HEARTS, or mixed

COOKING LIQUID

Measure the	[	ARTICHOKE LIQUID
Add enough	[	WATER to cook Peas and Limas
	[1/4-tp	SALT

- Place the PEAS/LIMAS in a heavy saucepan.
- Pour over the Cooking Liquid. Cook. Drain, set aside. Reserve the COOKING LIQUID.

Return saucepan to stove, medium heat, heat	[2 TB	BUTTER
When it sizzles, stir in	[(2) 10 oz-pkg	FROZEN CREAMED ONIONS

- When Onions are hot add the PEAS/LIMAS. If too thick, gradually add Cooking Liquid to obtain desired consistency. Season to taste. Optional: add 1 can Mushrooms, drained.
- Line up the ARTICHOKE BOTTOMS into a 9 x13 oven-proof dish.
- Pour over them the Bean Mixture. Cover with foil and refrigerate. Best the next day.

To serve - Bring to room temperature. Heat, covered with foil, in oven preheated to 350°
for 15-to-20 minutes. Before serving sprinkle with sliced toasted ALMONDS.
Optional - Optional, when adding the Onions, stir in any cooked Sausage thinly sliced.

ARTICHOKE QUICHE - MUSHROOMS QUICHE - "BASIC RECIPES"

Preheat oven to 375°. Drain	[1 can	ARTICHOKE BOTTOMS halve, slice thinly crosswise to obtain 1 cup.

In a nonstick skillet, over medium heat, heat	[1 TB	BUTTER + 1 TB VEGETABLE OIL
When it sizzles, sauté	[2 TB	SHALLOTS finely chopped
When Shallots soften, add	[6 oz	MUSHROOMS thinly sliced
When they have browned, add ARTICHOKES	[to taste	SALT, GROUND BLACK PEPPER

In a large bowl beat	[3	EGGS
Brush with a little of the beaten EGGS a	[9-inch	FROZEN UNCOOKED PIE SHELL

Set in the oven for 2 minutes only. Let cool.

Whisk into the Eggs	[3/4-cup	HEAVY CREAM + 1/4-cup MILK
	[1/4-tp	SALT, GROUND BLACK PEPPER
	[3 oz	SWISS CHEESE coarse-grated
	[1 oz	PARMESAN grated
	[2 TB	PARSLEY finely chopped

To assemble and bake - Place the PIE SHELL, in its foil pan, on a cookie sheet. Spread in it
the VEGETABLES. Spoon over the CUSTARD. Smooth the surface.
- Slide into oven, reduce heat to 350°. Bake as per "BASIC RECIPES".

326

ARTICHOKE - VICHYSSOISE

VICHYSSOISE see "BASIC RECIPES"

Prepare the	[	BASIC RECIPE
Simmer in their Liquid until quite tender	[1 can	ARTICHOKE BOTTOMS
	[1/4-tp	LEMON JUICE

- Drain. Reserve the ARTICHOKE LIQUID.
- Cut Artichokes into pieces. Put them into blender, add a little of the Vichyssoise. Blend.
- Add gradually more Vichyssoise, until the flavor is to your taste.
- If too thick, add gradually a little Artichoke Liquid. Season with SALT and WHITE PEPPER.
- Pass the Mixture through a fine sieve, using a wooden spoon to mash it. Discard fiber residue.

Serve chilled. Top with minced CHIVES, WATERCRESS, or a scoop of SALMON ROE CAVIAR.

ASPARAGUS - *Preparation and Cooking*

- Cut off hard stringy ends.   To serve whole, line up the Tips, cut Asparagus the same length.
- Wash them gently under cold water, avoid breaking the Tips. Spread on a dish towel, pat dry.

To peel thick Asparagus - Cut off stringy ends, wash, spread on a dish towel, pat dry.

- Fill a rectangular pan, long enough to hold the Asparagus, with 1-1/4 inches of cold Water.
- Put Asparagus on a dry towel. Place your fingers on its tip to protect from breaking. With a swivel vegetable peeler, start below the Tip, peel off the tough skin. Remove the tiny leaves.
- Place the peeled Asparagus in the pan of water. It will prevent their surface from toughening. Leave Asparagus in the water until ready to cook them. Dry with a dish towel.

Blanch Asparagus into bundles of 7-to-8. Tie at 1-inch below the Tips. At 2-inches above the ends.

- In a saucepan, wide enough to fit the Asparagus lying horizontally, add enough cold water to cover them by 1-1/2-to-2 inches. Add Salt. Bring Water to a boil. See BLANCHING.
- Place the bundle(s) in the boiling Water. Blanch until desired tenderness is obtained.
- To serve tender but firm without bending, cook 8-to-15 minutes, depending on thickness.
- With a slotted spoon or tongs, remove Asparagus from the boiling water. Plunge it into iced water to stop the cooking. Place on a dish towel. Untie, separate the spears to drain.

Steamed in microwave - *al dente:* thin Asparagus 1 minute. Thick 3-to-8 minutes.
                                    - This is the easiest way to cook Asparagus.

Salads, Pasta, Risotto - If the Tips are much thinner than stalks, slant-cut the Asparagus into
                                      1-inch or 1/2-inch pieces. Microwave separately thin and thick pieces.

ASPARAGUS - CROUSTADES

CROUSTADE see "SANDWICHES"

In a nonstick skillet, brown in a little BUTTER	[cooked	ASPARAGUS SPEARS	cut to fit Croustades
Brush CROUSTADES with Asparagus Butter	[top with	ASPARAGUS SPEARS	
	[sprinkle	PARMESAN grated	

- Pass under the broiler to melt the Parmesan.
- Optional - butter then first top the Croustade with a slice of HAM. Then add the Asparagus. Cover with a Béchamel Sauce and grated Parmesan. Pass under the broiler until golden brown.

ASPARAGUS - FRITTATA   *Serves 4*   FRITTATA see "BASIC RECIPES"

Steam in microwave for 2-1/2 minutes	[12 medium	ASPARAGUS (12 oz) then slant-cut into 1/2-inch pieces.
In a bowl, whisk	[4 large	EGGS
	[1/4-tp	SALT, GROUND BLACK PEPPER
When well blended, whisk in	[1/4-cup	PARMESAN grated
	[2 TB	SWISS CHEESE coarse-grated
	[2 TB	PARSLEY finely chopped
	[	the Asparagus
In a 10-inch skillet than can go under the broiler, over medium heat, heat	[2 TB	BUTTER + 1 TB VEGETABLE OIL
When it sizzles stir in	[3 TB	SHALLOTS finely chopped

- Sauté the Shallots until they have softened and begin to color.
- Pour into the skillet the EGG MIXTURE. Spread it evenly with a spatula. Reduce heat to low.
- Cook and pass the Frittata under preheated broiler, following directions in "BASIC RECIPES".

ASPARAGUS - MUSHROOMS and FARFALLE   *Serves 2*

Steam *al dente* in microwave	[6 oz	ASPARAGUS slant-cut 1-inch pieces
In a nonstick skillet, over medium heat, heat	[2 TB	BUTTER + 1/2-tp VEGETABLE OIL
When it sizzles, sauté	[1 TB	SHALLOTS finely chopped
When they soften, add	[3 oz	CREMINI MUSHROOMS sliced
When Mushrooms begin to brown, mix in	[	the Asparagus
Stir for 1 minute and	[sprinkle	SALT, GROUND BLACK PEPPER
Turn off heat.		
Add to salted boiling water	[3 oz	FARFALLE PASTA (Bow Ties)

Drain the PASTA.
Toss it into the Asparagus/Mushrooms.

Add	[to taste	PARMESAN grated
Optional, before adding Parmesan, drizzle with	[a little	LIGHT CREAM room temperature

VARIATIONS - Add chopped PROSCIUTTO, HAM. Omit Parmesan, add CRAB MEAT.

ASPARAGUS - CRAB MEAT in PHYLLO NESTS   *Serves 4*

Use 4 ramekins (1-cup size) to make	[4	PHYLLO NESTS see "BASIC RECIPES"
Steam *al dente* in microwave	[1 lb	ASPARAGUS cut into 1-inch pieces
In a nonstick skillet, over medium heat, heat	[3 TB	BUTTER + 1 tp VEGETABLE OIL
When it sizzles, sauté	[3 TB	SHALLOTS finely chopped
When Shallots have softened add	[	the Asparagus
Stir until the Shallots turn golden then add	[1/2-tp	LEMON JUICE
	[to taste	SALT, GROUND BLACK PEPPER
	[1 TB	PARSLEY finely chopped
	[1-3/4 cups	CRAB MEAT
Stir until Crab Meat is heated through. Fill	[	PHYLLO NESTS

ASPARAGUS - MUSHROOM QUICHE   QUICHE - "BASIC RECIPES"

Steam *al dente* in microwave	[8 oz	ASPARAGUS medium size
		Slant-cut into 1/2-inch pieces.
In a nonstick skillet, over medium heat, heat	[1 TB	BUTTER + 1/2-tp VEGETABLE OIL
When it sizzles, sauté	[1 cup	ONIONS coarsely chopped
When Onion begins to color, add	[6 oz	CREMINI MUSHROOMS sliced
When lightly brown mix in the ASPARAGUS	[a dash	NUTMEG grated
	[sprinkle	SALT, GROUND BLACK PEPPER

Preheat oven to 375°.

In a large bowl, beat	[3	EGGS
Brush with a little of the beaten EGGS a	[9-inch	FROZEN UNCOOKED PIE SHELL

Set in the oven for 2 minutes only. Let cool.

Whisk into the Eggs	[3/4-cup	HEAVY CREAM + 1/4-cup MILK
	[1/4-tp	SALT, GROUND BLACK PEPPER
	[3 oz	SWISS CHEESE coarse-grated
	[1 oz	PARMESAN grated

- Place the PIE SHELL on a cookie sheet.
- Remove VEGETABLES with slotted spoon and spread them in it. Ladle over the CUSTARD.
- Slide Quiche into oven. Reduce heat to 350°. Bake as per "BASIC RECIPES".

ASPARAGUS - RISOTTO   *Appetizer, serves 4*   RISOTTO - "BASIC RECIPES"

Wash, dry, cut off and save HARD ENDS, then steam in microwave for 3 minutes	[12 medium	ASPARAGUS

- Slant-cut 8 of them into 1/2-inch pieces, as well as the Tips of the remaining 4.
- Finely chop remaining 4 stems in processor.

In small saucepan place the HARD ENDS, add	[enough	WATER to cover + 1/4-tp SALT

Bring to a rapid boil. Cover, reduce heat to low, simmer for 30 minutes. Discard ENDS.

Measure this LIQUID into a saucepan and add	[enough	CHICKEN BROTH to obtain 6 cups
		(on the side a 1/2-cup if needed)
In a 10-inch nonstick skillet, medium heat, heat	[3-1/2 TB	BUTTER + 1 TB VEGETABLE OIL
When it sizzles, sauté	[2 TB	SHALLOTS finely chopped
When Shallots soften, stir in	[	chopped Asparagus and pieces
Sauté for 2 minutes and add	[1-1/2-cups	ARBORIO RICE

- Stir until the grains are coated and glisten.
- Add simmering BROTH, a 1/2-cup at a time.

When 6 cups have been absorbed, stir in	[1-1/2 TB	BUTTER diced small
Turn off heat and add	[4 TB	PARMESAN grated
	[to taste	SALT, GROUND BLACK PEPPER
Cover, let Risotto set for 5 minutes. Serve	[on the side	PARMESAN grated

BEANS - DRIED *Pre-cooking and Cooking* *1 cup Dried Beans serves 4*

- Spread a small amount of Dried Beans on a plate and sort out any impurities.
- Place the Beans in a sieve, wash, thoroughly under running cold Water. Drain.

TO SOAK   Follow package directions. If there are none:
- Place the rinsed Beans in a saucepan, cover with plenty of Water. Bring to a rapid boil and let boil for 3 minutes. Turn off heat, cover and soak for 1 hour or longer.
- Drain, rinse in a sieve under running cold Water. Drain. They are ready to cook.
- The longer they soak, the shorter the cooking, the less water they need to cook.

TO COOK   Add Liquid as per package directions. If there are none, follow the recipes below.

FOR SALADS   Wash and soak.

- The Beans must cook in plenty of Water, to remain separated.
- Place them in a saucepan, add plenty of Water. Optional, any of: 1 or 2 Celery ribs, 1 Onion, 1 or 2 Garlic cloves, a Carrot, a sprig Parsley. Discard after cooking.
- Bring the Water to a rapid boil. Cover the saucepan, reduce heat to low, simmer until the Beans are cooked. They should be tender, but whole, not mushy.
- Half-way through the cooking you can add a little Salt.
- Drain in a colander and let cool. Store in a sealed container, refrigerate.
- *Optional*: Reduce the Cooking Liquid by half. Use it to make a Soup or Sauce.

FOR CREAMY BEANS

- They need less Liquid. Add gradually a little Water or Broth if they get too dry.
- To make a Soup with Beans or Lentils, use more Water or Broth to cook them. You will need some of the Cooking Liquid to add to processor.
- The cooked Beans should be creamy. The little Liquid left is absorbed as they cool.
- Cooking time depends on the quality and type of Beans, and heat of your stove.
- If too much Liquid is left, uncover, simmer, letting the Liquid evaporate, stir often.
- Turn off heat, cover partially, let cool. Remaining Liquid will thicken and mostly get absorbed. Refrigerate overnight.

CREAMY BEANS   Blackeyed Peas, Cannellini, Flageolets, Limas, Navy Beans, other.

BASIC RECIPE	Place in a heavy saucepan	[1 cup	BEANS prepared for cooking
	Mix with	[2 TB	EXTRA-VIRGIN OLIVE OIL
		[1/2-cup	ONION finely chopped
	Optional	[1 or 2	GARLIC CLOVES whole or minced
Cover. Let stand for 1 or 2 hours.*			
	Add	[1-1/2 cups	COLD WATER or CHICKEN BROTH
			Or as per package directions
	Optional	[2 or 3 strips	BACON chopped or whole
		[to taste	GROUND BLACK PEPPER
Over medium high heat bring to a boil.			
	With Water add	[1 cube	BOUILLON Chicken or other
Cover. Reduce heat to low.			
Simmer 45 minutes or longer until done,			
depending on the kind.			
	Halfway through add	[to taste	SALT, PEPPER if needed
	When ready and creamy, optional add	[to taste	WORCESTERSHIRE, other

Let cool, partially covered. Store in sealed container. Refrigerate. They are best the next day.

* If they soak for 3 hours or longer, use 1-1/4 cups of Water. They will take less time to cook.

VARIATIONS - When the Beans are almost done, add to taste TOMATO or MARINARA SAUCE.
- Or add 2 TB TOMATO PASTE, or more, when adding Broth or Water.
- Refrigerate. Serve the next day.

BASIC PURÉE

Mash in processor	[	warm CREAMY BEANS
With processor on, drizzle gradually through the feeding tube, to obtain desired texture	[	BROTH, or MILK, or LIGHT CREAM
Heat and serve, adding to taste, a little	[	melted BUTTER
	[	grated PARMESAN, SALT, PEPPER

BASIC CREAMY SOUP   *Per cup of Creamy Beans*

Place in blender	[	1/2-cup	BROTH, MILK or LIGHT CREAM
	[	1 cup	warm CREAMY BEANS

- Liquefy until the MIXTURE is smooth.
- Add more Beans, then Broth, Milk, Cream, or a combination, to obtain the desired texture.

- Warm in a saucepan, adding to taste: Spices, Herbs, Cheese, a Seasoning Sauce.
- Serve sprinkled with finely chopped Watercress, and Croutons.

Optional - Add raw Oysters, cooked Mussels, cooked Sausage, Chicken or Turkey.

BLACK BEAN SOUP - Add Ground Cumin. Serve with a small scoop of Sour Cream.

BLACKEYED PEAS and ARTICHOKES (Speedy) *Serves 2 to 3*

Drain and reserve LIQUID from a	[	14 oz-can	SMALL ARTICHOKE HEARTS
In another sieve, proceed the same way with	[	14 oz-can	BLACKEYED PEAS
Combine both LIQUIDS. Dissolve	[	2 tp	FLOUR into combined Liquids
In a saucepan big enough to hold the Peas and Artichokes, over medium heat, heat	[	2 tp	VEGETABLE OIL
When a light haze forms, sauté until limp	[	1 small	ONION quartered, thinly sliced

- Pour over the Liquid with dissolved Flour. Stir with wooden spoon until it boils and begins to thicken. Add Artichokes and Peas. Cover, reduce heat to low, simmer for about 10 minutes.
- Stir 2 or 3 times. Season to taste with PEPPER. Salt if needed.

Can be prepared ahead, transferred to a dish, covered, refrigerated.
Optional: add cooked Sausage pieces.

NOTE - Also see ARTICHOKE CASSEROLE with BABY LIMAS and BLACKEYED PEAS.

BROWN FAVA BEANS   (Egypt)   "Foul Mudammas" (fool-moo-dahm-mahss)

A staple, usually eaten in Pita Bread with raw Onion. Also served at breakfast with or without Eggs. FOUL MUDAMMAS is sold canned, in Middle Eastern stores. Out of the can, they are whole, tough, and have to be cooked with Olive Oil or Butter. Their special flavor is delicious.

Pour into a small heavy saucepan a	[20 oz-can	FOUL MUDAMMAS with Liquid
Stir into the Beans	[5 TB	EXTRA-VIRGIN OLIVE OIL
	or	3 TB BUTTER
	[1-1/2 tp	GROUND CUMIN
	[to taste	GROUND BLACK PEPPER

- Over medium low heat, bring slowly to a boil.
- Reduce heat to low, cover, simmer for 10 minutes. Stir occasionally.
- After 10 minutes, with a fork mash randomly the Beans, leaving un-mashed bits to give texture.
- Cover. Simmer for 10 minutes. Mash coarsely again. Simmer, partially covered, for 5 minutes.
- When the Liquid has been absorbed and the Beans are creamy, taste, add SALT and PEPPER.
- Transfer to a bowl and serve. Or cover the surface with wax paper, let cool, refrigerate.

Cooked in Olive Oil
- Serve cold, at room temperature, or warmed in the microwave.
- Oil and Lemon Dressing can be added. Goes well with Chicken, Fish.

Cooked in Butter
- Serve warm or hot as a Vegetable side-dish.

Puréed in processor
- Drizzle over the Purée Extra-Virgin Olive Oil or melted Butter.

WITH FRIED EGGS
- Heat a little Oil or Butter in a nonstick skillet. Warm the Beans in it.
- Make a well in the center, fry 1 or 2 Eggs. Top with browned Onions.

FLAGEOLETS À LA GRECQUE   In a Sauce

In heavy saucepan, over medium heat, heat	[6 TB	EXTRA-VIRGIN OLIVE OIL
When a light haze forms, sauté	[1/2-cup	ONION finely chopped
Stir for 2 minutes and add	[1 clove	GARLIC mashed and minced
When Onions are translucent add	[1 cup	FLAGEOLETS prepare for cooking
Stir for 2 minutes and add	[1 cup	TOMATO SAUCE ready-made
When it comes to a boil, add	[1-1/4 cups	WATER
	[to taste	SALT, GROUND BLACK PEPPER

- Bring to a boil, cover, reduce heat to low.
- Simmer for 1 hour and 45 minutes, or until the Flageolets are tender. Stir once in a while.
- Turn off heat, let the Flageolets cool completely. Transfer them to a dish or bowl with a lid.

FLAVORING BEANS DURING or AFTER COOKING

Dressings   Use ready-made SALAD DRESSINGS. Also see "DRESSINGS".

Sauces			
BARBECUE	KETCHUP	SOY SAUCE	TABASCO
CHILI	JALAPEÑO JUICE	SWEET and SOUR (after)	TAHINI (after)
HORSERADISH	MAPLE SYRUP	TOMATO sauce and paste	WORCESTERSHIRE

Seasonings				
ALLSPICE	CUMIN ground	NUTMEG grated	CHERVIL	OREGANO
CHILI powder	CURRY powder	PEPPERCORNS	CILANTRO	PARSLEY
CREOLE powder	GARLIC	BASIL	DILL	THYME

332

BEANS - REFRIED

- To refry: heat in a skillet VEGETABLE or EXTRA-VIRGIN OLIVE OIL: 1 tp per cup of cooked Beans.
- Add the Beans, stir, mashing them with a fork. Moisten with a little BROTH or melted BUTTER.
- When well heated, season with minced Onion, shredded Cheese, Ground Cumin, Jalapeños.

Add LEFTOVERS: chopped Ham, Chorizo, Sausage, Chicken, Turkey. Serve with fried Eggs.

NOTE - Refried Beans are available canned. Add Seasonings. Microwave to warm them.

NAVY BEANS - SALAD   See "Preparation for BEANS used in SALADS"

Blanch in a sieve, for 2 minutes	[1 medium	ONION sections separated

Pat dry. Chop finely to obtain a 1/2-cup.

Mix in a bowl the chopped Onion with	[2 cups	COOKED NAVY BEANS for Salad
	[2 TB	PARSLEY, BASIL or DILL
The Dressing To serve with	[cold	LAMB, PORK, TURKEY, CHICKEN
add to taste	[	BALSAMIC VINAIGRETTE
With	[	FISH, SEAFOOD, CHICKEN
add to taste	[	OIL and LEMON DRESSING
As an appetizer Mix into the Salad	[	CRAB MEAT or SHRIMP

BEAN SOUP with VEGETABLES   *Yields about 9 cups.*

In a large heavy saucepan, heat	[2 TB	VEGETABLE OIL
Over medium heat, sauté	[3	SHALLOTS thinly sliced
When the Shallots soften, add	[2 stalks	CELERY sliced 1/4-inch thick
Optional	[1 or 2	GARLIC CLOVES mashed, minced
Sauté for 2 minutes, stir in	[1/2-cup	FROZEN CARROTS thawed, diced
	[1 cup frozen	BROCCOLI FLORETS thawed
(If Florets are too big, cut them)	[1 cup frozen	CAULIFLOWER FLORETS thawed
	[1 can	CANNELLINI BEANS drain, rinse
	[1 can	RED or BLACK BEANS drain, rinse
	[4 TB	PARSLEY finely chopped
Add	[1 can	CHICKEN BROTH + 1 can WATER
	[1 can	CREAM of MUSHROOM SOUP

Bring to a boil. Cover, reduce heat to low,
simmer for 25 minutes.

Add	[to taste	SALT, GROUND BLACK PEPPER
Stir in	[6 oz	SLICED MUSHROOMS

- Bring to a boil.
- If too thick, add gradually a little more Water or Broth and bring to a boil.
- Cover, reduce heat to low, simmer for 10 minutes. Vegetables should be slightly crunchy.
- Adjust seasonings. Serve with grated PARMESAN on the side. And CRUSTY BREAD.

WHAT TO DO with COOKED BEAN LEFTOVERS

CROSTINI and BRUSCHETTA   Mash Beans   [with   PESTO   ready-made
                                 Spread on   [CROSTINI or BRUSCHETTA
                                 Top with   [TOMATOES   seeded and diced

            Or top mashed Beans with slices of   [BRIE, CAMEMBERT or CHEDDAR
            Pass under the broiler.

CRÊPE FILLINGS   Fluff mashed Beans with   [a little LIGHT CREAM
                                          Add   [chopped HAM, grated CHEESE, HERBS

CROQUE-MONSIEUR Fill with mashed Beans   [CHEESE, HAM, SALAMI, SAUSAGE

DIPS   Mash Beans and mix with   [MAYONNAISE, TARTARE SAUCE, PICKLES
                                                        HERBS, ONIONS, SEASONINGS

EGGS   Spread oven proof dish with Beans   [Break EGGS on top and shirr
                                                           see EGGS - "BASIC RECIPES"

              Or spread Beans in a skillet,
                make a well in the center   [Melt in it a little BUTTER. Fry EGGS.

PHYLLO NESTS   Mix the Beans with   [SEAFOOD and a DRESSING
                 Fill the NESTS. Garnish with   [sliced AVOCADO

SALADS   Mix Beans with DRESSING. Serve   [on a bed of GREENS
                                 Top with   [TOMATOES diced or sliced
                              Surround with   [CHICKEN, TURKEY or HAM

SANDWICHES   Stuff the Beans into   [PITA BREAD
                                      Add   [TOMATOES, ONIONS, CHICKEN, HAM,
                                             [SAUSAGE, FETA CHEESE, OLIVES

WELSH RAREBIT   Prepare in a chafing dish   [WELSH RAREBIT see FONDUES in
                                                            "BASIC RECIPES"

    Mix in to taste, CREAMY BEANS. Serve with   ["DUNKS" or TORTILLA CHIPS

On TOAST   -   Spread the mashed Beans on Toast, top with Welsh Rarebit. Serve with a Salad.
                  -    Or top the Beans with shredded Cheddar, pass under the broiler.

BEETS - BORSCHT VICHYSSOISE   *2-1/2 cups before Yogurt*

COLD SOUP   Boil until tender a   [10 oz-can   SLICED BEETS   in their Liquid

Place Beets in blender with their Liquid. Add   [1-1/3 cups   VICHYSSOISE BASE
                                                                      see "BASIC RECIPES"

          Blend until smooth, pour into a bowl and
                gradually stir in with a wire whip   [1/2-cup   PLAIN YOGURT

- Gradually add more Yogurt, until desired consistency and flavor is obtained. The color should
  turn to a deep shocking pink. The sweetness of the Beets combined with the Yogurt is delicious.
- As an appetizer, 2/3-cup per person is plenty. Serve chilled. Top with minced CHIVES.

334

BEETS and ENDIVES   Appetizer   *Yields about 1-3/4 cups*

In a bowl, beat with a fork [1/2-cup SOUR CREAM + 1 TB WATER
Stir into the Sour Cream [1/4-cup BLUE CHEESE   crumbled
Optional [to taste PREPARED HORSERADISH
Mix into the Sour Cream Mixture [1 cup BOILED BEETS small dice

Center BEETS on salad plates. Before serving
surround the Beets with [BELGIAN ENDIVE SPEARS
Sprinkle the Beets with [WALNUTS or PECANS   chopped

BEETS - ROASTED

Method 1   -   Preheat oven to 375°.

- Wash and dry Beets. Rub skins with a little Vegetable Oil. Place them on a baking sheet.
- Slide on middle rack of oven. Roast for 45 minutes to 1 hour, or until tender when pierced
  with a pointed knife or skewer.. Peel Beets whilst still warm. Wrap in foil and refrigerate.

Method 2   -   Preheat oven to 450°.

- Wash and dry Beets. Wrap in heavy foil. Place on a baking sheet. Slide on middle rack
  of oven. Roast for 45 minutes to 1 hour, or until tender when pierced with a pointed knife.
- Unwrap carefully, avoiding the steam. Peel while still warm. Wrap in foil and refrigerate.

Method 3   -   Preheat oven to 375°.

- Peel and cut Beets into cubes. Place them in an oven-proof dish, in a single layer.
- Sprinkle with Extra-Virgin Olive Oil, Salt, Ground Black Pepper. Stir the cubes to coat them
  with the Oil. Cover with foil. Bake 30 minutes. Uncover, bake for 10 minutes or until tender.

BEETS - SALAD with FRISÉE LETTUCE and GOAT CHEESE

Cut into 1/2-inch thick slices a [GOAT CHEESE LOG
Coat the slices with [FINE BREADCRUMBS

Over high heat, in a nonstick skillet heat [VEGETABLE OIL 1/8-inch deep

When it sizzles, fry the Cheese rapidly on all sides to light golden brown. Serve with the SALAD.

Mix   [FRISÉE LETTUCE   bite-size pieces   The DRESSING
       [ROASTED CUBED BEETS as in Method 3
       [PECANS (plain, spicy or glazed)   Add to [WHITE WINE VINEGAR VINAIGRETTE
       [HERB CROUTONS   [CHIVES
       [FRIED BACON   chopped, optional

BEETS - SALAD with RADICCHIO and GORGONZOLA

Mix   [RADICCHIO   shredded or bite-size   The DRESSING
       [ROASTED CUBED BEETS as in Method 3
       [KIWI   diced   Add to [BALSAMIC VINEGAR VINAIGRETTE
       [GORGONZOLA or BLUE CHEESE   [FRESH BASIL finely chopped
       [PINE NUTS   toasted

335

BELGIAN ENDIVES - BRAISED
Serves 2

Discard any brown leaves from   [(1 lb) 4   BELGIAN ENDIVES medium thick
(thick ones take longer to cook)

- Wash, point sides down, under running water.
  Dry. Slice off thinly the dark part of base.
- Roll each in paper towel, squeeze out excess
  Water, keep wrapped.

Over low heat, melt   [1-1/2 TB   BUTTER
As soon as melted, turn off heat and add   [1/4-cup   WATER or CHICKEN BROTH
  [2 tp   LEMON JUICE + 1/8-tp SALT

- Put ENDIVES side-by-side in nonstick skillet.
- Pour over the Butter. Bring to a boil over medium heat, cover, reduce heat, simmer 20 minutes.
- Place Endives snugly in a sprayed baking dish. Pour over their Juice + 2 TB melted BUTTER.
- Cover tightly with foil. Bake in 350° oven for about 1 hour, or until tender. Test with a skewer.

BELGIAN ENDIVES with HAM - GRATINÉE
Serves 2 or 4

In a small saucepan, over low heat, melt   [1-1/2 TB   BUTTER
As soon as melted, turn off heat and add   [1/4-cup   WATER or CHICKEN BROTH
  [2 tp   LEMON JUICE + 1/8-tp SALT

In a saucepan or skillet, place side-by-side   [(1 lb) 4   BELGIAN ENDIVES washed and
trimmed as in above recipe

Pour over them the Butter Mixture, bring to
a boil. Cover pan tightly, reduce heat to low,
simmer for 40 minutes.

Meanwhile prepare   [1 cup   MEDIUM WHITE SAUCE ("SAUCES")
When it thickens, turn off heat and stir in   [3 TB   SWISS CHEESE coarse-grated
  [2 TB   PARMESAN grated
  [to taste   WHITE PEPPER, SALT if needed

Remove Endives with slotted spoon. Pat dry.
Wrap around each   [1 or 2 slices   HAM per Endive

Place them in a sprayed baking dish and
pour the SAUCE over them. Sprinkle with   [2 TB   SWISS CHEESE coarse-grated
and   [BREADCRUMBS
Dot with   [1 TB   BUTTER diced small

Bake in oven preheated to 375° for 15 minutes. Pass under the broiler to brown the top.

BELGIAN ENDIVES - SAUTÉED
Serves 3 or 4

Wash, trim, dry, cut into 1/2-inch slices   [4   BELGIAN ENDIVES
In a large skillet, medium high heat, heat   [3 TB   BUTTER
When it sizzles add the ENDIVES. Sprinkle   [1 tp   LEMON JUICE
Stir until they soften, and sprinkle with   [SALT, GROUND BLACK PEPPER
Mix in   [4 TB   GOLDEN RAISINS
Sauté the Endives until barely wilted. Add   [3 TB   PINE NUTS

Serve immediately, to accompany roasted Chicken, Veal Chops or Veal Roast, Pork Chops.

BELL PEPPERS - ROASTED

1 lb yields 1/2-lb trimmed and roasted.

1 large Bell Pepper = 10 oz   Cored, seeded, membranes trimmed = 7-1/2 oz. *approx.*
     Roasted and peeled = 4 oz   *approx.*

For roasting, large Bell Peppers are meatier. The elongated ones make more attractive wedges.

1.   - Spread aluminum foil on a cookie sheet or tray that can go under the broiler.
     - Wash and dry Bell Peppers. With a pointed knife cut around the core, pull it out.

2.   - Cut Bell Peppers lengthwise into wedges, following their ridges. Remove seeds.
     - Cut away ribs and membranes. If wedges are too wide, cut in half lengthwise.
     - Cut off the "turned in" ends of wedges for them to lay flat skin side up.

3.   - Preheat the broiler. Place the wedges SKIN SIDE UP on the foil.

4.   - Place cookie sheet on closer rack under the broiler. Broil until Bell Pepper skin is
     completely charred. About 15 minutes, depending on the broiler.

5.   - Remove and wrap the foil around the Bell Peppers. Place them in a saucepan.
     - Cover with a lid. Let them steam for 10 minutes to facilitate the peeling.

6.   - Take the wedges out, one at a time, leaving the others wrapped in the foil, and
     the saucepan covered with its lid. Peel off the charred skin.
     - Stack the wedges on a plate, or in a dish, cover with plastic wrap. Refrigerate.
     - Optional, drizzle with a little Extra-Virgin Olive Oil, depending on their use.

NOTE   - Peeling the charred Bell Peppers, particularly the red ones, will leave stains on
     your fingers or rubber gloves. It is advisable to use disposable latex gloves.

<u>Hors-d' oeuvre</u>   - Wrap Strips around Ham, Sausage, Shrimp, Cheese, skewer on toothpicks.

<u>Use in</u>   - Salads, Frittatas, Quiches, Pastas, Risotto. Serve with Antipasti.
     - Combine colors, drizzle with Extra-Virgin Olive Oil, serve in a salad bowl.

MARINADE for 2 LARGE ROASTED BELL PEPPERS

Mix in a small bowl   [2 TB   EXTRA-VIRGIN OLIVE OIL
     [1 TB   BALSAMIC VINEGAR   do not use Salt

- Spread a little of the Marinade on the bottom of the Bell Pepper dish.
- As you peel the wedges, place them in it, brushing or dabbing each with a little Marinade.
- Layer them on top of each other. If there is any Marinade left, pour it over the wedges.
- Cover with a lid, or seal with plastic wrap. Refrigerate for at least 24 hours before serving.

BELL PEPPERS with PASTA

Serves 2 as an appetizer

In nonstick 8-inch skillet, medium heat, heat   [2 TB   EXTRA-VIRGIN OLIVE OIL
When a light haze forms, sauté   [1 medium   YELLOW ONION halved, sliced
When Onion turns golden, add   [1/2-cup   ROASTED BELL PEPPERS   strips

Stir for 1 more minute and toss into skillet   [3 oz   hot PENNE
Drizzle with   [EXTRA-VIRGIN OLIVE OIL
Toss in   [1/4-cup   FETA CHEESE   crumbled

BELL PEPPERS - PEPERONATA

Yields about 3-1/3 cups

The traditional Peperonata is prepared with raw Bell Peppers. I prefer using them Roasted.

See BELL PEPPERS - ROASTED. Roast [4 large   BELL PEPPERS (2 red, 1 orange,
                                                                    1 yellow)

Cut roasted wedges lengthwise into strips
about 1-inch wide.

In nonstick 8-inch skillet, medium heat, heat [4 TB   EXTRA-VIRGIN OLIVE OIL
          When a light haze forms, sauté [10 oz   ONIONS halved and thinly sliced
     When Onions begin to color, add [14 oz-can   DICED TOMATOES   drained
                                      [1/2-tp   SALT, GROUND BLACK PEPPER
Reduce heat, stir until Tomatoes melt into
Onion. Add BELL PEPPERS.
                 Stir 2 minutes, add [1-1/2 tp   BALSAMIC VINEGAR
                                      [1/4-tp   DRIED THYME   or more to taste
Reduce heat to low.
Cover, simmer for 15 minutes. Adjust SEASONINGS. Stir, turn off heat, let cool in the skillet.
Transfer to a serving dish or bowl. Cover with a lid or plastic wrap. Refrigerate overnight.

Serve - At room temperature, with Antipasti, cold Chicken or Fish, Seafood, cold Veal or Pork.
       - Serve warm, as a side-dish with hot food.

BELL PEPPERS - QUICHE

QUICHE see "BASIC RECIPES"

See BELL PEPPERS - ROASTED. Roast [3 large   BELL PEPPERS   red and or
                                                                    yellow/orange

Cut wedges into 3/4-inch wide strips.

In nonstick 8-inch skillet, medium heat, heat [1-1/2 TB   EXTRA-VIRGIN OLIVE OIL
          When a light haze forms, sauté [1-1/2 cups   ONIONS   halved, thinly sliced
     When the Onion turns golden, stir in [3/4-cup   DICED TOMATOES canned, drain
                                      [a pinch   SALT
Stir until all moisture has evaporated.
                          Mix in [the Bell Peppers
                        Sprinkle [SALT, GROUND BLACK PEPPER
Set aside in the skillet.
Preheat oven to 375°.
               In a large bowl, beat [3   EGGS
  Brush with a little of the beaten EGGS a [9-inch   FROZEN UNCOOKED PIE SHELL

Set in the oven for 2 minutes only. Let cool.

               Whisk into the Egg [3/4-cup   MILK + 1/4-cup LIGHT CREAM
                        Crumbled [3 oz   GARLIC HERB BOURSIN CHEESE
                                  [1 oz   SWISS CHEESE   coarse-grated
                                  [1 TB   FRESH BASIL   finely chopped
                                  [1/4-tp   SALT, GROUND BLACK PEPPER
                     Stir in the [Onion/Bell Pepper Mixture

To assemble and bake - Place Pie Shell in its foil pan, on a cookie sheet. Ladle in the CUSTARD.
                     - Slide into oven. Reduce heat to 350°. Bake as per "BASIC RECIPES".

338

BELL PEPPERS - SALSA CRUDA   *Yields about 2-1/2 cups*

Combine in a bowl:

[1 small   RED BELL PEPPER   finely diced
[1 small   YELLOW BELL PEPPER   finely diced
[1 medium   TOMATO   peeled, seeded, diced
[4 TB   RED ONION   finely diced
[2 TB   CILANTRO   finely chopped
[1 tp   SERRANO CHILI   minced

Mix   [2 TB   LIME JUICE
        [2 TB   EXTRA-VIRGIN OLIVE OIL
        [1 TB   TOMATO JUICE
        [1/8-tp   GROUND CUMIN   or more
Optional [1   GARLIC CLOVE   minced

Add Dressing to Vegetables, SALT and PEPPER.
Serve with Fish, Seafood, Chicken, cold Pork.

BELL PEPPERS - STUFFED with SAFFRON RICE

Prepare 4 BELL PEPPERS - Green ones of medium size. Shaped to sit upright in a dish.

1. Wash and pat dry. Cut a circle at a 1/2-inch around the cap. Pull out the cap, cut off its stem.
2. Remove inside core of the caps, so they can sit flat on the Stuffing. Set them aside.
3. Remove all seeds. Use a grapefruit spoon to de-rib the Bell Peppers.
4. Rinse inside under running cold water. Turn Peppers upside down on paper towels to drain.

The STUFFING   Dissolve in simmering [1-1/2 cups   CHICKEN BROTH   lightly salted
                                  [1/4-tp   SAFFRON THREADS   or more

        In a nonstick 8-inch skillet,
      over medium heat, heat [1/3-cup   EXTRA-VIRGIN OLIVE OIL
   When a light haze forms, sauté [3/4-cup   ONION   finely chopped
                                  [1/4-cup   CELERY   finely chopped
  When Onion turns golden, add [2/3-cup   LONG GRAIN WHITE RICE
                                             Use "Converted"

Stir until the grains glisten and add [1-1/4 cups   of the Saffron Broth
                                  [1/4-cup   GOLDEN RAISINS
                                  [3 TB   PINE NUTS   toasted

Bring the Broth to a boil. Reduce heat to low,
cover, simmer until it is absorbed. The Rice
is partially cooked. Turn off heat.

                         Add [the rest of the Saffron Broth
                             [to taste   SALT, GROUND BLACK PEPPER

To ASSEMBLE   Sit in a sprayed baking dish [the 4   prepared GREEN BELL PEPPERS

- Preheat oven to 375°.
- Fill Bell Peppers, 3/4-full, leaving room for
  the Rice to swell. *There may be some Rice
  left, depending on the size of Bell Peppers*.
- Top with caps. They may sink in, but rise
  as Rice expands.
        Drizzle over each Pepper [1/2-TB   EXTRA-VIRGIN OLIVE OIL

COOKING LIQUID   Mix into [1 cup warm   CHICKEN BROTH   lightly salted
                                [1 TB   EXTRA-VIRGIN OLIVE OIL
Pour the Broth over and around Peppers then
      sprinkle over the tops [BREADCRUMBS

BAKE - For 1 hour, or longer, until Bell Peppers are tender but firm. They should not collapse.
      - Baste every 25 minutes. Prepare a day ahead. Cool, cover with foil refrigerate.
      - Warm in oven, covered with foil. Or serve at room temperature, or cold.

BROCCOLI - *Preparation and Cooking*

PREPARATION   - Cut the FLORETS at their base. Rinse gently under running cold water. Drain.
                            - Cut off tough end of STALKS. Split them longwise. Pare off dark green skin.

BLANCHING   - See "BLANCHING". Blanch Florets in a strainer for 4-to-5 minutes.
                            - Blanch Stalks separately: 7-to-8 minutes. Use in salads, sauté with Vegetables.

BOILING   - In a strainer, plunge Florets into <u>gently</u> boiling water for 7-to-8 minutes.
                            - Drain. Spread on a dish towel to cool and dry. They are ready to eat.

MICROWAVE   - Cook or steam the Florets. Either partially cooked, or ready to eat.

ROASTING   - In a dish, toss Florets with Extra-Virgin Olive Oil. Sprinkle with Salt and Pepper.
                            - Sprinkle a sprayed roasting pan with 2 or 3 TB of Water. Spread the Florets in
                               it. Roast 15-to-18 minutes in oven preheated to 400°. They remain crunchy.

BROCCOLI - *BAKED OMELET*   *Serves 2 to 4*   *Light Lunch with a Salad.*

Thaw, partially steam in microwave (*half cook*) [10 oz-pkg   FROZEN BROCCOLI FLORETS

In a nonstick skillet, over medium heat, heat [1 TB   BUTTER + 1 TB VEGETABLE OIL
When it sizzles, sauté [1/2-cup   ONION   finely chopped
When translucent, stir in BROCCOLI and [1/2-cup   RED BELL PEPPER   diced
Sauté for 2 minutes, add [6 oz   SLICED MUSHROOMS
Sauté for 1 minute.
In a large bowl whisk [3 large   EGGS
[1/2-cup   LIGHT CREAM + 1/4-cup MILK
[1/4-tp   SALT, GROUND BLACK PEPPER
[a dash   NUTMEG grated
[1/2-cup   PARMESAN grated
Add [the Broccoli Mixture
Preheat oven to 350°.
Pour MIXTURE into sprayed 4-cup baking dish. Bake until set in the center: 20-to-25 minutes.

BROCCOLI au *GRATIN*   *Serves 4 to 5*   GRATIN see "BASIC RECIPES"

Blanch for 5 minutes the Florets from a [1-1/2 lb   BROCCOLI BUNCH (4 to 5 cups)

See "SAUCES". Prepare [1-1/2 cups   SHALLOT MEDIUM WHITE SAUCE
Adding to the FLOUR [1/4-tp   DRY MUSTARD
When it thickens, stir in until melted [2 oz   CHEDDAR coarse-grated
Turn off heat, add [to taste   WORCESTERSHIRE SAUCE
[SALT and PEPPER

In a sprayed oven-dish that holds Broccoli in
one layer, spread 3 TB of SAUCE. Fill with
the BROCCOLI. Cover with the SAUCE and [plenty of   CHEDDAR coarse-grated
Sprinkle with [3 TB   BREADCRUMBS
Dot with [1-1/2 TB   BUTTER diced small

Bake in oven preheated to 350° for 30-to-35 minutes. Pass under the broiler. Serve immediately.

BROCCOLI - QUICHE CORFU

QUICHE see "BASIC RECIPES"

Thaw and drain in a sieve	[10 oz-pkg	FROZEN CHOPPED BROCCOLI Press to remove excess moisture.

In a nonstick skillet, over medium heat, heat	[1-1/2 TB	EXTRA-VIRGIN OLIVE OIL
When a light haze forms, sauté	[1-1/2 cups	RED ONION halved, thinly sliced
When Onion begins to color, add	[	the Broccoli

Sauté until Broccoli are cooked and all Liquid
has evaporated. Sprinkle   [SALT, GROUND BLACK PEPPER
Turn off heat.
Preheat oven to 375°.

In a large bowl beat	[3 large	EGGS
Brush with a little of the beaten EGGS a	[9-inch	FROZEN UNCOOKED PIE SHELL

Set in the oven for 2 minutes only. Let cool.

Whisk into the EGGS	[2/3-cup	HEAVY CREAM + 1/3-cup MILK
	[4 oz	FETA CHEESE crumbled
	[1 tp	DRIED OREGANO
	[1/4-cup	BLACK OLIVES chopped
Mix in	[	the Broccoli

<u>To assemble and bake</u> - Place the Pie Shell on a cookie sheet. Ladle the EGG MIXTURE into it.
- Slide into oven. Reduce heat to 350°. Bake as per "BASIC RECIPES".

BROCCOLI - RISOTTO   *Appetizer, serves 4*   RISOTTO - "BASIC RECIPES"

Thaw, drain	[10 oz-pkg	FROZEN CHOPPED BROCCOLI

Press to remove excess liquid.

Simmer	[6 cups	CHICKEN BROTH (+ 1/2-cup if needed)
In a 10-inch heavy skillet, medium heat, heat	[3-1/2 TB	BUTTER + 1 TB VEGETABLE OIL
When it sizzles, sauté	[1/4-cup	ONION finely chopped
When Onion softens add	[1 clove	GARLIC mashed
When Garlic is fragrant, discard and add	[	the Broccoli
Sauté for 4 minutes and sprinkle	[a little	SALT, GROUND BLACK PEPPER
Then add	[1-1/2 cups	ARBORIO RICE
Stir until grains are coated and glisten. Add	[4-to-6 TB	DRY WHITE WINE

- Stir until the Wine evaporates.
- Add <u>one ladle</u> (1/2-cup) at a time of BROTH.
- When 6 cups have been absorbed, the Rice
  should be tender, firm, creamy.

Turn off heat and stir in	[1-1/2 TB	BUTTER diced small
	[4 TB	PARMESAN grated
	[adjust	SALT, GROUND BLACK PEPPER
Cover, let Risotto set for 5 minutes. Serve	[on the side	PARMESAN grated

VARIATIONS - Before adding the last ladle of Broth, add cooked SHRIMP bite-size pieces or
cooked SEAFOOD, SMOKED SALMON, HAM, PROSCIUTTO, SAUSAGE.

BRUSSELS SPROUTS - *Preparation and Cooking*

PREPARATION   Trim stem ends. Remove wilted leaves. Wash the Sprouts thoroughly in cold water. Drain, dry in a dish towel. With a sharp knife cut a cross at the base.

BLANCHING   Plunge in salted boiling water: moderate boil, to avoid leaves peeling off. Completely cooked: 10-to-12 minutes. Partially: 7-to-8 minutes. Drain.

MICROWAVE   Raw: 7-to-9 minutes, will be completely cooked. Frozen: package directions.

BRUSSELS SPROUTS - BRAISED   *Serves 2, with Chestnuts serves 4*

Blanch for 7 minutes	[1/2-lb	BRUSSELS SPROUTS drain
In a skillet with a lid, medium heat, heat	[2 TB	BUTTER
When it sizzles add	[	the Sprouts "Prepared"
Stir to coat them well and sprinkle with	[3 TB	APPLE JUICE or APPLE CIDER
	[	SALT, GROUND BLACK PEPPER

Cover tightly, reduce heat to low. Simmer
for 20-to-25 minutes. Add Juice as needed.

With CHESTNUTS Parboil for 15 minutes	[1/2-lb	CHESTNUTS peeled
		(see CHESTNUTS)
Sizzle in the skillet	[4 TB	BUTTER
Add blanched SPROUTS and CHESTNUTS	[to taste	SALT, GROUND BLACK PEPPER
	[5 TB	APPLE JUICE or APPLE CIDER

Cook as above until tender, yet firm.

BRUSSELS SPROUTS and APPLES - SAUTÉED   *Serves 2 or 3*

Thaw, drain and microwave for 6 minutes	[10 oz-pkg	FROZEN BRUSSELS SPROUTS
In a nonstick skillet, over medium heat, heat	[2 TB	BUTTER + 1 tp VEGETABLE OIL
When it sizzles, add	[1 cup	GOLDEN APPLES 1/2-inch dice
When Apples soften and begin to brown, add	[	the Sprouts
Stir, sauté until tender. Sprinkle with	[	SALT, GROUND BLACK PEPPER
Turn off heat, add	[1/4-cup	PECANS or SPICY WALNUTS

BRUSSELS SPROUTS - SOUFFLÉ   SOUFFLÉ see "BASIC RECIPES"

1. Thaw, microwave until tender, 8 minutes	[10 oz-pkg	FROZEN BRUSSELS SPROUTS
2. Set out at room temperature	[5	EGGS you need 5 Whites, 4 Yolks
3. In a nonstick skillet, medium heat, heat	[1-1/2 TB	BUTTER
When it sizzles, sauté	[1-1/2 TB	SHALLOTS minced
When they begin to color, add the	[	Sprouts coarsely chopped
Stir for 1 minute and	[sprinkle	SALT, GROUND BLACK PEPPER

Purée in processor.

342

4.   Rub a 1-1/2 quarts soufflé dish with [BUTTER
          (or use 4 ramekins)   Dust with   [1-1/2 TB   PARMESAN   refrigerate the dish
                                                                    (1-1/4 tp per ramekin)

5.   In a heavy nonstick skillet, prepare a   [CREAMY BÉCHAMEL ("SAUCES")
                    mixing into the Flour   [1/4-tp   DRY MUSTARD

- When Béchamel thickens, remove from heat.
- Break 1 EGG, drop the WHITE into stainless
   steel bowl. The YOLK into the Béchamel.
- With a wire whip beat it into the Sauce.
- Repeat with 3 more Yolks, one at a time.
- Return saucepan to stove. Over <u>low heat</u>
   stir for 1 minute to bind the Eggs.

          Turn off heat. Stir into it, until melted   [1/2-cup   CHEDDAR coarse-grated
                                                                    (+ for later 1 TB, for ramekins 4 tp)

                    Then mix in   [3/4-cup of   the Sprout Purée
                                  [adjust   SALT, GROUND BLACK PEPPER
- Set aside to cool. Can be prepared ahead to
   this point. Cover the surface with wax paper.
- Barely warm before adding the EGG WHITES.

6. Preheat oven to 400°. Set out soufflé dish.

Add to the 4 EGG WHITES 1 EGG WHITE and   [1/8-tp   CREAM OF TARTAR

a)   Beat the EGG WHITES until stiff and glossy, but not dry.
     - Add one ladle of WHITES to the BÉCHAMEL. Gently fold them in with a rubber spatula.
     - Then gently pour the BÉCHAMEL into the remaining Egg Whites.
     - Fold in with the spatula, scooping from the bottom towards the top as you turn the bowl.
        Do not fold too much, it would keep the Soufflé from rising well. White spots do no harm.

b)   Pour MIXTURE into the soufflé dish. Smooth the surface with a spatula.
     - Sprinkle with the reserved 1 TB of CHEDDAR. Or for each ramekin 1 tp.

c)   Place on middle rack of oven. Immediately reduce heat to 375°. Bake for 25-to-30 minutes.
     - Less time for the ramekins. Do not open oven door until the Soufflé is well puffed.
     - Test by inserting a thin knife or metal skewer. If it comes out clean, the Soufflé is ready.
        If not, cook 5 minutes longer. It should have a light brown crust with a creamy center.

BRUSSELS SPROUTS - SOUP VELOUTÉ   With no Eggs

                    Microwave for 8 minutes   [10 oz-pkg   FROZEN BRUSSELS SPROUTS
When still hot, purée finely in processor, with   [1/2-tp   LEMON JUICE

          See "SAUCES. Prepare a   [SHALLOT THIN WHITE SAUCE

With a wire whip stir the PURÉE into the Sauce.

                    Add   [to taste   PARMESAN grated
                          [SALT, WHITE PEPPER
          Serve with   [CROUTONS

343

CABBAGE - *Preparation for Cooking*

Remove tough outer leaves and discard. Separate the Leaves by cutting them off at the core.
With a small sharp pointed knife, cut out the tough white veins of the large Leaves.
Wash the leaves in batches, in a colander, under running cold water. Drain.

JULIENNE — - Pat dry the Leaves in a towel. Stack them and roll them as in a jelly-roll.
— - Slice them into ribbons from very thin to 1/2-inch wide.

SHREDDED — - Roll the Leaves into bundles. Pass them through the feeder of a processor,
using the shredding blade.

OTHER CUT — - Remove outer and large Leaves until you reach the tender ones. Quarter the
Cabbage, remove the core, lay the quarters on their side, slice thinly. Place
in a colander, wash under running cold water. Squeeze out excess water.
— - Drain for 1 hour. Dry in a towel.

TO BLANCH — - See "BLANCHING". Plunge the LEAVES in a large pot of boiling water, until
partially tender or according to recipe. Pass under running cold water, drain.

— - JULIENNE or SHREDDED: place in the strainer of a pasta cooker. Plunge into
boiling water: limp but still crunchy 4-to-5 minutes. Rinse. Drain.

CABBAGE and APPLES   *Serves 4 to 6   Goes with Pork, Ham, Turkey, Game.*

Julienne into 1/2-inch wide ribbons a	[2 lb	HEAD of RED CABBAGE
		(7-to-8 cups)
In a Dutch oven or oven-proof saucepan,		
over medium heat, heat	[4 TB	BUTTER
When it sizzles, add gradually	[	the Cabbage, mixing it in with
		the Butter

Cover, reduce heat to medium low, simmer
for 10 minutes, until limp.

BAKED   Stir in [2 TB   RED WINE VINEGAR
                                                    [1/2-cup   CHICKEN BROTH
                                                    [1/8-tp   SALT, GROUND BLACK PEPPER
                                                    [1/8-tp   GROUND CLOVES
Cover tightly, bake in oven preheated to 350°.

              1 hour later cut into thick wedges [4   TART APPLES
Spread the wedges on a plate. Sprinkle with [a little GRANULATED SUGAR on all sides

Spread the Apples on top of the Cabbage. Replace tightly the lid, bake until the Cabbage has
cooked for 2-1/2 hours or until very tender and melting. Add if needed a little more Broth.

BRAISED   Simmer the Cabbage as above
                              then stir in [1 cup   RED WINE   or   APPLE CIDER
                                            [4   TART APPLES   diced
                                            [1/8-tp   GROUND CLOVES
                                            [1/4-tp   SALT, GROUND BLACK PEPPER
Bring to a boil. Cover tightly the saucepan.
Reduce heat to low. Simmer for 2 hours or until the Cabbage is melting and moist, with no
Liquid left in the saucepan. Adjust Seasonings. Optional: stir in 2 TB BUTTER.

344

CABBAGE - BRAISED in WINE

Serves 4 to 6

Julienne into 1/2-inch wide ribbons a	[2 lb	HEAD of RED or GREEN CABBAGE (7-to-8 cups)
In a large heavy saucepan, heat	[4 TB	BUTTER
Over medium heat, when it sizzles, sauté	[1 cup	ONION halved and thinly sliced
When Onion is translucent, add gradually	[	the Cabbage, mixing it in with the Butter

Cover, reduce heat to medium low, simmer
for 10 minutes, until limp.

Add	[1 cup	RED WINE for Red Cabbage
	or	DRY WHITE WINE for Green
	[1/4-tp	SALT, GROUND BLACK PEPPER

- Bring to a boil. Cover tightly with a lid.
- Reduce heat to low, simmer for about 2 hours until the Cabbage is melting and moist.
- Adjust Seasonings. Optional: stir in 1 or 2 TB BUTTER.

CARROTS

Serves 2 or 3

BRAISED

Soak	[3 TB	GOLDEN RAISINS
With just enough to cover	[	APPLE CIDER
Pare, wash, pat dry, slice with a mandolin	[1 lb medium	CARROTS 1/8-inch thick slices
In a nonstick skillet, over medium heat, heat	[2 TB	BUTTER + 1 tp VEGETABLE OIL
When it sizzles, stir in	[	the Sliced Carrots
When they begin to brown, add	[1/2-cup	APPLE CIDER
	[1/2-tp	BROWN SUGAR
Stir and sprinkle with	[1/4-tp	GROUND CINNAMON
	[1/4-tp	GROUND GINGER
	[1/4-tp	SALT, GROUND BLACK PEPPER

- Bring to a boil, cover tightly with a lid.
- Reduce heat to low, simmer for 10 minutes. Stir in the RAISINS, drained. If needed add 2 TB CIDER or the Raisin Soaking Liquid. Do not let the Carrots dry. Simmer until they are tender.
- When they are ready there should just be a little Liquid left in the skillet. Adjust SALT and GROUND BLACK PEPPER.

GLAZED

Put in a skillet	[1 lb	CARROTS thinly sliced
Add just enough to cover	[	APPLE CIDER
	[sprinkle	SALT, GROUND BLACK PEPPER

- Bring the CIDER to a rapid boil.
- Cover tightly the skillet, reduce heat to low, simmer until the Carrots are tender.
- If there is any liquid left, simmer uncovered until it has evaporated.

Melt	[3 TB	BUTTER
Pour it over the Carrots and sprinkle with	[3 TB	BROWN SUGAR
or	[2 TB	MAPLE SYRUP

Over medium heat stir the Carrots with a wooden spoon until they are coated with a brown glaze.

VARIATION -   Add 3 TB soaked RAISINS. For a contrast, add 2 TB TINY CAPERS, rinsed, dried.

CARROTS - CREAMY SOUP   (No Fat)

Pare, wash and cut into 1/2-inch thick slices [2 medium   CARROTS
Halve lengthwise, wash, cut into 1-inch pieces [2 medium   LEEKS   white and light green
                                                                      parts

Peel, wash, cut into small cubes [1 (4 oz)   YUKON GOLD POTATO

Combine Vegetables in a heavy saucepan and [cover with   WATER
When the Water comes to a boil, dissolve in it [1 cube   BOUILLON Chicken or Vegetable

- Reduce heat to medium low, cook until fork tender. Remove with slotted spoon into a blender.
- Add 1 cup Cooking Liquid. Blend until smooth. Gradually add more Liquid to obtain desired
  consistency. Add to taste, SALT, WHITE PEPPER. Blend once more.

To serve hot   Heat the Soup. Add to taste [grated PARMESAN, NUTMEG
                 You can also add a little [MILK, LIGHT CREAM, or SOUR CREAM
                            Top with [FRENCH FRIED ONIONS   canned
                                    [or CHIVES   finely chopped

To serve cold   Omit the Cheese. Add a little [CREAM if desired
                    Top with finely chopped [CHIVES, WATERCRESS or DILL

Or, as in a Gazpacho, top with finely diced [BELL PEPPER, CUCUMBER, CELERY, ONION

CAULIFLOWER - Preparation and Cooking   See "BLANCHING"

Wash thoroughly the Florets. Soak in cold water for 30 minutes to remove impurities. Rinse, drain.

BLANCHING   - Cooked: 10-to-12 minutes. Partially: 7-to-9 minutes. Use a strainer.

MICROWAVE   - Cooked: 10-to-11 minutes. Partially: 6-to-8 minutes.

CAULIFLOWER À LA GRECQUE   *Serve with Cold Cuts, Fish, Seafood.*

Blanch or microwave for 10 minutes [8 oz   CAULIFLOWER FLORETS cut large
                                                    ones in half
THE BROTH   Combine in a heavy saucepan [1 cup   WATER
                                          [1/4-cup   EXTRA-VIRGIN OLIVE OIL
                                          [1   GREEN ONION
                                          [1 TB   LEMON JUICE
                                          [1/4-tp   GARLIC POWDER
                                          [1 sprig of   THYME
                                          [1/4-tp   SALT, GROUND BLACK PEPPER
- Bring to a boil, cover, reduce heat to low.
- Simmer for 15 minutes. Taste. Add Salt if needed.
- Add the CAULIFLOWER. If not covered by the Broth, add just enough Water to cover.
- Bring to a boil. Cover, reduce heat to low, simmer for 15-to-20 minutes. Stir once or twice.

- The Cauliflower should be tender, yet crunchy. Remove with a slotted spoon into a serving dish.
- Discard Onion and Thyme. Bring the Broth to a boil, uncovered, until it is reduced to a 1/4-cup.
- Pour the Broth over the Cauliflower. Let cool. Cover, refrigerate overnight.

346

CAULIFLOWER au GRATIN   *Serves 4 to 6*   GRATIN - "BASIC RECIPES"

Blanch the FLORETS from a	[1-1/2 lb	head of CAULIFLOWER
See "SAUCES". Prepare	[1-1/2 cups	VELOUTÉ WHITE SAUCE
When it thickens, turn off heat and stir in	[2 oz	SWISS CHEESE coarse-grated
	[1 oz	CHEDDAR coarse-grated
When the Cheese has melted, add	[to taste	WHITE PEPPER, SALT if needed
	[a dash	NUTMEG and/or DRY SHERRY

Spread 3 TB of Sauce in a sprayed gratin dish where Florets fit in one layer. Put them in it.

Cover with the Sauce and sprinkle on top	[3 TB	SWISS CHEESE coarse-grated
	[2 TB	BREADCRUMBS
Dot with	[1-1/2 TB	BUTTER diced small

Bake 25-to-30 minutes in oven preheated to 350°. To improve browning, pass under the broiler.

CAULIFLOWER and POTATOES au GRATIN   *Serves 4 to 6*

Blanch for 8 minutes	[2-1/2 cups	CAULIFLOWER FLORETS and cut them in half
Cut into 3/4-inch cubes, parboil 10 minutes	[2-1/2 cups	YUKON GOLD POTATOES
See "SAUCES". Prepare	[1-1/2 cups	SHALLOT VELOUTÉ SAUCE
When it thickens, turn off heat, stir in	[2 oz	SWISS CHEESE coarse-grated
	[1 oz	PARMESAN grated
When the Cheese has melted, add	[a dash	NUTMEG, PEPPER, SALT if needed
Rub an 8 x 8 baking dish with	[1 clove	GARLIC cut in half lengthwise
Spray it and fil with	[	Potatoes and Cauliflower.
Cover with the Sauce and sprinkle on top	[3 TB	SWISS and PARMESAN combined
Dot with	[1-1/2 TB	BUTTER diced small

Preheat oven to 350°.
Bake for 25 minutes, or until Florets are tender. Pass under the broiler.

CAULIFLOWER and BROCCOLI - GRATINÉE   *Serves 4 to 6*

Microwave *al dente*	[2-1/2 cups	CAULIFLOWER FLORETS
Do the same with	[2-1/2 cups	BROCCOLI FLORETS
Prepare	[1-1/2 cups	MEDIUM WHITE SAUCE
When it thickens, turn off heat, stir in	[2 oz	CHEDDAR coarse-grated
	[1 oz	SWISS CHEESE coarse-grated
	[to taste	NUTMEG, WHITE PEPPER, SALT

Put the Vegetables in a sprayed 8 x 8 baking dish. Cover with the Sauce. Sprinkle on top

	[1 oz	SWISS CHEESE coarse-grated
Dot with	[1-1/2 TB	BUTTER diced small

Bake in oven preheated to 350° for 10-to-15 minutes. Pass under the broiler to brown the top.

CAULIFLOWER and POTATO - PURÉE

FINE PURÉE   Microwave until tender   [CAULIFLOWER FLORETS   cut in half

Boil a quarter of their weight in   [IDAHO POTATOES   peeled and cubed

Purée in processor Cauliflower and Potatoes.
Transfer the Purée into a heavy saucepan.

Over low heat, stir in to taste   [BUTTER, MILK, LIGHT or HEAVY CREAM
                                        [PARMESAN   grated
                                        [NUTMEG   grated
                                        [SALT, WHITE or BLACK PEPPER

RUSTIC PURÉE   Microwave until tender   [CAULIFLOWER FLORETS amount to taste
                                 Boil   [POTATOES   amount to taste
With a fork, mash them separately.
Then combine and mash them together.

Add to taste   [any of the above
                                 [CRUMBLED FRIED BACON
                                 [PARSLEY   chopped
and/or   [CHIVES

VARIATION   Rub mixing bowl with a   [GARLIC CLOVE
Omit Butter, Milk. Mash with   [EXTRA-VIRGIN OLIVE OIL
Add Seasonings to taste and   [PARSLEY   chopped, and/or   CHIVES

CAULIFLOWER and ONION - QUICHE

Steam in microwave until tender but firm a [10 oz-pkg   FROZEN CAULIFLOWER FLORETS
                                                        Let cool. Cut into thin slices.

In a nonstick skillet, over medium heat, heat [2 TB   BUTTER + 1 tp VEGETABLE OIL
            When it sizzles, sauté [12 oz   ONION   coarsely chopped
             When golden brown, add [the Cauliflower
Stir for 2 minutes. Turn off heat.   Sprinkle [SALT, GROUND BLACK PEPPER

Preheat oven to 375°.
                      In a bowl beat [3   EGGS
Brush with a little of the beaten EGGS a [9-inch   FROZEN UNCOOKED PIE SHELL

Set in the oven for 2 minutes only.   Let cool.

Whisk into the Eggs   [1 cup   LIGHT CREAM
                              [1/4-tp   SALT, GROUND BLACK PEPPER
                              [to taste   NUTMEG   grated
                              [3 oz   SWISS CHEESE coarse-grated
                              [1 oz   CHEDDAR   coarse-grated
When blended add   [Cauliflower and Onions

To assemble and bake   -   Place the PIE SHELL on cookie sheet. Ladle the CUSTARD into it.
                            -   Slide cookie sheet with Quiche into the oven. Reduce heat to 350°.
                            -   Bake following directions in "BASIC RECIPES".

348

CAULIFLOWER - ROASTED

- Spray a roasting pan. In it, toss Cauliflower Florets, whole or halved, with Extra-Virgin Olive Oil.
- Sprinkle and toss with Salt, Pepper. A pinch Garlic Powder, optional. Spread them in one layer.
- Roast in oven preheated to 400° for about 35 minutes, or until golden brown. Stir twice.

CAULIFLOWER - BORSCHT SOUP   Serves 4 or 5

THE BROTH   Combine in a stockpot [1 large   ONION   quartered
                                         [2 medium   BEETS   chopped
                                         [2 cloves   GARLIC   whole
                                         [1 stalk   CELERY   quartered
                                         [4 sprigs   FLAT LEAF PARSLEY
                                         [2 cans   BEEF BROTH
                                         [3-1/2 cups WATER

- Bring to a boil. Cover tightly. Reduce heat
  to medium, boil for 1 hour.
- Put over a large bowl a fine sieve lined with
  cheesecloth. Strain the Broth. Discard solids.

THE SOUP   Combine in the rinsed stock pot [2 cups   CAULIFLOWER FLORETS if large
                                                                              cut in half
                                             [1 cup   POTATOES cut into 1/2-inch dice
                                             [1 cup   CARROTS   diced
                                             [1-1/2 cups BEETS diced
                        Add the BROTH and   [2 TB   RED WINE VINEGAR
                                             [1 tp   SUGAR

- If the Broth doesn't cover the Vegetables by
  1-inch, add Water (allows for evaporation).
- Bring to a boil. Cover tightly, reduce heat
  to low, simmer about 45-to-50 minutes.
- Cauliflower should be tender crunchy.

Serve the Borscht in a tureen.   Sprinkle with [plenty of   FRESH DILL   snipped
                          Serve on the side a bowl of [SOUR CREAM
                                                      [CRUSTY BREAD
A Sour Cream dollop is added to each serving.
Optional: Serve Meats and/or Cured Meats. Top Meats with a serving of Borscht and Sour Cream.

CAULIFLOWER - VICHYSSOISE   VICHYSSOISE - "BASIC RECIPES"

                    Prepare the   [BASIC RECIPE

            Cut in half and boil until tender   [CAULIFLOWER FLORETS

- Drain and reserve the COOKING LIQUID. Put Cauliflower in a blender, add a little VICHYSSOISE.
- Blend. Add gradually more Vichyssoise until the flavor is to your taste.
- If too thick, add gradually a little of the Cooking Liquid. Season to taste.

COLD - Top with finely chopped WATERCRESS, CHIVES. Add a scoop of SALMON ROE CAVIAR.
HOT   - Top with grated PARMESAN, CROUTONS, CRISPY FRENCH FRIED ONIONS (canned).

CHESTNUTS - *Preparation and Cooking*

PEELING   With a small sharp pointed knife make an X incision on flat side of the shell. Place Chestnuts in oven preheated to 450°. Bake for 8-to-10 minutes until the shells open. Peel off, whilst still hot, the shell and skin.

BOILED   Peel Chestnuts. Add Water or Broth to cover. Bring to a boil, cover, reduce heat to low, simmer 25 minutes, or until fork tender without breaking. Drain.

ROASTED   Incise an X on flat side. Roast in oven preheated to 375° for 20-to-25 minutes.

CHESTNUTS - PURÉE   *Yields about 2-1/2 cups*

Combine in a saucepan   [1 lb   CHESTNUTS peeled
                         [1-1/4 cups   MILK
                         [1 TB   BROWN SUGAR
                         [2 TB   SHALLOTS finely chopped

- Bring to a boil. Cover, reduce heat to low, simmer for 20-to-30 minutes, or until the Chestnuts can be crumbled with a fork.
- Drain the Chestnuts. Strain the MILK.
- Purée the Chestnuts in processor.

Then add gradually through the feeding tube   [some of the   Cooking Milk until desired Purée texture is obtained

Transfer into a heavy saucepan and stir in   [to taste   SALT, PEPPER, NUTMEG

To serve   Heat the Purée over low heat, add   [2 TB   BUTTER or to taste
                                  Or   [1-to-2 TB   HEAVY CREAM
                                       [1-1/2 TB   BRANDY or to taste

Serve with Turkey, Goose, Game, Pork.

CHICK PEAS - CREAM SOUP   Garbanzos   *Yields about 3-1/2 to 4 cups*

In a heavy saucepan, medium heat, heat   [1 TB   BUTTER + 1 TB VEGETABLE OIL
When it sizzles, sauté   [1/3-cup   ONION finely chopped
When Onion softens, add   [2 cloves   GARLIC mashed and minced
When Garlic is fragrant, stir in   [2 cups   CHICK PEAS canned, drained, rinsed, drained

Stir and sprinkle with   [1 tp   GROUND CUMIN
Add   [3 cups   CHICKEN BROTH lightly salted

- Bring to a boil, reduce heat to low.
- Cover, simmer for 30 minutes or until the Peas are very tender. Turn off heat.
- Liquefy in blender the Peas with the Broth.

With blender on, add gradually   [1/2-cup   HEAVY CREAM
Add   [to taste   SALT and WHITE PEPPER

To serve hot   - Simmer until hot.
                - Top with CROUTONS, CHIVES, or WATERCRESS finely chopped.
Chilled   - As a Vichyssoise. Top with CHIVES or WATERCRESS finely chopped.

350

CORN - CREAMED

- Break in half Ears of Corn. Stand up broken ends. With a sharp knife saw off Kernels.
- Place Kernels in a saucepan. Add HEAVY CREAM, just enough to almost cover.
- Bring to a boil, reduce heat to low, cover, simmer for 10 minutes. Add Seasonings.
- Simmer 5 more minutes, until it thickens. Optional, add grated Cheddar, Parmesan.
    NOTE - Do not discard the Cobs. Boil, use the Broth to prepare a Sauce, Chowder, Soup.

CORN - FLAN   *Serves 6*   *Serve with Fish, Seafood, Ham, roast Pork or Veal.*

1.   Blanch for 2 minutes [2 cups   CORN KERNELS drain, spread in
                                                                              a pan to cool.
Transfer into a bowl.
                          Seal in a plastic bag [1-1/2 oz   SEASONED HERB CROUTONS

Place the bag on a counter. Beat it with a can
to crumble Croutons. Do not pulverize.

Mix the Croutons with the Kernels, as well as [1/2-cup   CHEDDAR   coarse-grated

            Spray a 1-1/2 quart ring-mold with [COOKING SPRAY   rub it all over

Spread the Kernel Mixture into it.

2.   In a heavy saucepan, combine [2 cups + 3 TB MILK *3 TB allow for evaporation*
                                                [1-1/2 oz   ONION chunks

- Bring to a boil. Cover, reduce heat to low
  and simmer for 20 minutes. Turn off heat.
- Preheat oven to 350°.

3.   In a wide bowl beat with a wire whip [3 large   EGGS

- Beat gradually into the Eggs 4 TB hot MILK.
- Then add a ladle of Milk and beat.
- Hold a sieve over the Eggs. Pour the rest of
  the Milk. Discard the Onion.
                                    Beat in [1/4-cup   CHEDDAR   coarse-grated
                                             [1/4-cup   PARMESAN   grated

TO BAKE   - Set the ring-mold on a cookie sheet and gently ladle the CUSTARD into it.
               - Slide cookie sheet with mold into the oven. Bake for 45 minutes to 1 hour.
               - The Flan will shrink slightly around the edges. Insert a thin knife. If it comes
                 out clean, the Flan is ready. Place it on a wire rack to cool.

TO UNMOLD   - When the Flan is cold shake the mold gently to make sure the Flan is loosened.
               - Run a thin knife around the edge. Top the mold with a serving platter.
                 Tap the mold on the counter two or three times, turn upside down, unmold.
               - Wash the mold, cover the Flan with it until ready to serve.
               - Can be refrigerated and brought to room temperature before serving.
To serve
warm or hot   - Unmold the Flan into an oven-proof dish or platter. Cover it with the clean
                 mold. If refrigerated, bring to room temperature.
               - Heat, covered with the mold, in a warm oven, for 20-to-30 minutes.

EGGPLANT - *Preparation for Cooking*

1. - Wash, dry the Eggplant. If the recipe requires paring, use a sharp knife or a peeler.
    - Cubed: no lesser than 3/4-inch. Sliced no lesser 1/3-inch thick. Thinner it will tear.

2. - To remove bitterness, sprinkle slices or cubes with Salt as you layer them in a colander.
    - Weight them down with an upside-down plate topped with a 16 oz-can. Set the
      colander over a bowl or plate. Press down occasionally to squeeze the water out.

3. - Let stand from 2-to-4 hours, depending on thickness of cubes or slices.

4. - Rinse Eggplant in colander under running cold Water. Drain. (It will be lightly salted)
    - Spread cubes or slices in a pan and lightly pat dry with paper towels.

BABY EGGPLANTS   as well as the Japanese variety need no peeling, nor the Salt treatment.
                    - They can be sliced as thin as a 1/4-inch and baked or fried.

   - However, when split lengthwise according to recipe, it is better to soak them in Salt
     Water. The Salt will tenderize them. Caps and stems are often left on for the look.
   - Wash, dry and split the Baby Eggplant lengthwise. Leave or remove stems and caps.
   - Lay them in a pan, cut side down. With a measuring cup pour water over them.
   - Count the cups of Water. Add 1 tp of Salt per 2 cups. Soak for 30 minutes.
   - Then, squeeze out lightly the moisture, let drain, cut side down, on a dish towel.

EGGPLANT - *Cooking*   Follow PREPARATION steps 1 through 4.

BAKED   - Brush slices or toss cubes with Olive Oil. Pepper to taste. Salt after cooking.
             - Lay them in one layer on a sprayed cookie sheet or in a baking pan.
             - Bake at 375° until golden brown. Cooking time depends on their thickness.

BROILED   - Brush slices on all sides with Olive Oil. Or a Marinade with Olive Oil, no Salt.
             - Lay the slices on a sprayed cookie sheet or in a baking pan.
             - Set under the broiler, broil to a golden brown. Turn and broil other side.
             - Adjust Seasonings. Serve sprinkled with Parmesan.
             - This method can be used instead of frying: preparation of casseroles or other.

DEEP-FRIED   - Eggplant absorbs a lot of Oil and gets very greasy. It is best to coat it with a
               batter and deep fry it in very hot Oil at a 350° temperature.

Option   1 - Dip in Flour, shake excess, deep fry to golden brown. Drain on paper towels.

            2 - Dip sliced Eggplant in EGG WASH, then in Flour seasoned with Salt, Pepper,
                Herbs, Spices. Shake off excess Flour, deep fry to golden brown. Drain.

            3 - Dip the sliced Eggplant in Flour, Egg Wash, and then Seasoned Breadcrumbs.
                HORS-D'OEUVRE   - Use this Option for 1/4-inch slices of Baby Eggplant.
                                 - Serve with a Marinara Sauce or a Tahini Sauce.

SKILLET-FRIED - Over high heat, in a heavy skillet, heat Olive Oil, 1/8-inch deep. Fry plain
                slices a few at a time, rapidly, to a golden brown, avoiding Oil absorption.
              - Or dip slices in Flour, as in above options. Skillet-fry, drain on paper towels.
              - Fry cubed Eggplant without crowding the skillet.
              - Add more Oil as you fry. Let the Oil get hot before adding more Eggplant.

EGGPLANT - *Methods to char the skin*   For a smoky pulp flavor

Smoky Eggplant is used in the preparation of Babaghanoush ("DIPS and SPREADS" - ETHNIC). As well as in Eggplant Caviar and Eggplant Yogurt (recipes in this chapter).

FIRST   -   Wash the Eggplant, pat dry, pierce with a fork in 3 spots, to allow steam to escape.

Method 1   Preheat oven to 475°.

1.   - Place the Eggplant in a small oven-pan lined with foil. Slide on middle rack of oven.
          - Reduce heat to 450°. Bake until the skin is wrinkled and the Eggplant collapses.
          - A one pound Eggplant will take about 1 hour and 20 minutes. Larger takes longer.

2.   - Take the Eggplant out of the oven, place it under the broiler until the skin is charred.
          - About 7-to-10 minutes, depending on your broiler.
          - When the "burnt aroma" starts invading your kitchen, broil 2 or 3 minutes longer.

3.   - Let the Eggplant cool in the pan for 5 minutes. The skin will harden.
          - Split it open with a knife. Use a dinner spoon to gently scrape the pulp out, and put
            it in a fine sieve. Do not leave any little pieces of hard charred skin in the pulp.

4.   - Let it drip for 15 minutes or longer, to rid of liquid. Spread the Pulp on a plate.
          - With a knife and fork chop it up. Let cool completely before adding other Ingredients.

NOTE   -   Following are other methods. I think the first one is the best and the easiest.

Method 2   - Char the Eggplant under the broiler, turning frequently. Then bake at 350°.

Method 3   - Cut off the stem. Drive a skewer through the stem side and a fork through the
              base. Hold Eggplant over the open flame of a gas burner, turn it until the skin
              is charred on all sides. This may take a long time. Then bake at 350°.

EGGPLANT alla PARMIGIANA   *Serves 4 to 5*

[2-1/4 cups	MARINARA SAUCE ready-made	
[10 oz	MOZZARELLA shredded	
[3/4-cup	PARMESAN grated	

Wash, peel and cut into 1/3-inch thick slices [2 medium   EGGPLANTS (in all about 2 lbs)

- Follow "Preparation for Cooking" steps 2, 3, 4.
- Dust with Flour, skillet-fry the slices to golden
  brown following directions in "Cooking".
- Preheat oven to 375°.

In a sprayed 8 x 8 baking dish, spread [MARINARA SAUCE
                    Sprinkle with [PARMESAN
               Overlap a layer of [Fried Eggplant
                    Sprinkle with [MOZZARELLA
      Sprinkle the Mozzarella with [PARMESAN

- Repeat until you have used all the Eggplant. Finish with a layer of MARINARA SAUCE.
- Top with plenty of MOZZARELLA. Sprinkle with PARMESAN. Cover tightly the dish with foil.
- Slide into oven, reduce heat to 350°. Bake 20 minutes. Remove foil, bake another 5 minutes.

EGGPLANT - BAKED as in GREECE   *Serves 4 to 6*

The TOMATO MIXTURE   Mix in a bowl   [28 oz-can   DICED TOMATOES   drained
                                           [4 cloves   GARLIC   mashed and minced
                                           [1/2-cup   EXTRA-VIRGIN OLIVE OIL
                                           [1/3-cup   FRESH PARSLEY   finely chopped
                                           [1-1/2 tp   DRIED OREGANO
                                           [a little   SALT and GROUND BLACK PEPPER

The VEGETABLES
                                    Slice [2 medium   ONIONS   1/4-inch thick slices
Wash, dry, trim, slice longwise 1/3-inch thick   [1 lb   ZUCCHINI   medium size
Wash, dry, slice crosswise 1/3-inch thick   [1 lb (4)   BABY EGGPLANTS
Peel, wash, dry, slice 1/3-inch thick   [1 lb   YUKON GOLD POTATOES

In a sprayed 8 x 8 baking dish: Part 1   **Part 2**

Spread [1/2-cup of   TOMATO MIXTURE   Top with [half of   ZUCCHINI
        [1/2-of   sliced ONIONS   [a little   Salt, Black Pepper
Sprinkle [a little   Salt, Ground Black Pepper
                                                  Top with [half of   EGGPLANT
Add   [half of   the POTATOES   [a little   Salt, Black Pepper
Sprinkle [a little   Salt, Ground Black Pepper Spread   [1/2-cup of   TOMATO MIXTURE
Spread [1/2-cup of   TOMATO MIXTURE   [the rest of ONIONS

Part 3   Repeat   - Potatoes, Seasoning, Tomato Mixture, Zucchini, Seasoning.
                      - Top with remaining Eggplant. Spread the remaining Tomato Mixture.
                      - Cover tightly the dish with foil. Bake in oven at 350° for 1-1/4 hours.
                      - Uncover and continue baking until the Vegetables are tender.
Optional   - Sprinkle baked Vegetables with FETA CHEESE. Pass rapidly under the broiler.

EGGPLANT - "IMAM BAYILDI"   (Turkey)   *Appetizer, serves 4 to 8*

                          Wash and dry   [4 thick   BABY EGGPLANTS 5-to-6 inches long
- Cut off the stems.
- Keep the leafy caps. Halve Eggplants longwise.
- On the cut side, with a knife, make 2 incisions
  longwise without touching the skin.

Place Eggplants in a pan, cut side down. Add   [enough   WATER to cover (measure it)
                                                [1 tp   SALT   per 2 cups of Water

- Soak Eggplants for 30 minutes.
- Remove and squeeze gently to rid of Water.
- Pat dry, set cut-side-down, on a dish towel.

In a large nonstick skillet, medium heat, heat   [1/4-cup   EXTRA-VIRGIN OLIVE OIL
When a light haze forms, sauté   [3 medium   ONIONS halved and thinly sliced
When Onions soften, add   [3 cloves   GARLIC   mashed and minced
When Onions turn golden, add   [14 oz-can   DICED TOMATOES   drained
                                 [1/2-cup   TOMATO SAUCE
Bring to a slow bubble, stir 2 minutes, add   [1 tp   GRANULATED SUGAR
                              Stir and add   [1/2-tp   ALLSPICE   or more to taste
                                             [1/4-tp   DRIED THYME crumbled
                                             [to taste   SALT, GROUND BLACK PEPPER
               Turn off heat and stir in   [1/4-cup   RAISINS loosen if stuck together
                                           [1/4-cup   PINE NUTS   *(continued)*

354

- Spray a 1-3/4 inch deep baking dish, in which the Eggplant halves can fit snugly.
- Arrange the Eggplant halves, cut side up, in it.
- With a pointed knife, make 2 crisscross incisions into the Pulp, to allow juices to seep in.

- Top each with a heap of ONION TOMATO MIXTURE. If there is any Mixture left, spread it around.
- Bake in oven preheated to 350° for 1 hour, or until Eggplants are tender. Let cool.
- Cover with foil, refrigerate. It tastes best the next day. Serve cold or at room temperature.

EGGPLANT - CAPONATA   Italian antipasto   *Yields 3-to-3-1/2 cups*

Wash, trim, pare and cut into 3/4-inch cubes	[1 lb	EGGPLANT
Follow steps 2, 3 and 4 of	[	"Preparation for Cooking"
In a large skillet, medium high heat, heat	[1/4-cup	EXTRA-VIRGIN OLIVE OIL
		(add more as needed)
When a light haze forms sauté the EGGPLANT		
until tender and browned on all sides	[sprinkle	GROUND BLACK PEPPER

Remove with a slotted spoon and set aside.

Return skillet to stove, medium heat, heat	[2 TB	EXTRA-VIRGIN OLIVE OIL
When a light haze forms, add	[1 cup	ONION quartered, thinly sliced
Sauté Onion to golden brown, then add	[1 cup	CELERY finely diced
Stir Onion and Celery then add	[1-1/2 cups	WHOLE TOMATOES canned,
		drained

Stir, break up the Tomatoes.
Bring to a bubble, reduce heat to low, cover,
simmer for 15 minutes.

Mix and add	[1 TB	TOMATO PASTE + 2 TB WATER
In a cup microwave a few seconds to dissolve	[1 TB	RED WINE VINEGAR
	[2 tp	SUGAR

Add the Vinegar.

Stir in the EGGPLANT and	[1 TB	TINY CAPERS rinsed, drained
	[8	PITTED BLACK OLIVES chopped
	[1 TB	PINE NUTS
	[to taste	GROUND BLACK PEPPER

Over medium heat stir until it bubbles.
Cover the skillet, reduce heat to low, simmer 20 minutes. Stir 2 or 3 times. Adjust Salt, Pepper.
Transfer to a serving dish or bowl. Let cool. Cover. Refrigerate overnight.

EGGPLANT CAVIAR - DIP   Mediterranean   *Yields about 1 cup*

As in METHOD 1 char a 1 lb EGGPLANT.

The next day:

Mix   the chopped Pulp
  [2 TB   EXTRA-VIRGIN OLIVE OIL
  [1/2-tp   RED WINE VINEGAR
    or LEMON JUICE or more to taste
  [to taste   GARLIC   powder or minced Clove
  [to taste   SALT and GROUND BLACK PEPPER

[add a little   EXTRA-VIRGIN OLIVE OIL
[adjust   Seasonings
[garnish with   TARRAGON or PARSLEY
               finely chopped
- Serve at room temperature
  with toasted PITA CHIPS.

Cover the surface with plastic wrap. Refrigerate overnight.

EGGPLANT GRATIN - ARTICHOKES and MUSHROOMS

Serves 4 to 6

Wash, trim, halve lengthwise, slice crosswise into 1/3-inch thick slices	[1 lb	EGGPLANT Follow "Preparation" steps 2 to 4.

See "Cooking" : dust with Flour and skillet-fry.

Prepare	[2 cups	MEDIUM WHITE SAUCE ("SAUCES")
mixing	[1/4-tp	ONION POWDER with the FLOUR
When the Sauce thickens, turn off heat, add	[to taste	SALT, BLACK PEPPER, NUTMEG

<u>Have ready</u>	[4 oz (1 cup)	SWISS CHEESE coarse-grated
	[1/2-cup	PARMESAN grated
	[8 oz	SLICED MUSHROOMS
Drain	[1 can	ARTICHOKE BOTTOMS slice a 1/4-inch thick

1. Layer   half of EGGPLANT in a sprayed 8 x 8 baking dish
2. Sprinkle   1/3-cup SWISS CHEESE   Top with   1/2-cup of the WHITE SAUCE
3. Layer   ARTICHOKES, MUSHROOMS   Top with   1/3-cup SWISS, 1/2-cup SAUCE
4. Layer   remaining EGGPLANT   Top with   1/3-cup SWISS, remaining SAUCE

Smooth the surface. Top with the grated PARMESAN.
Bake in oven preheated to 350°, 20-to-25 minutes until golden brown. Pass under the broiler.

EGGPLANT MOUSSAKA - MEATLESS   *Serves 6*

Wash, peel, cut crosswise into 1/2-inch slices	[2 elongated	EGGPLANTS (2 lbs)
Follow steps 2 to 4 of	[	"Preparation for Cooking"

Skillet-fry the slices dusted with Flour. Or broil.

<u>THE SAUCE</u> In a skillet, medium heat, heat	[2 TB	EXTRA-VIRGIN OLIVE OIL
When a light haze forms, sauté	[1-1/2 cups	ONION finely chopped
When Onion is translucent, add	[1 or 2	GARLIC CLOVES mashed, minced
When Onion begins to color, add	[14 oz-can	DICED TOMATOES with liquid
	[1 cup	TOMATO SAUCE
	[1-1/2 tp	GRANULATED SUGAR
	[2 tp	DRIED OREGANO
	[1/8-tp each	ALLSPICE, GROUND CINNAMON
	[to taste	SALT, GROUND BLACK PEPPER

Bring to a bubble, reduce heat to low, simmer for 20 minutes. Turn off heat and stir in	[1/4-cup	PARSLEY finely chopped

In a sprayed 8 x 8 baking dish splash a little
Sauce. Overlap half of the EGGPLANT.

Cover with half of the SAUCE and sprinkle	[1/4-cup	PARMESAN grated
Add remaining Eggplant, Sauce, and sprinkle	[1/4-cup	PARMESAN *

Bake in oven preheated to 350° for 30 minutes. Let cool. Serve warm or cold. Cut into squares.

* *VARIATION* - At this point top with 1-1/2 cups MEDIUM WHITE SAUCE, adding to it:
     6 TB PARMESAN, NUTMEG, SALT, PEPPER. After baking pass under the broiler.

356

EGGPLANT - RATATOUILLE   *Yields about 5-1/2 cups*

There are two ways to prepare a Ratatouille:

THE LONG WAY - is to sauté separately Eggplant and Zucchini. Sauté Bell Peppers, Onion,
Garlic, then add the Tomatoes. Assemble everything, add Seasonings,
finish the cooking. This takes too much time, utensils, and kitchen space.

HERE IS
THE SHORT WAY - cook everything together. The result tastes even better, as all flavors
are infused from the start.

Cut crosswise into slices 1-inch thick a	[1 lb	EGGPLANT do not peel

- Follow "Preparation for Cooking" steps 2 to 4.
- Then cut the slices into cubes.

Wash, cut off ends, slice into 3/4-inch pieces	[1 lb	LIGHT GREEN ZUCCHINI 3 large Smaller ones cook too fast.
Place the pieces in a bowl and sprinkle with	[	SALT

Transfer to a sieve. Weight down with a plate
and heavy can. Let stand for 1 hour.

Core, remove seeds and ribs from an	[8-oz (large)	GREEN BELL PEPPER cut into 3/4-inch squares
Split in half lengthwise, slice very thinly	[8 oz	YELLOW ONION peel then weigh
This is a rustic dish, chop not too finely	[1 TB	GARLIC or sauté 2 cloves in the Oil and discard
Remove leaves from stems to obtain	[2 tp	FRESH THYME
Drain a	[14 oz-can	DICED TOMATOES

THE COOKING   In a large heavy saucepan,

over medium high heat, heat	[6 TB	EXTRA-VIRGIN OLIVE OIL
When a light haze forms, sauté	[	the Onions
When Onions are translucent add	[	the Garlic
and	[	the Zucchini

Stir until Zucchini begin to soften.

Add	[	the Eggplant

Stir until Eggplant begins to brown.

Add	[	the Bell Peppers
Stir for 2 minutes and add	[	the Tomatoes
	[	Thyme
	[sprinkle	GROUND BLACK PEPPER

- Stir until the Mixture begins to bubble.
- Reduce heat to low, cover but keep the lid slightly ajar, and simmer for 45 minutes.
- Do not overcook. The Zucchini and Bell Pepper should have a slight crunch.
- When cooked, adjust SEASONINGS. Turn off heat. Let cool in the saucepan for 15 minutes.

- Transfer to a serving casserole with a lid, or cover with foil. Refrigerate overnight.
- It tastes best the next day. Serve cold, at room temperature, or warm.

Serve - As an appetizer with FISH, SEAFOOD. Garnish: OLIVES, PICKLES.
- As a side dish with grilled MEATS, SAUSAGE, CHICKEN.
- Heat the Ratatouille and toss it with PENNE or SPAGHETTINI.

EGGPLANT - RATATOUILLE LEFTOVERS

CRÊPES — Fill with RATATOUILLE. Serve with MARINARA or TOMATO SAUCE.

EGGS — Break Eggs on top of Ratatouille and shirr. Or melt a little Butter in a skillet, spread in it some Ratatouille, make a well in the center, fry in it the Eggs.

OMELET — Warm the RATATOUILLE and use it as a FILLING.

PIZZA — Prepare the PIZZA CRUST, see "PIZZAS". Spread it with Ratatouille.
— Top with shredded MOZZARELLA. Bake until the Cheese has melted.

QUICHE — Chop 1-1/2 cups of Ratatouille. Mix with the Custard and bake.

SANDWICHES — Fill Pita Bread with Ratatouille, chopped Olives. Wrap in foil. Warm in oven.

EGGPLANT - PATATOUILLE   Ratatouille variation   *Yields 5-1/2 cups*

Cut crosswise into slices 1-inch thick a [1 lb   EGGPLANT   do not peel

Follow "Preparation for Cooking" steps 2 to 4.
Then cut into cubes.
Parboil for 20 minutes [1 lb   YUKON GOLD POTATOES   then peel, cut into 1/2-inch cubes.

Cut into 3/4-inch squares an [8 oz (large) GREEN BELL PEPPER

Split in half lengthwise, slice very thinly [8 oz   YELLOW ONION   peel then weigh

Chop not to finely [1 TB   GARLIC or sauté 2 cloves in the Oil and discard

Remove leaves from stems to obtain [1 tp   FRESH THYME or 1/4-tp dried
[1/2-tp   FRESH ROSEMARY or 1/4-tp dried

Drain [14 oz-can   DICED TOMATOES reserve Liquid
Mix into the Tomato Liquid [1 TB   TOMATO PASTE

THE COOKING   In a large heavy saucepan,
over medium high heat, heat [6 TB   EXTRA-VIRGIN OLIVE OIL
When a light haze forms, sauté [the Onion
When Onion is translucent, add [the Garlic and Eggplant

Stir until Eggplant has lightly browned. Add [the Bell Pepper
Stir for 2 minutes. Add [the Potatoes
Stir for 1 minute. Add [the diced Tomatoes
[Thyme and Rosemary
[to taste   GROUND BLACK PEPPER
Pour over the Vegetables [1/4-cup of   the Tomato Liquid

- Stir until the Mixture begins to bubble. Reduce heat to low, cover, simmer for 45 minutes to 1 hour. Add if needed a little Tomato Liquid, or Water if you run out. Do not let the Mixture dry.
- Turn off heat. Adjust SALT, PEPPER. Transfer to a serving casserole with a lid, or cover with foil.
- Refrigerate. Tastes best the next day. Serve at room temperature or hot, as a side dish.

358

EGGPLANT - YOGURT   Dip or Sauce

Rub a bowl with 1 clove GARLIC. Mix in it:

[1 cup   SMOKY EGGPLANT PULP (Method 1)
[1/3-cup   PLAIN YOGURT
[2 TB   RED ONION   finely chopped
[1/2-tp   RED WINE VINEGAR
[1/2-tp   LEMON JUICE
[2 TB   PARSLEY   finely chopped
[to taste   GROUND CUMIN
[SALT, GROUND BLACK PEPPER

Add to taste more Lemon Juice or Vinegar. Cover, refrigerate.

Serve with:

[TOASTED PITA CHIPS

As a SAUCE with:

[grilled MEATS, KEBABS
[VEGETABLES

FENNEL - *Preparation and Cooking*

TRIMMING
- Cut off stems and base. If tough, discard outer sections. Wash thoroughly.
- Keep one or two sprigs of fronds for garnish. Snip them finely with scissors.

BLANCHED
- See - BLANCHING. With slotted spoon plunge whole, halves, or sections into the boiling Water for 7-to-8 minutes. Leave whole Bulbs longer.
- Remove with slotted spoon and plunge into iced Water to stop the cooking.
- This is not necessary if the Fennel is going to be cooked right away.

BOILED
- Plunge trimmed Bulbs into rapidly boiling salted water. Cook uncovered for about 30 minutes or until tender but firm.
- Remove with a slotted spoon, plunge into iced Water to stop the cooking.
- If the Bulbs are halved or quartered, cook for 10-to-20 minutes, or until desired tenderness is obtained. Plunge into iced Water to stop the cooking. Drain.

STEAMED
- If you don't have a steamer, use a collapsible colander in a pan of boiling Water.
- Arrange sections in it. Make sure the Water doesn't touch the Fennel.
- Sprinkle with Salt, Pepper, Herbs. Steam10 minutes or until desired doneness.

FENNEL à la GRECQUE   *For 1 lb Fennel, double the Broth amounts.*

Trim and slice off the hard base of an   [8-to-9 oz   FENNEL   cut longwise 8 wedges
                                                                     Wash under cold Water.

Combine in a 5-1/2 inch heavy saucepan   [1 cup   WATER
                                            [4 TB   EXTRA-VIRGIN OLIVE OIL
                                            [1   GREEN ONION trimmed
                                            [1 TB   LIME or LEMON JUICE
                                            [1 sprig of   THYME
                                            [1/4-tp   SALT, GROUND BLACK PEPPER

- Bring to a boil then reduce heat to low.
- Cover, simmer for 15 minutes. Turn off heat. Taste the Broth. Add to taste Salt, if needed.
- Arrange the Fennel wedges side by side in the Broth. Baste them. Bring to a rapid boil.
- Cover, reduce heat to low and simmer for 25-to-30 minutes, until the Fennel is tender.

- Remove it with tongs. Place the wedges side-by-side in a shallow serving dish.
- Bring the Broth to a boil and continue boiling, uncovered, until it is reduced to about 1/3-cup.
- Pour Broth over the Fennel, let cool. Cover, refrigerate overnight. Serve at room temperature.

FENNEL - BRAISED

Serves 4

Trim and slice off the hard base of [2   FENNEL BULBS   cut longwise into
                                                 8 wedges

Wash and blanch the wedges for 6 minutes.

In heavy nonstick skillet, medium heat, heat [2 TB   BUTTER
                                           [2 TB   EXTRA-VIRGIN OLIVE OIL
When it sizzles, add the Fennel and [sprinkle   SALT, GROUND BLACK PEPPER

Brown it lightly on all sides. *
                             Pour over it [1 cup   CHICKEN BROTH
Bring to a quick boil.
Reduce heat to low, cover, simmer for about
25 minutes, or until the Fennel is tender.

* *VARIATION* I   After browning add [2 or 3 TB   OUZO   or   PERNOD

Swirl it around, stir for 2 minutes to let it
evaporate, before adding the Broth.

* *VARIATION* II   Lay snugly browned Fennel
                  into an oven-dish, add [1 cup   CHICKEN BROTH
                   Top with plenty of [grated   PARMESAN

Bake in oven preheated to 350° until the Fennel is tender and the Parmesan golden brown.

FENNEL - GRILLED with RADICCHIO

Serves 2 to 4

Trim and slice off the hard base of [1 large   FENNEL BULB
Remove the outer leaves of [1 small   RADICCHIO

Quarter them lengthwise.   Wash, drain, pat dry.

Lay wedges in a pan, cut side up, drizzle with [plenty of   EXTRA-VIRGIN OLIVE OIL
And sprinkle with [SALT, GROUND BLACK PEPPER

                                    Mix [1 TB   BALSAMIC VINEGAR
                                           [1 tp   BROWN SUGAR
Sprinkle VINEGAR over the RADICCHIO.

Brush a grilling skillet with EXTRA-VIRGIN OLIVE OIL.
When the skillet is hot, grill Radicchio and Fennel on all sides, until tender yet crunchy.

<u>Serve as a side-dish with</u>   Fish, Meats, Poultry.

<u>As an appetizer</u>   place in a sprayed baking dish, side-by-side the grilled Fennel and Radicchio.

Sprinkle the wedges with [plenty of   PARMESAN   grated
Top with [plenty of   MOZZARELLA   shredded

Pass under the broiler until Mozzarella melts to golden.   Serve immediately.
Option - Remove from broiler and top the melted Mozzarella with slices of PROSCIUTTO.

360

GARLIC CLOVES - BRAISED

In a nonstick skillet, over medium heat, heat   [2 TB   EXTRA-VIRGIN OLIVE OIL
             When a light haze forms, stir in   [12 cloves   GARLIC   if pre-peeled pat dry
      Sauté to a golden brown then sprinkle   [optional   ALLSPICE   or   GROUND CUMIN
                              [to taste   SALT, GROUND BLACK PEPPER
                            Add [1/4-cup   WATER

Bring to a boil. Reduce heat to low.
Cover, cook until cloves are tender. Stir once in a while.
Add to Salads, mash into mashed Potatoes. As a Spread: mash with Olive Oil and Seasonings.

GARLIC HEAD - ROASTED

Remove outer loose skin, cut off pointed top,
              and cut in half crosswise   [large   GARLIC HEADS

Method 1   Spray a muffin tray, put into
           each cup a half Garlic Head   [drizzle   EXTRA-VIRGIN OLIVE OIL
                   Sprinkle with   [optional   SALT, GROUND BLACK PEPPER
                             [optional   ALLSPICE   a little

Cover and wrap the tray with aluminum foil.
Bake in oven preheated to 350° for 45 minutes to 1 hour, or until Cloves are tender to mushy.
Squeeze to extract Cloves. Combine with Vegetables, Pasta, Purées, Spreads.

Method 2 - Preheat oven to 400°. Brush cut sides with OLIVE OIL or melted BUTTER.
           - Lay cut side down in a pan, bake 15 minutes. Turn cut side up, bake 10 minutes.

Method 3 - Place 2 halves, cut side up, on heavy foil. Drizzle with Extra-Virgin Olive Oil.
           - Wrap well. Roast 45-to-60 minutes in oven preheated to 350°, or until tender.

LEEKS - Preparation and Cooking

TRIM   - Cut off green tops and root ends, leave white and light green parts only. Remove
           tough outer layers. Use green tops to make strong flavored Stock for Soup or Risotto.

WASH - Slice the Leeks in half lengthwise. Take the sections apart. To rid of grit, wash under
           running cold water. Soak for 10-to-15 minutes in a bowl of cold water.
     - Rinse in a colander, drain. Pat dry with paper towels. Cut according to recipe.

       To maintain sections attached Trim root end, leave a thin part to hold sections attached.

     - Split the Leeks lengthwise into quarters, or in half, to within 1-inch from the base.
     - Spread the attached sections under running cold water to rid of grit.
     - Soak in cold water 20 minutes, make sure all grit is removed. Rinse again.

BLANCH See "VEGETABLES" - BLANCHING
     - WHOLE LEEKS with sections attached: assemble them in bundles of three, tie them
        at both ends with trussing string. Blanch, cut string, drain on dish towel, pat dry.
     - Partially cooked: 7-to-9 minutes. Fully cooked: 10-to-14. Depends on thickness.

     - HALVES: Tie every 2 Halves, at both ends and in the middle with trussing string.

LEEKS - *Preparation for Salads*

- Trim, split LEEKS in half, keep them attached at the base. Wash. See Preparation.
- In a skillet bring to a boil just enough water to cover the Leeks. Add Seasonings.
- With slotted spoon plunge the Leeks, cut side down. Cook 10-to-15 minutes, until fork tender but firm. Remove with slotted spoon. Drain on a dish towel.

- When cool, lift the Leeks with your fingers, set them in a shallow dish cut side down.
- Cover with plastic wrap and refrigerate. The Leeks will render some liquid.
- Lift partially the wrap. Hold onto the Leeks with the wrap, tilt the platter, pour out the liquid. Absorb remaining liquid with paper towel. Add the Dressing before serving.

LEEKS - GRATINÉE   *Serves 3*   LEEKS see "Preparation and Cooking"

Prepare, cut in half with sections attached,
and blanch for 10 minutes [6 medium   LEEKS   white parts only
                                           Drain on a dish towel, pat dry.

See "SAUCES". Prepare [1 cup   VELOUTÉ WHITE SAUCE

When it thickens, turn off heat, stir in [4 TB   SWISS CHEESE   coarse-grated
                                          [2 TB   PARMESAN grated
When the Cheese has melted add [to taste   SALT and WHITE PEPPER
                                [a dash   NUTMEG   grated
Place the LEEKS snugly in sprayed baking dish.
Pour the SAUCE over them.
                    Sprinkle with [3 TB   SWISS CHEESE   coarse-grated
                    Dot with [1 TB   BUTTER cut in half, diced small

Bake in oven preheated to 375° for 20 minutes. Pass under the broiler to brown.
Option: prepare ahead Leeks and Sauce. Warm the Sauce. Assemble the dish, bake and serve.

VARIATION - Wrap each Leek with a slice of HAM or PROSCIUTTO. Then add the Sauce.

SMOTHERED GRATINÉE   Do not blanch the Leeks

In a skillet with a tight-fitting lid, melt [2 TB   BUTTER + 2 TB WATER
Put the LEEKS in it, turn them in the Liquid [sprinkle   SALT, GROUND BLACK PEPPER

- Cover tightly. Over medium low heat, cook the Leeks until tender but firm.
- Transfer to the baking dish. Cover with the Velouté Sauce and continue as above.

LEEKS - QUICHE   QUICHE see "BASIC RECIPES"

            Separate the sections and wash [3 large   LEEKS white and light green parts

Hold the sections in bunches, slice them
a 1/2-inch thick. Pat dry in a dish towel.

In a large nonstick skillet, medium heat, heat [1 TB   BUTTER + 1 TB VEGETABLE OIL
            Sauté the LEEKS until limp. Sprinkle [SALT, GROUND BLACK PEPPER

362

Preheat oven to 375°.

In a bowl, beat	[3	EGGS
Brush with a little of the beaten Eggs a	[9-inch	FROZEN UNCOOKED PIE SHELL

Set in the oven for 2 minutes only. Let cool.

Whisk into the Eggs	[3/4-cup	HEAVY CREAM + 1/4-cup MILK
Cut into tidbits and add	[3 oz	PHILADELPHIA CREAM CHEESE
	[2 oz	GRUYERE coarse-grated
	[1 oz	PARMESAN grated
	[a dash	NUTMEG grated
	[1/4-tp	SALT, GROUND BLACK PEPPER
Stir in	[	the Leeks

To assemble - Place the Pie Shell, in its foil pan, on a cookie sheet. Ladle CUSTARD into it.
              - Smooth the surface. Slide Quiche into the oven, reduce heat to 350°.
To bake   - Follow directions in "BASIC RECIPES".

VARIATION   - Add to Custard a 1/2-cup chopped Ham or Smoked Salmon.

LEEKS and ASPARAGUS - RISOTTO   RISOTTO - "BASIC RECIPES"
Serves 4 as an appetizer.

Trim, wash and set aside DARK GREEN PARTS of LEEKS.

Separate sections and wash	[2 medium	LEEKS white and light green parts

Drain.
Place in a dish towel, pat dry. Thinly slice.

BROTH   Combine in a saucepan   [DARK GREEN PARTS   in pieces
                                             [6 cups   WATER

Bring to a boil, cover, reduce heat to medium
low, simmer for 1 hour. Strain the Broth.

To obtain 6 cups add to a	[10.5 oz-can	CHICKEN BROTH
The BROTH from DARK GREENS and	[if needed	WATER to obtain the 6 cups

RISOTTO   Steam 3 minutes in microwave [8 medium   ASPARAGUS   then slant-cut into
                                                                          1/2-inch pieces

In a 10-inch heavy skillet, medium heat, heat	[3-1/2 TB	BUTTER + 1 TB VEGETABLE OIL
When it sizzles, add	[	the Leeks
Stir until wilted, then add	[	the Asparagus
Sauté for 2 minutes then stir in	[1-1/2 cups	ARBORIO RICE

- Stir until the grains are coated and glisten.
- Add one ladle (1/2-cup) at a time of BROTH.
- When 6 cups have been absorbed the Rice
  should be tender but firm, and creamy.

Turn off heat and stir in	[2-1/2 TB	BUTTER diced small
	[4 TB	PARMESAN grated
	[to taste	SALT, GROUND BLACK PEPPER

Cover, let Risotto set for 5 minutes.   Serve [on the side   PARMESAN   grated

LENTILS - *Preparation for Cooking*   *1 cup Dried Lentils serves 4 to 6*

- Spread the Lentils, a handful at a time, on a plate. Pick out any impurities.
- Place them in a sieve. Wash thoroughly under cold water. Drain.
- Soak if package directions indicate it. Then rinse and drain.

LENTILS used in SALADS - *Preparation*

For Salads, Lentils must always cook in plenty of Water to prevent them from sticking together.

In a heavy saucepan combine	[1 cup	LENTILS washed and drained
	[3-1/2 cups	COLD WATER
	[1	SMALL ONION whole
	[1	BAY LEAF
	[a pinch	SALT, GROUND BLACK PEPPER
	[1 or 2	GARLIC CLOVES whole, optional

Bring to a boil, reduce heat to low.
Simmer until Lentils are tender but firm. Drain, discard Onion, Garlic, Bay Leaf. Let cool.

BASIC RECIPE for CREAMY LENTILS   All kinds

Also use this recipe for the preparation of Lentil Purée and Creamy Soups. You can substitute the Olive Oil with Butter or Vegetable Oil.

Mix in a heavy saucepan	[1 cup	LENTILS washed and drained
	[1/2-cup	* ONION finely chopped
	[2 TB	EXTRA-VIRGIN OLIVE OIL
Optional	[1 clove	GARLIC minced

Cover, let marinate for 1 hour.

| Add to Lentils | [2-1/4 cups | WATER |
| Over medium heat, bring to a boil and add | [1 cube | CHICKEN BOUILLON   crumbled |

Reduce heat to low. Simmer 50 minutes, or
until tender and creamy. Add Water if needed.

| When Lentils are cooked and creamy, stir in | [1 tp | GROUND CUMIN   or to taste |
| | [to taste | SALT, GROUND BLACK PEPPER |

Stir. Simmer for 5 more minutes.
Transfer to a container with a lid. Cover the
Lentil surface with wax paper. Refrigerate.

<u>To serve cold as is</u>   Add to taste [1 or 2 TB   EXTRA-VIRGIN OLIVE OIL

<u>To serve hot as is</u>   Add [BUTTER   (optional)

* <u>Option</u>   - Sauté the Onion in the Oil. When it softens add the Garlic.
           - When the Onion begins to color, add the Lentils, the Broth, continue as above.

<u>VARIATIONS</u>   - When Lentils begin to simmer, add BACON STRIPS whole or chopped, or
             RAW SAUSAGE chunks, or both.
           - Half way through the cooking, add pieces of cooked HAM or SAUSAGE.

364

CREAMY LENTILS - PURÉE   Over-processing makes the Lentils pasty.

The Purée should be light and fluffy. Drizzle through the processor feeding tube any of: the Cooking Liquid, Broth, Milk, Cream, to obtain desired consistency. Add Seasonings.

BLACK BELUGA LENTILS   Poor Man's Caviar   *Serves 4 to 6*

Combine in a blender and blend	[2 TB	EXTRA-VIRGIN OLIVE OIL
and	[3-to-4 oz	ONION coarsely chopped

Mix in a heavy saucepan blended ONION with	[1 cup	BLACK BELUGA LENTILS
		washed, drained
Cover, let stand for 1 hour. Add to Lentils	[1-1/4 cups	WATER
	[1 cup	CHICKEN BROTH canned

- Bring to a boil. Reduce heat to low, simmer
  50 minutes or until Lentils are tender creamy.
- If needed, add a little Water. Stir occasionally.

Transfer the Lentils into a bowl and stir in	[2 TB	EXTRA-VIRGIN OLIVE OIL
	[	SALT, GROUND BLACK PEPPER

Cover the surface with wax paper. Refrigerate.

VARIATIONS - Add to taste Salmon Roe Caviar, creating a contrast of colors and flavors.
    - Mix in a little Lemon Juice. Top the Lentils with cold Seafood or Fish.

GREEN LENTILS with MINT   *Serves 4 to 6*

Follow the above Black Beluga recipe, substituting the Black Lentils with GREEN LENTILS.

Half way through the cooking, stir in	[2 TB	DRIED GARDEN MINT crumbled
or	[3 TB	FRESH MINT finely chopped
When Lentils are cooked and creamy, add	[to taste	SALT, GROUND BLACK PEPPER
	[1 TB	BUTTER or more, to taste

To heat add 1 or 2 tp of Water or Butter.
Serve with Fish, Lamb, Chicken, Salmon. (With Salmon, omit Mint, use 3 TB FRESH DILL).

LENTILS - SOUP   Cook 1 cup of CREAMY LENTILS as in the *Option*.

Use	[2 TB	BUTTER + 1 tp VEGETABLE OIL
When the ONION colors, mix in	[1 tp	* GROUND CUMIN, 1/2-tp CORIANDER
	[4 cups	WATER + 2 cubes BOUILLON

Simmer until Lentils are tender.
Liquefy in blender. Add SALT, PEPPER,
LEMON JUICE.

Serve hot topped with	[canned	FRENCH FRIED ONIONS, CROUTONS
Serve chilled topped with	[	CUCUMBER or BELL PEPPER diced

* Spices for Lentil Soup flavoring are sold in Middle Eastern stores. Omit Cumin and Coriander.

365

MOLOKHIA SOUP   (Middle East)

A traditional Sunday lunch and casual get-together for families and friends, to enjoy good food and company at a leisurely pace. The meal consists of the Soup, Rice and roasted Chicken. Varieties of Meats are sometimes served too. Individual large pasta bowls are the ideal size for it.

MOLOKHIA is a leafy vegetable similar to Spinach. It is sold, chopped or leaf, in frozen 14-oz packaged slabs, available in Middle Eastern stores. It has some of the sliminess of Okra, but so delicious, once you've tasted it, you'll love it. You need the chopped Molokhia for this Soup.

NOTE   - 2 cups of Soup would be the minimum amount per serving, which includes seconds.
   - Leftover Molokhia Soup can be refrigerated or frozen and reheated.
   - Package directions indicate using 2 cups of Broth. This makes the Soup too thick.
     I use 3-1/2 to 4 cups of Broth per package.
   - The cooked RICE: plan a 1/2-to-3/4 cup per 1 cup of Soup. Or according to appetites.

MOLOKHIA FOR TWO - AS A TRY-OUT

NOTE   - Do not thaw the Molokhia. Slide it frozen into the Broth. To cut a frozen slab, leave it
     out a few minutes. Break it by hand or cut with a pointed knife.. It separates easily.
   - For the Soup use a saucepan wide enough to fit the slab of frozen Molokhia, or cut it in
     half. Every slab will increase the Soup volume by about 2 cups.

THE SOUP   In the saucepan simmer   [4 cups   CHICKEN BROTH Salt to taste

In a small skillet, over medium heat, heat   [1 TB   BUTTER
                                             [1 TB   MARGARINE
When it sizzles, using a wooden spoon, sauté [1 TB + 1 tp GARLIC   finely minced

Do not brown the Garlic. Stir 2 or 3 minutes
                   until it softens then mix in [1 TB   GROUND CORIANDER

- Stir and sauté Garlic/Coriander for 3 minutes.
- Pour carefully a 1/2-ladle of simmering Broth
  into the skillet, stand back, it will splatter.
- Stir. Add another 1/2-ladle of Broth.
- Stir and pour the whole thing into the Broth.

        Bring the Broth to a boil and slide into it   [14 oz-pkg   FROZEN CHOPPED MOLOKHIA

- Reduce heat to medium low and let the slab loosen. Stir once in a while.
- When it has loosened, bring the Soup to a boil then cover and simmer for 10-to-15 minutes.
- Add Salt and Pepper to taste. Turn off heat, cover, let the Soup set for 20 minutes or longer.
- Cook the Rice. Heat the Soup. Serve it in a tureen.

THE CHICKEN   -   Roast or broil it, or use store-bought Plain or Lemon-Garlic rotisserie Chicken.

THE WHITE RICE   -   Use long or short grain Rice.

THE MOLOKHIA RITUAL   - Serve the Chicken on individual plates, next to individual bowl.
                         - Break into the bowl toasted Pita Bread   (see "SANDWICHES").
                         - Add the Rice, then the Soup.
                         - LEMON JUICE to taste.
                         - MINCED RED ONIONS in VINEGAR (with the following recipe)
                         - Cut up the Chicken into bite-size pieces, add them to the Soup.

MOLOKHIA PARTY   *Serves 6*

Prepare two days ahead

THE BROTH   Use a large Pasta Cooker with removable strainer. Or wire basket that fits in a
stockpot.

Combine in it	[3	CHICKEN DRUMSTICKS skinless
	[3	CHICKEN THIGHS skinless
	[1	ONION whole (medium size)
	[1	LARGE CARROT peeled, cut in 3
	[15 cups	WATER
	[1 tp	SALT, GROUND BLACK PEPPER

- Bring to a boil. Cover.
- Cook over medium heat for 2 hours or longer, until the meat begins to fall from the bones.
- Skim the scum as it forms on the surface. Evaporation will reduce the Broth to about 12 cups.
- Turn off heat. Remove strainer with Solids, let it drip into a bowl. Let the Broth cool.
- Discard Solids, add the drippings to the Broth. Pass the Broth through a fine sieve into a bowl.
- Add Salt to taste. When cold, cover, refrigerate. The next day skim off the Fat to de-grease.

Prepare the day before

4 LOAVES PITA BREAD   - Toast the Pita, see "SANDWICHES", store in a sealed container.

1 LARGE RED ONION   - Chop it finely in processor. Put in a glass jar or serving bowl.
- Add Red Wine Vinegar just to cover. Seal the jar. Refrigerate.
- Some like their Soup with Red Onion and a little of its Vinegar.
- Others, the Red Onion, the Vinegar, and Lemon Juice. So do I.

1/2-cup LEMON JUICE   - Strain the Juice, refrigerate. Serve it in a glass salad-oil server.

2 or 3 LEMONS   - Split lengthwise in quarters to scrub the Chicken.

2 or 3 ROASTING CHICKENS   - Quartered. Wash, pat dry. Sprinkle Salt, Pepper, a little Garlic
Powder. Scrub the Chicken pieces with the quartered Lemons.
- Stack them in a bowl. Cover. Refrigerate.

PARTY DAY

THE SOUP   Bring to a simmer the [12 cups of   Chicken Broth (de-greased)

In a small skillet, over medium heat, heat	[2 TB	BUTTER + 2 TB MARGARINE
When it sizzles, sauté	[4 TB	GARLIC minced finely in
		processor
Stir for 2 or 3 minutes, until it softens, mix in	[3 TB	GROUND CORIANDER
Stir for 3 minutes. Add, it will splatter	[1/2-ladle	of the Chicken Broth
Stir and add another	[1/2-ladle	of Broth

Pour Mixture into the Broth, bring to boil, add [3 slabs   FROZEN CHOPPED MOLOKHIA

Cook the Molokhia as in the previous recipe. Cover, let rest and re-heat when ready to serve.

THE CHICKEN   Lay it in a sprayed baking dish: 1-1/4 hours before serving, roast it golden brown.

THE RICE   Cook [3 cups   WHITE RICE = 9 cups cooked
Or according to appetites.

To serve   follow the MOLOKHIA RITUAL as in previous recipe.

367

MUSHROOMS - *Preparation for Cooking*

Cut off tough stems, reserve to make a Broth. When ready to use, wash the Mushrooms in a bowl of cold water. With a soft brush clean the gills. Rinse gently several times. Drain, pat dry.

The BROTH - Wash the stems. Chop and boil them: 2 cups Water per 1 cup stems.
                - Strain the Broth through a fine sieve lined with 2 layers of cheesecloth.

FRESH MUSHROOMS - 2 cups raw sliced = about 5-to-6 oz. Cooked = 1 cup.

CHANTERELLES   Must be carefully cleaned. Sometimes they are parboiled before sautéeing.

CHINESE DRIED MUSHROOMS Place in a bowl, cover with lukewarm Water, soak for 30 minutes.

- Remove with slotted spoon. Drain, pat dry on paper towels. Cut off the tough stems.
- Strain the Soaking Liquid through a sieve lined with 4 layers of cheese cloth, until quite clear. Use the Soaking Liquid to cook Rice, Risotto, or prepare a Sauce.

ITALIAN DRIED FUNGHI or PORCINI   To reconstitute, soak for 30 minutes, in warm WATER.

- A 1/2-oz Dried *weighs* 2-2/3 oz when reconstituted. Use 1 cup of Water per 1/2-oz.

- Lift the Mushrooms carefully out of the Water without stirring the grit at the bottom.
- Put them in a bowl. Reserve the SOAKING LIQUID.
- Rinse them in the bowl, several times, with lukewarm Water, until rid of impurities.
- Place them in a sieve, under gently running lukewarm Water, stir them with your hand.
- Drain on paper towels. Mushrooms are now ready for cooking.

- Strain the SOAKING LIQUID through a sieve lined with 4 layers of cheesecloth, until quite clear. Avoid pouring out the grit . Use this LIQUID to prepare a Sauce or Risotto.

To sauté	Over medium heat, heat	[1-1/2 TB	BUTTER or OLIVE OIL or mixed
	When it sizzles, sauté	[1 TB	SHALLOT/ONION finely chopped
	When translucent, sauté until tender	[1/2-oz	reconstituted FUNGHI

Or poach in Soaking Liquid (strained) until tender. Or sauté briefly after poaching.

MORELS - DRIED: In a bowl, cover with hot water. Soak 30 minutes. Drain, pat dry.
        - Reserve Soaking Liquid: strain through a sieve lined with cheesecloth.

- FRESH: Trim stems. Rinse many times in a bowl of cold water to rid of grit.
- Last rinse, add a little Salt. It brings out impurities. Soak 5 minutes.

PORTOBELLOS   Cut off stems. Wipe caps with damp paper towels.

- Rinse rapidly in a bowl of cold water, rubbing lightly to dislodge grit. If there is any left in the water, rinse again. Set on paper towels to drain, pat dry.
- To Grill marinate for 30 minutes to prevent the skin from getting leathery.

MARINADE for 4 large caps	[3 TB	RED WINE VINEGAR or LEMON JUICE
	[1/2-cup	EXTRA-VIRGIN OLIVE OIL
	[2 cloves	GARLIC crushed, or 2 TB SHALLOT sliced
FRESH HERBS	[to taste	BASIL, TARRAGON, THYME and CHIVES

SHIITAKE - (Japanese - Dried)   Place them in a bowl, cover with twice as much Water.
        - Soak for 30 minutes. Drain, rinse and dry on paper towels. Trim off hard stems.

MUSHROOM CAPS - STUFFED

Yields 2-1/2 cups: 3 TB per Cap

Cut off STEMS, clean, rinse and dry	[12	MUSHROOM CAPS 2" diameter
Clean, rinse and chop into small bits	[	the Stems
In nonstick 6-inch skillet , medium heat, heat	[1 TB	BUTTER + 1/2-tp VEGETABLE OIL
When it sizzles, sauté	[1	SHALLOT finely chopped
When Shallot softens add	[	the Mushroom Stems
Sauté until they are tender and stir in	[1 TB	PARSLEY finely chopped
See "SAUCES". Prepare	[1 cup	CREAMY BÉCHAMEL
When it thickens, stir in until melted	[3 TB	PARMESAN grated
	[3 TB	SWISS CHEESE coarse-grated
Turn off heat, add MUSHROOMS STEMS and	[1 cup	HAM chopped in processor
	[to taste	SALT, GROUND BLACK PEPPER
Fill the Caps	[sprinkle	BREADCRUMBS

Lay them in sprayed baking dish. Bake in 350° oven for 10 minutes. Pass under the broiler.

MUSHROOMS and LINGUINE

Serves 4 as an appetizer

Soak as in "Preparation for Cooking" a	[1/2-oz	DRIED ITALIAN FUNGHI
To obtain <u>1-1/2 cups</u> add to	[strained	FUNGHI SOAKING LIQUID
	[	CHICKEN BROTH
In an 8-inch skillet, over medium heat, heat	[2 TB	BUTTER + 2 tp VEGETABLE OIL
Sauté the FUNGHI for 2 minutes, then add	[6 oz	SLICED CREMINI MUSHROOMS
Sauté until browned and tender, then	[sprinkle	SALT, GROUND BLACK PEPPER

Turn off heat.

See "SAUCES". Prepare	[1-1/2 cups	THIN WHITE SAUCE
with	[	the Soaking Liquid/Chicken Broth
When the Sauce thickens, mix in	[6 TB	PARMESAN grated
Stir in the MUSHROOMS, turn off heat. Add	[to taste	GROUND BLACK PEPPER, SALT
Toss into the skillet with the Mushrooms	[6 oz	LINGUINE
Serve immediately. On the side	[grated	PARMESAN

MUSHROOMS - MINI QUICHES

MINI QUICHE - "BASIC RECIPES"

Spray a tray of 12 muffin cups (1/4-cup size) with a mist of Cooking Spray. Preheat oven to 375°.

In a bowl, whisk [4   EGGS
[1/4-cup   HEAVY CREAM
[2 TB   MASCARPONE
[4 TB   PARMESAN   grated
[2 TB   PARSLEY   finely chopped
[a pinch   ONION POWDER
[1/4-tp   SALT, BLACK PEPPER

Spread into each muffin cup:

[1 TB + 1 tp   MUSHROOMS sautéed, chopped
[1/8-cup of   EGG MIXTURE

Bake the Quiches following directions in
"BASIC RECIPES".

MUSHROOMS - RISOTTO with DRIED FUNGHI

*Serves 4 as an appetizer **

Soak as in "Preparation for Cooking" a	[1/2-oz	DRIED ITALIAN FUNGHI
Strain the	[	FUNGHI SOAKING LIQUID
and add to it	[enough	CHICKEN BROTH to obtain 1 cup
Bring to a simmer	[5 cups	CHICKEN BROTH
		(+ 1/2-cup if needed)
In a 10-inch heavy skillet, medium heat, heat	[3 TB	BUTTER
	[1-1/2 TB	VEGETABLE OIL
When a light haze forms, add	[	the Funghi
Sauté the Funghi for 3 minutes, and add	[1-1/2 cups	ARBORIO RICE
Stir until grains are coated and glisten. Add	[1/4-cup	DRY WHITE WINE

Stir until the Wine evaporates.
First add one ladle (1/2-cup) of BROTH.

Microwave for 10 seconds to heat the	[1 cup of	FUNGHI SOAKING LIQUID

- When the 1/2-cup has been absorbed add
  in 2 times the FUNGHI SOAKING LIQUID.
- Continue with remaining 4-1/2 cups.
- When absorbed, the Rice should be tender
  but firm and creamy.

Turn off heat, stir in	[1-1/2 TB	BUTTER diced small
	[4 TB	PARMESAN grated
	[to taste	SALT, GROUND BLACK PEPPER
Let the Risotto set for 5 minutes. Serve with	[grated	PARMESAN on the side

* Also serve as a side-dish with roasted Chicken, Chicken Paillard, Veal Scaloppine.

VARIATION - Transfer the Risotto to a serving dish and top it with sautéed CHICKEN SUPRÊMES.

DRIED FUNGHI RISOTTO in PORTOBELLO CAPS Serves 4

PORTOBELLOS	"Prepare for cooking" [4	PORTOBELLO CAPS
		3-1/2 inches in diameter
	[or use 8	of 2-1/2 to 3-inches in diameter
Brush caps and gills with	[	EXTRA-VIRGIN OLIVE OIL
Sprinkle	[lightly	SALT, GROUND BLACK PEPPER

Cover loosely with foil, let stand for 1 hour.

In nonstick 8-inch skillet, medium heat, heat	[enough	EXTRA-VIRGIN OLIVE OIL to
		cover the base of skillet
Sauté the Portobello Caps until tender, and	[sprinkle	SALT, GROUND BLACK PEPPER

- Place the CAPS in an oven-proof dish, cover with foil and keep in a warm oven.
- Prepare the RISOTTO. Heap it into the CAPS. Sprinkle with PARMESAN. Serve immediately.

RISOTTO with MIXED MUSHROOMS   *Serves 4 as an appetizer*

In a nonstick skillet, over medium heat, heat	[1 TB	BUTTER
When it sizzles, sauté	[2 tp	SHALLOTS finely chopped
When softened, sauté until tender, browned	[4 oz sliced	CREMINI or PORCINI
	[sprinkle	SALT, GROUND BLACK PEPPER

Transfer to a bowl.

Repeat with	[4 oz	FRESH MORELS "Prepared for Cooking"

Mix all the Mushrooms into the same bowl.

Bring to a simmer	[6 cups	CHICKEN BROTH (+ 1/2-cup)

In a 10-inch heavy skillet, medium heat, heat	[3-1/2 TB	BUTTER + 1 TB VEGETABLE OIL
When it sizzles, sauté	[2 TB	SHALLOTS finely chopped
When Shallots have softened, stir in	[3 oz	WHITE MUSHROOMS chopped into tidbits
Sauté the Mushrooms for 1 minute and add	[1-1/2 cups	ARBORIO RICE
Stir until grains are coated and glisten, add	[1/3-cup	DRY WHITE WINE

- Stir until the Wine has evaporated.
- Add, a 1/2-cup at a time, 5 cups of BROTH.
- Mix in MUSHROOMS. Add last cup of BROTH.

The Rice should be tender, firm, creamy, add	[2 TB	BUTTER diced small
	[4 TB	PARMESAN, SALT, PEPPER

Cover, let the Risotto set for 5 minutes.

MUSHROOMS - TOAST GRATINÉE   GRATINÉE - "BASIC RECIPES"

Serves 2

In a nonstick skillet, over medium heat, heat	[2 TB	BUTTER + 1 tp VEGETABLE OIL
When it sizzles, sauté	[2 TB	ONION finely chopped
When Onion begins to color, add	[6 oz	SLICED MUSHROOMS
Stir, cook the Mushrooms until tender, then	[sprinkle	SALT, GROUND BLACK PEPPER
	[a dash	NUTMEG grated

Turn off heat, cover.

Prepare a	[	WHITE SAUCE ("SAUCES")
with	[1 TB	BUTTER
	[1 TB + 1 tp	FLOUR
	[3/4-cup	MILK
When it thickens, stir in until melted	[1/4-cup	SWISS CHEESE coarse-grated
Turn off heat, add the MUSHROOMS	[to taste	GROUND BLACK PEPPER

Toast	[2 slices	CHALLAH BREAD 3/4-inch thick

Place slices in two sprayed individual
oven-proof dishes. Ladle on top the
MUSHROOM SAUCE.

Sprinkle with	[plenty of	SWISS and PARMESAN mixed

Set the dishes on a cookie sheet. Pass under the broiler to brown the top.

VARIATION - Add to the Mixture chopped Ham or Prosciutto. Or crumbled cooked Sausage.

ONIONS - Cutting and Peeling

To cut an Onion without tears, put it in the freezer for 30-to-45 minutes. Or refrigerate 2 hours.
To reduce Onion sharpness, soak it in salted cold Water for 10-to-15 minutes.

PEARL AND SMALL ONIONS   Blanch 2-to-3 minutes until the skins loosen. Drain, rinse under
running cold water. Cut off root base, slip off skins. Trim the tops.

ONIONS - CARAMELIZED   *Serve with Ham Steaks, Pork Chops.*

In large heavy skillet, over medium heat, heat [1 TB   BUTTER + 1 tp VEGETABLE OIL
When it sizzles, add to the skillet [2 lbs   ONIONS small size, to obtain
small rings. Slice 1/4-inch thick.
Stir until they begin to soften. Sprinkle with [2 tp   GRANULATED SUGAR

Over medium low heat cook slowly until caramelized, about 45-to-60 minutes. Stir occasionally.

VARIATIONS - When Onions soften, add gradually 1/2-cup Vermouth or White Wine. Stir as it
evaporates. When golden, before they caramelize, add Herbs, Seasonings.

With APPLES   Caramelize Onions as above. With slotted spoon transfer them to a plate.

Return skillet to stove, medium heat, heat [3 TB   BUTTER
With a wooden spoon deglaze the skillet, add [3 peeled   GRANNY SMITH APPLES   diced
[1/8-tp each   GROUND CUMIN and GINGER
Sauté Apples until golden brown but firm, add [Onions and Seasoning to taste

ONION SOUP GRATINÉE   *Yields about 4 cups, serves 2 or 3*

In a heavy saucepan, over medium heat, heat [3 TB   BUTTER + 1 tp VEGETABLE OIL
When it sizzles, add [2 lbs   ONIONS   small size, to obtain
small rings. Slice 1/4-inch thick.
Stir to coat the Onions. Reduce heat to
medium-low. Stir occasionally until Onions
begin to brown.
Then add gradually [1/2-cup   DRY WHITE WINE   optional
- Stir until it evaporates.
- When Onions are caramelized a few will
remain a lighter color, turn off heat.
- In all, about 45 minutes of cooking time.

Pour into the saucepan with the Onions a [10.5 oz-can   BEEF BROTH
[10.5 oz-can   BEEF CONSOMME (or Broth)
[1 can   COLD WATER

In a small cup dissolve [2 tp   ARROWROOT in 1/4-cup WATER

Bring the Broth to a boil. Add ARROWROOT
and stir until the Broth thickens, then add [to taste   GROUND BLACK PEPPER

Reduce heat to low, cover, simmer 30 minutes. Turn off heat. Adjust Seasonings. *(continued)*

To serve   Slant-cut and toast   [BAGUETTE slices a 1/2-inch thick

            Place in each oven-proof soup bowl
    2 slices of toasted BAGUETTE. Sprinkle   [plenty of   PARMESAN grated

Heat the Onion Soup and fill the bowls.

Top each with 2 slices Baguette, sprinkle with   [grated   PARMESAN
                    and cover with plenty of   [shredded   SWISS or EMMENTHAL CHEESE

Place the soup bowls under the broiler until the Cheese melts to a golden crust.
Serve immediately. With more Baguette to dunk.

VARIATION -   Before topping with Baguette slices, mix in pieces of cooked Sausage or Chicken.

POTATOES - Cooking Methods

BAKED   - Scrub, wash and dry Baking Potatoes. Rub the skin with a little Cooking Oil.
               - Bake 45-to-60 minutes in 450° oven, or until soft when squeezed.
               - The Potatoes can also be wrapped in foil and baked. Omit rubbing with Oil.

BOILED   - Whole: put in a saucepan, cover with plenty of Water. Add 1/2-tp Salt. Cover.
               - Over medium high heat bring to a boil. Reduce heat to medium. From this
                 point, count 25-to-40 minutes, depending on size. Test by inserting a knife.
               - Diced / sliced: 10-to-15 minutes. New Potatoes: 15-to-25 depending on size.

SAUTÉED   - Boil the Potatoes for about 15 minutes, leave them firm but not quite cooked.
                 Slice or dice. Sauté until golden brown, in Butter, Olive or Vegetable Oil.
               - To sauté raw Potatoes, sliced less than a 1/4-inch thick, they will break.

STEAMED   - Wash New Potatoes. Do not peel. Place them in a steamer in one layer, or
                 two, not more. Cooking time about 30-to-40 minutes.

POTATOES - ANNA   *Serves 4 to 6*

THE DISH   - Measure in cups of water the volume of the baking pie-dish. Or ramekins.

THE POTATOES   - YUKON GOLD: peel, slice 1/8-thick with a mandolin, to obtain the same
                 amount in cups. Wash in batches in a colander under running cold water.
               - Dry in a dish towel.

TO ASSEMBLE   Brush the baking dish with   [MELTED BUTTER

Overlap in it a layer of Potatoes, in concentric
circles, all the way to the center.
                        Sprinkle with   [MELTED BUTTER, SALT and PEPPER
    Repeat until you fill the dish. Brush top with   [MELTED BUTTER
            Optional: sprinkle between layers   [PARMESAN   grated

- Bake in oven preheated to 400° for 45-to-50 minutes, or until Potatoes are tender and underside
  has a golden brown crust. Loosen it with a spatula. Tilt, soak up any Butter with a paper towel.
- Place a serving platter over the dish and invert to unmold.

POTATOES in BROTH

BAKED PIE   Spray a 9-inch baking pie-dish, 1-to-1-1/2 inches deep.

In a skillet, over medium heat, heat   [1 TB   BUTTER
When it sizzles, sauté until golden brown [2 cups   ONION halved and thinly sliced

Set aside.

Peel, slice with a mandolin   [3 cups   YUKON GOLD POTATOES
                                             slices 1/8-inch thick

Dry them in a dish towel.
Layer Potatoes in the dish, scattering Onions
in-between, sprinkle with PEPPER.

Cover with   [boiling   CHICKEN BROTH salted to taste

Preheat oven to 400°.
Bake for about 45 minutes, or until Potatoes are soft, crusty on top and all Liquid has been
absorbed. If needed, add more Broth during the baking, do not let it dry.

ROASTED   Preheat oven to 375°. Peel, wash, dry small POTATOES or small YUKON GOLD.
- Place in a baking dish. Pour over CHICKEN BROTH, filling the pan half-way up.
- Bake 1 hour or more, until tender with golden brown tops. Baste once or twice.
- Serve as is or remove from Broth.

POTATOES - CROQUETTE BASE   *Yields 2 cups*

Peel, wash, cube, and boil until fork tender   [1 lb   IDAHO POTATOES
                                                 [1/2-tp   SALT   added to boiling Water

Drain. Over medium heat shake Potatoes in
a skillet to remove remaining moisture.

Purée the POTATOES in processor with   [1 TB   BUTTER   softened
                                        [1/4-tp   SALT, WHITE PEPPER to taste
                                        [1 tp   PARSLEY   very finely chopped
                                        [optional   ONION POWDER   barely a pinch
                            Optional   [1/4-cup   PARMESAN   grated

                             Beat   [1   EGG + 1 EGG YOLK
                                        [optional   NUTMEG grated, a dash

- Pour the beaten EGGS into the processor.
- With short pulses mix Eggs and Potatoes. Do not process excessively.
- Transfer the Mixture into a bowl. Cover the surface with plastic wrap and refrigerate.
- Shape and fry the Croquettes following directions in "BASIC RECIPES".

WITH FILLING - Mix 1 cup of CROQUETTE BASE with 1 cup of FILLING. See Fish, Salmon, Ham.
              - Or stuff the center with a piece of Goat cheese or Brie (rindless).

WITH A MEAT FILLING

In a nonstick skillet, over medium heat, heat [1/2-TB   BUTTER + 1 tp VEGETABLE OIL
                      When it sizzles, sauté   [1 medium   ONION   finely chopped
              When Onion is translucent add   [1/2-lb   LEAN GROUND ROUND   or mix
                                                            with raw Sausage Meat

Break up lumps, stir until the Meat loses its raw color.

374

When browned but not dry, add [2 TB   PARMESAN   grated
                              [to taste NUTMEG or ALLSPICE
              Stir in [1 TB   PARSLEY   finely chopped
                      [SALT, GROUND BLACK PEPPER

- Tilt the skillet , absorb Fat with paper towels.
- Refrigerate. Form with CROQUETTE BASE oval patties 2-1/2 x 3 x 1/3-inch thick. Put in the
  center 1-1/2-to-2 teaspoons of Filling. Seal, roll into ovals. Fry as per "BASIC RECIPES".

POTATOES - MOUSSAKA   (Greece)   *Serves 4 to 6*

               See "SAUCES". Prepare a [SPEEDY BOLOGNESE
          Just use to moisten the Meat [1 cup of   TOMATO PASTA SAUCE
                        Season with [to taste   ALLSPICE, CINNAMON, PARMESAN
Do not bring to a boil or simmer.
                        Have ready [1/2-cup   PARMESAN/SWISS mixed equally
                                   [1 cup   TOMATO PASTA SAUCE

    Boil for 20 minutes only, peel, let cool [6 large   YUKON GOLD POTATOES
            Slice them a 1/4-inch thick and [sprinkle   SALT, GROUND BLACK PEPPER

In a large nonstick skillet pour 1/8-inch deep [COOKING OLIVE OIL
Heat the Oil. Over medium high heat, sauté [the Potatoes *

- Proceed in 3 or 4 batches. Brown lightly on both sides. Drain on paper towels.
- Add more Oil as needed, heat well before adding Potatoes. Divide Potatoes into 3 equal stacks.

1. In a sprayed 8 x 8 baking dish: overlap 1/3-of the POTATOES.
2. Spread over them half of the MEAT   and   repeat: 1/3-of Potatoes, the rest of the MEAT.
3. Cover with the remaining Potatoes   -   top with the 1 cup of TOMATO PASTA SAUCE.
4. Sprinkle with the 1/2-cup of CHEESE   -   bake in oven preheated to 350° for 30 minutes.

* *NOTE* -   You can also use the partially cooked Potatoes without sautéing them in the Oil.

POTATOES - RÖSTI   Hash Brown Cake   (Switzerland)   *Serves 4*

If you have a 7-inch copper and stainless steel oven-to-table skillet use it. The Rösti can also be
cooked in a Frittata pan. It allows to crisp both sides without having to pass under the broiler.
(If the Frittata pan is larger than 7-inches, use more Potatoes and Butter).

       Peel, wash, dry and coarse-grate through
the large holes of a grater or processor blade [1-1/2 lbs   IDAHO POTATOES

Dry them in a dish towel, sprinkle and rub in [a little   SALT, GROUND BLACK PEPPER

    In the skillet, over medium heat, heat [6 TB   BUTTER

- When it sizzles sauté the Potatoes until lightly browned. Then, with a spatula flatten them
  into a cake. Reduce heat to medium low, cook slowly until underside is crispy golden brown.
- Pass under preheated broiler until the top is golden brown.
- To unmold from a regular oven-proof skillet, run a thin knife around the Rösti. Slide them onto
  a plate. Place a serving platter on top and invert.

SPANISH TORTILLA DE PATATA   Potato Omelet   *Serves 6 to 8*

The Spanish Tortilla de Patata has the appearance of a cake. It is a compact Omelet about 1-inch thick and has no relationship with the Mexican flat tortillas.

Peel, wash, dry and cut in half lengthwise [2 lbs   YUKON GOLD POTATOES

Slice crosswise, paper thin with a mandolin.

After peeling weigh [10 oz   ONION   slice 1/4-inch thick and
                                             chop, not too finely.
In a 10-inch skillet, medium high heat, heat [1/2-cup   EXTRA-VIRGIN OLIVE OIL
      When a light haze forms, add [the Potatoes

Stir with wooden spoon to coat well with Oil.
Keep stirring, sauté, breaking randomly the
Potatoes.
                When they begin to color, add [the Onions
                         Sprinkle with a [1/4-tp   SALT, GROUND BLACK PEPPER
- Reduce heat to medium.
  Sauté, breaking up the Potatoes, until tender
  and cooked. Stir often.
- To prevent sticking, add a little Oil if needed.
- When cooked, add Salt to taste.
- Transfer to a sieve for 30 minutes to cool
  and drain excess Oil.
                In a large bowl beat [6 large   EGGS
                                      [1/4-tp   SALT, GROUND BLACK PEPPER
When blended, mix in the POTATOES.
Let set for 10 minutes. Preheat broiler.

In an 8-inch skillet, that can go under the
         broiler, over medium heat, heat [3 TB   EXTRA-VIRGIN OLIVE OIL

- Swirl the Oil to coat base and sides of skillet. When a light haze forms pour in the MIXTURE.
- Spread it evenly with a spatula, sinking the spatula randomly into the Mixture to even it out.
- Reduce heat to medium low, cover the skillet and let the Omelet take its time to cook.
- Once or twice uncover and run a spatula around to loosen the edges, gently shake the skillet.
- When the Tortilla is almost set, the underside should be golden brown. The top still creamy.

Method 1   - At this point, pass under the broiler to brown and finish cooking the top.
                - Run a thin spatula around and shake the skillet gently to loosen the Tortilla.
                - Cool for 5 minutes. Slide the Tortilla onto a plate. Top with a platter, invert.

Method 2   - It doesn't need an oven-proof skillet. Use a regular 8-inch nonstick skillet.
                - Before starting to cook the Tortilla, place a larger skillet on another burner.
                - Dab the bottom with Extra-Virgin Olive Oil. Turn on heat to low.
                - When the underside of the Tortilla is golden brown, the top not quite set,
                  place the larger skillet upside down on top, invert the skillets.
                - Over low heat cook the Tortilla in the larger skillet, until the underside is set.
                - Shake the skillet gently to loosen the Tortilla. Slide it onto a platter.

Serve   - At room temperature. As an appetizer or a light lunch with a Salad.
                - Or cut into bite-size squares, stick with toothpicks, serve as an hors-d'oeuvre.
                - Add to the squares Smoked Salmon, Ham or Sausage, and a sliver of Pickle.
                - Wrap in foil and refrigerate Leftovers. Cold it is delicious.

376

RADICCHIO and PASTA - EXCELSIOR   *Appetizer, serves 2*

Trim, wash and blanch for 9 minutes	[6-to-8	BRUSSELS SPROUTS large to medium

Drain. Let cool. Chop coarsely in processor.

In a large nonstick skillet, medium heat, heat	[4 TB	EXTRA-VIRGIN OLIVE OIL
When a light haze forms, sauté	[2 cloves	GARLIC thinly sliced into slivers
When the Garlic turns golden add	[1-1/2 cups	RADICCHIO shredded

Stir to coat the Radicchio with Oil. Cover the
skillet, reduce heat to medium low, cook until
soft and wilted, not longer.

Mix in	[	the chopped Brussels Sprouts
	[to taste	SALT, GROUND BLACK PEPPER
Stir to heat the Sprouts, turn off heat, add	[2 TB	PINE NUTS toasted
Toss into the skillet with the Mixture	[3 oz	hot SPAGHETTINI
Serve immediately, with, on the side	[grated	PARMESAN

SPINACH - *Preparation and Blanching*   See - BLANCHING

TRIM   - Remove hard stems, wilted leaves. Wash under running cold water. Drain.

BLANCH   - Blanch until desired doneness. Completely cooked: blanch for 5 minutes.
          - Drain in a colander and pass under running cold water to stop the cooking.
          - Drain again. Squeeze gently to remove excess water. Pat dry in a dish towel.

NOTE 1 lb fresh Spinach cooked = about 1 cup. A 10 oz-pkg Frozen Spinach cooked = 1 cup.

CREAMED SPINACH   *Serves 2*

1.	In a nonstick skillet, medium heat, heat	[1 TB	BUTTER
	When it sizzles, add	[1-to-1-1/4 cups	SPINACH cooked

Stir for 2 or 3 minutes, until all moisture has evaporated, then mix in	[3 TB	HEAVY CREAM or more
Stir until the Mixture thickens, add	[a dash	NUTMEG, SALT, PEPPER
	[optional	PARMESAN grated, then add Salt

2.	Sauté in the Butter	[1/4-cup	ONION finely chopped
	When Onion begins to color, add	[1-to-1-1/4 cups	SPINACH cooked

Continue as above.

3.	See "SAUCES". Prepare a	[1/2-cup	VELOUTÉ WHITE SAUCE
	Stir the SAUCE into	[2 cups	SPINACH cooked
	Add	[to taste	PARMESAN grated
		[	NUTMEG, SALT, PEPPER

4. Sauté a 1/2-cup Onion, as in 2. Add 2 cups Spinach, then add White Sauce and Seasonings.

CREAMED SPINACH and PASTA - BAKED   *Serves 4 to 6*

Cook in salted boiling water, 6 minutes only [5 oz   PENNE   drain, let cool

Cook following package directions [(2) 10 oz-pkg FROZEN CREAMED SPINACH
When hot, add [2 TB   BUTTER
Mix in a bowl Pasta, Spinach.
Beat [2   EGGS
[1cup   MILK
When blended, stir in [1/2-cup   PARMESAN grated
[1/2-cup   SWISS coarse-grated
[to taste   GROUND BLACK PEPPER, SALT

Stir the EGG MIXTURE into PASTA/SPINACH.
Pour it into sprayed 8 x 8 baking-dish.
Mix [4 TB   BREADCRUMBS
with [2 TB each   PARMESAN and SWISS

Sprinkle Breadcrumbs over Pasta. Dot with [1 TB   BUTTER split in half, diced small

Bake 30 minutes in oven preheated to 375°. Top should be lightly browned. Serve immediately.

SPINACH - FILLING for CRÊPES   *Fillings yield about 2-1/4 cups*

FILLING I   Mix in processor:

[1-1/2 cups   CREAMED SPINACH drain if runny
[3 oz   GARLIC HERB BOURSIN CHEESE
[1/4-cup   MOZZARELLA coarse-grated
[1/4-cup   PARMESAN grated
[to taste   GROUND BLACK PEPPER

Optional, serve with Crêpes [ALFREDO SAUCE

FILLING II   Mix in processor:

[1-1/2 cups   CREAMED SPINACH
[3 oz   PHILADELPHIA CHEESE
[3 oz   FETA CHEESE
[2 TB   SWISS CHEESE
[1 TB   FRESH DILL,   PEPPER

No Sauce is needed for these Crêpes.

SPINACH MOUSSE   *Serves 2. Yields about 2 cups.*

Steam for 6 minutes in microwave a [10 oz-pkg   FROZEN LEAF SPINACH

In a nonstick skillet, over medium heat, heat [1 TB   BUTTER
When it sizzles, sauté [1/2-cup   ONION slice 1/4-inch thick, chop
When Onion begins to color, add [the Spinach

Stir for 1 minute, spread on a plate to cool.

Combine in processor the SPINACH [1 large   EGG
[3 oz   FETA CHEESE cut up
[2 oz   PHILADELPHIA CHEESE   cut up
[1/4-cup   PARMESAN grated
[1/8-tpNUTMEG, 1/4-tp BLACK PEPPER

- Process until smooth: 3 or 4 quick pulses.
- In a 2-to-3-cup BUTTERED casserole pour the MIXTURE. Bake in 375° oven for 30 minutes.
- With a skewer test doneness. If it comes out clean, the Mousse is ready. If sticky, bake longer.
- *Option*: cover the surface with wax paper, refrigerate. Bring to room temperature, bake.

SPINACH MOUSSE with CUSTARD TOPPING *Variation*

Pour SPINACH MIXTURE (previous recipe) into 3-cup casserole.
Cover with wax paper. Refrigerate overnight.
Bring to room temperature before adding the Custard and baking.

See "SAUCES. Prepare	[1 cup	VELOUTÉ WHITE SAUCE
with	[1/2-cup	MILK + 1/2-cup LIGHT CREAM

Remove from heat.

Beat in a small bowl	[1	EGG
	[a dash	NUTMEG grated

- Beat into the Egg 1 TB of hot Sauce.
- Repeat. Then whisk the Egg into the Sauce.
- Over low heat, stir until Egg is incorporated.

Stir in until melted	[1/4-cup	PARMESAN grated
	[to taste	SALT and WHITE PEPPER

Let the Sauce cool.

Pour it over the Mousse and sprinkle with	[1/4-cup	PARMESAN grated
and	[2 TB	PLAIN BREADCRUMBS

Slide into oven preheated to 375°.
Bake for 30 minutes. Test doneness. Pass under the broiler to golden brown the top.

SPINACH QUICHE with FETA CHEESE QUICHE - "BASIC RECIPES"

Steam separately for 6 minutes in microwave	[2-pkg	FROZEN LEAF SPINACH
		(10 oz each)

With a knife and fork chop it up coarsely.

In a nonstick skillet, over medium heat, heat	[1-1/2 TB	BUTTER
When it sizzles, sauté	[2/3-cup	ONION finely chopped
When Onion is translucent add	[1-2/3 cups	of the Spinach
Stir until all moisture has evaporated. Add	[to taste	SALT, GROUND BLACK PEPPER

Preheat oven to 375°.

In a large bowl, beat	[3	EGGS
Brush with a little of the beaten EGGS a	[9-inch	FROZEN UNCOOKED PIE SHELL

Set in the oven for 2 minutes only. Let cool.

Whisk into the Eggs	[3/4-cup	HEAVY CREAM + 1/4-cup MILK
	[1 oz	GRUYERE CHEESE grated
	[3 oz	FETA CHEESE crumbled
	[1/2-tp	DRIED OREGANO crumbled
	[1/2-tp	DRIED MINT crumbled
Add	[	the Spinach

<u>To assemble</u> - Place the Pie Shell in its foil pan on a cookie sheet. Ladle into it the CUSTARD.

<u>To bake</u> - Slide the Quiche into the oven. Reduce heat to 350°.
Bake as per "BASIC RECIPES".

SPINACH and RICE   *Serves 4 as a side dish*

Microwave following package directions	[10 oz-pkg	FROZEN CHOPPED SPINACH
In a heavy saucepan, over medium heat, heat	[2 TB	VEGETABLE OIL
When a light haze forms, sauté	[1/2-cup	ONION finely chopped
When Onion is translucent, add	[1 clove	GARLIC mashed and minced
When Onion begins to color, add	[	the Spinach
Sprinkle	[1/4-tp	GROUND CORIANDER
Stir for 1 minute and add	[1/2-tp	LEMON JUICE
	[a pinch	SALT, GROUND BLACK PEPPER
Stir and add	[1 cup	UNCOOKED WHITE RICE

Mix the Rice with the Spinach.

Then add	[	BROTH as per Rice package
	[1/4-tp	SALT (or as per Broth saltiness)

Bring to a boil then reduce heat to low.
Cover, simmer until the Rice is done.

Mix in	[1/4-cup	PINE NUTS toasted

Serve with   Meatballs and plain Yogurt. Roasted Chicken, grilled Meats or Fish.

TOMATOES - Peeling

1.   - Make an incision in the shape of an X on the base of the Tomatoes.
2.   - Bring to a boil a pot of water. Plunge the Tomatoes in it for 10-to-20 seconds,
         or longer, depending on their skin toughness. Remove with a slotted spoon.
      - Or insert a fork at the top of Tomatoes and plunge into the boiling water.
3.   - Peel them from the spot where the skin has separated at the X incision.

GAZPACHO   Cold Soup   (Spain)   *Yields 5-to-5-1/2 cups*

In a large bowl combine:

[1-1/2 lbs	TOMATOES peel, seed, coarsely chop
[1	KIRBY CUCUMBER peel, coarsely chop
[1 medium	GREEN BELL PEPPER coarsely chop
[2 oz	YELLOW ONION coarsely chop
[2 cups	WATER
[1/4-cup	EXTRA VIRGIN OLIVE OIL
[1 TB	SHERRY VINEGAR
[1 TB	LEMON JUICE
[1 or 2	SMALL GARLIC CLOVES optional

The GARNISHES

Serve in separate dishes:

[CELERY   finely diced
[RADISHES   finely diced
[GREEN BELL PEPPER   finely diced
[KIRBY CUCUMBER peel, finely dice

In a bowl, soak for 2 or 3 minutes in 2 TB WATER:

[1-1/2 oz   STALE WHITE BREAD weighed after removing the Crust

- Squeeze out moisture from the Bread and add it to the VEGETABLES.
- Liquefy in a blender until smooth. Proceed in two batches. Strain through a sieve.
- Add to taste SALT, BLACK PEPPER, LEMON JUICE
- Cover and refrigerate.
- Serve the Gazpacho in chilled bowls. Diners top their Soup with the Garnishes.

380

SPEEDY GAZPACHO

Combine in a blender:

[2 cans   V 8 or TOMATO JUICE
[2 tp   EXTRA-VIRGIN OLIVE OIL
[1/2-tp   SHERRY VINEGAR or to taste
[a pinch   GARLIC POWDER optional
[to taste   SALT, BLACK PEPPER, LEMON JUICE

Soak as in previous recipe, in 1 TB WATER

[1 slice   STALE WHITE BREAD crust removed

- Squeeze out moisture. Add the Bread and blend until smooth.
- Serve with Garnishes as in previous recipe.

TOMATO SNACK TOASTS

AEGEAN   Mix to taste:

[TOMATOES   seeded and diced
[EXTRA-VIRGIN OLIVE OIL   a little
[DRIED OREGANO or FRESH PARSLEY
[GROUND BLACK PEPPER
[FETA CHEESE, or crumble it after spreading the Tomatoes.

Toast slices of [COUNTRY BREAD   3/4-inch thick
Rub them with a [GARLIC CLOVE

VARIATION - Add to the Tomato Mixture:

[ANCHOVY FILLETS   chopped

BRUSCHETTA

CROSTINI and BRUSCHETTA see "BASIC RECIPES"

This popular Italian snack served all day in bars and cafés, is also a late evening comfort food.

Prepare the BRUSCHETTA with [CIABATTA or any other BREAD
Optional: rub the toasted Bread with a [GARLIC CLOVE

Version 1   Mix in a bowl [RIPE TOMATOES   seeded and diced
                                    [FRESH BASIL   finely chopped
When ready to serve, moisten with [EXTRA-VIRGIN OLIVE OIL
                                      [SALT and GROUND BLACK PEPPER
Spread the hot Toast with the Tomatoes.

Version 2   Toast the Bread. Top with [MOZZARELLA   sliced

Broil until melted. Top with the Tomatoes

Version 3   Mix into the Tomatoes chopped [ANCHOVIES, SARDINES, SMOKED SALMON,
                                      [PROSCIUTTO, HAM, CHICKEN.

PARISIENNE

Cut in half lengthwise [2 large   PLUM TOMATOES   seed them
Place them in a pan cut side up, sprinkle with [BLACK PEPPER and NUTMEG
Top with [plenty of   BREADCRUMBS   seasoned
Dot with [tidbits of   BUTTER
Broil to brown Breadcrumbs.

Meanwhile brown in 1 TB BUTTER [1/2-cup   ONION sliced, coarsely chopped
                                    [sprinkle   SALT, GROUND BLACK PEPPER
Chop the Tomatoes, tilt the plate, rid of fluid.
Mix in the Onions and [1/4-cup   GOAT CHEESE   tidbits
Mixture yields 1 cup.
Spread the Mixture on [toasted   BAGUETTE   slant-cut

TOMATOES - STUFFED with RICE   À la Grecque   *Serves 4*

Prepare 4 TOMATOES   Ripe but not soft, medium large, the regular kind. Their skin is more resistant and matches Bell Pepper cooking time when baked together.

1.   Remove stems and leaves. Wash and dry the Tomatoes with paper towels.
2.   Cut a circle around their tops, about 2-inches in diameter. Remove caps, set aside.
3.   Scoop out pulp, seeds, membranes with a grapefruit spoon, drop them into a blender.
4.   Place Tomatoes upside down on paper towels to drain.

BLENDER LIQUID   Add to pulp in blender   [enough   WATER to obtain 1-1/3 cups
                                              [1/8-tp   SALT, a twist BLACK PEPPER
Blend to liquefy.

The STUFFING   In an 8-inch nonstick skillet,
                    over medium heat, heat   [1/4-cup   EXTRA-VIRGIN OLIVE OIL
         When a light haze forms, sauté   [1/2-cup   ONION   finely chopped
When Onion begins to turn golden, add   [1/2-cup   LONG GRAIN WHITE RICE
                                                            Use "Converted" for this recipe.

      Stir until the grains glisten and add   [2/3-cup of   BLENDER LIQUID
                                              [2 TB   CURRANTS or GOLDEN RAISINS
                                              [1-1/2 TB   PINE NUTS   toasted

Bring LIQUID to a boil, cover and simmer
until it has been absorbed. Turn off heat.

   The Rice will be partially cooked. Stir into it   [2 TB of the   BLENDER LIQUID
                       Taste, adjust   [SALT, GROUND BLACK PEPPER
                   and stir in   [3 TB   FRESH DILL   snipped
Preheat oven to 375°.

The TOMATOES   In a sprayed baking dish
                   fit in snugly the   [4 prepared   TOMATOES
                          Put a   [1/4-tp of   GRANULATED SUGAR in each one

- Fill the Tomatoes, 3/4-full, with STUFFING,
  leaving space for the Rice to expand.
- Place caps over the Tomatoes.
                          Drizzle   [1/2-TB   EXTRA-VIRGIN OLIVE OIL over
                                                       each Tomato

BLENDER LIQUID   Add to remaining Liquid   [enough   WATER to obtain 1 cup
                                               [1-1/2 tp   TOMATO PASTE
                                               [1 TB   EXTRA-VIRGIN OLIVE OIL
                                               [1/8-tp   SALT, GROUND BLACK PEPPER
Blend to liquefy.
Pour slowly the Liquid over the Tomatoes.

                   Sprinkle over their tops   [BREADCRUMBS

BAKE   - From 40-to-45 minutes. Baste after 20 minutes. Then once again 15 minutes later.

Serve   - At room temperature. To heat in a warm oven, keep covered with foil.

NOTE   - This dish can be prepared ahead of time. Cool, cover with foil, refrigerate overnight.
             Best the next day. This is an excellent buffet dish. For 8 Tomatoes, double amounts.

TOMATOES and BELL PEPPERS - STUFFED with RICE

Prepare 4 TOMATOES as in previous recipe and add their Pulp to blender.

Prepare 4 GREEN BELL PEPPERS   Of a rather medium size. Shaped to sit upright and matching more or less the size of the Tomatoes.

1.   Wash, dry them. Cut a circle at a 1/2-inch around the cap. Pull it out, cut off the stem.
2.   Cut away the caps' inside core, so they can sit flat on the Stuffing. Set them aside.
3.   Remove all seeds. Use a grapefruit spoon to de-rib the Bell Peppers.
4.   Rinse inside under running cold water. Turn Peppers upside down on paper towels to drain.

BLENDER LIQUID   Add to the Tomato pulp   [1 medium   TOMATO   peeled and chopped
and   [enough   WATER to obtain 3 cups
[1/4-tp   SALT, GROUND BLACK PEPPER
Blend to liquefy.

The STUFFING   In a large nonstick skillet,
over medium heat, heat   [1/2-cup   EXTRA-VIRGIN OLIVE OIL
When a light haze forms, sauté   [1 cup   ONION   finely chopped
When Onion begins to turn golden add   [1-1/8 cups   LONG GRAIN WHITE RICE
Use "Converted" for this recipe.

Stir until the grains glisten and add   [2 cups of   BLENDER LIQUID
[4 TB   GOLDEN RAISINS
[3 TB   PINE NUTS   toasted

Bring to a boil, cover, simmer until Liquid has been absorbed. Turn off heat.

The Rice will be partially cooked. Stir into it   [1/3-cup of   BLENDER LIQUID
Stir in   [4 TB   FRESH DILL   snipped
[2 TB   PARSLEY   finely chopped

BLENDER LIQUID   Add to remaining Liquid   [enough   WATER   to obtain 2 cups
[2 TB   TOMATO PASTE
[2 TB   EXTRA-VIRGIN OLIVE OIL
[1/4-tp   SALT, GROUND BLACK PEPPER
Blend to liquefy.

To ASSEMBLE   In a sprayed baking dish
fit in snugly on one side the   [prepared   BELL PEPPERS
On the other the   [prepared   TOMATOES
Put into each Tomato a   [1/4-tp   GRANULATED SUGAR

Fill Tomatoes and Peppers with the STUFFING, 3/4-full, leaving space for the Rice to expand.

Place caps on Tomatoes and Peppers. Drizzle   [1/2-TB   EXTRA-VIRGIN OLIVE OIL over
each one

Pour slowly the BLENDER LIQUID over the Tomatoes and Peppers, then sprinkle on top   [BREADCRUMBS

- Bake in oven preheated to 350° for 1-1/2 hours, or until Vegetables are tender and browned.
- Baste every 20-to-25 minutes.
- This dish can be prepared ahead of time. Cool, cover with foil refrigerate overnight.

To serve   -   Heat, covered with foil, in a warm oven. Or serve at room temperature.

ZUCCHINI - FRITTATA

Serves 4 to 6　　FRITTATA - "BASIC RECIPES"

Cut off rough green tops and root ends of [2 medium　LEEKS keep white and light green
　　　　　　　　　　　　　　　　　　　　　　　　　　　　　parts only

Separate sections, wash thoroughly, dry in a
dish towel. Slice thinly.

Wash, pat dry, cut off ends and slice into
　　　　　　　　1/4-inch thick rounds [3 medium　ZUCCHINI light green, 5 oz each

In nonstick skillet, over medium heat, heat [1 TB　　BUTTER + 1/2-tp VEGETABLE OIL
When it sizzles, sauté until limp and tender [　　　　the Leeks

Remove with slotted spoon, set aside to cool.

Add to the skillet and heat over medium heat [2 TB　VEGETABLE OIL
　　　When hot, sauté to light golden brown [　　　the Zucchini
　　　　　　　　　　　　　　Sprinkle with [　　　SALT, GROUND BLACK PEPPER
Spread them in a sieve to drain.

In a large bowl whisk [5 large　EGGS
　　　　　　　　　　[　　　　　GROUND BLACK PEPPER
When well blended, whisk in [1/2-cup　PARMESAN grated
　　　　　　　　　　　　[2 TB　　SWISS CHEESE coarse-grated
　　　　　　　　Stir in [　　　　the Leeks and Zucchini
　　　　　　　　　　　[2 TB　　PARSLEY finely chopped
In a 10-inch skillet that can go under the
　broiler, over medium heat, heat [2 TB　BUTTER + 1 TB VEGETABLE OIL

- When it sizzles, pour in the EGG MIXTURE. Spread it evenly with a spatula. Reduce heat to low.
- Cook and pass the Frittata under preheated broiler following directions in "BASIC RECIPES".

ZUCCHINI - MOUSSE

Serves 4 to 6

Wash, dry, and slice thinly [1-1/2 lbs　ZUCCHINI light green color

In a large nonstick skillet heat [3 TB　BUTTER + 1 tp VEGETABLE OIL
　　　　　When it sizzles, add [4 oz　ONION slice 1/4-inch thick, dice
Stir the Onion in the Butter and add [　　the sliced Zucchini
Stir Zucchini until wilted and lightly browned [sprinkle　SALT, GROUND BLACK PEPPER

Preheat oven to 375°.

Purée the Zucchini in processor, then add [3　　EGGS
　Process until smooth. Add and process [2 oz　GARLIC HERB BOURSIN CHEESE
　　　　　　　　　　　　　　　　[1/3-cup　SWISS CHEESE coarse-grated
　　　　　　　　　　　　　　　　[1/4-cup　PARMESAN grated
　　　　　　　　　　　　　　　　[1/4-tp　SALT, GROUND BLACK PEPPER

Spray a 1-quart oven-proof casserole with [a mist of　COOKING SPRAY

- Pour ZUCCHINI MIXTURE into the casserole. Bake uncovered from 40-to-45 minutes.
- With a metal skewer test doneness. If clean, the Mousse is ready. If sticky, bake a little longer.
- Let the Mousse cool about 5 minutes. Serve hot.

ZUCCHINI - STUFFED with RICE   *Serves 4*

8 ZUCCHINI - of medium size. Fairly thick. Of a bright green color with no blemishes.
- Scrape lightly to remove any grit. Wash, dry and cut off the stem end.
- With a serrated corer remove the Pulp, leaving a 1/4-inch wall all around.
- Rinse inside under running cold water. Turn upside down on paper towels.
- Mash the PULP with a fork and set aside.

The BROTH   You will need   [1-1/2 cups   CHICKEN BROTH

The STUFFING   In a 6-inch nonstick skillet,

over medium heat, heat	[1/4-cup	EXTRA-VIRGIN OLIVE OIL
When a light haze forms, sauté	[1/2-cup	ONION finely chopped
When Onion is translucent, add	[1/2-cup	LONG GRAIN WHITE RICE Use "Converted" for this recipe.
Stir until the grains glisten and add	[2/3-cup	of the Broth
	[2 TB	GREEN ONION finely chopped

Bring the Broth to a boil. Cover and simmer
until it has been absorbed. Turn off heat.

The Rice will be partially cooked. Stir into it	[1/3-cup	of the Broth
	[1/2-cup	mashed Zucchini Pulp
	[1 TB	FRESH DILL snipped, or 1/4-tp DRIED
	[1/3-cup	PARMESAN grated
Adjust	[to taste	SALT, GROUND BLACK PEPPER

Flatten the Stuffing in the skillet.

The SAUCE

In a blender mix	[2 cups	MARINARA SAUCE ready-made
with	[	the remaining 1/2-cup of Broth
	[1 TB	EXTRA-VIRGIN OLIVE OIL
	[1 TB	FRESH DILL snipped, or 1/4-tp DRIED
	[adjust	SALT, GROUND BLACK PEPPER
You will need	[2 more cups	MARINARA SAUCE

STUFFING the ZUCCHINI - Divide STUFFING into quarters, like a pie: 2 Zucchini per quarter.

With a regular teaspoon stuff the Zucchini, leaving 1-inch of empty space at the top, to allow the
Rice to expand. With the end of a wooden spoon push down the Stuffing. Do not pack it too tight.

ASSEMBLING the DISH   -   Spray a baking dish in which the Zucchini fit snugly in one layer.

- Lay the Zucchini in it. Pour over the SAUCE to immerse them only to the level where
  the Stuffing begins. Avoid the Sauce running into the Stuffing, it will draw it out.
- Reserve remaining Sauce. During the cooking the Zucchini will give off some liquid.
- Cover tightly with foil. Pierce the foil once in each corner with a fork.

BAKE - In oven preheated to 375° for about 1-1/2 hours, or until Zucchini are fork tender.
- About 45 minutes into the cooking, lift foil, baste the Zucchini. Add a little more
  Sauce if needed. Cover again with foil and continue baking.

SERVE - Remove the foil and let the Zucchini cool 5-to-10 minutes.
- Pour a little Marinara Sauce over the Zucchini, serve the rest on the side.

VEGETABLES - MISCELLANEOUS

BAKED COUNTRY STYLE

- Combine Vegetables which take the same amount of time to cook. Wash, trim and dry.

- Mix the Vegetables into a sprayed baking-pan/dish. Drizzle with Extra-Virgin Olive Oil.
- Rub the Oil into the Vegetables. To taste, sprinkle with Spices, Rosemary, Thyme, other.

- Bake in oven preheated to 450° for 20 minutes, then reduce heat to 375° and bake for about 1 hour, or longer, until the Vegetables are tender, yet crunchy and golden brown.

- Half-way through, add Vegetables which take less time to cook, such as: ASPARAGUS, CAMPARI TOMATOES, whole MUSHROOMS.

- When done, add Salt to taste. Serve hot or at room temperature.

Combination I	*Amounts to taste*	**Combination II**
[BABY EGGPLANT	- slice crosswise 1/3-inch thick	[BROCCOLI FLORETS
[BELL PEPPERS	- multicolor, small, quartered	[CAULIFLOWER FLORETS
[SMALL ARTICHOKES	- remove outer leaves, cut points stems trimmed, quartered	[BRUSSELS SPROUTS
		[NEW POTATOES cut in half
[FENNEL	- trimmed, halved lengthwise cut into wedges a 1/2-inch thick	[GARLIC CLOVES
[CIPOLLINI ONIONS	- peeled	Half-way through add:
[GARLIC CLOVES	- whole	[TOMATOES, MUSHROOMS

For a PASTA PRIMAVERA - BASIC

- Blanch the Vegetables *al dente*, separately or together (according to kind). Dice them.
- In a nonstick skillet sauté Onion or Shallot in Butter or Extra-Virgin Olive Oil. Optional: Garlic.
- When it begins to color, add the Vegetables. Sauté to barely brown. Add Salt and Pepper.
- Toss into skillet the cooked Pasta with the Vegetables. Optional: drizzle Extra-Virgin Olive Oil.
- Or moisten with Light Cream or Tomato Sauce. Add to taste: grated Parmesan.

For a RISOTTO PRIMAVERA - BASIC   RISOTTO - "BASIC RECIPES"

THE BROTH	- Tomato Sauce can be mixed in it. Or stirred in, when the Risotto is ready.
Method 1.	- In a nonstick skillet sauté the Onion or Shallot. When translucent, add the diced Vegetables. Sauté until tender and slightly browned. Set aside. - Cook the Risotto. Before the last cup of Broth, add the Vegetables and Juices.
Method 2.	- Dice the Vegetables. Put them in a strainer. Plunge it into boiling water. - Blanch the Vegetables until firm and crunchy. Drain. - Sauté Onion or Shallot in Butter/Oil. Add the Vegetables. - Sauté the Vegetables for 2 or 3 minutes. Add the Rice.
Method 3.	- Blanch the Vegetables as in Method 2. Add them gradually as you cook the Risotto. Add frozen thawed Green Peas before adding the last cup of Broth.

A MINESTRONE for ALL SEASONS   *Serves 4*

Minestra in Italian means soup, Minestrone, a big soup. This thick Vegetable Soup with no "clear" Broth, includes Beans as well as Potatoes.

- Wash thoroughly all the Vegetables, trim, pare, peel, wash again if needed. Dry in a towel.
- Vegetables which take longer to cook go into the pot first. Do not brown the sautéed Vegetables.

In a stockpot, over medium heat, heat	[3 TB	BUTTER
	[3 TB	EXTRA-VIRGIN OLIVE OIL
When it sizzles, sauté	[1/2-cup	ONION slice 1/4-inch thick, chop
When translucent, add	[1 cup	CARROTS diced
Sauté for 3 minutes then add	[1-1/2 cups	POTATOES diced
Sauté for 3 minutes, then add	[1/2-cup	CELERY
and	[1 cup	ZUCCHINI diced
	[1/2-cup	BRUSSELS SPROUTS quartered
Stir for 3 minutes then add	[3 cups	CHICKEN or BEEF BROTH
Bring to a boil, then add	[1/2-cup	DICED TOMATOES canned, with their Liquid
	[2-inch piece	PARMESAN RIND
	[to taste	BLACK PEPPER, SALT if needed

- Bring to a boil. Cover, reduce heat to low, simmer for 1-1/4 hours.
- Stir occasionally. If it gets too thick add a little Broth.

After 1-1/4 hours add	[1 cup	CANNELLINI BEANS canned, rinsed, drained
	[1/2-cup	FROZEN PEAS thawed, drained
Cover, continue to simmer 15 minutes, then	[adjust	Seasonings
Serve in a tureen and sprinkle with	[2 or 3 TB	PARSLEY or BASIL finely chopped
On the side	[grated	PARMESAN, CRUSTY BREAD

MINESTRONE alla GENOVESE   Before serving stir in to taste 3 or 4 TB PESTO SAUCE.

MORE VEGETABLES FOR MINESTRONE

BEETS	CABBAGE	CORN	GREEN BEANS	MUSHROOMS	SQUASH
BROCCOLI	CAULIFLOWER	GARBANZOS	LEEKS	PARSNIPS	TURNIPS

MINESTRONE with ETHNIC FLAVORS   *As above, omit Parmesan.*

CARIBBEAN   Onions, Carrots, Sweet Potatoes, Green Beans, Celery, Squash, black/red Beans, Pimientos, Chilies. Sprinkle with Cilantro. Add diced Avocado before serving.

MEXICAN   Onions, Carrots, Broccoli, Celery, Parsnips, Corn, Garbanzos, Chilies, Jalapeños. Sprinkle with Cilantro and crumbled Tortilla Chips.

IBERIAN   Season the Broth with Saffron. Before serving add diced cooked Chorizo.

RUSSIAN   Onions, Beets, Potatoes, Green Beans, Squash, Celery, Turnips, White Beans, Pearl Barley. Sprinkle with Dill. Optional: a dollop of Sour Cream or Plain Yogurt.

VEGETABLE and FRUIT SALSAS

SALSAS   - Serve with cold Pork or Veal Roast, cold Chicken, Duck, Turkey.
                - Add to the SALSAS cold Seafood. Or toss them into Mixed Greens.
                - *Ingredient amounts are flexible, use them according to taste.*

DRESSINGS   - After blending adjust Seasonings. To avoid a watery Salsa or Salad, add a
                  <u>Salted</u> Dressing before serving. Stir it in gradually, you may not need all of it.

SALSA - ASIANA

Combine in a bowl:

[1 cup	PINK GRAPEFRUIT small chunks
[1 cup	LICHEES canned or fresh, cut in half
[1/2-cup	YELLOW RED PEPPER finely diced
[1/2-cup	SHELLED EDAMAME BEANS cooked
[2 TB	RED ONION finely diced
[2 TB	CILANTRO finely chopped
[to taste	GINGER grated

THE DRESSINGS
Blend

[4 TB	SESAME OIL	
[2 TB	SOY SAUCE	
[1 tp	LEMON JUICE	
[2 tp	MAYONNAISE	
[1/2-tp	MUSTARD mild/hot	
[1/4-tp	BROWN SUGAR	
[a pinch	GARLIC POWDER or	
[1/2-clove	GARLIC minced	

HAWAIIANA

[1 cup diced	PINEAPPLE, or use canned, drained
[1 cup	PAPAYA diced
[1/2-cup	GREEN BELL PEPPER finely diced
[1/2-cup	BLUE BERRIES
[2 TB	GREEN ONION very thinly sliced
[2 TB	CILANTRO finely chopped
[to taste	SWEET or HOT PIMIENTOS

Blend

[3 TB	SALAD OIL
[2 TB	MAYONNAISE
[2 tp	LEMON JUICE
[1/2-tp	HORSERADISH
[1 tp	LIGHT RUM
[1/4-tp	POPPY SEEDS

IBERIANA

[1 cup	CANTALOUP diced
[1 cup	ORANGE diced
[1/2-cup	ROASTED RED BELL PEPPERS cut into thin short strips
[1/2-cup	SPANISH or SWEET ONION chopped
[1/4-cup	RED RADISHES grated
[1/4-cup	PIMIENTO GREEN OLIVES chopped
[3 TB	FRESH BASIL finely chopped

Blend

[4 TB	EXTRA-VIRGIN OLIVE OIL
[3 TB	SHERRY VINEGAR
[1 TB	MAYONNAISE
[1 small	GARLIC CLOVE
[or a pinch	GARLIC POWDER
[1/4-tp	GROUND CUMIN
[a sprinkle	CAYENNE PEPPER

INDIANA

[1 cup	MANGO diced
[1 cup	HONEYDEW MELON diced
[1/2-cup	RED BELL PEPPER finely diced
[1/2-cup	CELERY thinly sliced
[1/4-cup	COCONUT shredded
[2 TB	RED ONION finely chopped
[2 TB	FRESH MINT finely chopped

Blend

[4 TB	SALAD OIL
[2 TB	MAYONNAISE
[1 TB	PLAIN YOGURT
[1 TB	LEMON JUICE
[1/4-tp	CURRY POWDER or more
[a pinch	GARLIC POWDER or Clove

TROPICANA

[1 cup	PAPAYA diced
[1 cup	AVOCADO diced, add before serving
[1/2-cup	CELERY finely diced
[4 TB	CRUSHED PINEAPPLE canned, drained
[2 or 3 TB	RED ONION finely chopped
[1 TB	CILANTRO finely chopped
[1 TB	CAPERS rinsed, drained, minced
[1/2-tp	POPPY SEEDS

Blend

[4 TB	EXTRA-VIRGIN OLIVE OIL
[3 TB	LIME or LEMON JUICE
[1 TB	MAYONNAISE
[1/4-tp	POPPY SEEDS
[1/8-tp	ALLSPICE
[1/8-tp	GROUND CINNAMON
[optional	HOT CHILI PEPPER minced

388

XV

FRUIT and CHEESE

"Say Cheese please."

Fruit and Cheese, with their sweet and salty contrasts, belong to a delicious world we often tend to bypass.

Crowning a heavy meal with Fruit, Cheese and thin Wafers, is still lighter than indulging in a calorie loaded dessert.

"Poets have been mysteriously silent on the subject of Cheese."

Gilbert K. Chesterton

"What a friend we have in cheeses!
For no food so subtly pleases ...."

William Cole

FRUIT and CHEESE

* NOTE

Omit the Apples. Use this recipe for a Cheese Soufflé.

APPLE - CRÊPES with BLUE CHEESE   CRÊPES - "BASIC RECIPES"

FILLING *for 8 Crêpes*   Peel, quarter, core [2 medium   APPLES halve quarters longwise,
                                                                            slice thinly crosswise

In a nonstick skillet, over medium heat, heat [1-1/2 TB   UNSALTED BUTTER
When it sizzles, stir in the APPLES, sprinkle [1 TB   LIGHT BROWN SUGAR
                                              [to taste   NUTMEG, BLACK PEPPER
When Apples are tender and browned, mix in [2 tp   CAPERS rinsed, dried, minced
                                            [2 TB   PINE NUTS toasted
Turn off heat.
                  With a fork, mash until smooth [3 oz   BLUE CHEESE crumbled
                                                  [2 TB   MASCARPONE + 1 tp MILK
- Spread CHEESE MIXTURE over the CRÊPES.
- Top with Apple Filling. Roll and place in a sprayed baking dish. Cover with foil. Refrigerate.
- Bring to room temperature. Warm in oven preheated to 250°.
- Serve as an Appetizer or Light Lunch with a Green Salad. Or to accompany Ham or Roast Pork.

APPLE - OMELET   *Serves 2*   OMELET - EGGS see "BASIC RECIPES"

THE FILLING   Peel, quarter lengthwise, core [1 medium   APPLE slice thinly crosswise

In a nonstick skillet, over medium heat, heat [2 TB   BUTTER salted or unsalted
                         When it sizzles, stir in [2 TB   ONION finely chopped
When Onion is translucent, add APPLES and [1 TB   BROWN SUGAR
                                            [to taste   NUTMEG or GROUND GINGER
                                            [optional   BRANDY to taste
When soft, lightly caramelized, turn off heat
                                and stir in [1/3-cup   CHEDDAR shredded
                                            [or 3 TB   BLUE CHEESE crumbled

THE OMELET   Beat with a fork [4 large   EGGS + 2 TB MILK
                                [1/8-tp   DRY MUSTARD, SALT, PEPPER

In a 6-1/2 to 7-inch nonstick skillet, heat [1-1/2 TB   BUTTER

When it sizzles, add the EGGS, cook the Omelet. Add the FILLING, as per "BASIC RECIPES".

APPLES in PHYLLO POCKETS   PHYLLO see "BASIC RECIPES"

THE APPLES Peel, slice into very thin wedges [GOLDEN APPLES as needed for pockets
                Place in a bowl, sprinkle with [GRANULATED SUGAR   a little
                              A few drops [LEMON JUICE
                                To taste [CHEDDAR coarse-grated

Cut out of paper a 5-inch square.   Butter [5 sheets   PHYLLO   stacked

- Use the paper square as a guide to cut the Phyllo into 6 squares.
- Place in the center, over a 3-inch square surface, the Apple wedges, 2 or 3 layers.
- Fold on top of the Apples the 4 corners of the square. Brush them with BUTTER.
- Lift pockets with a spatula onto a greased cookie sheet. Leave 1-inch in-between.
- Bake in oven preheated to 350° until puffed and golden.

APPLE and CHEESE SOUFFLÉ

SOUFFLÉ - "BASIC RECIPES"

APPLES	Peel, quarter, core, cut quarters		

APPLES Peel, quarter, core, cut quarters
crosswise into thin slices to obtain [2 cups   McINTOSH APPLES 2-to-2-1/2
Put them in a bowl and mix in [1 tp   LEMON JUICE

In a nonstick skillet, over medium heat, heat [2 TB   UNSALTED BUTTER
When it sizzles add the APPLES and sprinkle [1-1/2 TB   BROWN SUGAR
[a dash   NUTMEG   grated
Sauté Apples until lightly caramelized, add [2 TB   PINE NUTS   toasted
Turn off heat and mix in [2 TB   BLUE CHEESE   crumbled

EGGS Set out at room temperature [5   EGGS you need 5 Whites, 4 Yolks

SOUFFLÉ DISH 1-1/2 quarts   Rub it with [BUTTER   salted or unsalted
(or use 4 ramekins) Dust with [1-1/2 TB   PARMESAN   refrigerate the dish
(1-1/4 tp per ramekin)

BÉCHAMEL BASE Prepare a [CREAMY BÉCHAMEL ("SAUCES")

- When Béchamel thickens, remove from heat.
- Break 1 EGG, drop the WHITE into stainless
  steel bowl. The YOLK into the Béchamel.
- With a wire whisk beat it into the Sauce.
- Repeat with 3 more Yolks, one at a time.
- Return saucepan to stove. Over low heat
  stir 1 minute to bind the Eggs. Turn off heat.

CHEESE Stir into Béchamel until melted [1/2-cup   SWISS CHEESE   coarse-grated
(+ for later 1 TB, for ramekins 4 tp)

[2 TB   BLUE CHEESE   crumbled
[2 TB   PARMESAN,   to taste PEPPER
- Set aside to cool. Can be prepared ahead to
  this point. Cover the surface with wax paper.
- Warm barely before adding the EGG WHITES.

Preheat oven to 400°.
Spread on the bottom of the dish(es) the APPLES.

Add to the 4 EGG WHITES 1 EGG WHITE and [1/8-tp   CREAM of TARTAR

a) Beat the EGG WHITES until stiff and glossy, but not dry.
    - Add one ladle of WHITES to the BÉCHAMEL. Gently fold them in with a rubber spatula.
    - Then gently pour the BÉCHAMEL into remaining EGG WHITES.
    - Fold in with the spatula, scooping from the bottom towards the top, as you turn the bowl.
      Do not fold too much, it would keep the Soufflé from rising well. White spots do no harm.

b) Pour Mixture into Soufflé dish(es). Smooth the top. Sprinkle with reserved CHEESE.

c) Place on middle rack of oven. Immediately reduce heat to 375°. Bake for 25-to-30 minutes.
    - Less time for the ramekins. Do not open the oven door until the Soufflé is well puffed.
    - Test by inserting a thin knife or metal skewer. If it comes out clean, the Soufflé is ready.
      If not, cook 5 minutes longer. It should have a light brown crust with a creamy center.

NOTE - Omit the Apples. Serve as a Cheese Soufflé. Use 3/4-cup SWISS or mix with CHEDDAR.

393

APPLES with STILTON SPREAD   Hors-d'oeuvre

Mash in processor until smooth   [4 oz   STILTON   at room temperature
                                   [1-1/2 oz   UNSALTED BUTTER

Serve in a bowl or crock. Smooth the top,
cover with plastic wrap. Refrigerate.
Bring to room temperature before serving.

Just before serving   Peel, quarter and core   [APPLES   cut quarters into wedges

Surround the Stilton with the Apple wedges.
Add 2 or 3 butter knives.   Serve with   [PORT WINE

APRICOTS - BROILED   Dessert   *Serve with a Fruit Brandy or Champagne*

Place in a sprayed baking dish, cut side up   [canned   APRICOT HALVES   drained
                        Fill the cavities with [a chunk of   BRIE or CAMEMBERT
                            Sprinkle with   [chopped   SLIVERED ALMONDS   toasted
Pass under the broiler.
When the Cheese melts serve right away with [WAFERS

APRICOTS with FETA CHEESE   *Cheese Mixture yields about 1/3-cup*

Mash in processor until smooth   [1 oz   CREAM CHEESE room temperature
                           with [3 oz   FETA CHEESE   room temperature
                                 [1 TB   MILK
                                 [1/2-tp   DRIED MINT   crumbled
              Make a slit into   [pitted   DRIED PLUMP APRICOTS
          Stuff each APRICOT with [1 tp of   Feta Mixture
          Stick into Mixture   [PINE NUTS   toasted

Garnish a Salad with the Apricots. Any of   [ARUGULA, AVOCADO, BEETS, CELERY,
                                             [ENDIVE, FENNEL, FRISÉE, MUSHROOMS,
                                             [RADICCHIO, SPINACH, RED RADISH.

VARIATION   Substitute Feta with:
              GOAT CHEESE or BLUE CHEESE. Substitute Mint with FRESH BASIL.

DATES with BLUE CHEESE MOUSSE   *Dessert, serve with Kirsch or Grappa.*

Mash in processor until smooth: Slit and remove pits from:

[3 oz   BLUE CHEESE   [DRIED MEDJOOL DATES
[1 oz   MASCARPONE   Stuff with   [the Cheese Mousse
[1 TB   WHIPPING CREAM
[to taste   KIRSCH or GRAPPA   Substitute Dates with DRIED PLUMP FIGS.

DATES - BUTTERFLIED   *Dessert, serve with Brandy or Champagne.*

            Slit, pit and butterfly [DRIED MEDJOOL DATES or other kind
Lay the Dates in a baking dish. Top each with [BRIE, CAMEMBERT or PONT L'ÉVÊQUE
     Pass under the broiler. Sprinkle with [HAZELNUTS   toasted, chopped

FRUIT and CHEESE

To enjoy my Fruit and Cheese, I like to be seated at a table, with a plate, a knife, a fork, a napkin and a good glass of wine!

When the honorees are Fruit and Cheese, let's splurge and omit anything else on the menu. How about dinner for two on a TV evening, when cooking is not on the schedule?

Whether a buffet lunch, pre-theater dinner or post-theater supper, make it a Fruit and Cheese event, accompanied by 2 or 3 types of Wine, carefully selected to go with the Cheese.

The CHEESE   - Most important is its selection. Avoid the usual common variety.
             - Take your time to explore the world of Cheese, then make a choice.
             - Include mild and sharp flavors, and types from different countries of origin.
             - Combine soft and semi-hard Cheeses. Place a good knife by hard Cheese.
             - You may want to create name flags. Use bamboo skewers with fancy labels.

The FRUIT   Combine what is available in season with GRAPES and DRIED FRUIT.

Combine on platters a colorful mix of sliced [KIWI, MANGOES, MELON, ORANGES,
                                               [PAPAYA, PINEAPPLE, WATERMELON

                          Wedges of [APRICOTS, PLUMS, marinated PEACHES
             Serve in separate bowls [CHERRIES, RASPBERRIES, STRAWBERRIES

Fresh Apples and Pears oxidize. Serve [POACHED APPLES and PEARS   wedges
                                Add [LICHEE NUTS   canned, drained

The NUTS   -   Do not scatter them around the Fruit and Cheese. Present them in bowls.

The BREAD   -   A variety. Include crunchy, BAGUETTE, toasted BAGUETTE slices.

CRACKERS, WAFERS, BREAD STICKS   An assortment. Avoid the ones with Cheese.

FRUIT with CHEESE QUICHE   QUICHE see "BASIC RECIPES"

Preheat oven to 375°.
                    In a large bowl beat [3   EGGS
      Brush with a little of the beaten Eggs a [9-inch   FROZEN UNCOOKED PIE SHELL

Set in the oven for 2 minutes only. Let cool.

                    Whisk into the Eggs [3/4-cup   HEAVY CREAM + 1/4-cup MILK
                                         [1/4-tp   SALT
                                         [1/4-tp   DRY MUSTARD
                                         [a dash   NUTMEG   grated
                                         [3 oz   SWISS CHEESE   shredded
                                         [3 oz   CREAM CHEESE   tidbits
                                         [1 oz   PARMESAN grated

To assemble and bake   -   Place the Pie Shell in its foil on a cookie sheet. Pour in the CUSTARD.
                       -   Bake as per "BASIC RECIPES".   Serve at room temperature.

To serve top with: Apricots, Kiwis, Peaches, Pineapple, Blueberries, Raspberries, Strawberries.

PARMESAN BISCUITS

Knead with an electric mixer   [8 oz   FLOUR
  [8 oz   UNSALTED BUTTER   soft
  [8 oz   PARMESAN   grated
  [a pinch   SALT, PEPPER to taste

- When smooth, shape the Dough into a ball.
- Wrap in plastic wrap, refrigerate for 30 minutes. Spray a cookie sheet with COOKING SPRAY.
- On a floured pastry board, use a rolling pin to roll out the dough, about 1/4-inch thick.
- Cut out the Biscuits with a pastry wheel, or a cookie cutter dipped in Flour.
- Bake in oven preheated to 350° until golden. Let Biscuits cool completely. Store in cookie box.
- Serve with Fruit Salads and Compotes.

PEACH and CHEESE SOUFFLÉ

SOUFFLÉ - "BASIC RECIPES"

PEACHES   Peel, cut thin wedges to obtain   [2 cups   PEACHES or NECTARINES

Place the slices in a bowl and mix with   [2 tp   LEMON JUICE

In a nonstick skillet, over medium heat, heat   [1 TB   UNSALTED BUTTER
When it sizzles, add PEACHES and sprinkle   [1 TB   GRANULATED SUGAR
  [1 tp   MAPLE SYRUP
  [1 TB   BRANDY   or to taste

Sauté until Peaches are soft and syrupy.
Cover and set aside.

EGGS   Set out at room temperature   [5   EGGS you need 5 Whites, 4 Yolks

SOUFFLÉ DISH   1-1/2 quarts   Rub it with   [BUTTER
(or use 4 ramekins) Dust with   [1-1/2 TB   PARMESAN   refrigerate the dish
(1-1/4 tp per ramekin)

CHEESE   Mix in a bowl   [1/2-cup   SWISS CHEESE   coarse-grated
  [1/4-cup   SHARP CHEDDAR   coarse-grated
  [a dash   NUTMEG   grated

BÉCHAMEL BASE   Prepare a   [CREAMY BÉCHAMEL   ("SAUCES")

- When Béchamel thickens, remove from heat.
- Break 1 EGG. Drop the White into a stainless steel bowl. Drop the YOLK into the Béchamel.
- With a wire whisk beat it into the Sauce. Repeat with 3 more Egg Yolks, one at a time.
- Return saucepan to stove. Over low heat stir for 1 minute to bind the Eggs. Turn off heat.

- Gradually stir in until melted, the CHEESE MIXTURE.
- Set aside to cool. Can be prepared ahead to this point. Cover the surface with wax paper.
- Before adding the EGG WHITES warm barely, it must be tepid.

- Preheat oven to 400°. Set out soufflé dish(es).
- Spread on the bottom of the dish(es) the PEACHES.

Add to the 4 EGG WHITES 1 EGG WHITE and   [1/8-tp   CREAM of TARTAR

Follow the same directions as in APPLE and CHEESE SOUFFLÉ: from a) through c).

396

PEACH - CROUSTADES
Light Lunch   CROUSTADE - "SANDWICHES"

CHEDDAR   Place on cookie sheet [CROUSTADES
                        Top them with [RIPE PEACHES   peel, slice into wedges
                        Sprinkle with [WORCESTERSHIRE SAUCE
                          Cover with [SHARP CHEDDAR   shredded
Broil until the Cheese melts.

MOZZARELLA   Spread CROUSTADES with [DIJON or AMERICAN YELLOW MUSTARD
                   Lay on top wedges of [RIPE PEACHES or NECTARINES
                    Top with plenty of [MOZZARELLA   shredded
                        Sprinkle with [GROUND BLACK PEPPER
Broil until the Cheese melts.

PEAR - CROUSTADES
Light Lunch   *Serves 2*

MELTED CHEESE   Peel, quarter, core [1 large   PEAR cut quarters into 2 wedges

In a nonstick skillet, over medium heat, heat [1 TB   UNSALTED BUTTER
When it sizzles, stir in PEAR wedges, sprinkle [1-1/2 tp   GRANULATED SUGAR
                                        [a dash   NUTMEG   grated
                                        [sprinkle KIRSCH or PEAR BRANDY

Sauté the wedges until tender, golden brown.
Turn off heat. Cover.
                             Top [2   CROUSTADES   Challah or other
                            with [slices of BRIE, CAMEMBERT or CHEDDAR
Pass under the broiler until melted.

Top Croustades with the PEARS, sprinkle with [chopped   SLIVERED ALMONDS   toasted

ROQUEFORT   Mix in a blender [1/3-cup   LIGHT CREAM
                                    [1 oz   ROQUEFORT or BLUE CHEESE
                                    [2 tp   FRESH BASIL   finely chopped

Prepare as above PEARS and CROUSTADES,
        top with the Sauce and sprinkle [PECANS   chopped

PEAR - TARTLETS PARADISO
Serves 4   Mixture yields about 1 cup

                   Mix in processor [3 oz   CREAM CHEESE
                                [3 oz   BLUE CHEESE or GORGONZOLA
                                [4 leaves FRESH BASIL
              Transfer to a bowl and mix in [2 oz   MOZZARELLA   shredded

In a nonstick skillet, over medium heat, heat [2-1/2 TB   UNSALTED BUTTER
              When it sizzles, add, peeled [3 small   PEARS each cut into 8 wedges
                                [1 TB   GRANULATED SUGAR
Sauté until the Pears have softened.

Lay on cookie sheet, fill with Cheese Mixture [4   READY-MADE BAKED TARTLET SHELLS

Top with the PEAR wedges. Bake in oven preheated to 350° until the Cheese melts.

PINEAPPLE - GRILLED CHEESE OPEN-SANDWICH

Drain and cut in half [	CANNED PINEAPPLE SLICES or ripe fresh
Place on a cookie sheet [	RAISIN BREAD slices
Spread on them [	PREPARED HORSERADISH to taste
Top with [	Pineapple (3 half slices per Bread Slice)
Cover Pineapple with, per serving: 3 slices of [	CHEDDAR ready-packed
[	GROUND BLACK PEPPER

Pass under broiler until the Cheese has melted.

PINEAPPLE - TART with RICOTTA CHEESE   *Yields about 2-1/2 cups*

PIE FILLING

Mix in processor [	1 cup	RICOTTA CHEESE
[	3 oz	FETA CHEESE
[	(2) 8 oz-cans	CRUSHED PINEAPPLE drained

Spread the CHEESE MIXTURE in a [	9-inch	BAKED PIE SHELL or TARTLETS
Top with [	2 cups	FRESH FRUIT one kind or mixed
Brush with a [		FRUIT GLAZE see

"FRUIT DESSERTS"- TARTS and TARTLETS

PINEAPPLE - TARTLETS with CAMEMBERT

Drain [	CANNED PINEAPPLE SLICES
Mash with a little Pineapple Juice [	CREAM CHEESE until smooth to spread
To taste [	HORSERADISH prepared
Spread Cream Cheese into [	BAKED TARTLET SHELLS
Top it with a Pineapple slice. Top with [	sliced pieces of CAMEMBERT

Place in oven preheated to 350° until the Cheese has melted. Serve immediately.

TUTTI FRUTTI   *Serve with Cookies*

Version I   Combine in a bowl and refrigerate: Version II

Version I	Version II
[CANTALOUPE BALLS small size	[HONEYDEW BALLS small size
[HONEYDEW BALLS small size	[PEACHES or NECTARINES small chunks
[GREEN SEEDLESS GRAPES	[LEMON JUICE a little
[RAISINS soaked and drained	[BLUEBERRIES
[DRIED APRICOTS coarsely chopped	[DRIED FIGS coarsely chopped
[MEDJOOL DATES coarsely chopped	[CANDIED ORANGE PEEL diced

Before serving, toss in: Before serving, toss in:

[PECANS coarsely chopped	[PINE NUTS toasted
[BLUE CHEESE or ROQUEFORT crumbled	Diced [SMOKED MOZZARELLA or PROVOLONE

WATERMELON and FETA   *A delicious snack after a night on the town.*

A big favorite in Greece and the Middle East, where it is served at outdoor cafés.
Serve WATERMELON with FETA. Optional, sprinkle the Feta with fresh MINT LEAVES finely chopped.

398

XVI

FRUIT and FRUIT DESSERTS

FRUIT and FRUIT DESSERTS

401

FRUIT - BAKED

Yields Syrup for 2 lbs of Fruit

THE SYRUP | Boil until it thickens lightly | [1/4-cup | BROWN SUGAR + 3/4-cup WATER
| | [2 TB | MAPLE SYRUP or HONEY
| Optional, season to taste with | [any of | CINNAMON, GINGER, 5 CLOVES
| | [| BRANDY or RUM
| | | ORANGE or VANILLA EXTRACT

THE FRUIT
- Peel, core. Leave pits in whole Fruit.
- The Fruit can be halved or quartered. Lay it snugly in a baking dish. Pour over the Syrup. Bake in oven preheated to 375° until tender. Baste occasionally.

FRUIT - BAKED OMELET

Serves 6

In a large bowl whisk | [4 large | EGGS
| [1/2-cup | MILK + 1/2-cup LIGHT CREAM
| [4 TB | GRANULATED SUGAR
| [1 tp | VANILLA EXTRACT

Mix into the EGGS cut up Fruit, any of [3 cups APRICOTS, BANANAS, BERRIES, KIWIS, PEACHES, PINEAPPLE, CHERRIES pitted

Pour MIXTURE into a sprayed 8 x 8 oven-proof dish.
Bake in oven preheated to 350° until set in the center: about 25 minutes.
Serve at room temperature or cold, sprinkled with CONFECTIONERS' SUGAR. Cut into squares.

FRUIT - BASIC BAVAROISE

A molded Mousse   *Yields about 5-1/2 cups*

In a small bowl, sprinkle over 1/3-cup WATER | [2 TB | UNFLAVORED GELATINE POWDER
| | *(2 envelopes)*

In small saucepan, medium heat, bring to boil | [2/3-cup | WATER
| [1 cup | SUGAR

- Reduce heat to medium low. Let bubble just until it thickens. Stir in the Gelatine.
- Let cool completely.

Purée in processor | [1 lb | FRUIT
Add | [| the Gelatine Syrup, pulse again

In chilled bowl, with electric beater, whip stiff | [1 cup | chilled WHIPPING CREAM

- Fold PURÉE into the CREAM. Pour into a mold, refrigerate until set.
- To unmold, run a thin knife around the Bavaroise. Top with a platter, tap the mold on the counter and invert. Garnish with Fruit. Refrigerate until ready to serve.

FRUIT - CHARLOTTE   A Bavaroise surrounded with Lady Fingers

- The Charlotte mold is scalloped around the rim. Each scallop slants down into a half-cone.
- Each LADY FINGER fits into a half-cone, its rounded side against the mold. Use firm, dry LADY FINGERS, not the spongy kind. A large mold holds 14 Lady Fingers, and above Bavaroise.

- Place each Ladyfinger in a half-cone cavity. Cut to even them with the rim of the mold.
- With a ladle carefully pour into the mold the Bavaroise Mixture, avoid displacing the Ladyfingers.
- Refrigerate until the Bavaroise is firm and set. Unmold onto a serving platter. Garnish to taste.

THE EASY WAY Prepare the BAVAROISE in a 6-cup soufflé mold. Refrigerate, unmold. *(continued)*

- Stick the LADY FINGERS side-by-side around the unmolded Bavaroise, for them to stand a 1/4-inch higher. If needed, use a little Fruit Jelly on the back.
- If too tall, cut the bottom end. Pipe whipped Cream around the base and on top. Refrigerate.
- Garnish: Strawberries or other. See "MANGO BAVAROISE" and "STRAWBERRY BAVAROISE".

FRUIT - CLAFOUTIS   A Fruit Flan from France   *Serves 6 to 8*

BASIC CUSTARD Mix in blender, until smooth	[1-1/4 cups	MILK
	[1/3-cup	GRANULATED SUGAR
	[3	EGGS
	[2 tp	VANILLA EXTRACT
Optional	[1/2-tp	ALMOND or ORANGE EXTRACT
	[1 TB	KIRSCH, BRANDY, RUM, other
Then sift in gradually and blend until smooth	[4 flat TB	FLOUR

Spray an 8 x 8 baking dish. Spread in it   [3-1/2 cups FRUIT macerated with Sugar, drain

Pour over the Custard. Bake in a 350° oven, 40-to-60 minutes, until firm. Insert a skewer. If it comes out clean, it's ready. Serve warm or room temperature. Dust with Confectioners' Sugar.

FRUIT - CRÊPES   *Filling yields about 2-1/4 cups*   CRÊPES - "BASIC RECIPES"

THE FILLING	Macerate for 1 hour	[2-1/4 cups	FRUIT thinly sliced or small pieces
	with	[1-1/2 TB	GRANULATED SUGAR
		[to taste	GROUND CINNAMON, RUM, other

| In a nonstick skillet, over medium heat, heat | [1 TB | UNSALTED BUTTER |
| Add the | [| drained Fruit, reserve the SYRUP |

- Stir the Fruit for 4 or 5 minutes.
- When excess Liquid has evaporated, transfer to a bowl. Let cool. Refrigerate.
- Fill the Crêpes. Arrange them in a baking dish. Cover with foil. Refrigerate.
- To serve: bring to room temperature and lightly heat the Crêpes in a warm oven.

In a skillet, add to SYRUP   [1/3-cup   ORANGE JUICE + 2 TB SUGAR

Bring to a boil until medium thick. Pour the hot Syrup over the Crêpes and serve immediately.

FLAMBÉ Set on a plate a metal ladle, pour in [2 TB   RUM or LIQUEUR used in Fruit

Ignite and pour over the Crêpes. Baste with a long spoon. Serve when the flames die down.

FRUIT - FLAMBÉED OMELET   *Serves 2*   EGGS - "BASIC RECIPES"

In a cup, dissolve in microwave [3 TB   SUGAR in 3 TB MILK
Let cool.
In a bowl beat the MILK with [4   EGGS
and [1/4-tp   VANILLA EXTRACT
Cook the Omelet.
Add 1 cup of sautéed FRUIT FILLING. Fold, slide onto a platter. Flambé as above.

FRUIT - MOUSSE

FRESH RASPBERRIES or STRAWBERRIES

Yields about 2-1/2 cups

In a bowl, mix [1 pint   BERRIES
with [1/2-cup   GRANULATED SUGAR
Optional, to taste [1 TB   KIRSCH, COINTREAU,
or   GRAND MARNIER

- Macerate for 1 hour at room temperature.
- Drain the Berries, reserve their SYRUP.
- Purée them in processor.
- Place a fine sieve over a bowl.
- Pass through it the Purée to rid of seeds,
  mashing it with the back of a wooden spoon.
- Rinse processor. Return to it the Purée.

If needed, add to Syrup [enough   WATER to obtain 1/4-cup
Pour it into a small skillet, sprinkle with [1 TB   UNFLAVORED GELATINE POWDER
(1 envelope)

- Let it sit for 10 minutes.
- Heat the Syrup over low heat to dissolve the
  Gelatine. Pour it into the Purée and process
  with 1 or 2 quick pulses to mix well.

In a large chilled bowl, with an electric beater,
whip lightly [1/2-cup   WHIPPING CREAM   chilled

- Fold the PURÉE into the CREAM. Fill stem glasses, bowls, or a serving glass bowl.
- Refrigerate overnight for the Mousse to firm up. Serve garnished with whole Berries.

FROZEN BERRIES   Thaw in a colander [2 cups   FROZEN BERRIES   save the Juice

Place the BERRIES in a bowl and mix with [1/4-cup   GRANULATED SUGAR or to taste
[optional   KIRSCH or other, as above

- Let stand for 1 hour at room temperature.
- Drain, reserve the SYRUP. Add to it the
  Juice obtained from thawing.
- Purée the Berries as above, pass through
  a sieve and return to processor.
Prepare [as above   the SYRUP with GELATINE
Whip lightly [2/3-cup   WHIPPING CREAM   chilled

Fold the Purée into the Cream and continue as above.

FRESH APRICOTS and PEACHES   Mix [2 cups   FRUIT   peeled, cut small chunks
[1/2-cup   GRANULATED SUGAR
[1 tp   LEMON JUICE + 1-1/2 TB LIQUEUR

Macerate for 1 hour. Drain, purée as above.
Add the SYRUP with GELATINE.
Whip lightly [1/2-cup   WHIPPING CREAM   chilled
Fold the Purée into the Cream.

CANNED FRUIT   Drained.

For [2 cups of   cut up FRUIT puréed   (no sugar)
use [1/4-cup of   the FRUIT SYRUP, 1 TB GELATINE
[to taste   LIQUEUR
and [2/3-cup   WHIPPING CREAM   whipped stiff

404

FRUIT - POACHED   Compote   *Syrup yield for 2-to-2-1/2 lbs of Fruit*

THE FRUIT   - If the Fruit has to be blanched before peeling, do it before starting the Syrup.

	Fit into a saucepan	[2-to-2-1/2 lbs	FRUIT peeled, cored, cut or whole
THE SYRUP	Combine and bring to a boil	[2-1/2 cups	WATER
		[1 cup	GRANULATED SUGAR
		[1 tp	LEMON JUICE
		[optional	CINNAMON or 5-to-6 CLOVES

Reduce heat to medium low, simmer, stir
occasionally until thickened into a light Syrup.
Turn off heat.

Optional, add to taste any of   [ORANGE, ANISE or VANILLA EXTRACT,
BRANDY, LIQUEUR, RUM, WINE, PORT

- Pour the hot SYRUP over the FRUIT.
- It <u>must cover</u> it. If not, add just enough Water. Over medium heat bring to a simmer.
- Cover, simmer until the Fruit is tender: 15-to-30 minutes (depends on firmness, thickness).
- Cool, uncovered, in the saucepan. Transfer the Fruit with its Syrup into a bowl. Refrigerate.

FRUIT - SAUCES   For a smoother result strain the Sauces through a fine sieve.

LIGHT SYRUP	Combine in a saucepan	[1/2-cup	WATER
		[1/3-cup	GRANULATED SUGAR

- Bring to a boil.
- Reduce heat, simmer until thickened into a light Syrup. Use as much as needed for a Sauce.

THE FRUIT fresh, frozen, cooked, canned (drained). Purée in processor, transfer to a bowl.

BERRIES Purée, strain through fine sieve, mix [LIGHT SYRUP to obtain desired consistency

FRESH FRUIT   Add gradually to the Purée [LIGHT SYRUP to obtain desired consistency

FROZEN	Thaw in a fine sieve. Purée with	[a little	LEMON JUICE
	Add to obtain desired consistency	[	LIGHT SYRUP

COOKED OR CANNED   Add [some of   the FRUIT SYRUP

COULIS	Blend at medium speed	[8 oz	FRESH FRUIT
		[5 oz	GRANULATED SUGAR

JELLIES AND JAMS	Over low heat, melt	[1 cup	FRUIT JELLY or JAM PRESERVES
	with	[2 TB	WATER or FRUIT JUICE
		[1 TB	LEMON JUICE

Strain through a fine sieve to rid of skins.

To thicken SAUCES	Per 1 cup Sauce, dissolve	[1 tp	ARROWROOT
	in	[2 TB	COLD WATER

Add Arrowroot to the Sauce.
Over medium low heat, bring to boiling point and stir until the Sauce thickens. Serve hot or cold.

OPTIONAL   Add to Fruit Sauces, to taste [LIQUEUR, BRANDY, KIRSCH, RUM,
[EXTRACTS, CINNAMON, GINGER, CLOVES

FRUIT - SIMPLE SOUFFLÉ

Serves 4

Purée in processor to obtain	[1 cup	FRUIT PURÉE

Transfer to a saucepan, warm the Purée, add   [if needed   GRANULATED SUGAR
To taste   [any of   VANILLA EXTRACT, RUM, LIQUEUR
Transfer warm Purée to a bowl.

Beat   [4   EGG WHITES until stiff and glossy

- Fold gradually Whites into the Purée.
- Pour them into a 1-1/2 quart soufflé dish, buttered and dusted with Granulated Sugar.
- Set the dish in a pan of hot water. Bake in oven preheated to 375° for 25-to-30 minutes.
- Dust with CONFECTIONERS' SUGAR. Serve immediately, as this Soufflé will collapse quickly.

FRUIT - SOUFFLÉ OMELET

*Serves 4 **

The Soufflé Omelet can be served plain with a Fruit Sauce. Or it can have a Fruit Filling.

In 2 bowls, separate   [6   EGGS you need 5 Yolks, 6 Whites
at room temperature

With an electric beater, beat   [5 Yolks
with   [4 TB   GRANULATED SUGAR
When Yolks are thick, foamy and white, add   [1/4-tp   VANILLA EXTRACT
and/or   [1 TB   COINTREAU, or GRAND MARNIER
Wash the beater and dry it.

Then beat until very stiff   [6 Whites
with   [a pinch   SALT
Halfway through add   [1 TB   GRANULATED SUGAR

With a spatula fold them into the YOLKS.

In a large nonstick skillet, medium heat, heat   [1-1/2 TB   UNSALTED BUTTER

- When it sizzles, add the Eggs. Do not stir. Poke the Eggs randomly a few times with a spatula.
- Let the bottom cook until golden. The top must be creamy, not runny.
- Fold one half of the Omelet over the other, following directions in "BASIC RECIPES" - EGGS.
- Loosen the Omelet with the spatula, let it sit in the skillet for about 30 seconds.
- Slide the Omelet onto a warm platter. Sprinkle it with plenty of CONFECTIONERS' SUGAR.

To FLAMBÉ   Pour into a metal ladle   [2 TB   COINTREAU or GRAND MARNIER

Ignite and pour over the Omelet. Serve when the flames die down.

* *Serves 2:* 3 Yolks, 2-1/2 TB Sugar, 1/8-tp Vanilla Extract, 2 tp Liqueur, 3 Whites, 1/2-TB Sugar.

With FRUIT FILLING - Prepare 1 cup Fruit as in recipe: FRUIT - FLAMBÉED OMELET.
- Warm it before adding it to the Omelet.
- Or spread a Fruit Preserve over half of the Omelet, then fold it.

BAKED SOUFFLÉ OMELET   Butter and dust with Sugar a 10-inch baking dish: 1-1/2 inches deep.

- After folding the WHITES into the YOLKS, pour them into the dish. Smooth the top.
- Bake in oven preheated to 400° for about 18-to-20 minutes, until the Omelet has puffed up.
- Sprinkle with CONFECTIONERS' SUGAR. Flambé immediately and serve.

FRUIT - TARTS and TARTLETS

NOTE - To transfer a "PIE CRUST SHELL - FROZEN and UNCOOKED", from its foil pan, into an oven-proof pie dish, see "HELPFUL HINTS".

Preheat oven to 375°.   Beat [1   EGG with 1 TB WATER
                          Brush with it a [9-inch   FROZEN UNCOOKED PIE SHELL
                                     or [6 individual FROZEN UNCOOKED PIE SHELLS

- Set in the oven for 2 minutes only.
- Cut a round piece(s) of wax paper, a little
  larger than the bottom of the Pie Shell(s).

Place it in the Pie Shell(s), fill the bottom with [DRIED BEANS

- Place Shell(s), in their pan or dish, on a cookie sheet. Slide into oven, reduce heat to 350°.
- Bake until golden. Let Shells cool. Lift carefully the wax paper with the Beans.
- When Shells have cooled, brush them with the Fruit Glaze.

The GLAZE   Combine in a small saucepan [1-1/4 cups   FRUIT JELLY
                                                 [1 TB + 1 tp WATER

- Over low heat, warm until frothy and thickened, but still thin enough to run off a spoon.
- If needed strain through a fine sieve to rid of skins. Optional: add 1 TB KIRSCH, RUM or BRANDY.
- When still warm, use a pastry brush to brush lightly with it, inside and rim of Shells. Let dry.

The FRUIT   2 hours before serving, arrange
                 decoratively into the Pie Shell(s) [3 cups   FRUIT (one kind or mixed)

APRICOTS/PEACHES - Ripe. Peel. Cut into wedges. Arrange in concentric circles.
BLUEBERRIES   - Spread tightly over the Tart surface. Smooth the top evenly.
GRAPES   - Seedless. Mix with other Fruit.
KIWIS   - Slice into rounds. Mix with other Fruit.
PINEAPPLE   - Canned, sliced. Drain. Overlap slices. Mix with other Fruit.
STRAWBERRIES   - Remove stems, wash, dry. Sit on their flat end, in concentric circles.
CANNED FRUIT   - Drained. Mix 2 or 3 kinds.

Warm remaining FRUIT GLAZE, brush it over the Fruit.
Tarts can be refrigerated. Serve them at room temperature.

With CRÈME PÂTISSIÈRE   French Custard

                Prepare following recipe the [CRÈME PÂTISSIÈRE see "CREAMS"

        Spread the cold CRÈME PÂTISSIÈRE in [BAKED PIE SHELL or TARTLETS
                          Arrange on top [FRUIT   fresh, poached or canned

Brush over with the FRUIT GLAZE. Refrigerate the Tart(s) until ready to serve.

With STRAWBERRY MOUSSE

- Fill a BAKED PIE SHELL with 2 cups of STRAWBERRY MOUSSE see FRUIT - MOUSSE.
- Chill until the Mousse is firm. Arrange on top WHOLE STRAWBERRIES.
- Brush with STRAWBERRY GLAZE. Refrigerate until ready to serve.

FRUIT - TIRAMISU   "tira-mi-su" means in Italian "pull me up"   *Serves 6*

Espresso soaked Lady Fingers with Mascarpone are meant to give a "lift". Here is my version!

CUSTARD   See "CUSTARDS". Prepare an   [ENGLISH CUSTARD
                                    with   [3 cups   MILK
                                            [1-1/2 TB   VANILLA EXTRACT
                                            [6   EGG YOLKS
                                            [3/4-cup   GRANULATED
                                            [1-1/2 tp   CORNSTARCH
            After straining it into a bowl, stir in   [3 TB   GRAND MARNIER
                                                    Yields about 3-1/3 cups

Cover the surface with wax paper. Refrigerate.

LADY FINGERS   In an 8 x 8 glass dish,
                    lay side-by-side a row of   [5   LADY FINGERS
Cut off the ends, at the dish center, to fit a
                    second row of   [5   LADY FINGERS cut the same way

                    You will need another   [10   LADY FINGERS   for the top row

FRUIT   Slice into thin wedges to obtain   [2 cups   any of: ripe or canned (drained)
                                              [APRICOTS, PEACHES, PEARS,
                                                    NECTARINES, PINEAPPLE RINGS
                                              [or   STRAWBERRIES sliced

COFFEE   Prepare   [3/4-cup   COFFEE of your choice, or
                                                                        decaffeinated
            Or substitute the Coffee with   [3/4-cup   FRUIT JUICE

LIQUEUR   You need   [3/4-cup   GRAND MARNIER

To assemble

- With a teaspoon sprinkle half of the Coffee
  (or Fruit Juice) over the Lady Fingers.
- Do the same with half of the Grand Marnier.
- Spread evenly in 1 layer the Fruit.
- Cover with half of the Custard.
                        Sprinkle   [1/2-cup   SEMISWEET CHOCOLATE grated

- Cover with the rest of the Lady Fingers.
- Spread over them the remaining Custard.
- Cover the dish with plastic wrap, refrigerate
  overnight.
                    Before serving dust with   [COCOA POWDER use a small sieve

For a dish:	8-3/4 x 12 use:	9-1/2 x 14 use:	
LADYFINGERS	40 in 2 layers of 20, cut ends to fit	48 in 2 layers of 24, they fit in whole	
CUSTARD	double the recipe	CUSTARD	double the recipe + half
FRUIT	3 cups	FRUIT	4 cups
COFFEE	1 cup + 2 TB	COFFEE	1-1/3 cups
LIQUEUR	1 cup + 2 TB	LIQUEUR	1-1/3 cups
CHOCOLATE	2/3-cup grated	CHOCOLATE	1 cup grated

FRUIT - TRIFLE   English Dessert   *Create a Trifle*

Traditionally: layers of Pound Cake, Brandy and/or medium-dry Sherry, Jam, Raspberries, Custard and Whipped Cream.

1.   Line a deep glass bowl with a layer of [POUND CAKE sliced a 1/2-inch thick.
    [Also use FRUIT CAKE or a JELLY ROLL CAKE

2. Douse the Cake with any, or a mixture of [BRANDY, medium-dry SHERRY, RUM, LIQUEUR

3.   Spread on top of the cake [RASPBERRY or APRICOT JAM, OTHER to taste

4. Top with a packed layer of FRUIT, any of [RASPBERRIES, sliced PEACHES, APRICOTS,
    [halved or sliced STRAWBERRIES, or mix Fruit

5.   Top the Fruit with another layer of [CAKE

6.   Douse the CAKE with [the LIQUOR you have chosen

7.   With a spatula spread on top the [ENGLISH CUSTARD * see CUSTARDS

8.   Top the Custard with a layer of [RASPBERRIES

9.   With a pastry bag pipe on top [WHIPPED CREAM beat with Sugar, add Vanilla

    Garnish [RASPBERRIES or whole STRAWBERRIES

* Custard: prepare a day ahead.
   Refrigerate. Depending on the size of the Trifle, you may need to double the amount.

FRUIT - ZUPPA INGLESE   English Soup: the Italian version of the Trifle.

- See "CUSTARDS", prepare an ENGLISH CUSTARD. Refrigerate. You need 2 layers for the Zuppa.
- A large Zuppa Inglese, in a 9-inch bowl, will take about 2 cups of Custard for each layer.

1.   Cut horizontally into 3 layers a [SPONGE CAKE   each layer 3/4-inch thick
    Lay 1 slice of CAKE in a deep glass bowl
    and douse with [RUM or AMARETTO LIQUEUR

2.   Top with a layer, any of [RASPBERRIES, STRAWBERRIES, APRICOTS,
    PEACHES

3.   Top with half of the [CUSTARD   in a thick layer

4.   Repeat with [CAKE, LIQUOR and FRUIT

5.   Mix the rest of the CUSTARD with [canned CRUSHED PINEAPPLE   drained
    (1/2-cup Pineapple to 1 cup Custard)

6. Top the FRUIT with PINEAPPLE CUSTARD.

7. Top the CUSTARD with the third piece of [CAKE and douse with LIQUOR.

8.   Cover the CAKE with [WHIPPED CREAM   piped decoratively

9.   Garnish with [RASPBERRIES or whole STRAWBERRIES
    Refrigerate.

APPLE - CLAFOUTIS PUDDING

CLAFOUTIS see FRUIT - CLAFOUTIS

Peel, quarter, core, cut thin wedges, to obtain	[3 cups	APPLES (3-to-4 medium Apples)
In a nonstick skillet, over medium heat, heat	[2-1/2 TB	UNSALTED BUTTER
When it sizzles stir in the APPLES, sprinkle	[1 TB	GRANULATED SUGAR
	[1/4-tp	GROUND CINNAMON or to taste
Sauté until the Apples begin to soften, then turn off heat and mix in	[1/4-cup	RAISINS soaked, drained, dried
	[1/4-cup	PECANS coarsely chopped
	[1/4-cup	MAPLE SYRUP
	[to taste	DARK RUM or BRANDY
Prepare the CLAFOUTIS BASIC CUSTARD, adding	[2 tp	VANILLA EXTRACT,
	[to taste	DARK RUM or BRANDY
Line a sprayed 1-1/2 qt baking dish with	[a layer of	POUND CAKE slice 1/2-inch thick
Douse the Pound Cake with	[to taste	DARK RUM or BRANDY

Spread the APPLES on top. Pour over the CUSTARD. Bake following CLAFOUTIS recipe.

APPLE - CRÊPES SUZETTE

CRÊPES see "BASIC RECIPES"

Mix ready-made	[	APPLESAUCE 1-1/2 TB per Crêpe
with	[to taste	GROUND CINNAMON or GINGER
Optional, a few drops	[	BRANDY or DARK RUM
Spread the APPLESAUCE	[on each	CRÊPE
	[sprinkle	PECANS chopped

Fold each Crêpe in four, set them on a platter.

THE SAUCE   *Yields about 3/4-cup (for 9-to-12 Crêpes)*

In a chafing skillet over a table-top burner, melt	[4 TB	UNSALTED BUTTER small bits
When it sizzles, dissolve in it	[4 TB	GRANULATED SUGAR
Add	[1/2-tp	LEMON JUICE
	[1/3-cup	APPLE JUICE
	[2 TB	BRANDY or RUM

- Stir until bubbly. Place the CRÊPES in it.
- Simmer for 3 or 4 minutes. Baste the Crêpes with the Sauce, until they are heated through.
- To FLAMBÉ see FRUIT - CRÊPES. Serve with a scoop of VANILLA ICE CREAM on the side.

APPLE FILLING for CRÊPES

Yields about 2-1/2 cups

In a nonstick skillet, over medium heat, heat	[2 TB	UNSALTED BUTTER
When it sizzles, sauté	[2-1/4 cups	McINTOSH APPLES peeled, diced
When they begin to soften, sprinkle	[1 TB	LIGHT BROWN SUGAR
	[1/4-tp each	GROUND CINNAMON and GINGER
When Apples are lightly browned, add	[1/4-cup	GOLDEN RAISINS
	[1/3-cup	APPLE SAUCE
	[to taste	BRANDY or RUM *(continued)*

410

- Reduce heat to low, simmer 5-to-8 minutes. Refrigerate before filling the Crêpes.
- Warm the filled Crêpes in oven preheated to 300°.

Serve dusted with   [CONFECTIONERS' SUGAR
Optional, on the side   [a scoop of VANILLA ICE CREAM

APPLE - CUSTARD PIE   QUICHE see "BASIC RECIPES"

Over low heat, dissolve in a   [1/4-cup   MILK
                               [1/3-cup   GRANULATED SUGAR
Do not boil. Turn off heat and stir in   [3/4-cup   HEAVY CREAM
                               [1/2-tp   VANILLA EXTRACT
Set aside to cool.
Preheat oven to 375°.

Peel, quarter, core, slice quarters crosswise
          very thinly to obtain   [2 cups   GOLDEN DELICIOUS APPLES
Place them in a bowl and mix with   [1 tp   LEMON JUICE

In a nonstick skillet, over medium heat, heat   [1 TB   UNSALTED BUTTER
When it sizzles, stir in the APPLES, sprinkle   [1 TB   GRANULATED SUGAR
                               [1/4-tp   GROUND CINNAMON or GINGER

Stir until the Apples have softened lightly.
Remove from heat and let them cool.

In a large bowl, whisk   [4   EGGS
Brush with a little of the beaten Eggs a   [9-inch   FROZEN UNCOOKED PIE SHELL

Set in the oven for 2 minutes only. Let cool.

Gradually whisk into the Eggs   [the Milk/Cream

To assemble and bake   - Place the Pie Shell in its foil on a cookie sheet. Spread the Apples in it.
                       - Ladle the CUSTARD over it. Smooth the surface with a spatula.
                       - Slide into oven. Reduce heat to 350°. Bake as per "BASIC RECIPES".
Serve   - At room temperature or cold. Dust with CONFECTIONERS' SUGAR.

APPLE - STRUDEL   *Serves 6*   PHYLLO - STRUDEL see "BASIC RECIPES"

THE FILLING   Peel, quarter, core   [4   TART APPLES   cut small chunks
                    Mix APPLES in a bowl with   [1 tp   LEMON JUICE
                               Then stir in   [1/2-cup   BROWN SUGAR
                                              [1 tp   GROUND CINNAMON
                           When mixed, add   [1/2-cup   GOLDEN RAISINS
                                              [1/3-cup   PECANS or HAZELNUTS   chopped
                                              [1 tp   ORANGE ZEST   grated
THE STRUDEL
             Butter, including top sheet   [6   PHYLLO SHEETS
             Sprinkle over the top sheet   [PLAIN BREADCRUMBS
                                          [or, 3 or 4   GINGER COOKIES   finely grated
Add the FILLING, roll and bake.
                          To serve   [sprinkle   CONFECTIONER'S SUGAR

411

APPLE - "TARTE TATIN" - BASIC TECHNIQUE

This upside-down Apple Tart is attributed to the Tatin Damsels. Did they use quartered Apples, Apple wedges or slices? The recipes vary. However, their Apples were cooked and caramelized, then topped with raw Pastry, put in the oven to bake, and inverted onto a platter.

In some recipes the raw Apples, Butter and Sugar are put in a 2-inch deep baking dish, topped with the raw Pastry and baked. However, by baking the raw Apples and Pastry together, the Pastry will be cooked before the Apples are, unless very thinly sliced. Still, they won't be caramelized.

In other recipes, the Apples are baked in the dish, until browned, then the dish is removed from the oven. The Pastry placed on top and the dish returned to the oven.

By following the steps below, you can make a Tarte Tatin of any size: in a 5-inch skillet, or smaller.

1.   - Melt in a cast-iron skillet 1/8-inch deep of Butter. Brush the sides with it.

2.   - Line the skillet with a 1/4-inch thick layer of granulated Sugar. Melt it in the Butter.

3.   - Top the Sugar with Apple quarters (not larger), thick wedges or slices, placed tightly side-by-side in concentric circles. Start with outer circle all the way to the center.
     - With quarters, use 1 layer. Sit them on their peeled rounded side.
     - Overlap thick wedges in one layer.
     - For slices: 2 or 3 layers, not more. Total thickness of layers: 1-1/2 to 1-3/4 inches.
     - Drizzle between the layers a little melted Butter and a sprinkle of Sugar.

4.   - Without stirring, cook over medium heat until the Apples soften, using a bulb-baster to baste them, until the Syrup turns to caramel brown. Turn off heat. Set aside.
     - The Apples must hold their form. Press down with a spatula to even them, fill spaces.

5.   - Cover with a round sheet of raw Puff Pastry. Brush with Egg Wash. Tuck in edges.
     - Slit into the Pastry four 1-inch steam-vents.

6.   - Place the skillet on a cookie sheet. Bake until the Crust is golden.
     - Let stand 15 minutes. Loosen the Crust by running a thin knife around it.

7.   - Place over the pan a platter with a brim (to prevent the juice from running out).
     - Wear oven mitts. Hold the pan and platter together (they are heavy), quickly invert.

NOTE   - Do not let the "Tarte" cool in the pan, the caramelized fruit will stick to the bottom.

THIN "TARTE TATIN"   Basic for any size skillet

Pastry - Roll out the Puff Pastry 1/8-inch thick. Cut it out as in the next recipe, refrigerate.

Apples - Peel, quarter lengthwise and core. Slice quarters into wedges 1/8-inch thick.

Syrup - Melt enough BUTTER to line generously the skillet. Turn off heat. Brush the sides.
       - Add enough SUGAR to cover the bottom of the skillet: 1/8-inch deep.
       - Over medium heat stir Butter / Sugar until it bubbles to a golden Syrup. Turn off heat.

Tarte - Overlap in the Syrup a layer of Apple wedges in concentric circles.
       - Cook without stirring, basting the Apples until caramel brown. Turn off heat.
       - Place the Puff Pastry on top. Brush with Egg wash. Tuck in the edge.
       - Make slits in the Pastry as in the next recipe. Bake until golden. Invert.

412

APPLE - "La TARTE TATIN" (See Basic Technique) *Serves 6 to 8*

- On a sheet of wax paper, turn upside down a cast-iron 8-to-9-inch skillet.
- Make a pencil trace around it. Add 1/2-inch more around the periphery to make it wider.
- Cut out this paper disk.

                                    Thaw [1 sheet of   PUFF PASTRY (available frozen)
- Roll it out thinly on a pastry board.
- Place the disk on it, cut the Pastry around it.
- Set the Pastry on a cookie sheet lined with
  wax paper, dusted with Flour. Refrigerate.

    In the cast-iron skillet, over low heat, melt [1 stick (4 oz) UNSALTED BUTTER   sliced

Brush the skillet sides with it.

                    Melt into the Butter [1 cup   GRANULATED SUGAR
Turn off heat.
                    Peel, one at a time [8   GOLDEN DELICIOUS or GRANNY SMITH
                                                                    medium size
                                                    (you may not need all of them)

- Halve the Apples.
- Cut each half into 3 wedges. Core them.
- Start with outer circle, lay wedges in the
  skillet, tightly side-by-side, in concentric
  circles, until skillet is well packed and full.

                    Sprinkle with [1 TB   GRANULATED SUGAR
                                   [optional   GROUND CINNAMON
- Over medium heat, cook the Apples, do not
  stir, use a bulb-baster to baste them.
- When the Apples are tender and the Syrup
  turns to caramel brown, turn off heat before
  it burns. Set aside the skillet.
- Preheat oven to 400°.
                            Beat [1   EGG with 1 TB WATER
- Cover the Apples with the Puff Pastry.
- Be careful, the skillet is hot. Tuck the Pastry edge into the skillet. Brush with EGG WASH.

- Slit at 2-inches from edge, perpendicular to it, 1-inch steam-vents: right, left, top and bottom.
- Place the skillet on a cookie sheet. Slide it in the oven, bake until the Pastry Crust is golden.
- Let stand 15 minutes. Loosen the Crust by running a thin knife around it. Invert on a platter.

APRICOTS - *Peeling Apricots, Peaches and Plums*

Make an X incision on the base. Plunge into boiling Water from 20 seconds to 1 minute. Remove
with slotted spoon. Peel starting from the X incision. For unripe Fruit, use a sharp paring knife.

BROILED

- Drain canned APRICOTS. Mix into their Syrup a little APRICOT JELLY and KIRSCH or BRANDY.
- Line a sprayed baking dish with slices of POUND CAKE. Heat the Syrup, douse the Cake with it.
- Top with Apricots. Fill each cavity with a MARSHMALLOW. Pass under the broiler until melted

APRICOTS with CREAM PISTACHIO FILLING   *Yields a 1/2-cup*

Whip   [4 TB   MASCARPONE   Make a slit into
           [2 TB   SOUR CREAM
           [1/2-tp ORANGE BLOSSOM or ROSE WATER   [SOFT PLUMP DRIED APRICOTS
Add   [3 TB   PISTACHIOS skinned, chopped

Fill them with the Mixture, a little over a teaspoon per Apricot. Sprinkle with chopped PISTACHIOS.

APRICOT - CLAFOUTIS   *Serves 6 to 8*   See FRUIT - CLAFOUTIS

Macerate for 2 hours: Prepare the BASIC CLAFOUTIS CUSTARD with:

[2 cups   APRICOTS thick wedges   [1 tp   VANILLA EXTRACT
[2 TB   GRANULATED SUGAR   [1/2-tp ORANGE EXTRACT
[1/2-cup DRIED APRICOTS diced   [2 TB   KIRSCH or AMARETTO LIQUEUR
[1/4-cup GOLDEN RAISINS
[1/4-cup SLIVERED ALMONDS
[2 TB   KIRSCH or AMARETTO LIQUEUR

Drain and spread the APRICOTS into a sprayed 8 x 8 BAKING dish.   Pour over the CUSTARD.
Bake following directions in FRUIT CLAFOUTIS.

APRICOT - CUSTARD PIE   QUICHE see "BASIC RECIPES"

       Soak for 2 hours in lukewarm WATER [1-1/4 cups   DRIED APRICOTS not plump ones
                                      [1 or 2 TB   KIRSCH or AMARETTO LIQUEUR
Let drain for 30 minutes. Dry. Chop coarsely.

   Over low heat, do not boil, dissolve in a [1/4-cup   MILK
                                  [1/3-cup   GRANULATED SUGAR
           Turn off heat and stir in [3/4-cup   HEAVY CREAM
                                  [1/2-tp   VANILLA EXTRACT
Set aside to cool.
Preheat oven to 375°.
               In a large bowl beat [3   EGGS
     Brush with a little of the beaten EGGS a [9-inch   FROZEN UNCOOKED PIE SHELL

Set in the oven for 2 minutes only. Let cool.

         Gradually whisk into the Eggs [the Milk/Cream Mixture
            Cut into bits and mix in [3 oz   PHILADELPHIA CREAM CHEESE
   Then stir in the APRICOTS. Optional [1 TB   KIRSCH or AMARETTO LIQUEUR

<u>To assemble and bake</u> - Place the Pie Shell in its foil on a cookie sheet. Ladle in the Custard.
                     - Bake as per "BASIC RECIPES". Cool then brush with the GLAZE.

The GLAZE   Combine in a small saucepan [1/2-cup   APRICOT JELLY PRESERVE
                                [1 tp   LEMON JUICE + 1 TB WATER
                                [to taste   KIRSCH or AMARETTO LIQUEUR
- Heat until blended. Add Water if needed.
- The Glaze must be thin enough to run off a spoon. Strain through a fine sieve to rid of skins.
- When the Pie has cooled, with a pastry brush, brush the warm GLAZE over the Custard surface.
- The Pie can be refrigerated and brought to room temperature a half hour before serving.

414

APRICOTS - CHOCOLATE SOUFFLÉ

APRICOTS   Wash, dry, cut in half and pit [APRICOTS You need enough halves to line in
1 layer the bottom of soufflé dish.

In a skillet, where Apricots can fit in 1 layer,
heat to dissolve [1/2-cup   SUGAR in 1 cup WATER
[1/2-tp   LEMON JUICE

- Lay in it the Apricots, cut side down.
- Add just enough WATER to cover. Bring to a
  boil, reduce heat to low, simmer 15 minutes.
- With slotted spoon remove the Apricots and
  pour out the Water, return them to skillet.

[sprinkle   CONFECTIONERS' SUGAR

To flambé, put the skillet in a clear space
and set a ladle on its rim, pour into it [2 TB   DARK RUM or BRANDY

Ignite and pour over the Apricots. Set aside.

SOUFFLÉ - The Chocolate Soufflé Base is heavier. Large Chocolate Soufflés do not rise well.
    - This Soufflé can be plain, without Apricots. Optional, serve with a Custard Sauce.

Set out at room temperature [4   EGGS you need 3 Yolks , 4 Whites

Rub a 1-quart soufflé dish with [UNSALTED BUTTER
(or use 4 ramekins) and dust with [1-1/2 TB   GRANULATED SUGAR refrigerate
(1-1/4 tp per ramekin)

In a small saucepan, low heat, dissolve in [4 TB   MILK
[5 TB   GRANULATED SUGAR

With a wooden spoon stir, melting into it,
(do not let it boil) until texture is smooth [4 oz   SEMISWEET BAKING CHOCOLATE
coarse-grated

Add [2 tp   VANILLA EXTRACT
[1 TB   DARK RUM or BRANDY   optional

- Remove from heat, let stand 5 minutes.
- Break 1 EGG, drop the WHITE into stainless
  steel bowl. The YOLK into the Chocolate.
- With wooden spoon beat it into the Chocolate.
- Repeat with 2 more YOLKS.
- To add WHITES the Chocolate must be tepid.

- Preheat oven to 400°. Set out soufflé dish(es).
- Arrange in them the APRICOTS in 1 layer.

Add to the 3 EGG WHITES 1 EGG WHITE and [a pinch   SALT

Beat the WHITES until soft peaks form, add [1 TB   GRANULATED SUGAR

a) Continue beating until stiff peaks are formed. Add one ladle of the WHITES to the CHOCOLATE.
   - Gently fold them in with a spatula.
   - In 3 times, add the Chocolate to the rest of the WHITES, scooping from the bottom towards
     the top as you turn the bowl. Do not fold too much.

b) Pour Mixture into the soufflé dish(es). Smooth the top with a spatula. Place on middle rack
   of oven. Immediately reduce heat to 375°. Bake for about 25 minutes. Less for ramekins.
   - Insert a knife to test doneness. Sprinkle CONFECTIONERS' SUGAR. Serve immediately.

BANANAS - FLAMBÉ   Also called Bananas Foster   *Serves 2*

In a chafing skillet, stir until melted	[1-1/2 TB	UNSALTED BUTTER
with	[3 TB	BROWN SUGAR
Add and sauté	[2 ripe	BANANAS split in half lengthwise
When they soften, sprinkle with	[a dash of	GROUND CINNAMON
Have ready in two elongated dishes	[2 scoops	VANILLA ICE CREAM in each dish
Pour into a ladle and ignite	[2 TB	WHITE RUM

- Pour the Rum over the Bananas. Baste with a long spoon until the flames die down.
- Serve the Bananas over the Ice Cream. Top with the SYRUP. Garnish with RASPBERRIES.

BERRIES

CRÊPES	- Mix BERRIES with WHIPPED CREAM or CRÈME PÂTISSIÈRE (see "CREAMS").
	- Fill the Crêpes. Cover with foil. Barely warm in the oven.
	Sprinkle with CONFECTIONERS' SUGAR. Serve with a RASPBERRY SAUCE.
MERINGUE SHELLS	- Mix BERRIES with a little GRANULATED SUGAR and LIQUEUR to taste.
	- Refrigerate. Fill Shells with a scoop of ICE CREAM. Top with the Berries.

CANDIED FRUIT - CASSATA   Layered Ice Cream mold   (Italy)

PREPARATION - You need a rectangular loaf or pound cake mold. Size: according to servings.
- Measure in cups the mold content, then buy the Ice Cream accordingly.
- Substitute the flavors below with any of your choice, but make it colorful.
- Let the Ice Cream soften in the refrigerator, it will be easier to spread.

- FREEZE EACH LAYER before adding another, to prevent melting into each other.
- Cover the Ice Cream with wax paper before returning it every time to freezer.

For an 8-cup mold   9-1/2 x 5-1/2 x 2-3/4 inches deep, use 5 cups of Ice Cream, 3 cups of Filling.
Yields 10 slices

Needed	[2-1/2 cups	RASPBERRY or STRAWBERRY ICE CREAM
	[2-1/2 cups	PISTACHIO ICE CREAM
1st layer Spread into the mold	[half of	Raspberry or Strawberry Ice Cream
2nd Spread over it	[half of	Pistachio Ice Cream

3rd The Filling: in a large chilled bowl,

with electric beater, whip stiff	[1 cup cold	WHIPPING CREAM (it doubles in size)
	[1/2-tp	VANILLA EXTRACT
Fold in gradually	[1/4-cup	CONFECTIONERS' SUGAR
Then mix in	[1 cup	MIXED CANDIED FRUIT diced small
4 th Top the Filling with	[the rest of	Pistachio Ice Cream
5 th Top Pistachio with	[the rest of	Raspberry or Strawberry Ice Cream

To unmold   Dip the mold a few seconds in a sink of hot water. Dry it. Top with a platter, invert.
Freeze. Garnish with chopped PISTACHIOS, MARASCHINO CHERRIES. *(continued)*

FILLING VARIATION	Whip	[1/2-cup	WHIPPING CREAM
	Mix with	[1 cup	VANILLA ICE CREAM
	Add	[1 cup	MIXED CANDIED FRUIT diced

CARAMEL - BASIC RECIPE

The CARAMEL which lines molds becomes a Sauce when the Custard or Pudding is unmolded.
- As soon as the Caramel is ready you must pour it into the mold, before it hardens.
- Wear mitts to handle metal molds in which the Caramel is being poured.

| In a small heavy saucepan combine | [2 parts | SUGAR | (Example 1 cup) |
| and | [1 part | WATER | (1/2-cup) |

- Over medium heat let Sugar dissolve.
- Then, with a metal spoon stir once in a while, watching closely until it bubbles into a foam.
- The Caramel will turn golden and immediately darken. Remove from heat before it burns.

Large mold - Pour the Caramel into it. Holding the mold, swirl the Caramel around to coat it. Use the back of a metal spoon, if needed, to spread it on the sides.

Ramekins - Coat one at a time, leaving the rest of the Caramel in the saucepan.
- If you pour Caramel in all the molds at the same time, it will solidify whilst you are coating the first mold. If it gets too thick in the saucepan, heat it barely.

CHERRIES - CLAFOUTIS   See FRUIT - CLAFOUTIS

The Clafoutis originated in France as a peasant dish of Cherries and Custard.

Spray a 1-1/2 qt, 2-inch deep oven dish, add	[3 cups	BLACK CHERRIES pitted
		Spread them evenly.
Follow the BASIC CUSTARD RECIPE and use	[2 tp	VANILLA EXTRACT
	[1 tp	ALMOND EXTRACT
Optional	[1-1/2 TB	KIRSCH

| Then sift in gradually and blend until smooth | [4 flat TB | FLOUR |

Pour the CUSTARD over the CHERRIES. Bake following directions in FRUIT - CLAFOUTIS.

CHERRIES - JUBILEE

Drain	[1 lb can	PITTED BING CHERRIES
Dissolve in a 1/4-cup WATER	[1 TB	ARROWROOT
Pour in chafing skillet the Cherry Liquid, add	[1/4-tp	LEMON JUICE
	[1/8-tp	ALMOND EXTRACT

- Bring the Liquid to a boil. Thicken with the Arrowroot. Add the CHERRIES.
- Stir until heated.

| Ignite in a ladle | [1/4-cup | KIRSCH or CHERRY BRANDY |

- Pour it over the Cherries.
- Baste with a long spoon until the flames die down. Serve over Ice Cream or Cake.

417

CREAMS and CUSTARDS

CRÈME CHANTILLY   Vanilla flavored Whipped Cream

In large chilled bowl, with electric beater, beat [1 cup chilled WHIPPING or HEAVY CREAM
[2 tp   CONFECTIONERS' SUGAR
[1 tp   VANILLA EXTRACT
Beat until soft peaks are formed. Refrigerate.

CRÈME FRAÎCHE   Also called Crème d'Isigny.   *Available in some markets.*

It resembles a light Sour Cream with the taste of plain Cream. Used in salt and sweet recipes.
If Crème Fraîche is not available, to obtain a somewhat similar composition, proceed as follows:

In a chilled bowl, whisk just until it thickens [6 oz   HEAVY CREAM   (do not whip)
Then mix in [2 oz   SOUR CREAM
Refrigerate.
Remove from refrigerator about 20 minutes before serving. Serve over Berries or other Fruit.

CRÈME PÂTISSIÈRE   Thick French Custard   *Yields about 2-1/2 cups*

Used as a Filling for Pastry: Eclairs, Pies, Fruit Tarts, Napoleons, Crêpes, layered Cakes.

In a heavy saucepan, boil [2 cups   MILK
[1/2-of a   VANILLA BEAN*   split crosswise
Turn off heat, remove Vanilla Bean.

In a large bowl, with an electric beater, beat [5   EGG YOLKS
[2/3-cup   GRANULATED SUGAR
When Egg Mixture is foamy and whitens,
gradually sift in, stirring with a wire whip [4 TB   ALL-PURPOSE FLOUR

- Add gradually the hot MILK, continue stirring.
- When smooth, return Mixture to saucepan.
- Over medium heat bring to a boil, continue
  stirring with wire whip until the Custard is
  thick and smooth.
Optional, add to taste [1 TB   RUM, KIRSCH or a LIQUEUR
[ORANGE or LEMON ZEST   grated
Strain the Custard through a fine sieve into
a serving bowl. Refrigerate.

* Vanilla Bean can be substituted with 1 TB VANILLA EXTRACT after the Custard has thickened.

CRÈME PÂTISSIÈRE with CHOCOLATE   *See above recipe*

Melt slowly in a double boiler, until smooth [4 oz grated SEMISWEET BAKING CHOCOLATE
with [3 TB   WATER or 2 Water, 1 Liqueur/Rum

- When the Crème Pâtissière thickens add the melted Chocolate, stir well to mix.
- Remove from heat. Add Vanilla Extract, Liqueur to taste. Strain the Cream. Cool. Refrigerate.

CUSTARD - CRÈME BRÛLÉE   *Serves 4   (Prepare a day ahead)*

In the top of a double boiler, bring to simmer	[2 cups	HEAVY CREAM
In a large bowl, with electric beater, beat	[4	EGG YOLKS
	[4 TB	GRANULATED SUGAR
When Mixture is foamy and whitens, with a wire whip, gradually stir in	[2 tp	CORNSTARCH
Gradually add the hot Cream to Egg Yolks and continue beating until blended. Stir in	[1-1/2 tp	VANILLA EXTRACT

Version 1
- Spoon the Custard, through a fine sieve, into 4 individual oven-proof Crème Brûlée dishes. Place them in a pan. Pour around a 1/2-inch of hot water.
- Bake in oven preheated to 350° for 45 minutes. Let cool 5 minutes.

To caramelize
- Cover each Crème with a layer of GRANULATED SUGAR. Shake to distribute the Sugar evenly. Place the dishes in the pan with hot water.
- Pass under the broiler until the Sugar caramelizes. Do not let it burn.
- Let cool. Refrigerate until ready to serve.
  NOTE - The Sugar can also be caramelized with a culinary blowtorch.

Version 2
- After adding the Vanilla, strain the Custard, through a fine sieve, into the top of the double boiler, over hot but not boiling water. Stir constantly with a wooden spoon until it thickens to coat the back of the spoon.
- Remove from heat and continue stirring for 1 minute to cool the Custard.
- Spoon it into individual oven-proof Crème Brûlée dishes or a serving dish.
- Refrigerate until set. Bring to room temperature. Caramelize as in Version 1.

CUSTARD - CRÈME CARAMEL FLAN   *For a 5-cup ring mold*

For directions to make the Caramel and line the mold, see the CARAMEL - BASIC RECIPE.

THE CARAMEL	Use	[2/3-cup	GRANULATED SUGAR
		[1/3-cup	WATER
THE CUSTARD			
In a heavy saucepan, simmer		[3 cups	MILK
		[2/3-cups	GRANULATED SUGAR
		[1	VANILLA BEAN
Preheat oven to 350°.			
In a large bowl, whisk		[4	EGGS + 1 EGG YOLK

- Remove Vanilla Bean. Whisk 3 TB of MILK into the EGGS, then gradually whisk in all the MILK.
- Pour the Custard into the Caramel-lined ring mold. Place on a cookie sheet, slide into the oven.
- Bake for 40 minutes. Test by inserting a thin knife or metal skewer into the Custard. If it comes out clean the Flan is ready. If sticky, bake a little longer.
- Let it cool completely. Cover the mold with an upside-down plate and refrigerate overnight.

To unmold
- Run a thin knife around the Flan. Plunge the mold for 1 minute in a sink with hot water. Set it on a towel, dry it. Place a platter with a rim on top, invert.
  - If it resists, rap the mold on the table, or plunge it again into hot water.
  - The Caramel Sauce will spread around the Flan. Refrigerate until ready to serve.

ORANGE FLAN   Simmer in the Milk for 20 minutes, the PEEL (no pith) from 3 ORANGES.

CUSTARD - ENGLISH *Basic Vanilla Custard* *Yields 2-1/4 cups*

<u>Method 1</u>   Over medium heat, scald   [2 cups   MILK
                      with   [1   VANILLA BEAN or 1 TB EXTRACT

In a large bowl, with an electric beater, beat   [4   EGG YOLKS
                      with   [1/2-cup   GRANULATED SUGAR
When Mixture is foamy and whitens, beat in   [1 tp   CORN STARCH

- With a wire whip whisk 3 TB of boiling MILK into the EGGS, then gradually whisk in all the MILK,
- Pour it into a heavy saucepan. Over medium low heat, stir with a wooden spoon. Do not let it boil, it would curdle. The Custard is ready when thick enough to cover the back of the spoon.

- Strain the Custard through a fine sieve into a bowl.
- Add to taste 1 TB LIQUEUR, RUM or KIRSCH. Or grated ORANGE ZEST, or any other flavoring.
- Let cool. Ladle into individual custard bowls, ramekins, a serving bowl. Refrigerate overnight.

<u>Method 2</u>   Scald the Milk, Sugar and Vanilla. With a wire whip beat the Eggs and Cornstarch. Then gradually beat in the sweetened boiling Milk. Cook the Mixture as above.

<u>AS A WARM SAUCE</u>   Thin in double boiler with a little Milk. Cold: see SAUCES served with FRUIT.

CUSTARD VARIATIONS

CARAMEL   Combine in a heavy saucepan   [1/2-cup   GRANULATED SUGAR
                      [1/4-cup   WATER

- Over medium low heat let Caramel bubble until it begins to turn to a dark brown (do not burn).
- Remove immediately from heat. Gradually and carefully (it will spatter) stir in 2 cups of simmering Milk. Use this Milk to make the ENGLISH CUSTARD. Omit the Sugar in the recipe.

CHOCOLATE   In a heavy saucepan or
               double-boiler, melt   [4 oz grated   SEMISWEET BAKING CHOCOLATE
                      in   [2 cups   MILK
Bring to a simmer. Stir until smooth.
                      Add   [to taste   GRANULATED SUGAR
                      [VANILLA EXTRACT
                      [BRANDY or DARK RUM
Follow recipe as in <u>Method 2</u>.

COFFEE   Dissolve in the hot Milk   [to taste   INSTANT COFFEE
                      [or   concentrated ESPRESSO
Follow recipe as in <u>Methods 1 or 2</u>.

ORANGE   Combine in a saucepan   [2 cups   MILK
                      [1   VANILLA BEAN
               The grated ZEST of   [1   ORANGE

- Over medium low heat, bring to a boil then reduce heat to low and simmer for 20 minutes.
- Strain the Milk into a bowl, through a fine sieve lined with 2 layers of cheesecloth.
- Rinse the saucepan, bring the Milk to a boil before proceeding with <u>Methods 1 or 2</u>.
- Add to taste GRAND MARNIER, COINTREAU, or CURAÇAO.

420

CUSTARD - FLAN aux SAVOYARDS   *5-cup ring mold, serves 6 ***

Savoyards are Lady Fingers. Savoie, a region of France. A variation on the Crème Caramel Flan.

The CARAMEL   Line the ring mold with Caramel, see the CARAMEL - BASIC RECIPE.

	Use	[2/3-cup	GRANULATED SUGAR
		[1/3-cup	WATER

The FILLING   You need   [2 oz   LADY FINGERS**   hard not soft
[1/4-cup   SLIVERED ALMONDS
[1/4-cup   GOLDEN RAISINS

- Sprinkle in the mold Almonds and Raisins.
- Crumble some Lady Fingers. Continue with
  remaining Almonds, Raisins, Lady Fingers.

Douse with, optional [3 or 4 TB   KIRSCH or LIQUEUR   to taste
Preheat oven to 350°.

The CUSTARD   Bring to a simmer [1 pint   MILK
[4 TB   GRANULATED SUGAR
[1   VANILLA BEAN

In a bowl whisk [3   EGGS

- Remove Vanilla Bean. Whisk 3 TB of MILK into the EGGS, then gradually whisk in all the MILK.
- Ladle Custard into the ring mold. Place the mold on a cookie sheet and slide it into the oven.

- Bake for 40 minutes. Insert a thin knife or metal skewer into the Flan. If it comes out clean,
  the Flan is ready. If sticky, bake a little longer. It will separate from the mold around the edge.
- Let it cool completely. Cover the mold with an upside-down plate and refrigerate overnight.

To unmold   Run a thin knife between the Flan and the mold.

- Plunge the mold for 1 minute in a sink of hot water. Dry on a towel. Place a platter with a
  rim on top, invert. If it resists, rap the platter on the table. If it resists, plunge in hot water.
- The Caramel Sauce will spread around the Flan. Refrigerate until ready to serve.

- To dissolve any Caramel stuck in the mold, add to it 3-to-4 TB of boiling WATER.
- Place the mold in a skillet of simmering water. Scrape the Caramel with a spoon until it melts.
- Pour it over the Flan. Wash the mold, cover the Flan with it. Refrigerate.
- Serve the Flan as is, or with a Fruit Salad or Stewed Fruit.

**   You can substitute with Chocolate Chip Cookies or any other, as long as they are light and dry.

* *10-cup ring mold*   Caramel [1 cup Sugar, 1/2-cup Water
                       Filling [3-1/2-to-4 oz Lady Fingers, 1/2-cup Almonds, 1/2-cup Raisins
                       Custard [1 quart Milk, 1 Vanilla Bean, 7 TB Sugar, 6 Eggs

With AMARETTI di SARONNO   Italian Almond Cookies   *5-cup ring-mold*

Follow the above recipe for FLAN aux SAVOYARDS. Use 2 oz AMARETTI di SARONNO.
They are hard to crumble. Put them in a plastic bag, seal it. Hit with a heavy can to crumble.

Douse Amaretti, Almonds and Raisins with [4 TB   AMARETTO LIQUEUR

ORANGE BLOSSOM WHITE CUSTARD   (Middle East)   *Serves 4*

Mix into a paste	[2 TB + 1 tp	CORN STARCH
	[2 TB	WATER
In a heavy saucepan, over medium low heat, bring to a boil	[3 cups	MILK
Then add	[1/2-cup	GRANULATED SUGAR
Stir until the Milk begins to boil and mix in	[	the Cornstarch

Continue stirring with a wooden spoon until the Custard has well thickened. Then add   [1 tp   ORANGE BLOSSOM WATER
or more to taste

Stir for another minute. Spoon into cups or a bowl. Let cool. Refrigerate.

To serve [sprinkle with GROUND CINNAMON

RICE CUSTARD   *Serves 4 to 6*

Version 1 - no Eggs   Mix into a paste   [2 TB   CORNSTARCH
[4 TB   WATER

In a heavy saucepan, over medium heat, bring to a boil   [1 cup   WATER
Then stir in   [1/3-cup   SHORT GRAIN WHITE RICE

Reduce heat to low. Cover.
Simmer until water is absorbed.

Add   [1 quart   MILK

- Turn up to medium heat.
- With a wooden spoon, stir until the Milk boils.
- Reduce heat to low. Cover, simmer for
  20 minutes. Stir occasionally.

Mix in   [the Cornstarch
Stir until it has dissolved, then add   [1/2-cup   GRANULATED SUGAR

Stir until the Custard thickens into a cream.
At this point continue, or go to Version 2. *

Taste, only add Sugar if needed, and mix in   [1 tp   ORANGE BLOSSOM WATER
or more to taste

Spoon into custard cups or a bowl.
Refrigerate.

Serve sprinkled with   [GROUND CINNAMON
Also serve with   [STEWED FRUIT, BERRIES
Or top with   [CRUSHED PINEAPPLE   drained

VARIATIONS - Substitute Orange Blossom Water with, to taste: Rose Water or Vanilla Extract.
- Flavor with ANISE EXTRACT, add GOLDEN RAISINS before removing from heat.
  Serve sprinkled with chopped toasted ALMONDS.

* *Version 2 - with Eggs*   When the Custard has thickened into a cream, remove from heat.

In a small bowl beat   [2   EGGS

- Beat into the Eggs 2 TB of the hot Custard. Repeat. Stir the Eggs into the Custard, mix well.
- Return saucepan to stove. Over low heat stir for 2 minutes until blended. Add Sugar if needed.
- Stir until melted. Add 1 tp VANILLA EXTRACT, or to taste. Let cool. Serve in bowls. Refrigerate.

422

RICE CHOCOLATE CUSTARD   Prepare the RICE CUSTARD as in *Version* 1.

In a double-boiler, over low heat, melt in   [2 TB   MILK
                                              [4 oz   SEMI-SWEET CHOCOLATE grated
When Rice Custard thickens add the Chocolate.
Turn off heat. Optional: add 1/2-tp of Orange Extract. Serve in custard cups. Refrigerate.

DATES - STUFFED   *Yields about 1/3-cup*

Mix   [3 TB   MASCARPONE   Fill with the Mixture:
      [1-1/2 TB   HONEY
      [a light pinch ALLSPICE
      [2 TB   PECANS or PISTACHIOS chopped   [soft DRIED DATES
      [1 tp   BRANDY or LIGHT RUM

DRIED FRUIT - SALAD   *Serve with Ice Cream, Custard Sauce or Rice Custard.*

Amounts are flexible *   Combine in a bowl [1 cup   DRIED APRICOTS cut in half
                                              [1 cup   DRIED FIGS cut in half longwise
                                              [1 cup   DRIED PEARS cut into bite-size
                                              [1/2-cup   RAISINS
                 Cover the Fruit + 2-inches with [APPLE JUICE or APPLE CIDER
                                          Add   [1   CINNAMON STICK
                                       and/or   [4-to-8 CLOVES
                        Optional to taste   [2 or 3 TB   DARK RUM
                                        or   [1 TB   ORANGE BLOSSOM WATER
Cover the bowl. Refrigerate overnight.
                                          Add   [1/3-cup SLIVERED ALMONDS
Remove the Cinnamon stick.
Transfer to a glass bowl. Add more Apple Juice if needed. Refrigerate until ready to serve.

* Or use any of: Dried Apples, Dates, Peaches, Pineapple, Prunes. Cut large pieces before soaking.

GRAPEFRUIT with CUSTARD   *Serves 2*

Cut in half and scoop out wedges from   [1 large   PINK GRAPEFRUIT

Squeeze the JUICE out of membrane into a
measuring cup. It won't be much.

                 Add to the JUICE [UNFLAVORED GELATINE POWDER
                                              as per Juice amount

- In a small saucepan warm the Juice, dissolve
  in it the Gelatine. Add SUGAR if needed.
- Divide Grapefruit into sherbet glasses/bowls.
- When cooled, pour Juice over the Grapefruit.
- Refrigerate until set.
                 Top with cold [ENGLISH CUSTARD see "CUSTARDS"
Refrigerate.
          Before serving garnish with [COCONUT   shredded
                                        [or RASPBERRIES, or STRAWBERRIES

VARIATION - Substitute the Grapefruit with ORANGES. Top with a CHOCOLATE CUSTARD.

MANGO - BAVAROISE   A molded Mousse   Serves 6

Pour into a small bowl	[	1/3-cup	WATER
Sprinkle over it	[	2 TB	UNFLAVORED GELATIN POWDER
			(2 envelopes)
In a small saucepan, bring to a boil	[	2/3-cup	WATER
	[	1 cup	GRANULATED SUGAR

Reduce heat to medium low, let the Syrup
bubble. Stir occasionally, until it thickens but
remains clear and white.

Add	[		the Gelatine Mixture
Dissolve it in the Syrup, turn off heat, add	[	1 tp	LEMON JUICE
	[	1 tp	VANILLA EXTRACT

Cut ripe MANGOES into small pieces to obtain [2-1/2 cups   MANGO PULP 1/2-cup allows for
                                                                                    fiber residue
                                              If Pulp has no fiber, you need 2 cups.

- Purée the Pulp in processor.
- Place a fine sieve over a bowl. Pass through
  it the Purée, mashing with the back of a
  wooden spoon. Discard the stringy residue.
- Transfer to a bowl, mix in GELATINE SYRUP.

In a large chilled bowl, with electric beater,
                        whip stiff [1 cup   WHIPPING CREAM   chilled

Fold the MANGO PURÉE into the Cream. Pour it into a 6-cup mold. Refrigerate overnight.

To unmold   Run a thin knife around the Bavaroise. Place a platter on top, tap mold on the
             counter, invert. Refrigerate until ready to serve. Garnish with STRAWBERRIES.

MANGO - MOUSSE   *Yields about 4 cups*

As in previous recipe, cut Mangoes to obtain [2-1/2 cups   MANGO PULP   (2 cups of Purée)
                                Sprinkle with [1/2-cup   GRANULATED SUGAR or more
- Let stand for 2 hours. Drain.
- Reserve the SYRUP. Purée in processor.
- Pass through a sieve as above.
- Clean processor. Return Purée to it.
                                        Add [WATER to the SYRUP to obtain 1/4-cup

Pour it into a small skillet, sprinkle with [2 tp   UNFLAVORED GELATINE POWDER

- Let it stand for 10 minutes.
- Over medium low heat, heat the SYRUP
  until the Gelatine is dissolved.
- Add GELATINE to the MANGO PURÉE.
                                        Add [1 tp   VANILLA EXTRACT
Process with 2 quick pulses.

In a large chilled bowl, with an electric beater,
                        whip lightly [1 cup   WHIPPING CREAM   chilled
Fold the PURÉE into it.
Spoon into sherbet glasses or bowls. Refrigerate. To serve, sprinkle with CHOCOLATE CHIPS.

424

ORANGE - CRÊPES SUZETTE   Classic   CRÊPES - "BASIC RECIPES"

9 to 12 CRÊPES   Fold them in four to form a triangle. Lay them on a platter.

THE SAUCE   Wash well and dry [1   ORANGE and 1 LEMON

   Rub the ORANGE skin, to infuse on all sides [3 lumps   SUGAR
   Rub the LEMON skin, to infuse on all sides [1 lump   SUGAR
In a small bowl, dissolve the SUGAR lumps in [1/3-cup   ORANGE JUICE   strained

In chafing skillet, over table-top burner, heat [4 TB   UNSALTED BUTTER
        When it sizzles, dissolve in it [1 TB   GRANULATED SUGAR
          Add the ORANGE JUICE and [2 TB   GRAND MARNIER, COINTREAU,
                   or CURAÇAO

- Bring to a boil. Let the Syrup bubble until it
  thickens and reduces by half. *Or prepare on
  the stove, then pour into the chafing skillet.*
- With a cake server lift the Crêpes from their
  pointed end, and place them in the Sauce.
- Simmer for 2 minutes. Baste until heated.

FLAMBÉ   with 2 TB of the LIQUEUR you have used. To flambé see FRUIT - CRÊPES.

Option - Add to the Syrup, one at a time the unfolded Crêpe. Turn it in the Syrup, fold into a
        triangle, slide to the side, proceed with next Crêpe. When all are done, flambé.

ORANGE and DRUNKEN POUND CAKE

- Line a dish with a layer of 1/2-inch thick slices of POUND CAKE.
- Mix to taste ORANGE JUICE and any of above LIQUEURS. Douse the Cake with it. Top with
  overlapping ORANGE slices. Drizzle with LIQUEUR. Cover with plastic wrap, refrigerate.

ORANGE - SOUFFLÉ OMELET   See FRUIT - SOUFFLÉ OMELET
                                   Serves 2

THE FILLING Warm in a skillet, over low heat [3/4-cup   ORANGES   diced
                                  [2 TB   SHREDDED COCONUT
                                  [2 TB   GOLDEN RAISINS
                       Optional [1 TB   GRAND MARNIER

THE OMELET   In two bowls, separate [4   EGGS   at room temperature

With an electric beater, beat until they whiten [the Egg Yolks
                           with [3 TB   GRANULATED SUGAR
                                [1/4-tp   VANILLA EXTRACT
                     Then beat in [1 TB   ORANGE ZEST   grated

   Wash the beater, dry it. Beat until stiff [the Egg Whites
               Halfway through, add [1 TB   CONFECTIONERS SUGAR

Fold the Whites into the Yolks. Cook and add Filling as in FRUIT - SOUFFLÉ OMELET.

ORANGE - SOUFFLÉ au GRAND MARNIER   SOUFFLÉ see
                                        "BASIC RECIPES"

1.   Set out at room temperature   [5   EGGS you need 5 Whites, 4 Yolks

2.   Rub a 1-1/2 quarts soufflé dish, with   [UNSALTED BUTTER
         (or use 4 soufflé ramekins)   Dust with   [GRANULATED SUGAR refrigerate
                                                               (1-1/4 tp per ramekin)

3. BÉCHAMEL: Parboil for 5 minutes the   [skin of an   ORANGE   scrape off all the Pith

In a small heavy saucepan, add the Orange to   [1-1/2 cups   MILK

Bring to a boil. Reduce heat to low, simmer
uncovered for 10 minutes. Strain.
                          Prepare a   [CREAMY BÉCHAMEL ("SAUCES")
                          with the   [1-1/4 cups   of Orange Milk

     When reduced, thick and smooth, sprinkle   [1/3-cup   GRANULATED SUGAR

- Stir until dissolved. Remove from heat.
- Break 1 EGG, drop the WHITE into stainless
  steel bowl. The YOLK into the Béchamel.
- With a wire whip beat it into the Sauce.
- Repeat with 3 more YOLKS. One at a time.
- Return skillet to stove. Over <u>low heat</u> stir
  for 1 minute to bind the Eggs.
- Turn off heat.
                    Stir into the Béchamel   [1 tp   VANILLA EXTRACT
                                              [1 TB   ORANGE ZEST   grated
                                              [3 TB   GRAND MARNIER
                                              [1/4-cup   CANDIED ORANGE PEEL finely diced
- Set aside to cool. Can be prepared ahead to
  this point. Cover the surface with wax paper.
- Warm barely before adding the EGG WHITES.

4.   - Preheat oven to 400°.
            - Set out soufflé dish or ramekins.

Add to the 4 EGG WHITES 1 EGG WHITE and   [1/8-tp   CREAM OF TARTAR

a) Beat the WHITES until stiff and glossy, but not dry. Add on ladle of WHITES to the BÉCHAMEL.
   - Gently fold them in with a rubber spatula. Then gently pour the Béchamel into the WHITES
     scooping from the bottom towards the top as you turn the bowl. Do not fold too much.

b) Pour Mixture into the soufflé dish(es). Smooth the top with a spatula. Place on middle rack
   of oven. Immediately reduce heat to 375°. Bake 25-to-30 minutes. Less for ramekins.
   - Insert a skewer, test doneness. Sprinkle CONFECTIONERS' SUGAR. Serve immediately.

ORANGE ZEST   Also Lemon   *Peel with a vegetable peeler, avoid the Pith.*

- To flavor: parboil the Zest for 5 minutes. Boil it in the Milk or Sauce, discard. Strain if needed.
- If it is to remain in the Sauce: julienne the Zest, simmer in water for 6 minutes. Drain and
  dry. Cook in the Sauce.
- Or mash the simmered julienne Zest and add to a Dough, Custards, Milk, Sauces.

426

PEACHES - CRUSTLESS PIE

In a sprayed 9-inch pie-dish add a layer of   [broken   COCONUT COOKIES or MACAROONS

Mix   [1/3-cup   APPLE JUICE
           [3 TB   MAPLE SYRUP

Peel, slice into 1/4-inch thick wedges to obtain [3 cups   PEACHES or NECTARINES

- Top Cookies with half of the Peaches, arranged in concentric circles. Top with broken Cookies.
- Top with the rest of Peaches. Cover with broken Cookies. Pour over evenly Maple/Apple Juice.
- Bake in oven preheated to 350° for about 30 minutes, until all Liquid has evaporated.

Serve warm, with ICE CREAM. Or refrigerate and serve cold, with or without Ice Cream.

PEACHES - MAHARANEE

See FRUIT - POACHED

In each sherbet glass or glass bowl, serve:

		Or		
[2 scoops	MANGO ICE CREAM		[2 scoops	PISTACHIO ICE CREAM
[2 halves	POACHED PEACHES/NECTARINES		[2 halves	PEACHES / NECTARINES
[plenty of	SWEETENED COCONUT flaked		[sprinkle	CRUSHED PINEAPPLE drain
			[mixed with	LIGHT RUM

PEACHES - MARQUISE

Serves 6

Refrigerate for 2 or 3 days   [a loaf of   CINNAMON RAISIN BREAD

Blanch, peel, slice into thin wedges to obtain [3 cups   PEACHES or NECTARINES
Place them in a bowl, sprinkle and stir in [2 TB   GRANULATED SUGAR
                                 [1 tp   LEMON JUICE
Optional [1 TB   DARK RUM   or to taste

In a bowl, with wire whip beat [3 large   EGGS
Add and beat in [1 cup   MILK + 1/3-cup HALF-and-HALF
                              [1/3-cup   GRANULATED SUGAR
                              [1 tp   VANILLA EXTRACT
                              [1 TB   DARK RUM   or to taste

Pour the Custard into a measuring pitcher.

- In a sprayed 8 x 8 baking dish lay side-by-side 1/3-inch thick slices of CINNAMON BREAD.
- Douse the slices with 1/3-of the CUSTARD. Arrange on top half of the PEACHES.

- Repeat: a layer of Cinnamon Bread, 1/3-of the Custard, top with the rest of the Peaches.
- Cover with a third layer of Cinnamon Bread. Douse with the rest of the Custard.

- Place the baking dish in a pan. Fill the pan half-way up the baking dish with hot water.
- Bake until firm in oven preheated to 350°, about 30-to-35 minutes. Test by inserting a knife or skewer. If it comes out clean, the Marquise is ready. If not, bake a little longer.
- Let cool. Refrigerate. Serve at room temperature.
- Before serving dust with CONFECTIONERS' SUGAR mixed with GROUND CINNAMON.

VARIATION - Substitute Peaches with sliced PINEAPPLE canned, and STRAWBERRIES halved.

427

PEACHES - MELBA Named after the opera singer Dame Nellie Melba

Prepare a	[	RASPBERRY SAUCE see RASPBERRIES
In each sherbet glass or glass bowl serve	[2 scoops	VANILLA ICE CREAM
Top with	[2 halves	POACHED PEACHES/NECTARINES
Spoon over some	[	Raspberry Sauce
Optional, sprinkle with	[chopped	toasted ALMONDS or HAZELNUTS

PEARS - BELLE HÉLÈNE   Serves 4   See "FRUIT" - POACHED

Bring to a boil	[2 cups	WATER
	[1 cup	GRANULATED SUGAR
	[1 tp	LEMON JUICE
Reduce heat to medium low. Simmer until the Syrup has thickened. Turn off heat, add	[1/2-tp	VANILLA EXTRACT
Wash, dry, cut thinly a slice off the base of	[4 small	PEARS with stems *
Core Pears from the bottom. Peel, rub with	[half	LEMON squeezing a little Juice
Stand the Pears snugly in a saucepan, pour over the SYRUP and	[if needed	more WATER to cover them

- Cover the saucepan.
- Simmer until the Pears are tender, about 25 minutes. Cool. Refrigerate.

Have ready in the freezer 4 glass bowls with	[	VANILLA ICE CREAM a thick layer
To serve Heat in double boiler a	[	CHOCOLATE SAUCE see "SAUCES served with FRUIT"

- With a slotted spoon remove each PEAR from the Syrup.
- Place it on top of the Ice Cream. Pour over the hot Chocolate Sauce.   Serve immediately.

* For a less elaborate presentation, use stewed PEAR HALVES. Or even canned.

PEARS and DRUNKEN BROWNIES

Drain and reserve the SYRUP from	[1 can	PEARS slice them into wedges
Mix the Syrup with	[to taste	PEAR BRANDY or KIRSCH
Crumble in a pie-dish a thick layer of	[	BROWNIES

Douse them with the SYRUP. Top with the PEARS arranged in concentric circles. Cover with plastic wrap. Refrigerate overnight.

To serve, sprinkle with	[grated	CHOCOLATE
Serve with	[	VANILLA ICE-CREAM

428

PEARS - DUBARRY

RASPBERRY SAUCE see SAUCES

Prepare a VANILLA flavored [RICE CUSTARD see "CUSTARDS"

Serve it in a bowl, leaving space at the top
for the PEARS.

Top the Rice with drained [POACHED PEARS   halves or quarters
(Or canned Pears)

Refrigerate.   Before serving, top with a [RASPBERRY SAUCE

PEARS - POACHED in RED WINE   *Serves 4*

The saucepan - Use one that can fit snugly 4 small Pears standing upright. If they don't
stand upright, cut a thin slice off the base. Do not core them.

THE WINE SYRUP   Combine in the saucepan [2-1/2 cups   DRY RED WINE
[1/3-cup   GRANULATED SUGAR
[1 small stick CINNAMON

Boil for 5 minutes, turn off heat.

THE PEARS   Wash and dry [4 small   PEARS not too ripe, stems on

After peeling each Pear, rub it with a [quarter   LEMON   squeezing a little Juice

- Stand the Pears in the WINE SYRUP. If it doesn't cover them add Wine to cover.
- Bring to a boil. Cover the saucepan. Reduce heat to low.
- Simmer from 35-to-40 minutes, until tender. Let the Pears cool in their Syrup.
- Remove them with a slotted spoon and place them in a serving dish or bowl.
- Bring the Syrup to a boil then simmer until it thickens into a medium thickness.
- Let the Syrup cool for a few minutes then pour it over the Pears. Refrigerate.

Serve with   - Crème Chantilly (see CREAMS), or Vanilla Ice-Cream, or a Cold Custard.

VARIATION   - Poach Pear halves. To serve: fill cavities with Custard, Raisins, Nuts.

PINEAPPLE, GINGERBREAD - CLAFOUTIS

Spread in an 8 x 8 sprayed baking dish [1-1/2 cups   GINGER BREAD COOKIES
chopped into bits
Mix in a bowl and macerate for 1 hour [1-1/2 cups   FRESH PINEAPPLE   small cubes
[1/2-cup   BLUEBERRIES
[2 TB   GRANULATED SUGAR
[2 TB   KIRSCH

See FRUIT - CLAFOUTIS.   Prepare the [BASIC CUSTARD
adding [1 TB   KIRSCH
[1 tp   VANILLA EXTRACT

Top the GINGERBREAD with the PINEAPPLE MIXTURE.
Pour over evenly the CUSTARD. Bake following directions in FRUIT - CLAFOUTIS.

SAUCES SERVED WITH FRUIT and DESSERTS

CARAMEL

Combine in heavy saucepan	[1/2-cup	GRANULATED SUGAR
	[1/4-cup	WATER
Over medium low heat bring to a bubble, add	[1/2-tp	LEMON JUICE

When Caramel turns deep golden amber, remove from heat, add 1 TB Water, stand back as it will splatter. Stir, add 1 TB Water. If too thick, add a little Water. Caramel thickens as it cools.

CARAMEL CREAM   After adding the 2 TB of Water, stir in 1/2-cup of hot HEAVY CREAM. To taste LIGHT or DARK RUM, chopped PECANS. Serve warm or cold.

CHOCOLATE   *Yields about 1-1/3 cups*

In double boiler, over simmering water, melt	[8 oz	SEMISWEET BAKING CHOCOLATE
with	[2 TB	COLD WATER
When the Chocolate has melted, mix in	[1 TB	UNSALTED BUTTER
When melted, stir in	[3 TB	GRANULATED SUGAR
When the Sugar has dissolved, stir in	[1/2-cup	HEAVY CREAM * simmering hot
Continue stirring and add	[1/4-tp	VANILLA EXTRACT or to taste
When it bubbles, turn off heat, add	[1 or 2 TB	BRANDY, RUM, GRAND MARNIER

* For a lighter Chocolate Sauce use less Chocolate or add LIGHT or HEAVY CREAM to taste.
- To serve hot: warm in double boiler. If too thick: thin with Milk, Water or Liqueur.

CHOCOLATE MINT   *Serve hot or cold*

In the top of a double boiler, low heat, melt	[10	CHOCOLATE MINT PATTIES
with	[2-1/2 TB	MILK
Stir in, as desired	[	HEAVY CREAM

CUSTARD   *Cold Sauce*

In a heavy saucepan, over medium heat, boil	[1-1/4 cups	MILK
Then add	[1/2-tp	VANILLA EXTRACT or to taste
In the top of a double boiler, with an electric beater, beat until whitened	[2	EGG YOLKS
	[1/4-cup	GRANULATED SUGAR

Slowly whisk into YOLKS the boiling MILK.
In double boiler, over simmering water, stir until the Custard thickens, do not boil. It must coat the back of a spoon, yet run off the spoon. Strain through a fine sieve. Add LIQUEUR to taste.

HONEY CREAM SAUCE

Warm	[HONEY (1 part)
Add	[HEAVY or SOUR CREAM (2 or 3 parts)
	[GROUND CINNAMON
	[CHOPPED NUTS

HONEY SYRUP SAUCE

Warm	[HONEY (2 parts)
with	[BOILING WATER (1 part)
	[GROUND CINNAMON
Optional	[ORANGE BLOSSOM
	or ROSE WATER

430

MAPLE SAUCE

Combine in saucepan [1 cup   MAPLE SYRUP
[1/4-cup   WATER

- Over medium heat, bring to a boil.
- Reduce heat to medium low, stir occasionally until it thickens to form a thread when dropped from a spoon. Remove from heat.
- *Optional add*: 1/3-cup PECANS coarsely chopped. Before serving: 2 TB HEAVY CREAM.

PINEAPPLE ORANGE SAUCE

Add to   [CRUSHED PINEAPPLE   canned
[ORANGE ZEST   grated
[COINTREAU LIQUEUR
[TOASTED HAZELNUTS   chopped

PINEAPPLE RAISIN SAUCE

Add to   [CRUSHED PINEAPPLE   canned
[RAISINS   whole or chopped
[DARK RUM
[LEMON ZEST

RASPBERRY SAUCE

Add to blender [10 oz   FROZEN RASPBERRIES   thawed
Juice from thawed Raspberries and [1/3- cup   GRANULATED SUGAR
Any of [2 TB   ORANGE JUICE, COINTREAU, KIRSCH

Blend at high speed until smooth.
Pass through a fine sieve into a bowl, mashing with the back of a wooden spoon. Refrigerate.

To THIN   - Add gradually a little Orange Juice.
To THICKEN   - Use 1 tp Arrowroot dissolved in 1 TB Water.
           - Heat the Sauce, add the Arrowroot. Over medium low heat bring to a boil.
           - Stir until the Sauce thickens. Cool. Refrigerate. Serve at room temperature.

TUTTI FRUTTI

Chop into tidbits and mix:

[4   DRIED APRICOTS
[3   DRIED FIGS
[3   DRIED DATES
[2 TB   GOLDEN RAISINS

Any of [CANDIED GINGER, LEMON or ORANGE PEEL

Mix in blender, pour into a bowl, refrigerate:

[1/3-cup   VANILLA ICE CREAM
[4 TB   MASCARPONE

Before serving:

- Mix Fruit with Mascarpone Mixture.
- If too thick, add Vanilla Ice Cream

ZABAIONE   (zah-bah-yó-ney)   Italian hot Marsala Custard

- A frothy Custard, last minute preparation, served in stem glasses, with Cookies or Lady Fingers.
- The glasses can be half-filled with Mixed Berries, or other diced Fruit. The hot Zabaione poured on top. It can also be served as a Sauce with Cake and Strawberries, or other Fruit.

Serves 2   (Per person: divide recipe in half)

In the top part of a double boiler,
beat with a wire whisk or an electric beater [2   EGG YOLKS
with [2 TB   GRANULATED SUGAR
When the Mixture is thick and creamy, add [4 TB any of   MARSALA, KIRSCH, LIGHT RUM

- Place top part of boiler over simmering Water which must not touch it by at least a 1/2-inch.
- Continue beating, until the Mixture rises, increases in volume, becomes light, frothy, and thick enough to hold its shape in a spoon. Serve immediately.

SOUFFLÉ with FRUIT PURÉE - Basic Recipe

1.   Prepare adding flavors to taste   [3/4-cup of   FRUIT PURÉE   drain if needed

2.   Set out at room temperature   [5   EGGS you need 5 Whites, 4 Yolks

3.   Rub a 1-1/2 quarts soufflé dish, with   [UNSALTED BUTTER
       (or use 4 soufflé ramekins) Dust with   [1-1/2 TB   GRANULATED SUGAR refrigerate
                                                          (1-1/4 tp per ramekin)

4. **THE BASE**   See "SAUCES". Prepare a   [CREAMY BÉCHAMEL
                                       with   [3 TB   UNSALTED BUTTER
                                              [3 TB   FLOUR
                                              [1-1/4 cups   MILK

When the Sauce has reduced and is thick and
   smooth, sprinkle and stir in until dissolved   [1/3-cup   GRANULATED SUGAR

- Remove from heat.
- Break 1 EGG, drop the WHITE into stainless
  steel bowl. The YOLK into the Béchamel.
- With a wire whip beat it into the Sauce.
- Repeat with 3 more Yolks, one at a time.
- Return skillet to stove. Over low heat stir
  for 1 minute to bind the Eggs.
- Turn off heat.
                          Stir into Béchamel   [3/4-cup   FRUIT PURÉE   room temperature
                                              [1-1/2 tp   VANILLA EXTRACT
                              Optional, any of   [2 TB   LIQUEUR, BRANDY, KIRSCH, RUM
                                              [1/3-cup   diced CANDIED FRUIT   optional
- Set aside to cool. Can be prepared ahead to
  this point. Cover the surface with wax paper.
- Warm barely before adding the EGG WHITES.

5. Preheat oven to 400°. Set out soufflé dish(es).

Add to the 4 EGG WHITES 1 EGG WHITE and   [1/8-tp   CREAM OF TARTAR

a) Beat the WHITES until stiff and glossy, but not dry.
   - Add one ladle of WHITES to the BÉCHAMEL. Gently fold them in with a rubber spatula.
   - Then gently pour the BÉCHAMEL into the remaining WHITES.
   - Fold in with the spatula, scooping from the bottom towards the top as you turn the bowl.
     Do not fold too much, it would keep the Soufflé from rising well. White spots do no harm.

b) Pour MIXTURE into soufflé dish or ramekins. Smooth the top with a spatula.

c) Place on middle rack of oven. Immediately reduce heat to 375°. Bake for 25-to-30 minutes.
   - Less time for the ramekins. Don't open the oven door until the Soufflé is well puffed.
   - Test by inserting a thin knife or skewer. If it comes out clean, the Soufflé is ready.
     If not cook 5 minutes longer. It should have a light brown crust and creamy center.
   - Sprinkle with CONFECTIONERS' SUGAR. Serve immediately.

FRUIT SOUFFLÉS   can be served with a cool, not cold, SAUCE, see "SAUCES" in this chapter.

VARIATION   Butter and dust the soufflé dish with Sugar. Line it with LADY FINGERS.
               Douse with LIQUEUR. Pour over the SOUFFLÉ MIXTURE, bake as above.

432

SOUFFLÉS with FRUIT

If you have used a Liqueur in the Fruit Purée, do not add any to the Creamy Béchamel.
Or just use Liqueur in the Béchamel. Or use 1 TB in the Fruit Purée and 1 TB in the Béchamel.

APRICOT   Add Apricot Purée to the BASE.

Cut into small pieces to obtain	[1 cup	SOFT PLUMP DRIED APRICOTS
In a processor purée the Apricots with	[1/4-tp	ALMOND EXTRACT
Purée will reduce to about 3/4-cup. Optional	[2 TB	AMARETTO LIQUEUR
		or APRICOT BRANDY

BANANA

Purée in processor	[4	BANANAS not too ripe
with	[1 tp	LEMON JUICE
	[2 TB	GRAND MARNIER or RUM

If the Purée does not measure 3/4-cup, use
more Banana. Add Purée to the BASE.

Serve the Soufflé with a RASPBERRY JELLY SAUCE (see FRUIT - SAUCES).

CANDIED FRUIT - SOUFFLÉ ROTHSCHILD

Dice small to obtain	[1/3-cup	MIXED CANDIED FRUIT
Mix the diced Fruit with	[1 TB	BRANDY or KIRSCH optional
Add to the BASE	[1 TB	BRANDY or KIRSCH optional
and	[	the Candied Fruit

To serve	Dust the Soufflé with	[	CONFECTIONERS' SUGAR.
	Garnish around the edge with	[	CANDIED CHERRIES
		[	or FRESH STRAWBERRIES

PEACH   Add Peach Purée to the BASE.

Peel, cut into small pieces to obtain	[1 cup of	PEACHES ripe
Mix with	[1 TB	GRANULATED SUGAR

- Macerate for 1 hour.
- Drain in a sieve for 30 minutes. Purée.
- If less than 3/4-cup add more Peach.

Mix into 3/4-cup of Purée	[1/4-tp	GROUND GINGER
	[2 TB	GRAND MARNIER or COINTREAU

RASPBERRY or STRAWBERRY   Add Purée to the BASE.

Thaw and drain in a colander	[10 oz frozen	RASPBERRIES or STRAWBERRIES
Transfer to a bowl and mix in	[2 TB	GRANULATED SUGAR

- Place in a sieve to drain for 30 minutes. Purée in processor.
- Pass through a fine sieve to rid of seeds, mashing with the back of a wooden spoon.
- Use 3/4-cup of puréed BERRIES.
- Optional, add 2 TB KIRSCH or RASPBERRY BRANDY (with the Raspberries).

STRAWBERRY - BAVAROISE   A molded Mousse   *Serves 6*

Pour into a small bowl	[1/3-cup	WATER
Sprinkle over it	[2 TB	UNFLAVORED GELATINE POWDER
		(2 envelopes)
In a small saucepan, bring to a boil	[2/3-cup	WATER
	[1 cup	GRANULATED SUGAR

Reduce heat to medium low, let the Syrup
bubble, stirring occasionally, until it thickens
but remains clear and white.

Stir in	[	the Gelatine
Mix well, turn off heat, add	[1 tp	LEMON JUICE

Set aside to cool.

Hull, wash and pat dry	[1 lb + 10 oz	STRAWBERRIES (you need 2 lbs)
Wash, dry, set aside for garnish	[6 oz of the	Strawberries with stems
Chop into bits	[10 oz of the	hulled Strawberries
Purée in processor	[1 lb of the	hulled Strawberries
	[1 tp	VANILLA EXTRACT
Then add	[	the Gelatine Syrup, pulse again

With electric beater, in a large chilled bowl, whip stiff	[1 cup	WHIPPING CREAM chilled

- Fold STRAWBERRY PURÉE into it.
- Add the CHOPPED STRAWBERRIES. Pour Mixture into a 6-cup mold, or ring mold. Refrigerate.
- To unmold run a thin knife around the Bavaroise. Top with a platter. Tap mold on the counter, invert. Refrigerate. Garnish with the whole STRAWBERRIES and piped whipped CREAM.

STRAWBERRIES in CHAMPAGNE   *Serves 2*

Sprinkle [	1 cup	STRAWBERRIES sliced
with [	to taste	GRANULATED SUGAR
Add [	1/4-cup	CHAMPAGNE

Refrigerate.

Serve the Strawberries in sherbet glasses.

Add to taste	[	CHAMPAGNE
Top with	[	VANILLA ICE CREAM
Sprinkle with	[	SLIVERED ALMONDS toasted

STRAWBERRIES - CRÊPES SUZETTE   *For 1 cup sliced Strawberries*

Spread on half of each Crêpe a thin layer of	[	SOUR CREAM room temperature
Sprinkle with	[chopped	HAZELNUTS toasted

Fold Crêpes in four.
Arrange them on a platter. Cover.

In chafing skillet, over table-top burner, heat	[1/2-TB	UNSALTED BUTTER
When it sizzles, dissolve in it	[1 TB	GRANULATED SUGAR
Add	[2 TB	ORANGE JUICE
	[1 TB	GRAND MARNIER or more
When the Syrup thickens, add	[1 cup	STRAWBERRIES thinly sliced
Sprinkle	[1 TB	GRANULATED SUGAR
Pour into a ladle	[2 TB	GRAND MARNIER

Ignite, pour over the Strawberries. When the flame dies down, spoon Strawberries over the Crêpes.

434

STRAWBBERRY / RASPBERRY - NAPOLEONS

Prepare the Phyllo Napoleon sections following directions in PHYLLO - "BASIC RECIPES".

Mix to taste	[	sliced STRAWBERRIES, or RASPBERRIES
with	[	WHIPPED CREAM or COOL WHIP
Spread the Berries between 3 Phyllo sections	[	dust with CONFECTIONERS' SUGAR.

STRAWBERRIES - ROMANOFF

In a glass bowl macerate	[	1 pint	STRAWBERRIES
with	[	1/4-cup	ORANGE JUICE
	[	2 TB	COINTREAU or CURAÇAO
	[	2 TB	GRANULATED SUGAR

Refrigerate.

Pipe decoratively on top	[	CRÈME CHANTILLY see CREAMS (1/2-of recipe)

SWEET QUICHE   *All-purpose: bake, let cool, top with any kind of Fruit.*

In a large bowl whisk	[	3	EGGS
Brush with a little of the beaten Eggs a	[	9-inch	FROZEN UNCOOKED PIE SHELL

Set in the oven for 2 minutes only. Let cool.

Beat into the Eggs and mix well	[	1/2-cup	GRANULATED SUGAR
Then stir in	[	3/4-cup	HEAVY CREAM
	[	1/4-cup	MILK
	[	3 oz	PHILADELPHIA CREAM CHEESE cut into bits
	[	1 tp	VANILLA EXTRACT
	[	1/3-cup	SLIVERED ALMONDS

- Place Pie Shell in its foil, on a cookie sheet.
- Pour into it the CUSTARD. Smooth the top. Slide into a 375° oven. Reduce heat to 350°.
- Bake following directions in QUICHE - "BASIC RECIPES".
- When it has cooled, before serving top with Berries, fresh or poached Fruit. Brush with a Glaze.

SYRUP   *Serve at room temperature   Yields about 2/3-cup*

This thick Syrup is served over Fruit or Pastries. It is not a Syrup in which to cook Fruit.

Over medium heat, bring to a boil	[	1-1/2 cups	GRANULATED SUGAR
	[	1 cup	WATER
	[	1 stick	CINNAMON optional

Reduce heat to medium low. Stir occasionally.

When the Syrup thickens, add to taste any of	[	VANILLA / ORANGE EXTRACT, RUM, LIQUEUR,
	[	ROSE or ORANGE BLOSSOM WATER, HONEY
	[	(Honey goes with other flavorings)

Let cool. Store in a glass jar.

"Remember tonight, for it is the beginning of always."

Dante Alighieri

12531743R00252

Made in the USA
Lexington, KY
13 December 2011